797,885 Books
are available to read at

Forgotten Books

www.ForgottenBooks.com

Forgotten Books' App
Available for mobile, tablet & eReader

ISBN 978-1-331-97384-3
PIBN 10262713

This book is a reproduction of an important historical work. Forgotten Books uses state-of-the-art technology to digitally reconstruct the work, preserving the original format whilst repairing imperfections present in the aged copy. In rare cases, an imperfection in the original, such as a blemish or missing page, may be replicated in our edition. We do, however, repair the vast majority of imperfections successfully; any imperfections that remain are intentionally left to preserve the state of such historical works.

Forgotten Books is a registered trademark of FB &c Ltd.
Copyright © 2015 FB &c Ltd.
FB &c Ltd, Dalton House, 60 Windsor Avenue, London, SW19 2RR.
Company number 08720141. Registered in England and Wales.

For support please visit www.forgottenbooks.com

1 MONTH OF FREE READING

at
www.ForgottenBooks.com

By purchasing this book you are eligible for one month membership to ForgottenBooks.com, giving you unlimited access to our entire collection of over 700,000 titles via our web site and mobile apps.

To claim your free month visit:
www.forgottenbooks.com/free262713

* Offer is valid for 45 days from date of purchase. Terms and conditions apply.

Similar Books Are Available from
www.forgottenbooks.com

The Punjab Chiefs' Association
by Sirdar Partap Singh

Proceedings of the School Committee of the City of Boston, 1902
by Boston. School Committee

Proceedings of the Asiatic Society of Bengal, 1880
by Asiatic Society Of Bengal

Report of the Commissioner of Indian Affairs to the Secretary of the Interior
For the Year 1871, by United States. Office of Indian Affairs

Report of the Director, 1921
by Connecticut Agricultural Experiment Station

Social Work in London, 1869 to 1912
A History of the Charity Organisation Society, by Helen Bosanquet

Origin, Doctrine, Constitution, and Discipline of the United Brethren in Christ
by Church of the United Bethren in Christ

Annual Report of the North Carolina Society of the Colonial Dames of America, 1912
by North Carolina Society of the Colonial Dames Of America

Housing Betterment
February, 1918, by Lawrence Turnure Veiller

The Innkeepers Opinion of the Triennial Act
by Daniel Defoe

The Christian Movement
In Its Relation to the New Life in Japan, by Nihon Kirisutokyo Kyogikai

The Journal of Prison Discipline and Philanthropy, 1875
by Philadelphia Society for Alleviating the Miseries of Public Prisons

Minutes of the Annual Meeting, 1908
by General Association of the Congregational Churches of Massachusetts

The Half Century of California Odd Fellowship
Illustrated, by George H. Tinkham

Minutes of the Illinois Conference of the Methodist Episcopal Church
Ninety-Fifth Session; Held at Quincy, Ill., September 19-23, 1918, by A. B. Peck

Transactions of the Third Annual Meeting, Cleveland, Ohio, October, 2-5, 1912
by American Association for Study and Prevention of Infant Mortality

Minutes of the Fiftieth General Assembly of the Cumberland Presbyterian Church in the United States, 1880
by Cumberland Presbyterian Church. General Assembly

Minutes of the Particular Synod of New York
Convened at Montgomery, N.Y., May 3d, 1881, by Unknown Author

Bulletin of the Public Affairs Information Service
A Cooperative Clearing House of Public Affairs Information; Sixth Annual Cumulation, by Alice L. Jewett

JOURNAL

OF THE

HOUSE OF DELEGATES

OF THE

COMMONWEALTH OF VIRGINIA,

BEGUN AND HELD AT THE CAPITOL,

IN THE CITY OF RICHMOND,

ON MONDAY, THE SEVENTH DAY OF DECEMBER, ONE THOUSAND EIGHT HUNDRED AND THIRTY-FIVE.

RICHMOND:
PRINTED BY SAMUEL SHEPHERD, PRINTER TO THE COMMONWEALTH.
1835.

JOURNAL

OF THE

HOUSE OF DELEGATES, &c.

GENERAL ASSEMBLY of the Commonwealth of Virginia, begun and held at the Capitol, in the City of Richmond, on Monday, the seventh day of December, eighteen hundred and thirty-five, and in the sixtieth year of the Commonwealth.

A majority of the members elected to the house of delegates having appeared and been qualified according to law:

On motion of Mr. Garland of Amherst, *Resolved*, That George Wythe Munford be appointed clerk to this house.

On motion of Mr. Garland of Amherst, the house then proceeded to the election of a speaker; whereupon, he nominated Linn Banks, esq., the delegate from the county of Madison, and the names of the members being called by the clerk, the vote was, for Mr. Banks 121; for Fleming B. Miller 3; for George W. Wilson 1.

The names of the gentlemen who voted for Mr. Banks, are Messrs. Grinalds, Drummond, Gilmer, Wiley, Garland of Amherst, M'Clintic, Campbell, Henshaw, Miller, Wilson of Botetourt, Decamps, Turnbull, Mallory, Booker, Austin, Beuhring, Clay, Daniel, Samuel, Christian, Richardson, Johnson, Hill, Wilson of Cumberland, Scott, Servant, Hunter of Essex, Ball, Smith of Fauquier, Hickerson, Dickinson, Strange, Steger, Holland, Bowen, Davisson, Smith of Frederick, Watts, Watkins, Hail of Grayson, Wethered, Avent, Carrington, Coleman, Sloan, Nixon, Goodall, Mullen, Harrison, Kincheloe, Randolph, Fontaine, Holleman, Griggs, Berry, Fleet, Hooe, Robinson, Carter, Neill, Hays, Straton, Beard, Powell, Taylor of Loudoun, Harris, Ragsdale, Taylor of Mathews and Middlesex, Waggener, Rogers, Garland of Mecklenburg, Willey, Morgan, Chapman, Ingles, Sherrard, Benton, Brown of Nelson, Murdaugh, Parker, Leland, Fitzgerald, Masters, Woolfolk, Almond, Critz, M'Coy, Swanson, Witcher, Cackley, Hopkins, Carroll, Madison, Morris, Shands, Williams, Marteney, Nicklin, Dorman, Leyburn, Moffett, Conrad, Jessee, M'Mullen, Bare, Rinker, Harley, Butts, Crutchfield, Moncure, Spratley, Hargrave, Gillespie, Delashmutt, Gibson, Jett, Prentiss, Saunders, Cunningham, Brown of Petersburg, and Stanard.—121.

Messrs. Hunter of Berkeley, Smith of Gloucester, and Gregory, voted for Fleming B. Miller.—3.

And Mr. Hale of Franklin, voted for George W. Wilson.—1.

Whereupon, Linn Banks, esq. was declared duly elected speaker, and being conducted to the chair by Messrs. Garland of Amherst and Wilson of Cumberland, returned from thence his acknowledgments to the house.

On motion of Mr. Garland of Amherst, *Resolved*, That Samuel Jordan Winston be elected sergeant at arms.

On motion of Mr. Garland of Amherst, (the same having been amended on motion of Mr. Sherrard,) *Resolved*, That John Stubblefield, Thomas Davis and Robert Bradley, be elected doorkeepers to this house.

On motion of Mr. Brown of Petersburg, *Resolved*, That editors of newspapers in the city of Richmond be admitted to seats within the bar of the house, for the purpose of reporting the proceedings thereof.

On motion of Mr. Garland of Amherst, *Resolved*, That the several rules and regulations prescribed for the government of the house of delegates at its last session, be adopted for the government of the present session.

THE SAID RULES AND REGULATIONS ARE THE FOLLOWING:

1. No member shall absent himself from the service of the house, without leave, unless he be sick, and unable to attend.

2. When any member is about to speak in debate, or deliver any matter to the house, he shall rise from his seat, and without advancing, shall, with due respect, address "MR. SPEAKER," confining himself strictly to the point in debate, avoiding all indecent and disrespectful language.

3. When any member rises and addresses the chair, the speaker shall recognize him by his name; but no member shall designate another by name.

4. No member shall speak more than *twice* in the same debate, without leave.

5. A question being once determined, must stand as the judgment of the house, and cannot during the same session, be drawn again into debate.

6. While the speaker is reporting or putting a question, none shall entertain private discourse, read, stand up, walk into, out of, or across the house.

7. No member shall vote on any question, in the event of which he is immediately and personally interested; nor in any other case where he was not present when the question was put by the speaker or chairman in any committee.

8. Every member who shall be in the house when any question is put, shall, on a decision, be counted on one side or the other.

9. A majority of delegates shall be necessary to proceed to business; and every question shall be determined according to the vote of a majority of the members present, except where the constitution otherwise provides; any smaller number, together with the speaker, shall be sufficient to adjourn; twenty may call a house, send for absentees, and make any order for their censure or discharge.

10. When the house rises, every member shall remain in his seat until the speaker passes him.

11. On a call of the house, the doors shall not be closed against any member until his name shall have been once enrolled.

12. When any member shall continue in his seat two days after having obtained leave of absence, such leave shall be regarded as revoked. It shall be the special duty of the clerk, to enter on the journal, every leave of absence, and to disallow the pay of the member for the time during which he was absent.

13. Any member, sustained by seven others, shall have a right, before the question is put, to demand the ayes and noes on the decision of any question; and on such occasions, the names of the members shall be called over by the clerk, and the ayes and noes respectively entered on the journal, and the question decided as a majority shall thereupon appear. After the ayes and noes shall have been taken, and before they are counted, or entered on the journal, the clerk shall read over the names of those who voted in the affirmative, and of those who voted in the negative, at which time any member shall have the right to correct any mistake committed in enrolling *his* name.

14. No business shall be introduced, or considered after 12 o'clock, until the orders of the day be disposed of, except messages from the senate or executive. Among the orders of the day, those which are general in their nature, shall have precedence over such as are private or local.

15. The speaker may call any member to the chair, who shall exercise its functions for the time; but no member, by virtue of such appointment, shall preside for a longer time than one day.

16. The speaker shall set apart convenient seats for the use of the members of the senate and executive, and of the judges of the superior courts of this commonwealth and of the United States, and of such other persons as he may invite within the bar of the house.

17. All bills or other business shall be dispatched in the order in which they are introduced, unless the house shall direct otherwise in particular cases.

18. The clerk shall not permit any records or papers to be taken from the table, or out of his possession; but he may deliver to a member, any bills depending before the house, on taking his receipt for the same.

19. The journal of the house shall be drawn up by the clerk, on each day, and after being examined by the speaker, shall be printed and delivered without delay.

20. The clerk shall publish with the laws, all resolutions of a general nature, annex marginal notes to each law or resolution, and subjoin an index to the whole.

21. The clerks of the senate and house of delegates, may interchange messages at such time between the hour of adjournment, and that of meeting on the following day, as that the said messages may be read immediately after the orders of the day.

22. It shall be the duty of the clerk to make an alphabetical schedule of the petitions presented during the session, with a short analysis of each, for the information of succeeding legislatures.

23. No petition of a private nature having been once rejected, shall be acted on a second time, unless it be supported by new evidence; nor shall any such petition, after a third disallowance, be again acted on. The several clerks of committees shall keep alphabetical lists of all such petitions, specifying the sessions at which they were presented, and the determination of the house thereon; and shall deliver the original petitions to the clerk of the house, to be preserved in his office.

24. No petition or memorial shall be received, praying for the division of a county or parish, changing the place of holding any court, or other local matter, unless the purport of such petition or memorial, shall have been fixed up at the court-house door of the county where such alteration is proposed, at two different courts, and shall have remained there one day during the sitting of each court, and at least one month shall have passed after the holding of the last court, and before the petition or memorial is presented. And no petition or memorial shall be received, or bill brought in for establishing or discontinuing ferries, nor for any other purpose affecting private rights, or property, unless the parties interested shall have had one month's notice. And if they be not known to the petitioner or memorialist, the purport of the petition, memorial or bill, shall be set up at the court-house in the manner before directed, and *also* three times inserted in some newspaper in the state most convenient for conveying the intended information, one month before offering or moving the same.

25. No petition shall be received claiming a sum of money, or praying the settlement of unliquidated accounts, unless it be accompanied with a certificate of disallowance from the executive, or auditor, containing the reason why it was rejected. But this order shall extend to no person applying for a pension.

26. When any petition, or bill founded on one, is rejected, such petition shall not be withdrawn, but the petitioner, or member presenting his petition, or any member from the county or corporation in which the petitioner resides, may without leave, withdraw any document filed therewith; and a list of every document so withdrawn, shall be preserved by the clerk. All petitions not finally acted on, may, with the accompanying documents, be in like manner withdrawn, after the expiration of the session at which they were presented.

27. No petition shall be read in the house, unless particularly required by some member; but every member presenting one, shall announce the name of the petitioner, the nature of the application, and whether in his opinion a similar application had been before made by said petitioner. He shall also endorse on the back of the petition, his own name, as a pledge that it is drawn in respectful language: whereupon, it shall be delivered to the clerk, by whom it shall be laid before the proper committee.

28. At the commencement of each session, the following committees shall be appointed by the speaker:
  1. A committee of privileges and elections, to consist of not less than nine nor more than thirteen members.
  2. A committee for courts of justice, to consist of not less than nine nor more than thirteen members.
  3. A committee for schools and colleges, to consist of not less than nine nor more than thirteen members.
  4. A committee of propositions and grievances, to consist of not less than nine nor more than thirteen members.
  5. A committee of claims, to consist of not less than nine nor more than thirteen members.
  6. A committee of roads and internal navigation, to consist of not less than nine nor more than thirteen members.
  7. A committee on the militia laws, to consist of not less than five nor more than seven members.
  8. A committee of finance, to consist of not less than seven nor more than nine members.
  9. A committee on the penitentiary, to consist of not less than five nor more than seven members.
  10. A committee on the armory, to consist of not less than seven nor more than thirteen members.
  11. A committee on executive expenditures, to consist of not less than five nor more than seven members.
  12. A committee to examine first auditor's office, to consist of not less than five nor more than seven members.
  13. A committee to examine second auditor's office, to consist of not less than five nor more than seven members.
  14. A committee to examine clerk's office, to consist of not less than five nor more than seven members.
  15. A committee to examine the register's office, to consist of not less than five nor more than seven members.
  16. A joint committee to examine the treasurer's accounts, to consist of not less than five nor more than seven members.
  17. A joint committee to examine the bonds of public officers, to consist of not less than five nor more than seven members.
  18. A joint committee on the banks, to consist of not less than five nor more than seven members.
  19. A joint committee on the public library, to consist of not less than five nor more than seven members.
  20. A committee on agriculture and manufactures, to consist of not less than five nor more than thirteen members.
  21. A committee to examine enrolled bills, to consist of not less than five nor more than ten members.

29. Five members of any standing or select committee, shall be a quorum to proceed to business.

30. The several committees are instructed to report, in all cases to them referred, whether other cases may arise comprised within the principle of the petitioner: and if a bill be ordered, it shall be so drawn as to provide for all such cases, as well as that in which it originated.

31. Select committees shall not consist of less than five nor of more than thirteen members.

32. The committee of privileges and elections shall report, in all cases of privilege or contested elections, the principles and reasons on which their resolutions are founded.

33. The committee of privileges and elections shall examine the oaths taken by each member, and certificates of election furnished by the sheriffs, and report thereon to the house.

34. The committee for schools and colleges shall annually examine into the state and manner of administration of the literary fund, and make such report as they may deem proper.

35. The committee of finance shall annually examine into the state of the debts due from the commonwealth; of the revenue and expenditures of the preceding year, and prepare an estimate of the expenses of the succeeding year, and make such report thereon as they may deem proper.

36. Any person contesting the election of a member returned to serve in this house, will be entitled to receive his wages only from the day on which such person is declared duly elected.

37. Whenever by the equality of sound, a division of the house is rendered necessary in the opinion of the speaker, or of a member, the members shall be required to rise in their places; and if on a general view of the house, a doubt still exist on the mind of the speaker, or of a member, as to the side on which the majority voted, the members shall be counted standing in their places, either by the speaker, or by two members of opposite opinions on the question, to be deputed for the purpose by the speaker.

38. Documents printed by order of the house, shall be printed on paper of the same size with the journal, and

a copy shall be bound up with each journal, and furnished the members at the end of the session; and it shall be the duty of the public printer to furnish 185 additional copies to be used for that purpose.

39. Any person shall be at liberty to sue out an original writ, or subpœna in chancery, to prevent a bar by the statute of limitations, or to file any bill in equity, and examine witnesses thereupon, for the purpose of preserving their testimony against any member of this house: *Provided*, That the clerk, after having made out and signed such original writ, or subpœna, shall not deliver it to the party, nor to any other person, during the continuance of the member's privilege.

40. Any person summoned to attend this house, or any one of its committees, as a witness, shall be privileged from arrest, during his coming to, attendance on, or return from the house or committee: and no such witness shall be obliged to attend, until the party, at whose request he was summoned, shall pay, or secure to him, for his attendance and travelling, the same allowance which is made to witnesses attending the general court.

41. If any person shall tamper with a witness, in respect of his evidence to be given before this house, or one of its committees, or directly or indirectly endeavour to deter or hinder a person from appearing or giving evidence, it shall be deemed a high misdemeanor, which the house will severely punish.

42. No person shall be taken into custody by the sergeant at arms, on any complaint of breach of privilege, until the matter is examined by the committee of privileges and elections, and reported to the house.

43. In all elections, but one vacancy shall be filled at a time.

44. In elections by joint vote of the two houses of the general assembly, each house shall first communicate, by message to the other, the names of the persons who may be put in nomination for the said office in each house respectively; and then each house shall vote separately in its own chamber; and shall each appoint a committee on its part to meet a committee on the part of the other house, and communicate the result of the vote in each house respectively; and if upon such vote, any person have a majority of the whole number of votes, the same shall be reported by the committees to their respective houses, and the speaker of each house shall declare such person duly elected; and if no person shall have a majority of the whole number of votes, both houses shall in like manner proceed to another vote, dropping the person who shall have the smallest number of votes on the former vote; and so on till an election be made; and the results of each vote in each house shall, in like manner, be communicated by each house to the other, and reported by their respective committees; and the election, when made, shall, in like manner, be declared by the respective speakers of the two houses.

The speaker laid before the house a communication from Littleton W. Tazewell, esq. governor of the commonwealth, which was read as follows:

EXECUTIVE DEPARTMENT, December 7th, 1835.

SIR,—Inclosed is a communication to the house of delegates, which you will be pleased to lay before that body.

I am, very respectfully, your most ob't serv't,

LITT'N W. TAZEWELL.

To the Speaker of the House of Delegates.

Fellow-Citizens of the Senate and House of Delegates:

Since the last adjournment of the general assembly, matters of so much interest to this commonwealth have occurred, that when they first attracted my attention, I doubted whether my duty did not require of me to exert the authority given by the constitution, and to convene you at a much earlier period than that to which you had been adjourned. But after a most careful examination of all our laws applicable to the then existing state of things, I found the powers with which the ordinary functionaries of the commonwealth were thereby endowed, amply sufficient to prevent or punish any threatened disturbance of the public peace that might occur within our limits; and that even your powers would not suffice to repress such designs when conceived or attempted beyond our confines. To effect an object so desirable, the co-operation of other governments was requisite. Such co-operation could neither be asked nor expected, however, until the several legislatures of these governments should assemble; and as this would not happen until after the time of your own regular meeting, I thought it better to take no notice of what was then going on, than to add to the prevailing excitement by any official act of mine; or to expose you to the great inconvenience which would probably be occasioned by a sudden and unexpected call of the general assembly, especially at such a season.

That many of the citizens of the northern and eastern states, aided by a few foreigners sojourning within their limits, have devised a system, in which they still persevere, to produce a direct interference with the slave property of the southern and south-western states, is now a matter of such notoriety as to need no reference to any particular evidence to establish its truth. To effect this purpose, they have organized numerous societies—have subscribed large sums of money—and have established presses to print and disseminate the disorganizing, seditious and incendiary doctrines of the members of these associations. All this has been done, and is still doing, for the undisguised purpose of effecting the immediate emancipation of our slaves. The authors of such schemes abide without our limits, and are so beyond the reach of our municipal laws. They are thus enabled, with impunity, to scatter amongst us, materials, obviously designed and well calculated to lead to insurrection, rapine and murder. The post offices under the direction and control of the federal government, furnish a ready mode of transmitting and spreading their mischievous productions.

These fanatics do not stop here. They assert a right in the congress of the United States to interfere with our property in various other modes. They contend, that congress is endowed by the federal constitution, with plenary authority to emancipate every slave in the district of Columbia—that it may inhibit the transportation of slaves, as such, from one state to another—that it may emancipate all slaves within the territories of the United States, and interdict the future introduction of any into the same, as a precedent condition to the admission of such territories into the union, as component members of the United States—and they boldly announce their purpose of exhibiting these several propositions before the congress now about to convene, and to claim their decision of the same.

Under this aspect of our affairs, two questions demand your consideration, the prompt decision of which is required not less by the rights of the state, than by the security and interest of those you represent. The first of these questions refers to the condition of things now existing, and exacts of you to determine whether such a state shall longer be borne. The second regards the proposed change in our present relations, which relations have so long brought happiness and tranquillity to all. This demands of you to decide upon the course most proper to be pursued in the emergency of the threatened change.

It is in vain to turn away our eyes from the state of things that now exists. We have to meet it, in some form or other; and it belongs properly to you to decide as to the manner in which this shall be done. It is no time to temporize. Should any thing arrest the progress of the scheme devised, for the present, experience teaches that it will surely be revived hereafter, whenever any circumstance may arise promising to its authors a more favourable result; and in such a government as that of the United States, occasions will often present themselves, even if they are not made, when such projects may be agitated with some fancied or pretended prospect of success. It behooves you, therefore, to settle, at once, upon the course proper to be pursued in such a contingency; and to inform those whom you represent, either to prepare for the occasion as becomes men determined to peril all in defence of their known rights, or to hold their possessions at the mere courtesy of others who are unacquainted with their situation and indifferent to their interests. Feeling with the other citizens of this commonwealth, and honoured by the responsible situation conferred upon me, I must be excused for calling your attention to this great subject, in a manner more impressive than I should think myself at liberty to adopt under ordinary circumstances.

In regard to the first question, no one can doubt, that under the wise provisions of the public law, intended as this is to perpetuate the peace and harmony of all states, whenever an association exists within the territory of any state, the object of which association is to disturb the repose of another, the state whose tranquillity is jeoparded by such means, may rightfully demand of the other, the prompt suppression of all such associations. Such demands, when sustained by proper proofs, are never refused by any state which wishes to remain a member of the family of civilized communities, or desires to maintain amicable relations with the state making and sustaining the demand. There is no exception to this rule. To doubt it now, would be to replunge the civilized world into that barbarism from which it has emerged, and to justify every nation in the impudent attempt to regulate the affairs of others, by its own notions; which, although sometimes concealed beneath the guise of pretended philanthropy, may always be traced to considerations much less pure. Hence, the universal doctrine and practice of modern states, is never to obtrude even their advice, unasked, as to the mere internal concerns of others, so long as these do no injury to their neighbours. And what states may not do themselves, can never be tolerated by them as the acts of their citizens or subjects, unless they mean to adopt such acts as their own.

The different states of this confederacy, are surely entitled to expect from each other, at least the same courtesy and consideration which is always manifested by nations absolutely independent and unconnected. Every clause of the federal compact inculcates this lesson, which has sunk so deep into the heart of almost every native American, that it may be well regarded as constituting the strongest bond of our union. Then, the slaveholding states have a perfect right to require of all the others, that they should adopt prompt and efficient means to suppress all such associations existing within their respective limits. Nor ought it to be doubted, as I think, that such a demand, if made, will meet from each of the other states a ready compliance on its part. Not doubting this myself, I will not suggest to you now, any measures founded upon a contrary supposition. But I will content myself with recommending to you, at present, the adoption of such measures only, as may justify a strong application to each of our co-states within whose limits any of the associations referred to may exist, to suppress them speedily; and to establish such other regulations, as may be effectual to prevent or punish acts designed or calculated to disturb our tranquillity.

Although these are my impressions, it is due to the importance of the occasion that I should say to you, that many who have had much better opportunities of forming correct opinions upon the subject than I have had, do not concur with me in this respect. I have had much correspondence in relation to it, with persons upon the spot; which, a regard to the public good prevents me from exhibiting to you at this time. The prevailing opinion of most of those with whom I have communicated, is that no effectual legislative action need be expected on the part of our co-states, where it is most necessary; but that the southern and south-western states will have to rely upon themselves only, for the preservation of their own peace and tranquillity. Therefore, while making a strong appeal to our co-states to do their duty towards us, prudence will suggest to you the propriety of considering the neglect of such an appeal, as at least a possible event.

I send you herewith an extract from a letter I have received from one to whose veracity and intelligence all respect is due. This letter accompanied a package containing a great number of books, tracts and other publications, which I have retained in this department for your inspection. The letter itself will disclose to you its own object.

In regard to the federal government, so long as it is agreed by all, that the powers of this government are limited not merely by the terms in which these powers are granted, but also by the object for the accomplishment of which these powers were given, unless the grant of the power to establish post-offices, can be considered as designed to furnish easy means for the general dissemination of seditious and incendiary publications, well calculated to disturb the peace and union of the states, the employment of such an agency, for such a purpose, must be admitted to be a gross perversion of its intent. Therefore, the states whose tranquillity is put in jeopardy by such a practice, have a clear right to demand of their government, that it shall adopt the most speedy and effectual means to prevent and punish it; and so to aid in the preservation of their peace and welfare.

There is no reason to doubt, that the officers of the government of the United States view this subject in the same light in which it is here presented. But being mere executive officers, bound to execute existing laws, each at his own peril, legislative enactments are required to protect these officers, and to cause the laws of the land to conform more exactly to the spirit and objects of the constitution. An intimation of a wish on your part, that our senators and representatives in congress would call the attention of that body to this subject, and would propose some plan by which the evil complained of may be effectually remedied, will probably accomplish every thing we ought to desire, in this respect. But to give more certain effect to the expression of such a wish, I would recommend, that communications be opened speedily with all the slaveholding states, to invite their co-operation in any plan that you may think most wise to be adopted, not only in regard to the action of the federal government, but to the suggested application to our co-states. The subject is one of equal interest to them all, and all should be consulted and co-operate in every measure in reference to it, which it may become either necessary or useful to adopt.

Respecting the threatened application to congress to interfere in any way with our rights of property, as it may be unnecessary for you to provide, at this time, for any such possible contingency, I will only say, that while that body is, necessarily, the judge of its own constitutional powers, in the first instance, the states are made, by the like necessity, the final arbiters of all questions touching their reserved rights. It is much to be desired, that the forbearance of either party, may ever incline each, to avoid any near approach to what may be regarded by the other as a limit not precisely defined. Nothing short of the most obvious necessity can ever excuse such a course. But if it is pursued in mere wantonness, without any pretext of necessity for resorting to it, as in the case supposed, it will become your duty, as the faithful guardians of the rights of the state, to adopt at once the most effectual means to provide for the occurrence. To enable you to do so seasonably, I shall endeavour to obtain the earliest information in regard to this subject; and will promptly communicate to you hereafter, any thing I may learn, that may seem to me to require any action on your part.

An incident has occurred of late in the administration of justice, and in the due execution of the laws of this commonwealth, to which, as it may become of much importance hereafter, I think it necessary to call your attention, at this time. A few weeks since, I received a report from the sheriff of the county of Norfolk, informing me, that he had been forcibly prevented from performing his duty, by one of the naval commanders of the United States. Upon the receipt of this information, I forthwith transmitted a copy of the letter of the sheriff to the president of the United States. The only reply to this letter I have yet received, is contained in one from the secretary of the navy of the United States. I send herewith copies of the letter of the sheriff of Norfolk to me, of my letter to the president, and of that of the secretary of the navy to me. These documents will enable you to see the merits of the whole case, so far as the rights and character of this commonwealth are involved in it.

In making the communication I did to the president of the United States, I had no other purpose, than to bring to his knowledge, distinctly and in the most authentic form, what was represented to me by one of the sworn officers of this government. I thought, and I still think, that neither the laws nor policy of the United States, could countenance the idea, that the powers of the federal government were equal to abolish or render null the relations between debtor and creditor, so far only as its particular officers, whether civil or military, may be concerned; or so to convert one of their vessels, either armed or unarmed, into an asylum for the protection of those who may be unwilling to satisfy engagements previously contracted with their fellow citizens. Nor had I any doubt, that the discipline of the naval service must be highly offended, by the use of the intemperate language, and the exertion of such power as was practised upon this occasion, towards one of the most responsible officers known to the laws of this and of every other state in our confederacy. Therefore, I thought it to be my duty to bring such acts directly under the observation of the magistrate charged with the preservation of this discipline, and with the execution of these laws; leaving it to him to decide upon the course he might think proper to adopt, under such circumstances.

I had no idea, however, of referring even to this high magistrate, or to any other forum than those of this commonwealth itself, to decide what was due to the offended majesty of her laws, or what punishment should be awarded against any who may outrage her peace and dignity. Therefore, I forthwith directed the proper legal proceedings to be instituted against the offender, in our own courts; and an indictment preferred against him by the attorney of the commonwealth has been returned by the grand jury as "a true bill." His departure from the commonwealth, may possibly have prevented the necessary process from being served upon him, as yet. But it will be continued again and again, even to the last extremity, until it has produced its effect; unless the most satisfactory reparation is made for the wrong done. To a community like this, the members of which have been reared in habitual reverence of law, nothing is so odious as to witness the contempt of that which they have been taught to venerate; and when such contempt is manifested by those who derive their whole authority from the law, there is always hazard that such examples may be followed by others differently situated. But civil liberty must cease to exist, whenever any man or body of men, whether clothed with civil or military authority, or without authority of any kind, is suffered to violate the law with impunity.

The facts of this case induce me to recommend to you a revision of the statutes applicable to it, and to suggest the propriety of providing by law, that the commander of any armed vessel of the United States, who after being duly notified by a creditor that his debtor is on board such vessel, shall remove such debtor from out of this commonwealth, shall for so doing be held personally liable for the amount of such debt. I recommend to you also, to authorize the proper officers of the law, upon due proof made before them that a misdemeanor has been committed by any one about to depart from the commonwealth, to award a *capias* at once against such offender. The statutes upon this subject, now in force, will not be found to authorize any such prompt proceedings, although in many cases it is obviously necessary.

Early in the month of September last, I received a communication from the governor of Maryland, accompanied by the copy of a report of a special committee of the house of delegates of that state, which concludes with two resolutions on the subject of its boundaries. By the first of these resolutions, that passed at the December session of this body in the year 1833, (a copy of which is now on your journals) is expressly repealed, and the attorney general is required to discontinue the proceedings thereby directed. By the last, the governor of Maryland is requested to transmit a copy of the first resolution to the government of Virginia, and to communicate to it the earnest desire of the state of Maryland to close and finally adjust the question concerning the boundaries of that state, by amicable negotiation. The duty with which the governor of Maryland was so charged, was fulfilled by the letter stated. In this, I was invited to a renewal of the negotiation upon the subject referred to, and to accept of the proposals formally made by Maryland in the resolutions passed by its legislature at their December session 1831.

Having no authority to enter into any new negotiation upon this subject, I promptly replied to the letter I had received, stating this fact; and promising to submit the matter to you for your determination. As I doubted, however, whether the authority formerly given to the governor of Maryland, had not been subsequently revoked, with a view of preventing any delay in the negotiation hereafter, (should you think proper to grant the necessary power to any one to commence it) I stated my doubts to governor Thomas, to the end that every defect of this sort might be speedily removed. And I proposed to him, at the same time, that we should commence an informal discussion of the subject, that we might thereby learn what were the precise questions as to which any disagreement existed between our respective states, and so be prepared to recommend the same plan to each, for the final adjustment of such questions.

In answer to this communication, governor Thomas informed me, that unless our act of March 5th, 1833, made provision for the umpirage proposed in the Maryland resolutions of 1831, in case of a disagreement between the commissioners therein mentioned, he had no authority to continue the negotiation. This act contains no such provision certainly: and as a copy of it had been transmitted to the governor of Maryland very soon after its enaction, I could regard this annunciation in no other light than as a rejection of my proposal. This I stated in my reply, which induced some further correspondence between us, not changing in any way, however, the former position of Maryland.

I send herewith copies of all the letters and documents referred to. From these you will perceive that Maryland expects you to accept unconditionally, the singular proposal made in her resolutions of 1831, as preliminary to any new negotiation in regard to this matter. The act of March 5, 1833, was designed to be, and is, an acceptance of so much of this proposal as it was thought necessary to accept at that time. This is not deemed satisfactory, however, and it now remains with you to decide, whether you will consent to refer an unknown question, involving unknown interests, to an unknown umpire, bound by no prescribed rules, and to be guided by any unknown evidence and argument that may hereafter be exhibited. Such a proposition is thought by Maryland to be equal and reciprocal; but when the relative situation of the parties is considered, it is difficult to see in what its reciprocity consists; and the same equality would be furnished by a reference to any mere chance. It is not usual, however, for states to make or to accept such propositions; especially as preliminary to a negotiation invited by themselves—nor can I recommend to you the acceptance of this.

I have the satisfaction to inform you, that before the first day of September last past, all the claims for military bounty land which had been exhibited to the executive, were disposed of finally by that body. Since then, I have learned through the secretary of the treasury of the United States, that the warrants filed exceed the appropriation of six hundred and fifty thousand acres made by congress in the act of March 3, 1835, by ninety-four thousand five hundred and ninety-nine acres. This excess, (as the register informs me,) does not comprehend other allowances made by the executive of this commonwealth, upon which allowances, no warrants have yet been granted by the register, because none who could shew themselves properly authorized to receive such warrants have applied to him for the same. Since the first day of September last, a few additional claims for military bounty land have been presented. Upon none of these, however, have I yet proceeded to decide; nor, under the circumstances stated, shall I feel myself at liberty to act hereafter, unless directed to do so by some act or resolution of yours. Your attention is therefore again invited to this subject.

The expiration of the charter of the Bank of the United States, is an event now so near at hand, and one that may, possibly, be productive of results of so much interest to the community, in very many respects, that I should be unmindful of my duty, if on exhibiting to you the condition of the commonwealth, I should omit to call your attention to a circumstance of such importance.

That the sudden abduction of so great an amount of currency, must occasion a temporary vacuum in the circulation every where, is a proposition which seems to be self-evident. There is no reason to doubt, however, that the youthful vigour of our society, and the intelligence of its members, would soon enable them to accommodate all their dealings and all their wants to the new state of things, whatever this may be, provided it promised to be permanent, and they could be left to act as their own discretion would dictate. Some individual distress might be caused by the sudden change, probably; and the finances of the government itself might possibly sustain a temporary shock; yet no general and permanent mischief would ensue.

But, unfortunately, we cannot expect to be left to ourselves, to adjust our own dealings to any new and permanent system. The United States present the singular spectacle of an extended country and numerous population, closely connected with each other by many ties, whose currency is left subject to the regulation of many different governments. Under such circumstances, nothing like uniformity can be expected. The interest of each state, will induce it to supply, if possible, every want of others, by its own particular means; and the temporary vacuum in the circulation of this commonwealth, if not supplied by herself, will surely be filled by issues from some other quarter. These issues will crowd fast upon the heels of each other, the worst perpetually expelling the better currency, until depreciation attains a height apparent to the most dull sighted observer. At this point, the federal government, (which as we know, entertains no doubt of its authority to do so,) will certainly interfere, in some way or other, as heretofore, to correct the evil; and then a new system will necessarily produce a new revolution.

Exposed thus to various perils, your most prudent caution will be required, to protect the interests of this commonwealth—to render events which you cannot control, as little injurious as possible—and seasonably to provide for future probable occurrences, by the best means in your power, without putting too much at risk upon any single chance.

If it was practicable, as some have supposed it to be, to make our currency consist of nothing but the precious metals, the immediate distress which would necessarily result from such an experiment, might possibly be compensated hereafter, by the success that might then attend it. But when we reflect, that at no period of our history has the currency of Virginia been of this character; that her faith is already pledged to several corporations, to receive their paper as equivalent to gold or silver; and that the paper of other states, with whom we have much intercourse, will certainly flow in upon us, in despite of every effort to prevent it; the attempt to establish here a currency exclusively metallic, can only be considered as a visionary project, of impossible execution, even if it promised more desirable results than any that can be shewn as likely to flow from it.

Then, our present situation seems to be this. Our currency is compounded in part (and necessarily so) of paper of various descriptions. Only a portion of this pervades the United States, and is made, by law, receivable every where by the federal government in payment of the many and heavy demands it is authorized to exact. This very portion of the currency is about to be withdrawn from circulation speedily. Its loss will be sensibly felt every where, for a season, and must be supplied by some equivalent. If this equivalent is not furnished by ourselves, it will be furnished by others. In the latter event, should depreciation occur, (and we shall have no means to prevent it) our own people will bear the loss, without a corresponding benefit to any of them. But if we supply the vacuum ourselves, we may prevent depreciation by wise legislation; and should it unhappily occur, in despite of all our caution, the loss one portion of our community may sustain, will be compensated, in some degree, by the gain of another portion; and although some of her citizens may suffer, the commonwealth itself will sustain but little comparative injury.

If this be a faithful picture of our situation, there seems to be little reason to doubt the prudence of increasing the banking capital of the state, at least to an extent equal to the expected deficit. But if any question the accuracy of the description I have given, or the policy of meeting the impending danger by a course similar to that which will certainly be adopted by other states, caution will require all such to forbear any action, until time shall prove whether my forebodings are well or ill founded. The remedy (if such it may be called) will be more difficult of adoption hereafter, certainly: but it is much better to pause when we doubt, than to run rashly into untried experiment, where error may be productive of such serious effects.

Should you determine to increase the banking capital of the commonwealth, at this time, various schemes present themselves, by any of which, it is probable, the desired end may be attained—but while each of these holds out some peculiar advantages, all are obnoxious to several strong objections. It belongs to you only to compare these, and to select that which you may consider the most expedient, under present circumstances.

The mischief to be provided for, is that of a suddenly reduced currency, the vacuum in which will be supplied by others, and supplied probably by a depreciating paper, if it is not differently replenished by you. The great hazard to be guarded against in correcting this mischief, is the risk of running into excess in the application of the remedy—a risk that belongs to the subject every where, but which is much aggravated in a country and under a government like this. Such excess, under any circumstances, would be equally pernicious with the mischief designed to be prevented; and it would tend, necessarily, to the production of the evil of depreciation, which it is so desirable to avert. There is another peril too, of but little less importance than this. It arises principally, from the nature of our government, in which a ruling majority will sometimes regard its own interests as those of the whole, and so overlook the claims of a minority. When the mischief to be redressed is general, the partial application even of a proper remedy will be of little avail. It may produce excess somewhere, but this excess cannot supply the deficiency in other quarters. To make the remedy useful, the same caution is necessary in its distribution, that is required in its creation. This, while it will guard against excess any where, will also provide for deficiency every where.

There is still another danger, which ought not to be overlooked in any arrangement that may be adopted in reference to this subject. It proceeds from the fact, that any plan you may think it wise to establish, may, and most probably will be crushed, or put in jeopardy, at some time or other, by the action of the federal government. Therefore, common prudence requires, that any scheme you may see fit to adopt, should be but temporary; and that the immediate interests of the commonwealth should not be involved in its success, further than is indispensably necessary. The untiring vigilance of private interest, and the prompt sagacity of individuals, may perhaps be relied upon, to warn them of the coming danger, and to guard them against its effects: but nothing short of this will do. It would be rashness to stake the immediate interests of the commonwealth, voluntarily, upon any scheme subject to be defeated by another will than its own; or upon one, which, when established, must be placed beyond its control, except at distant intervals of time.

The sum of fifty thousand dollars appropriated by the act of the 10th of March last, as a sinking fund, to be applied to the redemption of such portions of the certificates of debt of this commonwealth as were held by individuals and corporate bodies, and could be purchased at par, has been received of the treasury, by the commissioners of the said fund, appointed by the said act. But the sum so received, still remains in the hands of the treasurer of the state, subject to the order of the said commissioners. The only certificates of debt of the commonwealth which are yet payable, are those held by the president and directors of the literary fund, amounting to $343,039 17. The redemption of any of these certificates, was positively prohibited, either by the act referred to, or by that under which a portion of them was vested in the literary fund; and as none of the other certificates of debt of the commonwealth held by individuals or other bodies corporate could be purchased at par, the requirements of the act referred to could not be satisfied by the redemption of any such. Nor has any opportunity yet occurred, when, in the judgment of the commissioners of the sinking fund, any temporary investment of the whole or of any part of the said fund so subject to their control, might have been advantageously made, in any other productive public stocks.

As the existence of this fund will contribute much to preserve the credit of the commonwealth, and to keep the price of its stocks of all kinds above par; and as none of its certificates of debt will become payable for some years yet to come, it is not probable that the act creating the sinking fund can be carried into effect for some time, unless some new legislation is had upon the subject. It belongs to you only to decide, whether the debts of the commonwealth now due, shall be satisfied out of the fund provided for that purpose; and if not, what disposition shall be made of it until others may become payable.

Two fifths of the capital stock of the James river and Kanawha company having been subscribed by other persons than the commonwealth, but not the whole stock, the residue of the same was taken for the commonwealth, in pursuance of the act of January 24th last; and a sum equal to one dollar upon each share of the two fifths subscribed as aforesaid, having been paid by the subscribers, they thereupon became a body corporate, in pursuance of the act of the 16th of March, 1832. The president and directors of the James river company, having ascertained these facts, made publication of the same in conformity with the provisions of the act last mentioned; and in their said publication they appointed a day for a general meeting of the stockholders in the city of Richmond, to the end that the new company might be duly organized. The stockholders met in pursuance of this notice; and having performed the duties required of them by the said act, they adjourned on the 28th day of May last. At the expiration of thirty days thereafter, the whole interest of the commonwealth in the works and property of the former James river company, was transferred by the said act, to the James river and Kanawha company thereby incorporated, subject to the conditions thereby prescribed. Thus the former James river company has become extinct, except for the necessary purposes required by the acts that created this company, and which cannot be performed by the new James river and Kanawha company.

The reports of the auditor and treasurer, which will be furnished to you hereafter, by those officers respectively, will exhibit the pleasing information, that the receipts of the treasury during the fiscal year ending with the 30th of September last, have considerably exceeded the amount at which they were estimated, either by the auditor or the committee of finance of the last general assembly; and that although the disbursements of the treasury during the same period have also exceeded the amount estimated for them, yet that the excess of the disbursements is less than that of the receipts. In consequence of this, you will find the balance remaining in the treasury on the 1st day of October last, greater than that which was there on the same day in the year 1834. This result, which plainly shews that the ordinary revenues of the commonwealth, are now amply sufficient to satisfy all its ordinary expenses, and that, therefore, no change in the present scheme of taxation is required, must be highly gratifying. An inspection too of the items composing the several heads of the disbursements, will probably satisfy you, that some of these may be still further reduced, with perfect propriety; while the natural increase to be expected in many of the subjects of taxation, will necessarily augment the amount of the ordinary revenue derived from thence, without any alteration in the present rate of the taxes.

It will be recollected, however, that the balance which remained in the treasury on the first day of October last, has been since reduced by the payment to the commissioners of the sinking fund of fifty thousand dollars. Should this appropriation be again continued, the annual balance in the treasury that may be hereafter expected, must necessarily be much diminished in amount. Indeed a similar appropriation for the current year, might possibly reduce that balance too low. I would, therefore, recommend, that the sum which may hereafter be applied to the sinking fund should not be defined, but should be made to depend upon the state of the public funds at the expiration of the fiscal year, taking care to reserve in the treasury always, a sufficient unappropriated surplus, to provide for probable emergencies.

The regulations prescribed by law for the government and discipline of the public guard stationed in this city, require revision and amendment; so far at least, as these regulations apply to courts martial for the trial of its officers. The number of members detailed for such duties, seems to be unnecessarily large; especially where all these are called from two particular regiments. The probable effect of this may be, that the character of the superior, will be committed, necessarily, to inferiors. Such a detail moreover, seems to imply a superiority and excellence in these two regiments over all the others, that is justified neither by the fact, nor in the theory of our military code. And if economy was consulted in prescribing this regulation, experience will shew, that even this object will not be attained by it.

Your attention is invited to this subject, as well as to the condition of the militia generally. The annual report of the adjutant general (which is herewith sent) will shew some of the defects of the present organization; and many others, requiring amendment, will probably be suggested by your own observation and experience. A provisional detachment of a portion of the militia, effected after the manner of the minute service of former times, would answer many useful purposes. Therefore, I beg leave to suggest such a scheme as worthy of your consideration.

Vacancies have occurred in several of the offices of the commonwealth, during the recess of the legislature, which it will be your duty to fill permanently. Except in cases where there existed a strong necessity for doing so, I have not exerted the power given by the constitution, to supply such vacancies. The death of the honourable James Semple, the judge of the fourth judicial circuit, occurring at the commencement of the autumnal sessions of the courts of this district, to prevent a delay in the administration of justice therein, I appointed John B. Christian, esq. the judge thereof, by a temporary commission. This, he accepted, and has ever since continued to perform the duties of that office.

The death of brigadier general William M'Coy has occasioned a vacancy in the eighteenth brigade, formerly commanded by this old officer, which it is necessary you should supply.

The duties that will devolve upon you, during the present session, may be both arduous and delicate; but you have brought with you the confidence of those you represent, which while it must serve to stimulate your efforts to advance and to secure their interests, will assure you of their honest approbation; the best reward a public agent can receive. Nothing will give me more pleasure than to co-operate with you, so far as I may, in the attainment of all such objects; and I beg leave to tender you for that purpose any aid in my power.

LITT'N W. TAZEWELL.

EXECUTIVE DEPARTMENT, December 7th, 1835.

On motion of Mr. Dorman, *Ordered*, That the same be laid upon the table.

On motion of Mr. Witcher, *Ordered*, That 500 copies of the said communication, and 185 copies of the accompanying documents, be printed for the use of the members of the general assembly.

The speaker also laid before the house two communications from the second auditor, transmitting in the one the accounts of the fund for internal improvement, for the year terminating the 30th September last, and the other the accounts for the literary fund for the same period, and statements relating to the transactions of the school commissioners of the preceding year; which, on motion of Mr. Garland of Amherst, were ordered to be laid upon the table, and that 185 copies thereof be printed for the use of the general assembly.

The speaker laid further before the house a communication from the auditor of public accounts, made in obedience to the several laws prescribing his official duties; which, on motion of Mr. Garland of Amherst, was ordered to be laid on the table, and that 185 copies be printed for the use of the general assembly.

The speaker laid before the house a communication from the treasurer, made in compliance with the several laws prescribing his duties; which was in like manner ordered to be laid upon the table and printed.

On motion of Mr. Garland of Amherst, *Resolved*, That when the house adjourns to-day, it will adjourn until to-morrow 12 o'clock.

And then, on his motion, the house adjourned accordingly.

TUESDAY, December 8th, 1835.

In compliance with the rules of the house, the speaker announced the following standing committees, viz:

A committee of privileges and elections, to be composed of Messrs. Holleman, Daniel, Wethered, Avent, Carrol, Servant, Bowen, Hooe, Harley, Craig, Mallory, Hargrave, and Hale of Franklin.

A committee for courts of justice, consisting of Messrs. Stanard, Booker, Dorman, Shands, Wilson of Botetourt, Berry, Summers, Woolfolk, Gilmer, Harrison, Leland, Hopkins and Austin.

A committee of schools and colleges, to be composed of Messrs. Garland of Mecklenburg, Southall, Cunningham, Randolph, Gregory, Hunter of Berkeley, Brooke, Hunter of Essex, Decamps, Leyburn, Garland of Amherst, Johnson and Ingles.

A committee of propositions and grievances, consisting of Messrs. Hill, Strange, Marteney, Rinker, Fontaine, Scott, Morgan, Nixon, Neill, Masters, Richardson, Samuel and Beuhring.

A committee of claims, to be composed of Messrs. Witcher, Christian, Bare, Sloan, Grinalds, Gibson, Spratley, Prentiss, Henshaw, Turnbull, Campbell, Straton and Conrad.

A committee of roads and internal navigation, to consist of Messrs. Watkins, Garland of Amherst, Miller, Murdaugh, Willey, Wilson of Cumberland, Kincheloe, Beard, Saunders, Hays, Dorman, Crutchfield, Chapman and Harris

A committee on the militia laws, consisting of Messrs. Parker, Smith of Frederick, Crutchfield, Ball, Kincheloe, Goodall, Carrington, and Wilson of Botetourt.

A committee of finance, to be composed of Messrs. Brown of Petersburg, Clay, Turnbull, Powell, Prentiss, Butts, Sherrard, M'Mullen, Griggs and Williams.

A committee to examine the penitentiary institution, to consist of Messrs. Hunter of Essex, Pate, Benton, Brown of Nelson, Hickerson, Critz and Morris.

A committee to examine the public armory; Messrs. Mallory, Waggener, Beard, Pate, Mullen, Almond, Watts, Williams, Nicklin, Jessee, Coleman and Fleet.

A committee to examine the executive expenditures for the current year; Messrs. Woolfolk, Smith of Gloucester, Steger, Rogers, Brown of Nelson, Fitzgerald, Dickinson and Hale of Grayson.

A committee to examine the first auditor's office; Messrs. Sherrard, Randolph, Smith of Fauquier, Taylor of Loudoun, Christian, Holland and Davison.

A committee to examine the second auditor's office; Messrs. Daniel, Swanson, Layne, Jett, Spratley, Gillespie and Delashmutt.

A committee to examine the clerk's office; Messrs. Christian, Layne, Taylor of Middlesex, Almond, Harley, Nicklin and Watts.

A committee to examine the register's office; Messrs. Summers, Mullen, Moncure, Rogers, Delashmutt, Cackley and Chapline.

A committee to act jointly with a committee from the senate to examine the treasurer's accounts; Messrs. Garland of Amherst, Johnson, Craig, Swanson, Harris, Leland and Powell.

A committee to examine the bonds of public officers; Messrs. Wethered, Servant, Robertson, Taylor of Middlesex, Goodall, M'Clintic and Morgan.

A committee to act jointly with a committee from the senate to examine the Bank of Virginia and Farmers bank of Virginia; Messrs. Carter, Brown of Petersburg, Cunningham, Cooke, Stanard, Moncure and Clay.

A committee to act jointly with a committee from the senate to examine the public library; Messrs. Brooke, Woolfolk, Wiley, Smith of Gloucester, Davison and Carter.

A committee of agriculture and manufactures; Messrs. Madison, Swanson, Drummond, Cackley, Hale of Grayson, Moffett, Henshaw, Chapline, Nicklin, Holland, Smith of Fauquier, Robertson and M'Clintic.

A committee to examine enrolled bills; Messrs. Mallory, Layne, Steger, Fleet, Butts, Samuel and Taylor of Loudoun.

On motion of Mr. Watkins, *Resolved*, That Hugh N. Pendleton be appointed clerk to the committees of roads and internal navigation, and of schools and colleges.

On motion of Mr. Woolfolk, *Resolved*, That Philip S. Fry be appointed clerk to the committee for courts of justice.

On motion of Mr. Strange, *Resolved*, That Thomas Vannerson be appointed clerk to the committees of propositions and grievances, and of finance.

On motion of Mr. Madison, *Resolved*, That Edward V. Sparhawk be appointed clerk to the committee of agriculture and manufactures.

On motion of Mr. Witcher, the appointment of clerk to the committees of privileges and elections, and of claims, was postponed until to-morrow.

Mr. Watkins presented the petition of Alexander Rives and Thomas J. Randolph, complaining of the undue election and return of Thomas W. Gilmer and Valentine W. Southall, the members from the county of Albemarle, and claiming the right to their seats.

Also, a petition of Isaac Adams, complaining of the undue election and return of Haman Critz, the member for the county of Patrick.

Mr. Stanard presented a petition of John M. Botts, complaining of the undue election of William B. Randolph, the member returned from the county of Henrico.

Mr. Wethered, a petition of Samuel Price, contesting the election of Hudson M. Dickinson, the returned member from the counties of Fayette and Nicholas.

Ordered, That the said petitions be referred to the committee of privileges and elections, that they do examine the matter thereof and report their opinion thereupon to the house.

Mr. Cunningham presented a memorial of the citizens of the borough of Norfolk, for the incorporation of a bank, to be established in the said borough, with liberty to establish one or more branches between the James and Roanoke rivers, which, on his motion, was ordered to be referred to a committee of Messrs. Cunningham, Murdaugh, Cooke, Parker, Rogers, Madison, Servant, Gregory, Holleman, Brown of Petersburg, and Shands, with leave to report thereon by bill or otherwise.

Mr. Murdaugh presented a petition of the citizens of the town of Portsmouth, asking for the establishment of a bank in said town, with the privilege of establishing branches on the line of the Roanoke navigation.

Mr. Madison, a petition of the citizens of the town of Farmville, for the establishment of a bank, or for the location of a branch of one of the present banks in said town.

Mr. Moncure, a petition of the citizens of the towns of Falmouth and Fredericksburg, and of the adjacent counties, asking for a bank or branch of one of the existing banks in the town of Falmouth.

Ordered, That the said petitions be referred to the committee to whom the memorial from the citizens of Norfolk, on the same subject, was referred.

Mr. Murdaugh also presented a petition of the Portsmouth and Roanoke rail-road company, for an increase in the amount of their capital stock, or for authority to borrow money on the credit of their existing capital.

Mr. Sloan, a petition of sundry citizens of the county of Hampshire, for a reduction of the tolls now allowed on the North-western turnpike road, and for other amendments to the charter of the company.

Mr. Mullen, a similar petition of sundry citizens of the county of Frederick.

Mr. Witcher presented a petition of the counties of Wythe, Floyd, Patrick, Henry, Franklin, Pittsylvania, Halifax, the towns of Petersburg, Portsmouth and Danville, and the borough of Norfolk, for a rail-road from Evansham in Wythe county, to the town of Danville in Pittsylvania, and thence to such place as may best secure the advantages of the Petersburg and Roanoke, Portsmouth and Roanoke, and Greensville and Roanoke rail-roads.

Mr. Garland of Mecklenburg, a petition of sundry citizens of the county of Mecklenburg, for the passage of laws to regulate the conduct of boatmen on the waters of the Roanoke river.

Mr. Holland, a petition of William Brown, to be allowed to increase the height of his mill-dam in the county of Franklin.

Ordered, That the said petitions be referred to the committee of roads and internal navigation, that they do examine the matter thereof, and report their opinion thereupon to the house.

Mr. Mullen presented a petition of Charlotte, a free woman of colour, asking to be permitted to remain in the commonwealth for a limited period, which was ordered to be referred to the committee for courts of justice, that they do examine the matter thereof, and report their opinion thereupon to the house.

Mr. Harley presented a petition of the school commissioners of the county of Smyth, praying that a law be passed authorizing the said commissioners to receive the quota due said county from the literary fund, which was ordered to be referred to the committee of schools and colleges, that they do examine the matter thereof, and report their opinion thereupon to the house.

Mr. Bare presented a petition of sundry citizens of the counties of Shenandoah and Frederick, asking for the formation of a new county out of parts of said counties.

Mr. Hunter of Berkeley, a petition of sundry citizens of the county of Berkeley, asking to change the place of holding a separate election from Robinson's mill to Lewis Grantham's school-house in said county.

Mr. Brown of Nelson, a petition of citizens of the county of Nelson, for the establishment of a separate election at Greenfield in said county.

Ordered, That the said petitions be referred to the committee of propositions and grievances, that they do examine the matter thereof, and report their opinion thereupon to the house.

Mr. Carter presented a petition of Joseph Palmer, administrator of Dominie Bennehan, deceased, praying that a sum of money recovered against the estate of his decedent, as security of David Greenlaw upon a forfeited recognizance, may be refunded to him, which was ordered to be referred to the committee of claims, that they do examine the matter thereof, and report their opinion thereupon to the house.

On motion of Mr. Johnson, *Ordered*, That leave be given to bring in a bill to amend an act, entitled, "an act to incorporate the Midlothian coal mining company," passed January 23d, 1835, and that Messrs. Johnson, Brown of Petersburg, Fitzgerald, Wiley, Hopkins, Holleman and Scott, prepare and bring in the same.

On motion of Mr. Fontaine, *Resolved*, That the committee of propositions and grievances be instructed to enquire into the expediency of establishing a separate election at the house of William Pulliam in the county of Henry, and that the said committee have leave to report by bill or otherwise.

On motion of Mr. Crutchfield, *Resolved*, That the committee of roads and internal navigation be instructed to enquire into the expediency of chartering a joint stock company to construct a rail-road from Fredericksburg to the eastern base of the Blue Ridge, or to some point in the valley, and that they report by bill or otherwise.

On motion of Mr. Murdaugh, *Resolved*, That a committee of twenty-one be raised on the subject of increasing the banking capital of this commonwealth, and that said committee take charge of all applications on that subject.

The speaker deferred announcing the said committee until to-morrow.

On motion of Shands, *Resolved*, That this house will, on Thursday the 10th instant, proceed by joint vote with the senate to the election of a public printer for one year.

Ordered, That the clerk communicate the same to the senate and request their concurrence.

Mr. Brown of Petersburg, presented a petition of sundry citizens of the town of Petersburg and its vicinity, for the passage of an act to incorporate the Ettrick Banks manufacturing company, which was ordered to be referred to the committee of agriculture and manufactures, that they do examine the matter thereof, and report their opinion thereupon to the house.

Also a petition of other citizens, merchants of said town, praying that the license tax on retail merchants may be graduated according to the extent of their capital and business, which was ordered to be referred to the committee of finance, that they do examine the matter thereof, and report their opinion thereupon to the house.

On motion of Mr. Hunter of Berkeley, the house adjourned until to-morrow 12 o'clock.

WEDNESDAY, December 9th, 1835.

In compliance with the resolution adopted on yesterday "on the subject of increasing the banking capital of the commonwealth," the speaker announced the following committee: Messrs. Carter, Murdaugh, Cunningham, Cooke, Madison, Stanard, Brown of Petersburg, Gilmer, Miller, Moncure, Craig, Hickerson, Carrington, Witcher, Parker, Steger, Griggs, Rogers, Daniel, Davison and Summers.

On motion of Mr. Brooke, *Ordered*, That leave be given to bring in a bill to amend an act, entitled, "an act to incorporate the Staunton and Potomac rail-road company," passed March 22d, 1831, and that Messrs. Brooke, Craig, Moffett, Almond, Bare, Hunter of Berkeley, Berry, Griggs, M'Coy, and Smith of Frederick, prepare and bring in the same.

On motion of Mr. Fontaine, *Resolved*, That the committee of schools and colleges be instructed to enquire into the expediency of incorporating the Martinsville academy, in the county of Henry, and that they have leave to report thereon by bill or otherwise.

On motion of Mr. Garland of Mecklenburg, *Resolved*, That so much of the governor's message as relates to the disorganizing, seditious and incendiary doctrines of certain associations created in the northern and eastern states for the purpose of producing a direct interference with the slave property of the south, and which assert a right in the United States to interfere with our property in various other modes, be referred to a select committee: that said committee be instructed to take also under consideration the sufficiency of the several acts of assembly intended to prevent or punish any threatened disturbance of the public peace within this commonwealth; and that they have leave to report by bill or otherwise.

And a committee was appointed of Messrs. Garland of Mecklenburg, Gilmer, Dorman, Hunter of Berkeley, Stanard, Wilson of Botetourt, Booker, Brown of Petersburg, Bowen, Parker, Hopkins, Holleman and Steger.

On motion of Mr. Moffett, *Ordered*, That leave be given to bring in a bill to amend the act, entitled, "an act establishing the town of Mount Crawford and for appointing trustees thereof," passed the 8th of January, 1825, and that Messrs. Moffett, Conrad, M'Coy, Brooke, Leyburn, Smith of Frederick, and M'Clintic, prepare and bring in the same.

On motion of Mr. Dorman, *Resolved*, That the committee of roads and internal navigation be instructed to enquire into the expediency of incorporating a joint stock company to construct a turnpike road from the town of Lexington, in the county of Rockbridge, to the city of Richmond; and that said committee have leave to report by bill or otherwise.

On motion of Mr. Clay, *Ordered*, That leave be given to bring in a bill to revive the inspection of tobacco at Spring warehouse, in the town of Lynchburg, and that Messrs. Clay, Daniel, Campbell, Pate, Garland of Amherst, Brown of Nelson, and Wiley, prepare and bring in the same.

On motion of Mr. Woolfolk, *Resolved*, That Joshua W. Fry be appointed clerk to the committees of privileges and elections, and of claims.

On motion of Mr. Harrison, *Resolved*, That the committee for courts of justice enquire into the expediency of so amending the act against fraudulent devises, as to subject lands and tenements devised to the contracts of the devisor in the same, and to the same extent, that lands and tenements descended are to the contracts of the ancestor, and that the said committee have leave to report by bill or otherwise.

On motion of Mr. Hunter of Berkeley, *Ordered*, That leave be given to bring in a bill to amend an act, passed March 5th, 1835, entitled, "an act to limit the assessment upon titheables, and to authorize a tax upon property, for the purpose of defraying county expenditures within the county of Berkeley," and that Messrs. Hunter of Berkeley, Henshaw, Berry, Nixon, Griggs, Sloan, and Smith of Frederick, prepare and bring in the same.

On motion of Mr. Booker, *Resolved*, That the committee for courts of justice enquire into the expediency of reducing the costs incident to the collection of money recovered by judgments and decrees, and that they report by bill or otherwise.

On motion of Mr. Smith of Gloucester, *Resolved*, That this house will, by joint vote with the senate, proceed on Saturday next, to elect a judge, to supply the vacancy occasioned by the death of the late judge James Semple, in the second district and fourth circuit.

Ordered, That the clerk communicate the same to the senate and request their concurrence.

On motion of Mr. Smith of Frederick, *Resolved*, That the committee upon the militia laws be instructed to bring in a bill explanatory of the 99th section of the act, entitled, "an act for the better organization of militia," passed March 8th, 1834.

On motion of Mr. Murdaugh, the same being amended on motion of Mr. Madison, *Ordered*, That the select committee to whom was referred on yesterday sundry petitions for establishing banks, be discharged from the consideration thereof, and that the same be referred to the general committee on the subject of banks, announced on to-day, that they do examine the matter thereof, and report their opinion thereupon to the house.

On motion of Mr. Watkins, *Resolved*, That the committee of privileges and elections be instructed to take into consideration on to-morrow, the several petitions referred to that committee contesting the elections of members returned to serve in this house.

On motion of Mr. Woolfolk, *Resolved*, That the committee for courts of justice be instructed to enquire into the expediency of providing by law for the removal of all persons confined in any county on any criminal charge, to any adjoining county, in cases where the jail of the county in which such persons are confined has been destroyed by fire or other accident, with leave to report by bill or otherwise.

Mr. Willey presented a petition of citizens of the town of Grandville, in the county of Monongalia, asking amendments to the act incorporating said town.

Mr. Griggs, a petition of citizens of the county of Frederick, asking for the formation of a new county from the eastern part of said county.

Mr. Carroll, a petition of citizens of the county of Preston, to change the place of holding the separate election held at the house of Isaac Criss, in said county.

Mr. Madison, a petition of the trustees of the town of Farmville, for the passage of an act extending the limits of said town, and vesting them with certain powers in relation thereto.

Mr. Powell, a petition of Ann M. Tutt, asking to be allowed the privilege of disposing of her property by a lottery.

Ordered, That the said petitions be referred to the committee of propositions and grievances, that they do examine the matter thereof, and report their opinion thereupon to the house.

Mr. Willey presented a petition of sundry inhabitants of the county of Monongalia, for the passage of a law authorizing the engineer of the state to make certain surveys and locations of roads in the counties of Monongalia and Preston.

Mr. Daniel a petition of citizens of the town of Lynchburg for the incorporation of a company for the construction of a rail-road from the town of Lynchburg, by Buford's gap in the Blue Ridge of mountains to some point on the Tennessee line.

Mr. M'Mullen, a petition of citizens of the county of Scott, to incorporate a company for the purpose of constructing a rail-road from some point on James river, to some point on the Tennessee line.

Mr. Hopkins, a petition of sundry citizens of the county of Powhatan, Cumberland and Amelia, for the incorporation of a company for the improvement of the Little and Big Deep creeks, from the Bellnemus mills in the county of Powhatan, to James river.

Mr. Harrison, a petition of Jesse Sturm, for the passage of an act, granting him leave to erect a mill dam across the west fork of the Monongalia river in the county of Harrison.

Mr. Moffett, a petition of citizens of the counties of Hardy and Rockingham, asking an appropriation from the treasury, to assist in constructing a road across the Shenandoah mountain in the counties of Rockingham and Hardy.

Mr. Daniel, a petition of citizens of the counties of Bedford and Campbell, for the incorporation of a company to construct a rail-road from Lynchburg to the Tennessee line, and for the privilege of extending the same to the city of Richmond, or that the same privilege may be granted to the James river and Kanawha company.

Ordered, That the said petitions be referred to the committee of roads and internal navigation, that they do examine the matter thereof, and report their opinion thereupon to the house.

Mr. Daniel also presented a petition of Milly Cooper for the relinquishment to her of the commonwealth's right in the estate of her son Archer Cooper, who died while confined in the lunatic hospital at Williamsburg.

Mr. Prentiss, a petition of George Johnson, asking to be relieved from the payment of certain fines and penalties imposed on him on a charge of unlawful gaming.

Mr. Hickerson, a petition of Berkeley Ward, asking to be relieved from the payment of a fine imposed on him by the superiour court of Fauquier county, for an alleged contempt of court, in failing to attend in the court-house to open court and execute its orders, and preserve order, or to have a deputy in the court-house to do the same.

Ordered, That the said petitions be referred to the committee of claims, that they do examine the matter thereof, and report their opinion thereupon to the house.

Mr. Daniel also presented a petition of Daniel Higginbotham, a free man of colour, and of citizens of the town of Lynchburg in his behalf, asking permission for him to remain in the commonwealth a limited time.

Mr. Brown of Petersburg, a petition of James Martin and others, praying that he may be authorized to hold certain real estate in anticipation of his becoming a naturalized citizen.

Mr. Moncure, a petition of Duff Green, praying the passage of a law discharging him from any liability under a bond executed by him to the executive, for arms furnished a rifle company under his command, the said arms having been accidentally partially destroyed by fire.

Mr. Murdaugh, petitions of Thomas Culpeper, and of Joseph Bailey, each praying to be divorced from his wife.

Ordered, That the said petitions be referred to the committee for courts of justice, that they do examine the matter thereof, and report their opinion thereupon to the house.

Mr. Davison presented a petition of the trustees of the Newtown and Stephensburg academy, asking an appropriation from the literary fund to relieve the academy from a debt, and to provide a salary for a teacher, which was ordered to be referred to the committee of schools and colleges, that they do examine the matter thereof, and report their opinion thereupon to the house.

Mr. Brown of Petersburg, presented a petition of sundry citizens of Petersburg and its vicinity, praying for the passage of an act to incorporate the Fleets manufacturing company, which was ordered to be referred to the committee of agriculture and manufactures, that they do examine the matter thereof, and report their opinion thereupon to the house.

Mr. Brown of Petersburg, also presented a petition of other citizens of said town, praying the passage of an act incorporating a company to run a line of packets between the said town and the city of New York, which was ordered to be referred to the committee of propositions and grievances, that they do examine the matter thereof, and report their opinion thereupon to the house.

Mr. Conrad presented a petition of the officers of the 58th regiment of militia, for a repeal of the act forming the 145th regiment, out of parts of the 58th and 116th regiments, in the county of Rockingham.

Mr. Carroll, a petition of citizens of the county of Preston, praying the formation of a new regiment out of the 114th regiment.

Mr. Powell presented a communication from the court of enquiry of the 132d regiment, for an amendment in the militia laws, providing for a battalion muster in the fall, in lieu of the October company muster now prescribed by law.

Ordered, That the said petitions and communication be referred to the committee on the militia laws, that they do examine the matter thereof, and report their opinion thereupon to the house.

Mr. Crutchfield presented a petition from citizens of the town of Fredericksburg, asking for the establishment of a bank in said town, which was ordered to be referred to the select committee on the subject of banks.

On motion of Mr. Gregory, the house adjourned until to-morrow 12 o'clock.

THURSDAY, December 10th, 1835.

A communication from the senate by their clerk:

IN SENATE, December 9th, 1835.

The senate have agreed to the resolution for proceeding on Thursday the 10th inst. to the election of a public printer.

On motion of Mr. Shands, the house proceeded to the execution of the joint order of the day for the election of public printer; whereupon, he nominated Thomas Ritchie, and Mr. Stanard nominated Samuel Shepherd; and the senate having been informed thereof by Mr. Shands, and no person being added to the nomination in that house, the names of the members were called by the clerk, when the vote was, for Ritchie 76, for Shepherd 55.

The names of the gentlemen who voted for Mr. Ritchie, are Messrs. Banks, (speaker,) Layne, Wiley, M'Clintic, Miller, Wilson of Botetourt, Decamps, Turnbull, Mallory, Booker, Austin, Clay, Daniel, Samuel, Richardson, Hill, Smith of Fauquier, Hickerson, Strange, Steger, Holland, Bowen, Davison, Watts, Watkins, Hail of Grayson, Avent, Carrington, Coleman, Sloan, Nixon, Goodall, Harrison, Kincheloe, Randolph, Fontaine, Holleman, Robinson, Hays, Straton, Harris, Ragsdale, Taylor of Mathews and Middlesex, Rogers, Garland of Mecklenburg, Willey, Morgan, Chapman, Sherrard, Brown of Nelson, Leland, Fitzgerald, Woolfolk, Almond, M'Coy, Cackley, Hopkins, Carroll, Madison, Shands, Williams, Marteney, Nicklin, Moffett, Conrad, Jessee, M'Mullen, Bare, Rinker, Harley, Crutchfield, Moncure, Spratley, Hargrave, Gillespie and Gibson—76.

The names of the gentlemen who voted for Mr. Shepherd, are Messrs. Grinalds, Drummond, Gilmer, Garland of Amherst, Brooke, Craig, Campbell, Pate, Hunter of Berkeley, Henshaw, Beuhring, Christian, Johnson, Servant, Hunter of Essex, Ball, Dickinson, Hale of Franklin, Smith of Frederick, Smith of Gloucester, Wethered, Mullen, Gregory, Griggs, Berry, Summers, Fleet, Hoce, Carter, Neill, Beard, Powell, Taylor of Loudoun, Waggener, Ingles, Benton, Murdaugh, Cooke, Parker, Chapline, Masters, Critz, Swanson, Witcher, Morris, Dorman, Leyburn, Butts, Delashmutt, Jett, Prentiss, Saunders, Cunningham, Brown of Petersburg, and Stanard—55.

Ordered, That Messrs. Shands, Stanard, Brown of Petersburg, Gilmer, Gregory, Powell, Witcher, Holleman, Parker, Watkins, Dorman and Prentiss, be a committee to act jointly with a committee from the senate, to ascertain the state of the joint vote; the committee then withdrew, and after some time returned into the house, and Mr. Shands reported that they had, according to order, ascertained the joint vote to be, for Ritchie 95, Shepherd 68; whereupon, Thomas Ritchie was declared duly elected public printer for one year.

Mr. Holleman presented sundry documents to be used as evidence in the contested elections from the counties of Albemarle and Henrico.

Mr. Wethered, documents to be used as evidence in the contested election from the counties of Fayette and Nicholas.

Ordered, That the same be referred to the committee of privileges and elections.

On motion of Mr. Holleman, *Resolved*, That authority be granted to the committee of privileges and elections, to send for persons and papers, in relation to the several contested elections before the said committee.

Mr. Watkins, from the committee of roads and internal navigation, presented a report upon the petitions of the Portsmouth and Roanoke rail-road company; of William Brown; of citizens of the counties of Monongalia, and of Powhatan, which was received and laid upon the table.

On motion of Mr. Leland, the house adjourned until to-morrow 12 o'clock.

FRIDAY, December 11th, 1835.

A communication from the senate by their clerk:

IN SENATE, December 10th, 1835.

The senate have appointed committees to act jointly with committees from the house of delegates, to examine the penitentiary institution, the armory, the treasurer's accounts, the Bank of Virginia and Farmers bank of Virginia, and the public library.

On motion of Mr. Moncure, *Ordered,* That leave be given to bring in a bill to incorporate the Falmouth mining company; and also, a bill to incorporate the Deep run mining company, and that Messrs. Moncure, Crutchfield, Hooe, Williams, Leland, Hill, Woolfolk, Harris and Nicklin, prepare and bring in the same.

On motion of Mr. Gregory, *Ordered,* That leave be given to bring in a bill to change the time of holding the courts in the third judicial circuit; and a bill to reorganize the first and second judicial districts of the circuit superior courts of law and chancery, and that Messrs. Gregory, Servant, Christian, Smith of Gloucester, Fleet, Robinson, Stanard, Murdaugh, Cunningham, Parker and Grinalds, prepare and bring in the same.

On motion of Mr. Parker, *Resolved,* That so much of the governor's message as relates to the militia, be referred to the committee on the militia laws.

On motion of Mr. Summers, *Resolved,* That the committee for courts of justice be instructed to enquire into the expediency of so amending the 5th section of the act, entitled, "an act for the limitation of actions, &c." passed February 25th, 1819, as to limit recoveries on judgments rendered in the courts of other states, in like manner, and to the same extent, that the remedies on judgments pronounced in the courts of this commonwealth are thereby limited, and that said committee have leave to report by bill or otherwise.

On motion of Mr. Fontaine, *Resolved,* That the committee of roads and internal navigation be instructed to enquire into the expediency of so amending the act incorporating the Smith's river navigation company, as to extend to the said company the benefit of the state subscription for stock, on the same conditions as is provided by law in similar cases, and that they have leave to report by bill or otherwise.

On motion of Mr. Shands, *Resolved,* That the executive council be requested to lay the journal of their proceedings for the last year before the general assembly.

On motion of Mr. Hickerson, *Resolved,* That the committee for courts of justice be instructed to enquire into the expediency of so amending the act, entitled, "an act requiring the clerks of the county and corporation courts to keep process books," passed the 11th day of March, 1835, as to authorize the clerks of the courts aforesaid to charge for such services the same fees which the clerks of the circuit superior courts of law and chancery are authorized to charge for similar services.

On motion of Mr. Hickerson, *Resolved,* That the committee for courts of justice be instructed to enquire into the expediency of extending magistrates' jurisdiction, and into the expediency of amending the several laws relating to constables.

On motion of Mr. Harris, *Resolved,* That the committee of roads and internal navigation be instructed to enquire into the expediency of incorporating a joint stock company to construct a rail-road from some point on the Richmond, Fredericksburg and Potomac rail-road, near Taylorsville, in Hanover county, by way of Louisa court-house, to some point, at or near the eastern base of the South-west mountains, in Orange county, and that they have leave to report by bill or otherwise.

On motion of Mr. Delashmutt, *Resolved,* That the committee of roads and internal navigation be instructed to enquire into the expediency of providing by law for the construction of a road from a point on the North-western turnpike, near the town of Clarksburg, in the county of Harrison, to Middlebourne, in the county of Tyler, and that they have leave to report by bill or otherwise.

On motion of Mr. Kincheloe, *Resolved,* That the committee of roads and internal navigation be instructed to enquire into the expediency of providing by law for the construction of a road from Wheeling to Clarksburg on the route designated by the engineer employed to survey the same, in pursuance of the resolution of the 27th of February, 1833; also to enquire into the expediency of constructing a road in like manner, from Clarksburg to Beverley, with leave to report by bill or otherwise.

Mr. M'Clintic presented a petition of sundry citizens of the county of Bath, asking the passage of an act giving the power to the court of said county to prescribe the location of a toll-gate upon the Huntersville and Warm spring turnpike road, or to prohibit the erection of a toll-gate on the eastern end of the said road in said county.

Mr. Ingles, a petition of sundry citizens of the county of Montgomery, asking to incorporate a company for the purpose of constructing a rail-road from the town of Lynchburg, by Buford's gap in the Blue Ridge of mountains, to some point on the Tennessee line.

Mr. Chapman, a petition of citizens of the county of Monroe, praying that a sum of money heretofore raised by lottery in said county may be invested in the stock of the company incorporated for the purpose of constructing a turnpike road from the White Sulphur springs in the county of Greenbrier, to the Salt Sulphur springs in the county of Monroe.

Also, petitions of John Shaver and others, and of William Booth and others, each praying the passage of acts allowing them to construct a road across the Sweet Springs and Price's mountains.

Mr. Ball presented a petition of sundry citizens of the county of Fairfax, praying a change in the rates of toll allowed upon the Little river turnpike road, so far as it relates to the county of Fairfax.

Ordered, That the said petitions be referred to the committee of roads and internal navigation, that they do examine the matter thereof, and report their opinion thereupon to the house.

Mr. Beard presented a petition of the officers of the 56th regiment, asking the passage of an act amending the law concerning the militia so as to restore the battalion musters.

Also, a resolution adopted by the regimental court of enquiry for the 57th regiment, asking the substitution of a battalion muster in the fall in lieu of the company muster now required by law to be held in the month of October.

Ordered, That the said petition and resolution be referred to the committee on the militia laws, that they do examine the matter thereof, and report their opinion thereupon to the house.

Mr. Woolfolk presented sundry documents to be used as evidence in the contested election from the district composed of the counties of Nicholas and Fayette.

Mr. Holleman presented documents to be used as evidence in the contested election from the county of Henrico.

Ordered, That the said documents be referred to the committee of privileges and elections.

Mr. Chapline presented a petition of the proprietors, lot holders and others of certain additions to the town of Wheeling, asking that the limits of said town may be extended so as to embrace the said additions, which on his motion was ordered to be referred to a committee of Messrs. Chapline, Masters, Decamps, Prentiss, Summers, Carroll and Willey, with leave to report thereon by bill or otherwise.

Mr. Ingles presented a petition of Celinda C. Wallace, praying to be divorced from her husband.

Mr. Mallory, a petition of James Haskins, committee of John Haskins, an insane person, asking the passage of an act authorizing a sale of the estate of the said Haskins.

Mr. Gilmer, a petition of Stephen, a free man of colour, and of sundry citizens of the county of Albemarle, in his favour, asking that he may be permitted to remain in the commonwealth.

Mr. Ball, a petition of Judy Johnson, a free woman of colour, for similar permission.

Mr. Mullen presented a petition of William Fisher, asking the relinquishment of the commonwealth's right to a tract of land in the county of Nicholas.

Ordered, That the said petitions be referred to the committee for courts of justice, that they do examine the matter thereof, and report their opinion thereupon to the house.

Mr. Moncure presented a petition of sundry citizens of the county of Stafford, for the establishment of a separate election at the store-house near the mill called Tackett's mill, in said county.

Mr. Chapline, a petition of sundry inhabitants of the county of Ohio, praying that the county court of said county may be authorized to select a suitable site within the town of Wheeling, or its additions, for the erection of a court-house, and other necessary buildings; also, sundry memorials in opposition to the prayer of said petition.

Mr. Saunders, a petition of citizens of the county of Wythe, asking to change the place of holding a separate election in the said county.

Mr. Beard, a petition of Noble S. Braden, and Fleming Hixon, praying for an act of incorporation authorizing them to erect a toll bridge across the Shenandoah river at Harper's ferry.

Mr. Carroll, petitions of citizens of the county of Preston, praying the passage of an act prohibiting farmers from other states from driving and herding stock in the county of Preston.

Mr. Morgan, a petition of sundry inhabitants of the county of Monongalia, to change the place of holding a separate election in said county.

Mr. Marteney presented a memorial of other citizens of said county, remonstrating against the prayer of the said petition.

Ordered, That the said petitions be referred to the committee of propositions and grievances, that they do examine the matter thereof, and report their opinion thereupon to the house.

Mr. Decamps presented a petition of Ephraim Wells, praying that the amount of certain taxes erroneously assessed against and paid by him for a number of years, may be refunded him.

Mr. Masters, a petition of Christopher Parriott and others, that the compensation allowed the commissioners of the revenue for the county of Marshall may be increased.

Ordered, That the said petitions be referred to the committee of finance, that they do examine the matter thereof, and report their opinion thereupon to the house.

Mr. Decamps also presented a petition of the trustees of the Brooke academy, in the county of Brooke, praying for an endowment of that institution from the literary fund, which was ordered to be referred to the committee of schools and colleges, that they do examine the matter thereof, and report their opinion thereupon to the house.

Mr. Campbell presented a petition of sundry citizens of the county of Bedford, for the pardon and release of Anderson Reed, a convict in the state penitentiary, which was ordered to be referred to the committee on the penitentiary institution, that they do examine the matter thereof, and report their opinion thereupon to the house.

Mr. Marteney presented a petition of sundry citizens of the counties of Preston and Randolph, for the passage of an act authorizing the survey and location of a road from the German settlement in the county of Preston, to the town of Beverley, in the county of Randolph.

Mr. Carroll presented a similar petition of other citizens of the said counties.

Ordered, That the said petitions be referred to the committee of roads and internal navigation, that they do examine the matter thereof, and report their opinion thereupon to the house.

A message from the senate by Mr. Page:

Mr. Speaker,—The senate have agreed to the resolution for the election of a judge in the fourth circuit, with an amendment, in which they request the concurrence of this house: And then he withdrew.

The said amendment proposed to postpone the said election from "Saturday next," until "the second Monday in January." The same being read,

On motion of Mr. Parker, it was amended, by striking out the words "the second Monday in January," and inserting in lieu thereof, the words "Monday week next," and as amended, was agreed to by the house.

Ordered, That the clerk inform the senate thereof and request their concurrence in the said amendment.

A report of the committee of roads and internal navigation, was taken up and read as follows:

The committee of roads and internal navigation have, according to order, had under consideration sundry petitions to them referred, and have come to the following resolutions thereupon:

1. *Resolved as the opinion of this committee,* That the petition of the president and directors of the Portsmouth and Roanoke rail-road company, praying that authority be given the said company to increase its capital stock, not exceeding one hundred and fifty thousand dollars, or to borrow an amount not exceeding that sum, on the credit of its existing capital, is reasonable.

2. *Resolved as the opinion of this committee,* That the petition of William Brown, senior, of the county of Franklin, praying the passage of an act authorizing the county court of said county to allow the petitioner to raise his mill dam across Blackwater river, one foot above its present elevation, and guarding the rights and privileges of individuals and corporate bodies, is reasonable.

3. *Resolved as the opinion of this committee,* That the petition of sundry citizens of the county of Monongalia, praying that the engineer of the state be authorized to locate a road from the Pennsylvania line, near the farm of Bushrod Hoge, by Morgantown, to some suitable point on the North-western turnpike, west of Cheat river; and also to locate a road from Morgantown to the Pennsylvania line, in the direction of Uniontown or Monroe, is reasonable.

4. *Resolved as the opinion of this committee,* That the memorial of sundry citizens of the counties of Powhatan and others, praying the incorporation of a company to improve the navigation of Little and Big Deep creeks, from the Bellnemus mills in Powhatan, to James river, by means of locks and dams, so as not to flow the water out of the natural channels, is reasonable.

The said resolutions were, on questions severally put thereupon, agreed to by the house, and bills were ordered to be brought in conformably therewith.

Mr. Watkins, from the committee of roads and internal navigation, presented a report, which was read as follows:

The committee of roads and internal navigation have, according to order, had under consideration sundry petitions to them referred, and have come to the following resolutions thereupon:

1. *Resolved as the opinion of this committee,* That the petition of sundry citizens of the county of Mecklenburg, praying that for the purpose of regulating the conduct of boatmen on the waters of the Roanoke river, an act be passed similar to the act passed February 9th, 1811, entitled, "an act to amend an act, entitled, 'an act for regulating the navigation of James river above the falls of the said river,'" with such amendments and alterations as may be suitable to the said Roanoke river, is reasonable.

2. *Resolved as the opinion of this committee,* That the petition of sundry citizens of the county of Harrison, praying that Jessee Sturm, of said county, be authorized by law to erect a mill dam across the west fork of Monongalia river, at the riffle immediately below the mouth of Feverbaugh creek, is reasonable.

3. *Resolved as the opinion of this committee,* That the petition of sundry citizens of the counties of Bedford, Campbell and Scott, and of the town of Lynchburg, praying that a joint stock company be incorporated for the purpose of constructing a rail-road from the town of Lynchburg, by Buford's gap, to such point on the Tennessee line as may serve to unite said road with such rail-road as the legislature of Tennessee may authorize to be formed from Nashville to the Virginia line, with the privilege to said company, or to the James river and Kanawha company, of extending a similar road from Lynchburg to the city of Richmond, so as to unite with the Richmond and Fredericksburg rail-road, is reasonable.

4. *Resolved as the opinion of this committee,* That the petition of sundry citizens of the counties of Wythe, Floyd, Patrick, Henry, Franklin, Pittsylvania and Halifax, of the towns of Petersburg, Portsmouth and Danville, and of the borough of Norfolk, praying the passage of an act to incorporate a joint stock company, with a capital of two millions of dollars, for the purpose of constructing a rail-road from the town of Evansham in the county of Wythe, by Danville in Virginia, through a portion of the territory of North Carolina on the Roanoke river, and intersecting the Petersburg and Roanoke, the Portsmouth and Roanoke, and the Greensville and Roanoke rail-roads, or to some point that may best secure to said route all the advantages of said rail-roads, is reasonable.

The said committee have also, according to order, enquired "into the expediency of incorporating a joint stock company to construct a turnpike road from the town of Lexington in the county of Rockbridge, to the city of Richmond:" Whereupon,

Resolved as the opinion of this committee, That it is expedient to incorporate a company for said purpose.

The said resolutions were, on questions severally put thereupon, agreed to by the house, and bills were ordered to be brought in conformably therewith.

Mr. Clay, according to order, presented a bill to revive the inspection of tobacco at Spring warehouse in the town of Lynchburg, which was read the first and ordered to be read a second time.

On motion of Mr. Daniel, *Resolved,* That the president and directors of the Bank of Virginia, and the president and directors of the Farmers bank of Virginia, be requested to prepare and furnish to this house a statement shewing the annual dividends declared by them on their capital stock since the dates of their respective incorporation; also the number, places and dates of the different branch banks located by each of them, and the amount of capital entrusted to, and the nett annual profits made by each of said branch banks since their establishment.

On motion of Mr. Holleman, *Ordered,* That he be excused from serving upon the committee to whom was referred so much of the governor's message as relates to the interference of certain societies in the northern states with the slave population of the south; and Mr. Coleman was ordered to be substituted in his stead, as a member of said committee.

On motion of Mr. Mullen, the house adjourned until to-morrow 12 o'clock.

SATURDAY, December 12th, 1835.

On motion of Mr. Garland of Mecklenburg, *Resolved*, That a committee be raised to collect and have printed for the use of the members of the general assembly, the proceedings of the meetings in the several counties on the subject of the proposed interference of the northern fanatics in the slave property of the south; that they also have collected and published such parts of proceedings in the non-slaveholding states, and of governor's messages which relate to the same subject.

And a committee was appointed of Messrs. Brown of Petersburg, Sherrard, Woolfolk, Garland of Mecklenburg, Turnbull, Harley, Clay, Austin, Brooke, Chapline and Madison.

On motion of Mr. Garland of Mecklenburg, *Resolved*, That the documents referred to in the governor's message, on the subject of the abolition of slavery, now in the executive department, be referred to the select committee on that subject.

On motion of Mr. Carter, *Resolved*, That so much of the governor's message as relates to the banking capital and currency of the commonwealth, be referred to the select committee on the subject of increasing the banking capital of this commonwealth.

On motion of Mr. Davison, *Resolved*, That the committee of roads and internal navigation be instructed to enquire into the expediency of extending the North-western turnpike road from the town of Winchester in the county of Frederick, to the termination of the Berryville turnpike at Berryville in said county, and that said committee have leave to report by bill or otherwise.

On motion of Mr. Smith of Fauquier, *Ordered*, That leave be given to bring in a bill to amend an act, entitled, "an act incorporating the Falmouth and Alexandria rail-road company," passed March the 9th, 1835, and that Messrs. Smith of Fauquier, Hickerson, Williams, Moncure, Powell, Beard, Hooe and Ball, prepare and bring in the same.

On motion of Mr. Holleman, *Ordered*, That the committee of privileges and elections have leave to sit during the session of this house.

On motion of Mr. Watkins, *Ordered*, That the committee of roads and internal navigation be discharged from the consideration of so much of the petition of sundry citizens of the counties of Preston and Randolph, as has not been acted upon by the said committee, and that the same be laid upon the table.

The speaker laid before the house a communication from John H. Smith, commissioner of revolutionary claims, transmitting "a report of his proceedings during the present year, as commissioner of revolutionary claims, and sundry papers accompanying it," which, on motion of Mr. Sherrard, was ordered to be laid on the table, and that 185 copies thereof, with the accompanying documents, be printed for the use of the general assembly.

On motion of Mr. Watkins, *Resolved*, That this house will, on Wednesday next, proceed by joint vote with the senate, to the election of a member of the executive council of this state, for three years from the 31st of March next, to supply the vacancy occasioned by the expiration of the term of service of Daniel A. Wilson, esq.

Ordered, That the clerk communicate the same to the senate and request their concurrence.

A message from the senate by Mr. Patteson:

Mr. Speaker,—The senate agree to the amendment proposed by the house of delegates to their amendment to the resolution for the election of a judge of the fourth circuit, with an amendment, in which they request the concurrence of the house of delegates.

And they have adopted a resolution "that when the senate adjourns on *Friday, the eighteenth* instant, it will, with the consent of the house of delegates, adjourn until Monday, the fourth day of January next," in which they very respectfully request the concurrence of this house: And then he withdrew.

The said amendment proposed by the senate to the amendment of the house of delegates to the senate's amendment to the resolution for the election of a judge in the fourth circuit, being read, was, on the question put thereupon, agreed to by the house.

Ordered, That the clerk inform the senate thereof.

The said resolution for the temporary adjournment of the senate being read, on motion of Mr. Parker, the same was amended by striking out the words "Friday, the 18th instant," and inserting in lieu thereof the words "Thursday, the 24th instant," and as amended was agreed to by the house.

Ordered, That the clerk inform the senate thereof and request their concurrence in the said amendment.

On motion of Mr. Hopkins, *Resolved*, That the committee for courts of justice be instructed to enquire into the expediency of so amending the 17th section of the act of assembly, entitled, "an act to reduce into one act the several acts and parts of acts concerning witnesses, and prescribing the manner of obtaining and executing commissions for taking their depositions in certain cases," passed January 10th, 1818, as to authorize the depositions of all witnesses in suits or cases now pending or hereafter to be instituted in any of the courts of this commonwealth, when they reside not less than one hundred miles from the court-house of the county, town or borough in which said suits or cases may be pending, to be taken upon reasonable notice, and to be read upon the trial of the same.

On motion of Mr. Masters, *Ordered*, That leave be given to bring in a bill changing the place of holding a separate election in the county of Marshall, and that Messrs. Masters, Chapline, Carroll, Prentiss, Decamps, Delashmutt, Summers and Morgan, prepare and bring in the same.

On motion of Mr. Morgan, *Resolved*, That the committee on the militia laws be instructed to enquire into the expediency of so amending the 65th section of the militia law as to grant the privilege to the commandant of the hundred and forty-seventh regiment to appoint a place for training the officers thereof within the bounds of said regiment.

Mr. Morgan presented a document connected with the said subject, which was ordered to be referred to the said committee.

Mr. Garland of Mecklenburg, presented a petition of sundry citizens of the county of Fayette, praying for a permanent location of the seat of justice for said county.

Mr. Holleman, a petition of Benjamin Ridgood, asking the relinquishment of the commonwealth's right to the estate of Betsy Ridgood, deceased, who died in the lunatic hospital.

Mr. Powell, a petition of William Weddeburn, asking remuneration for revolutionary services.

Ordered, That the said petitions be referred to the committee of propositions and grievances, that they do examine the matter thereof, and report their opinion thereupon to the house.

Mr. Stanard presented a petition of sundry citizens of the city of Richmond, asking for the establishment of a new bank in the said city, which was ordered to be referred to the select committee on banks, that they do examine the matter thereof, and report their opinion thereupon to the house.

Mr. Brown of Nelson, presented a petition of sundry citizens of Nelson and Albemarle counties, asking for the revival of the charter of the Nelson and Albemarle Union factory company, for the purpose of closing the concerns of said company, which was ordered to be referred to the committee of agriculture and manufactures, that they do examine the matter thereof, and report their opinion thereupon to the house.

Mr. Cunningham presented a petition of the mayor, recorder, aldermen and common council of the borough of Norfolk, praying the passage of an act to amend the charter of the Portsmouth and Roanoke rail-road company, so as to authorize said company to extend the said road to the said borough by means of steam boats, rail-way or otherwise, which, on motion of Mr. Cooke, was ordered to be laid upon the table.

Mr. Woolfolk presented a petition of the heirs of Thomas Carter, asking to be allowed compensation for his services as surgeon of cavalry in the Virginia line during the revolution, which was ordered to be referred to the committee of claims, that they do examine the matter thereof, and report their opinion thereupon to the house.

Mr. Summers presented a petition of sundry citizens of the counties of Kanawha and Fayette, praying the incorporation of a company to construct a turnpike road from the Narrow falls of New river, on the south side thereof, to a point opposite the town of Charlotte, in the county of Kanawha, with adequate capital to erect a bridge across New river, if found advisable by the company, which was ordered to be referred to the committee of roads and internal navigation, that they do examine the matter thereof, and report their opinion thereupon to the house.

Mr. Watkins, from the committee of roads and internal navigation, presented a report, which was read as follows:

The committee of roads and internal navigation have, according to order, had under consideration sundry petitions to them referred, and have come to the following resolutions thereupon:

1. *Resolved as the opinion of this committee,* That so much of the petition of sundry citizens of the counties of Preston and Randolph, as prays that a competent engineer may be directed to survey a route for a road from the North-western turnpike, at the German settlement, in the direction of Beverley, to the Tygart's Valley river, near the farm of Isaac Stalnaker, junior, is reasonable.

2. *Resolved as the opinion of this committee,* That the petition of sundry citizens of the counties of Rockingham and Hardy, asking an appropriation of five hundred dollars, in aid of private subscriptions, to construct a road from the Brock's Gap road on Starlick run in the county of Rockingham, across the Shenandoah mountain, to join the said Brock's Gap road below the Sulphur spring on Rarebagh run in the county of Hardy, be rejected.

The said resolutions were, on questions severally put thereupon, agreed to by the house, an *unsuccessful motion* having been made by Mr. Moffett, to amend the said last resolution, by striking therefrom the words "be rejected," and inserting in lieu thereof, the words "is reasonable," so as to reverse the decision of the committee.

Ordered, That a bill be brought in conformably with the said first resolution, and that the said committee prepare and bring in the same.

Mr. Watkins also, from the same committee, presented a bill to authorize the president and directors of the Portsmouth and Roanoke rail-road company to borrow a sum of money, which was read the first, and on his motion, the second time, and ordered to be committed to the said committee.

A bill to revive the inspection of tobacco at Spring warehouse in the town of Lynchburg, was read a second time, and ordered to be engrossed and read a third time.

On motion of Mr. Watkins, the house adjourned until Monday 12 o'clock.

MONDAY, December 14th, 1835.

Ordered, That Mr. Ragsdale be added to the committees of finance and on the public armory.

On motion of Mr. Sherrard, the 28th rule of the house was suspended, for the purpose of enlarging the committee appointed to examine the first auditor's office, and Messrs. Campbell, Ragsdale and Sloan, were ordered to be added to said committee.

On motion of Mr. Brown of Petersburg, *Resolved,* That the committee heretofore appointed to collect and have printed for the use of the members of the general assembly, certain proceedings of public meetings and other documents, respecting the interference of the northern fanatics with the slave property of the south, be discharged from the further consideration thereof, and that the subject matter of the same be referred to the general committee raised on that subject, with leave to said committee to employ a clerk or agent to make such collection, and to cause such portions of the same to be printed under the superintendence of the committee for the use of the members of the general assembly, as to the said committee may seem expedient.

On motion of Mr. Chapline, *Resolved*, That a special committee be appointed to enquire into the expediency of amending the acts incorporating the fire and marine company of Wheeling, with leave to report by bill or otherwise; and a committee was appointed of Messrs. Chapline, Masters, Prentiss, Carroll, Beuhring, Decamps and Morgan.

On motion of Mr. Chapman, *Ordered*, That leave be given to bring in a bill incorporating the Sweet springs company, and that Messrs. Chapman, Wilson of Botetourt, Wethered, M'Clintic, Brooke and Summers, prepare and bring in the same.

On motion of Mr. Stanard, *Resolved*, That the committee of roads and internal navigation enquire into the expediency of incorporating a company to construct a rail-road from the city of Richmond to the town of Petersburg, and that the said committee have leave to report by bill or otherwise.

On motion of Mr. Crutchfield, *Ordered*, That leave be given to bring in a bill incorporating the Phœnix mining company, and that Messrs. Crutchfield, Moncure, Woolfolk, Goodall, Robinson, Hooe and Hunter of Essex, prepare and bring in the same.

On motion of Mr. Layne, *Ordered*, That leave be given to bring in a bill to incorporate the Red spring company in the county of Alleghany, and that Messrs. Layne, Leyburn, Ingles, Harley, Miller, Chapman and Moffett, prepare and bring in the same.

On motion of Mr. Davison, *Ordered*, That leave be given to bring in a bill to alter the terms of the circuit superior courts of law and chancery in the 7th district and 13th circuit of this commonwealth, and that Messrs. Davison, Smith of Frederick, Hunter of Berkeley, Sherrard, Berry, Griggs, Rinker, Mullen, and Nixon, prepare and bring in the same.

The speaker submitted to the house a communication from the governor, transmitting a report of the superintendent of the penitentiary, which, on motion of Mr. M'Mullen, was ordered to be laid on the table, and that 185 copies thereof be printed for the use of the general assembly.

Mr. Watkins, from the committee of roads and internal navigation, presented a report, which was read as follows:

The committee of roads and internal navigation have, according to order, had under consideration sundry petitions to them referred, and have come to the following resolutions thereupon:

1. *Resolved as the opinion of this committee*, That the petition of sundry citizens of the county of Bath, representing that the Huntersville and Warm springs turnpike road leaves the Jackson's river turnpike about a quarter of a mile west of the Warm springs, and follows the Anthony's creek road through a narrow gap of the mountain, towards Huntersville, for about a quarter of a mile, and thence runs parallel with the said road one and an half or two miles, so that if the Huntersville and Warm springs turnpike company should erect a toll-gate on the eastern end of their road, in the gap, all persons will be compelled to pay toll on a section of five or ten miles, or more, as said company may think proper, when coming along the Anthony's creek road, although they will necessarily not travel more than about a quarter of a mile on the said turnpike; that a section of five miles of said turnpike is nearly completed; and praying the passage of an act to prevent the said company from erecting a toll-gate on the said turnpike, between the eastern end and the point of intersection of the Anthony's creek road, or to put it in the power of the court of said county to say where a toll-gate shall be erected; or to compel the county court to keep up so much of the turnpike road as is used by travellers on the Anthony's creek road, be rejected.

2. *Resolved as the opinion of this committee*, That the petition of John Shawver and other citizens of the county of Monroe, praying that the said John Shawver may be granted a charter to make and open a good road, or a turnpike, over the Sweet springs and Price's mountains, a distance of about eleven or twelve miles, with the privilege of charging thereon such tolls as may seem just, is reasonable.

3. *Resolved as the opinion of this committee*, That the petition of William Booth, of the county of Alleghany, and others, praying that the said William Booth may be authorized by law to graduate and improve the road from the eastern base of Price's mountain, in the county of Botetourt, to the Sweet springs, in the county of Monroe, for such moderate tolls as will enable him to complete and keep in repair the said road, is reasonable.

The first resolution being read, a motion was made by Mr. M'Clintic, to amend the same by striking therefrom the words "be rejected," and inserting in lieu thereof, the words "is reasonable."

On motion of Mr. Wethered, *Ordered*, That the said resolution and proposed amendment be laid upon the table.

The second and third resolutions were, on questions severally put thereupon, agreed to by the house, and bills were ordered to be brought in conformably therewith.

Mr. Watkins, from the same committee, presented a bill incorporating the stockholders of the Louisa rail-road company; and

A bill incorporating the stockholders of the Rappahannock and Blue Ridge rail-road company, which, on motions severally made, were ordered to be laid upon the table.

Also a bill to amend the act, entitled, "an act concerning William Brown;" and

A bill incorporating a company for the purpose of improving the navigation of Little and Big Deep creeks, in the county of Powhatan, which were severally read the first and ordered to be read a second time.

And a bill directing the survey and location of routes for certain roads therein mentioned, which was read the first and second times, on motion of Mr. Watkins, and ordered to be committed to the committee which brought it in.

Mr. Hill, from the committee of propositions and grievances, presented a report, which was read as follows:

The committee of propositions and grievances have, according to order, had under consideration the petition of a portion of the citizens and voters in the county of Nelson to them referred, praying that an act may pass authorising a separate election at Greenfield, on the lands of Mrs. Nancy Page, (who has certified her consent thereto:) Whereupon,

Resolved as the opinion of this committee, That the prayer of said petition, is reasonable.

The said resolution was, on the question put thereupon, agreed to by the house, and a bill was ordered to be brought in conformably therewith.

An engrossed bill to revive the inspection of tobacco at Spring warehouse in the town of Lynchburg, was read a third time:

Resolved, That the bill do pass, and that the title be, "an act to revive the inspection of tobacco at Spring warehouse in the town of Lynchburg."

Ordered, That the clerk communicate the same to the senate and request their concurrence.

Mr. Chapline presented a petition of certain inhabitants of the county of Marshall, asking the passage of an act to change the dividing line between the counties of Ohio and Marshall.

Also, a petition of certain inhabitants of the county of Ohio, for the establishment of a new election district in said county.

Mr. Hays presented a petition of sundry inhabitants of the counties of Lewis and Nicholas, asking for the formation of a new county out of parts of those counties.

Mr. Masters, a petition of William Chapline and others, for leave to erect wharves on Wheeling creek, and on the Ohio river, adjoining the town of South Wheeling.

Ordered, That the said petitions be referred to the committee of propositions and grievances, that they do examine the matter thereof, and report their opinion thereupon to the house.

Mr. Chapman presented a petition of sundry citizens of the county of Monroe, praying that a sum of money heretofore raised by lottery in said county, be applied to the erection of an academy in the town of Union, which was ordered to be referred to the committee of schools and colleges, that they do examine the matter thereof, and report their opinion thereupon to the house.

Mr. Fontaine presented a petition of James Johnson, asking to be allowed compensation for revolutionary services, which was ordered to be referred to the committee of claims, that they do examine the matter thereof, and report their opinion thereupon to the house.

Mr. Kincheloe presented a petition of sundry citizens of the county of Harrison opposing the prayer of the petition of Jessee Sturm, asking for leave to erect a dam across the west fork of Monongahela river, which was ordered to be referred to the committee of roads and internal navigation, that they do examine the matter thereof, and report their opinion thereupon to the house.

A motion was made by Mr. Watkins, that the house adopt the following resolution:

Resolved, That the resolution of the senate of the United States, passed March 28th, 1834, which declares, "that the president in the late executive proceedings in relation to the public revenue, has assumed upon himself authority and power not conferred by the constitution and laws, but in derogation of both," be referred to a select committee, with directions to enquire into the expediency of instructing the senators from this state, in the congress of the United States, to *introduce and vote* for a resolution, requiring the aforesaid resolution to be expunged from the journal of the senate.

Whereupon, a motion was made by Mr. Stanard, that the same be laid upon the table, and the question being put thereupon, was determined in the negative. Ayes 43, noes 83.

On motion of Mr. Dorman, (seven of the members present concurring,) *Ordered,* That the ayes and noes upon the said question be inserted in the journal.

The names of the gentlemen who voted in the affirmative, are Messrs. Grinalds, Drummond, Garland of Amherst, Craig, Campbell, Pate, Hunter of Berkeley, Henshaw, Christian, Johnson, Servant, Hunter of Essex, Ball, Hale of Franklin, Smith of Gloucester, Wethered, Mullen, Griggs, Berry, Summers, Hooe, Carter, Neill, Beard, Powell, Taylor of Loudoun, Ragsdale, Waggener, Cooke, Parker, Chapline, Masters, Critz, Swanson, Witcher, Dorman, Leyburn, Butts, Delashmutt, Jett, Prentiss, Cunningham and Stanard—43.

And the names of the gentlemen who voted in the negative, are Messrs. Banks, (speaker,) Gilmer, Layne, Wiley, Brooke, M'Clintic, Wilson of Botetourt, Decamps, Turnbull, Mallory, Booker, Austin, Beuhring, Clay, Daniel, Samuel, Richardson, Hill, Smith of Fauquier, Hickerson, Dickinson, Strange, Steger, Holland, Bowen, Davison, Smith of Frederick, Watts, Watkins, Hail of Grayson, Avent, Carrington, Coleman, Sloan, Nixon, Goodall, Harrison, Kincheloe, Randolph, Fontaine, Holleman, Gregory, Fleet, Robinson, Hays, Straton, Harris, Taylor of Mathews and Middlesex, Rogers, Garland of Mecklenburg, Willey, Morgan, Chapman, Ingles, Sherrard, Brown of Nelson, Leland, Fitzgerald, Woolfolk, Almond, M'Coy, Cackley, Hopkins, Carroll, Madison, Morris, Shands, Williams, Marteney, Nicklin, Moffett, Conrad, Jessee, M'Mullen, Bare, Rinker, Harley, Crutchfield, Moncure, Hargrave, Gillespie, Gibson and Saunders—83.

A motion was then made by Mr. Hickerson, to amend the said resolution, by inserting after the word "introduce," in the latter clause of the resolution, the word "support," so as to cause that part of the resolution to read "be referred to a select committee, with directions to enquire into the expediency of instructing the senators from this state in the congress of the United States, to *introduce, support and vote for* a resolution," &c.

And the question being put upon the said amendment, was determined in the negative. Ayes 6, noes 120.

On motion of Mr. Gregory, (seven of the members present concurring,) *Ordered*, That the ayes and noes upon the said question be inserted in the journal.

The names of the gentlemen who voted in the affirmative, are Messrs. Wilson of Botetourt, Booker, Austin, Hickerson, Smith of Frederick, and Moffett.—6.

And the names of the gentlemen who voted in the negative, are Messrs. Banks, (speaker,) Grinalds, Drummond, Gilmer, Layne, Wiley, Garland of Amherst, Brooke, Craig, M'Clintic, Campbell, Pate, Hunter of Berkeley, Henshaw, Decamps, Turnbull, Mallory, Beuhring, Clay, Daniel, Samuel, Christian, Richardson, Johnson, Hill, Servant, Hunter of Essex, Ball, Smith of Fauquier, Dickinson, Strange, Steger, Hale of Franklin, Holland, Bowen, Davison, Smith of Gloucester, Watkins, Hail of Grayson, Wethered, Avent, Carrington, Coleman, Sloan, Nixon, Goodall, Mullen, Harrison, Kincheloe, Randolph, Fontaine, Holleman, Gregory, Griggs, Berry, Summers, Fleet, Hooe, Robinson, Carter, Neill, Hays, Straton, Beard, Powell, Taylor of Loudoun, Harris, Ragsdale, Taylor of Mathews and Middlesex, Waggener, Rogers, Garland of Mecklenburg, Willey, Morgan, Chapman, Ingles, Sherrard, Brown of Nelson, Cooke, Parker, Leland, Fitzgerald, Chapline, Masters, Woolfolk, Almond, Critz, M'Coy, Swanson, Witcher, Cackley, Hopkins, Carroll, Madison, Morris, Shands, Williams, Marteney, Nicklin, Dorman, Leyburn, Conrad, Jessee, M'Mullen, Bare, Rinker, Harley, Butts, Crutchfield, Moncure, Hargrave, Gillespie, Delashmutt, Gibson, Jett, Prentiss, Saunders, Cunningham, Brown of Petersburg, and Stanard.—120.

The question was then put upon adopting the said resolution and was determined in the affirmative.

Ordered, That Messrs. Watkins, Parker, Stanard, Garland of Mecklenburg, Woolfolk, Brown of Petersburg, Booker, Wiley, Sherrard, Hooe, Wilson of Botetourt, Daniel and Harrison, compose the committee under the said resolution.

Mr. Holleman presented a document to be used in evidence in the contested election from the county of Henrico, which was ordered to be referred to the committee of privileges and elections.

The speaker submitted to the house a communication from the governor, which was read as follows:

EXECUTIVE DEPARTMENT, December 14th, 1835.

SIR,—Inclosed is a communication to the house of delegates, which you will please lay before that body.

I am, very respectfully, your ob't serv't,

LITT'N W. TAZEWELL.

To the Speaker of the House of Delegates.

EXECUTIVE DEPARTMENT, December 14th, 1835.

To the House of Delegates.

I have the honour to lay before you returns of the "Bank of the Valley in Virginia," exhibiting the condition of that institution, and its several branches, on the first days of August, October and December, 1835.

I am, very respectfully, your ob't serv't,

LITT'N W. TAZEWELL.

On motion of Mr. Carter, *Ordered*, That the said communication be referred to the committee on banks, that they do examine the matter thereof, and report their opinion thereupon to the house.

On motion of Mr. Sherrard, the house adjourned until to-morrow 12 o'clock.

TUESDAY, December 15th, 1835.

A communication from the senate by their clerk:

IN SENATE, December 14th, 1835.

The senate have agreed to the resolution for the election of a member of the executive council to supply the vacancy occasioned by the expiration of the term of service of Daniel A. Wilson, esq.

On motion of Mr. Chapman, *Resolved*, That the committee of roads and internal navigation be instructed to enquire into the expediency of incorporating a joint stock company to construct a turnpike road from the Blue Sulphur springs in the county of Greenbrier, to the Red Sulphur springs in the county of Monroe, and have leave to report by bill or otherwise.

On motion of Mr. Dorman, *Resolved*, That so much of the governor's message as relates to the interference by one of the naval commanders in the service of the United States with the due execution of the civil process of this commonwealth, and the revision of the various statutes applicable thereto, be referred to the committee for courts of justice.

On motion of Mr. Summers, *Ordered*, That leave be given to bring in a bill incorporating the Great Falls manufacturing company in the county of Fayette, and that Messrs. Summers, Dickinson, Chapline, Masters, Hays, Willey, Carroll and Prentiss, prepare and bring in the same.

On motion of Mr. Griggs, *Resolved*, That the committee of claims be instructed to enquire into the expediency of refunding to James Wysong the sum of twenty-five dollars, being so much overpaid by him as land tax in the county of Jefferson, and that said committee have leave to report by bill or otherwise.

On motion of Mr. Hays, *Resolved*, That the committee of roads and internal navigation be instructed to enquire into the expediency of providing by law for the construction of a road from Weston in the county of Lewis, to Charleston in the county of Kanawha, on the location made in pursuance of a resolution of the general assembly, and that they have leave to report by bill or otherwise.

On motion of Mr. Madison, *Resolved*, That the committee of roads and internal navigation be and they are hereby requested to enquire into the expediency of passing an act, authorizing the board of public works to subscribe on the part of the commonwealth for $28,000 of the stock of the Upper Appomattox company, provided the said company shall find it necessary to require such subscription, the said $28,000 being the balance of the stock which said company were authorized to raise by an act of the last legislature, passed the   day of   , 1835, and that the said committee report to this house.

On motion of Mr. Beuhring, *Ordered*, That leave be given to bring in a bill to amend the act, entitled, "an act to reduce into one the several acts for the settlement and regulation of ferries," passed January 30th, 1819, so far as said act relates to the ferry established from the lands of James Van Bibber, near the town of Guyandotte, across the Ohio river, and such other ferries as are now established by law across the rivers that are boundaries of this commonwealth, and that Messrs. Beuhring, Summers, Prentiss, Waggener, Chaplin, Decamps, Masters and Delashmutt, prepare and bring in the same.

Mr. Sherrard presented a petition of sundry citizens of the county of Berkeley, praying the establishment of a separate election at Hedgesville in said county.

Mr. Witcher, a petition of sundry citizens of the county of Bedford, asking that a portion of said county may be attached to the county of Pittsylvania.

Ordered, That the said petitions be referred to the committee of propositions and grievances, that they do examine the matter thereof, and report their opinion thereupon to the house.

Mr. Saunders presented a petition of Hugh M'Gavoc, asking to be allowed remuneration for revolutionary services.

Mr. Smith of Fauquier, presented a petition of Amos Johnson, praying to be paid the amount of sundry allowances made by the regimental court of enquiry of the 54th regiment to George Thayer, drummer to said regiment, which claims have been regularly assigned to him.

Ordered, That the said petitions be referred to the committee of claims, that they do examine the matter thereof, and report their opinion thereupon to the house.

Mr. Marteney presented a petition of sundry inhabitants of the counties of Randolph, Monongalia and Preston, that the engineer of the state may be directed to survey and locate a road from the Pennsylvania line through Morgantown, to intersect the road leading from Clarksburg to Beverley, at some point west of the Sorrel hill in Parker's settlement in the county of Randolph.

Mr. Drummond, a petition of Henry Parker, stating that Samuel C. White was required by an act of assembly establishing a ferry from the town of Onancock to Norfolk, to run a line of at least two packets between the said towns—that he has purchased of the said White his right and interest in the said ferry and packets, and praying that he may be authorized to run one packet instead of two, as required by the said act.

Mr. Wilson of Botetourt, a petition of James Shanks and John B. Lewis, to grant them an act of incorporation for the purpose of constructing a turnpike road across Price's and the Sweet spring mountains in the counties of Botetourt, Monroe and Alleghany.

Mr. Carroll, a petition of sundry citizens of the county of Preston, asking a change in the location of the North-western road through the town of Evansville in said county.

Ordered, That the said petitions be referred to the committee of roads and internal navigation, that they do examine the matter thereof, and report their opinion thereupon to the house.

Mr. Morris presented a petition of Jacob Boush and Tony Boush, free persons of colour and others, praying for leave to remain in the commonwealth.

Mr. Beuhring, a similar petition of Richard Bolling, a free man of colour.

Mr. Gillespie, a petition of John Barnes, praying to be divorced from his wife.

Ordered, That the said petitions be referred to the committee for courts of justice, that they do examine the matter thereof, and report their opinion thereupon to the house.

Mr. Dorman presented a petition of Henry Anderson, asking the relinquishment of the commonwealth's right to certain lands forfeited for the non-payment of taxes, which was ordered to be referred to the committee of finance, that they do examine the matter thereof, and report their opinion thereupon to the house.

Mr. M'Mullen presented a petition of sundry citizens of the town of Estillville in the county of Scott, for the passage of an act incorporating the trustees of said academy, and endowing the same out of the surplus in the literary fund, which was ordered to be referred to the committee of schools and colleges, that they do examine the matter thereof, and report their opinion thereupon to the house

Mr. Crutchfield, according to order, presented a bill to incorporate the Phœnix mining company.

Mr. Moncure, in like manner, a bill to incorporate the Falmouth mining company; and

A bill to incorporate the Deep run mining company.

Mr. Hill, from the committee of propositions and grievances, presented a bill to authorize a separate election at Greenfield, in the county of Nelson.

Mr. Smith of Fauquier, according to order, presented a bill to amend the act, entitled, "an act incorporating the Falmouth and Alexandria rail-road company."

Which several bills were received, read the first, and ordered to be read a second time.

A bill to amend the act, entitled, "an act concerning William Brown;" and

A bill incorporating a company for the purpose of improving the navigation of Little and Big Deep creeks, in the county of Powhatan, were severally read the second time and ordered to be engrossed and read a third time.

Mr. Hill, further from the committee of propositions and grievances, presented a report, which was read as follows:

The committee of propositions and grievances have, according to order, had under consideration the petition of sundry citizens of the town of Grandville, in the county of Monongalia, to them referred, praying that the general assembly will either appoint trustees for the government of said town, or authorize the citizens thereof to elect them; and that the owners of vacant lots in said town may be allowed further time for the improvement of the same, with such other regulations as may be deemed expedient: Whereupon,

Resolved as the opinion of this committee, That the prayer of the petition aforesaid, is reasonable.

The said resolution was, on the question put thereupon, agreed to by the house, and a bill was ordered to be brought in conformably therewith.

On motion of Mr. Crutchfield, a bill incorporating the stockholders of the Rappahannock and Blue Ridge railroad company, was taken up, read the first, and ordered to be read a second time.

On motion of Mr. Harris, a bill incorporating the stockholders of the Louisa rail-road company, was taken up, read the first, and ordered to be read a second time.

Mr. Chapman, according to order, presented a bill to incorporate the Sweet springs company, which was received and laid upon the table.

On motion of Mr. Henshaw, the house adjourned until to-morrow 12 o'clock.

WEDNESDAY, December 16th, 1835.

The house according to the joint order of the day, proceeded by joint vote with the senate to the election of a member of the executive council of this state for three years from the 31st of March next, to supply the vacancy occasioned by the expiration of the term of service of Daniel A. Wilson, esq.: whereupon, Mr. Sherrard nominated Peter V. Daniel, esq., and Mr. Murdaugh nominated Daniel A. Wilson, esq., and the senate being informed thereof by Mr. Sherrard, and no person being added to the nomination in that house, the names of the members were called by the clerk, when the vote was for Mr. Daniel 74; for Mr. Wilson 53; for Alexander W. Jones 1.

The names of the gentlemen who voted for Mr. Daniel, are Messrs. Banks, (speaker,) Layne, Wiley, Miller, Wilson of Botetourt, Decamps, Turnbull, Mallory, Booker, Austin, Clay, Daniel, Samuel, Richardson, Hill, Smith of Fauquier, Hickerson, Strange, Holland, Bowen, Davison, Watts, Watkins, Hail of Grayson, Avent, Carrington, Coleman, Sloan, Nixon, Goodall, Harrison, Kincheloe, Randolph, Fontaine, Holleman, Robinson, Hays, Straton, Harris, Ragsdale, Taylor of Mathews and Middlesex, Rogers, Garland of Mecklenburg, Willey, Morgan, Chapman, Ingles, Sherrard, Brown of Nelson, Leland, Fitzgerald, Woolfolk, Almond, M'Coy, Hopkins, Carroll, Madison, Shands, Williams, Marteney, Nicklin, Moffett, Conrad, Jessee, M'Mullen, Bare, Rinker, Harley, Crutchfield, Moncure, Hargrave, Gillespie, Gibson and Saunders.—74.

The names of the gentlemen who voted for Mr. Wilson, are Messrs. Grinalds, Drummond, Gilmer, Garland of Amherst, Brooke, Craig, M'Clintic, Campbell, Pate, Hunter of Berkeley, Henshaw, Beuhring, Christian, Johnson, Wilson of Cumberland, Servant, Hunter of Essex, Ball, Dickinson, Steger, Hale of Franklin, Smith of Gloucester, Wethered, Mullen, Griggs, Berry, Summers, Fleet, Hooe, Carter, Neill, Beard, Powell, Taylor of Loudoun, Waggener, Murdaugh, Cooke, Parker, Chapline, Masters, Critz, Swanson, Witcher, Morris, Dorman, Leyburn, Butts, Delashmutt, Jett, Prentiss, Cunningham, Brown of Petersburg, and Stanard.—53.

And Mr. Gregory voted for Alexander W. Jones.—1.

Ordered, That Messrs. Sherrard, Murdaugh, Parker, Carter, Brown of Petersburg, Mallory, Hooe and Jessee, be a committee to act jointly with a committee from the senate, to ascertain the state of the joint vote; the committee then withdrew, and after some time returned into the house, and Mr. Sherrard reported, that they had, according to order, ascertained the joint vote to be, for Daniel 91; for Wilson 64; scattering 1; whereupon, Peter V. Daniel, esq. was declared duly elected a member of the executive council for three years from the 31st of March next.

The speaker laid before the house a communication from the governor, transmitting two reports of the captain of the public guard, made in his capacity as superintendent of the armory and of public edifices for the present year, which, on motion of Mr. Miller, was ordered to be laid upon the table.

On motion of Mr. Wilson of Cumberland, the rule of the house limiting the number of the committee of schools and colleges, was suspended, and Mr. Madison was ordered to be added to the said committee.

Mr. Miller presented a petition of sundry citizens of the county of Botetourt, praying the incorporation of a company to construct a rail-road connecting with the James river and Kanawha improvement at Buchanan, and extending thence to the Tennessee line in the direction of Abingdon, to unite with a continuation of the New Orleans and Nashville rail-road.

Also, a petition of John Wood, for a charter authorizing him to continue to charge toll upon the road constructed by him over the Sweet spring mountain.

Ordered, That the said petitions be referred to the committee of roads and internal navigation, that they do examine the matter thereof, and report their opinion thereupon to the house.

A message from the senate by Mr. M'Carty:

MR. SPEAKER,—The senate have adopted a resolution for taking a recess from the 18th instant, until Monday the 4th day of January next, in which they most respectfully request the concurrence of this house: And then he withdrew.

The said resolution was read as follows:

"*Resolved*, That when the senate adjourns on Friday the eighteenth instant, it will, with the consent of the house of delegates, adjourn until Monday the fourth day of January next."

And the question being put upon concurring in the said resolution, was determined in the negative.

Ordered, That the clerk inform the senate thereof.

On motion of Mr. Campbell, (the same being amended on motion of Mr. M'Mullen) the rule of the house limiting the number of the committee of roads and internal navigation, was suspended for the purpose of adding five members to the said committee; and Messrs. Daniel, M'Mullen, Fontaine, Gillespie and Sloan were ordered to be added thereto.

Mr. Hoffeman presented sundry documents to be used as evidence in the contested election from the county of Henrico, which were ordered to be referred to the committee of privileges and elections.

On motion of Mr. Booker, *Resolved*, That the committee on agriculture and manufactures be instructed to enquire into the expediency of incorporating the Virginia mills manufacturing company in the county of Buckingham, and that they report by bill or otherwise.

On motion of Mr. Garland of Amherst, *Resolved*, That the committee on agriculture and manufactures be instructed to enquire into the expediency of enlarging the public warehouse in the city of Richmond, and that they have leave to report by bill or otherwise.

On motion of Mr. Harrison, *Resolved*, That the committee of claims be instructed to enquire into the expediency of allowing to Thomas Byrne of Lewis county, an annual sum for life, for certain wounds and permanent disabilities received by him in attempting to arrest one Dunahoo, charged with felony, and that the said committee have leave to report by bill or otherwise.

On motion of Mr. Chapline, *Ordered*, That leave be given to bring in a bill regulating the respective quotas of the primary school fund to which the counties of Ohio and Marshall are entitled, and for other purposes, and that Messrs. Chapline, Masters, Marteney, Decamps, Hays, Prentiss, Willey and Delashmutt, prepare and bring in the same.

On motion of Mr. Dickinson, *Resolved*, That the committee for courts of justice be instructed to enquire into the expediency of amending the 16th section of the act, entitled, "an act to reduce into one the several acts to regulate the solemnization of marriages, &c." and that they report by bill or otherwise.

On motion of Mr. Parker, the report of the adjutant general, accompanying the governor's message, was taken up, and ordered to be referred to the committee on the militia laws.

On motion of Mr. Delashmutt, (the rule of the house being suspended for that purpose,) *Ordered*, That leave be given to withdraw the petition of sundry citizens of the counties of Harrison and Tyler, presented to the last general assembly.

On motion of Mr. Brown of Petersburg, *Ordered*, That leave be given to bring in a bill to authorize the appointment of a third commissioner in chancery for the circuit superior court of law and chancery for the town of Petersburg, and that Messrs. Brown of Petersburg, Johnson, Shands, Mallory, Fitzgerald, Turnbull and Scott, prepare and bring in the same.

On motion of Mr. Madison, *Resolved*, That the committee of roads and internal navigation be instructed to enquire into the expediency of providing by law that the Upper Appomattox company be authorized to construct a towing path along the margin of Appomattox river from Farmville to Petersburg, whenever the said company may think proper to do so; also of amending the act of the last legislature in relation to lateral canals at the dams and locks of the company; also of authorizing the erection of mills at said dams; and also of authorizing the transfer of the old stock of the company in the manner prescribed for transferring the new stock, and that the said committee report to this house.

On motion of Mr. Chapline, *Ordered*, That leave be given to bring in a bill authorizing the mayor and commonalty of the town of Wheeling to take and subscribe for 2,500 shares of the capital stock of the Baltimore and Ohio rail-road company, and that Messrs. Chapline, Masters, Kincheloe, Hays, Prentiss, Berry, Mullen, Nixon, Griggs and Henshaw, prepare and bring in the same.

Mr. Brooke, according to order, presented a bill to amend an act, entitled, "an act to incorporate the Staunton and Potomac rail-road company."

Mr. Hill, from the committee of propositions and grievances, presented a report upon the petitions of citizens of the counties of Lewis and Nicholas; of Preston county; of the county of Monongalia; of citizens of Wythe county, and of owners of land in the town of Wheeling.

Mr. Stanard, from the committee for courts of justice, presented reports of resolutions of said committee upon the petitions of Judy Johnson, of James Haskins, of Charlotte Morgan, and of Duff Green.

Mr. Dorman from the committee of roads and internal navigation, presented a report upon the petition of sundry citizens of the counties of Randolph, Preston and Monongalia.

Also, a bill directing the survey of a route for a road from the North-western road in the direction of Beverley in the county of Randolph.

And a bill incorporating the stockholders of the Richmond and Petersburg rail-road company.

Mr. Madison, from the committee of agriculture and manufactures, presented a report upon petitions of citizens of the town of Petersburg.

Mr. Chapline, according to order, presented a bill to enlarge, define and establish the corporate boundaries and limits of the town of Wheeling in the county of Ohio.

Mr. Johnson in like manner, a bill to amend an act, entitled, "an act to incorporate the Midlothian coal mining company."

Which reports and bills were received and laid upon the table.

Mr. Gilmer submitted the following resolution:

Resolved, That the governor of this commonwealth be requested to open a correspondence with the executive authorities of those states within whose jurisdictions certain incendiary associations have been formed, for the purpose of abolishing slavery in the district of Columbia, and in the United States, with a view to ascertain as far as practicable, the disposition of those states to provide by adequate legal enactments for the suppression of such associations, and for arresting the circulation of their dangerous publications—also, with the executive authorities of other states, if he should deem it necessary, in order to ascertain the measures which have been taken or may be contemplated to counteract the fatal tendencies of these associations.

On motion of Mr. Wiley, the same was ordered to be laid upon the table.

Mr. Cooke presented a petition of sundry citizens of the town of Portsmouth, asking for the incorporation of a company for the purpose of navigating the waters of the Chesapeake bay and its tributaries, which was ordered to be referred to the committee of propositions and grievances, that they do examine the matter thereof, and report their opinion thereupon to the house.

Mr. Gibson presented a petition of John B. Findley and John Rogers, asking compensation for pursuing and apprehending a fugitive from justice.

Mr. Harrison, a petition of John J. Stackhouse and Nancy Stackhouse, deceased, praying the passage of an act, authorizing them to receive from the treasury the bounties promised their ancestor for his revolutionary services.

Mr. Willey, a petition of Shelton Ford, praying to be released from the payment of a fine imposed on him by the county court of Preston county.

Also, a petition of sundry citizens of the county of Preston upon the same subject.

Mr. Brown of Petersburg, presented a petition of William Fenn, asking to be allowed compensation for apprehending a certain James Alfriend, charged with horse-stealing.

Ordered, That the said petitions be referred to the committee of claims, that they do examine the matter thereof, and report their opinion thereupon to the house.

Mr. Clay presented a petition of sundry citizens of the town of Lynchburg, for the establishment of an independent bank in said town, to be called the bank of Lynchburg, with a capital of a million of dollars.

Mr. Brown of Petersburg, also presented a petition of sundry merchants and others of the town of Petersburg, for the establishment of an independent bank in that place, with the privilege of locating one or more branches thereof.

Ordered, That the said petitions be referred to the select committee on banks, that they do examine the matter thereof, and report their opinion thereupon to the house.

A motion was made by Mr. Gilmer, that the house do now take up the resolution submitted by him to-day, and which was then laid on the table on motion of Mr. Wiley, and demanded the ayes and noes upon the said motion, and the call having been seconded by the requisite number of members,

A motion was made by Mr. Miller, that the house do now adjourn, and the question being put thereupon, was determined in the affirmative. Ayes 68, noes 44.

On motion of Mr. Gilmer, (seven of the members present concurring,) *Ordered*, That the ayes and noes upon the said question be inserted in the journal.

The names of the gentlemen who voted in the affirmative, are Messrs. Banks, (speaker,) Wiley, M'Clintic, Miller, Wilson of Botetourt, Decamps, Turnbull, Mallory, Booker, Austin, Daniel, Christian, Hill, Smith of Fauquier, Hickerson, Strange, Steger, Bowen, Davison, Watts, Watkins, Hail of Grayson, Avent, Carrington, Coleman, Sloan, Nixon, Goodall, Harrison, Kincheloe, Randolph, Fontaine, Hays, Straton, Harris, Rogers, Garland of Mecklenburg, Willey, Morgan, Chapman, Ingles, Sherrard, Brown of Nelson, Murdaugh, Cooke, Fitzgerald, Almond, M'Coy, Cackley, Hopkins, Carroll, Madison, Shands, Williams, Marteney, Nicklin, Moffet, Conrad, Jessee, M'Mullen, Bare, Rinker, Crutchfield, Moncure, Gillespie, Delashmutt, Gibson and Prentiss.—68.

And the names of the gentlemen who voted in the negative, are Messrs. Grinalds, Gilmer, Garland of Amherst, Campbell, Pate, Hunter of Berkeley, Henshaw, Beuhring, Clay, Samuel, Johnson, Wilson of Cumberland, Servant,

Hunter of Essex, Dickinson, Holland, Smith of Gloucester, Gregory, Griggs, Berry, Summers, Fleet, Carter, Neill, Beard, Powell, Taylor of Loudoun, Taylor of Mathews and Middlesex, Waggener, Parker, Chapline, Masters, Critz, Swanson, Witcher, Morris, Dorman, Leyburn, Harley, Butts, Saunders, Cunningham, Brown of Petersburg, and Stanard.—44.

And then, at half past three o'clock, the house adjourned until to-morrow 12 o'clock.

THURSDAY, December 17th, 1835.

A communication from the senate by their clerk:

IN SENATE, December 16th, 1835.

The senate have passed the bill, entitled, "an act to revive the inspection of tobacco at Spring warehouse in the town of Lynchburg."

On motion of Mr. Wilson of Botetourt, the report of the committee of roads and internal navigation, upon the petition of sundry citizens of the county of Bath, was taken up, and ordered to be re-committed to the said committee.

Mr. Hill, from the committee of propositions and grievances, presented a report upon the petition of sundry citizens of the county of Marshall.

And a bill to amend the act establishing the town of Grandville in the county of Monongalia.

Mr. Watkins, from the committee of roads and internal navigation, presented a bill authorizing the board of public works to subscribe on behalf of the commonwealth to the stock of the Smith's river navigation company.

And reported with amendments, a bill to authorize the president and directors of the Portsmouth and Roanoke rail-road company to borrow a sum of money.

Mr. Brown of Petersburg, according to order, presented a bill to authorize the appointment of a third commissioner of the superior court of Petersburg.

Which reports and bills were received and laid upon the table.

An engrossed bill incorporating a company for the purpose of improving the navigation of Little and Big Deep creeks in the county of Powhatan, was read a third time:

Resolved, That the bill do pass, and that the title be, "an act incorporating a company for the purpose of improving the navigation of Little and Big Deep creeks in the county of Powhatan."

An engrossed bill to amend the act, entitled, "an act concerning William Brown," was read a third time:

Resolved, That the bill do pass, and that the title be, "an act to amend the act, entitled, 'an act concerning William Brown.'"

Ordered, That the clerk communicate the same to the senate and request their concurrence.

Mr. Chapline presented a petition of sundry citizens of the town of Wheeling, praying for the establishment of an independent bank at that place, with a capital of one million of dollars.

Also, a petition of the savings institution of the town of Wheeling, for a grant of banking privileges to the said institution.

Ordered, That the said petitions be referred to the select committee on banks, that they do examine the matter thereof, and report their opinion thereupon to the house.

Mr. Beard presented a petition of sundry citizens of the county of Loudoun, supporting the petition of Braden and Hixon, for an act to authorize the construction of a bridge across the Shenandoah river, which was ordered to be referred to the committee of propositions and grievances, that they do examine the matter thereof, and report their opinion thereupon to the house.

The following bills were read a second time, and ordered to be engrossed and read a third time, viz:

A bill to incorporate the Phœnix mining company.
A bill to incorporate the Falmouth mining company; and
A bill to incorporate the Deep run mining company.

A bill incorporating the stockholders of the Louisa rail-road company, was read a second time, and on motion of Mr. Watkins, ordered to be committed to the committee which brought it in.

A bill incorporating the stockholders of the Rappahannock and Blue Ridge rail-road company, was read a second time, amended on motion of Mr. Crutchfield, and as amended, ordered to be engrossed and read a third time.

Mr. Crutchfield presented a petition of sundry citizens of the town of Fredericksburg, praying for the incorporation of the said rail-road company, which was ordered to be laid upon the table.

On motion of Mr. Dorman, the resolution submitted by Mr. Gilmer on yesterday, requesting the governor to open a correspondence with the executive of other states to ascertain the disposition of those states to provide by law for the suppression of associations formed for the purpose of abolishing slavery, was taken up, and the same being amended on motion of Mr. Stanard, and being under discussion,

On motion of Mr. Dorman, the house adjourned until to-morrow 12 o'clock.

FRIDAY, December 18th, 1835.

A communication from the senate by their clerk:

IN SENATE, December 17th, 1835.

The senate have agreed to the amendment of the house of delegates to their resolution for a temporary adjournment.

The house according to the joint order of the day, proceeded by joint vote with the senate to the election of a judge of the general court to supply the vacancy occasioned by the death of the late judge James Semple: whereupon, Mr. Smith of Gloucester, nominated John B. Christian, esq'r, and the senate having been informed thereof by Mr. Gregory, and no person being added to the nomination in that house, the names of the members were called by the clerk, when Mr. Christian received 118 votes; James D. Halyburton 2; William H. Roy 1; John H. Peyton 1, and Joseph S. Watkins 1.

The names of the gentlemen thus voting, are Messrs. Banks, (speaker,) Drummond, Gilmer, Layne, Wiley, Garland of Amherst, Brooke, Craig, M'Clintic, Campbell, Pate, Hunter of Berkeley, Henshaw, Miller, Wilson of Botetourt, Decamps, Turnbull, Mallory, Booker, Austin, Beuhring, Clay, Daniel, Samuel, Christian, Richardson, Johnson, Hill, Wilson of Cumberland, Scott, Servant, Hunter of Essex, Ball, Smith of Fauquier, Hickerson, Dickinson, Strange, Steger, Hale of Franklin, Holland, Bowen, Davison, Smith of Frederick, Smith of Gloucester, Hail of Grayson, Wethered, Avent, Coleman, Sloan, Nixon, Goodall, Mullen, Harrison, Kincheloe, Randolph, Fontaine, Holleman, Gregory, Griggs, Berry, Summers, Fleet, Hooe, Robinson, Carter, Neill, Hays, Straton, Beard, Powell, Taylor of Loudoun, Harris, Taylor of Mathews and Middlesex, Waggener, Willey, Morgan, Chapman, Brown of Nelson, Cooke, Parker, Leland, Fitzgerald, Chapline, Masters, Woolfolk, Almond, Critz, Swanson, Witcher, Cackley, Hopkins, Carroll, Madison, Morris, Shands, Williams, Marteney, Nicklin, Dorman, Leyburn, Moffett, Conrad, Jessee, M'Mullen, Rinker, Harley, Butts, Crutchfield, Moncure, Hargrave, Gillespie, Delashmutt, Gibson, Jett, Saunders, Cunningham, Brown of Petersburg, and Stanard.—118.

Messrs. Watkins and Sherrard voted for James D. Halyburton.—2.

Mr. Murdaugh voted for William H. Roy.—1.

Mr. M'Coy voted for John H. Peyton.—1.

And Mr. Prentiss voted for Joseph S. Watkins.—1.

Ordered, That Messrs. Smith of Gloucester, Gregory, Taylor of Mathews and Middlesex, Fleet, Robinson, and Hunter of Essex, be a committee to act jointly with a committee from the senate to ascertain the state of the joint vote: the committee then withdrew, and after some time returned into the house, and Mr. Smith of Gloucester, reported that they had, according to order, ascertained the joint vote to be for Christian 136; scattering 13: whereupon, John B. Christian, esq'r, was declared duly elected a judge of the general court.

On motion of Mr. Prentiss, *Ordered*, That Mr. Chapline be added to the committee raised to enquire into the propriety of increasing the banking capital of the commonwealth.

Mr. Stanard, from the committee for courts of justice, presented a report upon the petition of William Fisher.

And a bill providing for the better security of persons charged with criminal offences.

Mr. Watkins, from the committee of roads and internal navigation, presented a report upon the petitions of sundry citizens of the counties of Kanawha and Fayette, and of citizens of the county of Preston

Also a bill authorizing Jesse Sturm to erect a dam across the west fork of Monongalia river, in the county of Harrison; and

A bill to regulate the conduct of boatmen on the Roanoke river and its branches.

And reported with amendment, a bill incorporating the stockholders of the Louisa rail-road company.

Mr. Christian, from the committee appointed to examine the clerk's office, presented a report upon the state of the said office.

Which reports and bills were received and laid upon the table.

On motion of Mr. Watkins, *Ordered*, That the committee of roads and internal navigation be discharged from the farther consideration of the petition of sundry citizens of the county of Bath, and the report of the said committee thereupon, and that the same be laid upon the table.

On motion of Mr. Murdaugh, a bill to authorize the president and directors of the Portsmouth and Roanoke rail-road company to borrow a sum of money, with the amendment thereto proposed by the committee of roads and internal navigation, was taken up, and the said amendment being read, was disagreed to by the house, and the said bill was ordered to be engrossed and read a third time.

Mr. Chapline, according to order, presented a bill concerning the fire and marine insurance company of Wheeling; and

A bill to authorize the mayor and commonalty of the town of Wheeling to subscribe for stock of the Baltimore and Ohio rail-road company.

Mr. Hill, from the committee of propositions and grievances, presented a report upon the petition of sundry citizens of the county of Berkeley.

Mr. Madison, from the committee of agriculture and manufactures, presented a bill to incorporate the Virginia mills manufacturing company.

Which bills and report were received and laid upon the table.

On motion of Mr. Brown of Petersburg, the communication of the auditor of public accounts was taken up and ordered to be referred to the committee of finance, with leave to the said committee to report thereon by bill or otherwise.

On motion of Mr. Smith of Frederick, *Ordered,* That leave be given to bring in a bill to amend an act, entitled, "an act for incorporating the stockholders of the Winchester and Potomac rail-road company, and that Messrs. Smith of Frederick, Davison, Bowen, Griggs, Berry, Henshaw, Mullen and Sherrard, prepare and bring in the same.

On motion of Mr. Powell, *Resolved,* That the committee for courts of justice be instructed to enquire into the expediency of so amending the laws in relation to slaves, free negroes and mulattoes, as to provide for the more summary trial of free negroes remaining in the commonwealth contrary to law.

An engrossed bill to incorporate the Phœnix mining company, was read a third time:

Resolved, That the bill do pass, and that the title be, "an act to incorporate the Phœnix mining company."

An engrossed bill to incorporate the Deep run mining company, was read a third time:

Resolved, That the bill do pass, and that the title be, "an act to incorporate the Deep run mining company."

An engrossed bill to incorporate the Falmouth mining company, was read a third time:

Resolved, That the bill do pass, and that the title be, "an act to incorporate the Falmouth mining company."

An engrossed bill incorporating the stockholders of the Rappahannock and Blue Ridge rail-road company, was read a third time, and sundry blanks therein were filled:

Resolved, That the bill do pass, and that the title be, "an act incorporating the stockholders of the Rappahannock and Blue Ridge rail-road company."

Ordered, That the clerk communicate the same to the senate and request their concurrence.

On motion of Mr. Woolfolk, a bill providing for the better security of persons charged with criminal offences, was taken up, read the first and second times, and ordered to be committed to the committee which brought it in.

Mr. Randolph presented a petition of Jesse Snead and others, for an act to incorporate a company to construct a rail-road from the coal mines in the county of Henrico, on the Tuckahœ valley, to the James river canal, which was ordered to be referred to the committee of roads and internal navigation, that they do examine the matter thereof, and report their opinion thereupon to the house.

On motion of Mr. Mullen, the house adjourned until to-morrow 12 o'clock.

SATURDAY, December 19th, 1835.

Mr. Witcher, from the committee of claims, presented reports upon the petitions of George Johnson and of Shelton Ford.

Mr. Hill, from the committee of propositions and grievances, presented a report upon the petitions of citizens of the town of Portsmouth, of citizens of Berkeley, and of citizens of the county of Stafford.

Mr. Watkins, from the committee of roads and internal navigation, presented reports upon the petitions of Henry P. Parker, and of citizens of the counties of Hampshire and Frederick.

And a bill incorporating the Lexington and Richmond turnpike company.

Mr. Davison, according to order, presented a bill to alter the terms of the circuit superior courts of law and chancery for the 7th district and 13th circuit of this commonwealth.

Which reports and bills were received and laid upon the table.

On motion of Mr. Watkins, *Ordered,* That the committee of roads and internal navigation be discharged from the further consideration of so much of the petition of sundry citizens of the county of Hampshire, as has not been acted upon by said committee, and that the same be laid upon the table.

An engrossed bill to authorize the president and directors of the Portsmouth and Roanoke rail-road company to borrow a sum of money, was read a third time:

Resolved, That the bill do pass, and (the title being amended on motion of Murdaugh,) that the title be, "an act to authorize the president and directors of the Portsmouth and Roanoke rail-road company *to increase their capital stock or* to borrow a sum of money."

Ordered, That the clerk communicate the same to the senate and request their concurrence.

Mr. Shands presented a petition of sundry citizens of the county of Prince George and the town of Petersburg, for the construction of a rail-road from the town of Petersburg to City Point, which was ordered to be referred to the committee of roads and internal navigation, that they do examine the matter thereof, and report their opinion thereupon to the house.

Mr. Crutchfield presented a petition of the managers of the female orphan asylum of Fredericksburg, asking for a donation of three hundred dollars per annum from the literary fund, for the education of children in the said asylum, which was ordered to be referred to the committee of schools and colleges, that they do examine the matter thereof, and report their opinion thereupon to the house.

Mr. Davison presented a petition of the stockholders of the Bank of the Valley in Virginia, by the president and directors thereof, praying an extension of its capital stock, which was ordered to be referred to the committee appointed to take into consideration the propriety of increasing the banking capital of the commonwealth, that they do examine the matter thereof, and report their opinion thereupon to the house.

Mr. M'Clintic presented a petition of Elisha B. Williams, for permission to erect a carding machine on Jackson's river in the county of Alleghany, which was ordered to be referred to the committee of propositions and grievances, that they do examine the matter thereof, and report their opinion thereupon to the house.

Mr. Parker presented a preamble and resolutions proceeding from a meeting of citizens of the county of Northampton, on the subject of the interference of the abolition societies of the north, with the slave property of the south, which was ordered to be referred to the select committee on that subject.

On motion of Mr. Dorman, the resolution submitted some days since by Mr. Gilmer, requesting the governor to open a correspondence with the executive of other states, with a view to ascertain the disposition of those states to provide by legal enactments for the suppression of incendiary associations for the abolition of slavery in the United States, was taken up; whereupon, a motion was made by Mr. Holleman, that the same be referred to the select committee upon that subject, and the ayes and noes upon the said motion having been demanded by Mr. Gregory, and the call having been sustained by the house,

On motion of Mr. Stanard, the house adjourned until Monday 12 o'clock.

MONDAY, December 21st, 1835.

A communication from the senate by their clerk:

IN SENATE, December 19th, 1835.

The senate have passed the bills, entitled,

"An act incorporating a company for the purpose of improving the navigation of Little and Big Deep creeks in the county of Powhatan;" and

"An act to amend the act, entitled, 'an act concerning William Brown.'"

On motion of Mr. Almond, *Resolved*, That the committee of roads and internal navigation be instructed to enquire into the expediency of granting to the counties of Madison and Page the sum of ———— dollars out of the public revenue of the said counties, to enable them to complete a public road across the Blue Ridge at Milam's gap, and that the said committee have leave to report by bill or otherwise.

On motion of Mr. Watkins, *Resolved*, That the committee of roads and internal navigation be instructed to enquire into the expediency of amending an act, entitled, "an act incorporating the Richmond rail-road company," and that they have leave to report by bill or otherwise.

Resolved, That the committee of roads and internal navigation be instructed to enquire into the expediency of incorporating a company to construct a turnpike road from the city of Richmond, to Tuckahoe bridge in the county of Henrico, with leave to report by bill or otherwise.

On motion of Mr. Harley, *Resolved*, That the committee of roads and internal navigation be instructed to enquire into the expediency of incorporating a joint stock company, with a capital of not less than thirty thousand dollars, for the purpose of improving the navigation of the north fork of Holstein river, from the Broadford in the county of Smyth, to the Tennessee line, and that they have leave to report by bill or otherwise.

On motion of Mr. Davison, *Ordered*, That leave be given to bring in a bill to incorporate the Newtown Stevensburg library company, and that Messrs. Davison, Smith of Frederick, Bowen, Berry, Sherrard, Hunter of Berkeley, M'Coy and Rinker, prepare and bring in the same.

Mr. Shands, from the committee for courts of justice, presented a report upon the petitions of Richard Bolling, and of Daniel Higginbotham.

And reported with amendments, a bill providing for the better security of persons charged with criminal offences.

Mr. Watkins, from the committee of roads and internal navigation, presented reports upon the petitions of James Shanks and John B. Lewis; of John Wood; and of citizens of the town of Petersburg and county of Prince George; and upon the resolution for a subscription to the stock of the Upper Appomattox company.

Mr. Masters, according to order, presented a bill to change the place of holding a separate election in the county of Marshall.

Which reports and bills were received and laid upon the table.

Mr. Gibson presented a petition of Lucy and Delila, free persons of colour, asking permission to remain in the commonwealth, which was ordered to be referred to the committee for courts of justice, that they do examine the matter thereof, and report their opinion thereupon to the house.

Also, a petition of sundry citizens of the town of Abingdon, and of others of the county of Washington, asking for the establishment of a branch of one of the state banks at the said town.

Mr. Craig presented a petition of citizens of the county of Augusta and town of Staunton, for the establishment of an independent bank in the said town.

Mr. Rogers, a petition of the inhabitants of the town of Clarksville, asking for the location of a branch of one of the banks of the state at the said town.

Ordered, That the said petitions be referred to the select committee on the subject of increasing the banking capital of the commonwealth, that they do examine the matter thereof, and report their opinion thereupon to the house.

Mr. Gilmer presented a petition of citizens of Scottsville in the county of Albemarle, and of the counties of Nelson, Buckingham and Fluvanna, asking the establishment of a branch of the Bank of Virginia, or of the Farmers bank of Virginia, at the town of Scottsville; which, on his motion, was ordered to be referred to the standing committee on banks, that they do examine the matter thereof, and report their opinion thereupon to the house.

Mr. Shands presented a petition of citizens of the town of Farmville, for the incorporation of a company to construct a rail-road from Petersburg to City Point, which was ordered to be laid upon the table.

Mr. Wilson of Cumberland, presented a petition of many voters of the county of Cumberland, asking the establishment of a separate election at Erving's tavern in said county.

Mr. Watkins, a petition of citizens of the counties of Caroline, King & Queen, and Essex, asking for the formation of a new county out of parts of said counties.

Mr. Chapline, a petition of the stockholders of the Wheeling and Belmont bridge company, asking for certain amendments to their charter of incorporation.

Also, a petition of citizens of Middle and East Wheeling, opposing the petition of other citizens of the town of Wheeling, for an extension of the limits of the said town.

Mr. Griggs, a petition of citizens of the county of Jefferson, for the incorporation of a company to construct a bridge across the Shenandoah river at the town of Harper's Ferry.

Also, a petition of other citizens of the town of Harper's Ferry, advocating the prayer of the petition of Noble S. Braden and Fleming Hixon, for permission to erect a bridge at the said town.

Mr. Samuels, a petition of citizens of the counties of Caroline, King & Queen and Essex, opposing the dismemberment of the said counties with a view to the formation of a new county therefrom.

Mr. Brown of Nelson, presented a petition of citizens of the county of Nelson, for the incorporation of a company to construct a rail-road from the town of Lynchburg to some point on the Tennessee line, which was ordered to be laid upon the table.

Mr. Wilson of Botetourt, presented a petition of Jacob Price, for leave to erect a toll-gate on Price's mountain, and for authority to improve the road over the same, and across the Sweet springs mountain, which was ordered to be referred to the committee of roads and internal navigation, that they do examine the matter thereof, and report their opinion thereupon to the house.

Mr. Coleman presented a petition of citizens of the county of Halifax, for the passage of an act incorporating the trustees of the Halifax academy.

Mr. Spratley, a petition of Richard H. Edwards, treasurer of the school commissioners of the county of Surry, asking that a sum of money paid by him as treasurer aforesaid may be refunded him.

Mr. Cunningham, a petition of the trustees of the Norfolk academy, asking for amendments to the act passed on the 19th of January, 1804, to confer explicit power upon the trustees of said academy to sell and dispose of their lot on Church street.

Ordered, That the said petitions be referred to the committee of schools and colleges, that they do examine the matter thereof, and report their opinion thereupon to the house.

Mr. Harrison presented sundry documents connected with the claim of Thomas Byrne, which was ordered to be referred to the committee of claims.

Mr. Cunningham also presented a petition of the vice president and others constituting the managing committee of the Norfolk and Portsmouth literary and scientific mechanics institute, for the passage of an act incorporating the said institute, which was ordered to be referred to the committee of schools and colleges, that they do examine the matter thereof, and report their opinion thereupon to the house.

On motion of Mr. Stanard, the resolution submitted by Mr. Gilmer requesting the governor to open a correspondence with the executive of other states to ascertain the disposition of those states to provide by legal enactments for the suppression of associations which exist in those states for the purpose of abolishing slavery in the United States, was taken up, and the same being under discussion,

On motion of Mr. Booker, the house adjourned until to-morrow 12 o'clock.

TUESDAY, December 22d, 1835.

The speaker laid before the house a communication from the governor, enclosing "returns of the North-western bank of Virginia, for the present year," which, on motion of Mr. Dorman, was ordered to be laid upon the table, and on motion of Mr. Chapline, 185 copies thereof were ordered to be printed for the use of the members of the general assembly.

A communication from the senate by their clerk:

IN SENATE, December 21st, 1835.

The senate have passed the bills, entitled,

"An act to incorporate the Phoenix mining company;" and

"An act to authorize the president and directors of the Portsmouth and Roanoke rail-road company to increase their capital stock or to borrow a sum of money."

They have also passed the bills, entitled,

"An act to incorporate the Falmouth mining company;" and

"An act to incorporate the Deep run mining company," with amendments, in which they request the concurrence of the house of delegates.

The said amendments being twice read, were, on questions severally put thereupon, agreed to by the house.

Ordered, That the clerk inform the senate thereof.

On motion of Mr. Murdaugh, *Ordered*, That leave be given to bring in a bill to vest the trustees of the town of Portsmouth with certain additional powers, and that Messrs. Murdaugh, Cooke, Cunningham, Servant, Gregory, Benton and Morris, prepare and bring in the same.

Mr. Smith of Frederick, according to order, presented a bill to amend an act, entitled, "an act for incorporating the stockholders of the Winchester and Potomac rail-road company."

Mr. Hill, from the committee of propositions and grievances, presented a report upon the petition of citizens of the town of Petersburg.

Mr. Witcher, from the committee of claims, presented a report upon the petition of James Wysong.

Mr. Watkins, from the committee of roads and internal navigation, presented a report upon the petition of citizens of the county of Halifax.

Which bill and reports were received and laid upon the table.

On motions severally made, *Ordered*, That leave of absence from the service of this house be granted to Mr. Carrington for ten days from yesterday; to Mr. Garland of Amherst, for ten days, and to Mr. Richardson for five days from Thursday next; to Mr. Brown of Nelson, for nine days from to-day; to Mr. Booker for six days from Wednesday next, and to Mr. Madison for five days from Friday next.

On motion of Mr. Garland of Mecklenburg, the rule of the house limiting the number of the committee of schools and colleges was suspended, and Mr. Murdaugh was ordered to be added to the said committee.

Mr. Smith of Frederick, presented a petition of certain citizens of the county of Frederick, opposing the division of the county.

Mr. Hunter of Essex, a petition of sundry citizens of the county of Essex, opposing the formation of a new county out of the counties of Caroline, King & Queen and Essex.

Ordered, That the said petitions be referred to the committee of propositions and grievances, that they do examine the matter thereof, and report their opinion thereupon to the house.

Mr. Smith of Frederick, also presented a petition of other citizens of the county of Frederick, asking for amendments to the charter incorporating the North-western turnpike road company.

Mr. Campbell, a petition of sundry citizens of the county of Bedford, for the incorporation of a company for the purpose of constructing a rail-road from the town of Lynchburg to the Tennessee line.

Mr. Wilson of Cumberland, a petition of citizens of the county of Cumberland, asking the incorporation of a company to construct a rail-road from the town of Farmville to the town of Cartersville.

Mr. Benton, a petition of citizens of the town of Suffolk, for the incorporation of a company to construct a rail-road from the upper part of the said town to the Nansemond river.

Ordered, That the said petitions be referred to the committee of roads and internal navigation, that they do examine the matter thereof, and report their opinion thereupon to the house.

Mr. Ball presented petitions of Charles Williams and of Daniel Starks, free men of colour, asking to be permitted to remain in the commonwealth for a limited period.

Mr. Murdaugh, a petition of Bernard O. Neill, administrator with the will annexed of Patrick Robertson, for authority to lease the lands of his testator for a term of years.

Ordered, That the said petitions be referred to the committee for courts of justice, that they do examine the matter thereof, and report their opinion thereupon to the house.

On motion of Mr. Parker, the resolution submitted some days since by Mr. Gilmer, requesting the governor to open a correspondence with the executive of other states to ascertain the disposition of those states to provide by legal enactments for the suppression of associations which have been formed for the purpose of abolishing slavery in the United States, was taken up; whereupon, a motion was made by Mr. Austin, that the farther consideration thereof be indefinitely postponed; and the same being under discussion,

On motion of Mr. Daniel, the house adjourned until to-morrow 12 o'clock.

WEDNESDAY, December 23d, 1835.

Mr. Hill, from the committee of propositions and grievances, presented a report upon the petitions of citizens of the county of Cumberland; of the county of Fayette, and of the county of Ohio.

Mr. Watkins, from the committee of roads and internal navigation, presented a report upon the petition of other citizens of the county of Cumberland.

Also, a bill incorporating the Red and Blue Sulphur springs turnpike company.

And a bill to revive and amend the act, entitled, "an act incorporating the Richmond rail-road company."

Mr. Summers, according to order, presented a bill incorporating the Great Falls manufacturing company in the county of Fayette.

On motion of Mr. Powell, *Ordered*, That 185 copies of the preamble and resolutions adopted by the general assembly in the year 1812, on the subject of the right of instruction, be printed for the use of the members of the general assembly.

On motion, *Ordered*, That leave of absence from the service of this house be granted to Mr. Jett and Mr. Ragsdale, for six days from Friday next.

The speaker laid before the house a report of the court of directors of the western lunatic hospital of Virginia, which, on motion of Mr. Mullen, was ordered to be laid upon the table, and that 185 copies thereof be printed for the use of the general assembly.

Mr. Ragsdale presented a petition of sundry citizens of the county of Lunenburg, praying that the separate election now holden at the house of Mrs. Fowlkes, may hereafter be holden at Pleasant Grove in said county.

Mr. Randolph, a petition of sundry citizens of the county of Henrico, for the establishment of two separate elections in said county.

Mr. Harrison presented a petition of citizens of the county of Harrison, for the establishment of a separate election at the house of Robert Reed in said county.

Ordered, That the said petitions be referred to the committee of propositions and grievances, that they do examine the matter thereof, and report their opinion thereupon to the house.

Mr. Ragsdale also presented a petition of Lucy Boomer, a free woman of colour, praying that if she is forced to be sold, she may be permitted the privilege of selecting her master.

Mr. Mullen, a petition of James Smith, a free man of colour, asking to be permitted to remain in the commonwealth.

Ordered, That the said petitions be referred to the committee for courts of justice, they do examine the matter thereof, and report their opinion thereupon to the house.

Mr. Madison presented a petition of the superintendents and trustees of the Upper Appomattox company, asking that the board of public works may be authorized to subscribe to the stock of the said company, and to authorize the construction of a tow-path on the bank of the Appomattox river, from the town of Farmville to the town of Petersburg, and for other amendments to the charter of the company.

Mr. Chapline presented a petition of a committee of the Brownsville convention, asking for a subscription by the state to the stock of the Baltimore and Ohio rail-road company.

Ordered, That the said petitions be referred to the committee of roads and internal navigation, that they do examine the matter thereof, and report their opinion thereupon to the house.

On motion of Mr. Sherrard, *Ordered*, That 185 copies of the said last memorial be printed for the use of the members of the general assembly.

Mr. Stanard presented a petition of Robert Briggs and others, for the passage of an act incorporating the petitioners and their successors, by the name of the medical college at Richmond, with the ordinary incidental powers of a corporation, which was ordered to be referred to the committee of schools and colleges, that they do examine the matter thereof, and report their opinion thereupon to the house.

Mr. Holleman, from the committee of privileges and elections, presented a report upon the contested election from the county of Henrico, which, on motion of Mr. Woolfolk, was ordered to be laid upon the table.

On motion of Mr. Daniel, the resolution submitted by Mr. Gilmer, which was under discussion on yesterday, was again taken up, and the question being upon the motion of Mr. Austin, that the farther consideration thereof be indefinitely postponed; and the same being under discussion,

On motion of Mr. Gregory, the house adjourned until to-morrow 12 o'clock.

THURSDAY, December 24th, 1835.

On motion of Mr. Fleet, *Resolved*, That the committee for courts of justice be instructed to enquire into the expediency of providing by law, that a certain portion of the property of debtors be exempted from execution for all debts hereafter contracted.

On motion of Mr. Woolfolk, the report of the committee of privileges and elections was taken up, and read as follows:

The committee of privileges and elections, to whom was referred the petition of John M. Botts, contesting the election of William B. Randolph, a delegate returned to serve in the present general assembly from the county of Henrico, have had the same under consideration, and have adopted the following general report, and a resolution thereupon, deeming it unnecessary, unless instructed by the house, to report specially the principles decided, or to state in detail the evidence adduced to sustain the votes contested by either party.

It appears to your committee from the poll-books of Henrico county, that at the close of the election the polls stood thus:

For Wm. B. Randolph,	419
For Jno. M. Botts.	380
Majority for Wm. B. Randolph,	39

John M. Botts contested one hundred and twenty-six votes on the poll of Wm. B. Randolph, of which number the objections to ninety-six were sustained by your committee. Of the said ninety-six votes, forty-two were decided to be illegal, or so admitted to be by William B. Randolph, and the remaining fifty-four were not attempted to be sustained by any evidence whatsoever. The remaining thirty votes were decided to be legal, or were so admitted by John M. Botts.

From William B. Randolph's poll of	419
Deduct the votes, the objections to which were sustained,	96
And there remains legal votes,	323

William B. Randolph contested on the poll of John M. Botts, one hundred and twenty votes, of which number the objections to thirty-eight were sustained by your committee. Of the said thirty-eight votes, twelve were decided to be illegal, or were so admitted to be by John M. Botts, and the remaining twenty-six were not attempted to be sustained by any evidence whatever.

The remaining eighty-two votes were decided to be legal, or were so admitted by William B. Randolph.

From John M. Botts's poll of	380
Deduct the votes, the objections to which were sustained,	38
And there remains legal votes,	342

The committee are, therefore, of the opinion, that the polls should stand thus:

For John M. Botts,	342
For William B. Randolph,	323
Majority for John M. Botts,	19

Resolved, therefore, as the opinion of this committee, That John M. Botts was duly elected a delegate from the county of Henrico to represent said county in the present general assembly.

The said resolution was, on the question put thereupon, agreed to by the house.

Ordered, That Mr. Botts be added to the several committees upon which Mr. Randolph was heretofore placed, in lieu of that gentleman.

On motions severally made, *Ordered,* That leave of absence from the service of this house be granted to Mr. Hopkins for two days; to Mr. Fitzgerald and to Mr. Wiley, for three days; to Mr. Booker for four days, and to Mr. Taylor of Middlesex, for six days each from Monday next.

Mr. Brown of Petersburg, presented a document to be used to support the petition of William Fenn; which was ordered to be referred to the committee of claims.

Mr. Stanard presented a petition of sundry citizens of the city of Richmond, for the incorporation of a company for the purpose of insuring property against destruction by fire, which was ordered to be referred to the committee of propositions and grievances, that they do examine the matter thereof, and report their opinion thereupon to the house.

On motion of Mr. Mullen, *Resolved,* That when this house adjourns to-day, it will adjourn until Monday next.

On motion of Mr. Garland of Mecklenburg, the resolution some days since submitted by Mr. Gilmer, and which was under discussion on yesterday, was taken up.

The same as amended is the following:

Resolved, by the general assembly of Virginia, That the governor of this commonwealth be requested to open a correspondence with the executive of those states within whose jurisdictions certain *fanatical or* incendiary associations have been formed, for the purpose of abolishing slavery in the district of Columbia, and in the United States, with a view to ascertain as far as practicable, the disposition of those states to provide by adequate legal enactments for the suppression of such associations and for arresting the circulation of their dangerous publications,—also with the executive authorities of other states, if he should deem it necessary, in order to ascertain the measures which have been taken or may be contemplated to counteract the fatal tendencies of these associations.

The question was put upon the motion made by Mr. Austin, that the farther consideration of the said resolution be indefinitely postponed, and was determined in the affirmative.—Ayes 66, noes 52.

On motion of Mr. Wilson of Botetourt, (seven of the members present concurring,) *Ordered,* That the ayes and noes upon the said question be inserted in the journal.

The names of the gentlemen who voted in the affirmative, are Messrs. Banks, (speaker,) Layne, Wiley, M'Clintic, Wilson of Botetourt, Decamps, Turnbull, Booker, Austin, Daniel, Richardson, Hill, Smith of Fauquier, Strange, Steger, Holland, Bowen, Davison, Watts, Watkins, Hail of Grayson, Coleman, Sloan, Nixon, Goodall, Harrison, Kincheloe, Fontaine, Holleman, Robinson, Hays, Straton, Harris, Taylor of Mathews & Middlesex, Rogers, Garland of Mecklenburg, Willey, Morgan, Chapman, Ingles, Sherrard, Leland, Fitzgerald, Woolfolk, Almond, M'Coy, Cackley, Hopkins, Carroll, Madison, Shands, Williams, Marteney, Nicklin, Moffett, Conrad, Jessee, M'Mullen, Bare, Rinker, Crutchfield, Moncure, Spratley, Hargrave, Gillespie and Gibson.—66.

And the names of the gentlemen who voted in the negative, are Messrs. Drummond, Gilmer, Brooke, Craig, Campbell, Pate, Henshaw, Beuhring, Clay, Christian, Johnson, Wilson of Cumberland, Servant, Hunter of Essex, Ball, Dickinson, Hale of Franklin, Smith of Frederick, Smith of Gloucester, Wethered, Mullen, Botts, Gregory, Griggs, Berry, Summers, Fleet, Hooe, Carter, Neill, Beard, Powell, Taylor of Loudoun, Ragsdale, Waggener, Parker, Chapline, Masters, Critz, Swanson, Witcher, Dorman, Leyburn, Harley, Butts, Delashmutt, Jett, Prentiss, Saunders, Cunningham, Brown of Petersburg, and Stanard.—52.

The speaker laid before the house a communication from the governor, which was read as follows:

EXECUTIVE DEPARTMENT, December 24th, 1835.

To the House of Delegates.

In compliance with their request, I have the honor to lay before you the accompanying report and resolutions in relation to the institution of domestic slavery, and the incendiary proceedings of the abolitionists in the non-slaveholding states, adopted unanimously, by both branches of the legislature of the state of South Carolina.

LITT'N W. TAZEWELL.

On motion of Mr. Dorman, *Ordered,* That the said communication and accompanying documents be laid upon the table, and that 185 copies thereof be printed for the use of the members of the general assembly.

On motion of Mr. Parker, the house then adjourned until Monday 12 o'clock.

MONDAY, December 28th, 1835.

Mr. Watkins from the committee of roads and internal navigation, reported with amendment a bill directing the survey and location of routes for certain roads therein mentioned.

And presented a bill to provide for the construction of a road between Weston in the county of Lewis and Charleston in the county of Kanawha.

Mr. Masters, according to order, presented a bill fixing the school quotas of the counties of Ohio and Marshall; which bills were severally received and laid upon the table.

Mr. M'Mullen presented sundry documents to be used as evidence in the contested election from the county of Patrick, which were ordered to be referred to the committee of privileges and elections.

Mr. Rogers presented a petition of sundry citizens of the town of Clarksville, for the passage of an act extending the boundaries of the said town, which was ordered to be referred to the committee of propositions and grievances, that they do examine the matter thereof, and report their opinion thereupon to the house.

Mr. Summers presented a petition of sundry citizens of the county of Kanawha, for the establishment of an independent bank at the town of Charleston.

Mr. Prentiss, a petition of a committee on behalf of the citizens of Parkersburg and its vicinity, praying for the establishment of a bank in said town.

Ordered, That the said petitions be referred to the committee on banks, that they do examine the matter thereof, and report their opinion thereupon to the house.

Mr. Layne presented a petition of Arthur Lee, a free man of colour, asking for permission to remain in the commonwealth, which was ordered to be referred to the committee for courts of justice, that they do examine the matter thereof, and report their opinion thereupon to the house.

Mr. Wilson of Botetourt, presented a petition of William Scott, praying for the passage of an act, authorizing him to construct a turnpike road across Price's and the Sweet springs mountains in the counties of Botetourt, Monroe and Alleghany.

Also, a petition of citizens of the counties of Rockbridge, Botetourt and Alleghany, for a company to construct a turnpike road from the head of the Blue Ridge canal to intersect the Lexington and Covington turnpike.

Ordered, That the said petitions be referred to the committee of roads and internal navigation, that they do examine the matter thereof, and report their opinion thereupon to the house.

Mr. Daniel presented a petition of John Jordan and F. H. Murrell, asking compensation for a horse which died in the service of the commonwealth; which was ordered to be referred to the committee of claims, that they do examine the matter thereof, and report their opinion thereupon to the house.

A bill to authorize a separate election at Greenfield, in the county of Nelson, was read a second time and ordered to be engrossed and read a third time.

A bill to amend the act, entitled "an act incorporating the Falmouth and Alexandria rail road company," was read the second time and ordered to be laid on the table on motion of Mr. Williams.

A bill incorporating the stockholders of the Louisa rail road company, with the amendments thereto proposed by the committee of roads and internal navigation, was taken up, and the said amendments being agreed to by the house with amendments, the same as amended, was ordered to be engrossed and read a third time.

A bill providing for the better security of persons charged with criminal offences, with the amendments thereto proposed by the committee for courts of justice, was taken up, and the said amendments being agreed to by the house, the same as amended, was ordered to be engrossed and read a third time.

The speaker laid before the house a communication from P. N. Nicholas, esq. president of the Farmers bank of Virginia, enclosing a statement giving the information called for by a resolution of the 11th instant, which on motion of Mr. Daniel was ordered to be laid upon the table, and that 185 copies thereof be printed for the use of the members of the general assembly.

A bill to amend an act, entitled, "an act to incorporate the Staunton and Potowmac rail-road company," was read the first, and ordered to be read a second time.

A bill directing the survey of a route for a road from the North-western road, in the direction of Beverley in the county of Randolph.

A bill to amend an act, entitled, "an act to incorporate the Midlothian coal mining company;" and

A bill to enlarge, define and establish, the corporate boundaries and limits of the town of Wheeling in the county of Ohio, were severally read the first, and on motions made, the second time, and ordered to be committed to the committees which brought them in respectively.

A bill incorporating the stockholders of the Richmond and Petersburg rail-road company, was also read the first and second times, and ordered to be committed to the committee which brought it in.

The following bills were read the first time, and ordered to be read a second time, viz:

A bill authorizing the board of public works to subscribe on behalf of the commonwealth to the stock of the Smith's river navigation company.

A bill to authorize the appointment of a third commissioner of the superior court of Petersburg.

A bill to regulate the conduct of boatmen on the Roanoke river and its branches.

A bill concerning the fire and marine insurance company of Wheeling.

A bill to authorize the mayor and commonalty of the town of Wheeling to subscribe for stock of the Baltimore and Ohio rail-road company.

A bill to incorporate the Virginia mills manufacturing company.

A bill incorporating the Lexington and Richmond turnpike company.

A bill to change the place of holding a separate election in the county of Marshall.

A bill to amend an act, entitled, "an act for incorporating the stockholders of the Winchester and Potowmac rail-road company;" and

A bill to amend the act establishing the town of Grandville in the county of Monongalia.

Ordered, That Mr. M'Coy be added to the committee of roads and internal navigation, and on the register's office.

A bill to alter the terms of the circuit superior courts of law and chancery for the seventh district and 13th circuit of this commonwealth; and

A bill to incorporate the Sweet springs company, were read the first and second times, and ordered to be committed to the committees which brought them in.

The speaker laid before the house a communication from John Brockenbrough, esq. president of the Bank of Virginia, enclosing a statement affording the information called for by a resolution of the house of delegates adopted on the 11th instant, which, on motion of Mr. Daniel, was ordered to be laid upon the table, and that 185 copies thereof be printed for the use of the general assembly.

Two reports of the committee of claims were read as follow:

The committee of claims have, according to order, had under consideration the petition of Shelton Ford, to them referred, praying to be released from a judgment rendered against him in the circuit superior court of law and chancery for the county of Preston, at the last term of the said county, for the sum of two hundred dollars and costs, for selling as a hawker and pedlar in the said county, clocks to sundry persons, without being duly licensed for such purpose: Whereupon,

Resolved as the opinion of this committee, That the prayer of the said petition is reasonable, so far as the commonwealth is interested.

The committee of claims have, according to order, had under consideration the petition of George Johnson, of Wood county, to them referred, praying to be released from a judgment rendered against him by the circuit superior court of law and chancery for the said county of Wood, upon an indictment against him for unlawful gaming: Whereupon,

Resolved as the opinion of this committee, That the prayer of the said petition is reasonable.

The said resolutions were, on questions severally put thereupon, agreed to by the house, and bills were ordered to be brought in conformably therewith.

A report of the committee of propositions and grievances, rejecting the petition of sundry citizens of the county of Marshall, for a change in the dividing lines between the counties of Ohio and Marshall, was, on motion of Mr. Chapline, ordered to be laid upon the table.

A report of the committee of propositions and grievances, was read as follows

The committee of propositions and grievances have, according to order, had under consideration sundry petitions to them referred, and have come to the following resolutions thereupon:

1. *Resolved as the opinion of this committee,* That the petition of sundry citizens of the counties of Lewis and Nicholas, praying for various reasons in the petition set forth, that a new county may be formed of parts of said counties within certain boundaries in the petition described, is reasonable.

2. *Resolved as the opinion of this committee,* That the petition of sundry citizens of Preston county, representing that for years past the inhabitants of Pennsylvania and Maryland have driven, every spring and summer, large herds of cattle to range and graze in the glades and prairies of said county, but protect themselves as to so much of such range as lies in the state of Maryland, by recent legislation upon the subject, the legislature of the said state of Maryland having about two years since, enacted laws directing the construction of public pounds, and

authorizing the detention therein of cattle found *damage feasant*; that the effect has been to cause very large herds of cattle to be brought to the said grazing lands in Virginia, which herds not unfrequently break enclosures and destroy whole crops of grain and grass; that wealthy men of Pennsylvania purchase poor spots of land in said county, and place a herdsman thereon to keep their stock within the range, to the very great injury of the inhabitants of Preston county; and praying thereupon, that laws similar to those of Maryland upon the subject, may be enacted by the general assembly of Virginia, or such other provisions made as will afford relief in the premises to the petitioners, is reasonable.

3. *Resolved as the opinion of this committee*, That the petition of sundry citizens of the county of Monongalia, praying that the separate election authorized to be holden at the house of Henry Ross, may be changed to the house of James B. Morgan, be rejected.

4. *Resolved also as the opinion of this committee*, That the remonstrance of sundry other citizens of said county against the removal of said separate election, is reasonable.

5. *Resolved as the opinion of this committee*, That the petition of sundry citizens of Preston county, praying that an act may pass changing the separate election now authorized to be holden at the house of Isaac Criss, to the house of Wick Johnson in the town of Evansville, is reasonable.

6. *Resolved as the opinion of this committee*, That the petition of sundry voters of the county of Wythe, praying that the separate election holden at the house of Joseph Graham may be changed to that of Harvey Shepherd, is reasonable.

7. *Resolved as the opinion of this committee*, That the petition of several owners of lands lying on Wheeling creek and the Ohio river, adjoining the town of South Wheeling, praying that an act may pass authorizing them respectively to erect wharves on their lands at their own expense, to receive such wharfage fees as the mayor and commonalty of the town of Wheeling are authorized to receive at their wharves, and that payment of said fees be enforced in the same manner as the fees due the said mayor and commonalty, is reasonable.

The said resolutions were, on questions severally put thereupon, agreed to by the house, and bills were ordered to be brought in conformably with the said first, second, fifth, sixth and seventh resolutions.

Sundry reports of the committee for courts of justice were read as follow:

The committee for courts of justice have, according to order, had under consideration the petition of Richard Bolling, a free man of colour, to them referred, praying to be permitted to remain in the commonwealth, and have come to the following resolution thereupon:

Resolved as the opinion of this committee, That the prayer of the said petition is reasonable.

The committee for courts of justice have, according to order, had under consideration the petition of William Fisher, of the county of Nicholas, to them referred, praying the release of the commonwealth's right to a tract of land lying in the said county, containing one thousand acres: Whereupon,

Resolved as the opinion of this committee, That the prayer of the said petition is reasonable.

The committee for courts of justice have, according to order, had under consideration the petition of Daniel Higginbotham, a free man of colour, to them referred, praying to be permitted to remain in the commonwealth for the term of four years: Whereupon,

Resolved as the opinion of this committee, That the prayer of the said petition is reasonable.

The committee for courts of justice have, according to order, had under consideration the petition of Duff Green of the county of Stafford, to them referred, praying that he may be released from a bond executed by him some time in the year 1818 or 1819, to the executive, conditioned for the safe return of arms, furnished for the use of a volunteer company commanded by the said Green, and that the said bond may be cancelled, in consequence of the said arms having been destroyed by fire: Whereupon,

Resolved as the opinion of this committee, That the prayer of the said petition is reasonable.

The said resolutions in each of said reports, were on questions severally put thereupon agreed to by the house, and bills were ordered to be brought in conformably therewith.

A report of the committee of roads and internal navigation was read as follows:

The committee of roads and internal navigation have, according to order, had under consideration the petition of sundry citizens of Randolph, Preston, and Monongalia counties, to them referred, and have come to the following resolution thereupon:

Resolved as the opinion of this committee, That the petition of sundry citizens of the counties of Randolph, Preston, and Monongalia, praying that the engineer of the state be directed to survey and locate a route for a road, during the present year, from the Pennsylvania line, through Morgantown, and near Evansville, to intersect the road leading from Clarksburg to Beverley, near the residence of Solomon Yeager, is reasonable.

The said resolution was, on the question put thereupon, agreed to by the house, and a bill was ordered to be brought in conformably therewith.

A report of the committee on agriculture and manufactures, was read as follows:

The committee of agriculture and manufactures, to whom was referred the petition of sundry citizens of the town of Petersburg and its vicinity, praying for the passage of an act of the general assembly to incorporate the "Ettrick banks manufacturing company," have had the same under consideration, and report the following resolution thereupon:

Resolved, That the prayer of the aforesaid petition is reasonable.

The same committee have had under consideration the petition of sundry citizens of the town of Petersburg, to them referred, praying for the passage of an act of assembly to incorporate "The Fleet's manufacturing company," and have come to the following resolution thereupon:

Resolved, That the prayer of the said petition is reasonable.

The said resolutions were, on questions severally put thereupon, agreed to by the house, and bills were ordered to be brought in conformably therewith.

Several reports of the committee for courts of justice, were read as follow:

The committee for courts of justice have, according to order, had under consideration the petition of Judy Johnson, a free woman of colour, to them referred, praying to be permitted to remain in the commonwealth: Whereupon,

Resolved as the opinion of this committee, That the prayer of the said petition is reasonable.

The committee for courts of justice have, according to order, had under consideration the petition of the inhabitants of Hardy county, to them referred, praying that Charlotte Morgan, a woman of colour, who has been emancipated by the last will and testament of James Stone, deceased, may be permitted to remain in the commonwealth: Whereupon,

Resolved as the opinion of this committee, That the prayer of the said petition is reasonable; and that the said Charlotte Morgan be permitted to remain in the commonwealth for the term of five years.

The committee for courts of justice have, according to order, had under consideration the petition of James Haskins, committee of John Haskins, senr., a lunatic, to them referred, praying that the estate of the said lunatic may be sold, and the proceeds arising from such sale invested in bank or other profitable stock: Whereupon,

Resolved as the opinion of this committee, That the prayer of the said petition is reasonable.

The said resolutions were, on questions put thereupon, agreed to by the house, and bills were ordered to be brought in conformably therewith.

Several reports of the committee of roads and internal navigation, were read as follow:

The committee of roads and internal navigation have, according to order, had under consideration the petition of sundry citizens of the counties of Hampshire and Frederick, praying that the tolls on the North-western turnpike be reduced to one half or one third of their present rates, and that persons going to mill, or residing within four miles of a turnpike gate, be exempt from payment of toll: Whereupon,

Resolved as the opinion of this committee, That so much of said petition as prays a reduction of the tolls on the North-western turnpike, is reasonable.

The committee of roads and internal navigation have, according to order, had under consideration the petition of sundry citizens of the towns of Petersburg and Farmville, and of the county of Prince George, praying the passage of an act incorporating a joint stock company to construct a rail-road from City Point in the county of Prince George to some point within the town of Petersburg: Whereupon,

Resolved as the opinion of this committee, That the said petition is reasonable.

The committee of roads and internal navigation have, according to order, had under consideration the petition of James Shanks and John B. Lewis, praying that they be authorized by law to construct a turnpike road from the eastern side of the Seven mile or Price's mountain to the Sweet springs in the county of Monroe, a distance of about twelve miles, for the same rates of toll as are now authorized on seven miles of the distance by a charter to Jacob Price and others, now about to expire: Whereupon,

Resolved as the opinion of this committee, That the said petition is reasonable.

The said committee have also, according to order, had under consideration the petition of John Wood, praying that he may be authorized by law to construct a turnpike road over Price's and the Sweet springs mountains, upon such terms as may be deemed reasonable: Whereupon,

Resolved as the opinion of this committee, That the said petition is reasonable.

The committee of roads and internal navigation have, according to order, had under consideration sundry petitions to them referred, and have come to the following resolutions thereupon:

1. *Resolved as the opinion of this committee,* That the petition of sundry citizens of the counties of Kanawha and Fayette, praying the incorporation of a company to construct a turnpike road from the Narrow falls of New river, to some point opposite the town of Charleston in the county of Kanawha, with an adequate amount of capital, and power to enlarge the same, if found necessary, and with authority to erect a bridge across New river, at or near the Narrow falls, if found expedient by the company, is reasonable.

2. *Resolved as the opinion of this committee,* That the petition of sundry citizens of the county of Preston, praying that the act passed February the 20th, 1834, entitled, "an act directing a change of location of that part of the North-western road passing through the town of Evansville," may be so amended as to make it obligatory on the president and directors of the road to make such change of location, after having the payment of any additional expense which may be incurred thereby secured to be paid by the citizens of said town, is reasonable.

The committee of roads and internal navigation have, according to order, enquired "into the expediency of passing an act authorizing the board of public works to subscribe, on the part of the commonwealth, for $28,000 of the stock of the Upper Appomattox company, provided the said company shall find it necessary to require such subscription; the said $28,000 being the balance of the stock which said company were authorized to raise by an act of the last legislature, passed the   day of   1835:" Whereupon,

Resolved as the opinion of this committee, That it is expedient to authorize the said subscription on the part of the commonwealth.

11

The committee of roads and internal navigation have, according to order, had under consideration the petition of Henry P. Parker of the county of Accomac, representing that the petitioner has purchased of a certain Samuel C. White his right, under an act of the general assembly, to run a line of packets from the town of Onancock in said county to Norfolk, being required by said act to keep two packets on the line; that the travelling between the two places will not support two regular packets, and that he cannot run them without great pecuniary loss; and praying that such an amendment of said act, as to authorize him to keep but one boat or vessel on the line: Whereupon,

Resolved as the opinion of this committee, That said petition is reasonable.

The said resolutions in each report were, on questions severally put thereupon, agreed to by the house, and bills were ordered to be brought in conformably therewith.

A report of the committee appointed to examine the clerk's office was read as follows:

The committee appointed to examine the clerk's office, have, in obedience to order, performed that duty, and beg leave to report,

That they have carefully examined into the condition of the books and papers of the office, and find them neatly and systematically arranged, so as to afford a ready and convenient reference to them. That the enrolled bills from the year 1776 inclusive, up to the present time, are carefully preserved in separate tin cases for each year respectively, and upon examination of some of the most ancient of them, they were found in a good state of preservation. The original petitions, executive communications, resolutions, rough bills and miscellaneous papers belonging to the office, were also found to be filed in regular succession and in neat order. The journals of the house of delegates up to the present time were also found carefully bound up and in good order.

Your committee have ascertained, by reference to the journal of the last year, that the committee appointed to examine the clerk's office, recommended that the clerk should be hereafter instructed to make out and prepare an index to the journal of the house, to be printed and bound up with the journal at the end of the session. And in accordance with this recommendation, the house adopted a resolution requiring the clerk to prepare such an index, and that a reasonable compensation be allowed him for this additional service.

In obedience to this instruction, the clerk has prepared an index to the journal of the last session, an examination of which will demonstrate at once its utility and absolute necessity.

This index is still in manuscript form only, no provision having been made for printing and binding it up according to the intention of the house, and your committee find that no compensation has been allowed the clerk for preparing the same, and as your committee still think it indispensable to the proper use of the journals that the index should be prepared, printed and bound up annually, and that such additional labour ought not to be imposed on the clerk without remuneration.

Resolved therefore as the opinion of this committee, That it is expedient to provide by law for the preparation and printing hereafter of an index to the journal of the house of delegates, and for allowing a compensation therefor.

The said resolution was, on the question put thereupon, agreed to by the house, and a bill was ordered to be brought in conformably therewith.

Several reports of the committee of propositions and grievances, were read as follow:

The committee of propositions and grievances have, according to order, had under consideration the petition of sundry citizens of the county of Berkeley, to them referred, praying that the separate election heretofore authorized to be holden at the mill of Thomas Robinson, may hereafter be holden at the stone school-house of Lewis Grantham: Whereupon,

Resolved as the opinion of this committee, That the prayer of said petition is reasonable.

The committee of propositions and grievances have, according to order, had under consideration several petitions to them referred, and have come to the following resolutions thereupon:

1. *Resolved as the opinion of this committee,* That the petition of sundry citizens of the town of Portsmouth, praying that a charter may be granted them with a capital of two hundred thousand dollars, for the formation of a steam-boat company, for the purpose of navigating the waters of the Chesapeake and its tributaries, is reasonable.

2. *Resolved as the opinion of this committee,* That the petition of sundry citizens of Berkeley county, praying that an act may pass authorizing a separate election at the tavern-house of Baley T. Hedges in the town of Hedgesville, is reasonable.

3. *Resolved as the opinion of this committee,* That the petition of sundry citizens of the county of Stafford, praying that an act may pass authorizing a separate election at the store-house, near the mill called Tackett's mill, in said county, be rejected for want of notice.

The said resolutions were, on questions put thereupon, agreed to by the house, and bills were ordered to be brought in conformably with all the said resolutions except the last.

On motion of Mr. Drummond, the house adjourned until to-morrow 12 o'clock.

TUESDAY, December 29th, 1835.

On motion, *Ordered,* That leave of absence from the service of this house be granted to Messrs. Holleman and Spratley for three days from to-day.

On motion of Mr. Williams, a bill to amend the act, entitled, "an act incorporating the Falmouth and Alexandria rail road company," was taken up and read a second time, and on motion of Mr. Smith of Fauquier, the same was ordered to be recommitted to the committee which brought it in.

A motion was made by Mr. M'Mullen that the house adopt the following resolution:

Resolved, That the committee on finance be instructed to enquire into the expediency of altering the taxes as at present imposed by law upon horses and mules: and the question being put thereupon, was determined in the negative.

On motion of Mr. Chapman, *Resolved,* That the committee on roads and internal navigation be requested to enquire into the expediency of incorporating a joint stock company to construct a turnpike road from the Red Sulphur springs in the county of Monroe, passing by Giles court-house, to the town of Newburn in the county of Montgomery, and have leave to report thereon by bill or otherwise.

Mr. Hill from the committee of propositions and grievances, presented a report upon the petition of sundry citizens of the city of Richmond, for an insurance company.

Also, a bill to change the place of holding a separate election in the county of Preston.

A bill to change the place of holding a separate election in the county of Wythe.

And a bill to authorize William Chapline and others to construct wharves on Wheeling creek and the Ohio river, adjoining the town of South Wheeling, in Ohio county, which were received and laid upon the table.

Mr. Neil presented a petition of John C. Olinger, asking to be authorized to redeem a part of a tract of land forfeited to the commonwealth for the non-payment of taxes, which was ordered to be referred to the committee of finance, that they do examine the matter thereof, and report their opinion thereupon to the house.

Mr. Willey presented a petition of sundry citizens of the counties of Preston and Monongalia and Tyler, asking aid to construct a road from Brandonville in the county of Preston to the mouth of Fishing creek in the county of Tyler.

Mr. Carroll, a similar petition of citizens of the county of Preston.

Ordered, That the said petitions be referred to the committee of roads and internal navigation, that they do examine the matter thereof, and report their opinion thereupon to the house.

Mr. Chapman presented a petition of sundry citizens living in the vicinity of Pearisburg, in the county of Giles, asking the repeal of so much of the law authorizing the election of trustees of the town of Pearisburg, as gives the said trustees power to impose fines or penalties on horses, hogs, or other stock which may be found in the limits of said town, and whose owners are non-residents of said town, which was ordered to be referred to the committee of propositions and grievances, that they do examine the matter thereof, and report their opinion thereupon to the house.

Mr. Daniel, from the committee of privileges and elections, presented a report upon the contested election from the counties of Fayette and Nicholas, which being read, was ordered to be recommitted to the said committee, on motion of Mr. Woolfolk, with instructions to report specially in such cases as the parties to the contest may desire a report upon.

An engrossed bill to authorize a separate election at Greenfield, in the county of Nelson, was read a third time:

Resolved, That the bill do pass, and that the title be, "an act to authorize a separate election at Greenfield, in the county of Nelson."

An engrossed bill providing for the better security of persons charged with criminal offences, was read a third time:

Resolved, That the bill do pass, and that the title be, "an act providing for the better security of persons charged with criminal offences."

Ordered, That the clerk communicate the same to the senate and request their concurrence.

An engrossed bill incorporating the stockholders of the Louisa rail-road company, was read a third time, and on motion of Mr. Woolfolk, ordered to be laid upon the table.

A bill directing the survey and location of routes for certain roads therein mentioned, with the amendments thereto proposed by the committee of roads and internal navigation, was taken up, and the said amendments being agreed to by the house with an amendment, the said bill as amended was ordered to be engrossed and read a third time.

A bill to amend an act, entitled, "an act to incorporate the Staunton and Potomac rail-road company," was read a second time, and on motion of Mr. Moffett, ordered to be committed to the committee which brought it in.

A bill to amend the act establishing the town of Grandville in the county of Monongalia.

A bill authorizing the board of public works to subscribe on behalf of the commonwealth to the stock of the Smith's river navigation company; and

A bill to authorize the appointment of a third commissioner of the superior court of Petersburg, were read a second time, and ordered to be engrossed and read a third time.

A bill to regulate the conduct of boatmen on the Roanoke river and its branches, was read a second time, and on motion of Mr. Dorman, ordered to be committed to the committee which brought it in.

A bill to incorporate the Virginia mills manufacturing company, was read a second time, and ordered to be engrossed and read a third time.

A bill incorporating the Lexington and Richmond turnpike company, was read a second time, amended on motion of Mr. Dorman, and ordered to be engrossed and read a third time.

A bill to change the place of holding a separate election in the county of Marshall.

A bill to amend an act, entitled, "an act for incorporating the stockholders of the Winchester and Potomac railroad company."

A bill concerning the fire and marine insurance company of Wheeling; and

A bill to authorize the mayor and commonalty of the town of Wheeling to subscribe for stock of the Baltimore and Ohio rail-road company, were severally read the second time, and ordered to be engrossed and read a third time.

A motion was made by Mr. Austin that this house do now adjourn, and the question being put thereupon, was determined in the negative. Ayes 34, noes 43.

On motion of Mr. Parker, (seven of the members present concurring,) *Ordered*, That the ayes and noes upon the said question be inserted in the journal.

The names of the gentlemen who voted in the affirmative, are Messrs. Southall, Layne, Brooke, Wilson of Botetourt, Austin, Daniel, Samuel, Hunter of Essex, Ball, Davison, Smith of Frederick, Watts, Smith of Gloucester, Nixon, Mullen, Harrison, Botts, Straton, Powell, Waggener, Rogers, Willey, Sherrard, Woolfolk, Swanson, Cackley, Carroll, M'Mullen, Bare, Harley, Gillespie, Delashmutt, Gibson and Cunningham.—34.

And the names of the gentlemen who voted in the negative, are Messrs. Banks, (speaker,) Grinalds, Drummond, Craig, Campbell, Henshaw, Decamps, Turnbull, Beuhring, Hill, Smith of Fauquier, Hickerson, Hale of Franklin, Holland, Bowen, Watkins, Hail of Grayson, Coleman, Goodall, Kincheloe, Berry, Summers, Fleet, Carter, Harris, Chapman, Parker, Chapline, Masters, Almond, M'Coy, Witcher, Williams, Nicklin, Dorman, Leyburn, Moffett, Conrad, Jessee, Butts, Moncure, Saunders and Stanard.—43.

The speaker laid before the house a communication from the governor, transmitting the copy of a letter just received from the governor of the state of Maryland, written by him on the 24th instant, in answer to a letter of the governor of the 10th ulto., relative to the boundaries of the state of Maryland, which, on motion of Mr. Wilson of Botetourt, was ordered to be laid upon the table, and that 185 copies thereof be printed for the use of the members of the general assembly.

A report of the committee of propositions and grievances, was read as follows:

The committee of propositions and grievances have, according to order, had under consideration the petition of the merchants, manufacturers, tradesmen and citizens of the town of Petersburg, to them referred, praying that a charter may be granted to them with the usual privileges of a corporate company, and under such guards and restrictions as may seem just and reasonable, for the purpose of establishing a navigation company to facilitate the commerce of said town with the northern cities: Whereupon,

Resolved as the opinion of this committee, That the prayer of the petition aforesaid is reasonable.

The said resolution was, on the question put thereupon, agreed to by the house, and a bill was ordered to be brought in conformably therewith.

A report of the committee of roads and internal navigation, rejecting the petition of sundry citizens of the county of Fairfax, for the repeal of the act imposing half tolls on return wagons, &c., on the Little river turnpike, was, on motion of Mr. Ball, ordered to be laid upon the table.

On motion of Mr. Mullen, the house adjourned until to-morrow 12 o'clock.

WEDNESDAY, December 30th, 1835.

On motion of Mr. Hunter of Essex, *Resolved*, That the committee for courts of justice be instructed to enquire into the expediency of so amending an act, entitled, "an act providing a method for making partition of real estate held in joint tenancy, tenancy in common or co-parcenery, where some of the parties interested are known, and their shares ascertained, and others of the parties are unknown or their shares are not ascertainable," as to extend its operation to personal as well as real estate.

On motion of Mr. Hopkins, *Resolved*, That the committee for courts of justice be instructed to enquire into the expediency of conferring upon the circuit superior courts of law and chancery, concurrent jurisdiction with the county and corporation courts, in all actions of forcible entry and detainer, and that they have leave to report by bill or otherwise.

Resolved, That the committee for courts of justice be instructed to enquire into the expediency of amending or explaining by legislative enactment, the 23d section of the act, entitled, "an act to reduce into one act, the several acts and parts of acts, concerning the county and other inferior courts, and the jurisdiction of justices of the peace within this commonwealth," and that they have leave to report by bill or otherwise.

On motion of Mr. Cunningham, *Resolved*, That the committee of roads and internal navigation be instructed to enquire into the expediency of amending an act, entitled, "an act for cutting a navigable canal from the waters of Elizabeth river, in the state of Virginia, to the waters of Pasquotank river in North Carolina," passed December the 1st, 1787; and that the said committee have leave to report by bill or otherwise.

On motion of Mr. Woolfolk, *Resolved*, That the committee of privileges and elections be instructed to enquire whether a stockholder in a corporation, which corporation holds lands, can by virtue of his stock be a freeholder or so possessed of said land or any part thereof, as to entitle him to the right of suffrage under the constitution, and report their opinion with their reasons to this house.

Mr. Brooke reported with amendment, a bill to amend an act, entitled, "an act to incorporate the Staunton and Potomac rail-road company."

Mr. Smith of Fauquier, reported with a substitute a bill to amend the act, entitled, "an act incorporating the Falmouth and Alexandria rail-road company."

Mr. Watkins, from the committee of roads and internal navigation, presented a bill further to amend the act, entitled, "an act to amend the act, entitled, 'an act establishing a ferry from Onancock town in the county of Accomack to Norfolk, and for other purposes,'" passed March 5th, 1833.

A bill directing the survey and location of a route for a road from the Pennsylvania line to its intersection with the road from Clarksburg to Beverley; and

A bill to incorporate the Narrow falls turnpike company.

Mr. Hill, from the committee of propositions and grievances, presented a report upon the petition of the trustees of the town of Clarkesville in Montgomery; also,

A bill to authorize a separate election at Hedgesville in the county of Berkeley; and

A bill to change the place of holding a separate election in the county of Berkeley.

Mr. Beuhring, according to order, presented a bill to amend the act, entitled, "an act to reduce into one the several acts for the settlement and regulation of ferries," passed January 30th, 1819.

Mr. Chapline reported without amendment, a bill to enlarge, define and establish the corporate boundaries and limits of the town of Wheeling in the county of Ohio.

Which bills and report were received and laid upon the table.

Mr. Henshaw presented a petition of sundry citizens of the county of Berkeley, praying the establishment of a town in said county, to be called the town of Hedgesville.

Mr. Beard, a petition of sundry citizens of the county of Loudoun, for an act incorporating a joint stock company to construct a bridge across the Shenandoah river at Harper's ferry.

Mr. Griggs, a petition of citizens of the county of Frederick, asking the formation of a new county out of said county.

Mr. Dorman a petition of John Ruff and John Jordan, asking leave to erect a toll-bridge across the Buffaloe creek in the county of Rockbridge.

Mr. Leyburn, a petition of citizens of the county of Rockbridge, opposing the petition of the said Ruff and Jordan.

Ordered, That the said petitions be referred to the committee of propositions and grievances, that they do examine the matter thereof, and report their opinion thereupon to the house.

Mr. Harley presented a petition of sundry citizens of the county of Smyth, for the establishment of a branch of one of the state banks in one of the south-western counties, on the main stage road between the New river and Tennessee line, which was ordered to be referred to the committee on banks, that they do examine the matter thereof, and report their opinion thereupon to the house.

On motion of Mr. Carter, *Resolved*, That the committee on increasing the banking capital of the commonwealth be authorized to employ a clerk to said committee.

Mr. Masters presented a petition of Isabella Anderson, asking to be divorced from her husband Robert Anderson, which was ordered to be referred to the committee for courts of justice, that they do examine the matter thereof, and report their opinion thereupon to the house.

On motion of Mr. Chapman, *Ordered*, That the committee of schools and colleges be discharged from the consideration of the petition of sundry citizens of the county of Monroe, and that the same be referred to the committee of roads and internal navigation, that they do examine the matter thereof, and report their opinion thereupon to the house.

Mr. Daniel, from the committee of privileges and elections, presented a report, which was taken up and read as follows:

The committee of privileges and elections, according to the following resolution passed by the house of delegates on the 29th December, 1835: "*Ordered*, That the committee of privileges and elections be instructed to report specially in the contested election from Fayette and Nicholas, in such cases as the parties to the contest may desire a report," have proceeded to report specially on the following votes, found on the poll of Hudson M. Dickinson, at his request.

In relation to the vote of George G. Mollohon, it appears by a patent produced, that on the 23d of February, 1835, a grant issued to George G. and James F. Mollohon, for one hundred and forty acres of land in Nicholas county:

1. *Resolved therefore as the opinion of this committee*, That the vote of said George G. Mollohon is illegal.

In relation to the vote of John Frame, it appears from the deposition of Robert Hamilton, clerk of Nicholas county, that a deed was recorded in that county on the 12th of March, 1828, from Robert Duffield to John Frame, Andrew Frame and three others, for 250 acres of land; that in the year 1832, this land was returned by the sheriff as unascertainable, and since has not been replaced on the commissioner's books. It appears further, from the evidence of Robert Duffield, that he purchased two thousand acres of land of Isaac Gregory, and that this land conveyed to John Frame and others was a part of that tract; that he gave eighty dollars for the 2,000 acre tract; that Gregory bought this land of the high sheriff of Randolph county, who sold it for the tax in 1816; and that said Gregory had brought a suit in chancery to quiet the title, but the result of the suit was not known; that the deponent believes the object in Frame's obtaining this deed was to obtain a right to vote. It appears from the deposition of John Frame, that he paid no consideration for this land, but that Duffield said it was made in consideration of his Duffield's having lived with him, but that the particular design was to entitle him to vote; that he did not consider the land of any great value, because he had never seen the land; and that he did suppose that he had a title to the land; and it appears by the deposition of Andrew B. Frame, that the design in making the deed was to entitle him to vote, and that he paid nothing for the land. It appears from the deposition of James M'Million, who states that he was deputy sheriff in Nicholas county for about seven years, and that he has been surveyor of the county near four years, that he believes the land was returned as unascertainable; and that he believes there is no such land:

2. *Resolved therefore as the opinion of this committee,* That the vote of said John Frame is illegal.

In relation to the votes of Hezekiah B. Copeland and Wilson Lloyd, it appears from their depositions, that they were housekeepers and heads of families more than twelve months preceding the election; and in answer to questions whether they were charged with any part of the revenue for 1834, and had paid the same, answered, they were charged with one horse each, and had paid the same, and had sheriff's receipts, but did not state at what time the tax was paid, whether before or after the election. These depositions were taken on the 28th September, 1835. And it appears from the deposition of William Tyree, deputy sheriff, that they had not paid the revenue before the election. It appears from the deposition of John P. Huddleston and Hiram Hill, that they were able to pay the revenue if the sheriff had used proper exertions; that according to the best belief these votes were considered legal upon the scrutiny of the poll for a site for the erection of the public buildings in said county; and that William Tyree was applied to as authority to know who had paid their taxes, and that no vote was allowed except such as he pronounced good:

3. *Resolved therefore as the opinion of this committee,* That the votes of Hezekiah B. Copeland and Wilson Lloyd, are illegal.

As relates to the votes of John Johnson, jr., James Johnson and Turly Foster, it appears by their own depositions that they were each a housekeeper and head of a family in the county more than twelve months before the election; that they each were charged with revenue, but had not paid the same though they were able to pay; and the testimony of John P. Huddleston and Hiram Hill, is the same as relates to Copeland and Lloyd:

4. *Resolved therefore,* That the votes of said John Johnson, jr. James Johnson and Turly Foster, are illegal.

The following votes were specially reported on at the request of Samuel Price, being found on the poll of Hudson M. Dickinson:

In relation to the vote of Israel A. Friend, it appears by the deposition of Andrew P. Friend, that he acknowledged a deed to said Israel A. Friend for 73 acres of land in Nicholas county, before two justices of the peace in 1830; that it was a deed of gift; that said Israel A. had been in possession of the land ever since; that it was Israel A.'s own fault that the deed had not been recorded; but the said Andrew P. Friend had ever held the deed, though he ever renounced title to the land:

5. *Resolved therefore as the opinion of this committee,* That the vote of Israel A. Friend is legal.

In relation to the vote of Hiram Hines, it appears from the deposition of Matthew Hines, that he acknowledged a deed to Hiram Hines in the fall of 1833, before two justices for land; the patent contained 455 acres; that it was delivered to a third person to carry to the clerk's office more than twelve months before the election:

6. *Resolved therefore as the opinion of this committee,* That the vote of Hiram Hines is legal.

In relation to the vote of James B. Cale, it appears from the deposition of said Cale, that he has a grant for two and a half acres of land, for which he would not take $100. And it appears from the deposition of Miles Manser, that he would not consider the land worth any thing. And it appears that this land was never charged on the commissioner's books, until 1835, when it was charged at $25. And it appears from said Cale's deposition, that he has been a housekeeper for six or seven years, and he appears charged on the commissioner's books with one horse in 1834, and no evidence of payment of taxes before the election:

7. *Resolved therefore as the opinion of this committee,* That the vote of James B. Cale is legal.

In relation to the vote of David M'Colgin, it appears that he is charged with revenue and paid the same in 1834; that he is a housekeeper, is not married, though there is a child bound to him and lives with him, and that a woman lives with him, as it is said in the neighbourhood, in illicit cohabitation:

8. *Resolved therefore as the opinion of this committee,* That the vote of David M'Colgin is legal.

At the request of Hudson M. Dickinson, the following votes are reported on specially, being found on the poll of Samuel Price:

In relation to the vote of Thomas Wells, it appears by a certificate of the clerk of Fayette county, that a deed from William T. Stockton for fifty acres of land in said county, was made to him, dated on the 24th day of August, 1834, and recorded the 21st day of April, 1835, and William T. Stockton is admitted to have been the owner of more than fifty acres of land in said county, though not charged with any on the commissioner's books of 1834:

9. *Resolved therefore,* That the vote of the said Thomas Wells is legal.

As relates to the vote of Andrew Lewis, it appears from the deposition of William Tyree, deputy sheriff, that he was charged with revenue for 1834, and paid the same before the election; that he had resided several years in the county; that since the death of his wife, he and his children lived with Abraham Price; and that he was the head of a family more than twelve months before the election; that he had a farm with a dwelling house thereon, near to Abraham Price; and it appears from the deposition of Abraham Price, that he considered Andrew Lewis a housekeeper for more than twelve months before the election; and it appears that his wife died in 1832:

10. *Resolved therefore,* That the vote of the said Andrew Lewis is legal.

As regards the vote of William Ryon, it appears from the deposition of Samuel Sparr, that on the 29th day of March, 1833, he sold to William Ryon a tract of land containing ninety some odd acres, ever since which time he has had it in possession, and that a deed was executed for said land by Sparr to Ryon on the day of the election:

11. *Resolved therefore,* That the vote of the said William Ryon is legal.

As regards the vote of William Terry, it appears from the depositions of William Tyree, deputy sheriff, and Thomas B. Hamilton, that he owns a farm; was charged with revenue for the year 1834, and paid the same before the election; that he had dwelled on his farm with his mother for more than twelve months before the election, and had the care and management of them, they alone keeping house :

12. *Resolved therefore,* That the vote of the said William Terry is legal.

As regards the vote of James R. Ramsey, it appears from the deposition of William Tyree, deputy sheriff, that he was charged with revenue for the year 1834, and paid the same before the election; and that he had been a housekeeper and head of a family in said county for more than twelve months before the election; but it appears that James Ramsey and not James R. Ramsey is charged on the commissioner's book:

13. *Resolved therefore,* That the vote of said James R. Ramsey is legal.

As regards the vote of Elisha Williams, it appears from the deposition of John M'Clung, deputy sheriff, that he resides and has resided in the county of Fayette, the county in which he voted, for more than twelve months before the election; had been a housekeeper and head of a family for more than twelve months before the election, and a freeholder in Nicholas county; was charged with 159 acres of land on the commissioner's books, and paid the tax before the election. Upon reference to the commissioner's books of the said county, Elisha Williams, Bath county, appears so charged :

14. *Resolved therefore,* That the vote of the said Elisha Williams is legal.

As regards the vote of George Underwood, it appears from the deposition of Robert Hamilton, that he is the son of James Underwood, deceased; that James Underwood is charged with 100 acres of land, valued at $50, of which he died possessed; and that since the death of said James Underwood, his heirs recovered 92 acres of land in said county of Elijah Lightner and others, before the election; and it appears that Elijah Lightner is charged with four tracts of land in said county, in all making 212½ acres, the average value of which, as charged on the commissioner's books, is 95 cents, and which make the value of 92 acres amount to $87 40 cents. It appears that four of the heirs of James Underwood, deceased, voted, two of whom were heads of families and housekeepers charged with revenue, and entitled so to vote if they had paid the same:

15. *Resolved therefore,* That the vote of the said George Underwood is legal.

As regards the vote of Peter Duffy, it is admitted that he had a freehold qualification to vote, and it appears that at the March term 1835 of the county court of Nicholas, he took the necessary oaths to entitle him to the rights of citizenship:

16. *Resolved therefore,* That the vote of the said Peter Duffy is legal.

As regards the vote of William S. Gregory, whose vote appears to be challenged in the following words : " William S. Gregory not qualified according to the constitution for same reason of Henry Jones ;" and the challenge to the vote of Henry Jones is in these words : " Henry Jones paid revenue on land conveyed by him to another more than one year preceding the election." The name of William S. Gregory appears on the polls to be entered William G. Gregory; but it is admitted that William S. Gregory, William G. Gregory, and William Gregory, are the same man. It appears from the deposition of Robert Hamilton, that William G. Gregory conveyed by deed to Ezra Clifton 95 acres of land, which deed was recorded in the clerk's office of Nicholas county on the 9th day of November, 1831. William Gregory appears charged on the commissioner's books of Nicholas county, for the year 1834, with 95 acres of land; and the aforesaid witness states, that he does not know whether this is the same land conveyed to Clifton or not; and it appears further from a certificate produced, signed by the first clerk in the register's office, that a grant for 95 acres of land issued to William Gregory on the 23d day of December, 1831, for land in Nicholas county. It appears that said Clifton is not charged on said books of 1834 with any land :

17. *Resolved therefore,* That the vote of said William S. Gregory is legal.

As regards the vote of Moses Caufield, it appears from the deposition of James M'Million, that he married a daughter of John Skidmore, deceased; that said Caufield and wife resided on the same farm with John Skidmore, and that said Skidmore recognized Caufield to be his son-in-law. It appears from the commissioner's book of Nicholas county, that the heirs of John Skidmore, in the year 1834, are charged with two tracts of land—one of 99 acres, valued at $99, and the other of 7 acres, valued at $3 50 cents, which the clerk of said county of Nicholas certifies have not been conveyed away. Said Caufield's name does not appear on said books :

18. *Resolved therefore,* That the vote of said Moses Caufield is legal.

At the request of Samuel Price, the votes of Joseph Young, John Sparr and James C. Warren, are specially reported on, they being found on his poll.

In relation to the vote of Joseph Young, it appears from a certificate of the register of the land office, that a grant issued to Joseph Young on the 7th of July, 1830, for fifty acres of land in Nicholas county; and it appears further, that this land calls to join the land of Robert Hughes, senior, on the north side of Gauley river, and it is admitted that Robert Hughes, senior, lives in that part of Fayette county which formed a portion of Nicholas in 1831, but that his land joins, or nearly joins, the county line. It also appears from the commissioner's books, that Robert Hughes, senior, is charged with land in Fayette county, and that he is not charged in Nicholas county with any land; and it is further admitted, that the land on the north side of Gauley river in Nicholas county, adjoining Robert Hughes, senior, is improved, and has been long in cultivation by others for one half mile:

19. *Resolved therefore as the opinion of this committee,* That the vote of Joseph Young is illegal.

In relation to the vote of John Sparr, it appears from the deposition of John Manix, that John Sparr has long been a housekeeper and head of a family in the county of Fayette, at least from its formation; that the deponent resides with said Sparr, and that when a demand was made for a list of taxable property in 1834, the property, one negro and one horse, belonging to John Sparr, was charged to him, the deponent, who is the principal manager of the business of the family; and that said revenue, thus charged, was paid by him before the election, and the sheriff's receipt given in his name:

20. *Resolved therefore,* That the vote of John Sparr is illegal.

In relation to the vote of James C. Warren, who voted in the county of Fayette, it is admitted that he has a freehold qualification to vote in Nicholas county, but none in Fayette

21. *Resolved therefore as the opinion of this committee,* That the vote of James C. Warren is illegal.

The first, second, third, fourth, sixth, eighth, ninth, eleventh, twelfth, thirteenth and fourteenth resolutions were on questions severally put thereupon agreed to by the house.

The said third resolution being under consideration, a motion was made by Mr. Woolfolk to amend the same by striking therefrom the word "illegal," and inserting in lieu thereof the word "legal," so as to reverse the decision of the committee, and the question being put thereupon was determined in the negative. Ayes 30, noes 71.

On motion of Mr. Hunter of Berkeley, (seven of the members present concurring,) *Ordered,* That the ayes and noes upon the said question be inserted in the journal.

The names of the gentlemen who voted in the affirmative, are Messrs. Pate, Miller, Wilson of Botetourt, Turnbull, Daniel, Steger, Hale of Franklin, Davison, Watts, Watkins, Hail of Grayson, Wethered, Nixon, Mullen, Kincheloe, Powell, Morgan, Ingles, Sherrard, Woolfolk, Almond, Cackley, Williams, Marteney, Dorman, Jessee, Bare, Rinker, Gillespie and Saunders.—30.

And the names of the gentlemen who voted in the negative, are Messrs Banks, (speaker,) Grinalds, Drummond, Layne, Brooke, Craig, M'Clintic, Campbell, Hunter of Berkeley, Henshaw, Decamps, Austin, Beuhring, Samuel, Christian, Hill, Hunter of Essex, Ball, Smith of Fauquier, Hickerson, Holland, Bowen, Smith of Gloucester, Coleman, Sloan, Goodall, Harrison, Botts, Griggs, Berry, Summers, Fleet, Hooe, Robinson, Carter, Neill, Hays, Straton, Beard, Taylor of Loudoun, Harris, Waggener, Rogers, Garland of Mecklenburg, Willey, Chapman, Murdaugh, Parker, Chapline, Masters, M'Coy, Swanson, Witcher, Hopkins, Carroll, Morris, Shands, Nicklin, Leyburn, Moffett, Conrad, M'Mullen, Harley, Butts, Crutchfield, Delashmutt, Gibson, Prentiss, Cunningham, Brown of Petersburg, and Stanard.—71.

The question then recurred upon concurring with the committee, and was decided in the affirmative.

The said fifth, seventh and tenth resolutions were, on questions severally put thereupon, disagreed to by the house.

Previous to these several questions, on motion of Mr. Southall, he was excused from voting thereupon.

On motion of Mr. Woolfolk, the residue of the said report was ordered to be laid upon the table, and the general report of the said committee was taken up. The same is the following:

The committee of privileges and elections have adopted the following general report, and a resolution thereupon, deeming it unnecessary, unless instructed by the house, to report specially the principles decided, or to state in detail the evidence adduced to sustain the votes contested by either party.

It appears to your committee, from a copy of the poll books of the said counties of Fayette and Nicholas, that at the close of the polls, the aggregate vote stood thus:

For Hudson M. Dickinson,	236
For Samuel Price, on face of poll,	223
For same on back of poll,	2
	225
Majority for Dickinson,	11

Samuel Price contested 47 votes of Hudson M. Dickinson, of which number the objections to 37 were sustained by your committee, or admitted to be illegal by the said Dickinson; the remaining 10 votes were decided to be legal, or were so admitted by Samuel Price.

From Hudson M. Dickinson's vote of	236
Deduct the illegal votes,	37
And his poll would stand	199

Hudson M. Dickinson contested on the poll book of Samuel Price 33 votes, of which number the objections to 17 were sustained by your committee; the remaining 16 were decided to be legal, or were so admitted by Hudson M. Dickinson.

From Samuel Price's poll of	225
Deduct the number decided to be illegal,	17
And his poll would stand thus,	208

The committee are, therefore, of opinion, that the polls should stand thus:

For Samuel Price,	208
For Hudson M. Dickinson.	199
Majority for Price,	9

Resolved therefore as the opinion of this committee, That Samuel Price was duly elected a delegate to represent the counties of Fayette and Nicholas in the present general assembly.

The said resolution was, on the question put thereupon, agreed to by the house.

Ordered, That Mr. Price be added to the several committees of which Mr. Dickinson was a member in his stead.

An engrossed bill directing the survey and location of routes for certain roads therein mentioned, was read a third time:

Resolved, That the bill do pass, and that the title be, "an act directing the survey and location of routes for certain roads therein mentioned."

An engrossed bill to amend the act establishing the town of Grandville in the county of Monongalia, was read a third time, and sundry blanks therein were filled:

Resolved, That the bill do pass, and that the title be, "an act to amend the act establishing the town of Grandville in the county of Monongalia."

Ordered, That the clerk communicate the same to the senate and request their concurrence.

An engrossed bill authorizing the board of public works to subscribe on behalf of the commonwealth to the stock of the Smith's river navigation company, was read a third time, and on motion of Mr. Holland, ordered to be laid upon the table.

An engrossed bill to authorize the appointment of a third commissioner of the superior court of Petersburg, was read a third time:

Resolved, That the bill do pass, and that the title be, "an act to authorize the appointment of a third commissioner of the superior court of Petersburg."

An engrossed bill to incorporate the Virginia mills manufacturing company, was read a third time:

Resolved, That the bill do pass, and that the title be, "an act to incorporate the Virginia mills manufacturing company."

Ordered, That the clerk communicate the same to the senate and request their concurrence.

On motion of Mr. Wilson of Botetourt, the house adjourned until to-morrow 12 o'clock.

THURSDAY, December 31st, 1835.

On motion of Mr. Strange, *Ordered,* That leave be given to bring in a bill to incorporate the Fluvanna mining company, and that Messrs. Strange, Watkins, Harris, Brown of Nelson, Goodall, Southall and Woolfolk prepare and bring in the same.

On motion of Mr. Sherrard, *Resolved,* That the committee on the militia laws be instructed to enquire into the expediency of allowing compensation to Peter Klipstine, for sundry stands of colours furnished to several regiments of militia within this commonwealth; that the said committee be authorized to report by bill or otherwise, and that the evidences of claim now presented be referred to said committee.

On motion of Mr. Shands, *Resolved,* That the committee for courts of justice enquire into the expediency of so amending the laws relating to slaves, free negroes and mulattoes as to provide that all slaves emancipated by any last will and testament, that do not leave this state in twelve months after their title to freedom shall accrue, shall forfeit their right to freedom, and descend and pass to the next of kin to the testator or testatrix, as if such testator or testatrix had died intestate as to such slave or slaves.

On motion of Mr. Masters, *Resolved,* That the committee of roads and internal navigation be instructed to enquire into the expediency of incorporating a company to construct a turnpike road from Elizabethtown in Marshall county, through the narrows to the town of Wheeling in the county of Ohio, and that they report by bill or otherwise.

On motion Mr. Brown of Petersburg, *Resolved,* That the committee on agriculture and manufactures be instructed to enquire into the expediency of incorporating the Mechanics manufacturing company for the manufacture of cotton, wool, hemp, flax, metals and wood, to be located at a site belonging to Robert Shanks on Swift creek, in the county of Chesterfield; and that the said committee have leave to report thereupon by bill or otherwise.

On motion of Mr. Murdaugh, *Resolved,* That the committee for courts of justice be instructed to enquire into the expediency of so amending the laws now in force concerning the jail fees of debtors, as to require security of the creditor for the fees whenever the jailor shall believe the creditor insolvent, or where the creditor resides out of the county, and upon failure to give such security, the jailor shall at his pleasure discharge the debtor.

Mr. Dorman submitted the following preamble and resolutions, which on his motion were ordered to be laid upon the table.

Whereas a period has arrived in our government history, when, in consequence of the payment of the public debt, and the financial prosperity of the United States, the government thereof is enabled to dispense with the revenue arising from the sales of the public lands, in order to meet the ordinary expenses of the government:

And whereas the receipts from the sale of the public lands during the present year, have gone beyond all former example, amounting to upwards of *eleven millions* of dollars, now lying idle in the national treasury:

And whereas the state of Virginia in the year 1784, prompted by a "magnanimous spirit of union and patriotism," ceded to the United States the whole of the territory lying north-west of the river Ohio, embracing at this time several large and prosperous states; which deed of cession, among other stipulations, provides, that the land thus ceded "shall be considered *a common fund for the use and benefit of such of the United States as have become, or shall become members of the confederation or federal alliance of the said states, Virginia inclusive,* according to their usual respective proportions in the general charge and expenditure, and shall be *faithfully* and *bona fide* disposed of for that purpose, and for no other use and purpose whatsoever:" thereby intending to provide, in the most clear and emphatic manner, that whensoever the ordinary and legitimate wants of the general government should not make it necessary to apply the proceeds of the sales of the public lands to those wants, that the same should be fairly distributed among the several states of this Union:

1. *Be it therefore resolved by the general assembly of Virginia,* That our senators in congress be instructed, and our representatives requested, to use their best efforts to obtain the passage of a law providing for the future distribution of the proceeds arising from the sale of the public lands among the several states of this Union, according to their federal representative population, to be limited at all times by the wants of the government arising out of a state of war with any foreign power.

2. *Resolved,* That the transfer or alienation of the public lands to the new states, within whose limits they are situate, would be regarded by the people of this commonwealth as an infraction of the compact entered into by the respective states in their deeds of cession to the United States, and as a flagrant breach of faith towards Virginia, whose munificence has greatly contributed to the discharge of the nation's debt, contracted in prosecuting the late war with England.

3. *Resolved,* That the governor of this commonwealth be requested to transmit a copy of the foregoing resolutions to each of our senators and representatives in the congress of the United States, with a request that the same be laid before their respective bodies.

On motion of Mr. Harrison, *Ordered,* That 185 copies of the said preamble and resolutions be printed for the use of the members of the general assembly.

Mr. Hill from the committee of propositions and grievances, presented a report upon petitions from the citizens of the counties of Shenandoah and Frederick for a new county; of Ann M. Tutt; and of William Wedderburn; and a bill to incorporate the Petersburg navigation company.

Mr. Stanard from the committee for courts of justice presented a report upon the petition of James Martin; which reports and bill were received and laid upon the table.

Mr. Harrison presented a petition of sundry citizens of the counties of Harrison, Randolph and Monongalia, praying the passage of an act, declaring Tygart's valley river a public highway from the mouth of Big Sandy creek to its junction with the west fork of the Monongalia river.

Mr. Stanard presented a petition of sundry citizens of the city of Richmond, for the incorporation of a company for the purpose of towing vessels navigating James river.

Mr. Berry, a remonstrance of the Tuckahœ canal company, opposing the petition of John G. Crouch and others.

Ordered, That the said petitions be referred to the committee of roads and internal navigation, that they do examine the matter thereof, and report their opinion thereupon to the house.

Mr. Brown of Petersburg presented a petition of the president and directors of the Merchants manufacturing company of Petersburg, praying to be authorized to increase their capital stock, which was ordered to be referred to the committee of agriculture and manufactures, that they do examine the matter thereof, and report their opinion thereupon to the house.

Mr. Stanard also presented a petition of Richard Lorton and others, praying the passage of an act relinquishing the right of the commonwealth to the property in which the Richmond museum is kept, to the petitioner; or that the commonwealth would resume the property granted for the use of the museum, under certain conditions, allowing compensation for the value of the improvements erected on the land, which was ordered to be referred to the committee of propositions and grievances, that they do examine the matter thereof, and report their opinion thereupon to the house.

Mr. Smith of Frederick presented a petition of Peter Kremer, asking to be allowed a reward offered by the executive for apprehending a negro slave, who was charged with having killed his overseer, the said slave having been apprehended by the petitioner, and the reward not allowed by the executive, which was ordered to be referred to the committee of claims, that they do examine the matter thereof, and report their opinion thereupon to the house.

On motion of Mr. Brooke, *Resolved,* That the committee of roads and internal navigation be instructed to enquire into the expediency of incorporating a company to construct a turnpike road from the town of Staunton to the Augusta springs, and to report by bill or otherwise.

On motion of Mr. Watkins, the rule of the house limiting the number of the committee of roads and internal navigation was suspended for the purpose of increasing the said committee, and Messrs. Cunningham and Price were ordered to be added thereto.

Mr. Watkins, from the committee of roads and internal navigation, presented several reports of said committee upon the petitions of citizens of the counties of Preston, Monongalia and Tyler, and of citizens of the county of Monroe, and on the resolution concerning the construction of roads from Wheeling to Clarksburg and from Clarksburg to Beverley.

And presented a bill to incorporate the stockholders of the Lynchburg and Tennessee rail road company, and to authorize them, or the James river and Kanawha company, to construct a rail road from Lynchburg to Richmond.

And reported with amendments, a bill directing the survey of a route for a road from the north-western road in the direction of Beverley in the county of Randolph.

And without amendment a bill incorporating the stockholders of the Richmond and Petersburg rail road company, which were severally received and laid upon the table.

On motion of Mr. Watkins, *Ordered*, That the committee of roads and internal navigation be discharged from the consideration of so much of the petitions of sundry citizens of the county of Monroe as has not been acted upon by the said committee, and that the same be laid upon the table.

An engrossed bill authorizing the board of public works to subscribe on behalf of the commonwealth to the stock of the Smith's river navigation company, was taken up; whereupon, on motion of Mr. Murdaugh, the rule of the house was suspended for the purpose of reconsidering the vote ordering the same to be engrossed and read a third time, and the said bill was then ordered to be recommitted to the committee which brought it in.

On motion of Mr. Harris, an engrossed bill incorporating the stockholders of the Louisa rail-road company, was taken up; whereupon, the rule of the house was suspended for the purpose of reconsidering the vote ordering the same to be engrossed and read a third time, and the said bill was then amended by the house on his motion, and ordered as amended, to be re-engrossed and read a third time.

A report of the committee of propositions and grievances was read as follows:

The committee of propositions and grievances have had under consideration the petition of Ann Mason Tutt, to them referred, and submit the following report and resolution:

The petition of Ann Mason Tutt of the county of Loudoun, prays that she may be allowed to dispose of certain lands by lottery, as the best mode of securing the full value of a trust estate, created for the benefit of herself and children, in which the trustees have the power of sale and re-investment: Whereupon,

Resolved as the opinion of this committee, That the prayer of said petition be rejected.

The said resolution was, on the question put thereupon, agreed to by the house.

Further reports of the same committee, rejecting the petition of William Weddeburn, and reporting reasonable the petition of citizens of Shenandoah and Frederick counties, for a new county out of parts of said counties, were, on motions severally made, ordered to be laid upon the table.

An engrossed bill incorporating the Lexington and Richmond turnpike company, was read a third time:

Resolved, That the bill do pass, and that the title be, "an act incorporating the Lexington and Richmond turnpike company."

An engrossed bill to change the place of holding a separate election in the county of Marshall, was read a third time:

Resolved, That the bill do pass, and that the title be, "an act to change the place of holding a separate election in the county of Marshall."

Ordered, That the clerk communicate the said bills to the senate and request their concurrence.

An engrossed bill to amend an act, entitled, "an act for incorporating the stockholders of the Winchester and Potomac rail-road company," was read a third time, and on motion of Mr. Crutchfield, ordered to be laid upon the table.

An engrossed bill to authorize the mayor and commonalty of the town of Wheeling to subscribe for stock of the Baltimore and Ohio rail-road company, was read a third time:

Resolved, That the bill do pass, and that the title be, "an act to authorize the mayor and commonalty of the town of Wheeling to subscribe for stock of the Baltimore and Ohio rail-road company."

Ordered, That the clerk communicate the same to the senate and request their concurrence.

An engrossed bill concerning the fire and marine insurance company of Wheeling, was read a third time; whereupon, on motion of Mr. Dorman, the rule of the house was suspended for the purpose of reconsidering the vote ordering the same to be engrossed and read a third time, and the said bill was then ordered to be committed to the committee which brought it in.

A bill to enlarge, define and establish the corporate boundaries and limits of the town of Wheeling, was taken up and ordered to be engrossed and read a third time.

A bill to amend the act, entitled, "an act incorporating the Falmouth and Alexandria rail-road company;" and

A bill to amend an act, entitled, "an act to incorporate the Staunton and Potomac rail-road company," together with the amendments thereto severally proposed by the respective committees to which the same had been committed, were taken up, and the said amendments being agreed to by the house, the said bills, as amended, were ordered to be engrossed and read a third time.

A bill authorizing Jesse Sturm to erect a dam across the West fork of Monongalia river in the county of Harrison, was, on motion of Mr. Kincheloe, ordered to be laid upon the table.

The speaker laid before the house a communication from the governor, transmitting, in compliance with their request, a preamble and resolutions on the subject of incendiary publications, adopted by the general assembly of the state of North Carolina, which, on motion of Mr. Henshaw, was ordered to be laid upon the table, and that 185 copies thereof be printed for the use of the members of the general assembly.

A bill incorporating the Red and Blue Sulphur springs turnpike company; and

A bill to revive and amend the act, entitled, "an act incorporating the Richmond rail-road company," were read the first and ordered to be read a second time.

A bill incorporating the Great Falls manufacturing company in the county of Fayette, was read the first and second times, and ordered to be committed to the committee which brought it in.

A bill fixing the school quotas of the counties of Ohio and Marshall, was read the first and ordered to be read a second time.

A bill to provide for the construction of a road between Weston in the county of Lewis, and Charleston in the county of Kanawha, was read the first and second times, and ordered to be committed to the committee which brought it in.

A bill to authorize William Chapline and others, to construct wharves on Wheeling creek and the Ohio river, adjoining the town of South Wheeling in Ohio county.

A bill to change the place of holding a separate election in the county of Preston; and

A bill to change the place of holding a separate election in the county of Wythe, were severally read the first and ordered to be read a second time.

A bill to incorporate the Narrow Falls turnpike company; and

A bill directing the survey and location of a route for a road from the Pennsylvania line to its intersection with the road from Clarksburg to Beverley, were severally read the first and second times, and ordered to be committed to the committees which brought them in.

A bill further to amend the act, entitled, "an act to amend the act, entitled, 'an act establishing a ferry from Onancock town in the county of Accomack, to Norfolk, and for other purposes," passed March the 5th, 1833; and

A bill to change the place of holding a separate election in the county of Berkeley, were read the first, and ordered to be read a second time.

A bill to authorize a separate election at Hedgesville in the county of Berkeley; and

A bill to amend the act, entitled, "an act to reduce into one the several acts for the settlement and regulation of ferries," passed January 30th, 1819, were severally read the first and second times, and ordered to be referred to the respective committees which brought them in.

A bill to incorporate the Petersburg navigation company, was read the first, and ordered to be read a second time.

A report of the committee for courts of justice was read as follows:

The committee for courts of justice have, according to order, had under consideration the petition of James Martin, to them referred, praying that he may be permitted to hold real estate, and have come to the following resolution thereupon:

Resolved as the opinion of this committee, That the prayer of the said petition is reasonable.

The said resolution was, on the question put thereupon, agreed to by the house, and a bill was ordered to be brought in conformably therewith.

A report of the committee of propositions and grievances was read as follows:

The committee of propositions and grievances have, according to order, had under consideration the petition of the trustees of the town of Clarkesville in the county of Mecklenburg, to them referred, praying that the boundaries of said town may be enlarged according to the plan in the petition set forth: Whereupon,

Resolved as the opinion of this committee, That the prayer of said petition is reasonable.

The said resolution was, on the question put thereupon, agreed to by the house, and a bill was ordered to be brought in conformably therewith.

A report of the committee of roads and internal navigation was read as follows:

The committee of roads and internal navigation have, according to order, had under consideration the petition of sundry citizens of the county of Cumberland, praying the incorporation of a joint stock company to construct a rail-road from the town of Cartersville, to Farmville in the county of Prince Edward: Whereupon,

Resolved as the opinion of this committee, That the said petition is reasonable.

The said resolution was, on the question put thereupon, agreed to by the house, and a bill was ordered to be brought in conformably therewith.

A report of the committee of claims was read as follows:

The committee of claims have, according to order, enquired into the expediency of refunding to James Wysong the sum of twenty-five dollars, being so much overpaid by him as land tax in the county of Jefferson: Whereupon,

Resolved as the opinion of this committee, That it is expedient to refund to the said James Wysong the amount so overpaid by him.

The said resolution was, on the question put thereupon, agreed to by the house, and a bill was ordered to be brought in conformably therewith.

A report of the committee of propositions and grievances was read as follows:

The committee of propositions and grievances have, according to order, had under consideration several petitions to them referred, and have come to the following resolutions thereupon:

1. *Resolved as the opinion of this committee,* That the petition of sundry citizens residing in the lower section of the county of Cumberland, praying the general assembly to establish a separate election at William Irwin's tavern, at the first fork of the stage road above Cartersville, is reasonable.

2. *Resolved as the opinion of this committee,* That the petition of sundry freeholders and other citizens of the county of Fayette, representing that the seat of justice of said county is not yet selected according to the satisfaction of the people thereof, and the true intent and meaning of the act of the general assembly, passed at the last session, submitting the question as to the most suitable place to the vote of the people of said county, and praying that an act may pass setting aside the proceedings had under the provisions of said act, and that another election by the vote of the people of the county be directed, in order to obtain the decisive opinion in relation to the three points in contest, is reasonable.

3. *Resolved also as the opinion of this committee,* That the residue of the prayer of said petition (in the alternative), "or that the said act be repealed, and the place selected at Abraham Vandal's by the five commissioners appointed at the session before the last, be the permanent place for erecting the courthouse for said county, the jail being already built at the place aforesaid," be rejected.

4. *Resolved as the opinion of this committee,* That the petition of sundry citizens of the county of Ohio, praying the general assembly to empower the county court of said county to select some suitable site within the town of Wheeling, or its additions, for the erection of a courthouse and other necessary buildings, and to obtain by purchase or otherwise, the site so selected, with authority to erect thereon all necessary and suitable buildings, be rejected.

5. *Resolved as the opinion of this committee,* That the petition of sundry other citizens of the county of Ohio, admitting the insufficiency of the present public buildings, and the unsuitableness of their site, and praying that an act may pass, appointing discreet and disinterested commissioners to select and obtain, within the town of Wheeling, or some of its additions, a suitable site for a courthouse, and such other public buildings as the convenience of the county requires, is reasonable.

The second resolution was, on motion of Mr. Hill, ordered to be recommitted to the said committee, together with the remonstrance of citizens of Fayette against the same.

The remaining resolutions were, on questions severally put thereupon, agreed to by the house, and bills were ordered to be brought in conformably with the said first and last resolutions.

A further report of the same committee was read as follows:

The committee of propositions and grievances have, according to order, had under consideration the petition of sundry citizens of the city of Richmond, to them referred, praying that an act may pass to incorporate a company, with sufficient capital, to be called the Virginia insurance company against fire on property other than houses, with such privileges as are usually granted to such companies: Whereupon,

Resolved as the opinion of this committee, That the prayer of the aforesaid petition is reasonable.

The said resolution was, on the question put thereupon, agreed to by the house, and a bill was ordered to be brought in conformably therewith.

On motion of Mr. Almond, the house adjourned until to-morrow 12 o'clock.

FRIDAY, January 1st, 1836.

On motion of Mr. Mullen, *Resolved,* That the committee of roads and internal navigation enquire into the expediency of directing the survey of a road from Moorfield to intersect the North-western turnpike at or near Charles Blue's in the county of Hampshire.

Mr. Decamps presented a petition of sundry citizens of the county of Brooke, for the passage of an act authorizing and requiring the county court of said county to assess a tax on the owners of dogs in said county, to be applied in aid of the county levy, which was ordered to be referred to the committee of finance, that they do examine the matter thereof, and report their opinion thereupon to the house.

Mr. Taylor of Loudoun, presented a petition of sundry citizens of the county of Loudoun, praying the incorporation of a joint stock company for erecting a bridge across the Shenandoah river, which was ordered to be referred to the committee of propositions and grievances, that they do examine the matter thereof, and report their opinion thereupon to the house.

Mr. Madison presented a petition of Thomas A. Morton, for leave to erect a mill-dam across Appomattox river, which was ordered to be referred to the committee of roads and internal navigation, that they do examine the matter thereof, and report their opinion thereupon to the house.

Mr. Hill, from the committee of propositions and grievances, reported with an amendment, a bill to authorize a separate election at Hedgesville in the county of Berkeley, which was subsequently taken up, and the said amendment being agreed to by the house, the same, as amended, was ordered to be engrossed and read a third time.

And presented a bill forming a new county out of parts of the counties of Lewis and Nicholas, which was subsequently taken up, read the first and second times, and ordered to be committed to the committee which brought it in, on motion of Mr. Price.

And a report, which was subsequently read as follows:

The committee of propositions and grievances have, according to order, had under consideration the petition of sundry citizens of the place called Hedgesville, in the county of Berkeley, to them referred, praying that an act may pass establishing a town by the name of Hedgesville at said place, on the lands of Josiah Hedges, senior, and Mrs. Mary Claycomb, according to a plan already laid off, and that trustees be appointed for the government thereof: Whereupon,

Resolved as the opinion of this committee, That the prayer of said petition is reasonable.

The said resolution was, on the question put thereupon, agreed to by the house, and a bill was ordered to be brought in conformably therewith.

Mr. Watkins, from the committee of roads and internal navigation, reported without amendment, a bill to incorporate the Narrow falls turnpike company.

And a bill to provide for the construction of a road between Weston, in the county of Lewis, and Charleston, in the county of Kanawha, which were subsequently taken up, and ordered to be engrossed and read a third time.

Mr. Watkins, also from the same committee, reported with amendments, a bill authorizing the board of public works to subscribe on behalf of the commonwealth to the stock of the Smith's river navigation company, which was subsequently taken up, and the said amendments being severally agreed to, and the said bill being further amended on motion of Mr. Brown, was, as amended, on motion of Mr. Murdaugh, ordered to be recommitted to the said committee.

Mr. Watkins also from the same committee, presented a bill directing a change of location of the North-western turnpike through the town of Evansville.

And a bill to amend an act, entitled, "an act for cutting a navigable canal from the waters of Elizabeth river, in the state of Virginia, to the waters of Pasquotank river in North Carolina; which were subsequently taken up, read the first and ordered to be read a second time.

Mr. Watkins also from the same committee, presented several reports, which were subsequently taken up and read as follow:

The committee of roads and internal navigation have, according to order, had under consideration the petition of Jacob Price, praying that he be permitted to make a turnpike road across Price's and the Sweet springs mountains, in the counties of Botetourt, Monroe and Alleghany: Whereupon,

Resolved as the opinion of this committee, That said petition is reasonable.

The said committee have also, according to order, had under consideration the petition of William Scott, praying authority to construct the said road across the said Price's and Sweet springs mountains: Whereupon,

Resolved as the opinion of this committee, That said petition is reasonable.

The committee of roads and internal navigation have, according to order, had under consideration the petition of sundry citizens of the town of Suffolk and others, praying the incorporation of a joint stock company to construct a rail-road from the upper part of said town to Nansemond river: Whereupon,

Resolved as the opinion of this committee, That said petition is reasonable.

The committee of roads and internal navigation have, according to order, enquired into "the expediency of extending the North-western turnpike road from the town of Winchester in the county of Frederick, to the termination of the Berryville turnpike, at Berryville, in said county:" Whereupon,

Resolved as the opinion of this committee, That it is not expedient to extend the said road.

The committee of roads and internal navigation have, according to order, enquired into "the expediency of providing by law for the construction of a road from Wheeling to Clarksburg, on the route designated by the engineer employed to survey the same, in pursuance of the resolution of the 27th February, 1833; also of constructing a road in like manner, from Clarksburg to Beverley:" Whereupon,

1. *Resolved as the opinion of this committee*, That it is inexpedient to provide for the construction of a road from Wheeling to Clarksburg.

2. *Resolved as the opinion of this committee*, That it is inexpedient to provide for the construction of a road from Clarksburg to Beverley.

The said resolutions were, on questions severally put thereupon, agreed to by the house, and bills were ordered to be brought in conformably with the said first, second and third resolutions

Mr. Madison, from the committee of agriculture and manufactures, presented a bill to provide for the enlargement of the public warehouse for the storage and inspection of tobacco in the city of Richmond, which was subsequently taken up, read the first, and ordered to be read a second time.

The following bills were read a second time and ordered to be engrossed and read a third time.

A bill incorporating the Red and Blue Sulphur springs turnpike company.

A bill to revive and amend the act, entitled, "an act incorporating the Richmond rail-road company."

A bill fixing the school quotas of the counties of Ohio and Marshall.

A bill to authorize William Chapline and others to construct wharves on Wheeling creek and the Ohio river, adjoining the town of South Wheeling in Ohio county.

A bill to change the place of holding a separate election in the county of Preston.

A bill to change the place of holding a separate election in the county of Wythe.

A bill further to amend the act, entitled, "an act to amend the act entitled, 'an act establishing a ferry from Onancock town in the county of Accomack, to Norfolk, and for other purposes,'" passed March 5th, 1833.

A bill to change the place of holding a separate election in the county of Berkeley; and

A bill to incorporate the Petersburg navigation company.

A bill to incorporate the stockholders of the Lynchburg and Tennessee rail-road company, and to authorize them, or the James river and Kanawha company, to construct a rail-road from Lynchburg to Richmond, was read the first, and on motion of Mr. Watkins, the second time, and ordered to be committed to the committee which brought it in.

The speaker laid before the house a communication from the governor, as president of the board of the literary fund, transmitting the report of the said board, affording the information respecting the University of Virginia, and the colleges and academies of the state, called for by a resolution of the general assembly of the 26th of February last, which, on motion of Mr. Garland of Mecklenburg, was ordered to be referred to the committee of schools and colleges; and, on motion of Mr. Dorman, 500 copies thereof were ordered to be printed for the use of the members of the general assembly.

The following reports of the committee of roads and internal navigation were read as follow:

The committee of roads and internal navigation have, according to order, had under consideration the petition of sundry citizens of the county of Monroe, representing that in pursuance of sundry acts of assembly authorizing money to be raised by lottery, for the purpose of building an academy in the town of Union, and of making a turnpike road from the White Sulphur springs to the Salt Sulphur springs, the sum of $1,400 was raised, which is now in the hands of James A. Dunlap, the treasurer appointed to receive the same; after which, further proceedings in relation to the lottery were declined by the contractor. That since the passage of said acts, a joint stock company has been incorporated to construct the said road, which could be speedily completed with the aid of the said sum of money; and praying either that the whole of said sum be invested in stock of the White and Salt Sulphur springs turnpike company, and that the dividends therefrom be applied to the building and support of an academy in the town of Union, or that one half of the said sum be appropriated to the completion of the said turnpike, and the residue to the academy: Whereupon,

Resolved as the opinion of this committee, That so much of said petition as prays that one half of said sum of money be appropriated to the completion of the said turnpike, and the residue to the said academy, is reasonable.

The committee of roads and internal navigation have, according to order, had under consideration the petition of sundry citizens of the counties of Preston, Monongalia, and Tyler, praying that an appropriation be made by law, in aid of the funds raised by the citizens directly interested, for the construction of a road from the mouth of Fishing creek in the county of Tyler, to Brandonvile in the county of Preston: Whereupon,

Resolved as the opinion of this committee, That said petition is reasonable.

The said resolutions were, on questions severally put thereupon, agreed to by the house, and bills were ordered to be brought in conformably therewith.

On motion of Mr. Stanard, *Ordered,* That leave be given to bring in a bill to revive and amend an act, entitled, "an act to incorporate the Belle Isle manufacturing company," passed 19th March, 1832, and that Messrs. Stanard, Botts, Watkins, Christian, Strange, Goodall and Johnson, prepare and bring in the same.

An engrossed bill incorporating the stockholders of the Louisa rail-road company, was read a third time:

Resolved, That the bill do pass, and that the title be, "an act incorporating the stockholders of the Louisa rail-road company."

Ordered, That the clerk communicate the same to the senate and request their concurrence.

An engrossed bill to amend an act, entitled, "an act to incorporate the Staunton and Potomac rail-road company," was read a third time, and on motion of Mr. Crutchfield, ordered to be laid upon the table.

An engrossed bill to enlarge, define and establish the corporate boundaries and limits of the town of Wheeling, in the county of Ohio, was read a third time:

Resolved, That the bill do pass, and that the title be, "an act to enlarge, define and establish the corporate boundaries and limits of the town of Wheeling, in the county of Ohio."

Ordered, That the clerk communicate the same to the senate and request their concurrence.

An engrossed bill to amend the act, entitled, "an act incorporating the Falmouth and Alexandria rail-road company," was read a third time, and on motion of Mr. Williams, ordered to be laid upon the table.

A bill directing the survey of a route for a road from the North-western road in the direction of Beverley, in the county of Randolph, with the amendments thereto proposed by the committee of roads and internal navigation, was taken up, and the said amendments being agreed to by the house, the said bill as amended was ordered to be engrossed and read a third time.

On motion of Mr. Leyburn, the rule of the house limiting the number of the committee of roads and internal navigation was suspended, and Mr. Brooke was ordered to be added to the said committee.

On motion of Mr. Mullen, *Resolved,* That the committee of roads and internal navigation enquire into the expediency of appropriating a sum of money to aid in the construction of a road from Moorfield to Wardensville, in the county of Hardy.

Mr. Watkins, from the committee of roads and internal navigation, presented a bill to reduce and regulate the tolls on the North-western turnpike, which was received and laid upon the table.

Mr. Watkins, from the select committee on that subject, presented a report, which was read as follows:

The committee, to whom was referred the following resolution,—"*Resolved,* That the resolution of the senate of the United States, passed March the 28th, 1834, which declares 'that the president, in the late executive proceedings in relation to the public revenue, has assumed upon himself authority and power not conferred by the constitution and laws, but in derogation of both,' be referred to a select committee, with directions to enquire into the expediency of instructing the senators from this state, in the congress of the United States, to introduce and vote for a resolution, requiring the aforesaid resolution to be expunged from the journal of the senate,"—have had the same under consideration, and beg leave to report the following preamble and resolutions:

Whereas the senate of the United States did, on the 28th day of March, 1834, adopt the following resolution: "*Resolved,* That the president, in the late executive proceedings in relation to the public revenue, has assumed upon himself authority and power not conferred by the constitution and laws, but in derogation of both;" which resolution now stands upon the journal of the senate:

And whereas the general assembly of Virginia regard this act of the senate as an assumption of power not warranted by the constitution, and calculated to subvert the rights of the house of representatives, and the fundamental principles of our free institutions:

And whereas this assembly deem it their solemn duty again to re-assert, in behalf of themselves and the people of Virginia, the right of the constituent to instruct, and the *duty* of the *representative to obey* or *resign :* Therefore,

1. *Resolved by the general assembly of Virginia*, That the senators from this state, in the congress of the United States, be and they are hereby instructed to introduce, and vote for, a resolution, directing the aforesaid resolution of the senate of the 28th day of March, 1834, declaring "that the president, in the late executive proceedings in relation to the public revenue, has assumed upon himself authority and power not conferred by the constitution and laws, but in derogation of both," TO BE EXPUNGED from the journal of the senate of the United States, by causing black lines to be drawn around the said resolution, as it stands on the original manuscript journal, and these words plainly written across the face of the said resolution and entry,—EXPUNGED *by order of the senate of the United States.*

2. *Resolved also*, That this assembly regard the right of instruction "as resting on the broad basis of the nature of representation," and one of the vital principles of our free institutions; and that it is the duty of the representative to obey the instructions of his constituents, or resign the trust with which *they* have clothed him, in order that it may be transferred into the hands of those who will carry into execution the wishes and instructions of the constituent body.

3. *Resolved*, That the governor of the commonwealth be requested to transmit the foregoing resolutions to each of the senators and representatives from Virginia, in the congress of the United States, with the request that they lay the same before their respective bodies.

On motion of Mr. Watkins, *Ordered*, That the said preamble and resolutions be laid upon the table, and that 185 copies thereof be printed for the use of the members of the general assembly.

On motion of Mr. Mullen, the house adjourned until to-morrow 12 o'clock.

SATURDAY, January 2d, 1836.

The speaker laid before the house the following letter :

PETERSBURG, 1st January, 1836.

SIR,—My bad state of health compels me to resign my seat in the house of delegates as member elect from the county of Dinwiddie. This resignation would have been tendered earlier but for the heretofore deceptive hope that I might be able soon to attend to the duties of my station. With sincere wishes for the safety and continued dignity of the commonwealth, I remain your most obedient servant,

JNO. L. SCOTT.

To the Speaker of the House of Delegates of Virginia.

On motion of Mr. Shands, *Ordered*, That the said letter be laid upon the table, and that a writ of election issue to the sheriff of the county of Dinwiddie, to supply the vacancy thus created.

On motion of Mr. Nixon, *Resolved*, That this house will, on Friday the 8th instant, proceed by joint vote with the senate, to the election of a brigadier general for the 18th brigade Virginia militia, to supply the vacancy occasioned by the death of general William M'Coy.

Ordered, That the clerk communicate the said resolution to the senate and request their concurrence.

A motion was made by Mr. Powell that the house adopt the following resolution :

Resolved, That a special committee be appointed to enquire into the expediency of making an appropriation for Elizabeth or Betsy Gary of Fairfax county, in the state of Virginia, and that they be instructed to report by bill or otherwise.

And the question being put thereupon, was determined in the negative.

On motion of Mr. Brown of Petersburg, *Resolved*, That leave be given to bring in a bill or bills to amend the charters of the Petersburg rail-road company, and the Greensville and Roanoke rail-road company, in conformity to certain resolutions adopted by the president and directors of those companies, so as to provide for a reduction and permanent regulation of the rates of transportation thereupon; and also to authorize an increase of their capital stock, with a view to the better accommodation of an increased trade and travel; and that Messrs. Brown of Petersburg, Shands, Smith, Mallory, Murdaugh, Turnbull, Cooke, Hargrave, Benton, Butts and Avent, prepare and bring in the same.

On motion of Mr. Cunningham, *Resolved*, That a committee be appointed to provide by law for paying to the legal representatives of Severn Eyre the amount of his losses occasioned by the burning of Norfolk in 1776, by order of the state convention, as ascertained by the report of the commissioners appointed for that purpose; and a committee was appointed of Messrs. Cunningham, Fontaine, Gilmer, Murdaugh, Waggener, Davison, Chapline, Hooe, Smith of Fauquier, Samuel, Harley, Saunders, and Hunter of Essex.

On motion of Mr. Booker, *Resolved*, That the committee on agriculture and manufactures be instructed to enquire into the expediency of requiring the inspectors of tobacco in this commonwealth to designate in their inspections the tobacco the produce of this state, and that of other states, and that said committee have leave to report by bill or otherwise.

On motion of Mr. Southall, *Resolved*, That the committee for courts of justice be instructed to enquire into the expediency of so amending the act, entitled, "an act to reduce into one act the several acts concerning executions, and for the relief of insolvent debtors," as to authorize the plaintiff in actions of detinue after judgment, to sue out and prosecute at his election either a distringas, or an execution for the specific property, if to be found, or any other execution necessary to recover the alternative value now authorized by law upon other judgments, and that they have leave to report by bill or otherwise.

Mr. Wilson of Botetourt, presented a petition of Thomas Rosson and James Carper, for a charter to construct a turnpike road across Price's and the Sweet springs mountains.

And a petition of sundry citizens of the counties of Botetourt, Bedford, Monroe and Greenbrier, in favour of the same object.

Mr. Watkins, a petition of sundry citizens of the county of Goochland, for the incorporation of a company to make a turnpike road from Richmond to Charlottesville.

Ordered, That the said petitions be referred to the committee of roads and internal navigation, that they do examine the matter thereof, and report their opinion thereupon to the house.

Mr. Brown of Petersburg, presented a petition of sundry citizens of the town of Petersburg, and stockholders in the Lower Appomattox company, remonstrating against the incorporation of a company to construct a rail-road from City Point to their said town, which, on his motion, was ordered to be laid upon the table.

Mr. Beard presented a petition of sundry citizens of the village of Lovettsville, asking that the said village may be established as a town, which was ordered to be referred to the committee of propositions and grievances, that they do examine the matter thereof, and report their opinion thereupon to the house.

Mr. Wilson of Botetourt, also presented a petition of sundry citizens of the counties of Botetourt and Rockbridge, to be authorized to construct a turnpike road from the Blue Ridge canal to intersect the Lexington and Covington turnpike, which was ordered to be referred to the committee of roads and internal navigation, that they do examine the matter thereof, and report their opinion thereupon to the house.

On motion of Mr. Botts, *Resolved,* That the committee for courts of justice be instructed to enquire into the expediency of farther amending the act to amend an act, entitled, " an act regulating the manner of granting licenses to retail ardent spirits, and for other purposes."

Mr. Watkins, from the committee of roads and internal navigation, reported with amendment, a bill authorizing the board of public works to subscribe on behalf of the commonwealth to the stock of the Smith's river navigation company, which was taken up, and the said amendment being agreed to by the house, the same, as amended, was ordered to be engrossed and read a third time.

Mr. Watkins, also from the same committee, presented a bill to incorporate the Suffolk rail-road company, which was subsequently read the first and second times, and ordered to be committed to the said committee.

Also a bill to incorporate the stockholders of the City Point rail-road company, which was read the first, and ordered to be read a second time.

And a bill to incorporate the stockholders of the Cartersville and Farmville rail-road company, which was received and laid upon the table.

Mr. Chapman reported without amendment, a bill to incorporate the Sweet springs company, which was subsequently taken up, and ordered to be engrossed and read a third time.

Mr. Brown of Petersburg, reported with amendment, a bill to amend an act, entitled, " an act to incorporate the Midlothian coal mining company," which was subsequently taken up, and the said amendment being agreed to by the house, the said bill as amended, was ordered to be engrossed and read a third time.

Mr. Summers reported with amendment, a bill incorporating the Great falls manufacturing company in the county of Fayette, which was in like manner taken up, and the said amendment being agreed to by the house, the same as amended, was ordered to be engrossed and read a third time.

Mr. Hill, from the committee of propositions and grievances, presented a bill to prevent trespasses by non-resident herdsmen in the county of Preston, which was received and laid upon the table.

A bill directing a change of location of the North-western turnpike through the town of Evansville.

A bill to amend an act, entitled, " an act for cutting a navigable canal from the waters of Elizabeth river, in the state of Virginia, to the waters of Pasquotank river, in North Carolina ;" and

A bill to provide for the enlargement of the public warehouse for the storage and inspection of tobacco in the city of Richmond, were read a second time, and ordered to be engrossed and read a third time.

A bill to reduce and regulate the tolls on the North-western turnpike, was read the first, and ordered to be read a second time.

An engrossed bill to amend an act, entitled, " an act for incorporating the stockholders of the Winchester and Potomac rail-road company," was taken up on motion of Mr. Crutchfield, and read a third time ; whereupon, a clause by way of ryder thereto, was proposed by Mr. Smith of Frederick, which was read the first and second times, and engrossed and read a third time :

Resolved, That the bill (with the ryder) do pass, and that the title be, " an act to amend an act, entitled, 'an act for incorporating the stockholders of the Winchester and Potomac rail-road company.'"

Ordered, That the clerk communicate the same to the senate and request their concurrence.

An engrossed bill to amend an act, entitled, " an act to incorporate the Staunton and Potomac rail-road company," was taken up, on motion of Mr. Crutchfield, and read a third time ; whereupon, a clause by way of ryder thereto, was proposed by him, which was read the first and second times, amended and engrossed and read a third time, and on motion of Mr. Watkins, was again ordered to be laid upon the table.

An engrossed bill to revive and amend the act, entitled, "an act incorporating the Richmond rail-road company," was read a third time:

Resolved, That the bill do pass, and that the title be, "an act to revive and amend the act, entitled, 'an act incorporating the Richmond rail-road company.'"

Ordered, That the clerk communicate the same to the senate and request their concurrence.

An engrossed bill to incorporate the Narrow falls turnpike company, was read a third time, and on motion of Mr. Stanard, ordered to be laid upon the table.

An engrossed bill directing the survey of a route for a road from the North-western road *in the direction of Beverley,* in the county of Randolph, was read a third time:

Resolved, That the bill do pass, and (the title being amended on motion of Mr. Marteney,) that the title be, "an act directing the survey of a route for a road from the North-western road *to some point on Leading creek,* in the county of Randolph."

Ordered, That the clerk communicate the same to the senate and request their concurrence.

An engrossed bill to provide for the construction of a road between Weston, in the county of Lewis, and Charleston, in the county of Kanawha, was taken up; whereupon, on motion of Mr. Summers, the rule of the house was suspended, and the vote ordering the said bill to be engrossed and read a third time, was reconsidered, and the said bill was then ordered to be committed to the committee which brought it in.

An engrossed bill to change the place of holding a separate election in the county of Wythe, was read a third time:

Resolved, That the bill do pass, and that the title be, "an act to change the place of holding a separate election in the county of Wythe."

Ordered, That the clerk communicate the same to the senate and request their concurrence.

An engrossed bill further to amend the act, entitled, "an act to amend the act, entitled, 'an act establishing a ferry from Onancock town, in the county of Accomack, to Norfolk, and for other purposes,'" passed March 5th, 1833, was read a third time, and on motion of Mr. Parker, ordered to be laid upon the table.

An engrossed bill incorporating the Red and Blue Sulphur springs turnpike company, was read a third time, and on motion of Mr. Wethered, ordered to be laid upon the table.

An engrossed bill fixing the school quotas of the counties of Ohio and Marshall, was read a third time:

Resolved, That the bill do pass, and that the title be, "an act fixing the school quotas of the counties of Ohio and Marshall."

An engrossed bill to authorize William Chapline and others to construct wharves on Wheeling creek and the Ohio river, adjoining the town of South Wheeling, in Ohio county, was read a third time, and a blank therein was filled:

Resolved, That the bill do pass, and that the title be, "an act to authorize William Chapline and others to construct wharves on Wheeling creek and the Ohio river, adjoining the town of South Wheeling, in Ohio county."

Ordered, That the clerk communicate the same to the senate and request their concurrence.

An engrossed bill to change the place of holding a separate election in the county of Berkeley, was read a third time, and on motion of Mr. Sherrard, ordered to be laid upon the table.

An engrossed bill to authorize a separate election at Hedgesville, in the county of Berkeley, was read a third time, and on motion of Mr. Henshaw, ordered to be laid upon the table.

An engrossed bill to incorporate the Petersburg navigation company, was read a third time:

Resolved, That the bill do pass, and that the title be, "an act to incorporate the Petersburg navigation company."

An engrossed bill to change the place of holding a separate election in the county of Preston, was read a third time:

Resolved, That the bill do pass, and that the title be, "an act to change the place of holding a separate election in the county of Preston."

Ordered, That the clerk communicate the said bills to the senate and request their concurrence.

Mr. Madison, from the committee on agriculture and manufactures, presented reports upon the petitions of the Nelson and Albemarle Union factory company, and of the Merchants manufacturing company of Petersburg.

Also a bill to incorporate the Ettrick Banks manufacturing company; and

A bill to incorporate the Fleets manufacturing company.

Mr. Stanard, according to order, presented a bill to revive and amend "an act incorporating the Bell Isle manufacturing company," passed 19th March, 1832.

Which reports and bills were received and laid upon the table.

On motion of Mr. Henshaw, the house adjourned until Monday 12 o'clock.

MONDAY, January 4th, 1836.

On motion of Mr. Sloan, *Ordered,* That leave be given to bring in a bill to change the place of holding the Cundiff precinct election in the county of Hampshire, and that Messrs. Sloan, Nixon, Henshaw, Mullen, Sherrard and Bowen prepare and bring in the same.

On motion of Mr. Craig, *Resolved*, That the committee for courts of justice be instructed to enquire into the expediency of providing by law, that in all criminal prosecutions for misdemeanors which may hereafter be commenced and prosecuted to a judgment in any of the county or corporation courts of this commonwealth, the defendant or defendants in said prosecutions may apply to any one of the judges of the general court of Virginia for a writ of error to said judgments in vacation, in the same manner that applications are now made in term time; and that the said judges may be empowered to award such writ in vacation in the same manner and upon the same terms that writs of error are awarded in term time, with leave to report by bill or otherwise.

On motion of Mr. Johnson, *Ordered*, That leave be given to bring in a bill to amend an act, entitled, "an act to incorporate the Cold Brook company of colliers," passed January 23d, 1835, and a bill to amend an act, entitled, "an act to incorporate the Manchester wool and cotton manufacturing company," passed March 13th, 1832, and that Messrs. Johnson, Botts, Brown of Petersburg, Shands, Wiley, Hopkins and Hargrave prepare and bring in the same.

On motion of Mr. Crutchfield, *Resolved*, That the select committee on banks be instructed to enquire into the expediency of so amending an act to incorporate the Mechanics association of Fredericksburg, passed February 16th, 1835, as to authorize an increase of the capital stock of said association to an amount not exceeding one hundred thousand dollars, and to extend to said association banking privileges, by issuing and circulating notes, &c., and that they report thereupon.

Resolved, That the committee for courts of justice be instructed to enquire into the expediency of so amending an act reducing into one the several acts against hog stealing, passed February 2d, 1819, as to repeal the penalties of said act on slaves, and substituting other penalties therefor, and that they report by bill or otherwise.

On motion of Mr. Holleman, *Resolved*, That the committee appointed to enquire into the expediency of paying a claim for losses sustained by the burning of Norfolk in the year 1776, be instructed to enquire into the expediency of repealing the act passed the 11th day of March, 1834, appointing a commissioner of revolutionary claims, and that they report by bill or otherwise.

On motion of Mr. Murdaugh, *Resolved*, That the auditor of public accounts be requested to furnish a copy of the journal and report of the commissioners appointed by act of 1777, to ascertain the losses occasioned to individuals by the burning of Norfolk and Portsmouth in the year 1776.

On motion of Mr. Rinker, *Resolved*, That the committee for courts of justice be instructed to enquire into the expediency of so amending the act passed April 8th, 1831, for reducing into one act, the several acts concerning the courts of appeals and special courts of appeals, as to provide that appeals taken from the courts of the counties of Shenandoah, Hardy and Page, shall be tried at the court of appeals holden at Lewisburg instead of the court of appeals held in the city of Richmond, with leave to report by bill or otherwise.

On motion of Mr. Holleman, *Resolved*, That the committee for courts of justice be instructed to enquire into the expediency of requiring by law that all free negroes, (if males,) under the age of twenty-one years, (and if females,) under the age of eighteen years, be hired out annually, to white masters, by the overseers of the poor, and the nett proceeds of hires to be paid over to the parents of said free negroes.

Resolved, That the said committee also enquire whether any further legislation be necessary to remove free negroes from the commonwealth, and report by bill or otherwise.

On motion of Mr. Harrison, (the same being amended on motion of Mr. Gilmer,) *Resolved*, That the committee for courts of justice be authorized to collect and have printed, such documents connected with the cession of the public lands from the state of Virginia to the United States as they may deem necessary.

On motion of Mr. Watkins, *Resolved*, That the committee of roads and internal navigation be authorized to send for persons and papers to aid them in the investigation of the petition of Jesse Snead.

Mr. Beard presented a petition of sundry citizens of the town of Waterford, for an amendment of the acts incorporating said town.

Also a petition of sundry citizens of the county of Loudoun, asking that Braden and Hixon may be authorized to construct a toll-bridge across the Shenandoah river at Harper's Ferry.

Mr. Benton a petition of sundry citizens of the county of Nansemond, for the passage of an act prohibiting the catching of oysters in Nansemond river and Chuckatuck creek during the summer months in every year.

Mr. Morgan a petition of sundry citizens of the county of Monongalia, for the establishment of a separate election at the house of Michael Snodgrass in said county.

Mr. Woolfolk a petition of a portion of the citizens of the county of Orange, asking that the said county may be divided and a new county formed therefrom.

Ordered, That the said petitions be referred to the committee of propositions and grievances, that they do examine the matter thereof, and report their opinion thereupon to the house.

Mr. Harley presented a petition of sundry citizens of the county of Smyth, for the incorporation of a company to construct a rail-road from Lynchburg to some point on the Tennessee line, and from Lynchburg to the city of Richmond, which was ordered to be referred to the committee of roads and internal navigation, that they do examine the matter thereof, and report their opinion thereupon to the house.

Mr. Smith of Frederick presented a petition of the president and common council of the borough of Winchester, praying the establishment of an inspection of flour, &c. in said town, and that the power of appointing and removing the inspector may be vested in the hustings court thereof, which was ordered to be referred to the committee of agriculture and manufactures, that they do examine the matter thereof, and report their opinion thereupon to the house.

Mr. Gilmer presented a petition of sundry citizens of the county of Albemarle, asking that the banks of James river may be declared by law to be a lawful enclosure, which on his motion was ordered to be referred to the committee for courts of justice, that they do examine the matter thereof, and report their opinion thereupon to the house.

Mr. Hill from the committee of propositions and grievances, reported with amendments, a bill forming a new county out of parts of the counties of Lewis and Nicholas; which was subsequently taken up, and the said amendments being agreed to by the house, the said bill as amended, was ordered to be engrossed and read a third time.

Mr. Watkins from the committee of roads and internal navigation, reported with amendments, a bill to provide for the construction of a road between Weston in the county of Lewis and Charleston in the county of Kanawha, which was subsequently taken up, and the said amendments being agreed to by the house, the said bill as amended was ordered to be engrossed and read a third time.

Mr. Watkins from the same committee presented a bill to incorporate the Newburn and Red Sulphur springs turnpike company.

A bill to authorize a subscription on behalf of the commonwealth to the enlarged capital stock of the Upper Appomattox company, which were severally read the first and ordered to be read a second time.

Also a bill to dispose of certain moneys heretofore raised by lottery in the county of Monroe, which was read the first and second times, and (by general consent) ordered to be engrossed and read a third time.

And a bill to enact an act of the general assembly of North Carolina, entitled, "an act to incorporate the Roanoke, Danville and Junction rail-road company, which was read the first and second times, and ordered to be committed to the committee which brought it in.

Mr. Watkins also, from the same committee, presented a report which was read as follows:

The committee of roads and internal navigation have, according to order, enquired into "the expediency of directing the survey of a road from Moorfield, to intersect the North-western turnpike at or near Charles Blue's in the county of Hampshire:" Whereupon,

Resolved as the opinion of this committee, That it is expedient to direct the said survey.

The said resolution was, on the question put thereupon, agreed to by the house, and a bill was ordered to be brought in conformably therewith.

Mr. Beuhring reported with amendments, a bill to amend the act, entitled, "an act to reduce into one the several acts for the settlement and regulation of ferries," passed January 30th, 1819, which was taken up, and the said amendments being agreed to by the house, the said bill, as amended, was ordered to be engrossed and read a third time.

Mr. Chapline reported with amendment, a bill concerning the fire and marine insurance company of Wheeling, which was received and laid upon the table.

An engrossed bill to incorporate the Sweet springs company, was read a third time; whereupon, on motion of Mr. Dorman, the rule of the house was suspended, and the vote ordering the said bill to be engrossed and read a third time, was reconsidered; the said bill was then amended on his motion, and as amended, was ordered to be re-engrossed and read a third time.

An engrossed bill incorporating the Red and Blue Sulphur springs turnpike company, was taken up, on motion of Mr. Chapman; whereupon, the rule of the house was suspended, and the vote ordering the said bill to be engrossed, was reconsidered, and the said bill was then ordered to be committed to the committee which brought it in.

An engrossed bill to amend an act, entitled, "an act to incorporate the Midlothian coal mining company," was read a third time:

Resolved, That the bill do pass, and that the title be, "an act to amend an act, entitled, 'an act to incorporate the Midlothian coal mining company.'"

An engrossed bill to amend an act, entitled, "an act for cutting a navigable canal from the waters of Elizabeth river in the state of Virginia, to the waters of Pasquotank river in North Carolina," was read a third time:

Resolved, That the bill do pass, and that the title be, "an act to amend an act, entitled, 'an act for cutting a navigable canal from the waters of Elizabeth river in the state of Virginia, to the waters of Pasquotank river in North Carolina."

An engrossed bill authorizing the board of public works to subscribe on behalf of the commonwealth to the stock of the Smith's river navigation company, was read a third time:

Resolved, That the bill do pass, and (the title being amended on motion of Mr. Fontaine) that the title be, "an *act concerning Smith's river*."

An engrossed bill directing a change of location of the North-western turnpike through the town of Evansville, was read a third time:

Resolved, That the bill do pass, and that the title be, "an act directing a change of location of the North-western turnpike through the town of Evansville."

An engrossed bill to provide for the enlargement of the public warehouse for the storage and inspection of tobacco in the city of Richmond, was read a third time

Resolved, That the bill do pass, and that the title be, "an act to provide for the enlargement of the public warehouse for the storage and inspection of tobacco in the city of Richmond."

An engrossed bill incorporating the Great Falls manufacturing company in the county of Fayette, was read a third time:

Resolved, That the bill do pass, and that the title be, "an act incorporating the Great Falls manufacturing company in the county of Fayette."

An engrossed bill to amend an act, entitled, "an act to incorporate the Staunton and Potowmac rail-road company," was taken up on motion of Mr. Watkins, and read a third time:

Resolved, That the bill do pass, and that the title be, "an act to amend an act, entitled, 'an act to incorporate the Staunton and Potowmac rail-road company.'"

Ordered, That the clerk communicate the said bills to the senate and request their concurrence.

Reports of the committee of agriculture and manufactures were read as follow:

The committee of agriculture and manufactures, to whom were referred the petition of the Nelson and Albemarle Union factory company, praying for a revival of the charter of said company, for the purpose of selling and distributing the property of said company, have had the same under consideration, and have come to the following resolution thereupon:

Resolved, That the prayer of the aforesaid petition is reasonable.

The committee of agriculture and manufactures, to whom was referred the petition of the president and directors of the "Merchants manufacturing company" of the town of Petersburg, praying authority to increase their capital stock, have had the same under consideration, and have come to the following resolution thereupon:

Resolved as the opinion of this committee, That the prayer of the aforesaid petition is reasonable.

The said resolutions were, on questions severally put thereupon, agreed to by the house, and bills were ordered to be brought in conformably therewith.

A bill to reduce and regulate the tolls on the North-western turnpike, was read a second time, and ordered to be committed to the committee which brought it in on motion of Mr. Mullen.

A bill to incorporate the stockholders of the City Point rail-road company, was read the second time, and ordered, on motion of Mr. Brown of Petersburg, to be laid upon the table.

A bill to incorporate the stockholders of the Cartersville and Farmville rail-road company, was read the first and second times, and ordered to be committed to the committee which brought it in.

A bill to prevent trespasses by non-resident herdsmen in the county of Preston.

A bill to incorporate the Ettrick banks manufacturing company.

A bill to incorporate the Fleets manufacturing company; and

A bill to revive and amend an act incorporating the Belle Isle manufacturing company, passed 19th March, 1832, were severally read the first, and ordered to be read a second time.

On motion of Mr. Mullen, the house adjourned until to-morrow 12 o'clock.

TUESDAY, January 5th, 1836.

On motion of Mr. Sherrard, *Resolved*, That the committee for courts of justice be instructed to enquire whether any, and if any, what amendments are necessary to the first section of the act, entitled, "an act to reduce into one the several acts concerning grand juries and petit juries," passed January 7th, 1819; and into the propriety of defining more particularly the qualifications of grand jurors, and that said committee have leave to report by bill or otherwise.

On motion of Mr. Wethered, *Ordered*, That leave be given to bring in a bill to amend an act, entitled, "an act incorporating the Spring creek turnpike company," and that Messrs. Wethered, Price, Summers, Waggener, Hays, Willey, Prentiss, Decamps and Masters, prepare and bring in the same.

Mr. Strange, according to order, presented a bill to incorporate the Fluvanna mining company.

Mr. Christian, from the committee on the clerk's office, presented a bill to provide an index to the journals of the house of delegates, which were received and laid upon the table.

Mr. Gibson presented a petition of John Hope, asking to be divorced from his wife.

Also a remonstrance of Thomas Montgomery, opposing the said divorce, which were ordered to be referred to the committee for courts of justice, that they do examine the matter thereof, and report their opinion thereupon to the house.

Mr. Witcher, from the committee of claims, presented a bill concerning Shelton Ford.

A bill concerning George Johnson; and

A bill concerning James Wysong, which were received and laid upon the table.

On motion of Mr. Witcher, *Ordered*, That the committee of claims be discharged from the further consideration of the petitions of James Johnson, of John Stackhouse, of Hugh M'Gavoc, and of the heirs of doctor Thomas Carter, and that the same be referred to the select committee on revolutionary claims, that they do examine the matter thereof, and report their opinion thereupon to the house.

On motion of Mr. Fontaine, (the same having been amended on motion of Mr. Gilmer,) *Resolved*, That the committee on the militia laws be instructed to enquire into the expediency of providing by law for the better instruction, discipline and organization of the militia of this commonwealth.

Mr. Garland of Mecklenburg, from the select committee on that subject, presented a report, which was read as follows:

The select committee to whom was referred "so much of the governor's message as relates to the disorganizing, seditious and incendiary doctrines of certain associations created in the northern and eastern states for the purpose of producing a direct interference with the slave property of the south," have had the same under consideration, and report in part the following resolutions:

1. *Resolved*, That the general assembly solemnly declares its warm attachment to the Union, and its firm conviction, that while the measures of the general government are kept within the limitations of the constitution, and those of the states directed by the spirit of which that union is the offspring, it is the surest safegard of the peace, prosperity and happiness of each member thereof.

2. *Resolved*, That each state had originally the sole and exclusive right to interfere with, control, or legislate upon the subject of domestic slavery within its jurisdictional limits—a right which, so far from being impaired, is recognized and guaranteed by the constitution of the United States—and that all interference therewith by the general government, the other states, or the citizens thereof, is invasive of the rights of the states, and violates the obligations of the constitution.

3. *Resolved*, That the general assembly faithfully expresses the sentiments of the people and its own, when it declares its just abhorrence and reprobation of the fanatical, or reckless or malignant zeal that has embodied so many societies in the non-slaveholding states, under the denomination of abolitionists, carrying on by concert and confederacy a common scheme, endangering the peace, prosperity and safety of this and the other slaveholding states, regardless of the moral, social and political obligations they violate, and the evils they bring on the objects of their pretended or mistaken philanthropy: and with this sentiment of abhorrence is mingled one of the profoundest regret, that amongst the mischiefs likely to flow from such societies and their enterprizes, if unchecked, is to be numbered the alienation of the members of this great confederacy from each other, and the decay if not destruction of the ties that bind them to their glorious and happy union.

4. *Resolved*, That the slaveholding states have a right to claim of the states in which such societies are found or projected, the suppression or prevention of them by laws, inflicting adequate penalties on those who form them, and who print or circulate the prints, pamphlets, tracts or pictorial representations, tending or intended to produce insubordination and revolt among the slaves of the southern states—and that this claim, justified by the acknowledged principle of international law acting on separate and independent states, derives a peculiar force and sanctity from the social, fraternal and political relations of the states of this Union to each other.

5. *Resolved*, That confiding in the justice and loyalty to the principles of the Union, of the non-slaveholding states, reinforced by the strong sympathies of common dangers, sufferings and triumphs, the identity of interests, great and multiform, the social and political ties that connect, and that ought to bind in fraternal concord, the states and the people of this Union, the danger with which that Union will be menaced, should these societies, emboldened by impunity, persevere in their infatuated or incendiary schemes, the general assembly of Virginia respectfully but earnestly request that the legislatures of the states in which such societies have been formed, or may be projected, will take prompt and effectual measures of penal inhibition to suppress or prevent the formation of them, and by adequate penalties, prevent or punish the printing or circulation of the prints, pamphlets and pictorial representations aforesaid.

6. *Resolved*, That it is a subject of lively felicitation, that the schemes of fanatics and incendiaries who have projected, or are united in the said societies, have been discountenanced, disavowed or reprobated by a large portion of the intelligent citizens of the states in which they have been formed or projected; that to that portion of the citizens of those states, the thanks of the people of this are due; and their generous and honourable support of the rights of this and the other southern states, and the respect evinced by them for the obligations, social and constitutional, on the non-slaveholding states, warrant the augury, and give confidence to the expectation, that the foregoing request for legal security against future assault on the peace, property and safety of the slaveholding states, will with alacrity be granted.

7. *Resolved*, That congress has no constitutional or rightful power to abolish slavery in the district of Columbia; that such a measure would be an assumption of power not covered by the right of exclusive jurisdiction claimed under the constitution; infractive of the rights guaranteed by the articles of cession,—an implied if not direct denunciation of the slaveholding states by the government they have contributed to create,—affording just grounds of apprehension that future schemes against the rights of the slaveholding states are meditated, and rendering it certain that thereby the schemes already formed will be fostered, and an advanced post secured, from which they may be carried on with surer aim and more mischievous activity and success.

8. *Resolved*, That it is highly expedient that the other slaveholding states should respectfully but earnestly urge the states in which the said societies are found, to provide the securities sought for by the foregoing resolutions; and their co-operation in making such a request of the other states, and also in passing such laws and regulations as may be suitable and effectual to prevent or suppress the circulation of any of the mischievous or incendiary publications emanating from the said societies, and to prevent the formation of such societies within their limits, is hereby respectfully invited.

9. *Resolved*, That the governor be requested to transmit a copy of the foregoing resolutions to each of the senators and representatives in congress from this state, and that he be further requested to transmit a copy to the executive of the several states, with a request to lay them before their respective legislatures, and invite their prompt attention to them.

On motion of Mr. Wilson of Botetourt, the said report was ordered to be laid upon the table, and on motion of Mr. Garland of Mecklenburg, 185 copies thereof were ordered to be printed for the use of the general assembly.

Mr. Garland of Mecklenburg, submitted a report on the part of the minority of said committee on the same subject, 185 copies of which, on his motion, were ordered to be printed in like manner.

Mr. Carter, from the committee on banks, presented a report upon the expediency of increasing the banking capital of the commonwealth, which was received and laid upon the table.

On motion, *Ordered*, That 500 copies of the said report and documents be printed for the use of the members of the general assembly.

On motion of Mr. Harrison, *Resolved*, That the committee for courts of justice enquire into the expediency of giving to the courts of law in this commonwealth, power to appoint guardians ad litem for infant defendants in said courts, with leave to the committee to report by bill or otherwise.

On motion of Mr. Cunningham, *Resolved*, That the committee of schools and colleges be instructed to enquire into the expediency of providing by law for the distribution of the surplus revenue of the literary fund, and also to provide how such surplus shall be distributed, with leave to report by bill or otherwise.

On motion of Mr. M'Mullen, *Resolved*, That the committee of propositions and grievances be instructed to enquire into the expediency of providing by law for paying to the trustees of Estillville academy, in the county of Scott, the quota of that county, out of the fund created by act of 1833, for the removal of free persons of colour, and that they report by bill or otherwise.

On motion of Mr. M'Coy, *Resolved*, That the committee of roads and internal navigation be instructed to enquire into the expediency of appropriating a sum of money to complete the construction of the Alleghany turnpike road in the counties of Pendleton and Pocahontas, on the line of the Staunton and Parkersburg road, and that they report by bill or otherwise.

Mr. Gregory, according to order, presented a bill to change the times of holding the courts in the third judicial circuit.

And a bill to reorganize the first and second judicial districts.

Mr. Sloan, in like manner, a bill to change the place of holding a separate election in the county of Hampshire.

Mr. Cunningham, from the committee of schools and colleges, presented reports upon the petitions of the Norfolk and Portsmouth literary and scientific mechanics' institute, and of citizens of the county of Scott.

Which bills and reports were received and laid upon the table.

An engrossed bill to amend the act, entitled, "an act to reduce into one the several acts for the settlement and regulation of ferries," passed January 30th, 1819, was read a third time:

Resolved, That the bill do pass, and that the title be, "an act to amend the act, entitled, 'an act to reduce into one the several acts for the settlement and regulation of ferries,'" passed January 30th, 1819.

An engrossed bill to dispose of certain moneys heretofore raised by lottery in the county of Monroe, was read a third time:

Resolved, That the bill do pass, and that the title be, "an act to dispose of certain moneys heretofore raised by lottery in the county of Monroe."

An engrossed bill to provide for the construction of a road between Weston, in the county of Lewis, and Charleston, in the county of Kanawha, was read a third time, and the question being put upon its passage, was determined in the affirmative. Ayes 66, noes 47.

On motion of Mr. Witcher, (seven of the members present concurring,) *Ordered*, That the ayes and noes upon the said question be inserted in the journal.

The names of the gentlemen who voted in the affirmative, are Messrs. Southall, Wiley, Craig, M'Clintic, Hunter of Berkeley, Henshaw, Miller, Wilson of Botetourt, Decamps, Beuhring, Smith of Fauquier, Hickerson, Price, Strange, Bowen, Davison, Smith of Frederick, Watkins, Wethered, Sloan, Nixon, Mullen, Harrison, Kincheloe, Fontaine, Gregory, Griggs, Summers, Carter, Hays, Straton, Board, Taylor of Loudoun, Waggener, Willey, Morgan, Chapman, Sherrard, Benton, Brown of Nelson, Murdaugh, Chapline, Masters, Almond, M'Coy, Cackley, Hopkins, Carroll, Morris, Shands, Marteney, Nicklin, Dorman, Leyburn, Moffett, Conrad, Jessee, Rinker, Harley, Crutchfield, Moncure, Gillespie, Delashmutt, Gibson, Prentiss and Saunders.—66.

And the names of the gentlemen who voted in the negative, are Messrs. Banks, (speaker,) Grinalds, Drummond, Gilmer, Layne, Campbell, Pate, Turnbull, Mallory, Booker, Austin, Samuel, Richardson, Johnson, Hill, Wilson of Cumberland, Ball, Steger, Hale of Franklin, Holland, Watts, Hail of Grayson, Avent, Coleman, Botts, Holleman, Fleet, Robinson, Harris, Ragsdale, Taylor of Mathews and Middlesex, Rogers, Cooke, Parker, Fitzgerald, Critz, Swanson, Witcher, Madison, Williams, M'Mullen, Bare, Butts, Hargrave, Cunningham, Brown of Petersburg, and Stanard.—47.

Resolved, That the bill do pass, and that the title be, "an act to provide for the construction of a road between Weston, in the county of Lewis, and Charleston, in the county of Kanawha."

Ordered, That the clerk communicate the said bills to the senate and request their concurrence.

On motion of Mr. Carroll, the house adjourned until to-morrow 12 o'clock.

WEDNESDAY, January 6th, 1836.

Mr. Watkins, from the committee of roads and internal navigation, presented several reports upon petitions of citizens of Harrison, Monongalia and Randolph; of citizens of Rockbridge, Botetourt and Alleghany; of citizens of the county of Goochland; and of R. Anderson and others, and on the resolution for a road from Elizabethtown to Wheeling.

He also presented a bill to provide for the construction of a road across the Blue Ridge at Milam's gap; and
A bill directing the survey and location of a route for a road from Moorfield to the North-western turnpike.
And reported with amendments a bill to reduce and regulate the tolls on the North-western turnpike; and
A bill incorporating the Red and Blue Sulphur springs turnpike company.
And without amendment a bill to incorporate the stockholders of the Cartersville and Farmville rail-road company.

Mr. Hill, from the committee of propositions and grievances, presented a report upon the petition of Michael Snodgrass; and
A bill to establish the town of Hedgesville, in the county of Berkeley.

Mr. Stanard, from the committee for courts of justice, presented a bill allowing Charlotte Morgan, a free woman of colour, to remain in the commonwealth.
A bill concerning Duff Green.
A bill allowing Richard Bolling, a free man of colour, to remain in the commonwealth.
A bill allowing Daniel Higginbotham, a free man of colour, to remain in the commonwealth a limited time.
A bill allowing Judy Johnson, a free woman of colour, to remain in the commonwealth.
A bill authorizing James Martin to hold and convey certain real estate.
A bill regulating and reducing the expenses incident to the collection of money under execution.
A bill authorizing the sale of the estate of John Haskins, senior, a lunatic; and
A bill releasing to William Fisher the commonwealth's right to one thousand acres of land in the county of Nicholas.

Which reports and bills were received and laid upon the table.

On motion of Mr. Masters, *Resolved*, That the committee for courts of justice be instructed to enquire into the expediency of providing by law for the publication of the county levy as annually made by the justices in the several counties of this commonwealth, stating in such publication the amount and specific object of such levy, with the special purpose to which the same is intended to be applied, including the name or names of those for whose benefit it may be intended; and that they report by bill or otherwise.

On motion of Mr. Price, *Resolved*, That the committee of roads and internal navigation be instructed to enquire into the expediency of opening the eastern portion of the road surveyed by the public engineer from Huntersville to the Ohio river, and that they have leave to report by bill or otherwise.

On motion of Mr. Parker, the rule of the house limiting the number of the committee on the militia laws, was suspended, and Messrs. Hunter of Berkeley, Taylor of Loudoun, and Benton, were ordered to be added thereto.

Mr. Holleman, from the committee of privileges and elections, presented a report upon the petition of Isaac Adams, contesting the election of Haman Critz, the delegate returned to represent the county of Patrick in the present house of delegates, which, on motion of Mr. Price, was ordered to be recommitted to the said committee.

A motion was made by Mr. Sherrard that the report of the minority of the committee to whom was referred so much of the governor's message as relates to the disorganizing, seditious and incendiary doctrines of certain associations created in the northern and eastern states, for the purpose of producing a direct interference with the slave property of the south, which report was presented on yesterday, be inserted in the journal; whereupon, on motion of Mr. Witcher, the said proposition was ordered to be laid upon the table.

On motion of Mr. Craig, *Resolved*, That the committee of roads and internal navigation be instructed to enquire into the expediency of amending an act, entitled, "an act incorporating a company to construct a turnpike road from the eastern side of the Warm spring mountain to Harrisonburg in the county of Rockingham," so as to authorize the said Warm springs and Harrisonburg turnpike company, at their option so to change the location of their said road as to make the Augusta springs in the county of Augusta, a point on the same; and so as to authorize the said Warm springs and Harrisonburg turnpike company, at their option to connect their road with the eastern and western points of termination of the road of the Augusta springs turnpike company, without continuing their road between the said points of termination.

A bill to incorporate the stockholders of the City Point rail-road company, was taken up on motion of Mr. Shands, and ordered to be committed to the committee which brought it in.

Mr. Garland of Mecklenburg presented a petition of William Townes, asking to be authorized to erect a toll-bridge across the Roanoke river.

Mr. Delashmutt, a petition of citizens of the county of Tyler, for a change in the location of a separate election in said county, from the house of Presley Martin to the school-house on the land of Jeremiah Williams.

Mr. Conrad, a petition of sundry citizens of the county of Rockingham, for the establishment of a separate election at the town of Magaheysville in said county.

Ordered, That the said petitions be referred to the committee of propositions and grievances, that they do examine the matter thereof, and report their opinion thereupon to the house.

Mr. Fontaine presented a petition of sundry citizens of the county of Patrick, for the repeal of the acts concerning the processioning of lands, which was ordered to be referred to the committee for courts of justice, that they do examine the matter thereof, and report their opinion thereupon to the house.

Mr. Austin presented a petition of John Nicholas, asking for an additional allowance of land in consideration of his services as an officer in the revolutionary war, which was ordered to be referred to the committee on revolutionary claims, that they do examine the matter thereof, and report their opinion thereupon to the house.

Mr. Miller presented a petition of citizens of the county of Botetourt, for the incorporation of a company for the construction of a rail-road from the city of Richmond, by the way of Lynchburg, to the Tennessee line, with a branch to the town of Fincastle, which was ordered to be referred to the committee of roads and internal navigation, that they do examine the matter thereof, and report their opinion thereupon to the house.

A bill to revive and amend an act incorporating the Belle Isle manufacturing company, passed 19th March, 1832; and

A bill to prevent trespasses by non-resident herdsmen in the county of Preston, were severally read the second time, and ordered to be engrossed and read a third time.

A bill to authorize a subscription on behalf of the commonwealth to the enlarged capital stock of the Upper Appomattox company, was read a second time, and on motion of Mr. Madison, ordered to be committed to the committee which brought it in.

A bill to incorporate the Ettrick banks manufacturing company; and

A bill to incorporate the Fleets manufacturing company, were read a second time, and ordered to be engrossed and read a third time.

An engrossed bill forming a new county out of parts of the counties of Lewis and Nicholas, was read a third time, and sundry blanks therein were filled:

Resolved, That the bill do pass, and that the title be, "an act forming a new county out of parts of the counties of Lewis and Nicholas."

Ordered, That the clerk communicate the same to the senate and request their concurrence.

A bill concerning the fire and marine insurance company of Wheeling, with the amendments thereto proposed by the committee to which the same had been committed, was taken up, and the said amendments being agreed to by the house, the said bill as amended was ordered to be engrossed and read a third time.

An engrossed bill to incorporate the Sweet springs company, was read a third time:

Resolved, That the bill do pass, and that the title be, "an act to incorporate the Sweet springs company."

Ordered, That the clerk communicate the same to the senate and request their concurrence.

On motion of Mr. Gregory, the house adjourned until to-morrow 12 o'clock.

THURSDAY, January 7th, 1836.

A communication from the senate by their clerk:

IN SENATE, January 6th, 1836.

The senate have passed the bills, entitled,

"An act incorporating the Great falls manufacturing company in the county of Fayette."

"An act to change the place of holding a separate election in the county of Wythe."

"An act to incorporate the Virginia mills manufacturing company."

"An act to change the place of holding a separate election in the county of Preston."

"An act to change the place of holding a separate election in the county of Marshall."

"An act to authorize William Chapline and others to construct wharves on Wheeling creek and the Ohio river, adjoining the town of South Wheeling in Ohio county."

"An act to authorize the appointment of a third commissioner of the superior court of Petersburg;" and

"An act to authorize the mayor and commonalty of the town of Wheeling to subscribe for stock of the Baltimore and Ohio rail-road company."

They have also passed the bills, entitled,

"An act to amend the act establishing the town of Grandville in the county of Monongalia;" and

"An act to enlarge, define and establish the corporate boundaries and limits of the town of Wheeling in the county of Ohio," with amendments, in which they request the concurrence of the house of delegates.

The said amendments being twice read, were, on questions severally put thereupon, agreed to by the house.

Ordered, That the clerk inform the senate thereof.

On motion of Mr. Chapman, *Ordered*, That leave be given to bring in a bill changing the time of holding certain courts in the eighth district and sixteenth circuit, and that Messrs. Chapman, Saunders, Watts, Hale of Grayson, Straton, Ingles and Summers, prepare and bring in the same.

On motion of Mr. Moffett, *Resolved*, That the committee of agriculture and manufactures be instructed to enquire into the expediency of establishing by law a grade of flour above that of superfine, and that they have leave to report by bill or otherwise.

On motion of Mr. Hickerson, *Ordered*, That leave be given to bring in a bill to authorize the incorporation of the trustees of the Upperville academy in the county of Fauquier, and that Messrs. Hickerson, Smith of Fauquier, Williams, Moncure, Hill, Woolfolk, Crutchfield and Nicklin, prepare and bring in the same.

Mr. Hill, from the committee of propositions and grievances, presented a report upon the petition of citizens of the county of Ohio.

Also a bill to authorize a separate election at the tavern house of William Irwin in the county of Cumberland; and

A bill to enlarge the town of Clarksville in the county of Mecklenburg.

Mr. Parker, from the committee on the militia laws, presented a report upon the petition of the officers of the 104th regiment.

Mr. Hunter of Berkeley, according to order, presented a bill to amend an act, entitled, "an act to limit the assessment upon titheables, and to authorize a tax upon property, for the purpose of defraying county expenditures within the county of Berkeley," passed March 5th, 1835.

Which were received and laid upon the table.

Mr. Sherrard presented a petition of sundry citizens of the county of Morgan, praying for an increase of the salaries of the judges of the general court.

Mr. Moffett, a petition of Isaac Brock a free man of colour, for permission to remain in the commonwealth for a limited time.

Ordered, That the said petitions be referred to the committee for courts of justice, that they do examine the matter thereof, and report their opinion thereupon to the house.

Mr. Taylor of Middlesex, presented a petition of the president and directors of the Dragon Swamp canal company for a subscription to the stock of the said company, by the board of public works on behalf of the commonwealth.

Mr. Murdaugh, a petition of Duff Green and others, for an act of incorporation to work certain mines of coal and iron ore, to establish manufactories, and to construct a canal or slack water navigation from the Chesapeake and Ohio canal near Cumberland up the North branch of the Potowmac river, to George's creek, to the site of the contemplated manufactories; and to construct a rail-road from the mines to the factories.

Ordered, That the said petitions be referred to the committee of roads and internal navigation, that they do examine the matter thereof, and report their opinion thereupon to the house.

Mr. Holleman, from the committee of privileges and elections, presented a report, which was read as follows:

The committee of privileges and elections, to whom was referred the petition of Isaac Adams, contesting the election of Haman Critz, a delegate returned to represent the county of Patrick, in the present general assembly, submit for the consideration of the house, the following report:

From an examination of the poll books of the county of Patrick, it appears to your committee, that Haman Critz and Isaac Adams received two hundred and eighty-one votes each, and the return was given to Haman Critz by the casting vote of the sheriff of said county.

Isaac Adams contested sixty-three votes on the poll of Haman Critz, of which three were admitted to be illegal by Haman Critz; one was rejected because it was not attempted to be sustained by any evidence whatever; four were rejected because the notice to take evidence did not correspond with the time when the depositions were taken; and twenty-one were decided to be illegal for want of qualification according to the constitution and laws. Fifteen votes were admitted to be legal by Isaac Adams; nineteen were decided to be legal by the committee, and one was added to the poll of Haman Critz, it being proved that the vote was given and omitted on the poll by mistake.

Number on Haman Critz's poll,	281
Omitted through mistake,	1
	282
No evidence to sustain — — 1	
Notice illegal, — — 4	
Admitted illegal, — — 3	
Decided illegal, — — 21	
	29
Number of legal votes on the poll of Haman Critz,	253

Haman Critz contested fifty-six votes on the poll of Isaac Adams, of which eight were admitted to be illegal by Isaac Adams, and eleven were decided to be illegal for want of qualification according to the constitution and laws. Two were admitted to be legal by Haman Critz; thirty-five were decided to be legal by the committee; two were added to the poll of Isaac Adams, it being proved that the votes were given and omitted on the poll by mistake, and one was struck off, the name being entered twice.

Number on Isaac Adams's poll,	281
Omitted through mistake,	2
	283
Struck off, — — — 1	
Admitted illegal, — — 8	
Decided illegal, — — 11	
	20
Number of legal votes on the poll of Isaac Adams,	263

The committee are of the opinion that the polls should stand thus:
For Isaac Adams, - - - 263
For Haman Critz, - - - 253
　　　　　　　　　　　　　　　　　　　　　　　　　　　　　 10
Admitted bad by Isaac Adams after report was drawn up,　 1

Majority for Adams, - - - 9

They therefore recommend to the house the adoption of the following resolution:
Resolved, That Isaac Adams was duly elected a delegate from the county of Patrick in the present general assembly.

The committee of privileges and elections, to whom was recommitted the report from said committee, in relation to the contested election from the county of Patrick, have again had the same under consideration, and Haman Critz, the sitting member, having expressed himself satisfied that he cannot reverse the said report, and stated to the committee that he is willing that they should make the same report without amendment, which the committee accordingly do. They therefore recommend to the house the adoption of the resolution contained in said report in the following words:

Resolved, That Isaac Adams was duly elected a delegate from the county of Patrick in the present general assembly.

The said resolution was, on the question put thereupon, agreed to by the house.

Ordered, That Mr. Adams be added to the several committees on which Mr. Critz was a member, in his stead.

An engrossed bill to incorporate the Fleets manufacturing company, was read a third time, and sundry blanks therein were filled:

Resolved, That the bill do pass, and that the title be, "an act to incorporate the Fleets manufacturing company."

An engrossed bill to incorporate the Ettrick banks manufacturing company, was read a third time, and sundry blanks therein were filled:

Resolved, That the bill do pass, and (the title being amended on motion of Mr. Brown of Petersburg,) that the title be, "an act to incorporate the Ettrick manufacturing company."

An engrossed bill to revive and amend an act incorporating the Belle Isle manufacturing company, passed 19th March, 1832, was read a third time:

Resolved, That the bill do pass, and that the title be, "an act to revive and amend an act, incorporating the Belle Isle manufacturing company, passed 19th March, 1832."

An engrossed bill concerning the fire and marine insurance company of Wheeling, was read a third time:

Resolved, That the bill do pass, and that the title be, "an act concerning the fire and marine insurance company of Wheeling."

An engrossed bill to prevent trespasses by non-resident herdsmen, in the county of Preston, was read a third time, and sundry blanks therein were filled:

Resolved, That the bill do pass, and that the title be, "an act to prevent trespasses by non-resident herdsmen, in the county of Preston."

Ordered, That the clerk communicate the said bills to the senate and request their concurrence.

On motion of Mr. Watkins, the report of the committee to whom was referred the expediency of instructing the senators from this state in the congress of the United States to introduce and vote for a resolution to expunge from the journal of the senate the resolution adopted by that body disapproving the acts of the president in relation to the public revenue, was taken up; whereupon, a motion was made by him that the said report be referred to a committee of the whole house on the state of the commonwealth; and the question being put thereupon, was determined in the affirmative. Ayes 70, noes 57.

On motion of Mr. Dorman, (seven of the members present concurring,) *Ordered*, That the ayes and noes upon the said question be inserted in the journal.

The names of the gentlemen who voted in the affirmative, are Messrs. Banks, (speaker,) Drummond, Layne, Wiley, M'Clintic, Miller, Wilson of Botetourt, Decamps, Turnbull, Booker, Austin, Samuel, Richardson, Hill, Smith of Fauquier, Hickerson, Strange, Steger, Holland, Bowen, Davison, Watts, Watkins, Hail of Grayson, Avent, Sloan, Nixon, Goodall, Harrison, Kincheloe, Fontaine, Hays, Straton, Harris, Taylor of Mathews and Middlesex, Garland of Mecklenburg, Willey, Morgan, Chapman, Ingles, Sherrard, Brown of Nelson, Murdaugh, Cooke, Fitzgerald, Woolfolk, Almond, Adams, M'Coy, Cackley, Hopkins, Carroll, Madison, Shands, Williams, Marteney, Nicklin, Moffett, Conrad, Jessee, M'Mullen, Bare, Rinker, Crutchfield, Moncure, Spratley, Hargrave, Gillespie, Gibson and Saunders.—70.

And the names of the gentlemen who voted in the negative, are Messrs. Gilmer, Southall, Brooke, Craig, Campbell, Pate, Hunter of Berkeley, Henshaw, Mallory, Beuhring, Daniel, Christian, Johnson, Wilson of Cumberland, Servant, Hunter of Essex, Ball, Price, Hale of Franklin, Smith of Frederick, Wethered, Coleman, Mullen, Botts, Holleman, Gregory, Griggs, Berry, Summers, Fleet, Hooe, Robinson, Carter, Neill, Beard, Powell, Taylor of Loudoun, Ragsdale, Waggener, Rogers, Benton, Parker, Chapline, Masters, Swanson, Witcher, Morris, Dorman, Leyburn, Harley, Butts, Delashmutt, Jett, Prentiss, Cunningham, Brown of Petersburg, and Stanard.—57.

On motion of Mr. Crutchfield, *Resolved*, That this house will on Monday next resolve itself into a committee of the whole house to take the said report into consideration.

Mr. Wilson of Botetourt submitted the following resolution:

Resolved, That leave be given to introduce a bill to arrange the electoral districts of Virginia for electors for president and vice-president of the United States.

On motion of Mr. Dorman, *Ordered,* That the same be laid upon the table.

On motion of Mr. Crutchfield, *Ordered,* That leave be given to bring in a bill to incorporate the Stafford gold mining company, and that Messrs. Crutchfield, Moncure, Hooe, Williams, Powell, Hill, Woolfolk, Nicklin, Goodall and Harris prepare and bring in the same.

Mr. Watkins, from the committee of roads and internal navigation, presented a report upon the petition of citizens of the county of Harrison; and

A bill further to provide for the construction of a turnpike road across the Alleghany mountain in the counties of Pendleton and Pocahontas.

And reported with amendment a bill to incorporate the stockholders of the City Point rail-road company.

Mr. Madison, from the committee of agriculture and manufactures, presented a report upon the petition of the president and common council of the borough of Winchester.

Also a bill authorizing an increase of the capital stock of the Merchants manufacturing company.

A bill to incorporate the Mechanics manufacturing company; and

A bill to revive the charter of the Nelson and Albemarle Union factory company.

Which reports and bills were received and laid upon the table.

On motion of Mr. Stanard, a bill incorporating the stockholders of the Richmond and Petersburg rail-road company, was taken up, and ordered to be recommitted to the committee which brought it in.

Mr. Johnson presented a memorial of the stockholders of the Manchester and Petersburg turnpike company, asking to be allowed the privilege of constructing a rail-road from Richmond to Petersburg, which was ordered to be referred to the committee of roads and internal navigation, that they do examine the matter thereof, and report their opinion thereupon to the house.

On motion of Mr. Crutchfield, the house adjourned until to-morrow 12 o'clock.

FRIDAY, January 8th, 1836.

The following communication was received from the senate by their clerk:

IN SENATE, January 7th, 1836.

The senate have passed the bills, entitled,

"An act concerning Smith's river."

"An act to incorporate the Petersburg navigation company."

"An act to amend an act, entitled, 'an act for cutting a navigable canal from the waters of Elizabeth river in the state of Virginia, to the waters of Pasquotank river in North Carolina.'"

"An act to revive and amend the act, entitled, 'an act incorporating the Richmond rail-road company;" and

"An act providing for the better security of persons charged with criminal offences.'"

They have also passed the bill, entitled,

"An act to amend an act, entitled, "an act to incorporate the Midlothian coal mining company," with an amendment, in which they request the concurrence of the house of delegates.

And they have agreed to the resolution for the election of a brigadier general for the eighteenth brigade, with an amendment, in which they also request the concurrence of the house of delegates.

The said amendments being twice read, were, on questions put thereupon, agreed to by the house

Ordered, That the clerk inform the senate thereof.

On motion of Mr. Shands, *Ordered,* That leave be given to bring in a bill to authorize the judge of the second circuit to appoint a time for holding the courts thereof in certain cases, and that Messrs. Shands, Brown of Petersburg, Hargrave, Avent, Mallory, Fitzgerald, Wiley and Turnbull, prepare and bring in the same.

On motion of Mr. Summers, *Ordered,* That leave be given to bring in a bill incorporating a society for the insurance of slaves in the county of Kanawha, and that Messrs. Summers, Waggener, Beuhring, Chapline, Prentiss, Decamps, Layne, Gibson and Chapman, prepare and bring in the same.

On motion of Mr. Botts, *Ordered,* That leave be given to bring in a bill to incorporate the Fauquier Sulphur springs, and that Messrs. Botts, Stanard, Smith of Fauquier, Hickerson, Hill, Beard, Ball, Moncure and Woolfolk, prepare and bring in the same.

On motion of Mr. Watkins, *Ordered,* That leave be given to bring in a bill to incorporate the Virginia insurance company, and that Messrs. Watkins, Stanard, Cunningham, Brown of Petersburg, Murdaugh, Crutchfield, Hunter of Berkeley, Dorman, Summers, Austin and Robinson, prepare and bring in the same.

Mr. Hopkins submitted the following resolution, which on motion of Mr. Dorman, was ordered to be laid upon the table:

Resolved, That so much of the governor's message as relates to the controversy between Maryland and Virginia, as to the question of boundary, be referred, with the accompanying documents therein mentioned, to a select committee, and that they have leave to report by bill or otherwise.

On motion of Mr. Shands, *Resolved*, That the committee for courts of justice enquire into the expediency of fixing by law the commissions or sales made under decrees in chancery.

On motion of Mr. Hunter of Berkeley, *Resolved*, That a select committee be appointed to enquire into the expediency of changing or altering the arrangement of the furniture in the hall of the house of delegates, so as to provide a desk or table and seat for each member thereof, providing in such arrangement for the suitable accommodation of senators, officers of the government, and visitors upon the floor of the house, and in the gallery, and that the said committee report to the house such plan as they may deem most expedient; and a committee was appointed of Messrs. Hunter of Berkeley, Parker, Fontaine, Madison, Harrison, Johnson, Moffett, Leyburn, Berry, Willey, Strange, M'Coy and Austin.

On motion of Mr. Wiley, *Resolved*, That the committee for courts of justice be instructed to enquire into the expediency of so amending the attachment laws as to authorize sheriffs and other officers to execute process against absconding debtors, in any county or corporation of the commonwealth in which the absconding debtor may be found, with leave to report by bill or otherwise.

On motion of Mr. Wiley, *Ordered*, That leave be given to bring in a bill for the purpose of regulating the conduct of boatmen navigating the Appomattox river above the town of Petersburg, and that Messrs. Wiley, Madison, Wilson of Cumberland, Hopkins, Fitzgerald, Austin, Booker, and Brown of Petersburg, prepare and bring in the same.

Mr. Beard presented a petition of citizens of the county of Loudoun, for the incorporation of a joint stock company to construct a bridge across the Shenandoah river at Harper's Ferry.

Mr. Smith of Frederick, petitions of citizens of the county of Frederick, against the division of the said county.

Ordered, That the said petitions be referred to the committee of propositions and grievances, that they do examine the matter thereof, and report their opinion thereupon to the house.

Mr. Smith of Frederick, also presented a petition of sundry other citizens of said county, for an increase of the salaries of the judges of the general court, which was ordered to be referred to the committee for courts of justice, that they do examine the matter thereof, and report their opinion thereupon to the house.

Also, a petition of citizens of said county, for a reduction of the tolls on the North-western turnpike, which was ordered to be laid upon the table.

Mr. Daniel presented a petition of sundry citizens of the county of Campbell, for the incorporation of a company to construct a turnpike road from Lynchburg to Campbell court-house, which was ordered to be referred to the committee of roads and internal navigation, that they do examine the matter thereof, and report their opinion thereupon to the house.

Mr. Brown of Petersburg, presented a petition of citizens of the town of Petersburg, for the incorporation of a savings institution in said town, which was ordered to be referred to the committee on banks, that they do examine the matter thereof, and report their opinion thereupon to the house.

Mr. Hill, from the committee of propositions and grievances, presented a report, which was subsequently read as follows:

The committee of propositions and grievances have, according to order, had under consideration several petitions to them referred, and have come to the following resolutions thereupon:

The petition of sundry citizens of the county of Tyler, residing near the mouth of Fishing creek, prays that the separate election now authorized to be holden at the house of Presley Martin, for the accommodation of that part of the county, may hereafter be holden at the school-house on the farm of Jeremiah Williams, in Fishing creek bottom: Whereupon,

1. *Resolved as the opinion of this committee*, That the prayer of said petition is reasonable.

The petition of Mrs. Mary Fowlkes of the county of Lunenburg, together with sundry freeholders of said county concurring therein, prays that the separate election now authorized to be holden at her house, in the upper end of said county, may be hereafter holden at some other place, and designates as the most suitable, the place called Pleasant Grove: Whereupon,

2. *Resolved as the opinion of this committee*, That the prayer of the petition of Mrs. Mary Fowlkes and others, is reasonable.

The petition of the stockholders in "the Wheeling and Belmont bridge company," represents, that since the passing of the said act incorporating a company to erect a toll-bridge over the Ohio river at Wheeling, several of the managers appointed to carry the same into effect have died and removed from the country, and that those remaining are mostly aged and infirm; that doubts have arisen whether the surviving managers are authorized to call a meeting of the stockholders in said company, so as to organize the same previous to the first Monday in June, 1836; and prays, therefore, that an act may pass amending their charter, so as to authorize the surviving managers, (or any three of them,) to call a meeting of the stockholders in said company, for the purpose of electing a board of managers to conduct the affairs of said company, in pursuance of their act of incorporation: Whereupon,

3. *Resolved as the opinion of this committee*, That the prayer of the stockholders in "the Wheeling and Belmont bridge company," is reasonable.

The said resolutions were, on questions severally put thereupon, agreed to by the house, and bills were ordered to be brought in conformably therewith.

Mr. Parker, from the committee on the militia laws, presented a report, which was subsequently read as follows:

The committee upon the militia laws have had under consideration the petition of the officers of 104th regiment, praying for the creation of a new regiment out of part of the said 104th regiment, and have come to the following resolution:

Resolved, That the prayer of the said petition is reasonable.

The said resolution was, on the question put thereupon, agreed to by the house, and a bill was ordered to be brought in conformably therewith.

Mr. Watkins from the committee of roads and internal navigation, presented a report, which was subsequently read as follows:

The committee of roads and internal navigation have, according to order, had under consideration the petition of Duff Green and others, to them referred, praying that an act of incorporation be granted them and others, who may hereafter be associated with them, for the purpose of working certain mines of coal, iron ore, and other minerals, near the mouth of Savage river, of establishing manufactories, and of constructing a canal or slack water navigation, and a rail-road or rail-roads, connecting their said mines and manufactories with the Chesapeake and Ohio canal, the Baltimore and Ohio rail-road, or such other rail-road or rail-roads as may be authorized by this state: Whereupon,

Resolved as the opinion of this committee, That said petition is reasonable.

The said resolution was, on the question put thereupon, agreed to by the house, and a bill was ordered to be brought in conformably therewith.

Mr. Watkins from the same committee, reported with amendment, a bill to authorize a subscription on behalf of the commonwealth to the enlarged capital stock of the Upper Appomattox company, which was taken up, and the said amendments being agreed to by the house, the said bill as amended, was ordered to be engrossed and read a third time.

A bill to re-organize the first and second judicial districts; and
A bill to provide for the construction of a road across the Blue Ridge at Milam's gap, were severally read the first and second times, and ordered to be committed to the respective committees which brought them in.
A bill to incorporate the stockholders of the City Point rail-road company.
A bill to reduce and regulate the tolls on the North-western turnpike; and
A bill incorporating the Red and Blue Sulphur springs turnpike company, with the amendments thereto proposed by the respective committees to which the same had been committed, were taken up, and the said amendments being agreed to by the house, the said bills as amended, were ordered to be engrossed and read a third time.

A bill to incorporate the stockholders of the Cartersville and Farmville rail-road company, was, on motion of Mr. Madison ordered to be laid upon the table.

A bill to incorporate the Newburn and Red Sulphur springs turnpike company, was read a second time, and ordered to be engrossed and read a third time.

The following bills were read the first and ordered to be read a second time, viz:
A bill to incorporate the Fluvanna mining company.
A bill to provide an index to the journals of the house of delegates.
A bill concerning George Johnson.
A bill concerning James Wysong.
A bill concerning Shelton Ford.
A bill to change the times of holding the courts in the third judicial circuit.
A bill to change the place of holding a separate election in the county of Hampshire.
A bill directing the survey and location of a route for a road from Moorfield to the North-western turnpike.
A bill to establish the town of Hedgesville in the county of Berkeley.
A bill releasing to William Fisher the commonwealth's right to one thousand acres of land in the county of Nicholas.
A bill authorizing the sale of the estate of John Haskins, sen'r, a lunatic.
A bill regulating and reducing the expenses incident to the collection of money under execution.
A bill authorizing James Martin to hold and convey certain real estate.
A bill allowing Judy Johnson, a free woman of colour, to remain in the commonwealth.
A bill allowing Daniel Higginbotham, a free man of colour, to remain in the commonwealth a limited time.
A bill allowing Richard Bolling, a free man of colour, to remain in the commonwealth.
A bill concerning Duff Green.
A bill allowing Charlotte Morgan, a free woman of colour, to remain in the commonwealth.
A bill to enlarge the town of Clarksville in the county of Mecklenburg.
A bill to authorize a separate election at the tavern house of William Irwin in the county of Cumberland.
A bill to amend an act, entitled, "an act to limit the assessment upon tithables, and to authorize a tax upon property, for the purpose of defraying county expenditures within the county of Berkeley," passed March 5th, 1835.
A bill further to provide for the construction of a turnpike road across the Alleghany mountain in the counties of Pendleton and Pocahontas.
A bill authorizing an increase of the capital stock of the Merchants manufacturing company.
A bill to revive the charter of the Nelson and Albemarle Union factory company; and
A bill to incorporate the Mechanics manufacturing company.

Reports of the committee of propositions and grievances were read as follow:

The committee of propositions and grievances have, according to order, had under consideration several petitions to them referred, and have come to the following resolutions thereupon:

The petition of several citizens of the county of Giles, residing in the vicinity of the town of Pearisburg, prays that an act may pass, repealing so much of the act of the 7th February, 1835, as authorizes the trustees of said town to impose a fine or penalty on horses, hogs or other stock, found within the limits thereof, the owners of which are non-residents of the town: Whereupon,

1. *Resolved as the opinion of this committee,* That the prayer of said petition be rejected.

The petition of the trustees of the town of Farmville, in the county of Prince Edward, prays that twenty-five acres of the lands of the estate of Judith Randolph, next adjoining said town, and forty acres of the lands of Josiah Chambers, also next adjoining said town, be vested by an act of the general assembly in the trustees of said town, or such other trustees as may seem best, with authority to lay the same off into lots and streets, and to sell the same at public auction, on certain terms in the petition described, for the benefit of said Randolph and Chambers, who are persons of insane mind, and whose trustees have no legal authority to dispose of the said lands; and that the trustees of said town be authorized to dispose of such lots or fractions of lots as have been heretofore laid off on the lands of the estate of said Judith Randolph and not sold: to which prayer, the trustees of said persons of unsound mind have consented, as appears by their certificate annexed to said petition: and the said petition further prays, that the corporate powers of said town be extended over the lands so added to the town, as also over all other lands heretofore laid off or sold as lots adjoining said town: Whereupon,

2. *Resolved as the opinion of this committee,* That the prayer or prayers of the petition aforesaid are reasonable.

The petition of sundry landholders and inhabitants of the place called Lovettsville and its vicinity, in the county of Loudoun, prays that an act may pass, establishing said village a town, with such privileges and restrictions as are usual in such cases, embracing within the boundary of the town, the lots heretofore laid off, and fifteen acres adjoining, making in the whole thirty-five acres: Whereupon,

3. *Resolved as the opinion of this committee,* That the prayer of said petition is reasonable.

The committee of propositions and grievances have, according to order, had under consideration the petition of sundry citizens of the county of Monongalia to them referred, praying that an act may pass, authorizing a separate election at the house of Michael Snodgrass on Pharoah's run, in the western part of said county: Whereupon,

Resolved as the opinion of this committee, That the prayer of said petition is reasonable.

The said resolutions were, on questions severally put thereupon, agreed to by the house, and bills were ordered to be brought in conformably therewith, except with the first resolution.

Reports of the committee of schools and colleges were read as follow:

The committee of schools and colleges have, according to order, had under consideration the petition of sundry citizens of the town of Estillville in the county of Scott, praying that an act be passed to incorporate an academy in said town, and that aid be extended to said academy from the surplus revenue of the literary fund: Whereupon,

Resolved as the opinion of this committee, That so much of said petition as relates to the incorporation of the academy, is reasonable.

The committee of schools and colleges have, according to order, had under consideration the petition of the vice-president and others, constituting the managing committee of the Norfolk and Portsmouth literary and scientific mechanics institute, praying the passage of an act to incorporate the said association, giving it perpetuity, and conferring on it the right to sue and be sued, and to hold real estate to such value as may seem proper: Whereupon,

Resolved as the opinion of this committee, That the said petition is reasonable.

The said resolutions were, on questions severally put thereupon, agreed to by the house, and bills were ordered to be brought in conformably therewith.

Reports of the committee of roads and internal navigation were read as follow:

The committee of roads and internal navigation have, according to order, had under consideration the petition of sundry citizens of the county of Goochland, praying the incorporation of a company or companies to construct a continuous turnpike road from the city of Richmond to the town of Charlottesville: Whereupon,

Resolved as the opinion of this committee, That said petition is reasonable.

The committee of roads and internal navigation have, according to order, had under consideration the petition of Richard Anderson and others, citizens of Richmond, praying the passage of an act conferring on them the powers and privileges of a corporation, for the purpose of towing vessels navigating James river: Whereupon,

Resolved as the opinion of this committee, That said petition is reasonable.

The committee of roads and internal navigation have, according to order, had under consideration the petition of sundry citizens of the counties of Rockbridge, Botetourt and Alleghany, asking the incorporation of a joint stock company to construct a turnpike road from the upper end of the Blue Ridge canal to its intersection with the Lexington and Covington turnpike at the Clifton forge: Whereupon,

Resolved as the opinion of this committee, That said petition is reasonable.

The committee of roads and internal navigation have, according to order, enquired into "the expediency of incorporating a company to construct a turnpike road from Elizabethtown, Marshall county, through the Narrows to the town of Wheeling in the county of Ohio:" Whereupon,

Resolved as the opinion of this committee, That it is expedient to incorporate a company for said purpose.

The committee of roads and internal navigation have, according to order, had under consideration the petition of sundry citizens of the counties of Harrison, Monongalia and Randolph, praying that the Tygart's valley river be declared a public highway, from the mouth of Big Sandy creek to its junction with the west fork of Monongahela river: Whereupon,

Resolved as the opinion of this committee, That said petition be rejected.

The said resolutions were, on questions severally put thereupon, agreed to by the house, and bills were ordered to be brought in conformably with all the said resolutions except the last.

Further reports of the committee of propositions and grievances were read as follow:

The committee of propositions and grievances have, according to order, had under consideration the petition of sundry citizens of the county of Ohio, to them referred, praying that an act may pass, establishing a separate election at the house of John D. Foster, in the town of Triadelphia, in said county: Whereupon,

Resolved as the opinion of this committee, That the prayer of said petition is reasonable.

The committee of propositions and grievances have, according to order, had under consideration the petition of Benjamin Bidgood, of the county of Isle of Wight, to them referred, representing that Micajah Bidgood, his brother, died about the 4th July, 1829, possessed of an estate in land and negroes, worth between fifteen hundred and two thousand dollars; that his only heirs at law, were the petitioner and his sister Betsey Bidgood, a lunatic, who was then, and had long been confined in the hospital at Williamsburg, and who died soon after the said Micajah, viz. about the 6th November, 1830, leaving the petitioner her only heir at law; that one John W. Jordan became the administrator on the estate of the said Micajah Bidgood, who still holds the estate, and is unwilling to pay over the same to the petitioner, unless he is indemnified against all liability that may arise. That whilst the petitioner could obtain possession of said estate by becoming administrator thereof, he is unable to do so, in consequence of a balance said to be due the commonwealth from said Betsey Bidgood for her support while in the lunatic hospital, thereby rendering it difficult or impracticable for him to give the necessary security, unless that balance was paid to, or released by the commonwealth: That the petitioner is advised that the estate of the said Betsey is not responsible for the balance aforesaid, amounting at the time of her death, to the sum of $580 48; inasmuch as she died before the passage of the act of assembly, (passed on the 22d day of March, 1831,) making the estate of lunatics dying in the hospital, liable for expenses incurred for their maintenance: praying therefore, that an act may pass, releasing any claim or demand the commonwealth may have against the estate of the said Betsey Bidgood by reason of the balance aforesaid: Whereupon,

Resolved as the opinion of this committee, That the prayer of the petition aforesaid is reasonable.

The said resolutions were, on questions put thereupon, agreed to by the house, and bills were ordered to be brought in conformably therewith.

A report of the committee on the militia laws was read as follows:

The committee upon the militia laws, have had under consideration the petition of the officers of the 58th regiment, praying for a repeal of the act passed at the last session, establishing the 145th regiment; or for the appointment of commissioners to establish the lines between the said 145th regiment, the 58th and 116th regiments, and have come to the following resolutions thereupon:

1. *Resolved,* That the prayer of said petition for the repeal of the said act be rejected.
2. *Resolved,* That the prayer of said petition for the appointment of commissioners to establish the limits of the said 145th, 58th and 116th regiments is reasonable.

The said resolution was, on the question put thereupon, agreed to by the house, and a bill was ordered to be brought in conformably therewith.

A report of the committee of roads and internal navigation was read as follows:

The committee of roads and internal navigation have, according to order, had under consideration the memorial of sundry citizens of the county of Harrison, in opposition to the petition of Jesse Sturm of said county, for leave to erect a dam across the west fork of the Monongahela river: Whereupon,

Resolved as the opinion of this committee, That said memorial be rejected.

The said resolution was, on the question put thereupon, agreed to by the house.

A report of the committee on agriculture and manufactures was read as follows:

The committee of agriculture and manufactures, to whom was referred a petition of the president and common council of the borough of Winchester, praying for the establishment of an inspection of flour and indian meal in the said borough, having considered the same, have come to the following resolution thereupon:

Resolved, That the prayer of the aforesaid petition is reasonable.

The said resolution was, on the question put thereupon, agreed to by the house, and a bill was ordered to be brought in conformably therewith.

Mr. Hickerson, according to order, presented a bill to incorporate the trustees of the Upperville academy in the county of Fauquier.

Mr. Stanard, from the committee for courts of justice, presented reports upon the petition of Arthur Lee, and upon the resolution for exempting certain portions of property from execution.

Which bills and reports were received and laid upon the table.

On motion of Mr. Parker, the house adjourned until to-morrow 12 o'clock.

SATURDAY, January 9th, 1836.

The following communication was received from the senate by their clerk:

IN SENATE, January 8th, 1836.

The senate have passed the bills, entitled,

"An act to amend the act, entitled, 'an act to reduce into one the several acts for the settlement and regulation of ferries, passed January 30th, 1819.'"

"An act to amend an act, entitled, 'an act to incorporate the Staunton and Potowmac rail-road company;'" and

"An act to authorize a separate election at Greenfield in the county of Nelson."

They have also passed the bills, entitled,

"An act fixing the school quotas of the counties of Ohio and Marshall;" and

"An act to revive and amend an act incorporating the Belle Isle manufacturing company, passed 19th March, 1832," with amendments, in which they request the concurrence of the house of delegates.

The said amendments being twice read, were, on questions severally put thereupon, agreed to by the house.

Ordered, That the clerk inform the senate thereof.

On motion of Mr. Dorman, *Resolved*, That the committee for courts of justice be instructed to enquire into the expediency of enacting a general law punishing offences committed on the rail-roads of this commonwealth, and that said committee have leave to report by bill or otherwise.

Mr. Witcher, from the committee of claims, presented reports upon petitions of William Fenn and of Berkeley Ward.

Mr. Davison, according to order, presented a bill to incorporate the Newtown Stephensburg library company.

Mr. Shands, in like manner, a bill to authorize the judge of the second circuit to appoint a time for holding the courts thereof in certain cases.

Mr. Chapman, a bill changing the time of holding the circuit superior courts of law and chancery for the counties of Monroe, Giles and Montgomery.

Mr. Watkins, from the committee of roads and internal navigation, presented a report upon the petition of citizens of the county of Campbell.

And a bill incorporating the Virginia towing company.

And reported with amendment, a bill to incorporate the Suffolk rail-road company.

And without amendment, a bill to provide for the construction of a road across the Blue Ridge at Milam's gap.

Mr. Brown of Petersburg, from the committee of finance, presented reports upon the petitions of Ephraim Wells, of C. Parriott of Marshall county, and of the farmers of Brooke county.

Mr. Johnson, according to order, presented a bill to amend an act, entitled, "an act to incorporate the Manchester wool and cotton manufacturing company," passed March 13th, 1832.

Which bills and reports were severally received and laid upon the table.

On motion of Mr. Watkins, *Ordered*, That the committee of roads and internal navigation be discharged from the farther consideration of the petitions of sundry citizens of the county of Frederick; of citizens of the county of Bedford; and of Thomas Rosser and Joseph Carper; and that the same be laid upon the table.

On motion of Mr. Watkins, *Resolved*, That the committee of roads and internal navigation be discharged from the duty of bringing in bills in conformity with the several petitions for authority to construct a turnpike road across Price's and the Sweet Springs mountains; and that said committee enquire into the expediency of incorporating a joint stock company to construct said road, with leave to report by bill or otherwise.

On motion of Mr. Watkins, a bill to incorporate the Suffolk rail-road company was taken up, and ordered to be recommitted to the committee which brought it in.

On motion of Mr. Hopkins, the resolution submitted by him on yesterday was taken up, and agreed to by the house as follows:

Resolved, That so much of the governor's message as relates to the controversy between Maryland and Virginia as to the question of boundary, be referred, with the accompanying documents therein mentioned, to a select committee, and that they have leave to report by bill or otherwise.

And a committee was appointed of Messrs. Hopkins, Dorman, Sherrard, Parker, Garland of Mecklenburg, Willey, Harrison, Carroll, Hunter of Berkeley, Decamps and Griggs.

Mr. Sherrard presented a memorial of the Chesapeake and Ohio canal company, asking further aid to that improvement, and others to be connected with it, which was ordered to be referred to the committee of roads and internal navigation.

Mr. Sherrard also presented a report of Charles B. Fisk, resident engineer on the Chesapeake and Ohio canal, to the president and directors of the company on the subject of that improvement, and others on the Cacapehon, south branch of Potowmac and Shenandoah rivers, to be connected with it, which was also ordered to be referred to the said committee; and 185 copies thereof were ordered to be printed for the use of the members of the general assembly.

Mr. Davison presented a petition from citizens of the county of Frederick, for a reduction of the tolls on the North-western turnpike, which was ordered to be laid upon the table.

Also, a petition of citizens of the counties of Frederick and Shenandoah, for the formation of a new county out of parts thereof, which was ordered to be referred to the committee of propositions and grievances, that they do examine the matter thereof, and report their opinion thereupon to the house.

On motion of Mr. Davison, a report of the committee of propositions and grievances upon petitions of other citizens of said counties, for the formation of the said county, was taken up, and ordered to be recommitted to the said committee.

Mr. Moncure presented a petition of sundry citizens of the counties of Stafford, Culpeper, Fauquier and Rappahannock, for a bank or branch of a bank in the town of Falmouth, which was ordered to be referred to the committee on banks, that they do examine the matter thereof, and report their opinion thereupon to the house.

Mr. Beuhring presented a petition of Jacob and William Hite, praying that certain moneys paid by them into the treasury for escheated land purchased by them, may be refunded, which was ordered to be referred to the committee of claims, that they do examine the matter thereof, and report their opinion thereupon to the house.

A motion was made by Mr. Garland of Mecklenburg, that the report of the committee to whom was referred so much of the governor's message as relates to the disorganizing, seditious and incendiary doctrines of certain associations created in the northern and eastern states for the purpose of producing a direct interference with the slave property of the south, be now taken up; and the question being put thereupon, was determined in the affirmative. Ayes 87, noes 40.

On motion of Mr. Gilmer, (seven of the members present concurring,) *Ordered*, That the ayes and noes upon the said question be inserted in the journal.

The names of the gentlemen who voted in the affirmative, are Messrs. Banks, (speaker,) Grinalds, Drummond, Gilmer, Southall, Layne, Wiley, Brooke, Craig, M'Clintic, Campbell, Pate, Hunter of Berkeley, Henshaw, Miller, Decampe, Turnbull, Mallory, Beuhring, Samuel, Christian, Johnson, Hill, Wilson of Cumberland, Servant, Hunter of Essex, Ball, Smith of Fauquier, Hickerson, Price, Hale of Franklin, Holland, Bowen, Wethered, Sloan, Nixon, Goodall, Mullen, Botts, Fontaine, Gregory, Griggs, Berry, Summers, Fleet, Hooe, Carter, Neill, Hays, Straton, Beard, Powell, Taylor of Loudoun, Harris, Ragsdale, Taylor of Mathews and Middlesex, Waggener, Benton, Brown of Nelson, Murdaugh, Parker, Leland, Chapline, Masters, Adams, M'Coy, Swanson, Witcher, Hopkins, Morris, Shanda, Marteney, Dorman, Leyburn, Harley, Butts, Crutchfield, Moncure, Spratley, Delashmutt, Gibson, Jett, Prentiss, Saunders, Cunningham, Brown of Petersburg, and Stanard.—87.

And the names of the gentlemen who voted in the negative, are Messrs. Wilson of Botetourt, Booker, Austin, Daniel, Richardson, Strange, Steger, Davison, Watts, Watkins, Hail of Grayson, Avent, Coleman, Harrison, Kincheloe, Holleman, Robinson, Rogers, Garland of Mecklenburg, Willey, Morgan, Chapman, Ingles, Sherrard, Fitzgerald, Woolfolk, Almond, Cackley, Carroll, Madison, Williams, Nicklin, Moffett, Conrad, Jessee, M'Mullen, Bare, Rinker, Hargrave and Gillespie.—40.

The first resolution of the committee was read as follows:

Resolved, That the general assembly solemnly declares its warm attachment to the Union, and its firm conviction that while the measures of the general government are kept within the limitations of the constitution, and those of the states directed by the spirit of which that Union is the offspring, it is the surest safeguard of the peace, prosperity and happiness of each member thereof.

The said resolution was, on the question put thereupon, agreed to unanimously by the house.

Mr. Garland of Mecklenburg then submitted a substitute for the residue of the said resolutions; whereupon,

On motion of Mr. Woolfolk, the further consideration of the said resolutions and substitute was ordered to be postponed until Monday, and that they have priority on that day over all other orders of the day.

An engrossed bill to incorporate the Newburn and Red Sulphur springs turnpike company, was read a third time:

Resolved, That the bill do pass, and that the title be, "an act to incorporate the Newburn and Red Sulphur springs turnpike company."

Ordered, That the clerk communicate the said bill to the senate and request their concurrence.

On motion of Mr. Hooe, the house adjourned until Monday 12 o'clock.

MONDAY, January 11th, 1836.

The following communication from the senate by their clerk was received:

IN SENATE, January 9th, 1836.

The senate have passed the bills, entitled,
"An act to incorporate the Ettrick manufacturing company;" and
"An act to incorporate the Fleets manufacturing company."

On motion of Mr. Marteney, *Resolved*, That the committee of roads and internal navigation be instructed to enquire into the expediency of providing by law for the construction of a road across the Laurel hill in the county of Randolph, from the farm of Archibald Earle to the farm of William Yager, on the location made by the public engineer in the year 1834, and that they have leave to report by bill or otherwise.

On motion of Mr. Grinalds, *Resolved*, That the select committee on revolutionary claims be required to enquire into the expediency of allowing the heirs of Robert Milliner bounty lands for his services as a lieutenant in the navy of Virginia during the revolutionary war, with leave to report by bill or otherwise.

Mr. Wilson of Botetourt presented a petition of sundry citizens of the county of Botetourt, for the incorporation of a company to construct a rail-road from the town of Lynchburg to some point on the Tennessee line.

On motion of Mr. Cooke, the petition of sundry citizens of the county of Norfolk for the extension of the Portsmouth and Roanoke rail-road company to the borough of Norfolk, was taken up.

Ordered, That the said petitions be referred to the committee of roads and internal navigation, that they do examine the matter thereof, and report their opinion thereupon to the house.

Mr. Kincheloe presented a memorial of the trustees of the Randolph academy in the county of Harrison, asking aid from the literary fund to further the objects of the said academy, which was ordered to be referred to the committee of schools and colleges, that they do examine the matter thereof, and report their opinion thereupon to the house.

Mr. Morris presented instructions from citizens of the county of Princess Anne, requiring him to vote for the extension of the Portsmouth and Roanoke rail-road to the borough of Norfolk, which were ordered to be laid upon the table.

Mr. Gibson presented a petition of George W. Goodman, asking that Stephen, a free man of colour, may be permitted to remain in the commonwealth, which was ordered to be referred to the committee for courts of justice, that they do examine the matter thereof, and report their opinion thereupon to the house.

Mr. Watkins, from the committee of roads and internal navigation, presented a bill to provide for the construction of the eastern section of the road on the route surveyed from Huntersville to Parkersburg.

Mr. Hill, from the committee of propositions and grievances, presented a bill to incorporate the Virginia fire insurance company.

Which bills were received and laid upon the table.

The report of the select committee, to whom was referred so much of the governor's message as relates to the interference of associations created in the northern and eastern states, for the purpose of producing a direct interference with the slave property of the south, together with the substitute therefor submitted by Mr. Garland of Mecklenburg, was taken up.

The second resolution of the committee was then read as follows:

Resolved, That each state had originally the sole and exclusive right to interfere with, control, or legislate upon the subject of domestic slavery within its jurisdictional limits; a right which, so far from being impaired, is recognized and guaranted by the constitution of the United States—and that all interference therewith by the general government, the other states, *or the citizens thereof,* is invasive of the rights of the states, and violates the obligations of the constitution.

The resolutions contained in the said substitute are the following:

1. *Resolved,* That Virginia alone has the right to legislate over the slaves in her territory, and any attempt to change their condition, whether made by congress, the legislatures, or the people of other states, will be regarded as an invasion of our rights.

2. *Resolved,* That according to the principles of the constitution, as discussed and developed in the Missouri question, congress is considered, even by the non-slaveholding states, as precluded from all interference with slave property in the territories of the United States, south of thirty-six degrees thirty minutes north latitude.

3. *Resolved,* That although by the constitution, exclusive jurisdiction over the district of Columbia is vested in the congress of the United States, yet we regard any action on the part of that body, toward liberating the slaves in that district, as an assumption of power not delegated to any legislative body, but reserved to the people, to be exercised by them, only in convention assembled, and that we regard all such interference as a violation of the rights of property—an infraction of the articles of cession which expressly guaranty those rights—as a breach of faith towards those states, by whom the territory was originally ceded—all the other slaveholding states which have entered into this confederacy—and as the first step towards an attempt to a general emancipation of the slaves of the south.

4. *Resolved,* That the thanks of this state are due to, and the kindest feelings of the citizens thereof are cherished towards their brethren of the north, who have magnanimously sustained the principles of our federal government, and recognized and maintained our rights against the fanatics of those states.

5. *Resolved,* That our sister non-slaveholding states are respectfully requested to enact laws prohibiting the printing within their respective limits of all such publications as may have a tendency to make our slaves discontented with their present condition, or incite them to insurrection.

6. *Resolved,* That it is highly expedient for the slaveholding states, and we hereby invite their co-operation, to pass such laws and regulations as may be necessary to suppress and prevent the circulation of any incendiary publications within any of the slaveholding states.

7. *Resolved,* That the governor be, and he is hereby requested to forward a copy of these resolutions to each of our senators and representatives in congress, and to the executive of each of the states of the Union, with a request that the same be submitted to their respective legislatures.

The question being upon striking out the second resolution and inserting the substitute, Mr. Stanard required it to be divided, so as to submit the question upon first striking out the said second resolution, and then upon inserting in lieu thereof the first resolution of the said substitute.

This question being pending, a motion was made by Mr. Garland of Mecklenburg, to amend the said second resolution by striking therefrom the words " or the citizens thereof," and the question being put thereupon, was determined in the negative. Ayes 20, noes 108.

On motion of Mr. Parker, (seven of the members present concurring,) *Ordered,* That the ayes and noes upon the said question be inserted in the journal.

The names of the gentlemen who voted in the affirmative, are Messrs. Layne, Wilson of Botetourt, Decamps, Smith of Fauquier, Hickerson, Bowen, Watts, Watkins, Hail of Grayson, Coleman, Sloan, Nixon, Kincheloe, Garland of Mecklenburg, Morgan, Cackley, Moffett, Jessee, Rinker and Prentiss.—20.

And the names of the gentlemen who voted in the negative, are Messrs. Banks, (speaker,) Grinalds, Drummond, Gilmer, Southall, Wiley, Brooke, Craig, M'Clintic, Campbell, Pate, Hunter of Berkeley, Henshaw, Miller, Turnbull, Mallory, Booker, Austin, Beuhring, Daniel, Samuel, Christian, Richardson, Johnson, Hill, Wilson of Cumberland, Servant, Hunter of Essex, Ball, Price, Strange, Steger, Hale of Franklin, Holland, Davison, Smith of Frederick, Smith of Gloucester, Wethered, Avent, Goodall, Mullen, Harrison, Botts, Fontaine, Holleman, Gregory, Griggs, Berry, Summers, Fleet, Hooe, Robinson, Carter, Neill, Hays, Straton, Beard, Powell, Taylor of Loudoun, Harris, Ragsdale, Taylor of Mathews and Middlesex, Waggener, Rogers, Willey, Chapman, Ingles, Sherrard, Benton, Brown of Nelson, Murdaugh, Cooke, Parker, Leland, Fitzgerald, Chapline, Masters, Woolfolk, Almond, Adams, M'Coy, Swanson, Witcher, Hopkins, Carroll, Madison, Morris, Shands, Williams, Marteney, Nicklin, Dorman, M'Mullen, Bare, Harley, Butts, Crutchfield, Moncure, Spratley, Hargrave, Gillespie, Delashmutt, Gibson, Jett, Saunders, Cunningham, Brown of Petersburg, and Stanard.—108.

The question then recurred upon striking out the said second resolution, and Mr. Parker demanded the ayes and noes thereupon; and the said proposition being under discussion,

On motion of Mr. Daniel, the house adjourned until to-morrow 12 o'clock

TUESDAY, January 12th, 1836.

The following communication was received from the senate by their clerk:

IN SENATE, January 11th, 1836.

The senate have passed the bill, entitled:

"An act to provide for the enlargement of the public warehouse for the storage and inspection of tobacco in the city of Richmond."

The speaker laid before the house a communication from the governor, transmitting a report of the geological reconnoissance, made in the state of Virginia, during the past year, by professor Rogers of the University of Virginia, which was ordered to be laid upon the table on motion of Mr. Wilson of Botetourt, and 1,000 copies thereof were ordered to be printed for the use of the members of the general assembly, on motion of Mr. Summers.

On motion of Mr. Mallory, *Ordered*, That 185 copies of the report of the superintendent of the armory be printed for the use of the general assembly.

On motion of Mr. Price, *Resolved*, That the committee for courts of justice be instructed to enquire into the expediency of repealing the seventh section of the act, to reduce into one the several acts, concerning counsel and attornies at law, passed February the 15th, 1819; and that they have leave to report by bill or otherwise.

On motion of Mr. Dorman, *Resolved*, That the committee for courts of justice be instructed to enquire into the expediency of amending the 44th section of the act, entitled, "an act for limitations of actions, for preventing frivolous and vexatious suits, concerning jeofails and certain proceedings in civil cases," passed February 25th, 1819; and that the committee have leave to report by bill or otherwise.

Mr. Summers from the committee on the register's office, presented a report on the condition of the said office.

Mr. Crutchfield according to order, presented a bill to incorporate the Stafford mining company.

Mr. Murdaugh, in like manner, a bill concerning the town of Portsmouth.

Mr. Hill, from the committee of propositions and grievances, presented a report upon petitions of citizens of the town of Waterford in the county of Loudoun; and

A bill to change the place of holding a separate election in the county of Lunenburg.

A bill to authorize a separate election at the house of Michael Snodgrass, in the county of Monongalia.

A bill to authorize a separate election at Triadelphia, in the county of Ohio.

A bill releasing the commonwealth's claim to a certain balance against the estate of Betsey Bidgood.

A bill to change the place of holding a separate election in the county of Tyler.

Mr. Watkins from the committee of roads and internal navigation, presented reports upon petitions of the Upper Appomattox company; and of Thomas A. Morton.

Mr. Stanard from the committee for courts of justice, presented a report upon the petitions of Thomas Culpeper and of Joseph Bailey; and upon the resolution directing an enquiry into the expediency of amending the laws in relation to slaves, free negroes and mulattoes.

Which bills and reports were received and laid upon the table.

On motion of Mr. Watkins, *Ordered*, That the committee of roads and internal navigation be discharged from the consideration of the petition of citizens of Botetourt county, and that the same be laid upon the table.

Mr. Crutchfield presented a petition of John Chew, asking to be allowed the sum of $1,350, being the emoluments of a colonel of cavalry for horses and servants, sanctioned by the laws of the United States when in service, whether the servants and horses are actually employed or not, which emoluments have been disallowed by the executive.

On motion of Mr. Crutchfield, *Resolved*, That the petition of John Chew, presented, be referred to the committee of claims, with authority to said committee to send for persons and papers for the investigation of said petition, and that they report by bill or otherwise.

Mr. Wilson of Botetourt presented a petition of sundry citizens of the counties of Botetourt and Franklin, for the remission of the residue of the imprisonment of Eli Blankenship, a convict confined in the penitentiary, which was ordered to be referred to the committee on the penitentiary, that they do examine the matter thereof, and report their opinion thereupon to the house.

Mr. Griggs presented a petition of citizens of Jefferson and Frederick, for an enlargement of the capital of the Bank of the Valley and of the branch of the Farmers bank of Virginia at Winchester, which was ordered to be referred to the committee on banks, that they do examine the matter thereof, and report their opinion thereupon to the house.

Also, a petition of citizens residing in the thirteenth circuit of the seventh judicial district, for an increase of the salaries of the judges of this commonwealth, which was ordered to be referred to the committee for courts of justice, that they do examine the matter thereof, and report their opinion thereupon to the house.

On motion of Mr. Cunningham, *Ordered*, That the select committee appointed to enquire into the expediency of providing for paying the representatives of Severn Eyre the amount of losses occasioned by the burning of Norfolk in 1776, be discharged from the consideration of the sundry petitions referred to the said committee relating to revolutionary claims; and the said petitions were ordered to be laid upon the table.

The report of the select committee to whom was referred so much of the governor's message as relates to associations in the northern and eastern states for producing a direct interference with the slave property of the south, together with the substitute therefor submitted by Mr. Garland of Mecklenburg, was taken up; and the question being upon amending the second resolution of the committee, by inserting in lieu thereof the first resolution of the said substitute, and upon first striking out the said resolution upon the division of the question, a motion was made by Mr. Watkins to amend the said amendment, by striking out the said second resolution, and inserting in lieu the entire resolutions contained in the said substitute; and pending this motion, a further motion was made by Mr. Watkins to lay the said report and proposed amendments upon the table; and the question being put thereupon, was determined in the negative. Ayes 64, noes 64.

On motion of Mr. Gilmer, (seven of the members present concurring,) *Ordered*, That the ayes and noes upon the said question be inserted in the journal.

The names of the gentlemen who voted in the affirmative, are Messrs. Banks, (speaker,) Layne, Wiley, Brooke, Craig, M'Clintic, Wilson of Botetourt, Decamps, Turnbull, Austin, Daniel, Samuel, Richardson, Hill, Hunter of Essex, Smith of Fauquier, Hickerson, Strange, Steger, Bowen, Davison, Watts, Watkins, Hail of Grayson, Avent, Carrington, Coleman, Sloan, Nixon, Goodall, Harrison, Kincheloe, Griggs, Hooe, Hays, Harris, Rogers, Garland of Mecklenburg, Willey, Morgan, Chapman, Sherrard, Brown of Nelson, Cooke, Woolfolk, Almond, Adams, M'Coy, Cackley, Carroll, Madison, Shands, Williams, Marteney, Nicklin, Moffett, Conrad, Jessee, M'Mullen, Bare, Rinker, Hargrave, Gillespie and Gibson.—64.

And the names of the gentlemen who voted in the negative, are Messrs. Grinalds, Drummond, Gilmer, Southall, Campbell, Pate, Hunter of Berkeley, Henshaw, Miller, Mallory, Booker, Beuhring, Christian, Johnson, Wilson of Cumberland, Servant, Ball, Price, Hale of Franklin, Holland, Smith of Frederick, Smith of Gloucester, Wethered, Mullen, Botts, Fontaine, Holleman, Gregory, Berry, Summers, Fleet, Robinson, Neill, Straton, Beard, Powell, Taylor of Loudoun, Ragsdale, Taylor of Mathews and Middlesex, Waggener, Ingles, Benton, Murdaugh, Parker, Leland, Fitzgerald, Chapline, Masters, Swanson, Witcher, Hopkins, Morris, Dorman, Harley, Butts, Crutchfield, Spratley, Delashmutt, Jett, Prentiss, Saunders, Cunningham, Brown of Petersburg, and Stanard.—64.

On motion of Mr. Watkins, the house then adjourned until to-morrow 12 o'clock.

WEDNESDAY, January 13th, 1836.

A communication from the senate by their clerk was read as follows:

IN SENATE, January 12th, 1836.

The senate have passed the bills, entitled,

"An act to amend an act, entitled, 'an act for incorporating the stockholders of the Winchester and Potowmac rail-road company.'"

"An act directing a change of location of the North-western turnpike through the town of Evansville."

"An act directing the survey and location of routes for certain roads therein mentioned."

"An act directing the survey of a route for a road from the North-western road to some point on Leading creek in the county of Randolph;" and

"An act to incorporate the Newburn and Red Sulphur springs turnpike company."

They have also passed the bill, entitled,

"An act to prevent trespasses by non-resident herdsmen in the county of Preston," with amendments, in which they request the concurrence of the house of delegates.

The said amendments being twice read, were, on questions severally put thereupon, agreed to by the house.

Ordered, That the clerk inform the senate thereof.

On motion of Mr. Goodall, *Resolved,* That the committee of roads and internal navigation be instructed to enquire into the expediency of increasing the capital stock of the Richmond, Fredericksburg and Potowmac rail-road company, and that they have leave to report by bill or otherwise.

On motion of Mr. Carter, *Resolved,* That the committee for courts of justice be instructed to enquire into the expediency of so amending the laws which relate to the expenses of arrests and prosecutions in cases of crime and misdemeanor, as to provide for the payment of guards which may be necessarily employed before commitment, with leave to report by bill or otherwise.

On motion of Mr. Taylor of Middlesex, *Resolved,* That the committee of roads and internal navigation be instructed to enquire into the expediency of directing a survey and report by some competent engineer of the practicability and probable cost of improving the navigation of the Dragon swamp, so as to afford batteaux transportation to the highest practicable point on said swamp, and that they be instructed to report by bill or otherwise.

On motion of Mr. Taylor of Middlesex, *Ordered,* That leave be given to bring in a bill to amend an act, entitled, "an act for opening and improving the navigation of the Dragon swamp," passed February 19th, 1829, and that Messrs. Taylor of Middlesex, Smith of Gloucester, Fleet, Robinson, Samuel, Botts, Goodall and Watkins, prepare and bring in the same.

On motion of Mr. Wethered, *Resolved,* That the committee for courts of justice be instructed to enquire into the expediency of appropriating a sum of money to enlarge, for the use of the judges of the court of appeals, the public library at Lewisburg, and that they have leave to report by bill or otherwise.

On motion of Mr. Wilson of Cumberland, *Resolved,* That the committee of roads and internal navigation be instructed to enquire into the expediency of amending the act incorporating the Cartersville bridge company, to enable them to hold real estate not exceeding five acres of land, and that they report by bill or otherwise.

On motion of Mr. Layne, *Ordered,* That leave be given to bring in a bill to change the time of holding the county court of Alleghany county, and that Messrs. Layne, Dorman, Miller, Ingles, Leyburn, Brooke, Craig and M'Clintic, prepare and bring in the same.

Mr. Watkins, from the committee of roads and internal navigation, reported without amendment, a bill to enact an act of the general assembly of North Carolina, entitled, "an act to incorporate the Roanoke, Danville, and Junction rail-road company."

And presented a bill to incorporate the Union Potowmac company; and

A bill to provide for the construction of a road from the line of Preston county to the Ohio river.

Mr. Botts, according to order, presented a bill to incorporate the Fauquier White Sulphur springs.

Mr. Johnson, in like manner, a bill to amend an act, entitled, "an act to incorporate the Cold Brook company of colliers," passed January 23d, 1835.

Mr. Hill, from the committee of propositions and grievances, presented a report upon the petition of citizens of Caroline, Essex, and King and Queen, for a new county.

Which bills and report were received and laid upon the table.

On motion of Mr. Watkins, *Ordered,* That the committee of roads and internal navigation be discharged from the consideration of the petition of the Dragon swamp canal company, and that the same be laid upon the table.

On motion of Mr. Hill, *Ordered,* That the committee of propositions and grievances be discharged from the consideration of the petition of sundry citizens of the town of Wheeling, and that the same be laid upon the table.

Mr. Smith of Gloucester presented a petition of sundry citizens of the county of Gloucester, asking permission to borrow a sum of money for the purpose of removing the free negroes from said county, which was ordered to be referred to a committee of Messrs. Smith of Gloucester, Gregory, Parker, Drummond, Taylor of Middlesex, Fleet and Robinson, with leave to report by bill or otherwise.

Mr. Parker presented a petition of the president and directors of the Roanoke navigation company, remonstrating against the incorporation of a company to construct a rail-road from Evansham to the western termination of the Petersburg and Norfolk rail-roads, so far as the said road may run parallel with the improvement of the said navigation company.

Mr. Gilmer presented a petition of citizens of the county of Albemarle, for the construction of a rail-road from the town of Lynchburg to the Tennessee line.

Mr. Stanard, a petition of citizens of the city of Richmond, for the incorporation of a company to construct a rail-way from Richmond, along the ridge country between the James and Appomattox rivers, to the town of Lynchburg.

Ordered, That the said petitions be referred to the committee of roads and internal navigation, that they do examine the matter thereof, and report their opinion thereupon to the house.

Mr. Wethered presented a petition of William Zoll, for the establishment of a town on his land in the county of Greenbrier.

Mr. Harrison, a petition of citizens of Harrison county, to change the place of holding the precinct election now held at James M'Intire's, to the house of William Black, in Shinston, in said county.

Mr. Gilmer, a petition of citizens of the counties of Fluvanna and Albemarle, that the banks of James river may be declared to constitute a lawful enclosure.

Ordered, That the said petitions be referred to the committee of propositions and grievances, that they do examine the matter thereof, and report their opinion thereupon to the house.

Mr. Gilmer also presented a petition of citizens of the county of Albemarle, for enlarging the banking capital of the commonwealth, and locating a portion thereof at the town of Charlottesville, which was ordered to be referred to the committee on banks, that they do examine the matter thereof, and report their opinion thereupon to the house.

Mr. Powell presented a petition of citizens of the counties of Loudoun and Fauquier, praying the passage of an act more effectually to inhibit free negroes from carrying on traffic with slaves, which was ordered to be referred to the committee for courts of justice, that they do examine the matter thereof, and report their opinion thereupon to the house.

Mr. Leyburn presented a petition of citizens of the town of Lexington and its vicinity, praying a change in the organization of the Lexington arsenal, so as to give that institution a collegiate as well as a military character.

Also a petition of citizens of the town of Fairfield and its vicinity, to the same effect with the preceding.

Ordered, That the said petitions be referred to the committee of schools and colleges, that they do examine the matter thereof, and report their opinion thereupon to the house.

On motion of Mr. Williams, an engrossed bill to amend the act, entitled, "an act incorporating the Falmouth and Alexandria rail-road company," was taken up; whereupon, the rule of the house was suspended, the vote ordering the said bill to be engrossed and read a third time was reconsidered, and the said bill was ordered to be recommitted to the committee which brought it in.

The report of the select committee to whom was referred so much of the governor's message as relates to certain associations in the northern and eastern states, for the purpose of producing a direct interference with the slave property of the south, together with the several amendments thereto proposed, was taken up; whereupon, a motion was made by Mr. Watkins, that the said report and amendments be recommitted to a select committee, and the question being put thereupon, was determined in the negative. Ayes 59, noes 69.

On motion of Mr. Gregory, (seven of the members present concurring,) *Ordered*, That the ayes and noes upon the said question be inserted in the journal.

The names of the gentlemen who voted in the affirmative, are Messrs. Layne, Wiley, M'Clintic, Wilson of Botetourt, Decamps, Turnbull, Austin, Daniel, Richardson, Smith of Fauquier, Hickerson, Strange, Steger, Bowen, Davison, Watts, Watkins, Hail of Grayson, Avent, Carrington, Coleman, Sloan, Nixon, Goodall, Harrison, Kincheloe, Holleman, Hays, Straton, Harris, Rogers, Garland of Mecklenburg, Willey, Morgan, Chapman, Sherrard, Brown of Nelson, Fitzgerald, Woolfolk, Almond, Adams, Cackley, Hopkins, Carroll, Madison, Shands, Williams, Marteney, Nicklin, Moffett, Conrad, Jessee, M'Mullen, Bare, Rinker, Spratley, Hargrave, Gillespie and Gibson.—59.

And the names of the gentlemen who voted in the negative, are Messrs. Banks, (speaker,) Grinalds, Drummond, Gilmer, Southall, Craig, Campbell, Pate, Hunter of Berkeley, Henshaw, Miller, Mallory, Booker, Beuhring, Samuel, Christian, Johnson, Hill, Wilson of Cumberland, Servant, Hunter of Essex, Ball, Price, Hale of Franklin, Holland, Smith of Frederick, Smith of Gloucester, Wethered, Mullen, Botts, Fontaine, Gregory, Griggs, Berry, Summers, Fleet, Hooe, Robinson, Carter, Neill, Beard, Powell, Taylor of Loudoun, Ragsdale, Taylor of Mathews and Middlesex, Waggener, Ingles, Benton, Murdaugh, Cooke, Parker, Chapline, Masters, M'Coy, Swanson, Witcher, Morris, Dorman, Leyburn, Harley, Butts, Crutchfield, Moncure, Jett, Prentiss, Saunders, Cunningham, Brown of Petersburg, and Stanard.—69.

Mr. Watkins then asked and obtained leave of the house to withdraw his amendment submitted on yesterday, to the amendment offered by Mr. Garland of Mecklenburg, and Mr. Garland obtained similar leave to withdraw his said amendment.

The question then recurred upon agreeing to the second resolution of the committee; whereupon, a motion was made by Mr. Watkins to strike out the said second resolution, and insert in lieu thereof, several other resolutions, which were amended on motions severally made; and the same being still under consideration,

On motion of Mr. Parker, the house adjourned until to-morrow 12 o'clock.

THURSDAY, January 14th, 1836.

The speaker laid before the house a communication from the auditor of public accounts, transmitting a list of balances remaining on the books of his office on the first day of October last, which, on motion of Mr. Sherrard was ordered to be laid upon the table, and 185 copies thereof were ordered to be printed for the use of the general assembly.

On motion of Mr. Summers, *Resolved*, That the governor's message, transmitting professor Rogers' report of a geological reconnoissance of the state, together with said report, and the accompanying profile, be referred to a select committee, with instructions, that they enquire into the expediency of providing by law, for a detailed geological survey of the state, and a chemical analysis of its ores, marls, soils, mineral waters, &c., and that they have leave to report thereon, by bill or otherwise.

And a committee was appointed of Messrs. Summers, Sherrard, Harrison, Brown of Petersburg, Murdaugh, Fontaine, Brooke, Miller, Southall, Crutchfield, Jessee, Carter, and Smith of Fauquier.

On motion of Mr. Gibson, the rule of the house was suspended, and leave was granted to Stephen, a free man of colour, to withdraw his petition presented to the last session of the legislature, and the same was ordered to be referred to the committee for courts of justice, that they do examine the matter thereof, and report their opinion thereupon to the house.

Mr. Hooe presented a petition of Stapleton Crutchfield, asking to be allowed additional compensation for his services as sheriff of the county of Spottsylvania, in attending the superior court thereof, which was ordered to be referred to the committee of claims, that they do examine the matter thereof, and report their opinion thereupon to the house.

Mr. Smith of Gloucester presented a petition of citizens of the county of Gloucester, for the establishment of a separate election in said county, which was ordered to be referred to the committee of propositions and grievances, that they do examine the matter thereof, and report their opinion thereupon to the house.

Mr. Sloan presented a petition of citizens of the county of Frederick, and the adjacent counties, asking for an increase of the capital of the Bank of the Valley and its branches, and of the branch of the Farmers bank situated at Winchester, which was ordered to be referred to the committee on banks, that they do examine the matter thereof, and report their opinion thereupon to the house.

Mr. Crutchfield presented a petition of the agricultural societies of Albemarle and Fredericksburg, and many other persons interested in agriculture, from various parts of the state, for the establishment of an agricultural professorship in the University, and for the purchase of an experimental farm to be connected therewith; or for the establishment of a board of agriculture, to report to the legislature such matters as they may deem worthy of legislative action on the subject of agriculture; or to provide for an agricultural survey of the Atlantic states, which petition was ordered to be referred to the committee of agriculture and manufactures, that they do examine the matter thereof, and report their opinion thereupon to the house.

On motion of Mr. Crutchfield, *Ordered*, That 185 copies thereof be printed for the use of the general assembly.

Mr. Johnson, from the committee appointed to examine the treasurer's accounts for the preceding year, presented a report, which was laid upon the table, and, on his motion, 185 copies thereof were ordered to be printed for the use of the general assembly.

Mr. Gregory reported without amendment, a bill to re-organize the first and second judicial districts.

Mr. Watkins, from the committee of roads and internal navigation, presented a bill incorporating the Natural bridge turnpike company.

Mr. Booker, from the committee for courts of justice, presented a bill to explain the act, entitled, "an act to reduce into one act the several acts and parts of acts concerning the county and other inferior courts, and the jurisdiction of justices of the peace within this commonwealth."

Mr. Hill, from the committee of propositions and grievances, presented a report upon the petition of Ruff and Jordan, and the memorial in opposition thereto.

Which bills and report were received and laid upon the table.

The report of the select committee to whom was referred so much of the governor's message as relates to certain associations created in the northern and eastern states for the purpose of producing a direct interference with the slave property of the south, together with the amendment thereto proposed by Mr. Watkins on yesterday, was taken up.

The said amendment was amended on motions severally made, and as amended is the following:

1. *Resolved*, That Virginia has the exclusive right to legislate over the slaves within her territory—a right guaranteed by the constitution of the United States—and any attempt to change their condition, whether made by the federal government or by the other states, will be regarded as an invasion of our rights under the federal compact.

2. *Resolved*, That this state has a right to demand prompt and efficient legislation by her co-states, to restrain, as far as may be, and to punish those of their citizens, who, in defiance of the obligations of social duty and of the constitution, assail her safety and tranquillity, by printing, and circulating through the mail or otherwise, seditious and incendiary publications; and that this right, founded as it is on the principles of international law, is peculiarly fortified by a just consideration of the intimate and sacred relations that exist between the states of this Union.

3. *Resolved*, That although exclusive legislation over the district of Columbia is vested in the congress of the United States, yet we should regard any attempt on the part of that body to liberate the slaves in that district, as a violation of the constitution and of the rights of property, a breach of faith to the slaveholding states, and as a precursor to a scheme for the abolition of slavery in the southern states.

4. *Resolved*, That the thanks of this state are due to, and the kindest feelings of the citizens thereof are cherished towards, their brethren of the north, who have magnanimously sustained the principles of our federal government, and recognized and maintained our rights against the fanatics of those states.

5. *Resolved*, That our sister non-slaveholding states are respectfully and earnestly requested to adopt such measures, as will effectually suppress all those associations within their respective limits, purporting to be, or having the character of, abolition societies; and that they will make it highly penal to print, publish, or distribute newspapers, pamphlets, or other publications, calculated and having a tendency to excite the slaves of the southern states to insurrection and revolt.

6. *Resolved*, That it is highly expedient for the slaveholding states, and we hereby invite their co-operation, to pass such laws and regulations as may be necessary to suppress and prevent the circulation of any incendiary publications within their respective limits.

7. *Resolved*, That the governor be, and he is hereby requested to forward a copy of these resolutions to each of our senators and representatives in congress, and to the executive of each of the states of the Union, with a request that the same may be submitted to their respective legislatures.

The question being upon striking out the second resolution of the committee and inserting the said amendment, a motion was made by Mr. Woolfolk, to amend the said amendment, by inserting after the word "violation" in the second resolution, the words "of the constitution and," so as to cause it to read "yet we should regard any attempt on the part of that body to liberate the slaves in that district as a *violation of the constitution and* of the rights of property," &c.; and the question being put thereupon, was determined in the affirmative. Ayes 115, noes 13.

On motion of Mr. Woolfolk, (seven of the members present concurring,) *Ordered*, That the ayes and noes upon the said question be inserted in the journal.

The names of the gentlemen who voted in the affirmative, are Messrs. Banks, (speaker,) Grinalds, Drummond, Gilmer, Southall, Layne, Wiley, Garland of Amherst, M'Clintic, Campbell, Pate, Miller, Wilson of Botetourt, Decamps, Turnbull, Mallory, Booker, Austin, Beuhring, Daniel, Samuel, Christian, Richardson, Johnson, Hill, Wilson of Cumberland, Servant, Hunter of Essex, Smith of Fauquier, Hickerson, Price, Strange, Steger, Hale of Franklin, Holland, Bowen, Davison, Watts, Smith of Gloucester, Watkins, Hail of Grayson, Wethered, Avent, Carrington, Coleman, Sloan, Nixon, Goodall, Harrison, Kincheloe, Botts, Fontaine, Holleman, Gregory, Fleet, Hooe, Robinson, Carter, Neill, Hays, Straton, Harris, Ragsdale, Taylor of Mathews and Middlesex, Waggener, Rogers, Garland of Mecklenburg, Willey, Morgan, Ingles, Sherrard, Benton, Brown of Nelson, Cooke, Parker, Leland, Fitzgerald, Chapline, Masters, Woolfolk, Almond, Adams, M'Coy, Swanson, Witcher, Cackley, Hopkins, Carroll, Madison, Morris, Shands, Williams, Marteney, Nicklin, Dorman, Moffett, Conrad, Jessee, M'Mullen, Bare, Rinker, Harley, Butts, Crutchfield, Moncure, Spratley, Hargrave, Gillespie, Delashmutt, Gibson, Jett, Saunders, Cunningham, Brown of Petersburg, and Stanard.—115.

And the names of the gentlemen who voted in the negative, are Messrs. Brooke, Craig, Hunter of Berkeley, Henshaw, Mullen, Griggs, Berry, Summers, Beard, Powell, Taylor of Loudoun, Leyburn and Prentiss.—13.

The question then recurred upon striking out the said second resolution of the committee as amended, and inserting the said amendment; whereupon, on motion of Mr. Dorman, the report of the committee and proposed amendment was ordered to be laid upon the table, and 185 copies of the said amendment were ordered to be printed for the use of the general assembly.

The speaker laid before the house a communication from the governor, transmitting "the report and resolutions of the general assembly of the state of Georgia, relative to the movements of the abolitionists of the north," which on motion of Mr. Dorman, was ordered to be laid upon the table, and 185 copies thereof were ordered to be printed for the use of the general assembly.

On motion of Mr. Dorman, the house adjourned until to-morrow 12 o'clock.

FRIDAY, January 15th, 1836.

The following communication was received from the senate by their clerk:

IN SENATE, January 14th, 1836.

The senate have passed the bill, entitled,
"An act concerning the fire and marine insurance company of Wheeling."

They have also passed the bill, entitled,
"An act forming a new county out of parts of the counties of Lewis and Nicholas," with an amendment to the title, in which they request the concurrence of the house of delegates.

The said amendment being twice read, was, on the question put thereupon, agreed to by the house.

Ordered, That the clerk inform the senate thereof.

Mr. Smith of Fauquier reported with an amendment, a bill to amend the act, entitled, "an act incorporating the Falmouth and Alexandria rail-road company."

Mr. Hill, from the committee of propositions and grievances, presented a report upon petitions of citizens of Loudoun; of Noble S. Braden; of sundry citizens of Jefferson county; of Richard Lorton, and of citizens of the county of Nansemond.

Mr. Madison, from the committee of agriculture and manufactures, presented a report upon the resolution on the subject of an extra grade of flour.

And a bill to establish an inspection of flour and indian meal at the town of Winchester.

Which bills and report were received and laid upon the table.

On motion of Mr. Booker, the committee for courts of justice were ordered to be discharged from the consideration of the petition of Isabella Anderson, and the same was ordered to be laid upon the table.

Mr. Strange presented the memorial of George Holeman and John W. Toney, remonstrating against the location of the James river and Kanawha company's canal through their land, and asking the legislature to interpose to prevent the canal from being located as proposed.

Mr. Powell, petitions of citizens of the counties of Loudoun and Fauquier, asking amendments to the charter of the Goose creek and Little river navigation companies, and praying the commonwealth to subscribe for the usual proportion of the capital stock of said companies.

Ordered, That the said petitions be referred to the committee of roads and internal navigation, that they do examine the matter thereof, and report their opinion thereupon to the house.

Mr. Watkins presented a petition of Simeon B. Jewett, asking the passage of an act giving authority to the Alabama lumber company to transact business in this state, which was ordered to be referred to the committee of propositions and grievances, that they do examine the matter thereof, and report their opinion thereupon to the house.

An engrossed bill incorporating the Red and Blue Sulphur springs turnpike company, was read a third time:

Resolved, That the bill do pass, and that the title be, "an act incorporating the Red and Blue Sulphur springs turnpike company."

An engrossed bill to reduce and regulate the tolls on the North-western turnpike, was read a third time:

Resolved, That the bill do pass, and that the title be, "an act to reduce and regulate the tolls on the North-western turnpike."

Ordered, That the clerk communicate the same to the senate and request their concurrence.

An engrossed bill to authorize a subscription on behalf of the commonwealth to the enlarged capital stock of the Upper Appomattox company, was, on motion of Mr. Hopkins, ordered to be laid upon the table.

The report of the select committee to whom was referred so much of the governor's message as relates to the movements of the abolitionists of the north, together with the amendment thereto proposed by Mr. Watkins, was taken up on motion of Mr. Stanard, and the question being upon striking out the second resolution of the committee, and the same being under discussion,

On motion of Mr. Madison, the house adjourned until to-morrow 12 o'clock.

SATURDAY, January 16th, 1836.

On motion of Mr. Hopkins, *Resolved*, That the committee on the militia laws be instructed to enquire into the expediency of amending or explaining by legislative enactment, the 96th and 100th sections of the act, entitled, "an act for the better organisation of the militia," passed March 8th, 1834, and that they have leave to report by bill or otherwise.

On motion of Mr. Murdaugh, *Resolved*, That a committee of revolutionary claims be added to the standing committees of this house.

And a committee was appointed of Messrs. Gilmer, Murdaugh, Chapline, Saunders, Austin, Southall, Woolfolk, Dorman, Crutchfield, Grinalds, Brown of Nelson, Ragsdale, Hickerson and M'Coy.

On motion of Mr. Murdaugh, *Ordered*, That the several petitions and resolutions heretofore referred to the select committee on the subject of revolutionary claims, be referred to the said standing committee, that they do examine the matter thereof, and report their opinion thereupon to the house.

On motion of Mr. Crutchfield, *Ordered*, That leave be given to bring in a bill to incorporate the United States copper mining company, for the purpose of mining in copper and other minerals in the state of Virginia, and that Messrs. Crutchfield, Woolfolk, Butts, Campbell, Griggs, Holland, Garland of Amherst, M'Clintic, Carrington, Shands, Prentiss, Samuel and Conrad, prepare and bring in the same.

On motion of Mr. Crutchfield, *Ordered*, That leave be given to bring in a bill incorporating the Great Kanawha land, timber, salt, coal and iron company, for mining and agricultural purposes, and that Messrs. Crutchfield, Summers, Layne, Wethered, Swanson, Rogers, Bowen, Henshaw, Jett and Prentiss, prepare and bring in the same.

On motion of Mr. Summers, *Resolved*, That a number of the profile accompanying professor Rogers' report of a geological reconnoissance of the state, equal to the number of said report, which may be printed for the use of the general assembly, be engraved and published under the superintendence of the professor, provided the said engraving shall not cost the state more than two hundred dollars.

On motion of Mr. Cunningham, *Resolved*, That the president and directors of the bank of Virginia, and the president and directors of the Farmers bank of Virginia, be requested to furnish to this house a statement of the amount of the actual capital since the year 1820, of the branches of the bank of Virginia and Farmers bank of Virginia at Norfolk; also, a statement of the nett profits of those branches respectively, on the actual capital employed by them during the year 1835; and that they be requested to state also, the precise amount of the contingent or reserved fund of each of those institutions on the first of January, 1836, and whether the profits of the mother banks have not been in part realized from said funds and credited only to the nominal capital of said banks.

On motion of Mr. Dorman, *Resolved*, That the committee of schools and colleges be instructed to enquire into the expediency of establishing, in connexion with Washington college in the county of Rockbridge, a military school, and substituting said school, in lieu of the public arsenal at that place, as the depositary of the public arms, and that said committee have leave to report by bill or otherwise.

Mr. Watkins, from the committee of roads and internal navigation, presented a report upon the petition of the Manchester and Petersburg turnpike company.

Mr. Booker, from the committee for courts of justice, presented reports upon the petition of Lucy Boomer, and upon the resolution concerning jail fees of debtors

Mr. Watkins, according to order, presented a bill to incorporate the Virginia insurance company.

Mr. Hill, from the committee of propositions and grievances, presented a report upon the petition of citizens of the county of Rockingham.

Mr. Taylor of Middlesex, according to order, presented a bill to amend an act, entitled, "an act for opening and improving the navigation of the Dragon swamp."

Which bills and reports were received and laid upon the table.

Mr. Wilson of Cumberland, presented a petition of citizens of the counties of Amelia, Prince Edward, and Cumberland, praying that proper restrictions may be imposed on the Appomattox company, as to the height of their dams.

Mr. Watkins, a memorial of sundry citizens of the county of Rockingham, asking for a change in the location of the Warm spring and Harrisonburg turnpike.

Ordered, That the said petitions be referred to the committee of roads and internal navigation, that they do examine the matter thereof, and report their opinion thereupon to the house.

Mr. Wethered presented a petition of the president and directors of the Lewisburg and Blue Sulphur springs turnpike company, asking for certain amendments to their act of incorporation, which was also ordered to be referred to the said committee in like manner.

Mr. Miller, a petition of citizens of the county of Botetourt, for the incorporation of the town of Salem in that county, which was ordered to be referred to the committee of propositions and grievances, that they do examine the matter thereof, and report their opinion thereupon to the house.

Mr. Smith of Frederick, presented a petition of citizens of the county of Frederick, praying for an increase of the banking capital of the commonwealth, which was ordered to be referred to the committee on banks, that they do examine the matter thereof, and report their opinion thereupon to the house.

The report of the committee to whom was referred so much of the governor's message as relates to the movements of the abolitionists of the north, together with the amendment thereto proposed by Mr. Watkins, was taken up, and the question being upon striking out the second resolution of the committee, with a view to insert the said amendment, and a division of the question having been required by Mr. Stanard, the question was first put upon striking out the said second resolution, and was determined in the affirmative. Ayes 67, noes 64.

The said second resolution is the following:

Resolved, That each state had originally the sole and exclusive right to control, or legislate upon the subject of domestic slavery within its jurisdictional limits; a right which, so far from being impaired, is recognized and guaranteed by the constitution of the United States; and that all interference therewith by the general government, the other states, or the citizens thereof, is invasive of the rights of the states, and violates the obligations of the constitution.

On motion of Mr. Stanard, (seven of the members present concurring,) *Ordered*, That the ayes and noes upon striking out as aforesaid, be inserted in the journal.

The names of the gentlemen who voted in the affirmative, are Messrs. Layne, M'Clintic, Wilson of Botetourt, Decamps, Turnbull, Mallory, Austin, Daniel, Samuel, Richardson, Hill, Smith of Fauquier, Hickerson, Strange, Stager, Holland, Bowen, Davison, Watts, Watkins, Hail of Grayson, Avent, Carrington, Coleman, Sloan, Nixon, Goodall, Harrison, Kincheloe, Fontaine, Holleman, Robinson, Hays, Straton, Harris, Taylor of Mathews and Middlesex, Rogers, Garland of Mecklenburg, Willey, Morgan, Chapman, Sherrard, Brown of Nelson, Woolfolk, Almond, Adams, M'Coy, Cackley, Hopkins, Carroll, Madison, Shands, Williams, Marteney, Nicklin, Moffett, Conrad, Jessee, M'Mullen, Bare, Rinker, Crutchfield, Moncure, Spratley, Hargrave, Gillespie and Gibson.—67.

And the names of the gentlemen who voted in the negative, are Messrs. Banks, (speaker,) Grinalds, Drummond, Gilmer, Southall, Wiley, Garland of Amherst, Brooke, Craig, Campbell, Pate, Hunter of Berkeley, Henshaw, Miller, Booker, Beuhring, Christian, Johnson, Wilson of Cumberland, Servant, Hunter of Essex, Price, Hale of Franklin, Smith of Frederick, Smith of Gloucester, Wethered, Mullen, Botts, Gregory, Griggs, Berry, Summers, Fleet, Hooe, Carter, Neill, Beard, Powell, Taylor of Loudoun, Ragsdale, Waggener, Ingles, Benton, Murdaugh, Cooke, Parker, Leland, Fitzgerald, Chapline, Masters, Swanson, Witcher, Morris, Dorman, Leyburn, Harley, Butts, Delashmutt, Jett, Prentiss, Saunders, Cunningham, Brown of Petersburg, and Stanard.—64.

A motion was then made by Mr. Stanard, to amend the said amendment offered by Mr. Watkins; and the same being under consideration,

On motion of Mr. Hopkins, the house adjourned until Monday 12 o'clock.

MONDAY, January 18th, 1836.

The following communication from the senate by their clerk was received and read:

IN SENATE, January 16th, 1836.

The senate have passed the bill, entitled,

"An act to incorporate the Sweet springs company."

They have also passed the bill, entitled,

"An act to dispose of certain moneys heretofore raised by lottery in the county of Monroe," with an amendment, in which they request the concurrence of house of delegates.

The said amendment being twice read, was, on the question put thereupon, agreed to by the house.

Ordered, That the clerk inform the senate thereof.

A motion was made by Mr. Mallory, that the house adopt the following resolution:

Resolved, That the speaker of this house set apart convenient seats for the use of the members of the senate and executive, and of the judges of the superior courts of this commonwealth and of the United States, and of such other persons as he may invite within the bar of the house, in conformity with the sixteenth rule thereof, and that no other person whatever be admitted within the bar of the house.

On motion of Mr. Gregory, the farther consideration thereof was indefinitely postponed.

Mr. Hill, from the committee of propositions and grievances, presented a report upon the petition of William Zull, which was received and laid upon the table.

Mr. Bare presented a petition of sundry persons of the county of Shenandoah, opposing the formation of a new county out of parts of the counties of Shenandoah, Frederick, Hardy and Hampshire.

Mr. Bowen presented remonstrances from citizens of the county of Frederick, against dividing the said county.

Ordered, That the said petitions be referred to the committee of propositions and grievances, that they do examine the matter thereof, and report their opinion thereupon to the house.

Mr. Chapline presented a petition of citizens of the town of Wheeling, for the passage of an act granting a new charter of incorporation to the said town and its additions, which on his motion, was ordered to be referred to a select committee of Messrs. Chapline, Masters, Decamps, Willey, Kincheloe, Delashmutt, Prentiss and Hays, with leave to report thereon by bill or otherwise.

Mr. Chapline also presented a petition of John Moore and William Hayes, the administrators of Laureut Buzadone, asking to be remunerated for goods seized for the public service during the Illinois campaign in 1778, which was ordered to be referred to the committee on revolutionary claims, that they do examine the matter thereof, and report their opinion thereupon to the house.

Mr. Hunter of Berkeley, presented a petition of sundry citizens of the county of Berkeley, for an increase of the capital of the Bank of the Valley in Virginia, and of its several branches, and also of the branch of the Farmers bank of Virginia at Winchester, which was ordered to be referred to the committee of banks, that they do examine the matter thereof, and report their opinion thereupon to the house.

The report of the committee to whom was referred so much of the governor's message as relates to the movements of the abolitionists of the north, together with the amendment thereto proposed by Mr. Watkins, was taken up; whereupon, Mr. Stanard proposed to amend the said amendment; the speaker decided that the question having been divided, and one branch of the question having been put, first upon striking out, with a view to insert the said amendment, that it was not in order now to submit an amendment to the said amendment; from which decision of the chair, Mr. Stanard appealed to the house; and the point of order being under discussion,

A motion was made by Mr. Gilmer, that the house do now adjourn, and the question being put thereupon, was decided in the affirmative. Ayes 84, noes 45.

On motion of Mr. Daniel, (seven of the members present concurring,) *Ordered*, That the ayes and noes upon the said question be inserted in the journal.

The names of the gentlemen who voted in the affirmative, are Messrs. Banks, (speaker,) Grinalds, Drummond, Gilmer, Southall, Layne, Wiley, Garland of Amherst, Brooke, Craig, M'Clintic, Campbell, Pate, Hunter of Berkeley, Henshaw, Miller, Beuhring, Samuel, Christian, Hill, Wilson of Cumberland, Hunter of Essex, Smith of Fauquier, Price, Hale of Franklin, Davison, Smith of Frederick, Smith of Gloucester, Wethered, Carrington, Coleman, Sloan, Nixon, Goodall, Mullen, Botts, Fontaine, Gregory, Griggs, Berry, Summers, Fleet, Hooe, Robinson, Carter, Neill, Hays, Straton, Beard, Taylor of Loudoun, Ragsdale, Waggener, Rogers, Morgan, Ingles, Sherrard, Brown of Nelson, Parker, Leland, Fitzgerald, Chapline, Masters, Woolfolk, Almond, M'Coy, Swanson, Witcher, Carroll, Morris, Dorman, Leyburn, Conrad, Harley, Butts, Crutchfield, Moncure, Spratley, Hargrave, Delashmutt, Jett, Prentiss, Saunders, Brown of Petersburg, and Stanard.—84.

And the names of the gentlemen who voted in the negative, are Messrs. Wilson of Botetourt, Decamps, Turnbull, Mallory, Booker, Austin, Daniel, Richardson, Johnson, Hickerson, Strange, Steger, Holland, Bowen, Watts, Watkins, Hail of Grayson, Avent, Harrison, Kincheloe, Holleman, Powell, Harris, Taylor of Mathews and Middlesex, Garland of Mecklenburg, Willey, Chapman, Adams, Cackley, Hopkins, Madison, Shands, Williams, Marteney, Nicklin, Moffett, Jessee, M'Mullen, Bare, Rinker and Gibson.—45.

And then the house adjourned until to-morrow 12 o'clock.

TUESDAY, January 19th, 1836.

A communication from the senate by their clerk:

IN SENATE, January 18th, 1836.

The senate have passed the bill, entitled,
"An act incorporating the Red and Blue Sulphur springs turnpike company."
They have also passed the bill, entitled,
"An act to reduce and regulate the tolls on the North-western turnpike," with an amendment, in which they request the concurrence of the house of delegates.

The said amendment being twice read, was, on the question put thereupon, agreed to by the house.

Ordered, That the clerk inform the senate thereof.

On motion of Mr. Crutchfield, *Resolved*, That the committee on banks be instructed to enquire into the expediency of further amending the act incorporating the Fredericksburg mechanics association, than now required under a former resolution, and that they report by bill or otherwise.

On motion of Mr. Summers, *Resolved*, That the committee for courts of justice be instructed to enquire into the expediency of so amending the 6th section of the act, entitled, "an act to alter and reform the mode of proceeding in the courts of chancery," passed the 7th of March, 1826, as to lessen the time within which causes may be heard and determined in said courts upon the reports of commissioners in chancery, and that they have leave to report thereon by bill or otherwise.

On motion of Mr. Moncure, *Ordered*, That leave be given to bring in a bill to incorporate the New Hope gold mining company, and that Messrs. Moncure, Crutchfield, Hooe, Harris, Hill, Woolfolk, Jett and Williams prepare and bring in the same.

On motion of Mr. Harrison, *Resolved*, That the committee of roads and internal navigation be instructed to enquire into the expediency of changing the mode of constructing the North-western turnpike road and the superintendance thereof, with leave to report by bill or otherwise.

On motion of Mr. Price, *Resolved*, That the committee for courts of justice be instructed to enquire into the expediency of providing by law for the procurement and distribution of a further number of the last edition of Hening's justice, and that said committee have leave to report by bill or otherwise.

On motion of Mr. Hays, *Resolved*, That the committee for courts of justice be instructed to enquire into the expediency of continuing in force, so much of the 17th section of the law concerning delinquent and escheated lands, passed April 1st, 1831, as expires by its own limitation in April, 1836, and that the said committee have leave to report by bill or otherwise.

On motion of Mr. Hunter of Essex, the rule of the house limiting the number of the committee on the penitentiary institution, was suspended, and Mr. Harrison was ordered to be added thereto.

On motion of Mr. Gilmer, *Resolved*, That Philip S. Fry, esq. be assigned as clerk to the committee on revolutionary claims in addition to his appointment as clerk to the committee for courts of justice.

On motion of Mr. Servant, *Ordered*, That leave be given to bring in a bill to amend an act, entitled, "an act reducing into one the several acts concerning pilots and regulating their fees," and that Messrs. Servant, Stanard, Brown of Petersburg, Cunningham, Smith of Gloucester, Gregory, Cooke, Morris, Butts, Drummond and Spradley, prepare and bring in the same.

Mr. Stanard presented a petition of citizens of Richmond and Petersburg upon the subject of the fees of pilots, which was ordered to be referred to the said committee.

On motion, *Ordered*, That leave of absence from the service of this house be granted to Mr. Clay for seventeen days from Friday last.

On motion of Mr. Garland of Amherst, *Resolved*, That the president and directors of the lunatic hospital at Williamsburg be requested to furnish this house (without delay,) with the number and names of the persons that constituted their board of directors on the first day of January, 1826; also, all the subsequent changes that have taken place in that board up to the first day of this month, January, 1836, and the cause of such changes, so as to shew the time that each director has continued in office subsequent to the period aforesaid; also, the number of officers in that institution receiving an annual salary, the amount of salary paid to each, and whether these officers receive any other perquisites in the way of provisions, fuel, houses or otherwise, at the expense of that institution, and if they do, say what they are and the authority under which they are furnished.

On motion of Mr. Watkins, a bill to incorporate the Union and Potowmac company, was taken up, read the first and second times and ordered to be committed to the committee which brought it in.

Mr. Witcher from the committee of claims, presented reports upon the petitions of John Chew and of Amos Johnson.

Mr. Hill from the committee of propositions and grievances, presented a report upon the petitions of Elisha Williams and of Simeon B. Jewett.

Also, a bill to authorize additions to the town of Farmville, in the county of Prince Edward; and

A bill to amend the act, entitled, "an act, incorporating a company to erect a toll bridge over the Ohio river at Wheeling," passed February 17th, 1816.

Mr. Layne according to order, presented a bill to change the time of holding the county court of Alleghany county.

Which reports and bills were received and laid upon the table.

Mr. Hunter of Berkeley, presented a petition of Edward Colston, praying that the Potowmac river, from dam No. 5, upon the Chesapeake and Ohio canal, to the upper line of his land on said river, may be declared a lawful fence; which was ordered to be referred to the committee of agriculture and manufactures, that they do examine the matter thereof, and report their opinion thereupon to the house.

Mr. Beard presented a petition of sundry citizens of the town of Leesburg, praying for an amendment of the several acts incorporating the said town.

Mr. Witcher, a petition of citizens of the county of Pittsylvania, that the precinct election heretofore holden at the house of Benjamin Watkins, shall be held hereafter at the house of Walter Fitzgerald in said county.

Ordered, That the said petitions be referred to the committee of propositions and grievances, that they do examine the matter thereof, and report their opinion thereupon to the house.

Mr. Price presented a petition of Patrick Keenan, praying for the re-assessment of certain lands, and to be allowed further time to pay taxes due thereon in order to redeem the same; which was ordered to be referred to the committee of finance, that they do examine the matter thereof, and report their opinion thereupon to the house.

Mr. Garland of Mecklenburg, presented a petition of Randal Chavis, to be allowed compensation for services rendered by his father and uncle during the revolution; which was ordered to be referred to the committee on revolutionary claims, that they do examine the matter thereof, and report their opinion thereupon to the house.

He also presented a petition of sundry citizens of the town of Clarksville, praying for the incorporation of a female academy in said town.

Mr. Dorman, a petition of citizens of the town of Lexington, praying for certain changes in the organization of the Lexington arsenal, so as to make it a military school, and for the endowment of an asylum for the deaf and dumb of the state.

Ordered, That the said petitions be referred to the committee of schools and colleges, that they do examine the matter thereof, and report their opinion thereupon to the house.

Mr. Stanard presented a remonstrance of citizens of Richmond, against the petition of the Manchester and Petersburg turnpike company, and praying for the incorporation of a company to construct a rail-road from the city of Richmond to the town of Petersburg; which was ordered to be laid upon the table.

Mr. Masters presented a petition of John M'Lure and others, asking for amendments to the act regulating the tolls upon the Cumberland road; which was ordered to be referred to the committee of roads and internal navigation, that they do examine the matter thereof, and report their opinion thereupon to the house.

The report of the committee to whom was referred so much of the governor's message as relates to the movements of the abolitionists of the north, together with the amendment thereto submitted by Mr. Watkins, was taken up; and the question being upon the appeal from the decision of the chair upon the point of order submitted by Mr. Stanard on yesterday, on motion of Mr. Miller, the whole subject was ordered to be laid upon the table.

Mr. Miller then submitted a preamble and resolutions, intended to be offered as an amendment to the said report of the committee, which on motion of Mr. Gilmer, was ordered to be laid upon the table, and 185 copies thereof were ordered to be printed for the use of the general assembly.

On motion of Mr. Crutchfield, the house adjourned until to-morrow 12 o'clock.

WEDNESDAY, January 20th, 1836.

A communication from the senate by their clerk:

IN SENATE, January 19th, 1836.

The senate have passed the bill, entitled,

"An act to provide for the construction of a road between Weston in the county of Lewis, and Charleston in the county of Kanawha."

On motion of Mr. Gregory, *Resolved by the legislature of Virginia*, That the board of public works be directed to cause a survey and location to be made of the most suitable route for a rail-road from the city of Richmond to Yorktown in Virginia, during the present year, by a competent engineer, and that said engineer report his proceedings, together with a profile of said route to the next legislature.

Ordered, That Mr. Gregory carry the same to the senate and request their concurrence.

Mr. Shands presented a petition of sundry citizens of the town of Petersburg and county of Prince George, for a rail-road from the said town to City Point, which was ordered to be laid upon the table.

On motion of Mr. Hays, *Ordered*, That the committee for courts of justice be discharged from the consideration of the resolution referred to said committee on yesterday, relating to delinquent lands, and that the same be referred to the committee of finance.

On motion of Mr. Murdaugh, a bill concerning the town of Portsmouth was taken up, read the first and second times, and ordered to be committed to the committee which brought it in.

On motion of Mr. Watkins, *Ordered*, That the committee of roads and internal navigation be discharged from the consideration of the petition of the president and directors of the Roanoke navigation company, and that the same be laid upon the table.

Mr. Watkins, from the committee of roads and internal navigation, presented reports upon petitions of the president and directors of the Lewisburg and Blue Sulphur springs turnpike company, and of George Holeman and J. W. Toney, which were received and laid upon the table.

He also reported with amendments, a bill to incorporate the Union and Potomac company, which, on his motion, was taken up, and the said amendments being agreed to by the house, and a motion having been made by Mr. Price, farther to amend the same, on motion of Mr. M'Mullen, the said bill and amendment was ordered to be laid upon the table.

A motion was made by Mr. Miller, that the preamble and resolutions submitted by him on yesterday, on the subject of the movements of the abolitionists of the north, detached from their connection with the report of the committee and the amendments thereto, be taken up; and the question being put thereupon, was determined in the affirmative. Ayes 118, noes 8.

On motion of Mr. Miller, (seven of the members present concurring,) *Ordered*, That the ayes and noes upon the said question be inserted in the journal.

The names of the gentlemen who voted in the affirmative, are Messrs. Banks, (speaker,) Grinalds, Drummond, Gilmer, Southall, Layne, Wiley, Garland of Amherst, Brooke, Craig, M'Clintic, Hunter of Berkeley, Henshaw, Miller, Wilson of Botetourt, Decamps, Turnbull, Mallory, Booker, Austin, Beuhring, Daniel, Samuel, Richardson, Johnson, Hill, Wilson of Cumberland, Servant, Hunter of Essex, Smith of Fauquier, Hickerson, Price, Strange, Steger, Hale of Franklin, Holland, Bowen, Davison, Smith of Frederick, Watts, Watkins, Hail of Grayson, Wethered, Avent, Carrington, Coleman, Sloan, Nixon, Goodall, Mullen, Harrison, Kincheloe, Fontaine, Holleman, Gregory, Griggs, Berry, Summers, Fleet, Hooe, Robinson, Carter, Neill, Hays, Straton, Beard, Powell, Taylor of Loudoun, Harris, Ragsdale, Taylor of Mathews and Middlesex, Waggener, Rogers, Garland of Mecklenburg, Willey, Morgan, Chapman, Ingles, Sherrard, Brown of Nelson, Murdaugh, Leland, Fitzgerald, Chapline, Masters, Woolfolk, Almond, Adams, M'Coy, Swanson, Witcher, Cackley, Hopkins, Carroll, Madison, Morris, Shands, Williams, Marteney, Nicklin, Dorman, Leyburn, Moffett, Conrad, Jessee, M'Mullen, Bare, Rinker, Butts, Crutchfield, Moncure, Spratley, Hargrave, Delashmutt, Gibson, Jett, Prentiss and Saunders.—118.

And the names of the gentlemen who voted in the negative, are Messrs. Campbell, Christian, Smith of Gloucester, Botts, Parker, Harley, Brown of Petersburg, and Stanard.—8.

The said preamble and resolutions are the following:

Whereas certain associations having been formed in several of the non-slaveholding states for the purpose of abolishing slavery in the United States, this general assembly feels itself called upon to declare, that the state of Virginia has a right to demand prompt and efficient legislation by her co-states, to restrain as far as may be, and to punish those of their citizens who, in defiance of the obligations of social duty and those of the constitution, assail her safety and tranquillity, by forming associations for the abolition of slavery, or printing, publishing, or circulating, through the mail or otherwise, seditious and incendiary publications; and that this right, founded as it is on the principles of international law, is peculiarly fortified by a just consideration of the intimate and sacred relations that exist between the states of this Union:

1. *Resolved*, That this commonwealth only, has the right to control, or interfere with, the subject of domestic slavery within its limits, and that this right will be maintained at all hazards.

2. *Resolved*, That the non-slaveholding states of the Union are respectfully but earnestly requested, promptly to adopt penal enactments, or such other measures as will effectually suppress all associations within their respective limits, purporting to be, or having the character of, abolition societies; and that they will make it highly penal, to print, publish or distribute newspapers, pamphlets or other publications, calculated or having a tendency to excite the slaves of the southern states to insurrection and revolt.

3. *Resolved*, That this general assembly would regard any act of congress, having for its object the abolition of slavery in the district of Columbia, or the territories of the United States, as affording just cause of alarm to the slaveholding states, and bringing the Union into imminent peril.

4. *Resolved*, That it is highly expedient for the slaveholding states to enact such laws and regulations as may be necessary to suppress and prevent the circulation of any incendiary publications within their respective limits.

5. *Resolved*, That confiding in the justice and loyalty of our northern brethren, to the principles of the Union, enforced by the sympathies of common dangers, sufferings and triumphs, that bind us together in fraternal concord, we are warranted in the expectation, that the foregoing requests will be received in the spirit in which they are made, and complied with.

6. *Resolved*, That the governor be, and he is hereby requested to forward a copy of these resolutions to each of our senators and representatives in congress, and to the executive of each of the states of the Union, with a request that the same may be submitted to their respective legislatures.

The first resolution was, on the question put thereupon, unanimously agreed to by the house.

A motion was made by Mr. Stanard, to amend the said preamble and resolutions, by inserting between the said first and second resolutions the following:

"That the formation of abolition or anti-slavery societies, and the acts and doings of certain fanatics calling themselves abolitionists in the non-slaveholding states of this confederacy, are in violation of the obligations of the constitution, dissocial and incendiary in the extreme, and that this state has a right to claim of the states in which they have been or may be formed, the passage of laws, with adequate penalties, to suppress or prevent them."

Whereupon, Mr. Watkins demanded that the previous question be now put.

And the question being, shall the main question be now put, and was determined in the affirmative. Ayes 67, noes 58.

On motion of Mr. Parker, (seven of the members present concurring,) *Ordered*, That the ayes and noes upon the said question be inserted in the journal.

The names of the gentlemen who voted in the affirmative, are Messrs. Banks, (speaker,) Drummond, Layne, Wiley, M'Clintic, Miller, Wilson of Botetourt, Decamps, Turnbull, Mallory, Booker, Austin, Daniel, Samuel, Richardson, Hill, Smith of Fauquier, Hickerson, Strange, Steger, Holland, Bowen, Watts, Watkins, Hail of Grayson, Avent, Carrington, Nixon, Goodall, Harrison, Kincheloe, Fontaine, Holleman, Robinson, Hays, Straton, Harris, Rogers, Garland of Mecklenburg, Willey, Chapman, Ingles, Sherrard, Fitzgerald, Woolfolk, Almond, Adams, M'Coy, Cackley, Hopkins, Carroll, Madison, Shands, Williams, Marteney, Nicklin, Moffett, Conrad, Jessee, M'Mullen, Bare, Rinker, Spratley, Hargrave, Gibson, Prentiss and Saunders.—67.

And the names of the gentlemen who voted in the negative, are Messrs. Grinalds, Gilmer, Southall, Garland of Amherst, Brooke, Craig, Campbell, Hunter of Berkeley, Henshaw, Beuhring, Christian, Johnson, Wilson of Cumberland, Servant, Hunter of Essex, Price, Hale of Franklin, Davison, Smith of Frederick, Smith of Gloucester, Wethered, Coleman, Sloan, Mullen, Botts, Gregory, Griggs, Berry, Summers, Fleet, Hooe, Carter, Neill, Beard, Powell, Taylor of Loudoun, Ragsdale, Taylor of Mathews and Middlesex, Waggener, Morgan, Brown of Nelson, Murdangh, Parker, Leland, Chapline, Masters, Swanson, Witcher, Morris, Dorman, Leyburn, Harley, Butts, Crutchfield, Delashmutt, Jett, Brown of Petersburg, and Stanard.—58.

The question was then put upon agreeing to the said amendment submitted by Mr. Stanard, and was determined in the negative. Ayes 33, noes 93.

On motion of Mr. Stanard, (seven of the members present concurring,) *Ordered*, That the ayes and noes upon the said question be inserted in the journal.

The names of the gentlemen who voted in the affirmative, are Messrs. Grinalds, Drummond, Southall, Garland of Amherst, Campbell, Beuhring, Christian, Johnson, Wilson of Cumberland, Servant, Hale of Franklin, Smith of Frederick, Smith of Gloucester, Wethered, Mullen, Botts, Gregory, Fleet, Hooe, Neill, Ragsdale, Waggener, Murdaugh, Parker, Woolfolk, Swanson, Witcher, Morris, Harley, Butts, Jett, Brown of Petersburg, and Stanard.—33.

And the names of the gentlemen who voted in the negative, are Messrs. Banks, (speaker,) Gilmer, Layne, Wiley, Brooke, Craig, M'Clintic, Hunter of Berkeley, Henshaw, Miller, Wilson of Botetourt, Decamps, Turnbull, Mallory, Booker, Austin, Daniel, Samuel, Richardson, Hill, Hunter of Essex, Smith of Fauquier, Hickerson, Price, Strange, Steger, Holland, Bowen, Davison, Watts, Watkins, Hail of Grayson, Avent, Carrington, Coleman, Sloan, Nixon, Goodall, Harrison, Kincheloe, Fontaine, Holleman, Griggs, Berry, Summers, Robinson, Carter, Hays, Straton, Beard, Powell, Taylor of Loudoun, Harris, Taylor of Mathews and Middlesex, Rogers, Garland of Mecklenburg, Willey, Morgan, Chapman, Ingles, Sherrard, Brown of Nelson, Leland, Fitzgerald, Chapline, Masters, Almond, Adams, M'Coy, Cackley, Hopkins, Carroll, Madison, Shands, Williams, Marteney, Nicklin, Dorman, Leyburn, Moffett, Conrad, Jessee, M'Mullen, Bare, Rinker, Crutchfield, Moncure, Spratley, Hargrave, Delashmutt, Gibson, Prentiss and Saunders.—93.

The question then recurred upon adopting the second resolution contained in the proposition submitted by Mr. Miller; whereupon, Mr. Woolfolk called the previous question.

The question was then put, "Shall the main question be now put?" and was determined in the negative. Ayes 57, noes 68.

On motion of Mr. Parker, (seven of the members present concurring,) *Ordered*, That the ayes and noes upon the said question be inserted in the journal.

The names of the gentlemen who voted in the affirmative, are Messrs. Layne, Wiley, M'Clintic, Wilson of Botetourt, Decamps, Turnbull, Mallory, Booker, Austin, Daniel, Richardson, Hickerson, Strange, Steger, Holland, Bowen, Watts, Watkins, Hail of Grayson, Avent, Nixon, Harrison, Kincheloe, Fontaine, Holleman, Robinson, Hays, Straton, Harris, Garland of Mecklenburg, Chapman, Ingles, Sherrard, Fitzgerald, Woolfolk, Almond, Adams, M'Coy, Cackley, Hopkins, Carroll, Madison, Shands, Williams, Marteney, Nicklin, Moffett, Conrad, Jessee, M'Mullen, Bare, Rinker, Moncure, Spratley, Hargrave, Gibson and Prentiss.—57.

And the names of the gentlemen who voted in the negative, are Messrs. Banks, (speaker,) Grinalds, Drummond, Gilmer, Southall, Garland of Amherst, Brooke, Craig, Campbell, Hunter of Berkeley, Henshaw, Miller, Beuhring, Samuel, Christian, Johnson, Hill, Wilson of Cumberland, Servant, Hunter of Essex, Smith of Fauquier, Price, Hale of Franklin, Davison, Smith of Frederick, Smith of Gloucester, Wethered, Carrington, Coleman, Sloan, Goodall, Botts, Gregory, Griggs, Berry, Summers, Fleet, Hooe, Carter, Neill, Beard, Powell, Taylor of Loudoun, Ragsdale, Taylor of Mathews and Middlesex, Waggener, Rogers, Willey, Morgan, Brown of Nelson, Murdaugh, Parker, Leland, Chapline, Masters, Swanson, Witcher, Morris, Dorman, Leyburn, Harley, Butts, Crutchfield, Delashmutt, Jett, Saunders, Brown of Petersburg, and Stanard.—68.

A motion was then made by Mr. Gregory, that the farther consideration of the said preamble and resolutions be indefinitely postponed, and the question being put thereupon, was determined in the negative. Ayes 5, noes 120.

On motion of Mr. Brown of Petersburg, (seven of the members present concurring,) *Ordered*, That the ayes and noes upon the said question be inserted in the journal.

The names of the gentlemen who voted in the affirmative, are Messrs. Campbell, Gregory, Murdaugh, Parker, and Brown of Petersburg.—5.

And the names of the gentlemen who voted in the negative, are Messrs. Banks, (speaker,) Grinalds, Drummond, Gilmer, Southall, Layne, Wiley, Garland of Amherst, Brooke, Craig, M'Clintic, Hunter of Berkeley, Henshaw, Miller, Wilson of Botetourt, Decamps, Turnbull, Mallory, Booker, Austin, Beuhring, Daniel, Samuel, Christian, Richardson, Johnson, Hill, Wilson of Cumberland, Servant, Hunter of Essex, Smith of Fauquier, Hickerson, Price, Strange, Steger, Hale of Franklin, Holland, Bowen, Davison, Smith of Frederick, Watts, Smith of Gloucester, Watkins, Hail of Grayson, Wethered, Avent, Carrington, Coleman, Sloan, Nixon, Goodall, Mullen, Harrison, Kincheloe, Botts, Fontaine, Holleman, Griggs, Berry, Summers, Fleet, Hooe, Robinson, Carter, Neill, Hays, Straton, Beard, Powell, Taylor of Loudoun, Harris, Ragsdale, Waggener, Rogers, Garland of Mecklenburg, Willey, Morgan, Chapman, Ingles, Sherrard, Brown of Nelson, Leland, Fitzgerald, Chapline, Masters, Woolfolk, Almond, Adams, M'Coy, Swanson, Witcher, Cackley, Hopkins, Carroll, Madison, Morris, Shands, Williams, Marteney, Nicklin, Dorman, Leyburn, Moffett, Conrad, Jessee, M'Mullen, Bare, Rinker, Harley, Butts, Crutchfield, Moncure, Spratley, Hargrave, Delashmutt, Gibson, Jett, Prentiss, Saunders and Stanard.—120.

The question then recurred upon adopting the second resolution of the said preamble and resolutions; whereupon, a motion was made by Mr. Parker, to amend the same by striking therefrom the words, "adopt penal enactments, *or such other measures*," and insert in lieu thereof, the words "pass such laws," so as to cause the resolution to read, "that the non-slaveholding states of the Union are respectfully, but earnestly requested, promptly to pass such laws as will effectually suppress all associations within their respective limits, &c.;" and the question being put upon striking out and inserting as aforesaid, was determined in the negative. Ayes 26, noes 99.

On motion of Mr. Parker, (seven of the members present concurring,) *Ordered*, That the ayes and noes on the said question be inserted in the journal.

The names of the gentlemen who voted in the affirmative, are Messrs. Grinalds, Garland of Amherst, Campbell, Pate, Christian, Johnson, Servant, Price, Hale of Franklin, Smith of Frederick, Smith of Gloucester, Wethered, Mullen, Botts, Gregory, Hooe, Neill, Parker, Masters, Swanson, Morris, Harley, Butts, Delashmutt, Brown of Petersburg, and Stanard.—26.

And the names of the gentlemen who voted in the negative, are Messrs. Banks, (speaker,) Drummond, Gilmer, Southall, Layne, Wiley, Brooke, Craig, M'Clintic, Hunter of Berkeley, Henshaw, Miller, Wilson of Botetourt, Decampe, Turnbull, Mallory, Booker, Austin, Beuhring, Daniel, Samuel, Richardson, Hill, Wilson of Cumberland, Hunter of Essex, Smith of Fauquier, Hickerson, Strange, Steger, Holland, Bowen, Davison, Watts, Watkins, Hail of Grayson, Avent, Carrington, Coleman, Sloan, Nixon, Goodall, Harrison, Kincheloe, Fontaine, Holleman, Griggs, Berry, Summers, Fleet, Robinson, Carter, Hays, Straton, Beard, Powell, Taylor of Loudoun, Harris, Ragsdale, Taylor of Mathews and Middlesex, Waggener, Rogers, Garland of Mecklenburg, Willey, Morgan, Chapman, Ingles, Sherrard, Brown of Nelson, Murdaugh, Leland, Fitzgerald, Woolfolk, Almond, Adams, M'Coy, Witcher, Cackley, Hopkins, Carroll, Madison, Shands, Williams, Marteney, Nicklin, Dorman, Leyburn, Moffett, Conrad, Jessee, M'Mullen, Bare, Rinker, Crutchfield, Moncure, Spratley, Hargrave, Jett, Prentiss and Saunders.—99.

The question was then put upon agreeing to the said second resolution, and was determined in the affirmative.

The question was put upon adopting the third resolution, and was determined in the affirmative. Ayes 122, noes 4.

The question recurred upon adopting the fourth resolution, and was agreed to unanimously.

The question was then put upon adopting the fifth resolution, and was determined in the affirmative.

A motion was made by Mr. Miller, to amend the said resolutions by inserting between the fifth and sixth resolutions, the following:

"*Resolved*, That congress has no constitutional power to abolish slavery in the district of Columbia, or in the territories of the United States."

And the question being put thereupon, was determined in the affirmative. Ayes 105, noes 13.

On motion of Mr. Powell, (seven of the members present concurring,) *Ordered*, That the ayes and noes upon the said question be inserted in the journal.

The names of the gentlemen who voted in the affirmative, are Messrs. Banks, (speaker,) Grinalds, Drummond, Gilmer, Southall, Layne, Wiley, Garland of Amherst, M'Clintic, Miller, Wilson of Botetourt, Turnbull, Mallory, Booker, Austin, Beuhring, Daniel, Samuel, Christian, Richardson, Johnson, Hill, Wilson of Cumberland, Servant, Hunter of Essex, Smith of Fauquier, Hickerson, Price, Strange, Steger, Hale of Franklin, Holland, Bowen, Davison, Smith of Frederick, Watts, Smith of Gloucester, Hail of Grayson, Wethered, Avent, Coleman, Sloan, Nixon, Goodall, Harrison, Kincheloe, Botts, Fontaine, Holleman, Gregory, Fleet, Hooe, Robinson, Carter, Neill, Hays, Straton, Harris, Ragsdale, Taylor of Mathews and Middlesex, Waggener, Rogers, Garland of Mecklenburg, Morgan, Ingles, Sherrard, Brown of Nelson, Murdaugh, Parker, Leland, Fitzgerald, Masters, Woolfolk, Almond, Adams, M'Coy, Swanson, Witcher, Cackley, Hopkins, Carroll, Madison, Morris, Shands, Williams, Marteney, Nicklin, Dorman, Moffett, Conrad, Jessee, M'Mullen, Bare, Rinker, Harley, Butts, Crutchfield, Moncure, Spratley, Hargrave, Delashmutt, Jett, Saunders, Brown of Petersburg, and Stanard.—105.

And the names of the gentlemen who voted in the negative, are Messrs. Brooke, Craig, Hunter of Berkeley, Henshaw, Griggs, Berry, Summers, Beard, Powell, Taylor of Loudoun, Chapman, Leyburn and Prentiss.—13.

The question recurred upon adopting the sixth resolution, and was determined in the affirmative.

The question then recurred upon adopting the said preamble; whereupon, it was amended by the house on the motion of Mr. Summers, by striking therefrom the words, "*Whereas certain associations having been formed in several of the non-slaveholding states for the purpose of abolishing slavery in the United States, this general assembly feels itself called upon to declare*," and inserting in lieu thereof the word "*Resolved*," so as to cause it to read,

Resolved, That the state of Virginia has a right to *demand* prompt and efficient legislation by her co-states, to restrain, &c.

The said resolution was then further amended, on motion of Mr. Prentiss, by striking therefrom the word "demand," and inserting in lieu thereof, the word "claim;" and as amended, was, on the question put thereupon, agreed to by the house. Ayes 108, noes 7.

On motion of Mr. Stanard, (seven of the members present concurring,) *Ordered*, That the ayes and noes upon the said question be inserted in the journal.

The names of the gentlemen who voted in the affirmative, are Messrs. Banks, (speaker,) Grinalds, Drummond, Gilmer, Southall, Layne, Wiley, Garland of Amherst, M'Clintic, Hunter of Berkeley, Henshaw, Miller, Wilson of Botetourt, Decampe, Turnbull, Mallory, Booker, Austin, Beuhring, Daniel, Samuel, Christian, Richardson, Johnson, Hill, Wilson of Cumberland, Servant, Hunter of Essex, Smith of Fauquier, Hickerson, Strange, Steger, Holland, Bowen, Davison, Smith of Frederick, Watts, Smith of Gloucester, Hail of Grayson, Wethered, Avent, Carrington, Coleman, Sloan, Nixon, Goodall, Harrison, Kincheloe, Botts, Fontaine, Holleman, Gregory, Berry, Summers, Fleet, Hooe, Robinson, Carter, Neill, Hays, Straton, Beard, Powell, Taylor of Loudoun, Harris, Ragsdale, Rogers, Ingles, Sherrard, Brown of Nelson, Murdaugh, Parker, Leland, Fitzgerald, Woolfolk, Almond, Adams, M'Coy, Swanson, Witcher, Cackley, Hopkins, Carroll, Madison, Morris, Williams, Marteney, Nicklin, Dorman, Moffett, Conrad, Jessee, M'Mullen, Bare, Rinker, Harley, Butts, Crutchfield, Moncure, Spratley, Hargrave, Delashmutt, Gibson, Jett, Prentiss, Saunders, Brown of Petersburg, and Stanard.—108.

And the names of the gentlemen who voted in the negative, are Messrs. Craig, Mullen, Garland of Mecklenburg, Willey, Morgan, Shands and Leyburn.—7.

The first and second resolutions were then ordered to be transposed, and the said resolutions as finally adopted, are the following:

1. *Resolved,* That this commonwealth only, has the right to control, or interfere with the subject of domestic slavery within its limits, and that this right will be maintained at all hazards.

2. *Resolved,* That the state of Virginia has a right to claim prompt and efficient legislation by her co-states, to restrain as far as may be, and to punish those of her citizens who, in defiance of the obligations of social duty and those of the constitution, assail her safety and tranquillity, by forming associations for the abolition of slavery, or printing, publishing, or circulating, through the mail or otherwise, seditious and incendiary publications; and that this right, founded as it is on the principles of international law, is peculiarly fortified by a just consideration of the intimate and sacred relations that exist between the states of this Union.

3. *Resolved,* That the non-slaveholding states of the Union are respectfully but earnestly requested, promptly to adopt penal enactments, or such other measures as will effectually suppress all associations within their respective limits, purporting to be, or having the character of, abolition societies; and that they will make it highly penal, to print, publish or distribute newspapers, pamphlets or other publications, calculated or having a tendency to excite the slaves of the southern states to insurrection and revolt.

4. *Resolved,* That this general assembly would regard any act of congress, having for its object the abolition of slavery in the district of Columbia, or the territories of the United States, as affording just cause of alarm to the slaveholding states, and bringing the Union into imminent peril.

5. *Resolved,* That it is highly expedient for the slaveholding states to enact such laws and regulations as may be necessary to suppress and prevent the circulation of any incendiary publications within their respective limits.

6. *Resolved,* That confiding in the justice and loyalty of our northern brethren, to the principles of the Union, enforced by the sympathies of common dangers, sufferings and triumphs, which ought to bind us together in fraternal concord, we are warranted in the expectation, that the foregoing requests will be received in the spirit in which they are made, and complied with.

7. *Resolved,* That congress has no constitutional power to abolish slavery in the district of Columbia, or in the territories of the United States.

8. *Resolved,* That the governor be, and he is hereby requested to forward a copy of these resolutions to each of our senators and representatives in congress, and to the executive of each of the states of the Union, with a request that the same may be submitted to their respective legislatures.

Ordered, That the clerk communicate the same to the senate and request their concurrence.

The speaker laid before the house a communication from the auditor of public accounts, transmitting copies of the reports of the commissioners appointed by the act of 1777, to ascertain the losses occasioned to individuals by the burning of Norfolk and Portsmouth in 1776, which, on motion of Mr. Wilson of Cumberland, was ordered to be laid upon the table.

On motion of Mr. Henshaw, the house adjourned until to-morrow 12 o'clock.

THURSDAY, January 21st, 1836.

A communication from the senate by their clerk:

IN SENATE, January 20th, 1836.

The senate have passed the bill, entitled,
"An act incorporating the stockholders of the Rappahannock and Blue Ridge rail-road company," with amendments, in which they request the concurrence of the house of delegates.

The said amendments being twice read, were, on questions severally put thereupon, agreed to by the house.

Ordered, That the clerk inform the senate thereof.

On motion of Mr. Sherrard, *Resolved,* That this house will proceed, jointly with the senate, on Wednesday, the 27th instant, to the election of an auditor of public accounts, second auditor, treasurer of the commonwealth, and register of the land office, for one year from the expiration of the term for which the present incumbents of those offices were elected.

Ordered, That the clerk communicate the same to the senate and request their concurrence.

On motion of Mr. Botts, *Resolved,* That the committee of roads and internal navigation be instructed to enquire into the expediency of incorporating a company for the purpose of holding Mayo's bridge as joint stock property, and that they have leave to report by bill or otherwise.

On motion of Mr. Steger, *Resolved*, That the committee on the militia laws be instructed to enquire into the expediency of amending the 32d section of the militia law, passed March 8th, 1834, so as to provide more effectually for the enrolment of persons subject to militia duty.

Mr. Murdaugh reported, without amendment, a bill concerning the town of Portsmouth.

Mr. Layne, according to order, presented a bill to incorporate the Red springs company.

Which were received and laid upon the table.

Mr. Shands presented a petition of citizens of the county of Prince George, and town of Petersburg, for the construction of a rail-road from Petersburg, to some point at or near Harrison's bar on James river.

Mr. Murdaugh presented a petition of citizens of the borough of Norfolk, and a portion of the citizens of Norfolk county, for the extension of the Portsmouth and Roanoke rail-road to the borough of Norfolk.

Also, memorials of the stockholders in the Portsmouth and Roanoke rail-road company, opposing the extension of the said road.

And of citizens of Norfolk county, opposing so much of the petition of citizens of Norfolk county, as prays the erection of a bridge across the southern branch of Elizabeth river.

And an expose of the petition for the extension of the said Portsmouth and Roanoke rail-road, made by the joint committee of the citizens, and of the court and common council of the borough of Norfolk, raised for the purpose of attending to the application of a majority of the stockholders of the said company, which were ordered to be referred to the committee of roads and internal navigation, that they do examine the matter thereof, and report their opinion thereupon to the house.

Mr. Chapline presented a petition of citizens of the county of Ohio, praying for the passage of an act authorizing limited partnerships; which was ordered to be referred to the committee for courts of justice, that they do examine the matter thereof, and report their opinion thereupon to the house.

Mr. Woolfolk presented a memorial of sundry citizens of the county of Orange, opposing the formation of a new county out of a part of the said county of Orange; which was ordered to be referred to the committee of propositions and grievances, that they do examine the matter thereof, and report their opinion thereupon to the house.

Mr. Parker, from the committee on the militia laws, presented a bill establishing a new regiment in the county of Preston.

Mr. Stanard, from the committee for courts of justice, presented reports upon the resolution giving courts of law the power of appointing guardians *ad litem*, and upon the petition of Isaac Brock.

Also a bill to amend the act concerning fraudulent devises.

A bill giving to the circuit superior courts of law and chancery concurrent jurisdiction with the county and corporation courts in all actions of forcible entry and detainer; and

A bill to amend the act, entitled, "an act to alter and reform the mode of proceeding in the courts of chancery."

Which bills and reports were received and laid upon the table.

An engrossed bill to incorporate the stockholders of the City Point rail-road company, was read a third time:

Resolved, That the bill do pass, and that the title be, "an act to incorporate the stockholders of the City Point rail-road company."

Ordered, That the clerk communicate the same to the senate and request their concurrence.

A bill concerning James Wysong, was read a second time, and on motion of Mr. Griggs, ordered to be laid upon the table.

A bill concerning the town of Portsmouth, was taken up on motion of Mr. Murdaugh, and ordered to be engrossed and read a third time.

A bill regulating and reducing the expenses incident to the collection of money under execution, was read a second time, amended on motion of Mr. Booker, and then, on motion of Mr. Crutchfield, ordered to be laid upon the table.

A bill to change the times of holding the courts in the third judicial circuit, was read a second time, and, on motion of Mr. Parker, ordered to be laid upon the table.

On motion of Mr. Murdaugh, the communication of the auditor of public accounts, transmitted to the house on yesterday, was taken up, and ordered to be referred to the committee on revolutionary claims.

The following bills heretofore reported without amendment from the respective committees to which the same had been committed, were taken up, and ordered to be engrossed and read a third time:

A bill to enact an act of the general assembly of North Carolina, entitled, "an act to incorporate the Roanoke, Danville, and Junction rail-road company."

A bill to provide for the construction of a road across the Blue Ridge at Milam's gap; and

A bill to reorganize the first and second judicial districts.

A bill to amend the act, entitled, "an act incorporating the Falmouth and Alexandria rail-road company," with the amendment thereto proposed by the committee to which the same had been committed, was taken up, and the said amendment being agreed to by the house, the said bill as amended, was ordered to be engrossed and read a third time.

A bill to incorporate the Union Potomac company, was taken up on motion of Mr. M'Mullen, and as heretofore amended, was ordered to be engrossed and read a third time.

The following bills were read a second time, and severally ordered to be engrossed and read a third time, viz:

A bill to incorporate the Fluvanna mining company.
A bill to provide an index to the journals of the house of delegates.
A bill concerning George Johnson.
A bill concerning Shelton Ford.
A bill to change the place of holding a separate election in the county of Hampshire.
A bill directing the survey and location of a route for a road from Moorfield to the North-western turnpike.
A bill to establish the town of Hedgesville in the county of Berkeley.
A bill releasing to William Fisher the commonwealth's right to one thousand acres of land in the county of Nicholas.
A bill authorizing the sale of the estate of John Haskins, sen'r, a lunatic.
A bill authorizing James Martin to hold and convey certain real estate.
A bill allowing Judy Johnson, a free woman of colour, to remain in the commonwealth.
A bill allowing Daniel Higginbotham, a free man of colour, to remain in the commonwealth a limited time.
A bill allowing Richard Bolling, a free man of colour, to remain in the commonwealth.
A bill concerning Duff Green.
A bill to enlarge the town of Clarksville in the county of Mecklenburg.
A bill to authorize a separate election at the tavern house of William Irwin in the county of Cumberland.
A bill to amend an act, entitled, "an act to limit the assessment upon tithables, and to authorize a tax upon property, for the purpose of defraying county expenditures within the county of Berkeley," passed March 5th, 1835.
A bill further to provide for the construction of a turnpike road across the Alleghany mountain in the counties of Pendleton and Pocahontas.
A bill authorizing an increase of the capital stock of the Merchants manufacturing company; and
A bill to revive the charter of the Nelson and Albemarle Union factory company.
A bill allowing Charlotte Morgan, a free woman of colour, to remain in the commonwealth, was read a second time, and ordered, on motion of Mr. Mullen, to be committed to the committee which brought it in.

Mr. Decamps from the committee of schools and colleges, presented several reports of said committee upon petitions of citizens of the county of Halifax; of Robert Briggs and others; of R. H. Edwards; and of citizens of the town of Clarksville, and upon the resolution for incorporating the Martinsville academy.

And a bill to incorporate the trustees of the Estillville academy.

Which were received and laid upon the table.

On motion of Mr. Decamps, *Ordered,* That the committee of schools and colleges be discharged from the consideration of petitions of citizens of the town of Lexington, relative to changing the Lexington arsenal into a military school, and to the endowment of a deaf and dumb asylum; and also from the resolution on the subject of the said arsenal; and that the said petitions and resolution be referred to the committee on the militia laws, that they do examine the matter thereof, and report their opinion thereupon to the house.

Mr. Stanard presented the petition of Richard B. Haxall, to be authorized to erect wharves at his own expense at such points as he may select between the road called the Bermuda Hundred road and the upper lines of his lands on James river, and to receive wharfage fees thereat, which was ordered to be referred to the committee of propositions and grievances, that they do examine the matter thereof, and report their opinion thereupon to the house.

Mr. Wilson of Botetourt presented petitions of citizens of the county of Botetourt, for a company to construct a rail-road connecting with the James river and Kanawha improvement at the town of Buchanan, and extending thence to the Tennessee line, to unite with the continuation of the New Orleans and Nashville rail-road.

Also, of other citizens of said county, for a company to construct a rail-road from Lynchburg, by Buford's Gap, to the Tennessee line, with the privilege to the James river and Kanawha company to extend the same to the city of Richmond.

Ordered, That the said petitions be referred to the committee of roads and internal navigation, that they do examine the matter thereof, and report their opinion thereupon to the house.

On motion of Mr. Mullen, the house adjourned until to-morrow 12 o'clock.

FRIDAY, January 22d, 1836.

The following communication from the senate by their clerk, was received and read:

IN SENATE, January 21st, 1836.

The senate have passed the bill, entitled,

"An act incorporating the stockholders of the Louisa rail-road company," with amendments, in which they request the concurrence of the house of delegates.

And they have agreed to the resolution for a survey of a route for a rail-road from the city of Richmond to Yorktown in Virginia, with amendments, in which they also request the concurrence of the house of delegates.

On motion of Mr. Crutchfield, the said bill and proposed amendments were ordered to be laid upon the table.

The said amendments to the said resolution being twice read, were, on questions severally put thereupon, agreed to by the house.

Ordered, That the clerk inform the senate thereof.

On motion of Mr. Prentiss, *Resolved,* That the committee of roads and internal navigation be instructed to enquire into the expediency of renewing the act, entitled, "an act making further provision for completing the road from Staunton to the mouth of the Little Kanawha," passed March 19th, 1832, so as to extend the time for completing the same, and that they have leave to report by bill or otherwise.

Mr. Crutchfield, according to order, presented a bill to incorporate the United States copper mining company.

Mr. Hill, from the committee of propositions and grievances, presented a report upon the petition of citizens of the counties of Shenandoah and Frederick, for a new county out of parts of said counties.

Mr. Madison, from the committee on agriculture and manufactures, presented a bill requiring of the inspectors of tobacco in this commonwealth to distinguish in their inspections between tobacco produced in Virginia, and that produced in other states.

Mr. Witcher, from the committee of claims, presented reports upon petitions of Stapleton Crutchfield and of Jacob and William Hite.

Which bills and reports were received and laid upon the table.

On motion of Mr. Stanard, *Ordered,* That the committee for courts of justice be discharged from the consideration of the petition of Bernard O'Neill, and that leave be granted to the petitioner to withdraw his said petition.

Mr. Sherrard presented a petition of citizens of the county of Berkeley, opposed to the removal of the separate election in said county from Thomas Robinson's mill, and in favour of the establishment of a separate election at Hedgesville, which was ordered to be laid upon the table.

Mr. Johnson presented a petition of John Heth and others, for the incorporation of a company to construct a rail-way from the Chesterfield coal mines to some point on James river above Bosher's dam.

Mr. Gilmer, a petition of citizens of the counties of Albemarle and Nelson, for the passage of an act empowering the county courts of said counties to cause to be constructed a road from the head waters of Rockfish river to the town of Scottsville.

Ordered, That the said petitions be referred to the committee of roads and internal navigation, that they do examine the matter thereof, and report their opinion thereupon to the house.

Mr. Woolfolk presented a petition of citizens of the county of Orange, asking for a division of said county, forming a new county out of the same.

Mr. Hail of Grayson, a petition of citizens of the county of Grayson, for an amendment to the act incorporating the Grayson Sulphur springs company.

Mr. Brown of Petersburg, presented a petition of citizens of Petersburg, praying for authority to the common hall to open a new street between Union and Market streets in said town.

Also a memorial of John T. Robertson, opposing the opening of said street in the said town.

Ordered, That the said petitions be referred to the committee of propositions and grievances, that they do examine the matter thereof, and report their opinion thereupon to the house.

Mr. Grinalds presented a petition of the heirs at law of Francis F. Dunlap, asking to be allowed the usual amount of bounty land for services rendered by their ancestor during the revolution, which was ordered to be referred to the committee on revolutionary claims, that they do examine the matter thereof, and report their opinion thereupon to the house.

The order of the day for the house to resolve itself into a committee of the whole house, to take into consideration the report of the select committee, upon the subject of expunging from the journals of the senate of the United States, a resolution of that body, being read, a motion was made by Mr. Carter, that the execution of the said order of the day be postponed until Monday next, and the question being put thereupon, was determined in the negative. Ayes 53, noes 70.

On motion of Mr. Woolfolk, (seven of the members present concurring,) *Ordered,* That the ayes and noes upon the said question be inserted in the journal.

The names of the gentlemen who voted in the affirmative, are Messrs. Grinalds, Drummond, Gilmer, Southall, Garland of Amherst, Brooke, Craig, Campbell, Pate, Hunter of Berkeley, Henshaw, Mallory, Beuhring, Johnson, Wilson of Cumberland, Servant, Hunter of Essex, Price, Hale of Franklin, Smith of Frederick, Smith of Gloucester, Wethered, Mullen, Botts, Gregory, Griggs, Berry, Summers, Fleet, Hooe, Carter, Neill, Beard, Powell, Taylor of Loudoun, Waggener, Murdaugh, Parker, Leland, Chapline, Masters, Swanson, Witcher, Morris, Dorman, Leyburn, Harley, Butts, Delashmutt, Jett, Prentiss, Brown of Petersburg, and Stanard.—53.

And the names of the gentlemen who voted in the negative, are Messrs. Banks, (speaker,) Layne, M'Clintic, Miller, Wilson of Botetourt, Decamps, Turnbull, Booker, Austin, Daniel, Samuel, Richardson, Hill, Smith of Fauquier, Hickerson, Strange, Steger, Holland, Bowen, Davison, Watts, Watkins, Hail of Grayson, Avent, Carrington, Coleman, Sloan, Nixon, Goodall, Harrison, Kincheloe, Fontaine, Holleman, Robinson, Hays, Straton, Harris, Ragsdale, Taylor of Mathews and Middlesex, Rogers, Garland of Mecklenburg, Willey, Morgan, Chapman, Ingles, Sherrard, Brown of Nelson, Fitzgerald, Woolfolk, Almond, Adams, M'Coy, Hopkins, Carroll, Madison, Shands, Williams, Nicklin, Moffett, Conrad, Jessee, M'Mullen, Bare, Rinker, Crutchfield, Moncure, Spratley, Hargrave, Gibson and Saunders.—70.

The house then resolved itself into a committee of the whole house, to take the said report into consideration; Mr. Miller in the chair; and after some time spent therein the speaker resumed the chair, and Mr. Miller reported that the said committee had taken the subject into consideration, and instructed him to report the said preamble and resolutions to the house without amendment.

The said report and resolutions were then taken up; and the same being under discussion,

On motion of Mr. Price, the house adjourned until to-morrow 12 o'clock.

SATURDAY, January 23d, 1836.

A communication from the senate by their clerk:

IN SENATE, January 22d, 1836.

The senate have agreed to the resolution for the election of an auditor of public accounts, second auditor, treasurer of the commonwealth and register of the land office.

Mr. Vaughan, the delegate from the county of Dinwiddie, appeared and took his seat.

Ordered, That he be added to the committee of propositions and grievances, in lieu of Mr. Scott, resigned.

On motion of Mr. Sherrard, *Resolved,* That the committee on the militia laws be instructed to enquire into the expediency of allowing to David Stickley, assignee of Peter Klipstine, the amount due him for three stands of colours to the 13th regiment of Virginia militia, and that said committee have leave to report by bill or otherwise.

Mr. Sherrard also presented a document to support the said claim, which was ordered to be referred to the said committee.

On motion of Mr. Fontaine, *Resolved by the general assembly,* That the board of public works be required to cause a survey of Smith's river, towards improving the navigation thereof, and to report the probable cost of making said improvement to the said board; and should the previous engagements of the state engineer or his assistants be such as will prevent them from performing the said work in the course of the next spring or summer, that the said board employ an engineer to make the said survey.

Ordered, That the clerk communicate the same to the senate and request their concurrence.

Mr. Gilmer submitted a resolution, which on his motion was laid upon the table: the same is the following:

Resolved by the general assembly of Virginia, That the board of public works are hereby directed to employ a competent engineer, to survey a route for a rail-road from Gordonsville, in the county of Orange, to Harrisonburg, in the county of Rockingham, and from Gordonsville to the Rivanna river, at or near Charlottesville in the county of Albemarle, and report to the next general assembly his estimate of the cost of constructing the same, and the advantages which, in his opinion, will result to the commonwealth.

On motion of Mr. Madison, a report of the committee on agriculture and manufactures, reporting it expedient to establish an extra grade of flour above that of superfine, was taken up, and ordered to be recommitted to the said committee.

Mr. Wethered, according to order, presented a bill to amend an act incorporating the Spring creek turnpike company.

Mr. Watkins, from the committee on roads and internal navigation, presented a report upon the petition of John Heth and others, citizens of the county of Chesterfield and city of Richmond, for a rail-road from the coal mines to James river.

And a bill incorporating the Laurel hill turnpike company.

Mr. Stanard, from the committee for courts of justice, presented a report upon the resolution concerning witnesses.

Which bills and reports were received and laid upon the table.

An engrossed bill concerning the town of Portsmouth, was taken up, on motion of Mr. Murdaugh, and read a third time:

Resolved, That the bill do pass, and that the title be, "an act concerning the town of Portsmouth."

Ordered, That Mr. Murdaugh carry the same to the senate and request their concurrence.

Mr. Crutchfield presented a petition of the representatives of Dr. William Rumney, asking to be allowed the bounty in land due to their ancestor for his services as a surgeon during the revolutionary war.

Also, a petition of the heirs of William Ramsay, a surgeon's mate, during the revolution, asking to be allowed the bounty in land due to their ancestor for his services.

Mr. Robinson presented similar petitions for land bounty, from the heirs of Reuben Butler; and of the heirs of Thomas Waring.

Mr. Carter, a similar petition of Henry Fauntleroy, devisee of the late Robert Fauntleroy.

Mr. Hickerson, similar petitions of the heirs of Lincefield Sharpe, and of the heirs of Joseph Blackwell.

Ordered, That the said petitions be referred to the committee on revolutionary claims, that they do examine the matter thereof, and report their opinion thereupon to the house.

Mr. Beuhring presented a petition of Ann, a free woman of colour, praying to be permitted to remain in the commonwealth, which was ordered to be referred to the committee for courts of justice, that they do examine the matter thereof, and report their opinion thereupon to the house.

Mr. Chapline presented a petition of Daniel and Ebenezer Zane, asking the repeal of the act defining the boundaries of the town of Wheeling.

Mr. Leland, a petition of citizens of the county of Northumberland, for the establishment of a separate election at the place called the Burned Chimnies in said county.

Ordered, That the said petitions be referred to the committee of propositions and grievances, that they do examine the matter thereof, and report their opinion thereupon to the house.

Mr. Bowen presented a petition of inhabitants of the county of Frederick, asking for an enlargement of the capital of the Bank of the Valley in Virginia and its branches, and of the branch of the Farmers bank situated at Winchester, which was ordered to be referred to the committee on banks, that they do examine the matter thereof, and report their opinion thereupon to the house.

Mr. Brown of Petersburg, presented a petition of sundry merchants and ship owners of the town of Petersburg, praying amendments of the law regulating the duties and fees of pilots on the James river, which was ordered to be referred to the select committee on that subject, that they do examine the matter thereof, and report their opinion thereupon to the house.

On motion of Mr. Price, the report of the committee upon the propriety of expunging from the journals of the senate of the United States, a resolution of that body condemning certain acts of the president of the United States, was taken up, and the question being upon adopting the first resolution, and Mr. Gregory having demanded the ayes and noes thereon,

On motion of Mr. Mullen, the house adjourned until Monday 12 o'clock.

MONDAY, January 25th, 1836.

On motion of Mr. Powell, *Resolved*, That so much of the annual message of the executive as refers to the subject of revolutionary land bounty claims, be referred to the committee on revolutionary claims.

Resolved, That the same committee be instructed to enquire into the expediency of amending the act of assembly passed on the 21st February, 1833; and also, the act which passed on the 11th March, 1834, so as to provide some other and more suitable tribunal for the examination and decision of claims for land bounties promised to the officers and soldiers of the army of the revolution, by the various acts of assembly, passed during the war of the revolution, and after that period, and that said committee have leave to report by bill or otherwise.

On motion of Mr. Brooke, *Resolved*, That this house will on Wednesday next, proceed jointly with the senate, to the election of a secretary to the commonwealth and librarian of the state for the ensuing year.

Ordered, That the clerk communicate the same to the senate and request their concurrence.

On motion of Mr. Dorman, *Resolved*, That the committee for courts of justice be instructed to enquire into the expediency of providing by law for furnishing the several county court offices with a transcript from the abstract books in the register's office, shewing the number and dates of all the patents which have issued and which shall hereafter issue for lands in this commonwealth, and that said committee have leave to report by bill or otherwise.

On motion of Mr. Butts, *Ordered*, That leave be given to bring in a bill to authorize the county court of Southampton county to appoint processioners of lands in said county, and that Messrs. Butts, Morris, Benton, Vaughan, Avent, Hargrave, Turnbull and Ragsdale prepare and bring in the same.

On motion of Mr. Almond, *Resolved*, That the committee for courts of justice be instructed to enquire into the expediency of so amending the act concerning slaves, free negroes and mulattoes, passed March 2d, 1819, as to secure more effectually to creditors and other persons their rights to the services of slaves emancipated by will or otherwise, where such slaves shall be chargeable, or in any way liable to creditors, with leave to report by bill or otherwise.

Mr. Hunter of Essex, from the committee on the penitentiary, presented a report upon the petition of citizens of the county of Bedford, for the release of Anderson Read, a convict in the penitentiary.

Mr. Hill, from the committee of propositions and grievances, presented a report upon the petitions of sundry citizens of the county of Orange, and of the town of Salem in the county of Botetourt.

Which were received and laid upon the table.

Mr. Chapline presented a petition of the president and directors of the North-western bank of Virginia, for an amendment of the charter of the said bank, so as to increase its capital and extend the time of its existence.

Mr. Beard, a petition of citizens of the county of Loudoun, for an increase of the capital of the Bank of the Valley in Virginia and its branches, and of the branch of the Farmers bank at Winchester.

Ordered, That the said petitions be referred to the committee on banks, that they do examine the matter thereof, and report their opinion thereupon to the house.

Mr. Ball presented a petition of the clerk of the superior court of Fairfax, and a portion of the bar of said county, asking for a change in the time of holding the superior courts for said county.

Mr. Stanard presented petitions of Bassett Saunders, and of Milley, free persons of colour, asking permission to remain in the commonwealth.

Mr. Davison, a petition of sundry citizens of the county of Frederick, praying that Jonas Baker, a free man of colour, may be permitted to remain in the commonwealth.

Mr. Hill, a petition of citizens of the counties of Culpeper and Madison, that Robin, a free man of colour, may be permitted to remain in the commonwealth.

Ordered, That the said petitions be referred to the committee for courts of justice, that they do examine the matter thereof, and report their opinion thereupon to the house.

Mr. Ball also presented a petition of the president and directors of the Fallsbridge turnpike company, asking for the passage of a law authorizing a lottery to raise a sum of money to pay their debts and to complete their road.

Mr. Willey, a petition of George Price and others, asking that James Kern may be authorized to increase the height of his mill dam across the Monongalia river, in the county of Monongalia.

Mr. Avent, a petition of citizens of the county of Greensville, praying that the charter of the Greensville and Wilkins' ferry rail-road company may be so amended as to give to the company the power to locate a public road on the side of their rail-road.

Ordered, That said petitions be referred to the committee of roads and internal navigation, that they do examine the matter thereof, and report their opinion thereupon to the house.

Mr. Daniel presented a petition of citizens of the town of Lynchburg, for the incorporation of the Lynchburg female academy; which was ordered to be referred to the committee of schools and colleges, that they do examine the matter thereof, and report their opinion thereupon to the house.

Mr. Cook presented a petition of Solomon Tomlinson, administrator of the estate of Richard Kelsick, unadministered by Richard Kelsick, the former administrator, stating that his intestate in 1773, was part owner of a vessel which was insured by certain merchants in the borough of Norfolk; that the vessel was afterwards lost, and these merchants became responsible for the insurance; that they afterwards joined the British, and their property was confiscated and paid into the public treasury; and asking that the amount thus due for the insurance of the said vessel may now be paid out of the treasury; which petition was ordered to be referred to the committee of claims, that they do examine the matter thereof, and report their opinion thereupon to the house.

On motion of Mr. Dorman, *Resolved,* That when this house adjourns to-day, it will adjourn until to-morrow 11 o'clock.

On motion of Mr. Gilmer, the report of the committee on the subject of expunging from the journals of the senate of the United States a resolution of that body, was taken up; and the question of adopting the first resolution being still under discussion,

On motion of Mr. Hopkins, the house adjourned until to-morrow 11 o'clock.

TUESDAY, January 26th, 1836.

On motion of Mr. Saunders, *Resolved by the general assembly of Virginia,* That the board of public works be directed to employ an engineer to survey a road from Evansham in the county of Wythe, to Jeffersonville in the county of Tazewell, that he do report the estimated cost of constructing the said road, and also the advantages which, in his opinion, will result to the public if the same shall be constructed.

Ordered, That the clerk communicate the same to the senate and request their concurrence.

On motion of Mr. Carrington, *Ordered,* That leave be given to bring in a bill incorporating the Gills' mountain gold mining company in the county of Halifax, and that Messrs. Carrington, Coleman, Swanson, Holland, Pate, Adams, Daniel and Campbell prepare and bring in the same.

On motion of Mr. Garland of Amherst, *Resolved,* That the committee of roads and internal navigation be directed to enquire into the expediency of authorizing the board of public works to dispose of any portion of the stock held by the state in any rail-road, turnpike road, or navigation company, whenever such stock will command its par value or more, with leave to report by bill or otherwise.

On motion of Mr. Murdaugh, *Resolved,* That the committee of roads and internal navigation be instructed to enquire into the expediency of providing by a general law, a form for all road and navigation companies hereafter to be incorporated, and that said committee report by bill or otherwise.

On motion of Mr. Taylor of Middlesex, *Resolved,* That a select committee be appointed to bring in a bill to amend the act, passed the 24th March, 1831, for the protection of the oysters in the waters of Ware river, Severn river and others, so as to extend the provisions of said act to the Piankatank river, Milford haven, East river and Horn harbour, in conformity with the petition of certain citizens of the county of Mathews.

And a committee was appointed of Messrs. Taylor of Middlesex, Smith of Gloucester, Hunter of Essex, Hooe, Leyburn, Leland, Crutchfield, Murdaugh, Servant, Drummond, Morris, Wilson of Botetourt, and Fleet.

Mr. Taylor of Middlesex also presented the said petition of citizens of the county of Mathews on the said subject, which was ordered to be referred to the said committee.

Mr. Watkins, from the committee of roads and internal navigation, presented a report upon the petition of the mayor and commonalty of the borough of Norfolk, for an extension of the Portsmouth and Roanoke rail-road to the said borough.

Mr. Moncure, according to order, presented a bill to incorporate the New Hope gold mine company.

Mr. Madison, from the committee on agriculture and manufactures, presented a report upon the petition of Edward Colston.

Mr. Summers, from the select committee on that subject, presented a bill providing for a geological survey of the state and for other purposes.

Which were severally received and laid upon the table.

Mr. Sherrard, from the committee appointed to examine the office of the auditor of public accounts, presented a report, which, on his motion, was read as follows:

The committee appointed to examine the first auditor's office, having in discharge of their duty closed the examination, respectfully submit the following report:

That soon after their appointment they commenced the performance of the arduous duty assigned them, and prosecuted it to its completion, with as much expedition as a due regard to other indispensable duties would permit.

The books, papers, condition of the office generally, and the manner of discharging the difficult, various and complicated duties of those employed in it, have received the careful attention of the committee, and enable them to report, that the duties of the auditor and of the clerks employed, have been faithfully discharged, and with due regard to the provisions of law.

The annual report of the auditor, made to the general assembly at the commencement of the session, has received the careful attention of the committee, been compared with the entries on the books of the office and found correct.

The immense number of vouchers upon which warrants have been granted for the payment of money from the treasury during the past year, is such as to preclude the possibility of a critical examination of each, as such an examination would require more time than an ordinary session of the legislature would afford, but as many have been selected for special examination, and in such a way, as to give, in the opinion of your committee, a just general idea of the whole. Those most important received special attention, and your committee are satisfied that in issuing the warrants, a due regard has been had to all the provisions of law relating to them.

The ability with which the books are kept, entries made, papers filed and arranged, have, with assistance rendered by the clerks, greatly aided your committee in the discharge of its duties, and were well calculated to lead to the detection of errors, should any exist.

The papers of the office, books and documents, are as well arranged, secured, and in as good order and state of preservation, as the defective condition of the room in which they are kept, will permit.

But your committee regret, that it has become its duty to report, that without any blame attributable to any one of the officers in this department, many valuable papers and documents are exposed to injury, in a gradual state of decay, and in a condition to be totally destroyed; and as no remedy can be applied to this state of things by those in charge of the office, it becomes the duty of the legislature speedily to provide one.

The present office was never well calculated for the purposes to which it is appropriated, and it is now more manifest than ever, that it does not answer those for which it is used; not only too small for the convenient arrangement and security of the public records and papers belonging to it, and for public accommodation, but it is often too dark for the transactions of public business. The thickness of its walls, its numerous angles and arches, obstruct the light, and a degree of darkness and dampness is experienced pernicious to the occupants and destructive of the public property in it. A want of fires and ventilation, renders it uncomfortable in winter, and the latter cause equally so in the warmer seasons, not only to those employed in it, but to all whose business calls them there; in one room there is no fire-place, and from its peculiar construction there can be none, and unless some change is speedily made, the transaction of public business must be materially retarded.

To the auditor is confided by law, the care and preservation of the public papers and property in his possession, and he is in a high degree responsible for their safety and preservation, most of which are of incalculable value not only to the commonwealth generally, but to almost every individual in it, as well as to many elsewhere; their destruction by fire, moisture and other causes to which they are daily and nightly exposed, would be of infinite injury to the whole country, and sound policy seems to require that existing defects should be enquired into by the legislature, and a speedy remedy applied, and this is due not only to the best interests of the commonwealth, but to those the legislature may select to discharge the duties of the office.

In no one of the departments of the government do the public documents accumulate as rapidly as in this; and it cannot have escaped the observation of any one, whose attention has been drawn to the subject, that the evils referred to, now almost intolerable, are daily increasing, and that valuable records are now exposed without any place to secure them in.

This subject has been brought to the notice of the legislature for the last several previous sessions, by committees charged with the examination of the office, as well as by several annual executive communications previous to the last; to all of which your committee would ask the attention of the legislature, shewing their entire concurrence with the views now presented, and founded as all have been on personal inspection, and seem to your committee to be perfectly correct.

The proper sort of substitute your committee would prefer, they forbear for the present to suggest, not doubting that, as the attention of the legislature is again earnestly drawn to this important subject, one may be devised that would meet the approbation of all; and as your committee is fully impressed, not only with the importance but the absolute necessity of providing one, submit the following resolution:

Resolved, That other and more convenient and safe apartments ought to be provided for the office of auditor of public accounts.

The said resolution was, on the question put thereupon, agreed to by the house, and on motion of Mr. Sherrard, was ordered to be referred to the committee of finance.

Mr. Butts, according to order, presented a bill to authorize the county court of Southampton to appoint processioners of lands, which was read the first, and on his motion the second time, and ordered to be recommitted to the committee which brought it in.

The speaker laid before the house a letter from Anthony M. Dupey, secretary to the Danville rail-road convention, enclosing the proceedings of that body, which, on motion of Mr. Murdaugh, was ordered to be referred to the committee of roads and internal navigation.

Mr. Cunningham presented a petition of the president and directors of the Dismal swamp canal company, for authority to increase the capital stock of said company, and to consolidate their debt to be converted into stock; which was also ordered to be referred to the said committee, that they do examine the matter thereof, and report their opinion thereupon to the house.

Mr. Henshaw presented a petition of the administrator of George and Thomas Walls, asking the appropriation of funds from the treasury, to satisfy judgments obtained against the commonwealth for the commutation pay due to major George Walls and lieutenant Thomas Walls, officers of Crockett's regiment in the revolutionary war.

Mr. Sloan, a petition of John J. Jacobs, administrator of colonel David Rogers, asking that the usual bounty in lands may be granted for the services of the said Rogers during the revolution.

Ordered, That the said petitions be referred to the committee on revolutionary claims, that they do examine the matter thereof, and report their opinion thereupon to the house.

Mr. Masters presented a petition of citizens of Elizabethtown and Moundsville in the county of Marshall, asking an amendment to the act incorporating a savings institution in said county, which was ordered to be referred to the committee on banks, that they do examine the matter thereof, and report their opinion thereupon to the house.

Mr. Johnson presented a petition of Albert Michaels and others, for an act incorporating a company to explore and mine for coal in the counties of Chesterfield and Powhatan, which was ordered to be referred to the committee on agriculture and manufactures, that they do examine the matter thereof, and report their opinion thereupon to the house.

Mr. M'Mullen presented a petition of J. D. Grigsby, asking to be divorced from his wife, which was ordered to be referred to the committee for courts of justice, that they do examine the matter thereof, and report their opinion thereupon to the house.

An engrossed bill to enact an act of the general assembly of North Carolina, entitled, "an act to incorporate the Roanoke, Danville and Junction rail-road company," was taken up; whereupon, a clause by way of ryder thereto, was offered by Mr. Witcher, which was read the first and second times, and ordered to be engrossed and read a third time; and the said bill and ryder was ordered to be laid upon the table.

An engrossed bill to provide for the construction of a road across the Blue Ridge at Milam's gap, was read a third time, and the question being put, "shall the said bill pass?" was determined in the negative. Ayes 48, noes 49

On motion of Mr. Adams, (seven of the members present concurring,) *Ordered*, That the ayes and noes upon the said question be inserted in the journal.

The names of the gentlemen who voted in the affirmative, are Messrs. Banks, (speaker,) Layne, Wiley, Garland of Amherst, Brooke, M'Clintic, Hunter of Berkeley, Wilson of Botetourt, Decampe, Beuhring, Hill, Hickerson, Price, Strange, Steger, Davison, Sloan, Mullen, Harrison, Kincheloe, Berry, Hooe, Carter, Hays, Straton, Powell, Taylor of Loudoun, Waggener, Willey, Morgan, Brown of Nelson, Chapline, Masters, Woolfolk, Almond, M'Coy, Cackley, Madison, Morris, Williams, Marteney, Moffett, Conrad, Jessee, Rinker, Harley, Delashmutt and Gibson.—48.

And the names of the gentlemen who voted in the negative, are Messrs. Grinalds, Drummond, Pate, Turnbull, Mallory, Booker, Austin, Samuel, Christian, Johnson, Wilson of Cumberland, Vaughan, Smith of Fauquier, Hale of Franklin, Holland, Smith of Gloucester, Hail of Grayson, Avent, Carrington, Coleman, Botts, Fontaine, Gregory, Fleet, Robinson, Neill, Harris, Garland of Mecklenburg, Ingles, Sherrard, Benton, Cooke, Parker, Leland, Fitzgerald, Adams, Swanson, Witcher, Hopkins, Shands, Dorman, Leyburn, M'Mullen, Butts, Jett, Saunders, Cunningham, Brown of Petersburg, and Stanard.—49.

Resolved, That the said bill be rejected.

The speaker laid before the house a communication from John Brockenbrough, president of the Bank of Virginia, furnishing the "information required of the president and directors of the bank by a resolution of the house of delegates, passed the 16th instant," which was received and laid upon the table.

The report of the committee on the subject of expunging from the journals of the senate of the United States a resolution of that body, was taken up on motion of Mr. Hopkins, and the question of adopting the first resolution being still under discussion,

On motion of Mr. Prentiss, the house adjourned until to-morrow 11 o'clock.

WEDNESDAY, January 27th, 1836.

A communication from the senate by their clerk:

IN SENATE, January 26th, 1836.

The senate have passed the bill, entitled,
"An act to incorporate the stockholders of the City Point rail-road company.".
And they have agreed to the resolution for the election of a secretary to the commonwealth and librarian.

Mr. Murdaugh submitted the following resolution, which, on motion of Mr. Cunningham, was ordered to be laid upon the table:

Resolved, That the committee of roads and internal navigation be instructed to enquire into the expediency of incorporating a joint stock company to construct one or more boats to transport produce, merchandize and other articles across Elizabeth river between Norfolk and Portsmouth, and that said committee report by bill or otherwise.

On motion of Mr. Cunningham, the communication submitted on yesterday from the president of the bank of Virginia was taken up, and ordered to be referred to the committee on banks, and that 185 copies thereof be printed for the use of the general assembly.

An engrossed bill to amend the act, entitled, "an act incorporating the Falmouth and Alexandria rail-road company," was read a third time:

Resolved, That the bill do pass, and that the title be, "an act to amend the act, entitled, 'an act incorporating the Falmouth and Alexandria rail-road company.'"

Ordered, That the clerk communicate the said bill to the senate and request their concurrence.

The house according to the joint orders of the day, proceeded by joint vote with the senate, to the election of an auditor of public accounts, the second auditor, the treasurer, the register of the land office, and secretary to the commonwealth and librarian, and the rule of the house requiring one election to be made at a time having been suspended, on motion of Mr. Sherrard, he nominated for the office of auditor of public accounts, James E. Heath, esq.; Mr. Dorman nominated for the office of second auditor, James Brown, jr. esq.; Mr. Garland of Amherst, nominated for the office of treasurer, Lawson Burfoot, esq.; Mr. Summers nominated for the office of register, William Selden, esq.; and Mr. Brooke nominated for the office of secretary to the commonwealth and librarian, William H. Richardson, esq.; and the senate having been informed thereof by Mr. Sherrard, and no person having been added to the nomination in that house, and they agreeing to the mode of election indicated, the names of the members were called by the clerk, when there appeared an unanimous vote for each person in nomination.

The names of the gentlemen thus voting, are Messrs. Banks, (speaker,) Grinalds, Drummond, Layne, Wiley, Garland of Amherst, Brooke, M'Clintic, Campbell, Pate, Hunter of Berkeley, Henshaw, Decampe, Turnbull, Mallory, Booker, Austin, Beuhring, Daniel, Samuel, Christian, Richardson, Johnson, Hill, Wilson of Cumberland, Vaughan, Servant, Hunter of Essex, Ball, Smith of Fauquier, Hickerson, Price, Strange, Steger, Hale of Franklin, Holland, Davison, Smith of Frederick, Watts, Smith of Gloucester, Carrington, Coleman, Sloan, Nixon, Mullen, Harrison, Kincheloe, Botts, Fontaine, Holleman, Gregory, Griggs, Berry, Summers, Fleet, Hooe, Robinson, Neill, Hays, Straton, Beard, Powell, Taylor of Loudoun, Harris, Ragsdale, Waggener, Rogers, Garland of Mecklenburg, Willey, Morgan, Chapman, Ingles, Sherrard, Benton, Brown of Nelson, Murdaugh, Cooke, Parker, Leland, Fitzgerald, Chapline, Masters, Almond, Adams, M'Coy, Swanson, Witcher, Cackley, Hopkins, Madison, Morris, Williams, Marteney, Nicklin, Conrad, Jessee, M'Mullen, Bare, Rinker, Harley, Butts, Crutchfield, Spratley, Gillespie, Delashmutt, Gibson, Jett, Prentiss, Cunningham, Brown of Petersburg, and Stanard.—111.

Ordered, That Messrs. Sherrard, Summers, Brooke, Garland of Amherst, Dorman, Jessee, Almond, Ingles, Robinson and Marteney, be a committee to act jointly with a committee from the senate to ascertain the result of the joint vote: the committee withdrew, and after some time returned into the house, and Mr. Sherrard reported that they had according to order, ascertained the joint vote to be for each person in nomination 137 votes; whereupon, James E. Heath, esq., was declared duly elected auditor of public accounts; James Brown, jr. esq., the second auditor; Lawson Burfoot, esq. the treasurer of the commonwealth; William Selden, esq., register of the land office, and William H. Richardson, esq., secretary to the commonwealth and librarian, each for one year from the expiration of their respective terms of office.

An engrossed bill to incorporate the Union Potomac company, was read a third time; whereupon, a clause by way of ryder thereto, was offered by Mr. Sherrard, which was read the first and second times, and the said bill and ryder was, on motion of Mr. Booker, ordered to be laid upon the table.

On motion of Mr. Crutchfield, *Resolved,* That the committee for courts of justice be instructed to enquire into the expediency of amending an act, entitled, "an act concerning the session of the circuit superior court of law and chancery for the county of Spottsylvania," passed January 19th, 1833; and also, into the propriety of changing the times of holding the superior courts of law and chancery of the third judicial district, and that they report thereon, together or separately, by bill or otherwise.

The speaker laid before the house a communication from Philip N. Nicholas, president of the Farmers bank of Virginia, furnishing the information required by a resolution of the house of delegates on the 16th instant, which, on motion of Mr. Carter, was ordered to be laid upon the table.

The report of the committee on the subject of expunging from the journal of the senate of the United States a resolution adopted by that body, was taken up, and the first resolution being under discussion,

On motion of Mr. Parker, the house adjourned until to-morrow 11 o'clock.

THURSDAY, January 28th, 1836.

A communication from the senate by their clerk:

IN SENATE, January 27th, 1836.

The senate have agreed to the resolution requiring the board of public works to cause a survey of Smith's river, with an amendment, in which they request the concurrence of the house of delegates.

The said amendment being twice read, was, on the question put thereupon, agreed to by the house.

Ordered, That the clerk inform the senate thereof.

On motion of Mr. Henshaw, *Ordered,* That the committee on revolutionary claims be discharged from the consideration of the petition of George and Thomas Walls, and that the same be referred to the committee of finance.

On motion of Mr. Cunningham, the communication of the president of the Farmers bank of Virginia, laid on the table on yesterday, was taken up and ordered to be referred to the committee on banks, and 185 copies thereof were ordered to be printed for the use of the general assembly.

On motion of Mr. Miller, *Resolved,* That the joint committee on the library, be instructed to enquire into the expediency of amending the existing regulations of the library.

On motion of Mr. Watkins, the report of the committee of roads and internal navigation, upon the petition of the superintendents and trustees of the Upper Appomattox company, was taken up, and ordered to be recommitted to the said committee.

On motion of Mr. Jessee, *Resolved,* That the committee for courts of justice be instructed to enquire into the expediency of requiring by law that the jailor of each county shall reside in the dwellings that are now or may hereafter be attached to said jails, for the better security of prisoners, and that they have leave to report by bill or otherwise.

On motion of Mr. Murdaugh, *Ordered,* That leave be given to bring in a bill to amend the sixth section of the act, passed March 11th, 1835, directing the governor to cause houses or shelters to be erected for the protection and preservation of the equipments of the Richmond Fayette, and the Portsmouth artillery companies; and that Messrs. Murdaugh, Gregory, Stanard, Cooke, Cunningham, Goodall, Botts and Robinson, prepare and bring in the same.

On motion of Mr. Ball, *Resolved,* That the select committee on abolition be instructed to enquire into the expediency of instructing our senators and requesting our representatives in the congress of the United States to use their best efforts to procure such alterations in the laws relating to the post office department, as may be best calculated to prevent the transmission through the mail of all incendiary publications.

Mr. Gregory submitted the following resolution, which, on motion of Mr. Parker, was ordered to be laid upon the table:

Resolved, That the select committee on abolition be instructed to enquire into the expediency of preventing free negroes and mulattoes who go from this state to non-slaveholding states, from returning into this state.

Mr. Watkins submitted the following resolutions:

Whereas the general assembly of Virginia did, on the eleventh day of February, in the year one thousand eight hundred and thirty-four, agree to a "preamble and resolutions on the subject of the removal of the public deposits from the Bank of the United States, and against the power claimed by congress to establish a United States bank," which are in the words and figures following, to wit:

"Whereas the general assembly of Virginia deem it of the utmost importance, that the power to control the public revenue should be made to abide, in practice, where it has been vested by the constitution, in the immediate representatives of the people, and of the states, in congress assembled; and all experience of the practical operation of governments has proved, that arbitrary assumptions of power by them, or any officer of them, if silently acquiesced in, become precedents for farther and still greater acts of usurpation: Therefore,

"1. *Resolved by the general assembly,* That the recent act of the president of the United States, exerting a control over the public deposits, by causing them to be withheld and withdrawn, on his own responsibility, from the United States bank, in which they had been ordered to be placed by the act of congress chartering the said bank, is, in the judgment of the general assembly, a dangerous and alarming assumption of power by that officer, which cannot be too strongly condemned.

"2. *Resolved,* That while the general assembly will ever be ready to sustain the president in the exercise of all such powers as the constitution has confided to him, they, nevertheless, cannot but regard, with apprehension and distrust, the disposition to extend his official authority beyond its just and proper limits, which he has so clearly manifested in his recent interference with the treasury department of the federal government, in the exercise of a sound discretion which congress had confided to the head of that department alone.

"3. *Resolved,* That our senators in congress be instructed, and our representatives requested, to use their best exertions to procure the adoption, by congress, of proper measures for restoring the public moneys to the Bank of the United States, or, at least, for causing them to be deposited therein for the future, according to the direction and stipulation of the act of congress chartering the said bank, if, at the time of their action on the subject, the said bank be, in their opinion, a safe depository of the public treasure.

"4. *Resolved,* That the general assembly cannot recognize as constitutional the power which has been claimed by congress to establish a United States bank, because, in the opinion of the general assembly, as they have heretofore solemnly declared, that power is not given to congress by the constitution of the United States.

"5. *Resolved,* That the general assembly do not intend, by the declaration of their opinion in regard to the unconstitutionality of the Bank of the United States, to qualify, or in any manner to impair the force of their disapprobation of the withholding and withdrawing of the public deposites.

"6. *Resolved,* That the governor of the commonwealth be requested to transmit a copy of these resolutions to each of our senators and representatives in the congress of the United States."

And whereas the general assembly had rightful authority to act upon the subject of the aforesaid preamble and resolutions, but the same having been, without just cause, improvidently adopted, (with the exception of the fourth resolution): Therefore,

Resolved by this general assembly of Virginia, That the said recited preamble and resolutions (except the fourth,) be, and the same are hereby rescinded, and declared null and void.

A motion was made by Mr. Watkins, that the said resolutions be laid upon the table, and the question being put thereupon, was determined in the affirmative. Ayes 77, noes 30.

On motion of Mr. Henshaw, (seven of the members present concurring,) *Ordered,* That the ayes and noes upon the said question be inserted in the journal.

The names of the gentlemen who voted in the affirmative, are Messrs. Banks, (speaker,) Layne, Wiley, M'Clintic, Miller, Decamps, Turnbull, Mallory, Booker, Austin, Samuel, Richardson, Johnson, Hill, Wilson of Cumberland, Vaughan, Hunter of Essex, Smith of Fauquier, Strange, Steger, Holland, Watkins, Hail of Grayson, Carrington, Coleman, Sloan, Nixon, Goodall, Harrison, Kincheloe, Fontaine, Gregory, Griggs, Berry, Fleet, Robinson, Hays, Beard, Taylor of Loudoun, Harris, Ragsdale, Taylor of Mathews and Middlesex, Rogers, Garland of Mecklenburg, Willey, Morgan, Chapman, Ingles, Sherrard, Brown of Nelson, Cooke, Leland, Fitzgerald, Woolfolk, Almond, Adams, M'Coy, Cackley, Hopkins, Carroll, Madison, Williams, Marteney, Moffett, Conrad, Jessee, M'Mullen, Bare, Rinker, Harley, Crutchfield, Moncure, Spratley, Gillespie, Gibson, Saunders, and Brown of Petersburg.—77.

And the names of the gentlemen who voted in the negative, are Messrs. Grinalds, Garland of Amherst, Brooke, Campbell, Hunter of Berkeley, Henshaw, Beuhring, Christian, Ball, Smith of Gloucester, Summers, Hooe, Carter, Powell, Waggener, Benton, Murdaugh, Parker, Chapline, Masters, Swanson, Witcher, Morris, Dorman, Leyburn, Butts, Jett, Prentiss, Cunningham and Stanard.—30.

On motion of Mr. Watkins, *Ordered,* That 185 copies thereof be printed for the use of the general assembly.

On motion of Gregory, (a member voting with the majority,) the rule of the house requiring a question once decided to remain as the judgment of the house, was suspended, and the vote rejecting an engrossed bill to provide for the construction of a road across the Blue Ridge at Milam's gap, was reconsidered; and the question being upon passing the said bill, on motion of Mr. Gregory, the same was ordered to be laid upon the table.

Mr. Watkins, from the committee of roads and internal navigation, presented reports upon the petition of the Dismal swamp canal company, and upon the resolution relating to the Warm springs and Harrisonburg turnpike company.

And a bill to amend the act, entitled, "an act making further provision for completing the road from Staunton to the mouth of the Little Kanawha."

Mr. Butts reported without amendment, a bill to authorize the county court of Southampton to appoint processioners of lands.

Mr. Hill, from the committee of propositions and grievances, presented a report upon the petition of citizens of the county of Grayson, and upon the petition of sundry citizens of the counties of Frederick and Shenandoah.

And a bill to establish the town of Lovettsville in the county of Loudoun.

Which were received and laid upon the table.

Mr. Layne presented a petition of sundry citizens of the county of Alleghany, asking a change in the location of the site for the contemplated bridge at Covington, which was ordered to be referred to the committee of roads and internal navigation, that they do examine the matter thereof, and report their opinion thereupon to the house.

Mr. Saunders presented a petition of citizens of the town of Evansham, that an act may be passed incorporating a company for the purpose of supplying the said town with water, which was ordered to be referred to the committee of propositions and grievances, that they do examine the matter thereof, and report their opinion thereupon to the house.

Mr. Stanard presented a petition of Nelly Hoomes, a free woman of colour, asking permission to remain in the commonwealth a limited time.

Mr. Wiley, a petition of David Skurry, a free man of colour, asking permission to remain in the commonwealth.

Ordered, That the said petitions be referred to the committee for courts of justice, that they do examine the matter thereof, and report their opinion thereupon to the house.

Mr. Holleman presented a petition of citizens of the county of Isle of Wight, for the passage of an act to incorporate the Smithfield savings institution, which was ordered to be referred to a committee of Messrs. Holleman, Hargrave, Shands, Avent, Turnbull, Vaughan, Benton and Morris, with leave to report by bill or otherwise.

On motion of Mr Sherrard, the engrossed bill to incorporate the Union, Potomac company was taken up; whereupon, the ryder submitted thereto by him on yesterday, was amended on motions severally made, and as amended, ordered to be engrossed and read a third time; and the said bill and ryder was again ordered to be laid upon the table.

On motion of Mr. Hunter of Berkeley, *Resolved,* That when this house adjourns to-day, it will adjourn until to-morrow 12 o'clock.

The report of the select committee upon the subject of expunging from the journals of the senate of the United States a resolution of that body, was taken up, and the first resolution having been under discussion, on motion of Mr. Holleman, the said report was ordered to be laid upon the table.

The engrossed bill to incorporate the Union Potomac company was taken up, on motion of Mr. Watkins, and the amended ryder having been engrossed, was read a third time:

Resolved, That the bill (with the ryder) do pass, and that the title be, "an act to incorporate the Union Potomac company."

Ordered, That the clerk communicate the same to the senate and request their concurrence.

On motion of Mr. Watkins, the house adjourned until to-morrow 12 o'clock.

FRIDAY, January 29th, 1836.

On motion of Mr. Gregory, the resolution submitted by him on yesterday, directing "the committee on abolition to enquire into the expediency of preventing free negroes and mulattoes who go from this state to non-slaveholding states, from returning into this state," was taken up, and being amended by the house on his motion, was, as amended, agreed to by the house, as follows:

Resolved, That the committee for courts of justice be instructed to enquire into the expediency of so amending the several laws concerning slaves, free negroes and mulattoes, as more effectually to prevent the return to this commonwealth of such free negroes, mulattoes, Indians or descendants of Indians, as may have left or may hereafter leave this state, and that said committee have leave to report by bill or otherwise.

On motion of Mr. Gregory, *Resolved,* That a select committee be raised for the purpose of enquiring into the most suitable and effectual way of removing the free negroes and mulattoes from this commonwealth.

Resolved, That said committee be required to enquire into the expediency of preventing slaves, free negroes and mulattoes from trading either in carts or boats from one county to another, or from a county to any of the towns of this commonwealth.

And a committee was appointed of Messrs. Gregory, Murdaugh, Botts, Goodall, Christian, Crutchfield, Turnbull, Cunningham, Layne, Watts, Delashmutt, Parker, M'Mullen, Hunter of Berkeley, and Hays.

On motion of Mr. Parker, *Resolved,* That leave be given to bring in a bill to amend and to extend the provisions of an act making appropriations for the removal of free persons of colour, and that the select committee just raised prepare and bring in the same.

Mr. Watkins, from the committee of roads and internal navigation, presented a report upon the petition of citizens of the counties of Loudoun and Fauquier, to amend the charter of the Goose creek navigation company.

Mr. Hill, from the committee of propositions and grievances, presented a report upon the petition of citizens of the town of Leesburg.

And a bill appointing commissioners to select a site for the seat of justice for the county of Ohio.

Which reports and bill were received and laid upon the table.

On motion of Mr. Watkins, the committee of roads and internal navigation were ordered to be discharged from the consideration of the petition of citizens of the county of Albemarle, for a rail-road from Lynchburg to the Tennessee line, and that the same be laid upon the table.

Mr. Goodall presented a petition of Jessee Winn, asking that the commonwealth's right to certain land may be released to him upon the payment of the arrears of taxes due thereon, which, on his motion was ordered to be referred to the committee for courts of justice, that they do examine the matter thereof, and report their opinion thereupon to the house.

The house according to the joint order of the day, proceeded by joint vote with the senate, to the election of a brigadier general for the eighteenth brigade of militia, to supply the vacancy occasioned by the death of general William M'Coy; whereupon, Mr. Sherrard nominated John Sloan, esq.; Mr. M'Coy nominated James Boggs, esq., and Mr. Mullen nominated Angus W. M'Donald, esq.; and the senate having been informed thereof by Mr. Sherrard, and no person having been added to the nomination in that house, the names of the members were called by the clerk, when the vote was for Sloan, 103; for Boggs, 8; for M'Donald, 18.

The names of the gentlemen who voted for Mr. Sloan, are Messrs. Banks, (speaker,) Grinalds, Gilmer, Layne, Wiley, Garland of Amherst, Brooke, M'Clintic, Henshaw, Miller, Wilson of Botetourt, Decamps, Turnbull, Mallory, Booker, Austin, Daniel, Samuel, Christian, Richardson, Johnson, Hill, Wilson of Cumberland, Vaughan, Servant, Hunter of Essex, Ball, Smith of Fauquier, Hickerson, Strange, Steger, Holland, Bowen, Davison, Smith of Frederick, Watkins, Hail of Grayson, Avent, Carrington, Coleman, Nixon, Goodall, Harrison, Kincheloe, Fontaine, Holleman, Fleet, Hooe, Robinson, Carter, Neill, Hays, Straton, Beard, Taylor of Loudoun, Harris, Ragsdale, Taylor of Mathews and Middlesex, Rogers, Garland of Mecklenburg, Willey, Morgan, Chapman, Ingles, Sherrard, Brown of Nelson, Murdaugh, Leland, Fitzgerald, Masters, Woolfolk, Almond, Adams, Swanson, Witcher, Hopkins, Carroll, Madison, Morris, Shands, Williams, Marteney, Nicklin, Dorman, Leyburn, Conrad, Jessee, M'Mullen, Bare, Rinker, Harley, Butts, Crutchfield, Moncure, Spratley, Hargrave, Gillespie, Delashmutt, Gibson, Jett, Prentiss, Saunders and Cunningham.—103.

The names of the gentlemen who voted for Mr. Boggs, are Messrs. Drummond, Craig, Price, Watts, Wethered, Waggener, M'Coy and Cackley.—8.

And the names of the gentlemen who voted for Mr. M'Donald, are Messrs. Southall, Campbell, Pate, Hunter of Berkeley, Hale of Franklin, Smith of Gloucester, Mullen, Botts, Gregory, Griggs, Berry, Summers, Powell, Cooke, Parker, Chaplne, Brown of Petersburg, and Stanard.—18.

Ordered, That Messrs. Sherrard, M'Coy, Mullen, Hunter of Berkeley, Craig, Brooke, Gilmer, Nixon, and Conrad, be a committee to act jointly with a committee from the senate, to ascertain the state of the joint vote; the committee then withdrew, and after some time returned into the house, and Mr. Sherrard reported that they had accordingly to order, ascertained the joint vote to be, for Sloan, 130; for Boggs, 9; for M'Donald, 20: whereupon, John Sloan, esq., was declared duly elected a brigadier general for the eighteenth brigade of militia.

Mr. Cunningham, from the select committee upon the petition of the representatives of Severn Eyre, presented a report, which was received and laid upon the table.

Mr. Stanard presented a memorial of the stockholders of the James river and Kanawha company, asking certain modifications of the charter of the said company, which was ordered to be referred to the committee of roads and internal navigation, that they do examine the matter thereof, and report their opinion thereupon to the house.

Mr. Southall presented a petition of the heirs of lieutenant William Lewis, praying compensation for revolutionary services performed by their ancestor, which was ordered to be referred to the committee on revolutionary claims, that they do examine the matter thereof, and report their opinion thereupon to the house.

On motion of Mr. M'Mullen, the report of the select committee on the subject of expunging from the journals of the senate of the United States a resolution of that body, was taken up, and the same being under discussion,

On motion of Mr. Parker, the house adjourned until to-morrow 12 o'clock.

SATURDAY, January 30th, 1836.

A communication from the senate by their clerk:

IN SENATE, January 29th, 1836.

The senate have agreed to the resolution for a survey of a road from Evansham in the county of Wythe, to Jeffersonville in the county of Tazewell.

On motion of Mr. Craig, *Resolved,* That the committee of roads and internal navigation be instructed to enquire into the expediency of incorporating a joint stock company to complete the road from Staunton to the Warm springs, commonly called the Free road, and known by that name, and that the said committee have leave to report by bill or otherwise.

On motion of Mr. Gregory, the following report of the committee of schools and colleges was taken up and read:

The committee of schools and colleges have, according to order, had under consideration the petition of Robert Briggs and others, doctors of medicine, resident in the city of Richmond, praying that the petitioners and their successors be incorporated by the name of "the medical college at Richmond, Virginia," with the powers suitable for such a corporation: Whereupon,

Resolved as the opinion of this committee, That said petition is reasonable.

The said resolution was, on the question put thereupon, agreed to by the house, and a bill was ordered to be brought in conformably therewith.

On motion of Mr. Carrington, the following report of the same committee was taken up and read:

The committee of schools and colleges have, according to order, had under consideration the petition of sundry citizens of the county of Halifax, praying the passage of an act incorporating certain persons in said petition named, as trustees of an academy, to be located at or near Halifax court-house: Whereupon,

Resolved as the opinion of this committee, That said petition is reasonable.

The said resolution was, on the question put thereupon, agreed to by the house, and a bill was ordered to be brought in conformably therewith.

On motion of Mr. Craig, a report of the committee of roads and internal navigation upon the resolution relating to the Warm springs and Harrisonburg turnpike company, was taken up and ordered to be recommitted to the said committee.

Mr. Hill from the committee of propositions and grievances, presented a report upon the petition for the formation of a new county of part of the county of Frederick.

Mr. Cunningham from the committee of schools and colleges, presented a report upon the petition of citizens of the town of Lynchburg, for a female academy in said town.

Mr. Carrington, according to order, presented a bill to incorporate the Gills' mountain mining company.

Which were severally received and laid upon the table.

Mr. Murdaugh from the committee on revolutionary claims, presented a resolution which was read as follows:

Resolved, That the executive of this commonwealth be requested to furnish to the committee on revolutionary claims, on application of its chairman, the reason of the rejection of any petition presented to the executive to be allowed land bounty or other compensation for revolutionary services.

On motion of Mr. Parker, the said resolution was ordered to be laid upon the table.

Mr. Sherrard presented a petition of Jane Carter, a free woman of colour, asking that her husband Richard Binns, may be allowed to reside in this state for life, or until he can obtain the means of removing his wife and family, which was ordered to be referred to the committee for courts of justice, that they do examine the matter thereof, and report their opinion thereupon to the house.

Mr. Beard presented a petition of citizens of the county of Loudoun, for an increase of the capital of the Bank of the Valley, and of the branch of the Farmers bank of Virginia located at Winchester, which was ordered to be referred to the committee on banks, that they do examine the matter thereof, and report their opinion thereupon to the house.

An engrossed bill to enact an act of the general assembly of North Carolina, entitled, "an act to incorporate the Roanoke, Danville and Junction rail-road company," was taken up on motion of Mr. Witcher, and (the rule of the house having been suspended for the purpose,) the vote ordering the same to be engrossed and read a third time, was reconsidered, and on motion of Mr. M'Mullen, the said bill was ordered to be recommitted to the committee which brought it in.

An engrossed bill to re-organize the first and second judicial districts, was read a third time, and on motion of Mr. Parker, ordered to be laid upon the table.

An engrossed bill concerning George Johnson, was read a third time, and on motion of Mr. Dorman, ordered to be laid upon the table.

An engrossed bill to incorporate the Fluvanna mining company, was read a third time :

Resolved, That the bill do pass, and that the title be, "an act to incorporate the Fluvanna mining company."

Ordered, That the clerk communicate the same to the senate and request their concurrence.

The report of the select committee upon the subject of expunging from the journals of the senate of the United States a resolution of that body, was taken up on motion of Mr. Summers, and the first resolution in said report being under discussion,

On motion of Mr. Brown, the house adjourned until Monday 12 o'clock.

MONDAY, February 1st, 1836.

A communication from the senate by their clerk :

IN SENATE, January 30th, 1836.

The senate have passed the bill, entitled,

"An act concerning the town of Portsmouth," with amendments, in which they request the concurrence of the house of delegates.

The said amendments being twice read, were, on questions severally put thereupon, agreed to by the house.

Ordered, That the clerk inform the senate thereof.

Mr. Gregory presented the report of the court of directors of the lunatic hospital at Williamsburg, which on his motion was ordered to be laid upon the table, and 185 copies thereof, were ordered to be printed for the use of the members of the general assembly.

On motion of Mr. Gregory, *Ordered,* That leave be granted to David Anderson to withdraw his petition presented to the last general assembly.

Mr. Chapline, according to order, presented a bill to incorporate the city of Wheeling in the county of Ohio.

Mr. Hill, from the committee of propositions and grievances, presented a report upon petitions of citizens of the county of Harrison ; of Richard Barton Haxall ; and of citizens of the town of Evansham.

Mr. Watkins from the committee of roads and internal navigation, presented a report upon the petition of citizens of the town of Covington.

Mr. Witcher from the committee of claims, presented a report upon the petition of Thomas Palmer, administrator of Dominie Bennehan, deceased.

Mr. Summers, according to order, presented a bill incorporating the Kanawha slave insurance company.

Which bills and reports were received and laid upon the table.

Mr. Moncure presented a petition of the heirs of William Brooke, to be allowed a bounty in land for his services in the revolutionary war, which was ordered to be referred to the committee on revolutionary claims, that they do examine the matter thereof, and report their opinion thereupon to the house.

Mr. Cooke presented a petition of the trustees of the town of Portsmouth, asking for certain amendments to the act of the tenth of March, 1832, for opening a street in said town, which was ordered to be referred to the committee of propositions and grievances, that they do examine the matter thereof, and report their opinion thereupon to the house.

Mr. Daniel presented a petition of the Lynchburg and Pittsylvania turnpike company, asking that a subscription may be made by the board of public works on behalf of the commonwealth, to the stock of the said company, which was ordered to be referred to the committee of roads and internal navigation, that they do examine the matter thereof, and report their opinion thereupon to the house.

On motion of Mr. Woolfolk, the bill entitled, "an act incorporating the stockholders of the Louisa rail-road company," together with the amendments thereto proposed by the senate, was taken up, and the said amendments being twice read, were, on questions severally put thereupon, agreed to by the house, except the third amendment, which was in like manner disagreed to.

Ordered, That Mr. Woolfolk inform the senate thereof.

Mr. Gregory, from the committee of schools and colleges, presented a bill for incorporating the medical college at Richmond in Virginia, which was received and laid upon the table.

The report of the committee on the subject of expunging from the journals of the senate of the United States a resolution of that body, was taken up, on motion of Mr. Brown of Petersburg; and the first resolution in said report being under discussion,

On motion of Mr. Brown of Petersburg, the house adjourned until to-morrow 12 o'clock.

TUESDAY, February 2d, 1836.

A communication from the senate by their clerk:

IN SENATE, February 1st, 1836.

The senate have passed the bills, entitled,

"An act to amend the act, entitled, 'an act incorporating the Falmouth and Alexandria rail-road company;'" and

"An act to incorporate the Union Potomac company," with amendments, in which they request the concurrence of the house of delegates.

The said amendments being twice read, were, on questions severally put thereupon, agreed to by the house.

Ordered, That the clerk inform the senate thereof.

On motion of Mr. M'Mullen, *Resolved*, That the committee of roads and internal navigation be instructed to enquire into the expediency of aiding in the construction of a bridge across the north fork of Holstein river in the county of Scott, and that said committee have leave to report by bill or otherwise.

On motion of Mr. Decamps, *Resolved*, That the committee of claims be instructed to enquire into the expediency of allowing to John Pittenger, late sheriff of Brooke county, the sum of $27, the amount of his delinquent list of militia fines for the years 1832 and 1833, with interest, and that they have leave to report by bill or otherwise.

On motion of Mr. Hunter of Berkeley, *Ordered*, That the committee to whom was referred so much of the communication of the governor as relates to the disputed boundary between the states of Virginia and Maryland, be discharged from the further consideration of the said subject, and that the same be laid upon the table.

Mr. Mallory, from the joint committee on the public armory, presented a report, which was received, and 185 copies of which were ordered on his motion, to be printed for the use of the general assembly.

On motion of Mr. Garland of Mecklenburg, a bill for incorporating the medical college at Richmond in Virginia, was taken up, read the first and second times, and ordered to be committed to the committee which brought it in.

Mr. Garland of Mecklenburg, from the committee of schools and colleges, presented a bill to incorporate the trustees of the Halifax academy, which, on his motion, was taken up, read the first and second times, and ordered to be committed to the said committee.

Mr. Garland also, from the same committee, presented a bill incorporating the literary and scientific mechanics institute of Norfolk and Portsmouth.

Mr. Madison, from the committee on agriculture and manufactures, presented a report upon the petition of Albert Michaels and others.

Mr. Taylor of Middlesex, according to order, presented a bill to amend the act, entitled, "an act to amend and reduce into one act all acts and parts of acts, to prevent the destruction of oysters," passed March 24th, 1831.

Which bills and report were received and laid upon the table.

On motion of Mr. Summers, a bill providing for a geological survey of the state, and for other purposes, was taken up, read the first and second times, and ordered to be committed to the committee which brought it in.

Mr. Henshaw presented a petition of citizens of the counties of Jefferson and Berkeley, praying the incorporation of a company to construct a rail-road from Smithfield, to intersect the Winchester and Potomac rail-road, which was ordered to be referred to the committee of roads and internal navigation, that they do examine the matter thereof, and report their opinion thereupon to the house.

Mr. Goodall presented a petition of Price Frazer and Mary Ann Anthony, asking the relinquishment of the commonwealth's right to certain lands forfeited for the non-payment of taxes, and that the said taxes may be remitted, which was ordered to be referred to the committee of finance, that they do examine the matter thereof, and report their opinion thereupon to the house.

Mr. Leland presented a petition of Ann Edmonds, asking to be divorced from her husband, which was ordered to be referred to the committee for courts of justice, that they do examine the matter thereof, and report their opinion thereupon to the house.

A message from the senate by Mr. Fontaine:

MR. SPEAKER,—The senate insist upon their third amendment to the bill, entitled, "an act incorporating the stockholders of the Louisa rail-road company," to which the house of delegates disagreed. And then he withdrew.

The said bill and amendment were received and laid upon the table.

The report of the select committee upon the subject of expunging from the journals of the senate of the United States a resolution of that body, was taken up on motion of Mr. Brown of Petersburg, and the first resolution in said report being under discussion,

On motion of Mr. Dorman, the house adjourned until to-morrow 12 o'clock.

WEDNESDAY, February 3d, 1836.

A communication from the senate by their clerk:

IN SENATE, February 2d, 1836.

The senate have passed the bill, entitled:

"An act incorporating the Lexington and Richmond turnpike company," with amendments, in which they request the concurrence of the house of delegates.

The said amendments being twice read, were, on questions severally put thereupon, agreed to by the house.

Ordered, That the clerk inform the senate thereof.

The bill, entitled "an act incorporating the stockholders of the Louisa rail-road company," together with the third amendment thereto proposed by the senate, to which the house of delegates disagreed, and to which the senate insisted, was taken up, and the same being again read, was, on motion of Mr. Harris, ordered to be laid upon the table.

On motion of Mr. Bowen, *Ordered,* That leave be given to bring in a bill, incorporating the Front Royal library society, in the county of Frederick, and that Messrs. Bowen, Davisson, Berry, Bare, M'Coy, Griggs, Mullen and Almond, prepare and bring in the same.

On motion of Mr. Summers, *Ordered,* That leave be given to bring in a bill, changing the place of holding the separate election at Colesmouth, in the county of Kanawha; and a bill, declaring Pocatallico river a public highway, and that Messrs. Summers, Waggener, Prentiss, Chapman, Straton, Beuhring, Neill and Watts, prepare and bring in the same.

On motion of Mr. Garland of Amherst, *Resolved,* That the committee of roads and internal navigation be directed to enquire into the expediency of so amending the law in relation to internal improvements, as to declare that the granting of an act of incorporation on the part of this commonwealth, does not create any obligation either legal or implied on the part of the state, to take any portion of the stock in the said company, unless it shall hereafter appear expedient to do so, and that they report by bill or otherwise.

On motion of Mr. Woolfolk, *Ordered,* That leave be given to bring in a bill, incorporating the Orange savings society in the county of Orange, and that Messrs. Woolfolk, Crutchfield, Hill, Harris, Southall, Nicklin, Moncure and Smith of Fauquier, prepare and bring in the same.

On motion of Mr. Crutchfield, the resolution submitted by Mr. Gilmer, on the twenty-third ultimo, "that the board of public works are hereby requested to employ a competent engineer to survey a route for a rail-road from Gordonsville in the county of Orange, to Harrisonburg in the county of Rockingham, and from Gordonsville to the Rivanna river, at or near Charlottesville, in the county of Albemarle, and report to the next general assembly, his estimate of the cost of constructing the same, and the advantages, which, in his opinion, will result to the commonwealth," was taken up: whereupon, the same was amended on his motion, and as amended, was agreed to by the house as follows:

Resolved by the general assembly of Virginia, That the board of public works are hereby directed as soon as practicable, to cause the principal engineer, or employ a competent engineer, to survey a route for a rail-road from Gordonsville in the county of Orange, to Harrisonburg in the county of Rockingham; and to survey a route for a rail-road from Fredericksburg through the county of Orange or as near thereto as practicable, and through the town of Charlottesville, to the eastern base of the Blue Ridge, uniting them with the Staunton and Scottsville rail-road, as contemplated by the charter of the Rappahannock and Blue Ridge rail-road company, and report to the next legislature an estimate of the cost of constructing those works, and the advantages which in his opinion will result to the commonwealth by their being constructed.

Ordered, That the clerk communicate the same to the senate and request their concurrence.

Mr. Gregory presented a communication from the court of directors of the lunatic hospital, in reply to the resolution of the house of delegates of the 19th January, 1836, relative to the directory and the officers of the institution; which was ordered to be laid upon the table, and 185 copies of which were ordered to be printed for the use of the general assembly.

Mr. Hill from the committee of propositions and grievances, presented a report upon petitions of the citizens of the county of Bedford, and of citizens of the county of Pittsylvania, which was received and laid upon the table.

Mr. Madison presented a petition of citizens of the town of Farmville, for increasing the salaries of the inspectors of tobacco in the said town, which was ordered to be referred to the committee on agriculture and manufactures, that they do examine the matter thereof, and report their opinion thereupon to the house.

The report of the select committee, on the subject of expunging from the journals of the senate of the United States, a resolution of that body, was taken up on motion of Mr. Brown of Petersburg, and the first resolution in said report being under discussion, on motion of Mr. Daniel, the same was ordered to be laid upon the table.

Mr. Watkins from the committee of roads and internal navigation, presented reports upon the petitions of citizens of the town of Smithfield; of citizens of the counties of Albemarle and Nelson; of John M'Clure and others; of the president and directors of the Fallsbridge turnpike company; of citizens of the county of Prince George and town of Petersburg; of citizens of the county of Greensville; of the Chesapeake and Ohio canal company; upon the resolutions for appropriating money to construct a road from Moorfield to Wardensville; for a survey of the Dragon swamp; and for an appropriation to aid in the erection of a bridge across the north fork of Holston river. He also reported with amendments, a bill to incorporate the stockholders of the Lynchburg and Tennessee rail-road company, and to authorize them, or the James river and Kanawha company, to construct a rail-road from Lynchburg to Richmond.

Which reports and bill were received and laid upon the table.

On motion of Mr. Watkins, *Ordered*, That the committee of roads and internal navigation, be discharged from the consideration of the several petitions and resolutions referred to that committee, relating to improvements to be made by the Upper Appomattox company, and that the same be laid upon the table.

On motion of Mr. Watkins, the house adjourned until to-morrow 12 o'clock.

THURSDAY, February 4th, 1836.

A communication from the senate by their clerk:

IN SENATE, February 3d, 1836.

The senate have passed the bill, entitled,
"An act to incorporate the Fluvanna mining company."

Mr. Mallory from the committee on enrolled bills, reported that the said committee had examined sundry such bills and found them truly enrolled.

Ordered, That the clerk communicate the same to the senate.

On motion of Mr. Johnson, *Ordered*, That leave be given to bring in a bill, to incorporate the coal working company of Richmond and Manchester, and that Messrs. Johnson, Botts, Stanard, Hopkins, Fitzgerald, Shands, Turnbull, Spratley and Hargrave, prepare and bring in the same.

On motion of Mr. Berry, *Ordered*, That leave be given to bring in a bill, incorporating the trustees of the Charlestown athenæum and female academy, and that Messrs. Berry, Griggs, Nixon, Sherrard, Mullen, Smith of Frederick and Davisson, prepare and bring in the same.

On motion of Mr. Botts, *Ordered*, That leave be given to bring in a bill, to amend the act, entitled, "an act to incorporate the Richmond manufacturing company," as to reduce the shares in said company from one thousand to one hundred dollars each, and that Messrs. Botts, Stanard, Goodall, Johnson, Robinson, Christian, Watkins and Servant, prepare and bring in the same.

On motion of Mr. Carter, *Resolved*, That the select committee on banking be instructed to enquire whether any of the chartered banks or savings institutions of this commonwealth, have so construed their chartered powers as to authorize them in any manner whatever, to deal in bonds or other instruments under seal, for more than the legal rate of interest, and that the said committee have leave to report specially thereon, or by bill, as it may seem to them most expedient.

Mr. Garland of Mecklenburg, from the committee of schools and colleges, reported without amendments, a bill incorporating the medical college at Richmond in Virginia; and

A bill to incorporate the trustees of the Halifax academy.

Mr. Smith of Gloucester, according to order, presented a bill, concerning the county of Gloucester.

Mr. Summers reported without amendment, a bill, providing for a geological survey of the state, and for other purposes.

And presented according to order, a bill, changing the place of holding a separate election in the county of Kanawha; and

A bill declaring Pocatallico river a public highway.

Which bills were severally received and laid upon the table.

Mr. Summers also presented a petition of sundry citizens of the county of Nicholas, praying that a portion of the said county may be attached to the county of Fayette, which was ordered to be referred to the committee of propositions and grievances, that they do examine the matter thereof, and report their opinion thereupon to the house.

Mr. Servant presented a petition of citizens of the county of Elizabeth City, praying that the trustees of the Hampton academy, may be authorized to apply a portion of the interest resulting from the funds of the said academy, to the establishment of two other schools in said county, which was ordered to be referred to the committee of schools and colleges, that they do examine the matter thereof, and report their opinion thereupon to the house.

On motion of Mr. Harris, a bill, entitled, "an act, incorporating the stockholders of the Louisa rail-road company, with the amendment of the senate to which the house had disagreed, and to which the senate had insisted, was taken up, whereupon, a motion was made by him that this house recede from their disagreement to the said amendment, and the question being put thereupon, was determined in the negative; and then on motion of Mr. Gilmer, the said bill and amendment were again ordered to be laid upon the table.

Mr. Botts, according to order, presented a bill to amend the act, entitled, "an act, to incorporate the Richmond manufacturing company," passed on the 12th of January, 1832.

Mr. Holleman in like manner, presented a bill, incorporating the Smithfield savings institution, in the county of Isle of Wight.

Mr. Booker, from the committee for courts of justice, presented several reports upon petitions of John Hope; of Celinda C. Wallace, and of citizens of the county of Patrick.

Which bills and reports were received and laid upon the table.

The report of the select committee on the subject of expunging from the journals of the senate of the United States a resolution of that body, was taken up on motion of Mr. Daniel, and the first resolution in the said report being under discussion,

On motion of Mr. Hunter of Essex, the house adjourned until to-morrow 12 o'clock.

FRIDAY, February 5th, 1836.

On motion of Mr. Crutchfield, *Ordered*, That leave be given to bring in a bill to amend "an act, incorporating the Hunting Run mining company," passed February 7th, 1834, and that Messrs. Crutchfield, Moncure, Williams, Samuel, Woolfolk, Hill and Hickerson prepare and bring in the same.

On motion of Mr. Harris, *Ordered*, That leave be given to bring in a bill, incorporating the Goochland mining company, and that Messrs. Harris, Watkins, Strange, Gilmer, Brown of Nelson, Hopkins, Johnson and Wiley, prepare and bring in the same.

On motion of Mr. Stanard, *Ordered*, That leave be given to bring in a bill, to revive and amend an act, entitled, "an act to incorporate the Gallego manufacturing company," passed the 20th of January, 1834, and that Messrs. Stanard, Botts, Goodall, Watkins, Austin, Garland of Amherst, Christian and Harris, prepare and bring in the same.

Mr. Stanard from the committee for courts of justice, presented a bill, changing the times of holding the spring terms of the circuit superior courts of law and chancery, in the fifth circuit and third judicial district, and for other purposes, which on his motion was taken up, read the first and second times, and (by general consent) ordered to be engrossed and read a third time.

Mr. Johnson, according to order, presented a bill to incorporate the coal working company of Richmond and Manchester.

Mr. Watkins, from the committee of roads and internal navigation, reported without amendment, a bill to regulate the conduct of boatmen on the Roanoke river and its branches.

And presented several reports upon the petition of the Pittsylvania and Lynchburg turnpike company; and upon the resolutions for increasing the capital of the Richmond, Fredericksburg and Potowmac rail-road company.

Also, a bill, incorporating the Staunton and Augusta springs turnpike company; and

A bill, directing the sale of the stock held by the state in joint stock companies incorporated for purposes of internal improvement.

Which bills and reports were received and laid upon the table.

On motion of Mr. Watkins, *Ordered*, That the committee of roads and internal navigation be discharged from the further consideration of the petition of sundry citizens of the county of Botetourt, relating to the proposed railroad from Lynchburg to the Tennessee line; from the memorial of citizens of the city of Richmond, opposing the petition of the Manchester and Petersburg turnpike company; and from the resolution of the Danville convention; and that the said petitions and resolution be laid upon the table.

Mr. Spratley presented a petition of William H. Riggan, asking the passage of an act to change his name to that of William H. Drewry, which was ordered to be referred to the committee of propositions and grievances, that they do examine the matter thereof, and report their opinion thereupon to the house.

On motion of Mr. Booker, *Resolved*, That when this house adjourns to-day, it will adjourn until to-morrow 11 o'clock.

The report of the select committee upon the subject of expunging from the journals of the senate of the United States, a resolution of that body, was taken up on motion of Mr. Watkins, and the first resolution in the said report being under discussion, on motion of Mr. Brown of Petersburg, the said report was again laid upon the table.

Mr. Brown of Petersburg then, from the committee of finance, presented several reports upon the petitions of the administrator of George and Thomas Walls; of sundry retail merchants of the town of Petersburg, and of Henry Anderson; which were received and laid upon the table.

On motion of Mr. Botts, the house adjourned until to-morrow 11 o'clock.

SATURDAY, February 6th, 1836.

Mr. Sherrard reported without amendment, a bill to alter the terms of the circuit superior courts of law and chancery for the seventh district and thirteenth circuit of this commonwealth.

Mr. Woolfolk, according to order, presented a bill incorporating the Orange savings society.

Which were received and laid upon the table

An engrossed bill authorizing the sale of the estate of John Haskins, senior, a lunatic, was taken up and read a third time:

Resolved, That the bill do pass, and that the title be, "an act authorizing the sale of the estate of John Haskins, senior, a lunatic."

Ordered, That Mr. Mallory carry the same to the senate and request their concurrence.

On motion of Mr. Parker, an engrossed bill further to amend the act, entitled, "an act to amend the act, entitled, 'an act, establishing a ferry from Onancock town, in the county of Accomac, to Norfolk, and for other purposes,'" passed March 5th, 1833, was taken up:

Resolved, That the bill do pass, and that the title be, "an act further to amend the act, entitled, an 'act to amend the act, entitled, 'an act establishing a ferry from Onancock town, in the county of Accomac, to Norfolk, and for other purposes,'" passed March 5th, 1833.

An engrossed bill to provide an index to the journals of the house of delegates, was read a third time:

Resolved, That the bill do pass, and that the title be, "an act to provide an index to the journals of the house of delegates."

Ordered, That the clerk communicate the same to the senate and request their concurrence.

On motion of Mr. Butts, a bill to authorize the county court of Southampton to appoint processioners of lands, was taken up and ordered to be engrossed and read a third time.

An engrossed bill concerning George Johnson, was taken up on motion of Mr. Witcher, and read a third time, and the question being put upon its passage, was determined in the negative.

Resolved, That the said bill be rejected.

Mr. Daniel presented petitions of sundry inspectors of tobacco of the city of Richmond, and towns of Lynchburg, Petersburg and Clarksville, asking for an increase of their compensation, which was ordered to be referred to the committee of agriculture and manufactures, that they do examine the matter thereof, and report their opinion thereupon to the house.

An engrossed bill concerning Shelton Ford, was read a third time, and the question being put upon its passage, was determined in the negative.

Resolved, That the said bill be rejected.

An engrossed bill to establish the town of Hedgesville in the county of Berkeley, was read a third time, and on motion of Mr. Hunter of Berkeley, was ordered to be laid upon the table.

An engrossed bill to change the place of holding a separate election in the county of Hampshire, was read a third time:

Resolved, That the bill do pass, and that the title be, "an act to change the place of holding a separate election in the county of Hampshire."

An engrossed bill directing the survey and location of a route for a road from Moorfield, to the North-western turnpike, was read a third time:

Resolved, That the bill do pass, and that the title be, "an act directing the survey and location of a route for a road from Moorfield, to the North-western turnpike."

An engrossed bill to amend an act, entitled, "an act to limit the assessment upon titheables, and to authorize a tax upon property for the purpose of defraying county expenditures within the county of Berkeley," passed March 5th, 1835, was read a third time:

Resolved, That the bill do pass, and that the title be, "an act to amend an act, entitled, 'an act to limit the assessment upon titheables, and to authorize a tax upon property for the purpose of defraying county expenditures within the county of Berkeley,'" passed March 5th, 1835.

Ordered, That the clerk communicate the said bills to the senate and request their concurrence.

The report of the select committee upon the subject of expunging from the journals of the senate of the United States a resolution of that body, was taken up on motion of Mr. Stanard, and the first resolution in the said report being under discussion,

On motion of Mr. Harrison, the house adjourned until Monday 11 o'clock.

MONDAY, February 8th, 1836.

A communication from the senate by their clerk:

IN SENATE, February 6th, 1836.

The senate have agreed to the resolutions relative to the interference of certain associations in the northern states with domestic slavery in the south, with amendments, in which they request the concurrence of the house of delegates.

On motion of Mr. Sherrard the resolutions and proposed amendments were ordered to be laid upon the table.

On motion of Mr. Gregory, *Ordered*, That 185 copies of the said resolution and proposed amendments, be printed for the use of the general assembly.

On motion of Mr. Harris, *Resolved*, That the committee appointed to bring in a bill incorporating the Goochland mining company, have leave also to bring in a bill incorporating the Big Bird mining company.

Mr. Sherrard presented a report of the probable revenue of the Chesapeake and Ohio canal company after it reaches the coal mines near Cumberland and after its completion to Pittsburg; which on his motion was laid upon the table and 185 copies thereof were ordered to be printed for the use of the general assembly.

On motion of Mr. Neill, *Resolved*, That the committee for courts of justice be instructed to enquire into the expediency of so amending the criminal laws of this commonwealth, as to authorize a conviction and sentence to the penitentiary, of persons charged with counterfeiting, or knowingly passing counterfeit bank paper, for a term less than that now limited by law, with a view to a greater certainty of punishment, and that they have leave to report by bill or otherwise.

On motion of Mr. Wilson of Botetourt, *Resolved*, That the committee of schools and colleges be instructed to enquire into the expediency of increasing the number of visitors of the University of Virginia, with leave to report by bill or otherwise.

On motion of Mr. Garland of Amherst, *Resolved*, That 250 copies of the report of certain commissioners appointed to ascertain the losses by fire in the borough and county of Norfolk, in 1776, transmitted to this house by the auditor, be printed for the use of the general assembly.

Mr. Crutchfield presented petitions of Thomas F. Knox and others, for the passage of an act incorporating the Potowmac silk and agricultural company.

And of William Browne and others, for an act incorporating a company for the culture, reeling and manufactury of silk.

Ordered, That the said petitions be referred to the committee on agriculture and manufactures, with leave to report thereon by bill or otherwise.

Mr. Crutchfield according to order, presented a bill changing the Hunting Run gold mining company into a company for mining and manufacturing iron and steel.

Mr. Carter from the committee on banks, presented a bill concerning savings institutions.

Mr. Witcher from the committee of claims, presented a report upon the petition of the administrator of Richard Kelsick.

Which bills and report were received and laid upon the table.

An engrossed bill to authorize the county court of Southampton to appoint processioners of lands, was taken up on motion of Mr. Butts and read a third time:

Resolved, That the bill do pass, and that the title be, "an act to authorize the county court of Southampton to appoint processioners of lands."

Ordered, That Mr. Butts carry the same to the senate and request their concurrence.

On motion of Mr. Carrington, a bill to incorporate the trustees of the Halifax academy, was taken up and ordered to be engrossed and read a third time.

On motion of Mr. Parker, the rule of the house requiring the appointment of a standing committee on the subject of revolutionary claims, was ordered to be rescinded, and the committee were discharged from the farther consideration of the several subjects heretofore referred to them.

Mr. Daniel presented a petition of the members of the Lynchburg bar and others, officers of the Lynchburg circuit superior court, asking that the time for holding the said superior court be changed to the spring and fall time of the year, and that the time for holding the Bedford superior court may be also changed to the fifth days of May and October; which was ordered to be referred to a committee of Messrs. Daniel, Wilson of Cumberland, Pate, Campbell, Adams, Booker, Austin and Coleman, with leave to report thereon by bill or otherwise.

Mr. Stanard from the committee for courts of justice, presented reports upon the petitions of John Barnes; of Ann Edmonds, and of Ann, a woman of colour, which were received and laid upon the table.

Mr. Hopkins presented a petition of sundry citizens of the county of Powhatan, praying the incorporation of a joint stock company to construct a rail-road from Richmond to Lynchburg, which was ordered to be referred to the committee of roads and internal navigation, that they do examine the matter thereof, and report their opinion thereon, upon to the house.

Mr. Moffett presented a petition of officers and privates of the 116th and 145th regiments, opposing the petition of the officers of the 58th regiment, asking a repeal of the act of the last legislature, establishing the said 145th regiment in the county of Rockingham, which was ordered to be referred to the committee on the militia laws, that they do examine the matter thereof, and report their opinion thereupon to the house.

The report of the select committee on the subject of expunging from the journals of the senate of the United States a resolution of that body, was taken up on motion of Mr. Harrison.

The same is the following:

The committee, to whom was referred the following resolution,—" *Resolved*, That the resolution of the senate of the United States, passed March the 28th, 1834, which declares ' that the president, in the late executive proceedings in relation to the public revenue, has assumed upon himself authority and power not conferred by the constitution and laws, but in derogation of both,' be referred to a select committee, with directions to enquire into the expediency of instructing the senators from this state, in the congress of the United States, to introduce and vote for a resolution, requiring the aforesaid resolution to be expunged from the journal of the senate,"—have had the same under consideration, and beg leave to report the following preamble and resolutions:

Whereas the senate of the United States did, on the 28th day of March, 1834, adopt the following resolution: "*Resolved*, That the president, in the late executive proceedings in relation to the public revenue, has assumed upon himself authority and power not conferred by the constitution and laws, but in derogation of both;" which resolution now stands upon the journal of the senate:

And whereas the general assembly of Virginia regard this act of the senate as an assumption of power not warranted by the constitution, and calculated to subvert the rights of the house of representatives, and the fundamental principles of our free institutions:

And whereas this assembly deem it their solemn duty again to re-assert, in behalf of themselves and the people of Virginia, the right of the constituent to instruct, and the *duty* of the *representative to obey or resign:* Therefore,

1. *Resolved by the general assembly of Virginia*, That the senators from this state, in the congress of the United States, be and they are hereby instructed to introduce, and vote for, a resolution, directing the aforesaid resolution of the senate of the 28th day of March, 1834, declaring "that the president, in the late executive proceedings in relation to the public revenue, has assumed upon himself authority and power not conferred by the constitution and laws, but in derogation of both," TO BE EXPUNGED from the journal of the senate of the United States, by causing black lines to be drawn around the said resolution, as it stands on the original manuscript journal, and these words plainly written across the face of the said resolution and entry,—EXPUNGED *by order of the senate of the United States.*

2. *Resolved also*, That this assembly regard the right of instruction "as resting on the broad basis of the nature of representation," and one of the vital principles of our free institutions; and that it is the duty of the representative to obey the instructions of his constituents, or resign the trust with which *they* have clothed him, in order that it may be transferred into the hands of those who will carry into execution the wishes and instructions of the constituent body.

3. *Resolved*, That the governor of the commonwealth be requested to transmit the foregoing resolutions to each of the senators and representatives from Virginia, in the congress of the United States, with the request that they lay the same before their respective bodies.

The first resolution in said report being under consideration,

A motion was made by Mr. Mallory to amend the same, by striking therefrom the words, "*To be expunged from the journal of the senate of the United States, by causing black lines to be drawn around the said resolution as it stands on the original manuscript journal, and these words plainly written across the face of the said resolution and entry,—expunged by order of the senate of the United States;*" and inserting in lieu thereof, the words, "to be repealed, rescinded and declared null and void;" and the question being upon adopting the said amendment,

On motion of Mr. Watkins, the house adjourned until to-morrow 11 o'clock.

TUESDAY, February 9th, 1836.

The speaker laid before the house a communication from the governor, enclosing the address and resolutions of the legislature of Alabama, upon the subject of abolition, which being read, was on motion of Mr. Parker, ordered to be laid upon the table, and on motion of Mr. Woolfolk, 185 copies thereof were ordered to be printed for the use of the general assembly.

A communication from the senate by their clerk was received and read as follows:

IN SENATE, February 8th, 1836.

The senate have agreed to the resolution directing surveys for rail-roads from Gordonsville in Orange, to Harrisonburg in Rockingham; and from Fredericksburg, through the towns of Orange and Charlottesville to the eastern base of the Blue Ridge, with an amendment, in which they request the concurrence of the house of delegates.

The said amendment being twice read, was, on the question put thereupon, agreed to by the house.

Ordered, That the clerk inform the senate thereof.

On motion of Mr. Chapman, *Ordered*, That leave be given to bring in a bill so to change the line dividing the counties of Giles and Tazewell, as to include within the county of Giles that portion of the farm formerly owned by Archibald Burditt, (now by George W. Pearis,) lying within the county of Tazewell, and that Messrs. Chapman, Watts, Gillespie, Hail of Grayson, Straton, Beuhring and Lane prepare and bring in the same.

On motion of Mr. Murdaugh, *Resolved*, That the committee of roads and internal navigation be instructed to enquire into the expediency of incorporating a company to construct a rail-road from some point near Cherrystone, in the county of Northampton, on the eastern shore, to or near Wilmington in the state of Delaware, and thence to Philadelphia, and that they report by bill or otherwise.

On motion of Mr. Morgan, *Resolved*, That the committee for courts of justice be instructed to enquire into the expediency of re-enacting the act, passed the 24th day of January, 1824, entitled, "an act concerning the processioning of lands in certain counties."

On motion of Mr. Kincheloe, *Ordered*, That leave be granted to Edward Goodwin to withdraw his petition presented to the legislature at its last session.

Mr. Parker from the committee on the militia laws, presented a bill to equalize the regimental districts in the county of Rockingham and for other purposes.

Mr. Hill from the committee of propositions and grievances, presented a report upon petitions of owners of property on James river, to make said river a lawful fence; and of William Townes.

Mr. Berry according to order, presented a bill to incorporate the trustees of the Charlestown athenæum and female academy.

Which bills and report were received and laid upon the table.

A bill for incorporating the medical college at Richmond in Virginia, was taken up on motion of Mr. Garland of Mecklenburg, and ordered to be engrossed and read a third time.

An engrossed bill, to establish the town of Hedgesville, in the county of Berkeley, was taken up on motion of Mr. Hunter of Berkeley:

Resolved, That the bill do pass, and that the title be, "an act to establish the town of Hedgesville, in the county of Berkeley."

An engrossed bill allowing Judy Johnson, a free woman of colour, to remain in the commonwealth, was read a third time:

Resolved, That the bill do pass, and that the title be, "an act allowing Judy Johnson, a free woman of colour, to remain in the commonwealth."

An engrossed bill allowing Daniel Higginbotham, a free man of colour, to remain in the commonwealth, a limited time, was read a third time:

Resolved, That the bill do pass, and that the title be, "an act allowing Daniel Higginbotham, a free man of colour, to remain in the commonwealth a limited time."

An engrossed bill allowing Richard Bolling, a free man of colour, to remain in the commonwealth, was read a third time:

Resolved, That the bill do pass, and that the title be, "an act allowing Richard Bolling, a free man of colour, to remain in the commonwealth."

An engrossed bill concerning Duff Green, was read a third time:

Resolved, That the bill do pass, and that the title be, "an act concerning Duff Green."

An engrossed bill releasing to William Fisher, the commonwealth's right to one thousand acres of land in the county of Nicholas, was read a third time:

Resolved, That the bill do pass, and that the title be, "an act releasing to William Fisher, the commonwealth's right to one thousand acres of land in the county of Nicholas."

An engrossed bill authorizing James Martin to hold and convey certain real estate, was read a third time:

Resolved, That the bill do pass, and that the title be, "an act authorizing James Martin to hold and convey certain real estate."

Ordered, That the clerk communicate the said bills to the senate and request their concurrence.

The report of the select committee upon the subject of expunging from the journals of the senate of the United States a resolution of that body, together with the amendment to the first resolution on yesterday offered by Mr. Mallory, was taken up.

The said first resolution is the following:

Resolved by the general assembly of Virginia, That the senators from this state in the congress of the United States, be and they are hereby instructed *to introduce*, and vote for, a resolution, directing the aforesaid resolution of the senate of the 28th day of March, 1834, declaring "that the president, in the late executive proceedings in relation to the public revenue, has assumed upon himself authority and power not conferred by the constitution and laws, but in derogation of both," *to be expunged* from the journal of the senate of the United States, by causing black lines to be drawn around the said resolution, as it stands on the original manuscript journal, and these words plainly written across the face of the said resolution and *entry*,—expunged by order of the senate of the United States.

The said amendment proposed to strike from the said resolution the words, "to be expunged from the journal of the senate of the United States, by causing black lines to be drawn around the said resolution, as it stands on the original manuscript journal, and these words plainly written across the face of the said resolution and entry,—expunged by order of the senate of the United States;"—and inserting in lieu thereof the words, "to be repealed, rescinded and declared null and void;" and also instructed to cause this resolution and the preamble preceding it, to be inserted on the journal of the senate; whereupon, Mr. Daniel called a division of the question, and thereupon the question was put upon striking out the words proposed, and was determined in the negative. Ayes 61, noes 72.

On motion of Mr. Daniel, (seven of the members present concurring,) *Ordered*, That the ayes and noes upon the said question be inserted in the journal.

The names of the gentlemen who voted in the affirmative, are Messrs. Grinalds, Drummond, Gilmer, Southall, Garland of Amherst, Brooke, Craig, Campbell, Pate, Hunter of Berkeley, Henshaw, Miller, Mallory, Beuhring, Christian, Johnson, Wilson of Cumberland, Servant, Hunter of Essex, Ball, Price, Hale of Franklin, Smith of Frederick, Smith of Gloucester, Wethered, Mullen, Botts, Gregory, Griggs, Berry, Summers, Fleet, Hooe, Carter, Neill, Beard, Powell, Taylor of Loudoun, Ragsdale, Waggener, Ingles, Benton, Murdaugh, Cooke, Parker, Chapline, Masters, Swanson, Witcher, Morris, Dorman, Leyburn, Harley, Butts, Delashmutt, Jett, Prentiss, Saunders, Cunningham, Brown of Petersburg, and Stanard.—61.

And the names of the gentlemen who voted in the negative, are Messrs. Banks, (speaker,) Layne, Wiley, M°Clintic, Wilson of Botetourt, Decamps, Turnbull, Booker, Austin, Daniel, Samuel, Richardson, Hill, Vaughan, Smith of Fauquier, Hickerson, Strange, Steger, Holland, Bowen, Davison, Watts, Watkins, Hail of Grayson, Avent, Carrington, Coleman, Sloan, Nixon, Goodall, Harrison, Kincheloe, Fontaine, Holleman, Robinson, Hays, Straton, Harris, Taylor of Mathews and Middlesex, Rogers, Garland of Mecklenburg, Willey, Morgan, Chapman, Sherrard, Brown of Nelson, Leland, Fitzgerald, Woolfolk, Almond, Adams, M'Coy, Cackley, Hopkins, Carroll, Madison, Shands, Williams, Marteney, Nicklin, Moffett, Conrad, Jessee, M'Mullen, Bare, Rinker, Crutchfield, Moncure, Spratley, Hargrave, Gillespie and Gibson.—72.

A motion was then made by Mr. Parker to amend the said first resolution by adding thereto the following, viz:
It is not intended hereby to instruct the senators from Virginia to cause or aid in any act, by which the record of the said resolution of the 28th March, 1834, shall be destroyed, obliterated or defaced; but that every word and letter of the said resolution is to be preserved, so as to be distinctly seen and read.

And the question being put thereupon, was determined in the negative. Ayes 60, noes 72.

On motion of Mr. Gregory, (seven of the members present concurring,) *Ordered*, That the ayes and noes upon the said question be inserted in the journal.

The names of the gentlemen who voted in the affirmative, are Messrs. Grinalds, Gilmer, Southall, Garland of Amherst, Brooke, Craig, Campbell, Pate, Hunter of Berkeley, Henshaw, Miller, Mallory, Beuhring, Christian, Johnson, Wilson of Cumberland, Servant, Hunter of Essex, Ball, Price, Hale of Franklin, Smith of Frederick, Smith of Gloucester, Wethered, Mullen, Botts, Gregory, Griggs, Berry, Summers, Fleet, Hooe, Carter, Neill, Beard, Powell, Taylor of Loudoun, Ragsdale, Waggener, Ingles, Benton, Murdaugh, Cooke, Parker, Chapline, Masters, Swanson, Witcher, Morris, Dorman, Leyburn, Harley, Butts, Delashmutt, Jett, Prentiss, Saunders, Cunningham, Brown of Petersburg, and Stanard.—60.

And the names of the gentlemen who voted in the negative, are Messrs. Banks, (speaker,) Layne, Wiley, M'Clintic, Wilson of Botetourt, Decamps, Turnbull, Booker, Austin, Daniel, Samuel, Richardson, Hill, Vaughan, Smith of Fauquier, Hickerson, Strange, Steger, Holland, Bowen, Davison, Watts, Watkins, Hail of Grayson, Avent, Carrington, Coleman, Sloan, Nixon, Goodall, Harrison, Kincheloe, Fontaine, Holleman, Robinson, Hays, Straton, Harris, Taylor of Mathews and Middlesex, Rogers, Garland of Mecklenburg, Willey, Morgan, Chapman, Sherrard, Brown of Nelson, Leland, Fitzgerald, Woolfolk, Almond, Adams, M'Coy, Cackley, Hopkins, Carroll, Madison, Shands, Williams, Marteney, Nicklin, Moffett, Conrad, Jessee, M'Mullen, Bare, Rinker, Crutchfield, Moncure, Spratley, Hargrave, Gillespie and Gibson.—72.

A motion was then made by Mr. Witcher, to amend the said first resolution by striking therefrom the word, "expunged," and the question being put thereupon, was determined in the negative. Ayes 60, noes 72.

On motion of Mr. Witcher, (seven of the members present concurring,) *Ordered*, That the ayes and noes upon the said question be inserted in the journal.

The names of the gentlemen who voted in the affirmative, are Messrs. Grinalds, Gilmer, Southall, Garland of Amherst, Brooke, Craig, Campbell, Pate, Hunter of Berkeley, Henshaw, Miller, Mallory, Beuhring, Christian, Johnson, Wilson of Cumberland, Servant, Hunter of Essex, Ball, Price, Hale of Franklin, Smith of Frederick, Smith of Gloucester, Wethered, Mullen, Botts, Gregory, Griggs, Berry, Summers, Fleet, Hooe, Carter, Neill, Beard, Powell, Taylor of Loudoun, Ragsdale, Waggener, Ingles, Benton, Murdaugh, Cooke, Parker, Chapline, Masters, Swanson, Witcher, Morris, Dorman, Leyburn, Harley, Butts, Delashmutt, Jett, Prentiss, Saunders, Cunningham, Brown of Petersburg, and Stanard.—60.

And the names of the gentlemen who voted in the negative, are Messrs. Banks, (speaker,) Layne, Wiley, M'Clintic, Wilson of Botetourt, Decamps, Turnbull, Booker, Austin, Daniel, Samuel, Richardson, Hill, Vaughan, Smith of Fauquier, Hickerson, Strange, Steger, Holland, Bowen, Davison, Watts, Watkins, Hail of Grayson, Avent, Carrington, Coleman, Sloan, Nixon, Goodall, Harrison, Kincheloe, Fontaine, Holleman, Robinson, Hays, Straton, Harris, Taylor of Mathews and Middlesex, Rogers, Garland of Mecklenburg, Willey, Morgan, Chapman, Sherrard, Brown of Nelson, Leland, Fitzgerald, Woolfolk, Almond, Adams, M'Coy, Cackley, Hopkins, Carroll, Madison, Shands, Williams, Marteney, Nicklin, Moffett, Conrad, Jessee, M'Mullen, Bare, Rinker, Crutchfield, Moncure, Spratley, Hargrave, Gillespie and Gibson.—72.

A motion was then made by Mr. Witcher to amend the said first resolution, by striking therefrom the words, "introduce and," and the question being put thereupon, was determined in the negative. Ayes 58, noes 74.

On motion of Mr. Witcher, (seven of the members present concurring,) *Ordered*, That the ayes and noes upon the said question be inserted in the journal.

The names of the gentlemen who voted in the affirmative, are Messrs. Grinalds, Gilmer, Southall, Garland of Amherst, Brooke, Craig, Campbell, Pate, Hunter of Berkeley, Henshaw, Mallory, Beuhring, Christian, Johnson, Wilson of Cumberland, Servant, Hunter of Essex, Ball, Price, Hale of Franklin, Smith of Frederick, Smith of Gloucester, Wethered, Mullen, Botts, Gregory, Griggs, Berry, Summers, Fleet, Hooe, Carter, Neill, Beard, Powell, Taylor of Loudoun, Ragsdale, Waggener, Ingles, Benton, Murdaugh, Cooke, Parker, Chapline, Masters, Swanson, Witcher, Morris, Dorman, Leyburn, Harley, Butts, Delashmutt, Jett, Prentiss, Cunningham, Brown of Petersburg, and Stanard.—58.

And the names of the gentlemen who voted in the negative, are Messrs. Banks, (speaker,) Layne, Wiley, M'Clintic, Miller, Wilson of Botetourt, Decamps, Turnbull, Booker, Austin, Daniel, Samuel, Richardson, Hill, Vaughan, Smith of Fauquier, Hickerson, Strange, Steger, Holland, Bowen, Davison, Watts, Watkins, Hail of Grayson, Avent, Carrington, Coleman, Sloan, Nixon, Goodall, Harrison, Kincheloe, Fontaine, Holleman, Robinson, Hays, Straton, Harris, Taylor of Mathews and Middlesex, Rogers, Garland of Mecklenburg, Willey, Morgan, Chapman, Sherrard,

Brown of Nelson, Leland, Fitzgerald, Woolfolk, Almond, Adams, M'Coy, Cackley, Hopkins, Carroll, Madison, Shands, Williams, Marteney, Nicklin, Moffett, Conrad, Jessee, M'Mullen, Bare, Rinker, Crutchfield, Moncure, Spratley, Hargrave, Gillespie, Gibson and Saunders.—74.

A motion was then made by Mr. Brown of Petersburg, to amend the said first resolution, by adding thereto the following: " *Provided*, That the said resolution and entry on the journal of the senate shall not thereby be obliterated or rendered illegible." And the question being put thereupon, was determined in the negative. Ayes 64, noes 68.

On motion of Mr. Wilson of Botetourt, (seven of the members present concurring,) *Ordered*, That the ayes and noes upon the said question be inserted in the journal.

The names of the gentlemen who voted in the affirmative, are Messrs. Grinalds, Gilmer, Southall, Garland of Amherst, Brooke, Craig, Campbell, Pate, Hunter of Berkeley, Henshaw, Miller, Mallory, Beuhring, Christian, Johnson, Wilson of Cumberland, Servant, Hunter of Essex, Ball, Price, Hale of Franklin, Smith of Frederick, Smith of Gloucester, Wethered, Carrington, Goodall, Mullen, Botts, Gregory, Griggs, Berry, Summers, Fleet, Hooe, Carter, Neill, Beard, Powell, Taylor of Loudoun, Ragsdale, Waggener, Rogers, Ingles, Benton, Murdaugh, Cooke, Parker, Leland, Chapline, Masters, Swanson, Witcher, Morris, Dorman, Leyburn, Harley, Butts, Delashmutt, Jett, Prentiss, Saunders, Cunningham, Brown of Petersburg, and Stanard.—64.

And the names of the gentlemen who voted in the negative, are Messrs. Banks, (speaker,) Layne, Wiley, M'Clintic, Wilson of Botetourt, Decamps, Turnbull, Booker, Austin, Daniel, Samuel, Richardson, Hill, Vaughan, Smith of Fauquier, Hickerson, Strange, Steger, Holland, Bowen, Davison, Watts, Watkins, Hail of Grayson, Avent, Coleman, Sloan, Nixon, Harrison, Kincheloe, Fontaine, Holleman, Robinson, Hays, Straton, Harris, Taylor of Mathews and Middlesex, Garland of Mecklenburg, Willey, Morgan, Chapman, Sherrard, Brown of Nelson, Fitzgerald, Woolfolk, Almond, Adams, M'Coy, Cackley, Hopkins, Carroll, Madison, Shands, Williams, Marteney, Nicklin, Moffett, Conrad, Jessee, M'Mullen, Bare, Rinker, Crutchfield, Moncure, Spratley, Hargrave, Gillespie and Gibson.—68.

A motion was then made by Mr. Hays, to amend the said resolution, by inserting after the word "entry," the words, "in such manner as to leave said resolution legible." And the question being put thereupon, was determined in the negative. Ayes 64, noes 68.

On motion of Mr. Parker, (seven of the members present concurring,) *Ordered*, That the ayes and noes upon the said question be inserted in the journal.

The names of the gentlemen who voted in the affirmative, are Messrs. Grinalds, Gilmer, Southall, Garland of Amherst, Brooke, Craig, Campbell, Pate, Hunter of Berkeley, Henshaw, Miller, Mallory, Beuhring, Christian, Johnson, Wilson of Cumberland, Servant, Hunter of Essex, Ball, Price, Hale of Franklin, Smith of Frederick, Smith of Gloucester, Wethered, Carrington, Goodall, Mullen, Botts, Gregory, Griggs, Berry, Summers, Fleet, Hooe, Carter, Neill, Hays, Beard, Taylor of Loudoun, Ragsdale, Waggener, Rogers, Ingles, Benton, Murdaugh, Cooke, Parker, Leland, Chapline, Masters, Swanson, Witcher, Morris, Dorman, Leyburn, Harley, Butts, Delashmutt, Jett, Prentiss, Saunders, Cunningham, Brown of Petersburg, and Stanard.—64.

And the names of the gentlemen who voted in the negative, are Messrs. Banks, (speaker,) Layne, Wiley, M'Clintic, Wilson of Botetourt, Decamps, Turnbull, Booker, Austin, Daniel, Samuel, Richardson, Hill, Vaughan, Smith of Fauquier, Hickerson, Strange, Steger, Holland, Bowen, Davison, Watts, Watkins, Hail of Grayson, Avent, Coleman, Sloan, Nixon, Harrison, Kincheloe, Fontaine, Holleman, Robinson, Straton, Powell, Harris, Taylor of Mathews and Middlesex, Garland of Mecklenburg, Willey, Morgan, Chapman, Sherrard, Brown of Nelson, Fitzgerald, Woolfolk, Almond, Adams, M'Coy, Cackley, Hopkins, Carroll, Madison, Shands, Williams, Marteney, Nicklin, Moffett, Conrad, Jessee, M'Mullen, Bare, Rinker, Crutchfield, Moncure, Spratley, Hargrave, Gillespie and Gibson.—68.

A motion was then made by Mr. Parker to amend the said resolution, by adding thereto the following:

Whereas the constitution of the United States requires in express terms, that the senate of the United States shall "keep a journal of its proceedings;" therefore,

Resolved, That any attempt to expunge such journal or to destroy it, is in direct conflict with the plain letter of the constitution.

And the question being put thereupon, was determined in the negative. Ayes 62, noes 70.

On motion of Mr. Parker, (seven of the members present concurring,) *Ordered*, That the ayes and noes upon the said question be inserted in the journal.

The names of the gentlemen who voted in the affirmative, are Messrs. Grinalds, Gilmer, Southall, Garland of Amherst, Brooke, Craig, Campbell, Pate, Hunter of Berkeley, Henshaw, Miller, Mallory, Beuhring, Christian, Johnson, Wilson of Cumberland, Servant, Hunter of Essex, Ball, Price, Hale of Franklin, Smith of Frederick, Smith of Gloucester, Wethered, Goodall, Mullen, Botts, Gregory, Griggs, Berry, Summers, Fleet, Hooe, Carter, Neill, Beard, Powell, Taylor of Loudoun, Ragsdale, Waggener, Rogers, Ingles, Benton, Murdaugh, Cooke, Parker, Chapline, Masters, Swanson, Witcher, Morris, Dorman, Leyburn, Harley, Butts, Delashmutt, Jett, Prentiss, Saunders, Cunningham, Brown of Petersburg, and Stanard.—62.

And the names of the gentlemen who voted in the negative, are Messrs. Banks, (speaker,) Layne, Wiley, M'Clintic, Wilson of Botetourt, Decamps, Turnbull, Booker, Austin, Daniel, Samuel, Richardson, Hill, Vaughan, Smith of Fauquier, Hickerson, Strange, Steger, Holland, Bowen, Davison, Watts, Watkins, Hail of Grayson, Avent, Carrington, Coleman, Sloan, Nixon, Harrison, Kincheloe, Fontaine, Holleman, Robinson, Hays, Straton, Harris, Taylor of Mathews and Middlesex, Garland of Mecklenburg, Willey, Morgan, Chapman, Sherrard, Brown of Nelson, Leland, Fitzgerald, Woolfolk, Almond, Adams, M'Coy, Cackley, Hopkins, Carroll, Madison, Shands, Williams, Marteney, Nicklin, Moffett, Conrad, Jessee, M'Mullen, Bare, Rinker, Crutchfield, Moncure, Spratley, Hargrave, Gillespie and Gibson.—70.

A motion was then made by Mr. Gilmer to amend the said first resolution by adding thereto the following:

Whereas the constitution of the United States requires in express terms that the senate of the United States shall keep a journal of its proceedings; therefore,

Resolved, That to expunge such journal or to destroy it by any act of the senate, is in direct conflict with the plain letter of the constitution.

And the question being put thereupon was determined in the negative. Ayes 60, noes 71.

On motion of Mr. Parker, (seven of the members present concurring,) *Ordered*, That the ayes and noes upon the said question be inserted in the journal.

The names of the gentlemen who voted in the affirmative, are Messrs. Grinalds, Gilmer, Southall, Garland of Amherst, Brooke, Craig, Campbell, Pate, Hunter of Berkeley, Henshaw, Miller, Mallory, Beuhring, Christian, Johnson, Wilson of Cumberland, Servant, Hunter of Essex, Ball, Price, Hale of Franklin, Smith of Frederick, Smith of Gloucester, Wethered, Mullen, Botts, Gregory, Griggs, Berry, Summers, Fleet, Hooe, Carter, Neill, Beard, Powell, Taylor of Loudoun, Ragsdale, Waggener, Ingles, Benton, Murdaugh, Cooke, Parker, Chapline, Masters, Swanson, Witcher, Morris, Dorman, Leyburn, Harley, Butts, Delashmutt, Jett, Prentiss, Saunders, Cunningham, Brown of Petersburg, and Stanard.—60.

And the names of the gentlemen who voted in the negative, are Messrs. Banks, (speaker,) Layne, Wiley, M'Clintic, Wilson of Botetourt, Decamps, Turnbull, Booker, Austin, Daniel, Samuel, Richardson, Hill, Vaughan, Smith of Fauquier, Hickerson, Strange, Steger, Holland, Bowen, Davison, Watts, Watkins, Hail of Grayson, Avent, Carrington, Coleman, Sloan, Nixon, Goodall, Harrison, Kincheloe, Fontaine, Holleman, Robinson, Straton, Harris, Taylor of Mathews and Middlesex, Rogers, Garland of Mecklenburg, Willey, Morgan, Chapman, Sherrard, Brown of Nelson, Leland, Fitzgerald, Woolfolk, Almond, Adams, M'Coy, Cackley, Hopkins, Carroll, Madison, Shands, Williams, Marteney, Nicklin, Moffett, Conrad, Jessee, M'Mullen, Bare, Rinker, Crutchfield, Moncure, Spratley, Hargrave, Gillespie and Gibson.—71.

A motion was then made by Mr. Craig, that the report and resolutions be laid upon the table, and the question being put thereupon, was determined in the negative. Ayes 56, noes 76.

On motion of Mr. Wilson of Botetourt, (seven of the members present concurring,) *Ordered*, That the ayes and noes upon the said question be inserted in the journal.

The names of the gentlemen who voted in the affirmative, are Messrs. Grinalds, Gilmer, Southall, Garland of Amherst, Brooke, Craig, Campbell, Pate, Hunter of Berkeley, Henshaw, Beuhring, Christian, Johnson, Wilson of Cumberland, Servant, Hunter of Essex, Ball, Price, Hale of Franklin, Smith of Frederick, Smith of Gloucester, Wethered, Mullen, Botts, Gregory, Griggs, Berry, Summers, Fleet, Hooe, Carter, Neill, Beard, Powell, Taylor of Loudoun, Ragsdale, Waggener, Benton, Murdaugh, Cooke, Parker, Chapline, Masters, Swanson, Witcher, Morris, Dorman, Leyburn, Harley, Butts, Delashmutt, Jett, Prentiss, Cunningham, Brown of Petersburg, and Stanard.—56.

And the names of the gentlemen who voted in the negative, are Messrs. Banks, (speaker,) Layne, Wiley, M'Clintic, Miller, Wilson of Botetourt, Decamps, Turnbull, Mallory, Booker, Austin, Daniel, Samuel, Richardson, Hill, Vaughan, Smith of Fauquier, Hickerson, Strange, Steger, Holland, Bowen, Davison, Watts, Watkins, Hail of Grayson, Avent, Carrington, Coleman, Sloan, Nixon, Goodall, Harrison, Kincheloe, Fontaine, Holleman, Robinson, Hays, Straton, Harris, Taylor of Mathews and Middlesex, Rogers, Garland of Mecklenburg, Willey, Morgan, Chapman, Ingles, Sherrard, Brown of Nelson, Leland, Fitzgerald, Woolfolk, Almond, Adams, M'Coy, Cackley, Hopkins, Carroll, Madison, Shands, Williams, Marteney, Nicklin, Moffett, Conrad, Jessee, M'Mullen, Bare, Rinker, Crutchfield, Moncure, Spratley, Hargrave, Gillespie, Gibson and Saunders.—76.

A motion was then made by Mr. Murdaugh, that the house adopt the following in lieu of the said first resolution:

Resolved by the general assembly, That the following preamble and resolutions be submitted to the voters of this commonwealth at the next election of delegates to the general assembly, and that a poll be held at the court-houses and election precincts in the several counties and towns entitled to representation, by the officers directed to hold the elections, for their adoption or rejection; and when the said poll shall be completed, the officers conducting the elections shall transmit the same to the executive; and if a majority of the voters shall adopt the preamble and resolutions, then the governor shall be and he is hereby requested to communicate the same to our senators in the congress of the United States, as the sense of the people and of the general assembly of this commonwealth:

Whereas the senate of the United States did, on the 28th day of March, 1834, adopt the following resolution: "*Resolved*, That the president, in the late executive proceedings in relation to the public revenue, has assumed upon himself authority and power not conferred by the constitution and laws, but in derogation of both;" which resolution now stands upon the journal of the senate:

And whereas the general assembly of Virginia regard this act of the senate as an assumption of power not warranted by the constitution, and calculated to subvert the rights of the house of representatives, and the fundamental principles of our free institutions:

And whereas this assembly deem it their solemn duty again to re-assert, in behalf of themselves and the people of Virginia, the right of the constituent to instruct, and the *duty of the representative to obey or resign:* Therefore,

1. *Resolved by the general assembly of Virginia*, That the senators from this state, in the congress of the United States, be and they are hereby instructed to introduce, and vote for, a resolution, directing the aforesaid resolution of the senate of the 28th day of March, 1834, declaring "that the president, in the late executive proceedings in relation to the public revenue, has assumed upon himself authority and power not conferred by the constitution and laws, but in derogation of both," TO BE EXPUNGED from the journal of the senate of the United States,

by causing black lines to be drawn around the said resolution, as it stands on the original manuscript journal, and these words plainly written across the face of the said resolution and entry,—EXPUNGED *by order of the senate of the United States.*

2. *Resolved also,* That this assembly regard the right of instruction "as resting on the broad basis of the nature of representation," and one of the vital principles of our free institutions; and that it is the duty of the representative to obey the instructions of his constituents, or resign the trust with which *they* have clothed him, in order that it may be transferred into the hands of those who will carry into execution the wishes and instructions of the constituent body.

3. *Resolved,* That the governor of the commonwealth be requested to transmit the foregoing resolutions to each of the senators and representatives from Virginia, in the congress of the United States, with the request that they lay the same before their respective bodies.

And the question being put thereupon was determined in the negative. Ayes 57, noes 75.

On motion of Mr. Gregory, (seven of the members present concurring,) *Ordered,* That the ayes and noes upon the said question be inserted in the journal.

The names of the gentlemen who voted in the affirmative, are Messrs. Grinalds, Gilmer, Southall, Garland of Amherst, Brooke, Craig, Campbell, Pate, Hunter of Berkeley, Henshaw, Mallory, Beuhring, Christian, Johnson, Wilson of Cumberland, Servant, Hunter of Essex, Ball, Price, Hale of Franklin, Smith of Frederick, Smith of Gloucester, Wethered, Mullen, Botts, Gregory, Griggs, Berry, Summers, Fleet, Hooe, Carter, Neill, Beard, Powell, Taylor of Loudoun, Ragsdale, Waggener, Benton, Murdaugh, Cooke, Parker, Chapline, Masters, Swanson, Witcher, Morris, Dorman, Leyburn, Harley, Butts, Delashmutt, Jett, Prentiss, Cunningham, Brown of Petersburg, and Stanard.—57.

And the names of the gentlemen who voted in the negative, are Messrs. Banks, (speaker,) Layne, Wiley, M'Clintic, Miller, Wilson of Botetourt, Decamps, Turnbull, Booker, Austin, Daniel, Samuel, Richardson, Hill, Vaughan, Smith of Fauquier, Hickerson, Strange, Steger, Holland, Bowen, Davison, Watts, Watkins, Hail of Grayson, Avent, Carrington, Coleman, Sloan, Nixon, Goodall, Harrison, Kincheloe, Fontaine, Holleman, Robinson, Hays, Straton, Harris, Taylor of Mathews and Middlesex, Rogers, Garland of Mecklenburg, Willey, Morgan, Chapman, Ingles, Sherrard, Brown of Nelson, Leland, Fitzgerald, Woolfolk, Almond, Adams, M'Coy, Cackley, Hopkins, Carroll, Madison, Shands, Williams, Marteney, Nicklin, Moffett, Conrad, Jessee, M'Mullen, Bare, Rinker, Crutchfield, Moncure, Spratley, Hargrave, Gillespie, Gibson and Saunders.—75.

Mr. Madison then demanded that the main question be now put, and the same having been sustained by the house,

The question was then put upon adopting the said first resolution, and was determined in the affirmative. Ayes 73, noes 59.

On motion of Mr. Gregory, (seven of the members present concurring,) *Ordered,* That the ayes and noes upon the said question be inserted in the journal.

The names of the gentlemen who voted in the affirmative, are Messrs Banks, (speaker,) Layne, Wiley, M'Clintic, Wilson of Botetourt, Decamps, Turnbull, Booker, Austin, Daniel, Samuel, Richardson, Hill, Vaughan, Smith of Fauquier, Hickerson, Strange, Steger, Holland, Bowen, Davison, Watts, Watkins, Hail of Grayson, Avent, Carrington, Coleman, Sloan, Nixon, Goodall, Harrison, Kincheloe, Fontaine, Holleman, Robinson, Hays, Straton, Harris, Taylor of Matthews & Middlesex, Rogers, Garland of Mecklenburg, Willey, Morgan, Chapman, Sherrard, Brown of Nelson, Leland, Fitzgerald, Woolfolk, Almond, Adams, M'Coy, Cackley, Hopkins, Carroll, Madison, Shands, Williams, Marteney, Nicklin, Moffett, Conrad, Jessee, M'Mullen, Bare, Rinker, Crutchfield, Moncure, Spratley, Hargrave, Gillespie, Gibson and Saunders.—73.

And the names of the gentlemen who voted in the negative, are Messrs. Grinalds, Gilmer, Southall, Garland of Amherst, Brooke, Craig, Campbell, Pate, Hunter of Berkeley, Henshaw, Miller, Mallory, Beuhring, Christian, Johnson, Wilson of Cumberland, Servant, Hunter of Essex, Ball, Price, Hale of Franklin, Smith of Frederick, Smith of Gloucester, Wethered, Mullen, Botts, Gregory, Griggs, Berry, Summers, Fleet, Hooe, Carter, Neill, Beard, Powell, Taylor of Loudoun, Ragsdale, Waggener, Ingles, Benton, Murdaugh, Cooke, Parker, Chapline, Masters, Swanson, Witcher, Morris, Dorman, Leyburn, Harley, Butts, Delashmutt, Jett, Prentiss, Cunningham, Brown of Petersburg, and Stanard.—59.

The second resolution was then read, and the question being upon adopting the same, Mr. M'Mullen required (and being seconded according to the rule of the house) that the ayes and noes upon the said question be inserted in the journal.

Mr. Madison then demanded that the main question be now put upon adopting the said resolution: Whereupon,

A motion was made by Mr. Gregory, that this house do now adjourn, and the question being put thereupon, was determined in the negative. Ayes 33, noes 97.

On motion of Mr. Wilson of Botetourt, (seven of the members present concurring,) *Ordered,* That the ayes and noes upon the said question be inserted in the journal.

The names of the gentlemen who voted in the affirmative, are Messrs. Garland of Amherst, Pate, Hunter of Berkeley, Henshaw, Beuhring, Johnson, Servant, Ball, Price, Hale of Franklin, Smith of Frederick, Smith of Gloucester, Wethered, Mullen, Botts, Gregory, Berry, Summers, Carter, Beard, Powell, Taylor of Loudoun, Waggener, Benton, Murdaugh, Masters, Morris, Leyburn, Delashmutt, Jett, Prentiss, Brown of Petersburg, and Stanard.—33.

And the names of the gentlemen who voted in the negative, are Messrs. Banks, (speaker,) Grinalds, Gilmer, Southall, Layne, Wiley, Brooke, Craig, M'Clintic, Campbell, Miller, Wilson of Botetourt, Decamps, Turnbull, Mallory, Booker, Austin, Daniel, Samuel, Richardson, Hill, Wilson of Cumberland, Vaughan, Hunter of Essex, Smith of Fauquier, Hickerson, Strange, Steger, Holland, Bowen, Davison, Watts, Watkins, Hail of Grayson, Avent, Carrington, Coleman, Sloan, Nixon, Goodall, Harrison, Kincheloe, Fontaine, Holleman, Griggs, Fleet, Robinson, Neill, Hays, Straton, Harris, Ragsdale, Taylor of Mathews and Middlesex, Rogers, Garland of Mecklenburg, Willey, Morgan, Chapman, Ingles, Sherrard, Brown of Nelson, Cooke, Parker, Leland, Fitzgerald, Chapline, Woolfolk, Almond, Adams, M'Coy, Swanson, Witcher, Cackley, Hopkins, Carroll, Madison, Shands, Williams, Marteney, Nicklin, Dorman, Moffett, Conrad, Jessee, M'Mullen, Bare, Rinker, Harley, Butts, Crutchfield, Moncure, Spratley, Hargrave, Gillespie, Gibson, Saunders and Cunningham.—97.

Mr. Madison then withdrew his call for the previous question.

The question then recurred upon adopting the second resolution, which is the following:

Resolved also, That this assembly regard the right of instruction " as resting on the broad basis of the nature of representation," and one of the vital principles of our free institutions; and that it is the duty of the representative to obey the instructions of his constituents, or resign the trust with which *they* have clothed him, in order that it may be transferred into the hands of those who will carry into execution the wishes and instructions of the constituent body.

Mr. Stanard moved to amend the said resolution by striking out the same, and inserting in lieu thereof the following:

Resolved, That it is the indubitable right of the state legislatures to instruct their senators in congress on all points, either constitutional or politic, whenever the magnitude of the occasion shall require such interference; and that by consequence it is the bounden duty of the senators to obey such instructions; provided the instructions to be given and obeyed, require not the senator to commit a violation of the constitution, or an act of moral turpitude.

Mr. Daniel required that the question be divided, and be put upon first striking out the said resolution; and being so divided and put, it was determined in the negative. Ayes 37, noes 90.

On motion of Mr. Hunter of Berkeley, (seven of the members present concurring,) *Ordered,* That the ayes and noes upon the said question be inserted in the journal.

The names of the gentlemen who voted in the affirmative, are Messrs. Grinalds, Garland of Amherst, Brooke, Craig, Campbell, Pate, Hunter of Berkeley, Henshaw, Beuhring, Servant, Ball, Price, Smith of Frederick, Wethered, Mullen, Botts, Gregory, Berry, Summers, Neill, Beard, Powell, Taylor of Loudoun, Waggener, Benton, Murdaugh, Parker, Chapline, Masters, Witcher, Morris, Leyburn, Butts, Delashmutt, Jett, Prentiss and Stanard.—37.

And the names of the gentlemen who voted in the negative, are Messrs. Banks, (speaker,) Gilmer, Southall, Layne, Wiley, M'Clintic, Miller, Wilson of Botetourt, Decamps, Turnbull, Mallory, Booker, Austin, Daniel, Samuel, Richardson, Johnson, Hill, Wilson of Cumberland, Vaughan, Hunter of Essex, Smith of Fauquier, Hickerson, Strange, Steger, Hale of Franklin, Holland, Bowen, Davison, Watts, Smith of Gloucester, Watkins, Hail of Grayson, Avent, Carrington, Coleman, Sloan, Nixon, Goodall, Harrison, Kincheloe, Fontaine, Holleman, Fleet, Robinson, Hays, Straton, Harris, Ragsdale, Taylor of Mathews and Middlesex, Rogers, Garland of Mecklenburg, Willey, Morgan, Chapman, Ingles, Sherrard, Brown of Nelson, Cooke, Leland, Fitzgerald, Woolfolk, Almond, Adams, M'Coy, Swanson, Cackley, Hopkins, Carroll, Madison, Shands, Williams, Marteney, Nicklin, Dorman, Moffett, Conrad, Jessee, M'Mullen, Bare, Rinker, Harley, Crutchfield, Moncure, Hargrave, Gillespie, Gibson, Saunders, Cunningham, and Brown of Petersburg.—90.

A motion was then made by Mr. Gregory, that this house do now adjourn; and the question being put thereupon, was determined in the negative. Ayes 39, noes 90.

On motion of Mr. Gregory, (seven of the members present concurring,) *Ordered,* That the ayes and noes upon the said question be inserted in the journal.

The names of the gentlemen who voted in the affirmative, are Messrs. Southall, Garland of Amherst, Brooke, Craig, Campbell, Pate, Hunter of Berkeley, Henshaw, Beuhring, Johnson, Servant, Ball, Price, Hale of Franklin, Smith of Frederick, Smith of Gloucester, Wethered, Mullen, Botts, Gregory, Griggs, Berry, Summers, Carter, Beard, Taylor of Loudoun, Ragsdale, Waggener, Benton, Murdaugh, Parker, Chapline, Masters, Swanson, Morris, Leyburn, Delashmutt, Jett and Prentiss.—39.

And the names of the gentlemen who voted in the negative, are Messrs. Banks, (speaker,) Grinalds, Gilmer, Layne, Wiley, M'Clintic, Miller, Wilson of Botetourt, Turnbull, Mallory, Booker, Austin, Daniel, Samuel, Richardson, Hill, Wilson of Cumberland, Vaughan, Hunter of Essex, Smith of Fauquier, Hickerson, Strange, Steger, Holland, Bowen, Davison, Watts, Watkins, Hail of Grayson, Avent, Carrington, Coleman, Sloan, Nixon, Goodall, Harrison, Kincheloe, Fontaine, Holleman, Fleet, Hooe, Robinson, Neill, Hays, Straton, Harris, Taylor of Mathews and Middlesex, Rogers, Garland of Mecklenburg, Willey, Morgan, Chapman, Ingles, Sherrard, Brown of Nelson, Cooke, Leland, Fitzgerald, Woolfolk, Almond, Adams, M'Coy, Witcher, Cackley, Hopkins, Carroll, Madison, Shands, Williams, Marteney, Nicklin, Dorman, Moffett, Conrad, Jessee, M'Mullen, Bare, Rinker, Harley, Butts, Crutchfield, Moncure, Spratley, Hargrave, Gillespie, Gibson, Saunders, Cunningham, Brown of Petersburg, and Stanard.—90.

And then, on motion of Mr. Botts, the house adjourned until to-morrow 11 o'clock.

WEDNESDAY, February 10th, 1836.

A communication from the senate by their clerk:

IN SENATE, February 9th, 1836.

The senate have passed the bills, entitled,

"An act to change the place of holding a separate election in the county of Hampshire;" and

"An act further to amend the act, entitled, 'an act to amend the act, entitled, 'an act establishing a ferry from Onancock town in the county of Accomack to Norfolk, and for other purposes, passed March 5th, 1833.'"

They have also passed the bills, entitled,

"An act to authorize the county court of Southampton to appoint processioners of lands;" and

"An act authorizing the sale of the estate of John Haskins, senior, a lunatic," with amendments, in which they request the concurrence of the house of delegates.

The said amendments being twice read, were, on questions severally put thereupon, agreed to by the house.

Ordered, That the clerk inform the senate thereof.

Mr. Ball presented a petition of Levi Simms, praying to be released from the payment of certain fines against him, which was ordered to be referred to the committee of claims, that they do examine the matter thereof, and report their opinion thereupon to the house.

Mr. Booker from the committee for courts of justice, reported with amendment, a bill allowing Charlotte Morgan, a free woman of colour, to remain in the commonwealth.

Mr. Servant, according to order, presented a bill to amend the several acts concerning pilots.

Mr. Brown of Petersburg, in like manner, presented a bill to amend an act, entitled, "an act to enact with amendments, an act of the general assembly of North Carolina, entitled, 'an act to incorporate the Greensville and Roanoke rail-road company,'" passed February 7th, 1834; and

A bill to amend the several acts concerning the Petersburg rail-road company.

Mr. Carter from the committee on banks, presented reports upon the memorials of the Elizabethtown and Wheeling savings institutions.

Which bills and reports were received and laid upon the table.

Mr. Harley presented a petition of citizens of the county of Smyth, praying the appropriation of the revenue of said county for the year 1836, to the completion of a wagon road from the court-house of that county across Walker's mountain to the plaister banks in said county.

Mr. Johnson, a memorial of the Chesterfield rail-road company, opposing the petition praying the incorporation of a company to construct a rail-way from the coal mines in Chesterfield, to some point on James river above Bosher's dam.

Ordered, That the said petitions be referred to the committee of roads and internal navigation, that they do examine the matter thereof, and report their opinion thereupon to the house.

On motion of Mr. Johnson, the report of the said committee upon the petition of citizens of Richmond and Chesterfield, for the construction of the said rail-road, was taken up, and ordered to be recommitted to the said committee.

Mr. Botts presented a petition of Samuel S. Pendleton, a convict in the penitentiary, praying to be pardoned and liberated from confinement, which was ordered to be referred to the committee on the penitentiary institution, that they do examine the matter thereof, and report their opinion thereupon to the house.

On motion of Mr. Brown of Nelson, *Resolved,* That the committee on the militia laws be instructed to enquire into the expediency of furnishing arms to one volunteer company (whether uniformed or not) in each regiment, and that they have leave to report by bill or otherwise.

The report of the select committee upon the subject of expunging from the journal of the senate of the United States a resolution of that body, was taken up on motion of Mr. Watkins, and the second resolution being read as follows:

Resolved also, That this assembly regard the right of instruction "as resting on the broad basis of the nature of representation," and one of the vital principles of our free institutions, and that it is the duty of the representative to obey *the instructions of his constituents, or resign the trust with which they have clothed him, in order that it may be transferred into the hands of those who will carry into execution the wishes and instructions of the constituent body.*

A motion was made by Mr. Parker, to amend the said resolution, by striking therefrom the words "the instructions of his constituents, or resign the trust with which they have clothed him, in order that it may be transferred into the hands of those who will carry into execution the wishes and instructions of the constituent body."

And the question being put thereupon was determined in the negative. Ayes 3, noes 124.

On motion of Mr. Parker, (seven of the members present concurring,) *Ordered,* That the ayes and noes upon the said question be inserted in the journal.

The names of the gentlemen who voted in the affirmative, are Messrs. Garland of Amherst, Parker and Stanard.—3.

And the names of the gentlemen who voted in the negative, are Messrs. Banks, (speaker,) Grinalds, Gilmer, Southall, Layne, Wiley, Brooke, Craig, M'Clintic, Campbell, Pate, Hunter of Berkeley, Henshaw, Miller, Wilson of

Botetourt, Decamps, Turnbull, Mallory, Booker, Austin, Beuhring, Daniel, Samuel, Christian, Richardson, Johnson, Hill, Wilson of Cumberland, Vaughan, Servant, Hunter of Essex, Ball, Smith of Fauquier, Hickerson, Price, Strange, Steger, Hale of Franklin, Holland, Bowen, Davison, Watts, Smith of Gloucester, Watkins, Hail of Grayson, Wethered, Avent, Carrington, Coleman, Sloan, Nixon, Goodall, Mullen, Harrison, Kincheloe, Botts, Fontaine, Holleman, Gregory, Summers, Fleet, Hooe, Robinson, Carter, Neill, Hays, Straton, Beard, Taylor of Loudoun, Harris, Ragsdale, Taylor of Mathews and Middlesex, Waggener, Rogers, Garland of Mecklenburg, Willey, Morgan, Chapman, Ingles, Sherrard, Benton, Brown of Nelson, Murdaugh, Cooke, Leland, Fitzgerald, Chapline, Masters, Woolfolk, Almond, Adams, M'Coy, Swanson, Witcher, Cackley, Hopkins, Carroll, Madison, Morris, Shands, Williams, Marteney, Nicklin, Dorman, Leyburn, Moffett, Conrad, Jessee, M'Mullen, Bare, Rinker, Harley, Butts, Crutchfield, Moncure, Hargrave, Gillespie, Delashmutt, Gibson, Jett, Prentiss, Saunders, Cunningham, and Brown of Petersburg.—124.

A motion was made by Mr. Price to amend the said resolution, by adding thereto the following: "but the legislature of a state has no right to instruct its senators to commit a violation of the constitution, or an act of moral turpitude."

And the question being put thereupon, was determined in the negative. Ayes 51, noes 75.

On motion of Mr. Wilson, of Botetourt, (seven of the members present concurring,) *Ordered*, That the ayes and noes upon the said question be inserted in the journal.

The names of the gentlemen who voted in the affirmative, are Messrs. Grinalds, Gilmer, Southall, Garland of Amherst, Brooke, Craig, Campbell, Pate, Hunter of Berkeley, Henshaw, Beuhring, Christian, Johnson, Wilson of Cumberland, Servant, Hunter of Essex, Ball, Price, Hale of Franklin, Smith of Gloucester, Wethered, Mullen, Botts, Gregory, Berry, Summers, Fleet, Hooe, Carter, Neill, Beard, Taylor of Loudoun, Ragsdale, Waggener, Benton, Parker, Chapline, Masters, Swanson, Witcher, Morris, Dorman, Leyburn, Harley, Butts, Delashmutt, Jett, Prentiss, Cunningham, Brown of Petersburg, and Stanard.—51.

And the names of the gentlemen who voted in the negative, are Messrs. Banks, (speaker,) Layne, Wiley, M'Clintic, Miller, Wilson of Botetourt, Decamps, Turnbull, Booker, Austin, Daniel, Samuel, Richardson, Hill, Vaughan, Smith of Fauquier, Hickerson, Strange, Steger, Holland, Bowen, Davison, Watts, Watkins, Hail of Grayson, Avent, Carrington, Coleman, Sloan, Nixon, Goodall, Harrison, Kincheloe, Fontaine, Holleman, Robinson, Hays, Straton, Harris, Taylor of Mathews and Middlesex, Rogers, Garland of Mecklenburg, Willey, Morgan, Chapman, Ingles, Sherrard, Brown of Nelson, Cooke, Leland, Fitzgerald, Woolfolk, Almond, Adams, M'Coy, Cackley, Hopkins, Carroll, Madison, Shands, Williams, Marteney, Nicklin, Moffett, Conrad, Jessee, M'Mullen, Bare, Rinker, Crutchfield, Moncure, Hargrave, Gillespie, Gibson and Saunders.—75.

The question then recurred upon adopting the said second resolution; whereupon, Mr. Watkins demanded that the main question be now put, and the question being put thereupon, was determined in the affirmative. Ayes 66, noes 62.

On motion of Mr. Parker, (seven of the members present concurring,) *Ordered*, That the ayes and noes upon the said question be inserted in the journal.

The names of the gentlemen who voted in the affirmative, are Messrs. Banks, (speaker,) Layne, Wiley, M'Clintic, Wilson of Botetourt, Decamps, Turnbull, Booker, Austin, Daniel, Richardson, Hill, Vaughan, Smith of Fauquier, Hickerson, Strange, Steger, Holland, Bowen, Davison, Watts, Watkins, Hail of Grayson, Avent, Carrington, Coleman, Sloan, Nixon, Goodall, Harrison, Kincheloe, Fontaine, Holleman, Robinson, Hays, Straton, Harris, Rogers, Garland of Mecklenburg, Willey, Chapman, Sherrard, Fitzgerald, Woolfolk, Almond, Adams, M'Coy, Cackley, Hopkins, Carroll, Madison, Shands, Williams, Marteney, Nicklin, Moffett, Conrad, Jessee, M'Mullen, Bare, Rinker, Crutchfield, Moncure, Hargrave, Gillespie and Gibson.—66.

And the names of the gentlemen who voted in the negative, are Messrs. Grinalds, Gilmer, Southall, Garland of Amherst, Brooke, Craig, Campbell, Pate, Hunter of Berkeley, Henshaw, Miller, Beuhring, Samuel, Christian, Johnson, Wilson of Cumberland, Servant, Hunter of Essex, Ball, Price, Hale of Franklin, Smith of Frederick, Smith of Gloucester, Wethered, Mullen, Botts, Gregory, Berry, Summers, Fleet, Hooe, Carter, Neill, Beard, Taylor of Loudoun, Ragsdale, Taylor of Mathews and Middlesex, Waggener, Morgan, Ingles, Benton, Brown of Nelson, Murdaugh, Cooke, Parker, Leland, Chapline, Masters, Swanson, Witcher, Morris, Dorman, Leyburn, Harley, Butts, Delashmutt, Jett, Prentiss, Saunders, Cunningham, Brown of Petersburg, and Stanard.—62.

The question was then put upon adopting the said second resolution, and was determined in the affirmative. Ayes 114, noes 14.

On motion of Mr. Sherrard, (seven of the members present concurring,) *Ordered*, That the ayes and noes upon the said question be inserted in the journal.

The names of the gentlemen who voted in the affirmative, are Messrs. Banks, (speaker,) Grinalds, Gilmer, Southall, Layne, Wiley, Garland of Amherst, M'Clintic, Campbell, Pate, Henshaw, Miller, Wilson of Botetourt, Decamps, Turnbull, Booker, Austin, Beuhring, Daniel, Samuel, Christian, Richardson, Johnson, Hill, Wilson of Cumberland, Vaughan, Servant, Hunter of Essex, Smith of Fauquier, Hickerson, Strange, Steger, Hale of Franklin, Holland, Bowen, Davison, Smith of Frederick, Watts, Smith of Gloucester, Watkins, Hail of Grayson, Wethered, Avent, Carrington, Coleman, Sloan, Nixon, Goodall, Harrison, Kincheloe, Fontaine, Holleman, Gregory, Berry, Fleet, Hooe, Robinson, Carter, Neill, Hays, Straton, Beard, Taylor of Loudoun, Harris, Ragsdale, Taylor of Mathews and Middlesex, Rogers, Garland of Mecklenburg, Willey, Morgan, Chapman, Ingles, Sherrard, Benton, Brown of Nelson, Murdaugh, Cooke, Leland, Fitzgerald, Masters, Woolfolk, Almond, Adams, M'Coy, Swanson, Witcher, Cackley, Hopkins, Carroll, Madison, Morris, Shands, Williams, Marteney, Nicklin, Dorman, Leyburn, Moffett, Conrad, Jessee,

M'Mullen, Bare, Rinker, Harley, Butts, Crutchfield, Moncure, Hargrave, Gillespie, Gibson, Jett, Saunders, Cunningham, and Brown of Petersburg.—114.

And the names of the gentlemen who voted in the negative, are Messrs. Brooke, Craig, Hunter of Berkeley, Ball, Price, Mullen, Botts, Summers, Waggener, Parker, Chapline, Delashmutt, Prentiss and Stanard.—14.

The third resolution was then amended by the house on motion of Mr. Watkins, so as to read :

Resolved, That the governor of the commonwealth be requested to transmit the foregoing resolutions to each of the senators in the congress of the United States, with a request that they lay the same before the senate.

A motion was then made by Mr. Parker to amend the said resolution, by striking out the same after the word "Resolved," and inserting in lieu thereof, the following:

"That the speaker of the house of delegates and the speaker of the senate sign the foregoing resolutions, and that the speaker of the house of delegates cause a copy thereof to be transmitted to each of our senators in the congress of the United States, with a request that they lay the same before the senate."

And the question being put thereupon was determined in the negative. Ayes 32, noes 95.

On motion of Mr. Gregory, (seven of the members present concurring,) *Ordered*, That the ayes and noes upon the said question be inserted in the journal.

The names of the gentlemen who voted in the affirmative, are Messrs. Grinalds, Garland of Amherst, Brooke, Craig, Campbell, Pate, Hunter of Berkeley, Henshaw, Beuhring, Wilson of Cumberland, Servant, Ball, Price, Hale of Franklin, Smith of Frederick, Smith of Gloucester, Wothered, Botts, Gregory, Berry, Summers, Carter, Beard, Taylor of Loudoun, Waggener, Benton, Parker, Witcher, Jett, Prentiss, Cunningham and Stanard.—32.

And the names of the gentlemen who voted in the negative, are Messrs. Banks, (speaker,) Gilmer, Southall, Layne, Wiley, M'Clintic, Miller, Wilson of Botetourt, Decamps, Turnbull, Booker, Austin, Daniel, Samuel, Christian, Richardson, Johnson, Hill, Vaughan, Hunter of Essex, Smith of Fauquier, Hickerson, Strange, Steger, Holland, Bowen, Davison, Watts, Watkins, Hail of Grayson, Avent, Carrington, Coleman, Sloan, Nixon, Goodall, Harrison, Kincheloe, Fontaine, Holleman, Fleet, Hooe, Robinson, Neill, Hays, Straton, Harris, Ragsdale, Taylor of Mathews and Middlesex, Rogers, Garland of Mecklenburg, Willey, Morgan, Chapman, Ingles, Sherrard, Brown of Nelson, Murdaugh, Cooke, Leland, Fitzgerald, Chapline, Masters, Woolfolk, Almond, Adams, M'Coy, Swanson, Cackley, Hopkins, Carroll, Madison, Morris, Shands, Williams, Marteney, Nicklin, Dorman, Leyburn, Moffett, Conrad, Jessee, M'Mullen, Bare, Rinker, Harley, Butts, Crutchfield, Moncure, Hargrave, Gillespie, Delashmutt, Gibson, Saunders, and Brown of Petersburg.—95.

The question was then put upon adopting the said third resolution, and was determined in the affirmative.

The question then recurred upon adopting the preamble to the said resolutions.

The same is the following :

Whereas the senate of the United States did, on the 28th day of March, 1834, adopt the following resolution : "*Resolved*, That the president, in the late executive proceedings in relation to the public revenue, has assumed upon himself authority and power not conferred by the constitution and laws, but in derogation of both ;" which resolution now stands upon the journal of the senate :

And whereas the general assembly of Virginia regard this act of the senate as an assumption of power not warranted by the constitution, and calculated to subvert the rights of the house of representatives, and the fundamental principles of our free institutions :

And whereas this assembly deem it their solemn duty again to re-assert, in behalf of themselves and the people of Virginia, the right of the constituent to instruct, and the *duty* of the *representative* to *obey* or *resign :* Therefore,

And being put thereupon, was decided in the affirmative. Ayes 73, noes 53.

On motion of Mr. Stanard, (seven of the members present concurring,) *Ordered*, That the ayes and noes upon the said question be inserted in the journal.

The names of the gentlemen who voted in the affirmative, are Messrs. Banks, (speaker,) Layne, Wiley, M'Clintic, Miller, Wilson of Botetourt, Decamps, Turnbull, Booker, Austin, Samuel, Richardson, Hill, Vaughan, Smith of Fauquier, Hickerson, Strange, Steger, Holland, Bowen, Davison, Watts, Watkins, Hail of Grayson, Avent, Carrington, Coleman, Sloan, Nixon, Goodall, Harrison, Kincheloe, Fontaine, Holleman, Robinson, Hays, Straton, Harris, Taylor of Mathews and Middlesex, Rogers, Garland of Mecklenburg, Willey, Morgan, Chapman, Ingles, Sherrard, Brown of Nelson, Leland, Fitzgerald, Woolfolk, Almond, Adams, M'Coy, Cackley, Hopkins, Carroll, Madison, Shands, Williams, Marteney, Nicklin, Moffett, Conrad, Jessee, M'Mullen, Bare, Rinker, Crutchfield, Moncure, Hargrave, Gillespie, Gibson and Saunders.—73.

And the names of the gentlemen who voted in the negative, are Messrs. Grinalds, Gilmer, Southall, Garland of Amherst, Brooke, Craig, Campbell, Hunter of Berkeley, Henshaw, Beuhring, Daniel, Christian, Johnson, Wilson of Cumberland, Servant, Hunter of Essex, Ball, Price, Hale of Franklin, Smith of Frederick, Smith of Gloucester, Wethered, Mullen, Botts, Gregory, Berry, Summers, Fleet, Hooe, Carter, Neill, Beard, Powell, Taylor of Loudoun, Ragsdale, Waggener, Benton, Murdaugh, Cooke, Parker, Masters, Swanson, Witcher, Morris, Dorman, Leyburn, Butts, Delashmutt, Jett, Prentiss, Cunningham, Brown of Petersburg, and Stanard.—53.

Ordered, That the clerk communicate the said preamble and resolutions to the senate and request their concurrence.

On motion of Mr. Watkins, the house adjourned until to-morrow 11 o'clock.

THURSDAY, February 11th, 1836.

A communication from the senate by their clerk:

IN SENATE, February 10th, 1836.

The senate have passed the bill, entitled,

"An act to amend an act entitled, 'an act to limit the assessment upon tithables, and to authorize a tax upon property for the purpose of defraying county expenditures within the county of Berkeley,'" passed March 5th, 1835.

On motion of Mr. Wilson of Botetourt, *Ordered*, That leave be given to bring in a bill authorizing the auditor to issue a warrant in favour of James Paxton, and that Messrs. Wilson of Botetourt, Miller, Leyburn, Brown of Nelson, Nicklin, Henshaw, Rogers, Southall, Harris and Madison, prepare and bring in the same.

On motion of Mr. Crutchfield, *Ordered*, That leave be given to bring in bills incorporating the Rappahannock marine and fire insurance company; the Fredericksburg Union manufacturing company, and the American mining company, and that Messrs. Crutchfield, Ball, Williams, Moncure, Smith of Fauquier, Harris, Hill and Woolfolk, prepare and bring in the same.

On motion of Mr. Parker, *Ordered*, That the committee on the militia laws be discharged from the farther consideration of the petition of officers and privates of the 116th and 145th regiments, and that the same be laid upon the table.

Mr. Parker, from the committee on the militia laws, presented a report upon the petition of Peter Klipstine, and upon the resolution for furnishing arms to volunteer companies.

Mr. Madison, from the committee of agriculture and manufactures, presented a bill to establish an additional grade of flour in the inspections of flour in this commonwealth.

Mr. Harris, according to order, presented a bill to incorporate the Big Bird mining company; and

A bill to incorporate the Goochland mining company.

Which report and bills were received and laid upon the table.

On motion of Mr. Goodall, a report of the committee of roads and internal navigation on the resolution for increasing the capital of the Richmond, Fredericksburg and Potomac rail-road company, was taken up, and ordered to be recommitted to the said committee.

Mr. Gregory submitted a resolution proposing to refer to the committee for courts of justice the several propositions lately referred to the committee on revolutionary claims, with certain instructions to said committee, which, on his motion, was ordered to be laid upon the table.

Mr. Kincheloe presented a petition of Edward Goodwin, praying compensation for revolutionary services, which was ordered to be referred to the committee of claims, that they do examine the matter thereof, and report their opinion thereupon to the house.

Mr. Summers presented a petition of sundry citizens of the county of Kanawha, for the incorporation of a company to construct a rail-road from Cole river to the Great Kanawha river, for the transportation of timber, coal, &c. which was ordered to be referred to the committee of roads and internal navigation, that they do examine the matter thereof, and report their opinion thereupon to the house.

Mr. Gillespie presented a petition of sundry citizens of the county of Tazewell for the establishment of a separate election on the Louisa fork of Sandy river in said county, which was ordered to be referred to the committee of propositions and grievances, that they do examine the matter thereof, and report their opinion thereupon to the house.

On motion, *Ordered*, That leave of absence from the service of this house be granted to Mr. Fleet for two days from to-morrow, and to Mr. Samuel for two days from to-day.

An engrossed bill to authorize a separate election at Hedgesville in the county of Berkeley, was taken up on motion of Mr. Hunter of Berkeley, and read a third time:

Resolved, That the bill do pass, and that the title be, "an act to authorize a separate election at Hedgesville in the county of Berkeley."

An engrossed bill for incorporating the Medical college at Richmond in Virginia, was read a third time:

Resolved, That the bill do pass, and that the title be, "an act for incorporating the Medical college at Richmond in Virginia."

An engrossed bill to enlarge the town of Clarksville in the county of Mecklenburg, was read a third time:

Resolved, That the bill do pass, and that the title be, "an act to enlarge the town of Clarksville in the county of Mecklenburg."

A engrossed bill to incorporate the trustees of the Halifax academy, was read a third time:

Resolved, That the bill do pass, and that the title be, "an act to incorporate the trustees of the Halifax academy."

An engrossed bill to authorize a separate election at the tavern house of William Irwin in the county of Cumberland, was read a third time:

Resolved, That the bill do pass, and that the title be, "an act to authorize a separate election at the tavern house of William Irwin in the county of Cumberland."

An engrossed bill to revive the charter of the Nelson and Albemarle Union factory company, was read a third time:

Resolved, That the bill do pass, and that the title be, "an act to revive the charter of the Nelson and Albemarle Union factory company."

122   JOURNAL OF THE HOUSE OF DELEGATES.

An engrossed bill authorizing an increase of the capital stock of the Merchants manufacturing company, was read a third time:

Resolved, That the bill do pass, and that the title be, "an act authorizing an increase of the capital stock of the Merchants manufacturing company."

Ordered, That the clerk communicate the said bills to the senate and request their concurrence.

An engrossed bill further to provide for the construction of a turnpike road across the Alleghany mountain in the counties of Pendleton and Pocahontas, was, on motion of Mr. M'Coy, ordered to be laid upon the table.

An engrossed bill changing the times of holding the spring terms of the circuit superior courts of law and chancery in the fifth circuit and third judicial district, and for other purposes, was, on motion of Mr. Crutchfield, ordered to be laid upon the table.

A bill to incorporate the stockholders of the Lynchburg and Tennessee rail-road company, and to authorize them or the James river and Kanawha company to construct a rail-road from Lynchburg to Richmond, was, on motion of Mr. M'Mullen, ordered to be laid upon the table.

A bill allowing Charlotte Morgan, a free woman of colour, to remain in the commonwealth, with the amendment thereto proposed by the committee for courts of justice, was taken up, and the said amendment being agreed to by the house, the said bill as amended was ordered to be engrossed and read a third time.

A bill to regulate the conduct of boatmen on the Roanoke river and its branches; and

A bill providing for a geological survey of the state, and for other purposes, were taken up, and ordered to be engrossed and read a third time.

A bill to alter the terms of the circuit superior courts of law and chancery for the 7th district and 13th circuit of this commonwealth, was taken up, amended on motion of Mr. Sherrard, and ordered, as amended, to be engrossed and read a third time.

A bill to incorporate the Mechanics manufacturing company, was read a second time, and ordered to be engrossed and read a third time.

On motion of Mr. Brown of Petersburg, the following reports of the committee of finance, were taken up, and read:

The committee of finance have, according to order, had under consideration the petition of the administrator of George and Thomas Walls, to them referred, representing that he has obtained judgments against the commonwealth in the court of appeals, in the case of major George Walls, and in the circuit superior court of law and chancery for the county of Henrico, in the case of lieutenant Thomas Walls, for five years full pay to each, with interest from the 22d of April, 1783, until paid, they having been officers in Crockett's regiment of the state line, in the army of the revolution; and praying, therefore, that the general assembly will make the appropriation necessary for the payment of said judgments: Whereupon,

Resolved as the opinion of this committee, That the prayer of said petition is reasonable.

The committee of finance have, according to order, had under consideration the petition of sundry retail merchants of the town of Petersburg to them referred, praying that instead of being required to pay the same tax, without regard to their capital in trade, retail merchants may be divided into classes according to the extent of their capital and business, and the tax graduated and proportioned in such manner and under such guards and precautions as may seem equitable and just: Whereupon,

Resolved as the opinion of this committee, That the prayer of said petition is reasonable.

The said resolutions were, on questions severally put thereupon, agreed to by the house, and bills were ordered to be brought in conformably therewith.

On motion of Mr. Parker, the resolutions relative to the interference of certain associations in the northern states with domestic slavery in the south, together with the amendments thereto proposed by the senate, were taken up, and the first amendment being read, a motion was made by Mr. Parker, that this house disagree thereto.

The first resolution as it passed this house was,

"*Resolved,* That this commonwealth only, has the right to control or interfere with the subject of domestic slavery within its limits, *and that this right will be maintained at all hazards.*"

The senate proposed to strike out after the word "limits," the words "and that this right will be maintained at all hazards."

And the question being put upon disagreeing to the said amendment, was determined in the affirmative. Ayes 68, noes 58.

On motion of Mr. Parker, (seven of the members present concurring,) *Ordered,* That the ayes and noes upon the said question be inserted in the journal.

The names of the gentlemen who voted in the affirmative, are Messrs. Grinalds, Drummond, Gilmer, Southall, Wiley, Garland of Amherst, Campbell, Hunter of Berkeley, Henshaw, Miller, Booker, Beuhring, Daniel, Samuel, Johnson, Wilson of Cumberland, Servant, Hunter of Essex, Ball, Hale of Franklin, Smith of Frederick, Smith of Gloucester, Wethered, Carrington, Coleman, Goodall, Mullen, Harrison, Botts, Gregory, Griggs, Berry, Summers, Fleet, Hooe, Robinson, Carter, Neill, Beard, Powell, Harris, Ragsdale, Taylor of Mathews and Middlesex, Waggener, Garland of Mecklenburg, Ingles, Benton, Brown of Nelson, Murdaugh, Cooke, Parker, Chapline, Masters, Woolfolk, Swanson, Hopkins, Morris, Marteney, Leyburn, Harley, Butts, Moncure, Delashmutt, Jett, Saunders, Cunningham, Brown of Petersburg, and Stanard.—68.

And the names of the gentlemen who voted in the negative, are Messrs. Banks, (speaker,) Layne, Brooke, Craig,

M'Clintic, Wilson of Botetourt, Decamps, Turnbull, Austin, Richardson, Hill, Vaughan, Smith of Fauquier, Hickerson, Price, Strange, Steger, Holland, Bowen, Davison, Watts, Watkins, Hail of Grayson, Avent, Sloan, Nixon, Kincheloe, Fontaine, Holleman, Hays, Straton, Taylor of Loudoun, Rogers, Willey, Morgan, Chapman, Sherrard, Fitzgerald, Almond, Adams, M'Coy, Cackley, Carroll, Madison, Shands, Williams, Nicklin, Moffett, Conrad, Jessee, M'Mullen, Bare, Rinker, Crutchfield, Hargrave, Gillespie, Gibson and Prentiss.—58.

The second resolution as it passed this house was,

Resolved, That the state of Virginia has a right to claim prompt and efficient legislation by her co-states, to restrain as far as may be, and to punish, those of their citizens who, in defiance of the obligations of social duty and those of the constitution, assail her safety and tranquillity, by forming associations for the abolition of slavery, or printing, publishing, or circulating through the mail or otherwise, seditious and incendiary publications, and that this right, founded as it is on the principles of international law, is peculiarly fortified by a just consideration of the intimate and sacred relations that exist between the states of this Union.

The senate proposed to amend the same, by inserting after the word "publications," the words "designed, calculated or having a tendency to operate on her population."

The said amendment was, on the question put thereupon, agreed to by the house.

The third resolution as it passed this house was,

Resolved, That the non-slaveholding states of the Union are respectfully but earnestly requested promptly to adopt penal enactments, or such other measures as will effectually suppress all associations within their respective limits, purporting to be, or having the character of, abolition societies; and that they will make it highly penal to print, publish, or distribute newspapers, pamphlets, or other publications, calculated or having a tendency to excite the slaves of the southern states to insurrection and revolt.

The senate proposed to amend the same by striking out all after the word "that," in the first line, and inserting "the non-slaveholding states of the Union are respectfully but earnestly requested to adopt such measures as will effectually suppress all associations within their respective limits, purporting to be, or having the character of, abolition societies, and the publishing or circulating of newspapers, pamphlets or other publications, calculated or having a tendency to excite the slaves of the southern states to insurrection and revolt."

On motion of Mr. Parker, the house disagreed to the said amendment. Ayes 70, noes 55.

On motion of Mr. Parker, (seven of the members present concurring,) *Ordered*, That the ayes and noes upon the said question be inserted in the journal.

The names of the gentlemen who voted in the affirmative, are Messrs. Grinalds, Drummond, Gilmer, Southall, Garland of Amherst, Brooke, Craig, Campbell, Hunter of Berkeley, Henshaw, Miller, Booker, Beuhring, Samuel, Johnson, Wilson of Cumberland, Servant, Hunter of Essex, Ball, Price, Hale of Franklin, Davison, Smith of Frederick, Smith of Gloucester, Wethered, Carrington, Goodall, Mullen, Harrison, Botts, Gregory, Griggs, Berry, Summers, Fleet, Hooe, Robinson, Carter, Neill, Beard, Powell, Taylor of Loudoun, Harris, Ragsdale, Taylor of Mathews and Middlesex, Waggener, Rogers, Ingles, Benton, Brown of Nelson, Murdaugh, Cooke, Parker, Chapline, Masters, Swanson, Hopkins, Madison, Morris, Marteney, Leyburn, Harley, Butts, Moncure, Delashmutt, Jett, Saunders, Cunningham, Brown of Petersburg, and Stanard.—70.

And the names of the gentlemen who voted in the negative, are Messrs. Banks, (speaker,) Layne, Wiley, M'Clintic, Wilson of Botetourt, Decamps, Turnbull, Austin, Daniel, Richardson, Hill, Vaughan, Smith of Fauquier, Hickerson, Strange, Steger, Holland, Bowen, Watts, Watkins, Hail of Grayson, Avent, Coleman, Sloan, Nixon, Kincheloe, Fontaine, Holleman, Hays, Straton, Garland of Mecklenburg, Willey, Morgan, Chapman, Sherrard, Fitzgerald, Woolfolk, Almond, Adams, M'Coy, Cackley, Carroll, Shands, Williams, Nicklin, Moffett, Conrad, M'Mullen, Bare, Rinker, Crutchfield, Hargrave, Gillespie, Gibson and Prentiss.—55.

The sixth resolution as it passed this house was,

Resolved, That confiding in the justice and loyalty of our northern brethren to the principles of the Union, enforced by the sympathies of common dangers, sufferings and triumphs, which ought to bind us together in fraternal concord, we are warranted in the expectation that the foregoing requests will be received in the spirit in which they are made, and complied with.

The senate proposed to amend the same by striking therefrom all after the word "that," in the first line, and inserting in lieu thereof, "we have seen with great satisfaction the expressions of public opinion of our northern brethren respecting the proceedings of the abolitionists among them; and that confiding in their justice and attachment to the principles of the Union, enforced by the sympathies of common dangers, sufferings and triumphs, which ought to bind us together in fraternal concord, we are warranted in the expectation that the foregoing request will be received and complied with in the spirit in which it is made."

On motion of Mr. Parker, the house disagreed to the said amendment. Ayes 69, noes 56.

On motion of Mr. Parker, (seven of the members present concurring,) *Ordered*, That the ayes and noes upon the said question be inserted in the journal.

The names of the gentlemen who voted in the affirmative, are Messrs. Grinalds, Drummond, Gilmer, Southall, Garland of Amherst, Brooke, Craig, Campbell, Hunter of Berkeley, Henshaw, Miller, Beuhring, Daniel, Samuel, Johnson, Wilson of Cumberland, Vaughan, Servant, Hunter of Essex, Ball, Price, Hale of Franklin, Bowen, Smith of Frederick, Smith of Gloucester, Wethered, Carrington, Sloan, Mullen, Harrison, Botts, Gregory, Griggs, Berry, Summers, Fleet, Hooe, Robinson, Carter, Neill, Beard, Powell, Taylor of Loudoun, Ragsdale, Taylor of Mathews and Middlesex, Waggener, Rogers, Ingles, Benton, Brown of Nelson, Murdaugh, Cooke, Parker, Chapline, Masters, Swanson, Morris; Shands, Leyburn, Harley, Butts, Moncure, Hargrave, Delashmutt, Jett, Saunders, Cunningham, Brown of Petersburg, and Stanard.—69.

And the names of the gentlemen who voted in the negative, are Messrs. Banks, (speaker,) Layne, Wiley, M'Clintic, Wilson of Botetourt, Decamps, Turnbull, Booker, Austin, Richardson, Hill, Smith of Fauquier, Hickerson, Steger, Holland, Davison, Watts, Watkins, Hail of Grayson, Avent, Coleman, Nixon, Goodall, Kincheloe, Fontaine, Holleman, Hays, Straton, Harris, Garland of Mecklenburg, Willey, Morgan, Chapman, Sherrard, Fitzgerald, Woolfolk, Almond, Adams, M'Coy, Cackley, Hopkins, Carroll, Madison, Williams, Marteney, Nicklin, Moffett, Conrad, Jessee, M'Mullen, Bare, Rinker, Crutchfield, Gillespie, Gibson and Prentiss.—56.

The senate proposed in their fifth amendment to insert the fourth and fifth resolutions as they were originally adopted by this house, after the seventh resolution, and the question being put thereupon, was determined in the affirmative.

Ordered, That the clerk inform the senate that this house disagree to their first, third and fourth amendments, and agree to their second and fifth amendments to the said resolutions.

Mr. Botts submitted to the house a protest by himself against the preamble and resolutions upon the subject of expunging from the journals of the senate of the United States a resolution of that body, and moved that the same be inserted on the journal; whereupon, on motion of Mr. Miller, the said protest was ordered to be laid upon the table.

Mr. Stanard, according to order, presented a bill to revive and amend an act, entitled, "an act to incorporate the Gallego manufacturing company," passed 20th January, 1834, which was received and laid upon the table.

On motion of Mr. Booker, the rule of the house limiting the number of the committee for courts of justice was suspended, and Mr. Price was ordered to be added to the said committee.

Mr. Woolfolk submitted a resolution requesting Mr. Moncure Robinson to furnish or cause to be furnished to this house a copy of the estimates of the cost of constructing a rail-road from some point in Hanover, by Louisa court-house, to Gordonsville, together with a copy of the estimates furnished from his office to the member from Louisa, which resolution, on his motion, was ordered to be laid upon the table.

The report of the select committee on the subject of increasing the banking capital of the commonwealth, was taken up, and, on motion of Mr. Stanard, the consideration thereof was ordered to be postponed until to-morrow.

Several reports of the committee for courts of justice were read as follow :

The committee for courts of justice have, according to order, enquired into the expediency of providing by law that a certain portion of the property of debtors be exempted from execution, for all debts hereafter contracted : Whereupon,

Resolved as the opinion of this committee, That it is expedient to make the provision aforesaid.

The committee for courts of justice have, according to order, had under consideration the petition of Arthur Lee, a free man of colour, to them referred, praying that himself and family may be permitted to remain in the commonwealth, and have come to the following resolution thereupon :

Resolved as the opinion of this committee, That the prayer of the said petition be rejected.

The said resolutions were, on questions severally put thereupon, agreed to by the house, and a bill was ordered to be brought in conformably with the said first resolution.

A report of the committee of roads and internal navigation was read as follows :

The committee of roads and internal navigation have, according to order, had under consideration the petition of sundry citizens of the county of Campbell, praying the passage of an act incorporating a joint stock company to construct a turnpike road from Lynchburg to Campbell court-house : Whereupon,

Resolved as the opinion of this committee, That said petition is reasonable.

The said resolution was, on the question put thereupon, agreed to by the house, and a bill was ordered to be brought in conformably therewith.

Several reports of the committee of finance were read as follow :

The committee of finance have, according to order, had under consideration the petition of Ephraim Wells, of the county of Brooke, to them referred, praying on behalf of himself and the heir of Elijah Wells, his deceased brother, that the sum of seven dollars and eighty cents be refunded to them, being the tax on land, (as the petitioner alleges,) which they the said brothers never owned, and was therefore erroneously charged to them by the commissioner of the revenue for said county, and paid by them : Whereupon,

Resolved as the opinion of this committee, That the prayer of the petition aforesaid be rejected.

The committee of finance have, according to order, had under consideration several petitions to them referred, and have come to the following resolutions thereupon :

The petition of Christopher Parriott, of the county of Marshall, represents that he was lately appointed commissioner of the revenue therein, complains of the inadequacy of the compensation of one hundred and fifty dollars allowed for the duties required, and therefore prays "that the general assembly will, upon consideration of the subject, allow such compensation for the services which he is bound to perform, as is reasonable and just :" Whereupon,

1. *Resolved as the opinion of this committee*, That the compensation of one hundred and fifty dollars, now allowed said commissioner, is reasonable and just, and therefore needs no alteration.

The petition of a large portion of the farmers of the county of Brooke, prays that an act may pass, to authorise and make it the duty of the justices of the county court of said county, to assess a tax on the owners of dogs therein, to be applied in aid of the county levy, to subject the owners of dogs to an action for damages, for the first as well as for the second offence, also, to authorize the owner or tenant of any farm to kill any dog that may be found running at large on his premises: Whereupon,

2. *Resolved as the opinion of this committee,* That the prayer of said petition is reasonable.

The said resolutions were, on questions severally put thereupon, agreed to by the house, except the last resolution which was disagreed to.

A report of the committee of claims, rejecting the petition of Berkeley Ward, was read, and on motion of Mr. Hickerson, ordered to be recommitted to the said committee.

A further report of the same committee was read as follows:

The committee of claims have, according to order, had under consideration the petition of William Fenn, to them referred, praying compensation for arresting a horse thief, and have come to the following resolution thereupon:

Resolved as the opinion of this committee, That the prayer of the said petition is reasonable.

The said resolution was, on the question put thereupon, agreed to by the house, and a bill was ordered to be brought in conformably therewith.

The following bills were read the first and ordered to be read a second time, viz:

A bill to incorporate the trustees of the Upperville academy in the county of Fauquier.

A bill to incorporate the Newtown Stephensburg library company.

A bill to authorize the judge of the second circuit to appoint a time for holding the courts thereof, in certain cases.

A bill changing the time of holding the circuit superior courts of law and chancery for the counties of Monroe, Giles and Montgomery.

A bill incorporating the Virginia towing company; and

A bill to amend an act, entitled, "an act to incorporate the Manchester wool and cotton manufacturing company," passed March 13th, 1832.

A bill to change the place of holding a separate election in the county of Tyler; and

A bill to incorporate the Virginia fire insurance company; were severally read the first, and on motions made, the second times, and ordered to be committed to the committees which brought them in.

On motion of Mr. Ball, *Resolved,* That when this house adjourns to-day, it will adjourn until to-morrow 12 o'clock.

And then on motion Mr. Mullen, the house adjourned accordingly.

FRIDAY, February 12th, 1836.

A communication from the senate by their clerk:

IN SENATE, February 11th, 1836.

The senate have passed the bills, entitled,

"An act authorizing James Martin to hold and convey certain real estate."

"An act releasing to William Fisher the commonwealth's right to one thousand acres of land in the county of Nicholas;" and

"An act to establish the town of Hedgesville in the county of Berkeley."

They have also passed the bills, entitled,

"An act to provide an index to the journals of the house of delegates," with an amendment, in which they request the concurrence of the house of delegates.

The said amendment being twice read, was, on the question put thereupon, agreed to by the house.

Ordered, That the clerk inform the senate thereof.

On motion of Mr. Harrison, *Resolved,* That the committee for courts of justice enquire into the expediency of providing by law for the confinement in the penitentiary of this commonwealth, of convicts in the federal courts in this state, who may be sentenced by the said courts to confinement and hard labour, and that the said committee have leave to report by bill or otherwise.

On motion of Mr. Crutchfield, *Ordered,* That leave be given to bring in a bill to incorporate the Fredericksburg mining company, and that Messrs. Crutchfield, Moncure, Hill, Smith of Fauquier, Woolfolk, Harris, Samuel and Nicklin, prepare and bring in the same.

On motion of Mr. Cunningham, *Resolved,* That the committee appointed by the house of delegates to examine into the condition of the Bank of Virginia and Farmers bank of Virginia, be instructed to enquire into the expediency of providing by a declaratory law, that the president and directors of the Farmers bank at Richmond shall so distribute the surplus fund of the bank, intended to meet losses from bad and doubtful debts, as to place the bank at Richmond and the several branches thereof, in point of capital, upon the footing required by the act of incorporation; and that the said committee also enquire and report particularly to this house how the surplus or contingent fund of the Bank of Virginia has been administered.

On motion of Mr. Watkins, *Resolved,* That the committee of roads and internal navigation be instructed to enquire into the expediency of so amending the act authorizing a subscription on behalf of the state to the stock of the Richmond, Fredericksburg and Potomac rail-road company, passed January 23d, 1835, as to specify more accurately the amount of stock to be taken by the board of public works, with leave to report by bill or otherwise.

On motion of Mr. Davison, *Resolved,* That the petition of Hugh M'Gavoc of the county of Wythe, and the accompanying documents, be referred to the committee for courts of justice, with leave to report by bill or otherwise.

On motion of Mr. Garland of Amherst, *Ordered,* That leave be given to bring in a bill appointing trustees for the town of New Glasgow in the county of Amherst, and for other purposes, and that Messrs. Garland of Amherst, Brown of Nelson, Daniel, Pate, Campbell, Austin, Booker and Adams, prepare and bring in the same.

On motion of Mr. Wilson of Botetourt, the rule of the house was suspended, and the vote agreeing to the report of the committee for courts of justice, rejecting the petition of Arthur Lee, a free man of colour, was reconsidered, and then, on motion of Mr. Layne, the said report was ordered to be laid upon the table.

Mr. Garland of Mecklenburg, according to order, presented a bill to suppress the circulation of incendiary publications, and for other purposes.

Mr. Booker, from the committee for courts of justice, presented reports upon the petition of Robin, a free man of colour, and upon the resolution concerning commissions on sales under decrees in chancery.

Mr. Hill, from the committee of propositions and grievances, reported without amendment, a bill to change the place of holding a separate election in the county of Tyler.

And presented a report upon the petition of William H. Riggan, and upon the resolution concerning the Estillville academy.

And a bill to incorporate the Portsmouth and Chesapeake steam-boat company.

Mr. Wilson of Botetourt, according to order, presented a bill authorizing the auditor to issue a warrant in favour of James Paxton.

Mr. Crutchfield, according to order, presented a bill incorporating the Fredericksburg Union manufacturing company.

A bill incorporating the Great Kanawha mining, timber and lumber company.

A bill incorporating the American mining company; and

A bill incorporating the Rappahannock marine and fire insurance company.

Mr. Watkins, from the committee of roads and internal navigation, presented a report upon the petition of citizens of Kanawha county.

And a bill to explain the act authorizing subscriptions on the part of the commonwealth to the capital of joint stock companies.

Mr. Brown of Petersburg, from the committee of finance, presented a bill to authorize the auditor to issue warrants on the treasury in satisfaction of certain judgments against the commonwealth.

Which bills and reports were received and laid upon the table.

On motion of Mr. Watkins, *Ordered,* That the committee of roads and internal navigation be discharged from the farther consideration of the petition of George Price and others, and that the same be laid upon the table.

On motion of Mr. Stanard, a bill to revive and amend an act, entitled, "an act to incorporate the Gallego manufacturing company," passed 20th of January, 1834, was taken up, read the first and second times, and (by general consent,) ordered to be engrossed and read a third time.

Mr. Crutchfield presented a petition of the stockholders of the Rappahannock canal company, praying that the commonwealth may make a further advance upon, or dispose of its stock in said company, which was ordered to be referred to the committee of roads and internal navigation, that they do examine the matter thereof, and report their opinion thereupon to the house.

Mr. Leyburn presented a petition of T. W. Graves, asking that the amount paid by him for a license to vend lottery tickets may be refunded to him, which was ordered to be referred to the committee of finance, that they do examine the matter thereof, and report their opinion thereupon to the house.

On motion of Mr. Booker, *Ordered,* That 185 copies of a bill regulating and reducing the expenses incident to the collection of money under execution, be printed for the use of the members of the general assembly.

An engrossed bill to alter the terms of the circuit superior courts of law and chancery for the seventh district and thirteenth circuit of this commonwealth, was read a third time:

Resolved, That the bill do pass, and that the title be, "an act to alter the terms of the circuit superior courts of law and chancery for the seventh district and thirteenth circuit of this commonwealth."

Ordered, That Mr. Hunter of Berkeley, carry the same to the senate and request their concurrence.

On motion of Mr. Carter, the following report was taken up and read:

The select committee, to whom was referred the subject of increasing the banking capital of this commonwealth, and so much of the governor's message as relates to the banking capital and currency of the commonwealth, respectfully present on these subjects the following report and resolutions:

The committee have come to the all-important subject which has been submitted to their consideration by the house of delegates, with great diffidence, and under a strong sense of its importance to every portion of the community. The interests which are involved, extend themselves to every branch of trade and commerce, as well as to every profession of the country—the banker, who looks solely to the interests of stockholders—the merchant, who covers the sea with vessels freighted with the commodities of commerce—and the honest ploughman, engaged in the humble though useful cultivation of the earth, participate, in a greater or less degree, in these various and complicated interests. They are all connected by the same chain—one link of which being struck, the vibration is felt throughout.

The first and most important question which presents itself to the deliberation of the committee, is, whether the banking capital of the commonwealth shall be *augmented*? In the consideration of this question, the committee deem it not important to enter at large into the policy of banking institutions: these have already, for more than forty years, been established in the state of Virginia; and the circulation of this, as well as of every other state of the American confederacy, is composed in part of the precious metals, and to a much greater extent, of paper, which has become the representative of coin. It may be reasonably doubted, whether the commercial exchanges of the American community could, in the present condition of the currency, be restored to the exclusive use of the precious metals, or, if this were practicable, whether it would not, in the transmission of large amounts of metal from one place to another, produce increased expense and great inconvenience. It was in consequence of this expense and inconvenience, in the transmission of metals from one place to another, that banks of deposite were at first established, where deposites were made of the precious metals, and certificates of deposite issued. Such was the bank of Amsterdam and others. These certificates of deposite were equivalent to the metal deposited: they thus became the representative of such metal, and when payments were to be made from one country to another, these certificates were transmitted in lieu of the metal they represented. It soon became known that a small amount of metal would authorize the issue of a greater amount of paper, yet that it would be practicable to redeem all the paper which would at any time be presented at bank for payment. The difference between the amounts of metal which a bank may have at any time on hand, and the amount of its notes in circulation, has been termed the "circulating credit" of the country. It increases by so much the money of the country, and enables those who are engaged in buying and selling, to extend their commercial operations much further than they could do, if the circulation of the country were confined alone to metal.

All that we can with propriety do in the present state of things, is so to regulate the banking institutions of the country, as to prevent, as far as it is practicable by legislation, that reckless over issue of paper, by which the currency of the country may be deranged and finally depreciated, while at the same time we provide for the necessary and reasonable wants of the community.

It is necessary that the amount of paper in circulation should at all times be so far within the control of the banks, as to render its redemption in specie practicable. The adoption of a paper currency can never be injurious to a country so long as it is convertible at option into specie or bullion. The temptation to banks to over issue, will always be sufficiently checked, by the fact, that whenever a bank is so imprudent as to issue notes over and above the wants of the country, the currency would depreciate, and the paper of the bank would be returned to be exchanged for coin. This drain of the precious metals from the banks will continue until the bank diminishes the number of its notes, and brings back the currency to its natural level. It is obvious, that as the nominal prices of commodities will increase by the over issue of currency, so, for the same reasons, the contraction below the natural wants of circulation will diminish the nominal prices in the same proportion. This is an event not likely to occur, however, if there be a sufficiency of banking capital; for as the profits of a bank that issues paper, depend upon the quantity it can circulate, the directors will always endeavour to make the supply equal to the demand.

It is thus that the value of the currency is made to correspond with that of the precious metals, of which it is composed, or into which it is convertible, and as long as they continue to be the standard by which the value of other commodities is estimated, the circulating medium of the country will suffer no permanent depreciation, but only such as may arise from the intrinsic value of the precious metals themselves.

The rapid control over bank issues, will receive illustration by reference to certain facts developed in the report of the bullion committee made to the English house of commons in the year 1809, on an inquiry produced by the high rate of exchange, which, at the time, was against England, and by the writings of Ricardo, shewing a depreciation in the paper currency, and the high price of bullion. During the examination of the bank directors, before that committee, the question occurs—"What is the criterion which enables the bank to keep the issues of notes within the limit which the occasion of the public requires, and to guard against excess in the circulation of the country?" The answer is—"First, The paper would revert to us, if there were a redundancy in circulation; secondly, By discounting only solid paper, given, as far as we can judge, for real transactions."

If we refer to the actual condition of the currency, and observe its fluctuations whenever there is an over issue, the fact that the paper will revert to the bank will appear. For example: "In April 1809, immediately preceding the payment of dividends, the amount of notes of £5 and upwards, was £ 13,000,000. Subsequently to the 11th of April, an issue took place of £ 4,000,000, yet, on the 7th of May, the amount in circulation was only £ 13,100,000."

"On the 7th of July, the amount of £ 5 notes was £ 12,800,000; and of the issue of seven millions between the 11th and the end of the month, no evidence appeared on the 7th of August beyond a circulation of £ 13,100,000."

If this, then, be considered as an axiom, and it is sanctioned by the authority of great names, it would seem that there is no ground for great fear that the banks of this state will, for any length of time, issue beyond the regular wants of the community, as long as they are required to redeem their notes on demand with specie; because it is evident, that if these over issues did occur, bank notes would immediately depreciate, and that specie being worth more than notes, the bank paper would be rapidly thrown back upon the bank, and metal demanded for them.

Another principle seems also to be illustrated by the facts quoted in regard to the English currency, and if true there, it would, beyond doubt, be true here also.

It is the difficulty that exists (if indeed it be not impossible) to keep in circulation an amount, either of paper or of metal, beyond the demands of the community. In this quality, the community may be compared to a sponge, which has the power of absorbing only a given quantity of any fluid, and whenever it is in excess, it parts with it, or refuses to take up more.

Another check which may be somewhat relied upon to keep the banks within the legitimate and prudent exercise of the power they possess to issue paper, is the frequent expositions which they are called upon and required to make under their charters, as to the actual condition of their outstanding debt, the specie on hand, and the amount of their circulation.

The committee think it perfectly demonstrable, that unless it can be proven that the capital employed by the banks at present existing in the state, is greater than the demands of the community require, (and that it is, no one, it is believed, will contend,) that a considerable deficiency will be produced in the currency, when the offices of the United States bank, now doing business in the state, shall have ceased their banking operations. The charter of the bank of the United States will expire on the 3d of March, 1836; the branch located in Richmond has a capital employed of one million of dollars, and the branch at Norfolk half a million of dollars. It will appear by reference to "extracts from the semi-annual statement of the office of the bank of the United States at Norfolk," that on the 31st of May, 1835, the circulation of the branch in that borough, was $ 668,390, and its active debt amounted to $ 460,055. Your committee have no means of ascertaining the precise amount of either the circulation or the active debt of the branch situated in Richmond. By reference to the report of the select committee, made to the house of delegates at the last session of the legislature, the debt due to the Richmond branch amounted to "little short of" $ 1,500,000; but in this estimate there must be some error, as it would employ no more than the capital of the bank. But let us suppose it to be correct. The debt due to the two branches of the United States bank in Virginia, would amount to nearly two millions of dollars, and the circulation, if in the same ratio with the branch at Norfolk, would be $ 2,005,170, making the total circulation of the United States bank in the state $ 2,673,560.

Under these circumstances, the present banks must increase the circulation by an additional issue of two millions of dollars, or the space now filled in the circulation of the country by the notes of the United States bank, will be left unfilled. It is contrary to the principles which regulate the currency, to suppose that a vacuum in the circulating medium will remain for any length of time unfilled; if, therefore, it be not filled by the notes of our own state banks, as it may be gradually created by the withdrawal of the notes of the United States bank, the notes of foreign banks will be imported into the state, until the circulation regains its former level.

Is it probable that the existing state banks, can, with perfect safety, if indeed at all, with their present capital, so increase their issues? Your committee are confidently of opinion that they cannot; for as it is always the interest of these institutions, as it has been before stated, to keep as much of their paper in circulation as possible, in order to increase the profits of the stockholders, it is probable they have at the present moment extended their business as far as it is prudent for them to extend it.

The whole circulation of bank notes, issued by banks located within the state, is, at the present time, nearly as follows:

The bank of Virginia and its branches have at this time in circulation,	$ 2,984,895
Farmers bank of Virginia and its branches,	1,855,298
Bank of the Valley and its branches,	944,445
North-western bank of Virginia,	152,810
To which, if the circulation of the U. S. bank be estimated at	2,673,560
We have a circulation of notes belonging to banks within the state, amounting to the sum of	$ 8,611,008

The circulation of state bank notes, then, being estimated at eight millions and a half of dollars, and the circulation of the United States bank being withdrawn, would diminish the circulation of the country about *one fourth*.

It may be objected to the above mode of calculation, that although we may accurately ascertain the amount of notes issued by the banks, yet we cannot so well know the amount actually retained in circulation within the state. This is certainly to some extent true, but it may be reasonably inferred, that as many notes of foreign banks come into the state as will equalize the amount of our own notes, having a foreign circulation.

Let us also inquire how the United States bank can call in her outstanding debt, due within the state of Virginia, estimated at two millions, without collecting large amounts of the notes of the state banks. The state bank notes are inevitably thus to be used, by those who owe debts to the bank of the United States, and as they are daily collected by that bank, they will be sent into the state banks, and paid either in United States bank notes, in precious metal, or in bills drawn upon the north.

Under this view of the subject, your committee are so impressed with the necessity of increasing the banking capital of the state, that they may be permitted to consider it a proposition which requires no further illustration.

But let us take a rapid and superficial view of the condition of our own state, in relation to some others of the confederacy. First, in regard to *banking capital*. Second, *population*, at different periods. Third, *as to* the value of real estate. And lastly, in relation to their *exports* and *imports*; and we shall find that in the three last, which may be deemed essentials of national wealth, we have been outstripped by other states. From the best information within reach of the committee,

The banking capital of New York in 1835, amounted to	$ 31,780,264
Pennsylvania,	17,061,944
Maryland,	9,270,091
Whilst the state of Virginia has a banking capital, real and authorized, of	6,706,000

If reference be made to the statement appended to this report, shewing the banking capital of the United States and the population of each state according to the census of 1830, it will be found that the population of the above-named states stood thus:

New York had a population of	-	1,913,006
Pennsylvania,	"		1,384,233
Maryland,	"	-	-	447,040
Virginia,	"		-	1,211,405

By a comparison of the banking capital and the population of these several states, we shall obtain the following results: 1st, That New York has an excess of population over Virginia of 701,595 souls, while she has an excess of banking capital over Virginia of more than $25,385,000; 2dly, That Pennsylvania has an excess of population over Virginia of 172,828 souls, while her excess in banking capital amounts to $10,689,944; 3rdly, But as Maryland is, like Virginia, a slave-holding state, the comparison between her and Virginia may be considered as more appropriate; here, too, the same results are attained, for Maryland with a population *under* that of Virginia of 764,445 souls, has a banking capital *over* that of Virginia, of $2,875,491. The comparison, if extended further, would only exhibit the same results.

It may not be uninteresting to refer to the amount of circulation generally in the United States, as well as in England and France, for 1834. On the 1st of December, 1834, it was estimated that the circulation of paper, gold and silver, in the United States, amounted to ninety-eight millions, which, divided among a population of fourteen millions, would give an active circulation per head of seven dollars only. While in England, for the same year, the circulation is estimated by Marshall to have been 281 millions, which divided among a population of 15¼ millions, would give a circulation per head equal to 18¼. In France, in the same year, the circulation is estimated at 557, which, distributed through a population of 29 millions, would give per head 19.

It is unquestionably true, that if we extend our view beyond Virginia, into the states composing the northern portion of our confederacy, we shall on all sides be presented with the evidences of an activity and improvement, in all the departments of human industry, which will convince the most superficial observer, that they have advanced much more rapidly than we have, in population, wealth and commerce. But while your committee are ready to admit, that we find there the indications of great and increasing prosperity, they do not fully concur in the arguments of those, who attempt to prove that this prosperity is to be attributed *solely* to the large amount of banking capital that has been created in those states, whilst they readily acknowledge that bank capital may have been the spring which has pressed into action, energies, which, without its impetus, may have remained for a long time dormant.

It has been just stated, that New York, by the census of 1830, has an excess of population over Virginia, of 701,595 souls, and that Pennsylvania has a like excess of 172,828 souls. If we refer to the census of 1790 and 1800, we shall find that the relative amounts of population were very different. It then stood thus:

New York,	318,796
Pennsylvania and Delaware,	480,893
Virginia,	454,983

If we compare this population with the superficial extent of each of these states, we shall find that the population compared to the square mile, was nearly the same in each of them, and if the slave population of Virginia be embraced in the calculation, she will be found to have been the most densely peopled of the three.

The number of persons to the square mile in New York, Pennsylvania and Virginia, stood thus:

	In 1790.	In 1800.	In 1810.
New York,	7.56	13.02	21.31
Pennsylvania,	9.28	12.87	17.30
Virginia,	10.68	12.65	13.92

Your committee are induced to believe, that the increase of the population, both of New York and Pennsylvania, may be attributed, in part, to the fact that large cities were to be found in each of these states, inducing immigration, whereas Virginia had none. But granting this to be so, does it not shew that a like advantage would result to Virginia, if she had upon her seaboard or her fine navigable rivers, some emporium of commerce? To shew the influence upon the population of these states, which has been produced by their cities alone, let us refer to their population at different periods:

The population of the *city* of New York in 1696, was estimated so low as 4,302, whereas in 1830, its population was found to be as much as 202,589, making the increase, in the *city alone*, amount to 198,287 souls.

The population of Philadelphia in 1790, stood at 42,500, while in 1830, it was found to be 167,811, exhibiting an increase in the city of Philadelphia, of 125,311 souls.

The influence shewn to have been exercised on the population of New York and Pennsylvania, though considerable, is not the only point of view in which the benefits derived from their cities have been felt. Commerce and wealth, and luxury, may be said to be companions almost inseparable. Though the natural wants of man are few, and generally within his reach, yet as he advances in civilization and refinement, his demands are multiplied until they cannot be enumerated. Thousands of persons, mechanical, agricultural and professional, are employed to administer to his comfort, his pleasure, and his taste. These large cities not only attract to them a large population from abroad, and afford employment to thousands in the various mechanical occupations of life, but by creating a ready mart and offering high prices for all the productions of the earth, agriculture is stimulated widely around them, and by the superabundant wealth and luxury of the city, the country is beautified and adorned.

We shall feel more convinced of this influence, if we institute a comparison of the value of real estate between Virginia and other states. From an estimate of real estate, made for purposes of taxation in 1799 and 1815, it will be seen that the real estate of Pennsylvania in 1799, amounted to $102,145,900, and in the year 1815, to $346,633,889. New York, at the same periods, had of real estate $100,380,706, and $269,370,900, while the estimate at like periods in Virginia, was $71,225,127, and $165,608,179.

The commercial prospects of Virginia, when viewed in relation to other states of the Union, are equally, if not more gloomy, than in regard to population or the estimated value of real estate.

The average exports from 1802 to 1812, as stated by Seybert, were as follows:

Massachusetts exported merchandize of all descriptions, valued at	$13,451,241
New York,	15,516,150
Pennsylvania,	10,634,740
Maryland,	8,252,678
And Virginia, only	4,358,058

The value of exports and imports from the abovementioned states, for the year ending September 30th, 1834, and for nine months ending June 30th, 1835, were, as stated below, viz:

	30th September, 1834.		9 months, to June 30th, 1835.
Massachusetts, Imports,	$17,672,129	Imports,	$12,194,449
" Exports,	10,148,820	Exports,	6,717,858
New York, Imports,	73,188,594	Imports,	54,349,558
" Exports,	25,349,568	Exports,	21,259,275
Pennsylvania, Imports,	10,479,268	Imports,	8,214,614
" Exports,	3,989,746	Exports,	2,663,075
Virginia, Imports,	837,325	Imports,	398,873
" Exports,	5,483,098	Exports,	3,568,100

It may not be improper here to remark, that the produce shipped coastwise, is not taken into the estimate of exports, including only the foreign trade; of course, it may be calculated with certainty, that a considerable portion of the flour and other products of Virginia, is included in the amount of exports from foreign states. These estimates are presented, not solely with a view of contrasting the foreign trade of Virginia with that carried on by her sister states, but to shew what a large portion of foreign articles, finally sold and consumed in Virginia, are imported by other merchants than their own.

During twenty-one months previous to the 30th day of June, 1835, the exports of Virginia, exceeded her imports by $7,815,000, by which it appears that Virginia received goods or commodities of some sort, which were imported by other states to that amount. If we suppose the profit paid by Virginia upon these importations of $7,815 000, to have been at the rate of ten per cent. profit on the first cost of the article in a foreign market, then we have a loss accruing to Virginia of $781,500, in the shape of profits to foreign importers, which she would have saved, if she had had capital of her own to enable her to make these shipments directly to her own ports. If our state, then, had capital to carry on this trade directly with foreign nations, how great would be her saving, and to what an immense amount is she now tributary to the commercial enterprise and capital of New York or some other northern state!

If we look to the extent and geographical situation of Virginia, to her numerous navigable waters, sending their branches into a considerable portion of the state, to her climate, her soil, and great command of water power, as an agent for propelling machinery, we are of the opinion that in none of these can we discover inferiority to our neighbours. It seems to your committee, that with the same enterprise, the same persevering and untiring industry, and the same capital to put these agents into action, our state may prove herself the rival of the most fortunate of her sisters, in advancing to the goal of national wealth.

Under some of the disadvantages which are at present known and felt, cheering prospects yet present themselves, auguring for the future auspicious results. Our country will shortly be traversed by rail-roads in various directions, and our manufactories are multiplying and yielding handsome profits to those who have made investments in them. As our rail-roads reach the borders of our coterminous states, much of the produce of these countries will be conveyed into the state, which has heretofore seldom, and but in small quantities, reached our markets. As the commodities of commerce increase, either in quantity or price, so is it required to increase the capital of the country—money being the universal equivalent by which exchanges are made.

The public interests that recommend, according to the foregoing views, the augmentation of the bank capital of the state, demand, in the opinion of your committee, the exercise of the utmost caution and circumspection on the part of the legislature, in guarding against the mischiefs that may result from the course of action to which banking establishments have been most prone. There is a constant tendency in such institutions, especially in times of great apparent commercial prosperity, and activity in the various classes of industry and enterprise, to yield to solicitations for accommodation, and thus swell the issues of the banks to the verge of danger, from the frequent and often sudden and unforeseen vicissitudes to which commercial and other enterprises in which the capital supplied by such issues may be engaged, are exposed, and when those vicissitudes occur, the sudden contraction of those issues that self-security may require of the banks, causes fluctuations in the value of property and of money, always mischievous, and in many instances ruinous. Banks should not be established for the benefit of those who may chance to get their stock. When established, they become connected with public interests of great magnitude and importance, and the most vigilant care should be excited, by prudent and judicious restraints, to guard those interests from evils to which the mismanagement of those institutions may expose them. As those institutions will supply, by their notes or bills of credit, a large portion of the currency of the country, the paramount consideration with the legislature should be, so to organize them as to take all proper guarantees to keep the currency that may be supplied sound and convertible at all times into specie, and of general credit through the state, so that it may circulate without discount or depreciation. To this end, it seems fit to your committee, that restraints more strict than those imposed by the charters of the existing banks in this state, on the discounts of the new institutions, should be imposed. By those charters, the existing banks are authorized to discount to an amount equal to three fold of the capital stock paid in and deposites. Your committee think that discounts beyond twice the amount of capital and deposites should not be authorized; and they have the less difficulty in recommending this restriction, because that limit, it is believed, has been rarely transcended by the existing banks.

Another consideration is deemed worthy of notice in this connection. It is desirable to preserve and enlarge the metallic basis on which the bank circulation ought to repose, as a means of securing that circulation from depreciation, and mingling with it a convenient and useful portion of specie. For this object, it would be prudent at least to reserve to the legislature the power, to be exercised in its discretion at any future time, to prevent the issue of notes of less than ten dollars, and should it seem fit, after the lapse of a reasonable time, to prevent the circulation of notes of less than twenty dollars.

1. *Resolved therefore as the opinion of this committee,* That it is expedient at this time to augment the banking capital of this state.

2. *Resolved,* That in making such augmentation, it is expedient that restraints more strict than those imposed by the charters of the existing banks, to prevent excessive issues, and to give additional security for the soundness of the currency that such issues may supply, and its general credit throughout the state, should be carefully provided.

The said resolutions were, on questions severally put thereupon, agreed to by the house, and bills were ordered to be brought in conformably therewith.

A bill to incorporate the stockholders of the Lynchburg and Tennessee rail-road company, and to authorize them or the James river and Kanawha company to construct a rail-road from Lynchburg to Richmond, with the amendments thereto proposed by the committee of roads and internal navigation, was taken up on motion of Mr. M'Mullen, and the said amendments being severally agreed to, except the fifth amendment, which was disagreed to by the house, and the said bill being further amended on motions made by Mr. Stanard and Mr. M'Mullen, was, as amended, ordered on motion of Mr. Hopkins, to be laid upon the table.

On motion of Mr. Gilmer, the house adjourned until to-morrow 12 o'clock.

SATURDAY, February 13th, 1836.

A communication from the senate by their clerk:

IN SENATE, February 12th, 1836.

The senate recede from their first and third, and insist on their fourth amendment to the resolutions relative to the interference of certain associations in the northern states with domestic slavery in the south.

On motion of Mr. Hill, *Ordered,* That the said resolutions and amendments be laid upon the table.

On motion of Mr. Price, *Ordered,* That leave be given to bring in a bill to authorize the common council of the town of Fredericksburg to make an advancement upon the stock of the corporation in the Rappahannock canal company, and that Messrs. Crutchfield, Price, Moncure, Hill, Nicklin, Williams, Woolfolk, Smith of Fauquier, and Harris, prepare and bring in the same.

Mr. Parker, from the committee on the militia laws, presented a bill to amend the several acts concerning the public guard in the city of Richmond, which was received and laid upon the table.

Mr. Murdaugh presented a petition of John Benson, praying that citizens of the northern and eastern states may be prohibited from removing oysters at certain seasons of the year from the waters of the commonwealth, which was ordered to be referred to the select committee on that subject, that they do examine the matter thereof, and report their opinion thereupon to the house.

Mr. Booker presented a petition of citizens of the county of Buckingham, for the incorporation of a company to make a rail-road from Richmond to Lynchburg, which was ordered to be laid upon the table.

Mr. Decamps presented a petition of Benjamin Ramsay and others, for an act to incorporate the Wellsburg lyceum society, which was ordered to be referred to the committee of schools and colleges, with leave to report thereon by bill.

A bill to change the place of holding a separate election in the county of Tyler, was taken up, and ordered to be engrossed and read a third time.

The following bills were read the second time and ordered to be engrossed and read a third time, vis:

A bill incorporating the Virginia towing company.

A bill to incorporate the Newtown Stephensburg library company.

A bill changing the time of holding the circuit superior courts of law and chancery for the counties of Monroe, Giles and Montgomery.

A bill to amend an act, entitled, "an act to incorporate the Manchester wool and cotton manufacturing company," passed March 13th, 1832.

A bill to authorize the judge of the second circuit to appoint a time for holding the courts thereof in certain cases; and

A bill to incorporate the trustees of the Upperville academy, in the county of Fauquier.

The following bills were read the first time and ordered to be read a second time, viz:

A bill to change the place of holding a separate election in the county of Lunenburg.

A bill to authorize a separate election at the house of Michael Snodgrass, in the county of Monongalia.

A bill to incorporate the Stafford mining company.

A bill to authorize a separate election at Triadelphia, in the county of Ohio.

A bill to amend an act, entitled, "an act to incorporate the Cold Brook company of colliers," passed January 23d, 1835.

A bill to incorporate the Fauquier White Sulphur springs.

A bill to explain the act, entitled, "an act to reduce into one act the several acts and parts of acts, concerning the county and other inferior courts, and the jurisdiction of justices of the peace within this commonwealth."

A bill incorporating the Natural bridge turnpike company.

A bill to establish an inspection of flour and Indian meal at the town of Winchester.

A bill to incorporate the Virginia insurance company.

A bill to amend the act, entitled, "an act for opening and improving the navigation of the Dragon swamp."

A bill to change the time of holding the county court of Alleghany county.

A bill to authorize additions to the town of Farmville in the county of Prince Edward.

A bill to amend the act, entitled, "an act incorporating a company to erect a toll bridge over the Ohio river at Wheeling," passed February 17th, 1816.

A bill to incorporate the Red springs company.

A bill establishing a new regiment in the county of Preston.

A bill to amend the act concerning fraudulent devises.

A bill to amend the act, entitled, "an act to alter and reform the mode of proceeding in the courts of chancery."

A bill to incorporate the trustees of the Estillville academy.

A bill requiring of the inspectors of tobacco in this commonwealth, to distinguish in their inspections between tobacco produced in Virginia, and that produced in other states.

A bill to incorporate the United States copper mining company.

A bill to amend an act incorporating the Spring creek turnpike company.

A bill incorporating the Laurel Hill turnpike company.

A bill to amend the act, entitled, "an act, making further provision for completing the road from Staunton to the mouth of the Little Kanawha."

A bill to establish the town of Lovettsville in the county of Loudoun.

A bill to incorporate the New Hope gold mine company.

A bill appointing commissioners to select a site for the seat of justice for the county of Ohio.

A bill to incorporate the Gill's mountain mining company.

A bill to incorporate the city of Wheeling in Ohio county.

A bill to amend the act, entitled, "an act to amend and reduce into one act, all acts and parts of acts to prevent the destruction of oysters," passed March 24th, 1831.

A bill incorporating the Literary and Scientific mechanics institute of Norfolk and Portsmouth.

A bill concerning the county of Gloucester.

A bill changing the place of holding a separate election in the county of Kanawha.

A bill declaring Pocatallico river a public highway.

A bill to amend the act, entitled, "an act to incorporate the Richmond manufacturing company," passed on the 12th January, 1832.

A bill to incorporate the coal working company of Richmond and Manchester.

A bill incorporating the Staunton and Augusta springs turnpike company; and

A bill directing the sale of the stock held by the state in joint stock companies incorporated for purposes of internal improvement.

A report of the committee of propositions and grievances, rejecting the petition of citizens of Caroline, Essex, and King & Queen counties for a new county out of parts of said counties, was, on motion, ordered to be laid upon the table.

A report of the committee on the register's office, was read as follows:

The committee appointed to examine the register's office, have performed that duty, and respectfully submit the following report:

The accounts furnished by the register, shew the amount of fees received in the land office, for the year ending on the 4th day of November, 1835, to be $4,158 62¼. These accounts are rendered semi-annually, and embrace since the last settlement, the following items:

Fees received in the land office between the 4th day of November, 1834, and the 4th day of May, 1835:

Fees received on surveys,	1,757 25
On Northern Neck surveys,	164 94
On land office treasury warrants,	220 63
On exchange treasury warrants,	16 00
On military warrants, including exchange and duplicate military warrants,	270 92
On searches, copies and certificates,	104 66
On caveats,	7 50
	$2,541 91

Fees received between the 4th of May, 1835, and the 4th of November, 1835:

On surveys,	435 26
On Northern Neck surveys,	17 44
On treasury warrants,	204 34¼
On exchange treasury warrants,	10 00
On military warrants, including exchange and duplicate warrants,	850 58
On copies, searches and certificates,	90 09
On caveats,	9 00
	1,616 71¼
To amount of the first half year,	2,541 91
	$4,158 62¼

These accounts are verified by the affidavits of the register, and certified to have been examined by J. Jackson, clerk of accounts. The committee, however, on examining the entries on the books of the office, find a trifling error in the amount of fees received on surveys, of $1 54, undercharged, caused by some inadvertence in extending the additions. This will be carried into the accounts of the present year, and adjusted at the next settlement.

The amount above exhibited, of $4,158 62¼ has been duly paid into the treasury, as appears by proper receipts from the auditor's office in the possession of the register, the first being dated on the 4th day of May,

1835, for	2,541 91
And the other on the 4th day of November, 1835, for	1,614 00
	4,155 91
Amount due the register, as appears by the report of last year, and which was deducted from the payment made 4th November, 1835,	2 71¼
	$4,158 62¼

During the past year there have been issued from the land office,
    175 Treasury warrants,
    26 Exchange treasury warrants,
    263 Military warrants,
    37 Military exchange warrants, and
    11 Caveats.

The committee find, that within the same period, 807 grants for lands have been recorded, and 100 grants for land in the Northern Neck, and that all surveys have been recorded upon which grants could have issued according to law.

The committee take pleasure in stating, that they found the books and papers of the office well arranged, and generally in a good state of preservation. They observe a mouldy appearance about some of the cases, owing to the humid atmosphere of the room in which they are placed. To avoid serious injury to the records of the office, in the course of time from this cause, a frequent exposure of them to the sun and a drier air, is in the opinion of the committee, indispensable.

On motion of Mr. Summers, ordered that the same be laid upon the table.

Several reports of the committee of propositions and grievances were read as follow:

The committee of propositions and grievances have, according to order, had under consideration sundry petitions to them referred, and have come to the following resolutions thereupon:

1. *Resolved as the opinion of this committee,* That the petition of sundry citizens of the county of Loudoun, praying that an act may pass, incorporating a joint stock company, for the purpose of constructing a bridge across the Shenandoah river at Harper's Ferry, with a capital of six thousand dollars, and with the liberty of increasing it if necessary; that after declaring a dividend of not exceeding ten per cent. in any one year, the surplus tolls to be

appropriated in the nature of a sinking fund, for the redemption of the capital stock, so as ultimately to make the same a free bridge, is reasonable.

2. *Resolved as the opinion of this committee*, That the petition of Noble S. Braden, of the county of Loudoun, and Fleming Hixon, of the county of Jefferson, (together with the petitions of sundry citizens of the county of Loudoun, and of the town of Harper's Ferry and country adjacent thereto, in their behalf,) praying for an act of incorporation, authorizing them to erect a toll bridge across the Shenandoah river at Harper's Ferry, be rejected.

3. *Resolved also as the opinion of this committee*, That the petition of sundry citizens of the county of Jefferson, praying that an act may pass, incorporating a company to construct a bridge across the Shenandoah river at Harper's Ferry, be rejected.

4. *Resolved as the opinion of this committee*, That the petition of Richard Lorton of the county of Henrico, representing that under peculiar circumstances, he became in the year 1833, sole owner of the building on the capitol square, called the museum, and that the establishment having failed as a museum, he proposed to lease the property for years, but as this could only be done, subject to the conditions of the grant of the ground from the commonwealth, he has been unable to find any one willing to take a lease of the same, and proposing that the general assembly resume the grant of the land, allowing the petitioner the value of the improvements erected thereon, or that an act may pass, relinquishing the right of the commonwealth to the said property, or that such alterations be made in the conditions of the grant, as that the petitioner, his heirs, &c., may be enabled to lease the property for purposes other than those designated in the grant from the commonwealth, or to make such other disposition of the same, compatible with the reversionary right of the commonwealth, as he or they may find most beneficial, or that such other relief be extended to the petitioner as may seem proper, is reasonable.

5. *Resolved as the opinion of this committee*, That the petition of sundry citizens of the county of Nansemond, asking that an act may pass, to prevent the taking of oysters from the waters of Nansemond river, and Chuckatuck creek, above Logan's shoals in Nansemond river, and Edwin Goodwin's landing on Chuckatuck creek, between the first day of May, and the first day of September, in each and every year, is reasonable.

The committee of propositions and grievances have, according to order, had under consideration the petition of sundry voters of the county of Rockingham, to them referred, praying that an act may pass, establishing a separate election in the town of M'Gaheysville, in said county: Whereupon,

Resolved as the opinion of this committee, That the prayer of said petition is reasonable.

The committee of propositions and grievances have, according to order, had under consideration the petition of William Zull, of the county of Greenbrier, to them referred, praying that a town be established on his land, at the junction of the Blue sulphur turnpike road, (leading west,) with the Kanawha turnpike road, in Walker's meadows in said county, to include about forty acres of land, on the usual terms of establishing towns: Whereupon,

Resolved as the opinion of this committee, That the prayer of said petition is reasonable.

The committee of propositions and grievances have, according to order, had under consideration the petition of sundry citizens of the town of Waterford in the county of Loudoun, to them referred, praying that an act may pass, amending former acts in relation to said town, so as to authorise the citizens thereof to elect a mayor, recorder and other officers, in the manner that incorporated towns elect such officers; and that they be vested with such powers as may be necessary for the well ordering and governing the affairs of said town: Whereupon,

Resolved as the opinion of this committee, That the prayer of said petition is reasonable.

The committee of propositions and grievances have, according to order, had under consideration the petition of Elisha B. Williams, of the county of Alleghany, to them referred, representing that, inasmuch as Jackson's river in said county, is considered a public highway, it is not competent to him to interfere therewith without legislative authority, and being desirous of erecting a wool carding machine near the town of Covington in said county, prays that the general assembly will grant him the privilege, (either above or below high water mark,) to erect suitable buildings for his machinery, at a little fall in the river opposite said town, which fall will answer his purpose without a dam, or otherwise interfering with the navigation of said river, or the rights and privileges of others: Whereupon,

1. *Resolved as the opinion of this committee*, That the prayer of said petition is reasonable.

The said committee have, also, had under consideration, the petition of Simeon B. Jewett and others, his associates, asking the passage of an act, allowing them to establish a lumber yard and office in this commonwealth, and to transact business in their corporate name, (except the use of a seal,) in the same manner and to the same extent, as is allowed them by the act incorporating their company in the state of Alabama, and except also, as to their power to hold real estate, of which they ask to hold only three acres, but with the privilege of holding all such lands as they may find it necessary to purchase in payment of a debt charged thereon: Whereupon,

2. *Resolved as the opinion of this committee*, That the prayer of the petition of Simeon B. Jewett and others be rejected.

The said resolutions were, on questions put thereupon, agreed to by the house, and bills were ordered to be brought in conformably with the first, fourth and fifth resolutions in the first report, and with the resolutions in the other reports, except the last resolution.

Several reports of the committee of roads and internal navigation were read as follow:

The committee of roads and internal navigation have, according to order, had under consideration the petition of Thomas A. Morton, praying that the county courts of Prince Edward and Cumberland, or either of them, be authorized by law to grant him the privilege of erecting a dam across the Appomattox river, from his land in the town of Farmville, to the lands of Richard Randolph's estate on the opposite side, agreeably to the provisions of the general law in relation to mills and mill-dams: Whereupon,

Resolved as the opinion of this committee, That said petition is reasonable.

The committee of roads and internal navigation have, according to order, had under consideration the memorial of the president and directors of the Manchester and Petersburg turnpike company, praying that they be authorized by law to raise an additional capital of $400,000, for the purpose of constructing a rail-road from the city of Richmond to the town of Petersburg; or if a new company be incorporated for such purpose, that such indemnity be provided for the said turnpike company, and the state as a stockholder therein, as may be just and equitable: Whereupon,

Resolved as the opinion of this committee, That said petition is reasonable.

The committee of roads and internal navigation have, according to order, had under consideration the petition of the president and directors of the Lewisburg and Blue Sulphur springs turnpike company, praying a subscription on the part of the state for two fifths of the capital stock of the said company: Whereupon,

Resolved as the opinion of this committee, That said petition is reasonable.

The said resolutions were, on questions put thereupon, agreed to by the house, and bills were ordered to be brought in conformably therewith.

The following reports of the committee for courts of justice were read:

The committee for courts of justice have, according to order, had under consideration the petition of Thomas Culpeper, to them referred, praying to be divorced from his wife Caroline, and have come to the following resolution thereupon:

Resolved as the opinion of this committee, That the prayer of the said petition be rejected.

The committee for courts of justice have, according to order, had under consideration the petition of Joseph Bailey, to them referred, praying to be divorced from his wife Eliza, and have come to the following resolution thereupon:

Resolved as the opinion of this committee, That the prayer of the said petition be rejected.

The committee for courts of justice have, according to order, enquired into the expediency of so amending the laws relating to slaves, free negroes and mulattoes, as to provide that all slaves emancipated by any last will and testament that do not leave this state in twelve months after their title to freedom shall accrue, shall forfeit their right to freedom, and descend and pass to the next of kin to the testator or testatrix, as if such testator or testatrix had died intestate as to such slave or slaves: Whereupon,

Resolved as the opinion of this committee, That it is expedient so to amend the said laws.

The committee for courts of justice have, according to order, enquired into the expediency of so amending the laws now in force concerning the jail fees of debtors, as to require security of the creditor for the fees, whenever the jailor shall believe the creditor insolvent, or where the creditor resides out of the county, and upon failure to give such security, the jailor shall, at his pleasure, discharge the debtor: Whereupon,

Resolved as the opinion of this committee, That it is expedient so to amend the said laws.

The committee for courts of justice have, according to order, had under consideration the petition of sundry citizens of the county of Patrick, to them referred, praying that the acts of the general assembly, passed in the years 1819 and 1824, requiring the county courts of this commonwealth to appoint processioners of land, and specifying their duties, &c. may be repealed; and in the event of the legislature thinking the laws on this subject ought not to be repealed, praying that the same may be repealed so far as regards the said county of Patrick, and have come to the following resolutions thereupon:

1. *Resolved as the opinion of this committee,* That so much of the prayer of the said petition as asks a repeal of the laws generally, in relation to processioning lands in this commonwealth, be rejected.

2. *Resolved as the opinion of this committee,* That so much of the prayer of the said petition as asks a repeal of the laws aforesaid, so far as the county of Patrick is concerned, is reasonable.

The committee for courts of justice have, according to order, enquired into the expediency of giving to the courts of law in this commonwealth, power to appoint guardians *ad litem* for infant defendants in said courts: Whereupon,

Resolved as the opinion of this committee, That it is inexpedient to legislate upon the said subject, the courts of law possessing already that power.

The committee for courts of justice have, according to order, had under consideration the petition of Isaac Brock, a free man of colour, to them referred, praying that he may be permitted to remain in the commonwealth until the death of his mother, who is at this time about the age of fifty years, and have come to the following resolution thereupon:

Resolved as the opinion of this committee, That the prayer of the said petition be rejected.

The committee for courts of justice have, according to order, enquired into the expediency of so amending the 17th section of the act of assembly, entitled, "an act to reduce into one act the several acts and parts of acts concerning witnesses, and prescribing the manner of obtaining and executing commissions for taking their depositions in certain cases," passed January 10, 1818, as to authorize the depositions of all witnesses in suits or causes now pending or hereafter to be instituted in any of the courts of this commonwealth, when they reside one hundred miles from the court-house of the county, town or borough in which said suits or cases may be pending, to be taken upon reasonable notice, and to be read upon the trial of the same: Whereupon,

Resolved as the opinion of this committee, That it is expedient so to amend the said section.

The committee for courts of justice have, according to order, had under consideration the petition of Lucy Boomer, a woman of colour, who has been emancipated by the will of John Winn, deceased, to them referred, praying that if she is compelled to be sold, she may be permitted to make choice of a master, and have come to the following resolution thereupon:

Resolved as the opinion of this committee, That the prayer of the said petition be rejected.

The said resolutions were, on questions severally put thereupon, agreed to by the house, and bills were ordered to be brought in conformably with such of said resolutions as were reported reasonable or expedient by said committee.

A report of the committee of propositions and grievances, rejecting the petition of John Ruff and John Jordan of the county of Rockbridge, was, on motion of Mr. Watkins, ordered to be laid upon the table.

A report of the committee of roads and internal navigation, rejecting the petition of George Holleman, and John W. Toney, was, on motion of Mr. Strange, ordered to be laid upon the table.

Several reports of the committee of claims were read as follow:

The committee of claims have, according to order, had under consideration the petition of John Chew, to them referred, and have come to the following resolutions thereupon:

1. *Resolved as the opinion of this committee,* That so much of the prayer of the said petition as asks to be allowed the sum of thirteen hundred and fifty dollars, a balance claimed to be due him, in consideration of services rendered by the petitioner, as commissioner for adjusting the claims of this state against the United States, for military expenditures during the late war, is reasonable.

2. *Resolved as the opinion of this committee,* That so much of the prayer of the said petition as asks an allowance of interest upon the sum aforesaid, be rejected.

The committee of claims have, according to order, had under consideration the petition of Amos Johnson, to them referred, and have come to the following resolution thereupon:

Resolved as the opinion of this committee, That so much of the prayer of the said petitioner, as asks to be allowed certain claims held by him as assignee of George Thayer, drummer in the 44th regiment, is, to the amount of ten dollars, reasonable, and that the remainder thereof be rejected.

The committee of claims have, according to order, had under consideration the petition of Thomas Palmer, administrator of Dominie Bennehan, deceased, to them referred, praying to be refunded the sum of seven hundred and sixty-two dollars and ninety-one cents, being so much paid by the petitioner as administrator of the said Bennehan, who was a joint security with James Shepherd and Richard O. Jeffries, of one David Greenlaw of Richmond county, in a recognizance for his appearance before an examining court, upon a charge of having passed counterfeit money, over and above his co-securities, and have come to the following resolution thereupon:

Resolved as the opinion of this committee, That the prayer of the petitioner is reasonable.

The said resolutions were, on questions put thereupon, agreed to by the house, and bills were ordered to be brought in conformably with the said first and last resolutions.

Reports of the same committee, rejecting the petitions of Stapleton Crutchfield and of Jacob and William Hite, were, on motions severally made, ordered to be laid upon the table.

A report of the committee for courts of justice, rejecting the petition of Celinda C. Wallace, was, on motion of Mr Watkins, ordered to be laid upon the table.

Several reports of the committee of roads and internal navigation, rejecting petitions from Norfolk borough, for an extension of the Portsmouth and Roanoke rail-road to said borough; of the Chesapeake and Ohio canal company; and of the citizens of Albemarle and Nelson, for authority to their county courts to make a road from the head of Rockfish river to Scottsville, were, on motions severally made, ordered to be laid upon the table.

Several further reports of the committee of roads and internal navigation were read as follow:

The committee of roads and internal navigation have, according to order, had under consideration the petition of sundry citizens of the counties of Loudoun and Fauquier, praying sundry amendments to the act incorporating the Goose creek navigation company, and have come to the following resolutions thereupon:

1. *Resolved as the opinion of this committee,* That so much of said petition as prays that each stockholder be required to pay interest on all sums in arrears, after due notice of a call for the same, be rejected.

2. *Resolved as the opinion of this committee,* That so much of said petition as asks a subscription to the stock of said company on the part of the state, be rejected.

3. *Resolved as the opinion of this committee,* That the residue of said petition, praying that power be given said company to augment their capital to sixty thousand dollars; to extend their improvement to the intersection of the Ashby's gap turnpike with Goose creek, and as much higher as their funds will permit; to borrow money; to convert into stock all tolls applied to the construction of their works, and all sums paid as premiums or interest on loans; to erect dams, and to repair, at the expense of the proprietor, any private dam required for the works of the company, if it be beneficial to the proprietor; and that a further time of four years be allowed for the formation of the company, is reasonable.

The committee of roads and internal navigation have, according to order, had under consideration the petition of the Dismal Swamp canal company, by the president and directors thereof, praying that act be passed to authorise the debt due by the company to the commonwealth, and the bank stock loaned the company, to be converted into stock to be held by the state; that the board of public works be authorized to subscribe for 460 shares of stock in said company, which, in addition to the 256 shares proposed to be created as aforesaid, will be less than two fifths of the amount to which the said company ask their capital to be increased; and that the stock of the company be enlarged to $475,000 for the purposes aforesaid: Whereupon,

Resolved as the opinion of this committee, That said petition is reasonable.

The committee of roads and internal navigation have, according to order, had under consideration the petition of sundry citizens of the town of Covington, in the county of Alleghany, praying a change in the location of the contemplated bridge across Jackson's river at the said town, from Second to Third street, and have agreed on the following resolution in relation thereto:

Resolved as the opinion of this committee, That said petition is reasonable, upon the following conditions, to wit: that said bridge be constructed for the sum appropriated therefor by law; and that it be so built at the upper site, as, in the estimation of the principal engineer, to be rendered safe against the operation of freshets.

The committee of roads and internal navigation have, according to order, had under consideration the petition of John M'Clure and others, praying sundry amendments to the act regulating the tolls on the National road passing through Virginia: Whereupon,

Resolved as the opinion of this committee, That said petition is reasonable.

The committee of roads and internal navigation have, according to order, had under consideration the petition of sundry citizens of the town of Smithfield, in the county of Jefferson, praying the incorporation of a joint stock company to construct a rail-road from said town to a suitable point of intersection with the Winchester and Potomac rail-road: Whereupon,

Resolved as the opinion of this committee, That said petition is reasonable.

The committee of roads and internal navigation have, according to order, enquired into "the expediency of appropriating a sum of money to aid in the construction of a road from Moorfield to Wardensville, in the county of Hardy: Whereupon,

Resolved as the opinion of this committee, That it is not expedient to make such appropriation.

The committee of roads and internal navigation have, according to order, had under consideration the petition of the president and directors of the Fallsbridge turnpike company, praying the passage of a law to raise a sum of money by lottery to relieve the said company from their embarrassments: Whereupon,

Resolved as the opinion of this committee, That said petition be rejected.

The said resolutions were, on questions severally put thereupon, agreed to by the house, and bills were ordered to be brought in conformably with such of said resolutions as were reported reasonable.

A report of the committee for courts of justice was read as follows:

The committee for courts of justice have, according to order, had under consideration the petition of John Hope, to them referred, praying to be divorced from his wife Mary S. Hope, and have come to the following resolution thereupon:

Resolved as the opinion of this committee, That the prayer of the said petition be rejected.

The said resolution was, on the question put thereupon, agreed to by the house.

Several further reports of the committee of propositions and grievances were read as follow:

The committee of propositions and grievances have, according to order, had under consideration several petitions to them referred, and have come to the following resolutions thereupon:

1. *Resolved as the opinion of this committee,* That the petition of sundry voters in the northern part of the county of Harrison, praying that the separate election authorized to be holden at the house of James M'Intire, may hereafter be holden at the house of William Black, at Shinnston, in the neighbourhood of said M'Intire's is reasonable.

2. *Resolved as the opinion of this committee,* That the petition of Richard Barton Haxall, representing that he is the proprietor of three contiguous tracts of land, lying on James river, at the Bermuda Hundred in the county of Chesterfield; that a public landing has been from a very early period established there; praying that an act may pass, authorizing him to erect wharves at his own expense, at such convenient points as he may select, between the road called the Bermuda Hundred road, and the upper line of his lands on James river, and that he be allowed to demand and receive such rates of wharfage as shall be deemed proper, is reasonable.

3. *Resolved as the opinion of this committee,* That the petition of sundry citizens of the town of Evansham, in the county of Wythe, praying that an act may pass incorporating a company on the joint stock system, to be called "The Wythe Watering Company," with the privilege of having a capital of six thousand dollars, and the power to organize the company when half that sum shall be subscribed, and that the county court of Wythe be authorized to subscribe a sum not exceeding fifteen hundred dollars in said company, for the purpose of supplying said town with water, to be conveyed in iron or leaden pipes, is reasonable.

The committee of propositions and grievances have, according to order, had under consideration the petition of sundry citizens of the town of Leesburg in the county of Loudoun, to them referred, praying that the act passed at the last session, changing the mode of electing the mayor, recorder and sergeant of said town, may be repealed, and the former law restored; that the act incorporating said town may be amended, so as to prevent all persons, who shall not have been assessed with, and paid their portion of the corporation tax, from voting at their elections; that the time of holding their elections, may be changed from the first Monday in April to the first Monday in May: Whereupon,

Resolved as the opinion of this committee, That the prayer of said petition is reasonable.

The said resolutions were, on questions put thereupon agreed to by the house, and bills were ordered to be borught in conformably therewith.

A report of the committee on the treasurer's accounts was read as follows:

TREASURY OFFICE, January 14th, 1836.

The joint committee of the senate and house of delegates, appointed to examine the treasurer's accounts, have, according to order, performed the duty assigned them, and beg leave to submit the following report to their respective houses:

The annual report of the treasurer for the last fiscal year, terminating on the 30th day of September, 1835, has already put the general assembly in possession of the state of the finances of the commonwealth at that time, and exhibits the true balances on hand on the morning of the 1st day of October, 1835, the commencement of the present fiscal year. This statement is confirmed by information derived from the presidents of the Bank of Virginia and Farmers bank of Virginia.

The joint committee have examined every voucher, both of receipts and disbursements, during the year mentioned, compared them with the entries on the books of the treasurer, find them to be regular, and to correspond with great exactness. The additions were made, and the balances found correct—Indeed it is but just to remark, that the books and accounts of the treasurer manifest great accuracy, as well as great simplicity and method of arrangement.

The joint committee have thought it their duty to ascertain how much money has been paid into the treasury, and how much has been disbursed, from the 30th September, 1835, up to the morning of the 12th instant, and whether or not the proper sum was in bank to the credit of the commonwealth on that day.

To enable your committee to ascertain that fact, their chairmen addressed letters to the auditor and second auditor, requesting to be furnished with statements, shewing the amount of receipts and disbursements from the 30th September, 1835, to the morning of the 12th instant, and the balances on hand at that time. (See documents Nos. 1 and 2.) From the statements furnished by those officers, your committee make the following. (See Nos. 3 and 4.)

	Commonwealth.	Literary Fund.	James River Company.	Board of Public Works.	N. W. Turnpike Road.	Com'rs Sinking Fund.
Balances on hand 1st October, 1835,	118,253 07	68,390 33	4,409 06	76,135 45	42,313 14	—
Received in October, November and December, 1835, and to 12th January, 1836,	347,334 86	6,345 07	10,500 00	21,238 58	—	50,000 00
	465,587 93	74,735 40	14,909 06	97,374 63	42,313 14	50,000 00
Disbursed during same time,	178,933 39	21,374 63	1,662 04	34,868 33	8,353 75	—
Balances on 12th January, 1836,	$286,654 54	53,360 77	13,247 02	62,505 70	33,959 39	50,000 00

RECAPITULATION.

To the credit of the Commonwealth,	286,654 54
Literary fund,	53,360 77
James river company,	13,247 02
Board of public works,	62,505 70
North-western turnpike road,	33,959 39
Commissioners of the sinking fund,	50,000 00
	$499,727 42

It appears from the foregoing statements, that there should have been in the treasury on the morning of the 12th instant, the sum of $499,727 42. For the purpose of ascertaining that fact, the chairmen of the joint committee addressed a letter to each of the presidents of the banks, (see documents Nos. 5 and 6,) requesting to be informed how much money was on deposit to the credit of the treasurer of the commonwealth on the 30th of September, 1835, and on the morning of the 12th instant.

The answers to those letters (see Nos. 7 and 8,) furnish the following information:

In the Bank of Virginia on the morning of the 12th, the amount to the credit of the treasurer of the commonwealth was	250,496 84
In the Farmers bank at the same time,	250,878 57
Total in both banks,	501,375 41
From which deduct the amounts called for by the statements of the first and second auditors,	499,725 10
Leaving an excess in the two banks of	$1,650 31

Which is sufficient to pay the checks drawn by the treasurer on warrants issued by the two auditors previous to, and not presented at the banks for payment at, the time to which this statement has reference.

In conclusion, the joint committee remark that it fully appears, on a full and minute examination of the treasurer's accounts, that all the money which has come to his hands is duly accounted for, according to law.

WM. M. M'CARTY, *C. C. S.*
W. R. JOHNSON, *C. C. H. D.*

Ordered, That the said report be laid upon the table.

The following report of a select committee was read:

The select committee appointed to enquire into the expediency of providing by law for paying to the legal representatives of Severn Eyre the amount of his losses occasioned by the burning of Norfolk in 1776, have, according to order, had the same under consideration, and beg leave to submit the following resolution:

Resolved, That it is expedient to provide by law for paying to the legal representatives of Severn Eyre the amount of his losses, occasioned by the burning of Norfolk in 1776.

The said resolution was, on the question put thereupon, agreed to by the house, and a bill was ordered to be brought in conformably therewith.

Several reports of the committee of propositions and grievances were read as follow:

The committee of propositions and grievances have, according to order, had under consideration several petitions to them referred, and have come to the following resolutions thereupon:

1. *Resolved as the opinion of this committee,* That the petition of sundry citizens of the county of Bedford, praying that so much of the county of Bedford as lies next to the county of Pittsylvania, and is comprehended within a line running from the gap of Smith's mountain, along the ridge of said mountain to Cliff creek, thence down said creek to its junction with Staunton river, may be attached to and made a part of the county of Pittsylvania, be rejected, for want of notice.

2. *Resolved as the opinion of this committee,* That the petition of sundry citizens of the county of Pittsylvania, praying that the separate election now authorized to be holden at the storehouse of Benjamin Watkins, may be removed to the place called Sugar Tree, the residence of Walter Fitzgerald, is reasonable.

The petition of William Wedderburn, of Alexandria, D. C. (a native of Virginia) represents various revolutionary services rendered by him, but without any voucher, save his own affidavit, and prays that the general assembly will grant him such assistance as may seem just, as all the compensation he ever received was a certificate worth two or three dollars, in the year 1783—that he is now 71 years old, in feeble health and straitened circumstances, with two other persons (a wife and child) to support: Whereupon,

3. *Resolved as the opinion of this committee,* That the prayer of the petition of said Wedderburn, be rejected.

The said committee have also had under consideration the petition of the citizens of the town Salem in the county of Botetourt, to them referred, praying that an act may pass incorporating said town: Whereupon,

4. *Resolved as the opinion of this committee,* That the prayer of the citizens of the town of Salem in the county Botetourt, is reasonable.

The committee of propositions and grievances have, according to order, had under consideration the petition of sundry persons associated for the purpose of improving a mineral spring in the county of Grayson, to them referred, praying that the act passed at the last session of the general assembly, entitled, "an act to incorporate the Grayson Sulphur springs company," may be so amended as to incorporate the said persons so associated and signing said petition, as a joint stock company, with twenty shares of one hundred dollars each, with the privilege of increasing the number of shares, not exceeding one hundred, as said company may determine, and that such additional shares may be taken exclusively by the petitioners or others, at the election of the company—that if such additional stock shall be confined to the company, each member shall be at liberty to take an equal number of shares: Whereupon,

Resolved as the opinion of this committee, That the prayer of said petition is reasonable.

The said resolutions were, on questions severally put thereupon, agreed to by the house, and bills were ordered to be brought in conformably with the said second and fourth resolutions in the said first report, and with the resolution in the said last report.

A report of the committee on the penitentiary institution was read as follows:

The committee appointed to examine the penitentiary institution, to whom was referred the petition of sundry citizens of the county of Bedford, have taken the same under consideration, and submit the following resolution:

Resolved as the opinion of this committee, That the said petition, praying that Anderson Read, a convict confined in the penitentiary, may be released from confinement, and pardoned the offence of which he was convicted, be rejected.

The said resolution was, on the question put thereupon, agreed to by the house.

Further reports of the committee of roads and internal navigation were read as follow:

The committee of roads and internal navigation have, according to order, enquired "into the expediency of directing a survey and report by some competent engineer, of the practicability and probable cost of improving the navigation of the Dragon swamp, so as to afford batteaux transportation to the highest practicable point on said swamp:" Whereupon,

Resolved as the opinion of this committee, That it is expedient to direct such survey and report.

The committee of roads and internal navigation have, according to order, had under consideration the petition of sundry citizens of the county of Greensville, praying that the charter of the Greensville and Roanoke rail-road company be so amended, as to authorize the said company to change the location of the public road crossing their rail-road, where it may be deemed expedient: Whereupon,

Resolved as the opinion of this committee, That said petition is reasonable.

The committee of roads and internal navigation have, according to order, had under consideration the memorial of the president and directors of the Pittsylvania and Lynchburg turnpike company, representing that three fifths of the amount of capital necessary to construct their road, have been subscribed by individuals, and praying that a subscription be made on behalf of the state for the remaining two fifths: Whereupon,

Resolved as the opinion of this committee, That said petition is reasonable.

The committee of roads and internal navigation have, according to order, had under consideration the petition of sundry citizens of the county of Prince George and town of Petersburg, praying the incorporation of a joint stock company to construct a rail-road from Petersburg to some point on James river at or in the vicinity of Harrison's bar: Whereupon,

Resolved as the opinion of this committee, That said petition be rejected.

The committee of roads and internal navigation have, according to order, enquired "into the expediency of aiding in the construction of a bridge across the North Fork of Holstein river in the county of Scott:" Whereupon,

Resolved as the opinion of this committee, That it is not expedient to aid in the construction of such bridge.

The said resolutions were, on questions put thereupon, agreed to by the house, and bills were ordered to be brought in conformably with such of said resolutions as were reported reasonable or expedient.

Reports of the committee on agriculture and manufactures were read as follow:

The committee of agriculture and manufactures, to whom was referred the petition of Edward Colston, praying that the banks of the Potomac river, from dam No. 5 of the Chesapeake and Ohio canal, to the upper line of his land on said river, may be declared a lawful fence, having had the same under consideration, have come to the following resolution thereupon:

Resolved, That the prayer of the said petition is reasonable.

The committee of agriculture and manufactures, to whom was referred the petition of Albert Michaels and others, praying for the incorporation of a company to explore and mine for coal in the counties of Chesterfield and Powhatan, having had the same under consideration, have come to the following resolution thereupon:

Resolved, That the prayer of the said petition is reasonable.

The said resolutions were, on questions severally put thereupon, agreed to by the house, and bills were ordered to be brought in conformably therewith.

Reports of the committee of propositions and grievances, reporting reasonable petitions of citizens of Frederick and Shenandoah, for a new county out of parts of said counties, and of other citizens of said counties for another new county, of which Middletown is to be the seat of justice; and of citizens of the eastern part of said county of Frederick for a new county of said portion of the county, were severally ordered to be laid upon the table.

A further report of said committee, rejecting the petition of citizens of the county of Orange for a new county of parts thereof, was on motion, ordered to be laid upon the table.

A report of the committee of finance, rejecting the petition of Henry Anderson, was, on motion of Mr. Hopkins, ordered to be laid upon the table.

A report of the committee of schools and colleges, rejecting the petition of Richard H. Edwards, was, on motion of Mr. Holleman, ordered to be laid upon the table.

Further reports of the said committee were read as follow:

The committee of schools and colleges have, according to order, had under consideration the petition of sundry citizens of the town of Clarksville in the county of Mecklenburg, praying that certain persons in said petition mentioned be incorporated a board of trustees, for the purpose of establishing a female academy in said town: Whereupon,

Resolved as the opinion of this committee, That said petition is reasonable.

The committee of schools and colleges have, according to order, enquired into "the expediency of incorporating the Martinsville academy in the county of Henry:" Whereupon,

Resolved as the opinion of this committee, That it is expedient to incorporate the said academy.

The committee of schools and colleges have, according to order, had under consideration the petition of sundry citizens of the town of Lynchburg, praying the incorporation of trustees of an academy in said town, to be denominated "The Lynchburg female academy:" Whereupon,

Resolved as the opinion of this committee, That said petition is reasonable.

The said resolutions were, on questions severally put thereupon, agreed to by the house, and bills were ordered to be brought in conformably therewith.

The following bills were read the first and second times, and ordered to be committed to the several committees which brought them in, viz:

A bill incorporating the Orange savings society.

A bill incorporating the Smithfield savings institution in the county of Isle of Wight.

A bill releasing the commonwealth's claim to a certain balance against the estate of Betsy Bidgood.

A bill giving to the circuit superior courts of law and chancery concurrent jurisdiction with the county and corporation courts in all actions of forcible entry and detainer.

A bill to provide for the construction of the eastern section of the road on the route surveyed from Huntersville to Parkersburg; and

A bill to provide for the construction of a road from the line of Preston county to the Ohio river.

On motion of Mr. Madison, *Ordered,* That 185 copies of a bill, entitled, a bill to incorporate the stockholders of the Lynchburg and Tennessee rail-road company, and to authorize them, or the James river and Kanawha company to construct a rail-road from Lynchburg to Richmond, be printed for the use of the members of the general assembly.

A bill incorporating the Kanawha slave insurance company, was read the first and second times, and (by general consent,) ordered to be engrossed and read a third time.

On motion of Mr. Mullen, the house adjourned until Monday 12 o'clock.

MONDAY, February 15th, 1836.

Mr. Watkins, from the committee of roads and internal navigation, presented a report upon the memorial on behalf of a convention at Brownsburg, for a subscription by the state to the stock of the Baltimore and Ohio rail-road company.

Also a bill to amend the act, entitled, "an act concerning the Cumberland road."

A bill to amend an act, entitled, "an act to enact with amendments, an act of the general assembly of North Carolina, entitled, 'an act to incorporate the Greensville and Roanoke rail-road company.'"

A bill directing a survey of the Dragon swamp.

A bill to authorize a subscription on behalf of the state to the stock of the Pittsylvania and Lynchburg turnpike company, and for other purposes; and

A bill to authorize a subscription on behalf of the state to the stock of the Lewisburg and Blue Sulphur springs turnpike company.

And reported with amendments, a bill to enact an act of the general assembly of North Carolina, entitled, "an act to incorporate the Roanoke, Danville and Junction rail-road company."

A bill to provide for the construction of a road from the line of Preston county to the Ohio river.

And reported without amendment, a bill to provide for the construction of the eastern section of the road on the route surveyed from Huntersville to Parkersburg.

Mr. Stanard, from the committee for courts of justice, presented a bill to amend and explain the act, entitled, "an act to reduce into one the several acts to regulate the solemnization of marriages, &c." passed 1st March, 1819.

Also from a select committee, reported without amendment, a bill to incorporate the Virginia fire insurance company.

Mr. Hill, from the committee of propositions and grievances, reported with an amendment, a bill releasing the commonwealth's claim to a certain balance against the estate of Betsy Bidgood.

And presented a report upon the petition of citizens of Tazewell county for a separate election in said county.

And a bill to authorize a separate election at M'Gaheysville, in the county of Rockingham.

Mr. Cunningham, from a select committee, presented a bill concerning the legal representatives of Severn Eyre, deceased.

Mr. Carter, from the committee on banks, presented a report upon the petition of citizens of Petersburg, for a savings institution in said town.

Mr. Bowen, according to order, presented a bill to incorporate the Front Royal library society, in the county of Frederick.

Mr. Smith of Gloucester, from the committee on the executive expenditures for the current year, presented a report thereupon.

Which bills and reports were received and laid upon the table.

On motion of Mr. Wilson of Botetourt, *Resolved,* That the committee of privileges and elections enquire into the expediency of so amending the general election law as to provide that all the elections in this commonwealth be held on the same day, and that said committee have leave to report by bill or otherwise.

On motion of Mr. Stanard, *Resolved,* That the committee for courts of justice enquire into the expediency of amending the laws respecting the inspection of fish, so as to change the dimensions of the barrels, and in other respects to conform those laws to those of the other states, and that the said committee have leave to report by bill or otherwise.

On motion of Mr. Hunter of Berkeley, *Ordered,* That leave be given to bring in a bill to incorporate the Berkeley coal mining and rail-road company, and that Messrs. Hunter of Berkeley, Mullen, Smith of Frederick, Henshaw, Berry, Williams and Bare, prepare and bring in the same.

On motion of Mr. Brooke, *Ordered,* That leave be given to bring in a bill to amend an act, entitled, "an act to incorporate the Augusta springs company," so as to add to the number of commissioners appointed under the second section of said act, and that Messrs. Brooke, Gilmer, Dorman, Daniel, Woolfolk, Strange and Goodall, prepare and bring in the same.

On motion of Mr. Murdaugh, *Resolved,* That the committee of schools and colleges be instructed to enquire into the expediency of incorporating the Saint Bride's academy, in Norfolk county, and that they report by bill or otherwise.

Mr. Murdaugh presented a petition of the trustees of the Saint Bride's academy, asking for aid from the literary fund to complete their buildings and to further the objects of the said academy, which was ordered to be referred to the said committee, that they do examine the matter thereof, and report their opinion thereupon to the house.

Mr. Cunningham presented proceedings and resolutions of a meeting of the inhabitants of the borough of Norfolk, in answer to "the explanatory remarks" contained in a communication to this house, made by the president of the Bank of Virginia, in reply to a resolution passed on the 16th of January last; which resolutions were ordered to be referred to the select committee on banks.

On motion of Mr. Brown of Petersburg, *Resolved*, That the committee of finance be instructed to enquire into the expediency of amending the several acts respecting the restraint, support and maintenance of idiots and lunatics, and the preservation and management of their estates, with leave to report thereupon by bill or otherwise.

Mr. Crutchfield, according to order, presented a bill to authorize the common council of the town of Fredericksburg to make an advancement upon the stock of the corporation in the Rappahannock canal company, which, on his motion, was read the first and second times, and (by general consent) ordered to be engrossed and read a third time.

On motion of Mr. Crutchfield, a bill to amend an act, entitled, "an act for opening and improving the navigation of the Dragon swamp," was taken up, read the second time, and ordered to be committed to the committee which brought it in.

On motion of Mr. Booker, the petition of citizens of the county of Buckingham, for the incorporation of an independent joint stock company to construct a rail-road from Richmond to the town of Lynchburg, was taken up, and ordered to be referred to the committee of roads and internal navigation, that they do examine the matter thereof, and report their opinion thereupon to the house.

Mr. Stanard presented a petition of citizens of Richmond, opposing the incorporation of the said joint stock company.

And Mr. Hopkins, a similar petition of inhabitants of the county of Powhatan.

Which petitions were referred to the said committee in like manner.

On motion of Mr. Hays, *Ordered*, That leave be given to bring in a bill changing the time of holding the courts in the counties of Lewis and Braxton, and that Messrs. Hays, M'Mullen, Wethered, Saunders, Jessee, Price and Ingles, prepare and bring in the same.

On motion of Mr. Beuhring, *Ordered*, That leave be given to bring in a bill to change the place of holding a separate election in the county of Cabell, and that Messrs. Beuhring, Summers, Straton, Waggener and Price, prepare and bring in the same.

Mr. Garland of Amherst, presented a petition of Stephen Turner, praying that he may be authorized to appoint a trustee to hold certain property devised to him by his father, under certain limitations, with power to dispose of the same as the trustees appointed by the will of his father were authorized.

Mr. Dorman presented a petition of Andy, a free man of colour, asking permission to remain in the commonwealth.

Mr. Butts, a petition of Littlepage Anderson and his wife, praying to be divorced.

Ordered, That the said petitions be referred to the committee for courts of justice, that they do examine the matter thereof, and report their opinion thereupon to the house.

Mr. Almond presented a petition of sundry inhabitants of the county of Page, praying for a change of the time of holding their county court, which on his motion, was ordered to be referred to the committee of propositions and grievances, that they do examine the matter thereof, and report their opinion thereupon to the house.

Mr. Morris, a petition of citizens of Princess Anne county for the repeal of the act establishing a separate election at Kempsville, in said county; which was ordered to be referred to the said committee.

Mr. Servant presented a memorial of citizens of Elizabeth City county, opposing the petition of other citizens of said county, for dividing the funds of the Hampton academy and establishing therewith two other schools in said county; which was ordered to be referred to the committee of schools and colleges.

Mr. Stanard presented a petition of Peter J. Chevallie, praying the passage of an act for refunding to him the amount paid to the James river company for grants of water for the use of his mill, from the 6th of February, 1833, to the 1st of July, 1834, being the period during which he could not use the said water, in consequence of the burning of his said mill; which was ordered to be referred to the committee of claims, that they do examine the matter thereof, and report their opinion thereupon to the house.

Mr. Harrison submitted certain charges preferred by himself against Edwin S. Duncan, a judge of the general court, assigned to the 18th circuit of this commonwealth, which, on motion of Mr. Dorman, were ordered to be laid upon the table.

Mr. Dorman then presented a memorial of Edwin S. Duncan, praying that the said charges may be investigated, and that measures may be taken to effect that purpose, which was in like manner ordered to be laid upon the table.

On motion of Mr. Dorman, *Ordered*, That 185 copies of the said charges and of the said memorial and accompanying documents, be printed for the use of the general assembly.

Mr. Booker, from the committee for courts of justice, presented a bill making further provision for taking depositions in certain cases.

Mr. Madison, from the committee on agriculture and manufactures, presented a report upon the petition of the inspectors of tobacco at Farmville, for an increase of their salaries.

Which bill and report were received and laid upon the table.

On motion of Mr. Wilson of Cumberland, a bill to incorporate the stockholders of the Cartersville and Farmville rail-road company was taken up, and ordered to be engrossed and read a third time.

A bill authorizing Jesse Sturm to erect a dam across the west fork of Monongalia river in the county of Harrison, was taken up, on motion of Mr. Willey, read the first and second times, and ordered to be committed to the committee which brought it in.

A bill to change the times of holding the courts in the third judicial circuit was taken up on motion of Mr. Parker, read a second time, and in like manner ordered to be committed.

On motion of Mr. Parker, the rule of the house was suspended, and the vote agreeing to the resolutions of the committee on banks, for an increase of the banking capital of the commonwealth, was reconsidered, and the question being upon again agreeing to the first resolution of the said committee, a motion was made by Mr. M'Mullen, that the further consideration thereof be indefinitely postponed, and the question being put thereupon, was determined in the negative. Ayes 35, noes 86.

On motion of Mr. M'Mullen, (seven of the members present concurring,) *Ordered*, That the ayes and noes upon the said question be inserted in the journal.

The names of the gentlemen who voted in the affirmative, are Messrs. Gilmer, Southall, Wiley, M'Clintic, Turnbull, Booker, Austin, Richardson, Wilson of Cumberland, Vaughan, Hunter of Essex, Watkins, Hail of Grayson, Carrington, Coleman, Sloan, Nixon, Holleman, Fleet, Hooe, Robinson, Neill, Ragsdale, Taylor of Mathews and Middlesex, Woolfolk, Hopkins, Shands, Williams, Nicklin, Jessee, M'Mullen, Bare, Butts, Hargrave and Gillespie.—35.

And the names of the gentlemen who voted in the negative, are Messrs. Grinalds, Layne, Garland of Amherst, Brooke, Craig, Campbell, Hunter of Berkeley, Henshaw, Miller, Wilson of Botetourt, Decamps, Beuhring, Daniel, Hill, Servant, Ball, Smith of Fauquier, Hickerson, Price, Strange, Steger, Hale of Franklin, Holland, Bowen, Davison, Smith of Frederick, Watts, Smith of Gloucester, Wethered, Goodall, Mullen, Harrison, Kincheloe, Botts, Fontaine, Gregory, Griggs, Berry, Summers, Carter, Hays, Straton, Beard, Taylor of Loudoun, Waggener, Rogers, Garland of Mecklenburg, Willey, Morgan, Chapman, Ingles, Sherrard, Benton, Brown of Nelson, Murdaugh, Cooke, Parker, Fitzgerald, Chapline, Masters, Almond, Adams, M'Coy, Swanson, Witcher, Cackley, Carroll, Madison, Morris, Marteney, Dorman, Leyburn, Moffett, Conrad, Rinker, Harley, Crutchfield, Moncure, Delashmutt, Gibson, Jett, Prentiss, Saunders, Cunningham, Brown of Petersburg, and Stanard.—86.

The question then recurred upon adopting the said first resolution, which is the following:

Resolved therefore as the opinion of this committee, That it is expedient at this time to augment the banking capital of this state.

And being put thereupon, was determined in the affirmative. Ayes 82, noes 39.

On motion of Mr. Parker, (seven of the members present concurring,) *Ordered*, That the ayes and noes upon the said question be inserted in the journal.

The names of the gentlemen who voted in the affirmative, are Messrs. Grinalds, Layne, Garland of Amherst, Brooke, Craig, Campbell, Hunter of Berkeley, Henshaw, Miller, Wilson of Botetourt, Decamps, Beuhring, Daniel, Servant, Ball, Hickerson, Price, Strange, Steger, Hale of Franklin, Holland, Bowen, Davison, Smith of Frederick, Watts, Smith of Gloucester, Wethered, Goodall, Mullen, Harrison, Kincheloe, Botts, Fontaine, Gregory, Griggs, Berry, Summers, Carter, Hays, Straton, Beard, Taylor of Loudoun, Waggener, Rogers, Garland of Mecklenburg, Willey, Morgan, Chapman, Ingles, Sherrard, Benton, Brown of Nelson, Murdaugh, Cooke, Parker, Fitzgerald, Masters, Almond, Adams, M'Coy, Swanson, Witcher, Cackley, Carroll, Madison, Morris, Marteney, Dorman, Leyburn, Rinker, Harley, Crutchfield, Moncure, Delashmutt, Gibson, Jett, Prentiss, Saunders, Cunningham, Brown of Petersburg, and Stanard.—82.

And the names of the gentlemen who voted in the negative, are Messrs. Gilmer, Southall, Wiley, M'Clintic, Turnbull, Booker, Austin, Richardson, Hill, Wilson of Cumberland, Vaughan, Hunter of Essex, Smith of Fauquier, Watkins, Hail of Grayson, Carrington, Coleman, Sloan, Nixon, Holleman, Fleet, Hooe, Robinson, Neill, Ragsdale, Taylor of Mathews and Middlesex, Woolfolk, Hopkins, Shands, Williams, Nicklin, Moffett, Conrad, Jessee, M'Mullen, Bare, Butts, Hargrave and Gillespie.—39.

The second resolution was then again concurred in by the house, as follows:

Resolved, That in making such augmentation, it is expedient that restraints more strict than those imposed by the charters of the existing banks, to prevent excessive issues, and to give additional security for the soundness of the currency that such issues may supply, and its general credit throughout the state, should be carefully provided.

Ordered, That bills be brought in conformably therewith, and that the said committee prepare and bring in the same.

An engrossed bill to incorporate the Kanawha slave insurance company, was read a third time:

Resolved, That the bill do pass, and that the title be, "an act to incorporate the Kanawha slave insurance company."

An engrossed bill providing for a geological survey of the state, and for other purposes, was read a third time:

Resolved, That the bill do pass, and that the title be, "an act providing for a geological survey of the state, and for other purposes."

Ordered, That the clerk communicate the said bills to the senate and request their concurrence.

An engrossed bill allowing Charlotte Morgan, a free woman of colour, to remain in the commonwealth, was read a third time, and on motion of Mr. Dorman, ordered to be laid upon the table.

An engrossed bill to regulate the conduct of boatmen on the Roanoke river and its branches, was read a third time, and the question being put upon its passage, was determined in the negative
Resolved, That the bill be rejected.
On motion of Mr. Hunter of Berkeley, the house adjourned until to-morrow 12 o'clock.

TUESDAY, February 16th, 1836.

A communication from the senate by their clerk:

IN SENATE, February 15th, 1836.

The senate have passed the bills, entitled,
" An act to enlarge the town of Clarksville in the county of Mecklenburg."
" An act to authorize a separate election at Hedgesville in the county of Berkeley."
" An act to incorporate the trustees of the Halifax academy;" and
" An act to authorize a separate election at the tavern house of William Irwin in the county of Cumberland."
The speaker laid before the house a communication from the governor, enclosing the "annual statement of the Merchants and Mechanics bank of Wheeling, and of its office of discount and deposit at Morgantown," which being read, was, on motion of Mr. Gregory, ordered to be laid upon the table, and 185 copies thereof were ordered to be printed for the use of the general assembly.
On motion of Mr. Smith of Frederick, the following report of the committee of propositions and grievances was taken up and read:
The committee of propositions and grievances have, according to order, had under consideration a petition to them referred, and thereupon submit the following report and resolution:
The petition of sundry inhabitants of the counties of Frederick and Shenandoah, represents various grievances under which they labour, and have for years suffered, as distance from their respective court-houses, and separation from them by rivers and mountains, with rough roads and consequent detention at their court-houses, when called there on public or private business; and prays therefore, that the territory which they occupy, may be formed into a new county, according to certain boundaries in the petition described: Whereupon,
Resolved as the opinion of this committee, That the prayer of the aforesaid petition is reasonable.
The said resolution was, on the question put thereupon, agreed to by the house, and a bill was ordered to be brought in conformably therewith.
On motion of Mr. Williams, *Resolved by the general assembly of Virginia*, That the board of public works be requested to employ a competent engineer to survey a route for a rail-road from Falmouth in the county of Stafford, to Alexandria in the District of Columbia, and from Warrenton in the county of Fauquier, to some point of intersection and union with the route from Falmouth to Alexandria, provided the point of union be not nearer than twelve miles north of Falmouth and eighteen miles south of Alexandria, and that the said engineer report to the next legislature, the practicability, the advantages to the community, and the probable costs of such improvements.
Ordered, That the clerk communicate the same to the senate and request their concurrence.
Mr. Garland of Mecklenburg, from the committee of schools and colleges, presented a report, which, on his motion, was taken up and read as follows:
The committee of schools and colleges have, according to order, had under consideration the petition of sundry citizens of the county of Elizabeth City, praying that one third of the interest arising from the funds of Hampton academy, be appropriated by law, in equal portions, to two other schools, to be located in such places in said county as the trustees of the academy may select: Whereupon,
Resolved as the opinion of this committee, That the said petition be rejected, because the committee, after a full investigation of the subject, think that the said funds were, by a former legislature, appropriated for the sole benefit of said academy, and cannot, consistently with the principles of justice, be diverted from that institution, by this or any subsequent legislature, unless on the application of all the citizens of Elizabeth City county.
The said resolution was, on the question put thereupon, agreed to by the house.
Mr. Garland of Mecklenburg, also from the same committee, presented a bill incorporating the trustees of the Clarksville female academy; and
A bill to incorporate the proprietors of the Wellsburg lyceum.
Mr. Witcher, from the committee of claims, presented a report upon the petition of Berkeley Ward.
Also a bill concerning William Fenn; and
A bill concerning John Chew.
Mr. Hunter of Berkeley, according to order, presented a bill to incorporate the Berkeley coal mining and railroad company.
Mr. Watkins, from the committee of roads and internal navigation, presented a report upon the memorial of the stockholders of the James river and Kanawha company.
And a bill for the construction of a bridge across Jackson's river at the town of Covington.
Mr. Taylor of Middlesex, reported with amendment, a bill to amend an act, entitled, "an act for opening and improving the navigation of the Dragon swamp."

Which bills and reports were received and laid upon the table.

An engrossed bill to incorporate the Narrow falls turnpike company, was taken up on motion of Mr. Summers, whereupon, he offered a clause by way of ryder thereto, which was read the first and second times, and forthwith engrossed and read a third time, and then, on motion of Mr. Watkins, the said bill and ryder was ordered to be laid upon the table.

On motion of Mr. Parker, the resolutions relative to the interference of certain associations in the northern states with domestic slavery in the south, together with the amendments thereto proposed by the senate, was taken up.

The senate had insisted upon their fourth amendment to the said resolutions, to which the house of delegates had disagreed; on motion of Mr. Parker, the house receded from their disagreement to the said amendment, and then the same was amended on his motion, and as amended, was agreed to by the house.

Ordered, That Mr. Parker inform the senate thereof and request their concurrence in the said amendment to their fourth amendment.

An engrossed bill to authorize the common council of the town of Fredericksburg to make an advancement upon the stock of the corporation in the Rappahannock canal company, was taken up on motion of Mr. Crutchfield, and read a third time:

Resolved, That the bill do pass, and that the title be, "an act to authorize the common council of the town of Fredericksburg to make an advancement upon the stock of the corporation in the Rappahannock canal company."

Ordered, That Mr. Parker carry the same to the senate and request their concurrence.

An engrossed bill to amend the act, entitled, "an act to authorize the Upper Appomattox company to enlarge their capital stock, and for other purposes," passed February 23d, 1835, was taken up, on motion of Mr. Madison, read a third time, and sundry blanks therein were filled; and the question being put upon its passage, was determined in the negative. Ayes 38, noes 66.

On motion of Mr. Dorman, (seven of the members present concurring,) *Ordered,* That the ayes and noes upon the said question be inserted in the journal.

The names of the gentlemen who voted in the affirmative, are Messrs. Drummond, Southall, Layne, Wiley, M'Clintic, Hunter of Berkeley, Miller, Wilson of Botetourt, Beuhring, Price, Watts, Watkins, Wethered, Sloan, Holleman, Gregory, Griggs, Hooe, Beard, Taylor of Loudoun, Ragsdale, Waggener, Willey, Morgan, Sherrard, Parker, Fitzgerald, Masters, Almond, M'Coy, Cackley, Hopkins, Carroll, Madison, Harley, Gibson, Prentiss, and Brown of Petersburg.—38.

And the names of the gentlemen who voted in the negative, are Messrs. Banks, (speaker,) Grinalds, Gilmer, Craig, Campbell, Decamps, Turnbull, Booker, Austin, Samuel, Christian, Hill, Wilson of Cumberland, Vaughan, Smith of Fauquier, Hickerson, Strange, Steger, Hale of Franklin, Holland, Bowen, Smith of Gloucester, Hail of Grayson, Carrington, Nixon, Goodall, Mullen, Harrison, Kincheloe, Fontaine, Summers, Fleet, Robinson, Neill, Hays, Straton, Powell, Taylor of Mathews and Middlesex, Rogers, Garland of Mecklenburg, Chapman, Ingles, Benton, Brown of Nelson, Cooke, Woolfolk, Adams, Swanson, Witcher, Morris, Williams, Marteney, Nicklin, Dorman, Leyburn, Moffett, Jessee, M'Mullen, Bare, Rinker, Butts, Moncure, Gillespie, Delashmutt, Jett and Saunders.—66.

Resolved, That the said bill be rejected.

On motion of Mr. Griggs, the following report of the committee of propositions and grievances was taken up and read as follows:

The committee of propositions and grievances have, according to order, had under consideration the petition and documents of sundry citizens residing in the north-eastern part of Frederick county, to them referred, praying for a division of said county, so as to form a new county of the said north-eastern part, according to certain boundary lines referred to, as set forth and described in their former petition: Whereupon,

1. *Resolved as the opinion of this committee,* That the prayer of said petition is reasonable.

The said committee have also had under consideration the memorials of sundry other citizens of said county, remonstrating against any division thereof for the purpose of forming a new county: Whereupon,

2. *Resolved as the opinion of this committee,* That the said memorials, remonstrating as aforesaid, be rejected.

The said resolutions were, on questions severally put thereupon, agreed to by the house, and a bill was ordered to be brought in conformably with the said first resolution.

The speaker laid before the house a communication from the governor, enclosing "the twentieth annual report of the board of public works," which, on motion of Mr. Dorman, was ordered to be laid upon the table, and 185 copies thereof were ordered to be printed for the use of the general assembly.

On motion of Mr. Sherrard, a report of the committee of roads and internal navigation, upon the petition of the Chesapeake and Ohio canal company, was taken up, and ordered to be recommitted to the said committee.

On motion of Mr. Sherrard, the report of the probable revenue of the Chesapeake and Ohio canal, was taken up, and ordered to be referred to the said committee.

An engrossed bill to incorporate the Mechanics manufacturing company, was read a third time, and sundry blanks therein were filled:

Resolved, That the bill do pass, and that the title be, "an act to incorporate the Mechanics manufacturing company."

Ordered, That the clerk communicate the same to the senate and request their concurrence.

An engrossed bill to revive and amend an act, entitled, "an act to incorporate the Gallego manufacturing company," passed 20th January, 1834, was read a third time, and on motion of Mr. Watkins, ordered to be laid upon the table.

An engrossed bill to change the place of holding a separate election in the county of Tyler, was read a third time :

Resolved, That the bill do pass, and that the title be, "an act to change the place of holding a separate election in the county of Tyler."

An engrossed bill to incorporate the Newtown Stephensburg library company, was read a third time :

Resolved, That the bill do pass, and that the title be, " an act to incorporate the Newtown Stephensburg library company."

An engrossed bill to authorize the judge of the second circuit to appoint a time for holding the court thereof in certain cases, was read a third time :

Resolved, That the bill do pass, and that the title be, "an act to authorize the judge of the second circuit to appoint a time for holding the court thereof in certain cases."

An engrossed bill changing the time of holding the circuit superior courts of law and chancery for the counties of Monroe, Giles and Montgomery, was read a third time:

Resolved, That the bill do pass, and that the title be, "an act changing the time of holding the circuit superior courts of law and chancery for the counties of Monroe, Giles and Montgomery."

An engrossed bill to incorporate the trustees of the Upperville academy in the county of Fauquier, was read a third time :

Resolved, That the bill do pass, and that the title be, "an act to incorporate the trustees of the Upperville academy in the county of Fauquier."

Ordered, That the clerk communicate the said bills to the senate and request their concurrence.

The speaker laid before the house a letter from John Brockenbrough, president of the bank of Virginia, in answer to the proceedings and resolutions of a meeting of citizens of the borough of Norfolk, submitted to the house on yesterday by Mr. Cunningham, which being read, was, on motion of Mr. Carter, ordered to be referred to the committee on banks.

And then, on motion of Mr. Wethered, the house adjourned until to-morrow 12 o'clock.

WEDNESDAY, February 17th, 1836.

A communication from the senate by their clerk :

IN SENATE, February 16th, 1836.

The senate have passed the bill, entitled,
" An act concerning Duff Green."

They have also passed the bill, entitled,
" An act to alter the terms of the circuit superior courts of law and chancery for the seventh district and thirteenth circuit of this commonwealth," with amendments, in which they request the concurrence of the house of delegates.

And they have agreed to the amendment proposed by the house of delegates to their fourth amendment to the resolutions relative to the interference of certain associations in the northern states with domestic slavery in the south.

The said amendments being twice read, were, on questions severally put thereupon, agreed to by the house.

Ordered, That the clerk inform the senate thereof.

On motion of Mr. Dorman, *Ordered*, That leave be given to bring in a bill extending the time for the commencement of the work of the Greensville and Panther gap turnpike company, and that Messrs. Dorman, Leyburn, M'Coy, M'Clintic, Wilson of Botetourt, Steger and Brooke, prepare and bring in the same.

On motion of Mr. Morris, *Resolved by the general assembly*, That the board of public works be instructed to employ a competent engineer to survey and make estimates of the cost of opening communications between the head waters of Back bay and Linkhorn bay, and between the head waters of the northern branch of the North river and the head waters of the southern branch of Lynhaven river, in the county of Princess Anne.

Ordered, That the clerk communicate the same to the senate and request their concurrence.

On motion of Mr. Carter, *Ordered*, That leave be given to the select committee on banks to sit during the session of this house.

On motion of Mr. Brown of Petersburg, *Ordered*, That leave be given to bring in a bill to prevent frauds in the packing of cotton, by requiring the person at whose gin it may be packed to mark his or her name and residence upon the bale, and also providing suitable penalties for false packing, and that Messrs. Brown of Petersburg, Johnson, Shands, Vaughan, Turnbull, Fitzgerald, Avent, Butts and Morris, prepare and bring in the same.

On motion of Mr. Austin, *Resolved*, That leave be given to enquire into the expediency of amending an act to incorporate Booker's gold mine company, and that they have leave to report by bill or otherwise.

And a committee was appointed therefor of Messrs. Austin, Booker, Campbell, Daniel, Hopkins, Pate, Fontaine, Swanson and Wiley.

Mr. Brooke, according to order, presented a bill to amend the act, entitled, "an act to incorporate the Augusta springs company."

Mr. Chapman, in like manner, a bill to add a part of the county of Tazewell to the county of Giles.

Mr. Parker, from the committee on the militia laws, presented a report upon the petitions of the citizens of Lexington and the county of Rockbridge, and of the town of Fairfield; of Cornelius C. Baldwin and others; and upon a resolution for permitting the commandant of the 147th regiment to appoint a place for training the officers thereof.

Mr. Booker, from the committee for courts of justice, presented a bill securing to debtors a certain portion of their property.

A bill repealing the law requiring lands in this commonwealth to be processioned, so far as the same may apply to the county of Patrick.

A bill to amend the act, entitled, "an act reducing into one the several acts for punishing persons guilty of certain thefts and forgeries, and the destruction or concealment of wills;" and

A bill amending the laws concerning slaves, free negroes and mulattoes.

And a report upon a resolution in relation to the processioning of lands in certain counties.

Mr. Hays, according to order, presented a bill to change the time of holding the county courts of the counties of Lewis and Braxton.

Mr. Watkins, from the committee of roads and internal navigation, reported with amendments, a bill to incorporate the Suffolk rail-road company.

And presented a bill incorporating the Lynchburg and Campbell court-house turnpike company.

A bill concerning the subscription on behalf of the commonwealth to the stock of the Richmond, Fredericksburg and Potowmac rail-road company.

A bill to authorize Thomas A. Morton to erect a dam across Appomattox river.

A bill to amend the act, entitled, "an act incorporating the Goose creek navigation company;" and

A bill concerning the Rappahannock company.

Mr. Hill, from the committee of propositions and grievances, presented a report upon the petition of freeholders and other citizens of the county of Fayette.

And a bill to establish the town of Meadowville in the county of Greenbrier.

A bill to authorize a separate election at the house of William Pulliam in the county of Henry; and

A bill to authorize Richard Barton Haxall to construct additional wharves at and near the town of Bermuda Hundred.

Mr. Moffett, from the committee of agriculture and manufactures, presented a bill to incorporate the Potowmac silk and agricultural company.

And a bill to incorporate the Ætna coal company.

Which reports and bills were received and laid upon the table.

On motion of Mr. Parker, *Ordered*, That the committee on the militia laws be discharged from the consideration of the resolution directing said committee to enquire into the expediency of amending the 32d section of the militia law, passed March 8th, 1834, so as to provide more effectually for the enrolment of persons subject to militia duty, and that the same be laid upon the table.

On motion of Mr. Crutchfield, a bill concerning the Rappahannock company, was taken up, read the first and second times, and ordered to be committed to the committee which brought it in.

On motion of Mr. Watkins, *Ordered*, That 185 copies of a bill now pending before the committee of roads and internal navigation, entitled, "a bill to amend the charter of the James river and Kanawha company," be printed for the use of the general assembly.

Mr. Watkins presented a petition of sundry citizens of the county of Goochland, remonstrating against the application of the Cartersville bridge company, to be allowed to hold real estate.

Mr. Wilson of Cumberland, presented a similar petition of citizens of the county of Cumberland.

Ordered, That the said petitions be referred to the committee of roads and internal navigation, that they do examine the matter thereof, and report their opinion thereupon to the house.

A bill to authorize the auditor to issue warrants on the treasury in satisfaction of certain judgments against the commonwealth, was taken up on motion of Mr. Ball, read the first and second times, and ordered to be committed to the committee which brought it in.

An engrossed bill to revive and amend an act, entitled, "an act to incorporate the Gallego manufacturing company," passed 20th of January, 1834, was taken up on motion of Mr. Stanard; whereupon a clause by way of ryder thereto was offered by him, which was read the first and second times, and forthwith engrossed and read a third time.

Resolved, That the bill (with the ryder,) do pass, and (the title being amended on motion of Mr. Stanard,) that the title be, "*an act to incorporate the Heth manufacturing company.*"

An engrossed bill to provide for the construction of a road across the Blue Ridge at Milam's gap, was taken up on motion of Mr. Almond, and read a third time, and the question being put upon its passage, was determined in the affirmative. Ayes 58, noes 46.

On motion of Mr. Gregory, (seven of the members present concurring,) *Ordered*, That the ayes and noes upon the said question be inserted in the journal.

The names of the gentlemen who voted in the affirmative, are Messrs. Banks, (speaker,) Layne, Garland of Amherst, Brooke, M'Clintic, Hunter of Berkeley, Wilson of Botetourt, Hill, Servant, Smith of Fauquier, Hickerson, Price, Strange, Steger, Bowen, Davison, Smith of Frederick, Watts, Watkins, Wethered, Sloan, Nixon, Harrison, Kincheloe, Fontaine, Berry, Hooe, Robinson, Hays, Straton, Powell, Waggener, Willey, Morgan, Chapman, Sherrard,

Masters, Woolfolk, Almond, M'Coy, Cackley, Carroll, Morris, Williams, Marteney, Nicklin, Leyburn, Moffett, Conrad, Jessee, Bare, Rinker, Harley, Crutchfield, Gillespie, Delashmutt, Gibson and Prentiss.—58.

And the names of the gentlemen who voted in the negative, are Messrs. Grinalds, Drummond, Gilmer, Southall, Wiley, Campbell, Decamps, Turnbull, Booker, Austin, Samuel, Christian, Richardson, Wilson of Cumberland, Vaughan, Hunter of Essex, Ball, Hale of Franklin, Holland, Smith of Gloucester, Hail of Grayson, Goodall, Mullen, Holleman, Gregory, Fleet, Neill, Taylor of Loudoun, Harris, Ragsdale, Taylor of Mathews and Middlesex, Garland of Mecklenburg, Ingles, Benton, Brown of Nelson, Parker, Fitzgerald, Adams, Swanson, Hopkins, Shands, Dorman, M'Mullen, Butts, Jett and Saunders.—46.

Resolved, That the bill do pass, and that the title be, "an act to provide for the construction of a road across the Blue Ridge at Milam's gap."

Ordered, That Mr. Powell carry the said bills to the senate and request their concurrence.

A message from the senate by Mr. Basye.

Mr. SPEAKER,—The senate have passed the bill, entitled, "an act to authorize the common council of the town of Fredericksburg to make an advancement upon the stock of the corporation in the Rappahannock canal company." And then he withdrew.

An engrossed bill to re-organize the first and second judicial districts, was taken up, on motion of Mr. Parker, and read a third time, and the question being put upon its passage, was determined in the negative.

Resolved, That the said bill be rejected.

Mr. Holleman, from the committee of privileges and elections, presented a report upon the resolution directing them to enquire into the expediency of providing that all the elections in this commonwealth be held on the same day, which was received and laid upon the table.

An engrossed bill incorporating the Virginia towing company, was read a third time:

Resolved, That the bill do pass, and that the title be, "an act incorporating the Virginia towing company."

An engrossed bill to amend an act, entitled, "an act to incorporate the Manchester wool and cotton manufacturing company," passed March 13th, 1832, was read a third time:

Resolved, That the bill do pass, and that the title be, "an act to amend an act, entitled, 'an act to incorporate the Manchester wool and cotton manufacturing company,' passed March 13th, 1832.

Ordered, That the clerk communicate the said bills to the senate and request their concurrence.

An engrossed bill to incorporate the stockholders of the Cartersville and Farmville rail-road company, was, on motion of Mr. Wilson of Cumberland, ordered to be laid upon the table.

The following bills heretofore reported from the respective committees to which the same had been committed, with amendments, were taken up, and the said amendments being agreed to by the house, the said bills, as amended, were ordered to be engrossed and read a third time, viz:

A bill to provide for the construction of a road from the line of Preston county to the Ohio river.

A bill releasing the commonwealth's claim to a certain balance against the estate of Betsy Bidgood; and

A bill to amend an act, entitled, "an act for opening and improving the navigation of the Dragon swamp."

The following bills heretofore reported without amendment, from the respective committees to which the same had been committed, were taken up and ordered to be engrossed and read a third time, viz:

A bill to incorporate the Virginia fire insurance company; and

A bill to provide for the construction of the eastern section of the road on the route surveyed from Huntersville to Parkersburg.

A bill to enact an act of the general assembly of North Carolina, entitled, "an act to incorporate the Roanoke, Danville and Junction rail-road company," with the amendment thereto proposed by the committee of roads and internal navigation, was taken up, and the said amendment having been agreed to by the house, the same, as amended, was ordered to be engrossed and read a third time.

On motion of Mr. Watkins, the following report of the committee of roads and internal navigation, was taken up and read:

The committee of roads and internal navigation have, according to order, had under consideration the petition of sundry citizens of the counties of Albemarle and Nelson, praying the passage of a law empowering the county courts of those counties to construct a road from the head waters of Rockfish river to the town of Scottsville, upon the like terms on which the county courts of Albemarle and Rockingham were authorized by act of assembly to open a road from Charlottesville to Harrisonburg: Whereupon,

Resolved as the opinion of this committee, That said petition is reasonable.

The said resolution was, on the question put thereupon, agreed to by the house, and a bill was ordered to be brought in conformably therewith.

The following bills were read a second time, and ordered to be engrossed and read a third time, viz:

A bill to incorporate the Stafford mining company.

A bill to change the place of holding a separate election in the county of Lunenburg.

A bill to authorize a separate election at the house of Michael Snodgrass in the county of Monongalia.

A bill to authorize a separate election at Triadelphia in the county of Ohio.

A bill to amend an act, entitled, "an act to incorporate the Cold Brook company of colliers," passed January 23d, 1835.

A bill to incorporate the Fauquier White Sulphur springs.

A bill incorporating the Natural bridge turnpike company; and
A bill to establish an inspection of flour and Indian meal at the town of Winchester.
A bill to explain the act, entitled, "an act to reduce into one act the several acts and parts of acts concerning the county and other inferior courts, and the jurisdiction of justices of the peace within this commonwealth," was read a second time, and ordered, on motion of Mr. Witcher, to be laid upon the table.
On motion of Mr. Watkins, the house adjourned until to-morrow 12 o'clock.

THURSDAY, February 18th, 1836.

On motion of Mr. Sherrard, *Resolved*, That the committee of finance be instructed to enquire into the expediency of furnishing a room in the capitol for the use of the attorney general, and that said committee have leave to report by bill or otherwise.

On motion of Mr. Mallory, the following report was taken up and read:
The joint committee of the senate and house of delegates, appointed to examine the armory, have performed that duty, and submit the following report and resolutions:

Your committee first directed their attention to that portion of the arms put away in boxes, containing twenty each, making in the whole 7,840. Their condition is apparently good, but upon a close examination, your committee are of opinion that they require overhauling and repolishing, with some slight repairs. From this parcel the last year's work was taken; and by the report of the superintendent, it appears that 1,540 were overhauled, repaired, repolished and repacked during that time, leaving of that parcel 5,140. Your committee think that the future operations of the armory should be confined to that portion of the public arms until they are all overhauled, examined, and put in complete order.

Your committee next examined a parcel of muskets, received from the United States, neatly and securely packed away in boxes, of twenty each, making in all 15,216. They had several boxes opened, and from a partial inspection, presuming that they were a fair specimen of the whole, appeared to be free from rust, in excellent order, of good manufacture, and would, no doubt, be efficient arms in actual service. These, together with the parcel first alluded to, when completed, will make an aggregate of 23,056 effective stand of arms.

The further examination of your committee was extended to a quantity of old arms, in different rooms, thrown together indiscriminately, and reported by the superintendent to amount to 10,893; also 3,585 muskets, designated small calibre, making in all 14,478. These arms are in a miserable state of decay, and totally unfit for use: some without locks, some without stocks, others without ramrods, and all rusty. If these arms are permitted to remain in their present condition, they will, in the end, be a loss of considerable amount to the state. If it be the part of wisdom to prepare for war, in time of peace, and if it be desirable to make these arms available in a case of emergency, your committee beg leave to suggest the propriety, as soon as the other operations of the armory, before alluded to, will admit of it, of requiring the whole of the arms thus injured, to be rigidly examined; that such of them as in the opinion of the superintendent can be repaired with advantage to the state, shall be selected and carefully set aside with a view to that object.

Your committee will further state, that agreeably to the superintendent's report, there are in the armory 380 rifles, Virginia manufacture, in good order, in boxes; 1,580 received from the United States, in boxes as received, also in good order. Besides these two parcels, there are 270 fit for repair, and 228 without locks, and otherwise in very bad order, omitted in the superintendent's report.

There are also 239 pistols of different kinds, repaired and packed away, and 468 of different kinds, out of order, but capable of being repaired.

Your committee will further report, on this branch of their duty, that there are 976 swords for cavalry, with scabbards, in good order; 455 without scabbards, also in good order, and 1,782 of different kinds, out of order. Your committee are of opinion, that the rifles, pistols and swords, or such part of them as will justify it, should be repaired as early as the limited operations of the armory will admit of it, and as soon as the other repairs before suggested shall have been made.

From this view of the condition of the public arms, your committee are of opinion, that true policy requires that the number of artificers should be increased to twenty, with an increase of wages, in order to insure the repairs of said arms as promptly as possible, and thereby prevent greater injury to them, by remaining exposed as they are at present.

They also think it expedient, if the number of artificers hereby recommended can be obtained, to authorize the executive to employ a competent master armorer, to superintend the mechanical operations of the armory, if in his opinion the public good require it, to be paid a salary not exceeding eight hundred dollars per annum.

Your committee, with a view to ascertain the probable cost of employing twenty artificers for the present year, called on the superintendent of the armory for information; and in compliance therewith, he furnished an estimate, which puts the whole cost at eight thousand dollars.

Your committee are of opinion, that the roofs of the foundery and boring mill should be covered with tin; also the machinery in the buffing room repaired, upon which the mechanical operations mainly depend. The cost of these repairs is estimated by the superintendent at one thousand seven hundred and fifty dollars.

The foundery and boring mill, being of little or no use to the armory institution under its limited operations, the committee think might be leased out with much advantage to the commonwealth, provided it be done for a term of years; and in the event that a lease should be effected, then the superintendent should be required to have a shed or shelter, or some other protection, built on the public land west of the armory, for the safe keeping and preservation of the cannon and gun carriages in the armory.

It appears from the report of the superintendent, that during the last year he expended in the repairs of the buildings, the sum of $403 81, leaving an unexpended balance of the appropriation to that object of $296 19; and of the appropriation of three thousand dollars made for the pay of artificers, he has expended the sum of $2,427 95, leaving a balance of that appropriation of $572 05.

Your committee, during their examination, discovered, and were shewn by the superintendent, a parcel of old wheels and other parts of cannon carriages, also some old irons, cast wheels, and mill-stones, and a parcel of old cartouch boxes; all of which they think the superintendent, under the direction of the executive, should be authorized to sell, or transfer to the superintendent of the penitentiary, the irons attached to the wheels, or such portion of them, as he may find conducive to the public interest.

1. *Resolved therefore*, That it is expedient that the residue of the 7,840 muskets, out of which the last year's work was taken, should be first overhauled and repaired.

2. *Resolved*, That the superintendent cause the 14,478 muskets to be examined, and select such of them as can, in his opinion, be repaired with advantage to the state; also such rifles, pistols and swords as are worthy of being repaired or cleaned.

3. *Resolved*, That the superintendent, under the direction of the executive, be authorized to employ twenty artificers for the year 1836.

4. *Resolved*, That the superintendent, under the direction of the executive, be also authorized to employ a competent master armorer to superintend the mechanical operations of the armory, if in the opinion of the executive, it should be deemed expedient.

5. *Resolved*, That the superintendent cause the roofs to the foundery and boring mill to be covered with tin; also, that he cause the machinery in the buffing room to be repaired.

6. *Resolved*, That the superintendent, under the direction of the executive, lease out the foundery and boring mill for a term of years, not less than five nor more than ten years, and that he is hereby authorized to make the necessary trunks and wastes for furnishing the lessee with water.

7. *Resolved*, That the superintendent, under the direction of the executive, sell at public auction, the old wheels, gun carriages, old irons, cast wheels, mill-stones, and a parcel of old cartouch boxes; or transfer to the superintendent of the penitentiary the irons attached to the wheels, or such portion of them as he may find conducive to the public interest.

8. *Resolved*, That in the event the foundery and boring mill shall be leased out, then the superintendent be authorized to have a shed or shelter built on the public land west of the armory, for the preservation of the cannon and gun carriages in the armory; and that he have made a plank fence and grating, so as to separate the armory building from the foundery.

9. *Resolved*, That the superintendent hereafter add to his annual report, all the cannon, gun carriages, and every description of public property in the armory.

CH'S HUNTON, *C. S.*
J. B. MALLORY, *C. H. D.*

The said resolutions were, on questions severally put thereupon, agreed to by the house, and the committee of finance were ordered to prepare and bring in a bill or bills conformably therewith.

Mr. Parker reported with amendment, a bill to change the times of holding the courts in the third judicial circuit.

And from the committee on the militia laws, presented a bill to amend and explain the 96th, 99th and 100th sections of an act for the better organization of the militia, passed March 8th, 1834.

Mr. Gregory, according to order, presented a bill to prevent slaves, free negroes and mulattoes from trading beyond the limits of the city, county or town in which they reside.

Mr. Hill, from the committee of propositions and grievances, presented a bill forming a new county out of parts of the counties of Shenandoah and Frederick; and

A bill forming a new county out of the county of Frederick.

Mr. Decamps, from the committee of schools and colleges, presented a bill to incorporate the trustees of the Lynchburg female academy; and

A bill incorporating the trustees of the Martinsville academy.

Mr. Benhring, according to order, presented a bill to change the place of holding a separate election in the county of Cabell.

Mr. Booker, from the committee for courts of justice, presented reports upon the petitions of James D. Grigsby, and of Jacob Boush and Toney Boush; and upon the resolution in relation to process books in county courts.

And reported with amendment, a bill giving to the circuit superior courts of law chancery concurrent jurisdiction with the county and corporation courts in all actions of forcible entry and detainer.

Mr. Crutchfield, according to order, presented a bill incorporating the Fredericksburg mining company.

Mr. Watkins, from the committee of roads and internal navigation, reported with amendments, a bill incorporating the stockholders of the Richmond and Petersburg rail-road company.

Also, presented a report upon the petition of John Crouch and others.

And a bill to enlarge the powers of the county courts of Albemarle and Nelson, for the purpose of opening a road from Scottsville to the head waters of Rock fish river.

A bill incorporating the Marshall and Ohio turnpike company.

A bill to authorize the Dismal Swamp canal company to increase their capital stock, and to authorize the loans of the state to said company to be converted into stock.

A bill incorporating the stockholders of the Smithfield rail-road company; and

A bill incorporating the stockholders of the Eastern Shore rail-road company.

Which bills and reports were received and laid upon the table.

Mr. Dorman, according to order, presented a bill relating to the Greensville and Panther gap turnpike road, which on his motion was taken up, read the first and second times, and (by general consent,) ordered to be engrossed and read a third time.

On motion of Mr. Hooe, a report of the committee of claims rejecting the petition of Stapleton Crutchfield, was taken up and ordered to be committed to the committee for courts of justice.

Mr. Garland of Amherst, presented a petition of Samuel S. Williams and Henry A. Evans, contractors for the construction of the turnpike road at the canal of the Blue Ridge, in the counties of Rockbridge, Amherst and Bedford, stating that they had sustained losses in complying with their contracts, and asking to be remunerated therefor, which was ordered to be referred to the committee of roads and internal navigation, that they do examine the matter thereof, and report their opinion thereupon to the house.

On motion of Mr. Harris, a bill, entitled, "an act incorporating the stockholders of the Louisa rail-road company," together with the amendments thereto proposed by the senate, was taken up: the house of delegates had disagreed to the third amendment of the senate, and the senate had insisted upon the said amendment, and a motion had been made by Mr. Woolfolk that this house do insist upon their disagreement, and the question being now put thereupon, was determined in the negative; and on motion of Mr. Harris the house receded from their disagreement and agreed to the said amendment.

Ordered, That the clerk inform the senate thereof.

On motion of Mr. Woolfolk, the charges preferred by Mr. Harrison against Edwin S. Duncan, a judge of the general court of Virginia, together with the memorial of the judge and the accompanying document, were taken up; whereupon, on his motion, the house adopted the following resolution:

Resolved, That the charges preferred by the member from Harrison against judge Duncan, together with the memorial of the judge and his accompanying explanations, be referred to the committee for courts of justice, with instructions to enquire into the expediency of enquiring into the truth of the said charges, and if in their opinion it is expedient to make the enquiry, then to enquire into the most regular and convenient mode of conducting the enquiry, and report their opinion to this house.

Mr. Witcher, from the committee of claims, presented reports upon petitions of Levi Simms, and of Jordan and Murrell; and upon the resolution concerning Thomas Byrne.

Also a bill concerning John Pittinger, late sheriff of Brooke county.

And a bill concerning the administrator of Dominie Bennehan, deceased.

Mr. Watkins, from the committee of roads and internal navigation, reported with amendments, a bill authorizing Jessee Sturm to erect a dam across the West Fork of Monongalia river in the county of Harrison.

Which reports and bills were received and laid upon the table.

A bill to explain the act, entitled, "an act to reduce into one act the several acts and parts of acts concerning the county and other inferior courts, and the jurisdiction of justices of the peace within this commonwealth," was taken up on motion of Mr. Witcher, and ordered to be recommitted to the committee which brought it in.

An engrossed bill to enact an act of the general assembly of North Carolina, entitled, "an act to incorporate the Roanoke, Danville and Junction rail-road company," was read a third time:

Resolved, That the bill do pass, and that the title be, "an act to enact an act of the general assembly of North Carolina, entitled, 'an act to incorporate the Roanoke, Danville and Junction rail-road company.'"

Ordered, That the clerk communicate the same to the senate and request their concurrence.

An engrossed bill releasing the commonwealth's claim to a certain balance against the estate of Betsy Bidgood, was read a third time, and on motion of Mr. Shands, was ordered to be laid upon the table.

An engrossed bill to amend an act, entitled, "an act for opening and improving the navigation of the Dragon swamp," was read a third time:

Resolved, That the bill do pass, and that the title be, "an act to amend an act, entitled, 'an act for opening and improving the navigation of the Dragon swamp.'"

Ordered, That the clerk communicate the same to the senate and request their concurrence.

An engrossed bill to provide for the construction of the eastern section of the road on the route surveyed from Huntersville to Parkersburg, was, on motion of Mr. Price, ordered to be laid upon the table.

On motion of Mr. Wethered, the house adjourned until to-morrow 12 o'clock.

FRIDAY, February 19th, 1836.

A communication from the senate by their clerk:

IN SENATE, February 18th, 1836.

The senate have passed the bills, entitled,
"An act authorizing an increase of the capital stock of the Merchants manufacturing company."
"An act to authorize the judge of the second circuit to appoint a time for holding the courts thereof in certain cases."
"An act to incorporate the Mechanics manufacturing company."
"An act to incorporate the trustees of the Upperville academy in the county of Fauquier."
"An act changing the time of holding the circuit superior courts of law and chancery for the counties of Monroe, Giles and Montgomery."
"An act to change the place of holding a separate election in the county of Tyler;" and
"An act to incorporate the Kanawha slave insurance company."
They have also passed the bills, entitled,
"An act to incorporate the Newtown Stephensburg library company;" and
"An act to revive the charter of the Nelson and Albemarle Union factory company," with amendments, in which they request the concurrence of the house of delegates.

The said amendments being twice read, were, on questions severally put thereupon, agreed to by the house.

Ordered, That the clerk inform the senate thereof.

On motion of Mr. Powell, *Resolved*, That the committee for courts of justice be instructed to enquire into the expediency of passing a law authorizing the clerks of courts to deliver original wills and other documents under certain restrictions, to be used as evidence in courts of other states, and that they report by bill or otherwise.

On motion of Mr. Gregory, *Ordered*, That leave be given to bring in a bill to amend the charter incorporating the stockholders of the Richmond and Yorktown rail-road company, and that Messrs. Gregory, Servant, Christian, Botts, Hooe, Powell, Goodall, Jett and Smith of Gloucester, prepare and bring in the same.

On motion of Mr. Rinker, *Resolved*, That leave be given to bring in a bill to change the quarterly court of Shenandoah county to June instead of May, and that Messrs. Rinker, Bare, Almond, Sherrard, Henshaw, M'Coy and Mullen, prepare and bring in the same.

On motion of Mr. Brown of Petersburg, *Ordered*, That leave be given to bring in a bill to authorize the Matoaca manufacturing company to increase their capital stock, and that Messrs. Brown of Petersburg, Shands, Mallory, Vaughan, Turnbull, Fitzgerald, Holleman and Johnson, prepare and bring in the same.

On motion of Mr. Masters, *Ordered*, That leave be given to bring in a bill changing the time of holding the county courts in the counties of Marshall and Ohio; and also to amend an act, entitled, "an act establishing the town of Moundsville in the county of Ohio," passed January 28th, 1832, and that Messrs. Masters, Chapline, Willey, Morgan, Delashmutt, Prentiss and Marteney, prepare and bring in the same.

On motion of Mr. Brown of Nelson, *Resolved*, That the committee of roads and internal navigation be directed to enquire into the expediency of authorizing Lavender Landon and William H. Garland to erect a dam across Tye river in the county of Nelson, from their own land, for the purpose of working a saw mill and other machinery, and that they report by bill or otherwise.

On motion of Mr. Summers, *Resolved*, That Professor Rogers be authorized to publish on his own account, an edition of his report made to the present legislature on the geology of the state, and for that purpose to use the plate of the profile and physical sections accompanying said report, when the same shall have been engraved as ordered by this house.

On motion of Mr. Southall, *Resolved*, That the committee for courts of justice be instructed to enquire into the expediency of so amending the act, entitled, "an act for the relief of creditors against fraudulent devises," passed 18th December, 1789, as to authorize the plaintiff in any judgment heretofore, or which may hereafter be rendered against any heir or heirs, devisee or devisees, jointly or severally, to be satisfied of the lands, tenements or other assets of the ancestor or testator, descended or devised, to supersede any execution in case the issues and profits of the lands, tenements or other assets so descended or devised, will not in a reasonable time satisfy the judgment, and to apply for and obtain execution of *fieri facias*, whereby the lands, tenements and other assets so descended and devised, may be sold in satisfaction of the judgment, in like manner as the lands and tenements of sheriffs and other public collectors may be sold in satisfaction of debts due to the commonwealth, and that they have leave to report by bill or otherwise.

Mr. Brown of Petersburg, according to order, presented a bill to prevent frauds in the packing of cotton, which was received and laid upon the table.

An engrossed bill releasing the commonwealth's claim to a certain balance against the estate of Betsy Bidgood, was taken up, on motion of Mr. Holleman, and read a third time:

Resolved, That the bill do pass, and that the title be, "an act releasing the commonwealth's claim to a certain balance against the estate of Betsy Bidgood."

An engrossed bill to incorporate the Virginia fire insurance company, was read a third time, and a blank therein was filled:

Resolved, That the bill do pass, and that the title be, "an act to incorporate the Virginia fire insurance company."

An engrossed bill to incorporate the Stafford mining company, was read a third time:
Resolved, That the bill do pass, and that the title be, "an act to incorporate the Stafford mining company."
An engrossed bill to change the place of holding a separate election in the county of Lunenburg, was read a third time:
Resolved, That the bill do pass, and that the title be, "an act to change the place of holding a separate election in the county of Lunenburg."
An engrossed bill to authorize a separate election at the house of Michael Snodgrass in the county of Monongalia, was read a third time:
Resolved, That the bill do pass, and that the title be, "an act to authorize a separate election at the house of Michael Snodgrass in the county of Monongalia."
An engrossed bill to authorize a separate election at Triadelphia in the county of Ohio, was read a third time:
Resolved, That the bill do pass, and that the title be, "an act to authorize a separate election at Triadelphia in the county of Ohio."
An engrossed bill to amend an act, entitled, "an act to incorporate the Cold Brook company of colliers," passed January 23d, 1835, was read a third time:
Resolved, That the bill do pass, and that the title be, "an act to amend an act, entitled, 'an act to incorporate the Cold Brook company of colliers,'" passed January 23d, 1835.
An engrossed bill to incorporate the Fauquier White Sulphur springs, was read a third time:
Resolved, That the bill do pass, and that the title be, "an act to incorporate the Fauquier White Sulphur springs."
An engrossed bill to establish an inspection of flour and Indian meal at the town of Winchester, was read a third time:
Resolved, That the bill do pass, and that the title be, "an act to establish an inspection of flour and Indian meal at the town of Winchester."
An engrossed bill to incorporate the Natural Bridge turnpike company, was read a third time:
Resolved, That the bill do pass, and that the title be, "an act to incorporate the Natural Bridge turnpike company."
An engrossed bill relating to the Greensville and Panther gap turnpike road, was read a third time:
Resolved, That the bill do pass, and that the title be, "an act relating to the Greensville and Panther gap turnpike road."
An engrossed bill to provide for the construction of a road from the line of Preston county to the Ohio river, was read a third time, and a blank therein was filled:
Resolved, That the bill do pass, and (the title being amended on motion of Mr. Willey,) that the title be, "an act to provide for the construction of a road from *the Ohio river by Morgantown to the Maryland line.*"
Ordered, That the clerk communicate the said bills to the senate and request their concurrence.
A bill authorizing Jesse Sturm to erect a dam across the west fork of Monongalia river in the county of Harrison.
And a bill giving to the circuit superior courts of law and chancery concurrent jurisdiction with the county and corporation courts in all actions of forcible entry and detainer, together with the amendments thereto proposed by the respective committees to which the same had been committed, were taken up, and the said amendments being agreed to by the house, the said bills, as amended, were ordered to be engrossed and read a third time.
A bill incorporating the stockholders of the Richmond and Petersburg rail-road company, was, on motion of Mr. Mallory, ordered to be laid upon the table.
The speaker laid before the house a communication from the governor, enclosing "a report and resolutions in relation to the interference of certain citizens of the non-slaveholding states, usually denominated abolitionists, with the institution of domestic slavery, adopted by the legislature of the state of Mississippi," which, on motion of Mr. Dorman, was ordered to be laid upon the table, and 185 copies thereof were ordered to be printed for the use of the general assembly.
A bill to incorporate the Suffolk rail-road company, with the amendments thereto proposed by the committee of roads and internal navigation, was taken up, and the said amendments being agreed to by the house, the said bill, as amended, was ordered to be engrossed and read a third time.
The following bills were read a second time, and ordered to be engrossed and read a third time, viz:
A bill to incorporate the city of Wheeling in Ohio county; and
A bill incorporating the literary and scientific mechanics institute of Norfolk and Portsmouth.
A bill to change the times of holding the courts in the third judicial circuit, with the amendments thereto proposed by the select committee to which the same had been committed, was taken up, and the said amendments being agreed to by the house, the said bill as amended, was ordered to be engrossed and read a third time.
Mr. M'Mullen, from the committee of finance, reported without amendment, a bill to authorize the auditor to issue warrants on the treasury in satisfaction of certain judgments against the commonwealth, which on motion of Mr. Ball, was taken up and ordered to be engrossed and read a third time.
Mr. Watkins, from the committee of roads and internal navigation, presented a report upon the expediency of changing the mode of constructing the North-western road.
And reported with amendment a bill concerning the Rappahannock company.

Which report and bill was received and laid upon the table.

Mr. Harrison submitted an additional specification to one of the charges made by him against Judge Edwin S. Duncan, which was ordered to be referred to the committee for courts of justice.

Mr. Garland of Amherst, presented a petition of sundry landholders on James river, praying that the legislature will reject the proposed modification of the charter of the James river and Kanawha company, by which a larger quantity of land may be condemned for the use of the company than has hitherto been allowed, and a new mode of appointing commissioners provided for, which was ordered to be referred to the committee of roads and internal navigation, that they do examine the matter thereof, and report their opinion thereupon to the house.

On motion of Mr. Watkins, the house adjourned until to-morrow 12 o'clock.

SATURDAY, February 20th, 1836.

A communication from the senate by their clerk:

IN SENATE, February 19th, 1836.

The senate have passed the bill, entitled,

"An act to amend an act, entitled, 'an act to incorporate the Manchester wool and cotton manufacturing company,'" passed March 13th, 1832.

On motion of Mr. Smith of Fauquier, *Resolved*, That the committee for courts of justice be instructed to enquire into the expediency of so amending the existing laws in relation to special bail, as to authorize the sheriffs or other officers to take the body of the principal upon the written authority and direction of the bail, in the same way and for the same purposes that the bail himself might deliver him according to the present laws.

On motion of Mr. Campbell, *Ordered*, That leave be given to bring in a bill to amend an act, entitled, "an act incorporating the trustees of the Bedford female academy," and that Messrs. Campbell, Pate, Garland of Amherst, Swanson, Fontaine, Adams and Daniel, prepare and bring in the same.

On motion of Mr. Goodall, *Resolved*, That the committee of roads and internal navigation be instructed to enquire into the expediency of incorporating a company to improve the navigation of the Pamunkey river from Hanover town in the county of Hanover, to the junction of the North and South branches, and also the South branch of the Pamunkey to the bridge across the said stream, erected by the Richmond, Fredericksburg and Potowmac railroad company, with discretion to extend the improvement to Darracot's mill, and also with discretion to commence the improvement, if it shall be deemed advisable by the company, at New Castle, and that they have leave to report a bill for the same.

On motion of Mr. Garland of Amherst, *Resolved*, That the committee of roads and internal navigation be directed to enquire into the expediency of authorizing the board of public works to subscribe for two fifths of the capital stock of the Lexington and Richmond turnpike company, and that they report by bill or otherwise.

On motion of Mr. Moncure, *Resolved*, That the committee of propositions and grievances be requested to enquire into the expediency of increasing the wages of the inspectors of tobacco at Dixon's warehouse in the town of Falmouth, and report by bill or otherwise.

On motion of Mr. Hunter of Essex, *Resolved*, That leave be given to bring in a bill authorizing the auditor of public accounts to issue a warrant on the treasury, in favour of John H. Gwathmey, administrator of Richard Clarke, deceased, in pursuance of a judgment of the superior court of Henrico county, for commutation of five years full pay, and that Messrs. Hunter of Essex, Robinson, Fleet, Goodall, Dorman, Straton, Fitzgerald, Strange and Ingles, prepare and bring in the same.

On motion of Mr. Crutchfield, *Resolved*, That the committee of finance be instructed to enquire into the expediency of providing a proper apartment, as an office in or out of the capitol, for the use of the principal engineer of the state and his assistants, and that they report thereupon by bill or otherwise.

On motion of Mr. Harrison, *Resolved*, That the register of the land office of Virginia report to this house as early as practicable, the quantity of land bounty allowed by Virginia to such of her officers and soldiers as have not yet received their military warrants.

On motion of Mr. Witcher, *Resolved*, That the committee on the militia laws enquire into the expediency of increasing the pay of musicians, with leave to report by bill or otherwise.

Mr. Garland of Mecklenburg, from the committee of schools and colleges, presented a report upon the petition of the trustees of the Female Orphan asylum of Fredericksburg.

Mr. Hill, from the committee of propositions and grievances, presented a bill to authorize Richard Lorton to surrender his interest in the museum property.

Mr. Moffett, according to order, presented a bill incorporating the Virginia silk company.

Which report and bills were received and laid upon the table.

Mr. Smith of Fauquier, presented a petition of citizens of the town of Upperville, asking for an appropriation from the literary fund to aid in erecting buildings for literary institutions in said town, which was ordered to be referred to the committee of schools and colleges, that they do examine the matter thereof, and report their opinion thereupon to the house.

Also a petition of other citizens of Fauquier, praying the passage of a law excluding free persons of colour from the state, and that such as remain after the first of January, 1837, shall be subject to public sale for the benefit of the literary fund, which was ordered to be referred to the committee for courts of justice, that they do examine the matter thereof, and report their opinion thereupon to the house.

An engrossed bill to incorporate the Suffolk rail-road company, was read a third time, and on motion of Mr. Price, ordered to be laid upon the table.

Mr. Holleman, from committee of privileges and elections, presented a report upon the petitions of Alexander Rives and Thomas J. Randolph, contesting the elections of Thomas W. Gilmer and Valentine W. Southall, delegates from the county of Albemarle, which was read; whereupon, on motion of Mr. Holleman,

Resolved, That the report of the committee of privileges and elections on the contested election from the county of Albemarle, be recommitted to that committee, with instructions to report specially on those votes only on which either of the parties interested have good reason to believe the house ought to reverse the decisions of the committee.

A bill to incorporate the stockholders of the Lynchburg and Tennessee rail-road company, and to authorize them, or the James river and Kanawha company, to construct a rail-road from Lynchburg to Richmond, was taken up, on motion of Mr. Daniel, and having been amended on motions severally made, a motion was made by Mr. Wiley, further to amend the same, by striking therefrom the nineteenth and twentieth sections; and the ayes and noes having been demanded by Mr. Woolfolk, and the call having been sustained by the house, on motion of Mr. Carter, the said bill and amendment was ordered to be laid upon the table.

Mr. Carter, from the committee on banks, reported with amendments, a bill incorporating the Orange savings society.

And a bill incorporating the Smithfield savings institution in the county of Isle of Wight.

Which were received and laid upon the table.

On motion of Mr. Watkins, *Resolved*, That when this house adjourns to-day, it will adjourn until Monday 11 o'clock.

On motion of Mr. Booker, the house adjourned accordingly.

MONDAY, February 22d, 1836.

A communication from the senate by their clerk:

IN SENATE, February 20th, 1836.

The senate have agreed to the preamble and resolutions upon the subject of expunging from the journals of the senate of the United States a resolution of that body, and relative to the right of instruction.

On motion of Mr. Dorman, *Ordered*, That leave be given to bring in a bill authorizing certain changes in the road law, passed March 3d, 1835, so far as the county of Rockbridge is concerned, and that Messrs. Dorman, Leyburn, Miller, Layne, Brooke, M'Clintic and Ingles, prepare and bring in the same.

On motion of Mr. Cook, *Ordered*, That leave be given to bring in a bill to alter and increase the terms of the circuit superior court of law and chancery for the county of Norfolk, and that Messrs. Cooke, Murdaugh, Cunningham, Morris, Butts, Holleman and Servant, prepare and bring in the same.

On motion of Mr. M'Mullen, *Resolved by the general assembly of Virginia*, That the board of public works be, and they are hereby authorized and directed to have surveyed as early as practicable, by the state engineer, or if his engagements shall be such as to prevent it, then to employ a competent engineer to survey a route for a rail-road from Buford's gap to the Tennessee line, by Walker's creek in the county of   , and the north fork of Holstein, in the county of Scott.

Ordered, That the clerk communicate the same to the senate and request their concurrence.

Mr. Booker, from the committee for courts of justice, presented reports upon the petitions of Charles Williams; of Stephen; and of Daniel Starks.

And a bill providing further security for the payment of jailors' fees.

Mr. Dorman, according to order, presented a bill authorizing the auditor of public accounts to issue a warrant on the treasury in favour of John H. Gwathmey, administrator of Richard Clark, deceased, in pursuance of a judgment of the superior court of Henrico county, for commutation of five years full pay, with interest.

Which reports and bill were received and laid upon the table.

Mr. Beard presented a remonstrance of citizens of Leesburg, against the petition of other citizens of said town, asking for an amendment of the acts incorporating that town, which was ordered to be referred to the committee of propositions and grievances, that they do examine the matter thereof, and report their opinion thereupon to the house.

A motion was made by Mr. Taylor of Middlesex, that the house adopt the following resolution:

Resolved, That the superintendent of public buildings be requested forthwith, to have displayed on the capitol the flag of the United States, as heretofore, on the 22d of February.

Whereupon, a motion was made by Mr. Parker, that this house do now adjourn, and the question being put thereupon, was determined in the negative. Ayes 19, noes 79.

On motion of Mr. Parker, (seven of the members present concurring,) *Ordered*, That the ayes and noes upon the said question be inserted in the journal.

The names of the gentlemen who voted in the affirmative, are Messrs. Drummond, M'Clintic, Hunter of Berkeley, Henshaw, Hale of Franklin, Smith of Gloucester, Mullen, Berry, Waggener, Willey, Cooke, Parker, Chapline, Masters, Harley, Delashmutt, Jett, Prentiss and Cunningham.—19.

And the names of the gentlemen who voted in the negative, are Messrs. Banks, (speaker,) Southall, Layne, Wiley, Brooke, Wilson of Botetourt, Decamps, Turnbull, Mallory, Booker, Austin, Beuhring, Daniel, Samuel, Richardson, Johnson, Hill, Vaughan, Hunter of Essex, Ball, Smith of Fauquier, Hickerson, Price, Strange, Steger, Holland, Bowen, Watts, Watkins, Hail of Grayson, Wethered, Carrington, Coleman, Sloan, Nixon, Harrison, Kincheloe, Fontaine, Griggs, Summers, Fleet, Hooe, Hays, Straton, Beard, Harris, Ragsdale, Taylor of Mathews and Middlesex, Rogers, Garland of Mecklenburg, Morgan, Chapman, Ingles, Sherrard, Brown of Nelson, Fitzgerald, Almond, Adams, M'Coy, Swanson, Hopkins, Carroll, Madison, Morris, Williams, Marteney, Nicklin, Dorman, Leyburn, Moffett, Conrad, Jessee, M'Mullen, Bare, Rinker, Crutchfield, Moncure, Gibson and Saunders.—79.

Mr. Taylor of Middlesex, then, with the permission of the house, withdrew his said resolution.

Whereupon, a motion was made by Mr. Watkins, that the house adopt the following resolution:

Resolved, That the speaker direct the sergeant-at-arms to request the superintendent of the public buildings to display the flag of the Union on the capitol.

A motion was made by Mr. Hunter of Berkeley, that the same be laid upon the table, and the question being put thereupon, was determined in the negative. Ayes 11, noes 90.

On motion of Mr. Hunter of Berkeley, (seven of the members present concurring,) *Ordered*, That the ayes and noes upon the said question be inserted in the journal.

The names of the gentlemen who voted in the affirmative, are Messrs. Campbell, Pate, Hunter of Berkeley, Henshaw, Mullen, Powell, Cooke, Parker, Masters, Delashmutt and Cunningham.—11.

And the names of the gentlemen who voted in the negative, are Messrs. Banks, (speaker,) Grinalds, Drummond, Gilmer, Southall, Layne, Wiley, Garland of Amherst, Brooke, Craig, Wilson of Botetourt, Decamps, Turnbull, Mallory, Booker, Austin, Beuhring, Daniel, Samuel, Christian, Richardson, Johnson, Hill, Vaughan, Ball, Smith of Fauquier, Hickerson, Strange, Steger, Hale of Franklin, Holland, Bowen, Davison, Smith of Gloucester, Watkins, Hail of Grayson, Wethered, Coleman, Sloan, Nixon, Harrison, Kincheloe, Fontaine, Summers, Fleet, Hooe, Carter, Hays, Straton, Harris, Ragsdale, Taylor of Mathews and Middlesex, Garland of Mecklenburg, Willey, Morgan, Chapman, Ingles, Sherrard, Brown of Nelson, Murdaugh, Chapline, Almond, Adams, M'Coy, Swanson, Witcher, Cackley, Hopkins, Carroll, Madison, Morris, Williams, Marteney, Nicklin, Dorman, Leyburn, Moffett, Conrad, Jessee, M'Mullen, Bare, Rinker, Butts, Crutchfield, Moncure, Gillespie, Gibson, Jett, Prentiss and Saunders.—90.

The said resolution was then agreed to by the house.

And on motion of Mr. Daniel, the house adjourned until to-morrow 11 o'clock.

TUESDAY, February 23d, 1836.

A communication from the senate by their clerk:

IN SENATE, February 22d, 1836.

The senate have passed the bill, entitled,

"An act to establish an inspection of flour and Indian meal at the town of Winchester."

On motion of Mr. Dorman, *Resolved*, That the governor cause to be procured for the use of this commonwealth, a handsome flag of the United States, to be displayed by the public authorities on all proper occasions; and that the costs of the same be defrayed out of any money in the treasury not otherwise appropriated.

On motion of Mr. Cooke, *Ordered*, That leave be given to bring in a bill to increase the number of trustees in the town of Portsmouth, and to enlarge their powers and privileges, and that Messrs. Cooke, Murdaugh, Cunningham, Butts, Morris, Servant, Drummond, Smith of Gloucester, and Fleet, prepare and bring in the same.

Mr. Hill, from the committee of propositions and grievances, presented reports upon petitions of citizens of Princess Anne county; of Page county; of citizens of Petersburg; of John T. Robertson, and upon the memorial of Daniel and Ebenezer Zane.

Mr. Carter, from the committee on banks, presented a bill to amend an act incorporating the Fredericksburg Mechanics association.

Mr. Witcher from the committee of claims, presented a bill concerning Amos Johnson.

Mr. Madison, from the committee on agriculture and manufactures, presented a bill constituting a portion of the margin of the Potowmac river in Berkeley county a legal fence.

Which report and bills were received and laid upon the table.

Mr. Stanard presented a petition of Abner Robinson, stating that he purchased from the executive one of the slaves confined in the penitentiary, to be transported beyond the commonwealth; that the said slave escaped from him and was subsequently apprehended and returned to the penitentiary, and praying that the amount paid by him for the said slave may be refunded, which was ordered to be referred to the committee of claims, that they do examine the matter thereof, and report their opinion thereupon to the house.

Mr. Southall presented a petition of sundry citizens of the county of Albemarle, praying the location of a bank at the town of Charlottesville in said county, which was ordered to be referred to the committee on banks, that they do examine the matter thereof, and report their opinion thereupon to the house.

Mr. Madison presented a petition of citizens of Farmville, for the passage of an act authorizing the trustees of the town to appoint officers to weigh loose and unprized tobacco sold in said town, which was ordered to be referred to the committee on agriculture and manufactures, that they do examine matter thereof, and report their opinion thereupon to the house.

An engrossed bill to authorize the auditor to issue warrants on the treasury in satisfaction of certain judgments against the commonwealth, was read a third time, and on motion of Mr. Dorman, ordered to be laid upon the table.

A bill to incorporate the stockholders of the Lynchburg and Tennessee rail-road company, and to authorize them, or the James river and Kanawha company, to construct a rail-road from Lynchburg to Richmond, was taken up, on motion of Mr. Dorman, together with the proposed amendment submitted by Mr. Wiley on Saturday. It was proposed by him to amend the bill by striking therefrom the nineteenth and twentieth sections, which are the following:

19. When the Lynchburg and Tennessee rail-road company shall have commenced the construction of their rail-road, pursuant to the provisions of this act, it shall be lawful for the James river and Kanawha company to construct a similar rail-road, with one set of tracks, or more at their election, from the town of Lynchburg, by the towns of Scottsville in Albemarle, and Cartersville, provided that the company shall not be obliged to bring the road on the north side of the river, to the city of Richmond, and to connect the same with the road of the Richmond, Fredericksburg and Potomac rail-road company, in such manner as may be agreed upon by the said two companies, or as may be hereafter prescribed by the general assembly; and for this purpose the James river and Kanawha company may enlarge their capital stock, in the manner prescribed by the twenty-eighth section of the act passed on the sixteenth of March, eighteen hundred and thirty-two, entitled, "an act incorporating the stockholders of the James river and Kanawha company." But no part of the present capital stock of said company shall be employed in the location or construction of the said rail-road hereby provided for, or any part thereof. In the construction, use and enjoyment of such rail-road, and in relation to the tolls which may be taken upon it, the rights, privileges and exemptions, the duties and liabilities of the James river and Kanawha company, shall be regulated by the provisions of the above recited act, and other acts of assembly amendatory thereto, and shall be the same to all intents and purposes, except as is herein otherwise provided, as if the rail-road by this section authorized, had been provided for by the acts aforesaid: *Provided however*, That the tolls which may be demanded and received by the James river and Kanawha company shall be regulated by that part of the forty-eighth section of the said act, which prescribes the tolls west of Crow's ferry, except for the transportation of passengers, and that the company may demand and receive for the transportation of passengers tolls not exceeding six cents per mile for each person. But if the James river and Kanawha company shall not elect to construct the rail-road from Lynchburg to Richmond, hereby authorized, and six months before the said road from Lynchburg to Tennessee shall have been completed, actually and *bona fide* commence the construction of the aforesaid road from Lynchburg to Richmond, and diligently prosecute the work, so that the same shall be completed within five years thereafter, then the privilege hereby granted to the James river and Kanawha company shall cease, and all the land which they may have acquired for the use of the said road, and all the works which they may have constructed thereon, shall be vested in the commonwealth, to be disposed of as the general assembly may deem expedient.

20. If the James river and Kanawha company shall not make their election, and commence the work within the time, and in the manner above prescribed, then it shall be lawful for the Lynchburg and Tennessee rail-road company to continue their rail-road from Lynchburg, by the towns of Scottsville and Cartersville aforesaid, to the city of Richmond, and to connect the same with the road of the Richmond, Fredericksburg and Potomac rail-road company, in such manner as may be agreed upon between the two last mentioned companies, or as may hereafter be prescribed by the general assembly: *Provided*, That the Lynchburg and Tennessee rail-road company shall actually and *bona fide* commence the said extended road within six months after their right to construct the same shall have accrued, and diligently prosecute the work, so that within five years thereafter it shall be completed, in the style and manner herein prescribed for the construction of the road from Lynchburg to the Tennessee line: *And provided moreover*, That the said extended road shall in no manner obstruct the canal or other works of the James river and Kanawha company, or occupy any of the grounds of the said company, except upon such terms as the said two companies may agree upon, or as the general assembly may hereafter prescribe.

And the question being put upon striking out the said sections, was determined in the negative. Ayes 36, noes 81.

On motion of Mr. Woolfolk, (seven of the members present concurring,) *Ordered*, That the ayes and noes upon the said question be inserted in the journal.

The names of the gentlemen who voted in the affirmative, are Messrs. Banks, (speaker,) Wiley, M'Clintic, Campbell, Booker, Austin, Samuel, Richardson, Hill, Smith of Fauquier, Steger, Bowen, Hail of Grayson, Sloan, Nixon, Harrison, Kincheloe, Fontaine, Robinson, Straton, Beard, Ragsdale, Sherrard, Woolfolk, M'Coy, Hopkins, Madison, Williams, Nicklin, Moffett, Conrad, Bare, Moncure, Hargrave, Delashmutt and Gibson.—36.

And the names of the gentlemen who voted in the negative, are Messrs. Grinalds, Drummond, Gilmer, Southall, Layne, Garland of Amherst, Brooke, Craig, Hunter of Berkeley, Miller, Wilson of Botetourt, Decamps, Turnbull, Mallory, Beuhring, Daniel, Christian, Johnson, Vaughan, Hunter of Essex, Ball, Price, Strange, Hale of Franklin, Holland, Davison, Watts, Smith of Gloucester, Watkins, Coleman, Goodall, Mullen, Botts, Gregory, Griggs, Berry, Summers, Fleet, Hooe, Neill, Hays, Powell, Taylor of Loudoun, Harris, Taylor of Mathews and Middlesex, Waggener, Rogers, Garland of Mecklenburg, Chapman, Ingles, Benton, Brown of Nelson, Murdaugh, Cooke, Parker,

Leland, Masters, Almond, Adams, Swanson, Witcher, Cackley, Carroll, Morris, Shands, Marteney, Dorman, Leyburn, Jessee, M'Mullen, Rinker, Harley, Butts, Crutchfield, Gillespie, Jett, Prentiss, Saunders, Cunningham, Brown of Petersburg, and Stanard.—81.

The speaker laid before the house a communication from the governor, which was read as follows:

EXECUTIVE DEPARTMENT, February 22, 1836.

SIR,—Enclosed is a communication for the house of delegates, which you will be pleased to lay before that body.

Respectfully, your obedient servant,

LITT'N W. TAZEWELL.

To the Speaker of the House of Delegates.

To the House of Delegates.

I have just received a paper containing the preamble and resolutions adopted by the general assembly, upon the subject of expunging from the journal of the senate of the United States a resolution of that body.

By the last of the resolutions contained in this paper, I am requested to perform two several acts. I am desired to transmit these resolutions to each of the senators from Virginia in the congress of the United States, and also, to accompany this communication with a request to these senators, on my part, that they would lay the same before the body of which they are members.

Neither of the acts I am thus requested to perform, is embraced within the sphere of any duty assigned to the governor of this commonwealth, either by its constitution or laws; but as neither is thereby prohibited to him, I should not have hesitated to comply with the requests of the general assembly, if in doing so, I was not obliged to add my approbation to their resolves, and to unite my solicitation to their commands. Such a conclusion, however, is inevitable; for the terms employed in the resolutions, as well as the very nature of one of the acts I am thereby requested to perform, announce plainly, that both these acts are considered by the general assembly as merely voluntary on my part, to the performance of which acts, I am not compelled by the obligations of my legal duties. Therefore, it would be impossible for me to avoid the conclusions I have stated, should I comply with these requests. Even an addition to the communication I am requested to make, of such a disclaimer as might suffice to acquit me of this imputation, would be in direct conflict with the expressed wishes of the general assembly, and therefore, would not comport, as I think, with that respectful consideration which is due to that body, especially by every other department of this government.

Placed thus in a situation where my voluntary compliance with the wishes of the general assembly must expose me to an imputation, that in justice to myself I ought to disclaim; and should I do so, being constrained to depart from the course which my respect for them would induce me to adopt, no alternative is left but for me to decline a compliance with their requests. This I beg leave to do in the most respectful manner; and I hasten to communicate to them, this, my determination, to the end, that if the general assembly think it proper, the tasks which I have been requested to perform may be promptly assigned to some other agent, whose situation or opinions in this respect may be different from mine.

No ordinary circumstances would justify me, even to myself, in declining to co-operate with the general assembly, by the performance of any act on my part, that they might think useful to give effect to their wishes, and in that mode which to them might seem most proper. But I should be justly regarded by all as unworthy of the high trusts confided to me, if I were capable of permitting any consideration whatever, even my sincere wish to comply with the requests of the general assembly, to cause me to disregard my most sacred obligations. And as I cannot consider the resolutions I am requested to transmit, otherwise than as requiring a palpable violation of the constitution of the United States, I should incur guilt from which not even the approving voice of the present general assembly would suffice to absolve me, were I to lend my aid knowingly, in any way, to give effect to such a purpose. Greatly indeed, would this guilt be aggravated, if, while entertaining these opinions, I should dare to request others to incur such criminality on their part.

I may be mistaken in these opinions, but they are approved by my most deliberate judgment; and while so approved, it is my duty to act in conformity with them. Should I not do so, I should offend against my own conscience; and as by this I should justly merit the scorn and contempt of my fellow-citizens, I presume I should also incur that of the general assembly itself.

The courtesy and respect due to a co-ordinate department of the government, restrains me from stating here the various considerations which have induced me to entertain the opinion I have expressed, that the resolutions I am requested to transmit require a palpable violation of the constitution of the United States. The same motives induce me to abstain from characterizing the act I am requested to perform, in soliciting honourable and high-minded functionaries of Virginia to do that, which, if it is their duty to do, they will surely perform, without any officious request from me; and if it is contrary to their duty, none ought to desire of them to perform it, especially one who cannot claim authority of any kind to determine such a question for them.

The adoption of these resolutions must be considered by all as sufficient evidence that they who have sanctioned them by their approving votes, think differently from me in these particulars. This, their opinion, has now passed into an irreversible judgment. Therefore, it would ill become me to address an argument to the body itself which has so decided, to shew that this, its solemn and recorded and promulgated judgment was erroneous. It was necessary for my own justification, to state the fact that I did not concur in this judgment; but to do more than this, would be as improper as it would be now useless. Hence, I am restrained from presenting my own views of this subject to the general assembly, for the sincerity of whose expressed opinions I entertain the same respect that I claim for my own.

But if it should please the general assembly, either in kindness to me, or in justice to the people of Virginia, our common sovereign, to permit me to spread upon their journals a document respectful to those to whom it will be addressed, and dutiful to that sovereign to which only our allegiance is due, I should be gratified by such a permission; and I will gladly avail myself of it, to state in that way, the various considerations which have induced me to dissent from the opinions of the general assembly, as set forth in these resolutions. Without such permission, however, not even my own vindication can tempt me to be guilty of what I should consider as indecorous to any co-ordinate department of the government of my country, by which department I am addressed in terms of such courtesy as it has pleased the general assembly to employ in these resolutions towards me.

LITT'N W. TAZEWELL.

EXECUTIVE DEPARTMENT, *Richmond, February 22d,* 1836.

On motion of Mr. Watkins, *Ordered,* That the said communication be laid upon the table.

A motion was made by Mr. Watkins that the house adopt the following preamble and resolution.

Whereas a "preamble and resolutions upon the subject of expunging from the journals of the senate of the United States, a resolution of that body, and relative to the right of instruction," were passed by this general assembly, on the 20th day of the present month, (February, 1836;) and by one of the said resolutions, the governor of this commonwealth was requested to transmit the same "to each of the senators from Virginia, in the congress of the United States, with a request that they lay the same before the senate:" And whereas the governor of this commonwealth has refused to transmit the aforesaid preamble and resolutions in pursuance of the request aforesaid, and contrary to the usage of the executive of this state: Therefore,

Resolved by the general assembly of Virginia, That the speakers of the senate and house of delegates be, and they are hereby requested forthwith to transmit the aforesaid preamble and resolutions to each of the senators from Virginia in the congress of the United States, with a request that they lay the same before the senate of the United States.

The said resolution was, on the question put thereupon, agreed to by the house.

The question then recurred upon adopting the said preamble, and was determined in the affirmative. Ayes 79, noes 40.

The ayes and noes on that question being required by Mr. Botts, (and supported according to the rule of the house,) were as follow:

Ayes, Messrs. Banks, (speaker,) Layne, Wiley, Garland of Amherst, M'Clintic, Miller, Wilson of Botetourt, Decamps, Turnbull, Mallory, Booker, Austin, Beuhring, Daniel, Samuel, Richardson, Hill, Vaughan, Smith of Fauquier, Price, Strange, Steger, Holland, Bowen, Davison, Watts, Watkins, Hail of Grayson, Coleman, Sloan, Nixon, Goodall, Harrison, Kincheloe, Fontaine, Fleet, Hooe, Robinson, Neill, Hays, Straton, Harris, Ragsdale, Taylor of Mathews and Middlesex, Rogers, Garland of Mecklenburg, Willey, Morgan, Chapman, Ingles, Sherrard, Brown of Nelson, Cooke, Leland, Woolfolk, Almond, Adams, M'Coy, Cackley, Hopkins, Carroll, Madison, Shands, Williams, Marteney, Nicklin, Moffett, Conrad, Jessee, M'Mullen, Bare, Rinker, Harley, Crutchfield, Moncure, Hargrave, Gillespie, Gibson and Saunders.—79.

Noes, Messrs. Grinalds, Drummond, Gilmer, Southall, Brooke, Craig, Campbell, Hunter of Berkeley, Christian, Johnson, Servant, Hunter of Essex, Ball, Hale of Franklin, Smith of Gloucester, Mullen, Botts, Gregory, Berry, Summers, Carter, Beard, Powell, Taylor of Loudoun, Waggener, Benton, Parker, Chapline, Masters, Swanson, Witcher, Morris, Dorman, Butts, Delashmutt, Jett, Prentiss, Cunningham, Brown of Petersburg, and Stanard.—40.

Ordered, That the clerk communicate the said preamble and resolutions to the senate and request their concurrence.

Mr. Garland of Mecklenburg, from the committee of schools and colleges, presented a bill appropriating the surplus revenue of the literary fund; and

A bill to incorporate the trustees of Saint Bride's academy in Norfolk.

Mr. Brown of Petersburg, according to order, presented a bill concerning the Matoaca manufacturing company.

Mr. Brooke, from the committee of roads and internal navigation, presented a report upon the petition of the Chesapeake and Ohio canal company.

Which bills and report were received and laid upon the table.

On motion of Mr. Carroll, the house adjourned until to-morrow 11 o'clock.

WEDNESDAY, February 24th, 1836.

A communication from the senate by their clerk:

IN SENATE, February 23d, 1836.

The senate have passed the bills, entitled,
"An act to amend an act, entitled, 'an act for opening and improving the navigation of the Dragon swamp.'"
"An act relating to the Greensville and Panther gap turnpike road."
"An act to authorize a separate election at Triadelphia, in the county of Ohio."
"An act to authorize a separate election at the house of Michael Snodgrass, in the county of Monongalia;" and
"An act to incorporate the Stafford mining company."
They have also passed the bill, entitled,
"An act to incorporate the Heth manufacturing company," with an amendment, in which they request the concurrence of the house of delegates.

And they have agreed to the resolutions for the survey of a route for a rail-road from Falmouth to Alexandria, and from Warrenton to some point of intersection and union with the route from Falmouth to Alexandria; and for the survey between the head waters of Back bay and Linkhorn bay, and between the Northern branch of North river and the head waters of Lynhaven river.

The said amendment being twice read, was, on the question put thereupon, agreed to by the house.

Ordered, That the clerk inform the senate thereof.

On motion of Mr. Moncure, *Ordered*, That leave be given to bring in a bill to change the terms of the circuit superior court of law and chancery in and for the county of Stafford, and that Messrs. Moncure, Ball, Williams, Beard, Powell, Smith of Fauquier, Hooe and Hickerson, prepare and bring in the same.

On motion of Mr. Kincheloe, (the same having been amended on motion of Mr. Gilmer,)
Resolved, That this house will proceed on Saturday the 27th instant, by joint vote with the senate, to the election of a principal engineer, and of a superintendent and a general agent or storekeeper of the penitentiary institution.

Ordered, That the clerk communicate the same to the senate and request their concurrence.

On motion of Mr. Gregory, *Ordered*, That the select committee who were authorized to bring in a bill to amend the charter of the Richmond and Yorktown rail-road company, be discharged from the farther consideration of the same, and that the committee of roads and internal navigation prepare and bring in the said bill.

Mr. Dorman, from the committee for courts of justice, presented a bill changing the punishment of slaves convicted of hog stealing.

Mr. Cunningham, according to order, presented a bill to repeal the act to provide for the appointment of a commissioner to examine and report upon claims for unsatisfied military land bounties, and for other purposes, passed March 11th, 1834.

Mr. Watkins, from the committee of roads and internal navigation, presented reports upon petitions of citizens of Richmond, Buckingham and Powhatan, for a rail-road on the ridge from Richmond to Lynchburg; of citizens of Chesterfield and Richmond, for a rail-road from the Chesterfield coal mines to James river; and upon the resolution for incorporating a joint stock company to complete the free road from Staunton to the Warm springs.

And a bill incorporating the Mayo's bridge company.

Mr. Rinker, according to order, presented a bill to change the time of holding a quarterly term of the county court of the county of Shenandoah.

Mr. Hunter of Essex, from the committee on the penitentiary institution, presented a report upon petitions of citizens of Botetourt and Franklin, in favour of pardoning Eli Blankenship.

Mr. Masters, according to order, presented a bill changing the time of holding the county courts in the counties of Marshall and Ohio, and to amend the act establishing the town of Moundsville, in Ohio (now Marshall) county.

Which bills and reports were received and laid upon the table.

On motion of Mr. Wilson of Botetourt, the petition of the heirs of Lauriet Buzadone was taken up; whereupon a motion was made by him that the same be referred to a select committee; a motion was then made by Mr. Gregory that the same be referred to the committee for courts of justice; with instructions to report to this house, whether there be any general law authorizing the payment of such claims, and if there be such law, whether there be any tribunal for the adjustment and satisfaction of the same.

On motion of Mr. Garland of Amherst, the said petition and motions were ordered to be laid upon the table.

On motion of Mr. Gregory, the resolution submitted by him on the eleventh instant, was taken up and agreed to as follows:

Resolved, That the claims which were referred to the late committee on revolutionary claims, be referred to the committee for courts of justice, with instructions that said committee examine said claims, and report to this house, whether any claim has been presented, which, in its opinion ought to be paid, and for the settlement of which the existing laws, either of this state or the United States, have constituted a tribunal. And that said committee also enquire into the expediency of limiting by law, the time within which all applications for compensation for military services rendered during the revolutionary war, may be made, and that said committee have leave to report by bill or otherwise.

Mr. Southall presented a petition of citizens of the county of Albemarle, for the establishment of a bank at the town of Charlottesville, which was ordered to be referred to the committee on banks, that they do examine the matter thereof, and report their opinion thereupon to the house.

On motion of Mr. Murdaugh, *Resolved by the general assembly*, That the board of public works be instructed to cause a survey and examination to be made by a competent engineer, of the Nottoway river, from the point where it is crossed by the Petersburg and Roanoke rail-road, down to its mouth or where it empties into the Meherrin, and report the nature of the obstructions to navigation in that part of said river, and an estimate of the probable costs of removing those obstructions.

Ordered, That the clerk communicate the same to the senate and request their concurrence.

On motion of Mr. Layne, *Resolved*, That the committee of claims be instructed to enquire into the expediency of authorizing the auditor of public accounts to issue a warrant in favour of James Burk, in payment of two stands of colours, furnished the 128th regiment, should the fines of said regiment be sufficient; if not, for such amount as may have been paid in by said regiment, and that they report thereon by bill or otherwise.

A message from the senate by Mr. Rives:

Mr. Speaker,—The senate have adopted the preamble and resolution providing for the transmission to the senators from Virginia in the congress of the United States, of a preamble and resolutions upon the subject of expunging from the journals of the senate of the United States a resolution of that body, and relative to the right of instruction. And then he withdrew.

On motion of Mr. Dorman, the rule of the house was suspended, and the vote on yesterday, adopting a resolution for procuring a flag of the United States for the use of the commonwealth, was reconsidered; whereupon, the said resolution was amended, on motions severally made, and as amended, was agreed to by the house as follows:

Resolved by the general assembly, That the governor cause to be procured for the use of this commonwealth, a handsome flag of the United States, to be displayed by the superintendent of public buildings on the 22d day of February, and on the 4th of July, annually, and on all other proper occasions, and that the cost of the same be defrayed out of the contingent fund.

Ordered, That the clerk communicate the same to the senate and request their concurrence.

On motion of Mr. Bowen, *Resolved*, That the committee on the militia laws be instructed to enquire into the expediency of authorizing the auditor of public accounts to pay Peter Klipstine for three stand of colours purchased of him on the first of March, 1834, by Jacob Myers, lieutenant colonel commandant of the 67th regiment of Virginia militia, for the use of said regiment, and that they have leave to report by bill or otherwise.

The speaker laid before the house a communication from the register of the land office, made in obedience to the resolution of the house of delegates, requesting him to report the quantity of land bounty allowed by Virginia to such of her officers and soldiers as have not yet received their military warrants, and reporting that there are executive orders for land bounty filed in his office, and not yet acted on, for want of the requisite proof of heirship, amounting to fifty-five thousand acres of land, which being read, was, on motion ordered to be referred to the committee for courts of justice.

On motion of Mr. Chapman, *Resolved*, That the committee for courts of justice be instructed to enquire into the expediency of supplying the justices of the peace more generally with a copy of the revised code and supplement, and that said committee have leave to report by bill or otherwise.

Mr. Crutchfield presented a petition of citizens of the town of Fredericksburg, praying an amendment to the statute of limitation to real actions, passed April, 1831, which was ordered to be referred to the committee for courts of justice, that they do examine the matter thereof, and report their opinion thereupon to the house.

Mr. Renhring presented a petition of Frederick Moore, praying the relinquishment to him of the commonwealth's right to certain lands in the county of Cabell, which was ordered, in like manner, to be referred to said committee.

Also, a petition of John M'Henry, praying that a certain sum of money improperly collected of him and paid into the treasury, may be refunded to him, which was ordered to be referred to the committee of finance, that they do examine the matter thereof, and report their opinion thereupon to the house.

Mr. Daniel presented a petition of citizens of the town of Lynchburg, praying the passage of an act giving to the hustings court of said town power to let out the public roads within the corporation for the purpose of keeping the same in good repair, which was ordered to be referred to the committee of roads and internal navigation, that they do examine the matter thereof, and report their opinion thereupon to the house.

An engrossed bill to incorporate the Suffolk rail-road company, was taken up, on motion of Mr. Benton, and a blank therein was filled:

Resolved, That the bill do pass, and that the title be, "an act to incorporate the Suffolk rail-road company."

Ordered, That the clerk communicate the same to the senate and request their concurrence.

An engrossed bill to incorporate the city of Wheeling in Ohio county, was read a third time, and on motion of Mr. Watkins, ordered to be laid upon the table.

An engrossed bill incorporating the literary and scientific mechanics institute of Norfolk and Portsmouth, was read a third time:

Resolved, That the bill do pass, and that the title be, "an act incorporating the literary and scientific mechanics institute of Norfolk and Portsmouth."

Ordered, That the clerk communicate the same to the senate and request their concurrence.

An engrossed bill authorizing Jesse Sturm to erect a dam across the west fork of Monongalia river in the county of Harrison, was, on motion of Mr. Kincheloe, ordered to be laid upon the table.

An engrossed bill to change the times of holding the courts in the third judicial circuit, was read a third time:

Resolved, That the bill do pass, and (the title being amended on motion of Mr. Campbell,) that the title be, "an act to change the times of holding the courts in the third judicial circuit, and for other purposes"

Ordered, That the clerk communicate the same to the senate and request their concurrence.

On motion of Mr. Wilson of Botetourt, the house adjourned until to-morrow 11 o'clock.

THURSDAY, February 25th, 1836.

A motion was made by Mr. Watkins that the house adopt the following resolution:

Resolved by this house, That no resolution shall be received by the speaker and presented to the house on any day during the remainder of this session, unless the said resolution be offered within one hour after the meeting of the house.

On motion of Mr. Wiley, *Ordered,* That the farther consideration thereof be indefinitely postponed.

A motion was made by Mr. Summers that the house adopt the following resolution:

Resolved, That the committee for courts of justice be instructed to enquire into the expediency of more clearly defining by law, the duties of the attorney general, and regulating his fees, and that they have leave to report thereon by bill or otherwise.

And the question being put thereupon, was determined in the negative.

A motion was made by Mr. Straton that the house adopt the following resolution:

Resolved, That the committee on finance be instructed to enquire into the expediency of allowing to James Jenks, deputy sheriff of Logan county, the sum of thirty dollars and four cents, being the amount of sundry insolvent tickets in the militia fines of 1833, and of certain claims not presented in time in consequence of the death of said Jenks.

And the question being put thereupon, was determined in the negative.

Mr. Dorman, from the committee for courts of justice, presented reports upon the petitions of Hugh M'Gavoc; of Jim Smith; and of the clerk of the circuit superior court of Fairfax, and attorneys practising in that court.

Mr. Hill, from the committee of propositions and grievances, presented a report upon petitions of citizens of Henrico; and of citizens of Harrison county.

And a bill to change the place of holding a separate election in the county of Pittsylvania.

Which reports and bill were received and laid upon the table.

On motion of Mr. Bare, a bill forming a new county out of parts of the counties of Shenandoah and Frederick, was taken up, read the first and second times, and ordered to be committed to the committee which brought it in.

On motion of Mr. Griggs, a bill forming a new county out of the county of Frederick, was taken up, read the first and second times, and ordered to be committed to the committee which brought it in.

A bill regulating and reducing the expenses incident to the collection of money under execution, was taken up on motion of Mr. Crutchfield, and on motion of Mr. Mallory, the farther consideration thereof was indefinitely postponed.

Resolved, That the said bill be rejected.

Mr. Moncure, according to order, presented a bill changing the terms of the circuit superior court of law and chancery in and for the county of Stafford, which was received and laid upon the table.

The speaker laid before the house the following communication, which was read, and on motion of Mr. Booker, ordered to be laid upon the table:

RICHMOND, 24th February, 1836.

To the Speaker and Members of the House of Delegates.

GENTLEMEN,—Having at a late hour to-day, been asked by a member of your body, if I did not intend to report my reasons for failing to comply with your resolution addressed to me as superintendent of public edifices, on the 22d instant, requesting me to hoist the United States flag on the capitol, and at the same time informing me that there were many others who expected me to do so:

I feel myself, therefore, called upon to report, and am not disposed to withhold from you, (for whom I entertain unfeigned respect,) a candid statement of facts, and the motives which actuated me on the occasion.

I was in uniform, and on parade at the head of my corps, when the request above mentioned, was communicated to me, verbally, by Major Winston, your sergeant-at-arms, who was then in full uniform, and mounted; who addressed me as he usually does, viz: Captain, I have a request to deliver to you, from the house of delegates, that you will hoist the flag of the United States on the capitol; to which I replied, there is no flag staff on the capitol, but that I would see the governor forthwith, and report to him, not dreaming that the request was addressed to me in any other capacity than that of a military officer, it being a military occasion, and the article in question being strictly military.

I accordingly saw the governor, who advised me to ask, that the request be made in writing and shew it to him, which I did, and have not received any instructions from him relative to it.

I have, however, been informed that he wrote, and had despatched a communication to me, but upon examining the resolution itself, for the first time perceived that it was addressed to me as superintendent of public edifices, and not as captain of the public guard, and recalled it before it reached me. It is proper for me here further to remark, that the flag I was requested to display, was in my custody only as a military officer, in which character alone I am charged with the care of it, by the executive, and that under such circumstances, with no more propriety than any other citizen, could I use the flag without the governor's permission.

I beg the legislature to believe, that nothing was further from my design, than to disobey or slight in the least degree any direction given by them, still less one, that as a private citizen, I should have taken pleasure in executing, and trust they will find in the explanation I have thought it my duty to make, good grounds to absolve me from any charge of intended disrespect or disregard of their wishes.

I am, very respectfully,

BLAIR BOLLING,
Superintendent of Public Edifices.

An engrossed bill authorizing Jesse Sturm to erect a dam across the West fork of Monongalia river in the county of Harrison, was taken up on motion of Mr. Kincheloe, and read a third time; and the question being put upon its passage, was determined in the affirmative.

Resolved, That the bill do pass, and that the title be, "an act authorizing Jesse Sturm to erect a dam across the West fork of Monongalia river in the county of Harrison."

Ordered, That the clerk communicate the same to the senate and request their concurrence.

On motion, *Ordered,* That leave of absence from the service of this house, be granted to Mr. Parker for the remainder of the session.

An engrossed bill to incorporate the stockholders of the Lynchburg and Tennessee rail-road company, and to authorize them, or the James river and Kanawha company, to construct a rail-road from Lynchburg to Richmond, was read a third time, and sundry blanks therein were filled; and, on motion of Mr. Miller, ordered to be laid upon the table.

An engrossed bill giving to the circuit superior courts of law and chancery concurrent jurisdiction with the county and corporation courts in all actions of forcible entry and detainer, was read a third time: whereupon, a motion was made by Mr. Crutchfield, that the farther consideration of the same be indefinitely postponed; and the question being put thereupon, was determined in the affirmative. Ayes 71, noes 27.

The ayes and noes on said question being required by Mr. Hopkins, (and sustained according to the rule of the house,) were as follow:

Ayes, Messrs. Banks, (speaker,) Gilmer, Southall, Layne, Wiley, Garland of Amherst, M'Clintic, Henshaw, Miller, Wilson of Botetourt, Decamps, Turnbull, Mallory, Booker, Austin, Daniel, Samuel, Christian, Richardson, Hill, Vaughan, Servant, Ball, Smith of Fauquier, Hickerson, Strange, Hale of Franklin, Bowen, Smith of Gloucester, Watkins, Hail of Grayson, Carrington, Coleman, Sloan, Goodall, Mullen, Botts, Gregory, Fleet, Hooe, Robinson, Neill, Taylor of Loudoun, Harris, Ragsdale, Taylor of Mathews and Middlesex, Ingles, Benton, Brown of Nelson, Fitzgerald, Almond, M'Coy, Swanson, Cackley, Williams, Marteney, Dorman, Leyburn, Moffett, Conrad, Jessee, Rinker, Harley, Butts, Crutchfield, Hargrave, Gillespie, Jett, Prentiss, Saunders and Stanard.—71.

Noes, Messrs. Grinalds, Drummond, Campbell, Hunter of Berkeley, Beuhring, Wilson of Cumberland, Price, Holland, Watts, Nixon, Harrison, Kincheloe, Fontaine, Berry, Summers, Hays, Willey, Chapman, Sherrard, Leland, Chapline, Masters, Adams, Hopkins, Shands, M'Mullen and Spradey.—27.

Resolved, That the said bill be rejected.

Mr. Watkins, from the committee of roads and internal navigation, presented reports upon petitions of citizens of Lynchburg; of citizens of Smyth; of Samuel S. Williams and Henry H. Evans; and upon the resolution to allow Lavender London and William H. Garland to erect a dam across Tye river.

Also, a bill to amend the act, entitled, "an act to incorporate a rail-road company from the city of Richmond to the town of York;" and

A bill incorporating the Sweet springs and Price's mountain turnpike company.

Which were severally received and laid upon the table.

On motion of Mr. Watkins, *Ordered,* That the said committee be discharged from the farther consideration of the petitions of landholders on James river; of citizens of Goochland; and of citizens of Cumberland; and that the said petitions be laid upon the table.

Mr. Carter, from the committee on banks, presented a bill increasing the banking capital of this commonwealth, which, on his motion, was read the first and second times, and ordered to be committed to a committee of the whole house on the state of the commonwealth; and 185 copies thereof were ordered to be printed for the use of the general assembly.

Resolved, That this house will, on Monday next, resolve itself into a committee of the whole house to take the said bill into consideration.

On motion of Mr. Miller, the house adjourned until to-morrow 11 o'clock.

FRIDAY, February 26th, 1836.

A communication from the senate by their clerk:

IN SENATE, February 25th, 1836.

The senate have passed the bills, entitled,
" An act to incorporate the Fauquier White Sulphur springs."
" An act to incorporate the Virginia fire insurance company ;" and
" An act to provide for the construction of a road across the Blue Ridge at Milam's gap."
And they have agreed to the resolution for the election of a principal engineer, and of a superintendent and a general agent or storekeeper of the penitentiary institution.

On motion of Mr. Christian, *Ordered*, That leave be given to bring in a bill to authorize Robert W. Christian, treasurer of the late charity school of Charles City county, to pay over to the overseers of the poor of that county the funds in his hands of that institution, and that Messrs. Christian, Gregory, Servant, Botts, Spratley, Smith of Gloucester, and Taylor of Middlesex, prepare and bring in the same.

On motion of Mr. Garland of Mecklenburg, a bill appropriating the surplus revenue of the literary fund was taken up, read the first and second times, and ordered to be committed to the committee which brought it in.

Mr. Campbell, according to order, presented a bill to amend an act, entitled, " an act incorporating the trustees of the Bedford female academy;" which was received and laid upon the table.

Mr. Wilson of Botetourt, submitted the following resolution, which, on his motion, was ordered to be laid upon the table:

Resolved by the general assembly of Virginia, That the superintendent of the penitentiary institution be added to the committee or board of revisors appointed by an act to provide for a revision of the criminal code, passed March 12th, 1834.

An engrossed bill to authorize the auditor to issue warrants on the treasury in satisfaction of certain judgments against the commonwealth, was taken up, on motion of Mr. Ball, and read a third time:

Resolved, That the bill do pass, and that the title be, " an act to authorize the auditor to issue warrants on the treasury in satisfaction of certain judgments against the commonwealth."

Ordered, That Mr. Ball carry the same to the senate and request their concurrence.

An engrossed bill to incorporate the stockholders of the Cartersville and Farmville rail-road company, was taken up, on motion of Mr. Wilson of Cumberland, and read a third time, and a blank therein was filled, and the question being put upon its passage, was determined in the affirmative. Ayes 70, noes 44.

The ayes and noes thereupon being required by Mr. Madison, (and sustained according to the rule of the house,) were as follow :

Ayes, Messrs. Grinalds, Drummond, Gilmer, Southall, Layne, Garland of Amherst, Brooke, Craig, Campbell, Hunter of Berkeley, Wilson of Botetourt, Decamps, Mallory, Beuhring, Daniel, Christian, Wilson of Cumberland, Servant, Ball, Hickerson, Price, Strange, Hale of Franklin, Smith of Frederick, Watts, Watkins, Wethered, Goodall, Mullen, Harrison, Kincheloe, Botts, Gregory, Berry, Summers, Robinson, Neill, Hays, Straton, Beard, Powell, Taylor of Loudoun, Harris, Willey, Chapman, Ingles, Benton, Brown of Nelson, Cooke, Masters, Woolfolk, M'Coy, Swanson, Witcher, Cackley, Hopkins, Morris, Marteney, Dorman, Leyburn, Jessee, M'Mullen, Harley, Crutchfield, Moncure, Gibson, Prentiss, Saunders, Cunningham and Stanard.—70.

Noes, Messrs. Banks, (speaker,) Wiley, Miller, Turnbull, Booker, Austin, Samuel, Richardson, Hill, Vaughan, Smith of Fauquier, Holland, Bowen, Davison, Smith of Gloucester, Carrington, Coleman, Sloan, Nixon, Fleet, Hooe, Ragsdale, Taylor of Mathews and Middlesex, Waggener, Rogers, Garland of Mecklenburg, Sherrard, Fitzgerald, Almond, Adams, Carroll, Madisen, Shands, Williams, Nicklin, Moffett, Conrad, Rinker, Butts, Spratley, Hargrave, Delashmutt, Jett, and Brown of Petersburg.—44.

Resolved, That the bill do pass, and that the title be, " an act to incorporate the stockholders of the Cartersville and Farmville rail-road company."

Ordered, That the clerk communicate the same to the senate and request their concurrence.

On motion of Mr. Brown of Petersburg, the rule of the house limiting the number of the committee of finance was suspended, and Mr. Vaughan was ordered to be added to the said committee.

On motion of Mr. Daniel, an engrossed bill to incorporate the stockholders of the Lynchburg and Tennessee rail-road company, and to authorize them, or the James river and Kanawha company, to construct a rail-road from Lynchburg to Richmond, was taken up; whereupon, a clause by way of ryder thereto, was offered by Mr. Booker, which was read the first and second times. The same is the following:

" *Provided however*, That nothing herein before contained, shall in any wise impair the right of the general assembly of Virginia, at any time before the location and actual commencement of the construction of the rail-road from Lynchburg to Richmond, to locate the said road wherever in the opinion of the general assembly the public good and convenience may require it; and also to require the James river and Kanawha company, or the Lynchburg and Tennessee rail-road company, to commence and construct the same at earlier periods than herein before provided."

A motion was made by Mr. Harrison, to amend the same by adding thereto the following:

" *And provided also*, That the passage of this bill shall not be regarded as an implied pledge by the commonwealth to subscribe hereafter for the stock of the said company."

And the question being put upon the said amendment, was determined in the negative. Ayes 32, noes 75.

The ayes and noes thereupon being required by Mr. Harrison, (and sustained according to the rule of the house,) were as follow:

Ayes, Messrs. Grinalds, Drummond, Wiley, Decamps, Turnbull, Vaughan, Smith of Fauquier, Hickerson, Bowen, Smith of Gloucester, Hail of Grayson, Sloan, Nixon, Mullen, Harrison, Kincheloe, Fleet, Robinson, Rogers, Garland of Mecklenburg, Sherrard, Fitzgerald, Woolfolk, M'Coy, Shands, Nicklin, Moffett, Conrad, Rinker, Hargrave, Delashmutt and Prentiss.—32.

Noes, Messrs. Banks, (speaker,) Gilmer, Southall, Layne, Garland of Amherst, Craig, Campbell, Hunter of Berkeley, Henshaw, Miller, Wilson of Botetourt, Mallory, Booker, Austin, Beuhring, Daniel, Samuel, Christian, Richardson, Hill, Wilson of Cumberland, Price, Strange, Steger, Hale of Franklin, Holland, Smith of Frederick, Watts, Watkins, Wethered, Carrington, Coleman, Goodall, Botts, Gregory, Berry, Summers, Hooe, Neill, Hays, Straton, Beard, Taylor of Loudoun, Harris, Ragsdale, Willey, Chapman, Ingles, Brown of Nelson, Murdaugh, Cooke, Masters, Almond, Adams, Swanson, Witcher, Cackley, Hopkins, Madison, Morris, Dorman, Leyburn, Jessee, M'Mullen, Harley, Butts, Crutchfield, Moncure, Spratley, Gibson, Jett, Saunders, Cunningham, Brown of Petersburg, and Stanard.—75.

The question was then put upon engrossing the said ryder and reading it a third time, and was determined in the negative.

The question then recurred upon the passage of the said bill, and was determined in the affirmative. Ayes 66, noes 47.

The ayes and noes thereupon being required by Mr. Booker, (and sustained according to the rule of the house,) were as follow:

Ayes, Messrs. Gilmer, Southall, Layne, Garland of Amherst, Craig, Campbell, Hunter of Berkeley, Henshaw, Miller, Wilson of Botetourt, Mallory, Beuhring, Daniel, Hunter of Essex, Ball, Price, Strange, Hale of Franklin, Holland, Watts, Watkins, Hail of Grayson, Wethered, Goodall, Botts, Gregory, Berry, Summers, Neill, Hays, Straton, Beard, Powell, Taylor of Loudoun, Harris, Taylor of Mathews and Middlesex, Waggener, Chapman, Ingles, Benton, Brown of Nelson, Murdaugh, Cooke, Fitzgerald, Masters, Adams, Swanson, Witcher, Cackley, Morris, Marteney, Dorman, Leyburn, Jessee, M'Mullen, Rinker, Harley, Crutchfield, Spratley, Gillespie, Gibson, Jett, Saunders, Cunningham, Brown of Petersburg, and Stanard.—66.

Noes, Messrs. Banks, (speaker,) Wiley, Decamps, Turnbull, Booker, Austin, Samuel, Christian, Richardson, Hill, Wilson of Cumberland, Vaughan, Smith of Fauquier, Hickerson, Steger, Bowen, Smith of Gloucester, Carrington, Coleman, Sloan, Nixon, Mullen, Harrison, Kincheloe, Fleet, Robinson, Ragsdale, Rogers, Garland of Mecklenburg, Willey, Morgan, Sherrard, Almond, Hopkins, Carroll, Madison, Shands, Williams, Nicklin, Moffett, Conrad, Bare, Butts, Moncure, Hargrave, Delashmutt and Prentiss.—47.

Resolved, That the bill do pass, and that the title be, "an act to incorporate the stockholders of the Lynchburg and Tennessee rail-road company, and to authorize them, or the James river and Kanawha company, to construct a rail-road from Lynchburg to Richmond."

Ordered, That the clerk communicate the same to the senate and request their concurrence.

Mr. Christian, according to order, presented a bill concerning Robert W. Christian, treasurer of the late charity school of Charles City, and the overseers of the poor of said county, which was received and laid upon the table.

On motion of Mr. Hunter of Berkeley, the house adjourned until to-morrow 11 o'clock.

SATURDAY, February 27th, 1836.

A communication from the senate by their clerk:

IN SENATE, February 26th, 1836.

The senate have passed the bills, entitled,

"An act to change the place of holding a separate election in the county of Lunenburg;" and

"An act to incorporate the Suffolk rail-road company."

They have also passed the bills, entitled,

"An act incorporating the literary and scientific mechanics institute of Norfolk and Portsmouth;" and

"An act to amend an act, entitled, 'an act to incorporate the Cold Brook company of colliers,'" passed January 23d, 1835, with amendments, in which they request the concurrence of the house of delegates.

And their committee appointed to examine the enrolled bills, have examined all such bills as have been received from the house of delegates, and which being found truly enrolled, are herewith returned.

The said amendments being twice read, were, on questions severally put thereupon, agreed to by the house.

Ordered, That the clerk inform the senate thereof.

Mr. Mallory, from the committee on enrolled bills, reported that the said committee had examined sundry other such bills, and had found them truly enrolled.

Ordered, That the clerk communicate the same to the senate.

On motion of Mr. Crutchfield, *Ordered*, That leave be given to bring in a bill to incorporate the Deane iron and steel manufacturing company, and that Messrs. Crutchfield, Moncure, Williams, Samuel, Hooe, Woolfolk, Goodall, Hill and Smith of Fauquier, prepare and bring in the same.

On motion of Mr. Watkins, the rule of the house was suspended for the purpose of reconsidering the vote rejecting a resolution submitted by Mr. Summers, day before yesterday, and the said resolution was agreed to by the house as follows:

Resolved, That the committee for courts of justice be instructed to enquire into the expediency of more clearly defining by law the duties of the attorney general, and regulating his fees, and that they have leave to report thereon, by bill or otherwise.

Mr. Watkins, from the committee of roads and internal navigation, presented a report upon the resolution for increasing the capital of the Richmond, Fredericksburg and Potowmac rail-road company.

Mr. Hill, from the committee of propositions and grievances, reported with amendments, a bill forming a new county out of parts of the counties of Shenandoah and Frederick.

And a bill forming a new county out of the county of Frederick.

And presented a bill to incorporate the town of Waterford in the county of Loudoun.

A bill to prevent the destruction of oysters in Nansemond river, and Chuckatuck creek in the county of Nansemond; and

A bill to incorporate a company to construct a toll bridge across the Shenandoah river at Harper's Ferry.

Which report and bills were severally received and laid upon the table.

Mr. Gilmer presented a petition of citizens of the county of Albemarle, for the establishment of a bank at the town of Charlottesville, which was ordered to be referred to the committee on banks, that they do examine the matter thereof, and report their opinion thereupon to the house.

A bill incorporating the trustees of the Martinsville academy, was taken up on motion of Mr. Fontaine, read the first and second times, and ordered to be committed to the committee which brought it in.

A bill incorporating the stockholders of the Richmond and Petersburg rail-road company, together with the amendments thereto proposed by the committee of roads and internal navigation, was taken up on motion of Mr. Stanard, and the said amendments being amended on motions severally made, and as amended, agreed to by the house, a motion was made by Mr. Brown of Petersburg, further to amend the said bill by striking out a part of the first section: The part proposed to be stricken out, is the following:

"And for extending a branch or branches of the said rail-road, should the company hereby incorporated, at the commencement of the work, or at any time afterwards, deem it advisable to do so, from a point or points on the line of the said rail-road to Bermuda Hundred : *Provided,* nothing herein contained shall be construed as granting the privilege of extending the rail-road along any of the streets of the said city of Richmond or town of Petersburg, except with the consent of the common council of the said city or town, or along any of the streets of the town of Manchester, except with the consent of the trustees of the said town."

In lieu of the part so proposed to be stricken out, he proposed to insert the following:

"*Provided,* That the said rail-road shall terminate at the corporation line of Petersburg on the north bank of the Appomattox river to the eastward of the site of M'Neill's bridge, or at such point within the said corporation as may be designated and agreed to by a majority of two-thirds of the citizens of the town of Petersburg qualified by existing laws to vote for members of the common hall of said town, in general meeting assembled, after two weeks public notice thereof, in the newspapers printed in said town. But in no case shall any house, yard, garden or curtilage within the said corporation be invaded, without the consent of the owner or owners thereof."

And the question being put upon the said amendment, was determined in the negative. Ayes 47, noes 50.

The ayes and noes thereupon being required by Mr. Brown of Petersburg, (and sustained according to the rule of the house,) were as follow:

Ayes, Messrs. Grinalds, Drummond, Gilmer, Layne, Wiley, M'Clintic, Miller, Wilson of Botetourt, Decamps, Turnbull, Mallory, Booker, Austin, Hill, Vaughan, Servant, Holland, Bowen, Davison, Smith of Gloucester, Carrington, Coleman, Sloan, Nixon, Gregory, Ragsdale, Rogers, Willey, Chapman, Benton, Brown of Nelson, Murdaugh, Leland, Almond, Adams, M'Coy, Swanson, Hopkins, Madison, Shands, Nicklin, Moffett, Bare, Rinker, Butts, Hargrave, and Brown of Petersburg.—47.

Noes, Messrs. Banks, (speaker,) Southall, Garland of Amherst, Craig, Hunter of Berkeley, Henshaw, Daniel, Christian, Wilson of Cumberland, Hunter of Essex, Smith of Fauquier, Price, Strange, Watts, Wethered, Harrison, Kincheloe, Botts, Fontaine, Holleman, Griggs, Berry, Summers, Hooe, Carter, Hays, Taylor of Loudoun, Harris, Waggener, Ingles, Sherrard, Fitzgerald, Masters, Witcher, Morris, Marteney, Dorman, Leyburn, Jessee, M'Mullen, Crutchfield, Moncure, Spratley, Delashmutt, Gibson, Jett, Prentiss, Saunders, Cunningham and Stanard.—50.

The said bill was then further amended, on motion of Mr. Brown of Petersburg, and as amended, was ordered to be engrossed and read a third time.

The house, according to the joint orders of the day, proceeded by joint vote with the senate, to the election of a principal engineer, and of a superintendent and a general agent or storekeeper of the penitentiary for one year; and the rule of the house requiring but one election to be made at a time having been suspended, Mr. Kincheloe nominated Charles B. Shaw, esq'r, as principal engineer; Mr. Wilson of Botetourt, nominated Charles S. Morgan, esq'r, as superintendent of the penitentiary, and Mr. Ball nominated Thomas G. Moncure, esq'r, as general agent or storekeeper of the penitentiary; and the senate having been informed thereof by Mr. Kincheloe, and agreeing to the mode of election indicated by this house, the names of the members were called by the clerk, when the vote was for each of the nominees 107.

The names of the gentlemen thus voting, are Messrs. Banks, (speaker,) Grinalds, Gilmer, Southall, Layne, Wiley, Craig, M'Clintic, Hunter of Berkeley, Henshaw, Wilson of Botetourt, Decamps, Turnbull, Mallory, Booker, Austin, Beuhring, Daniel, Christian, Hill, Wilson of Cumberland, Vaughan, Servant, Ball, Smith of Fauquier, Hickerson, Price, Strange, Hale of Franklin, Holland, Bowen, Davison, Watts, Smith of Gloucester, Watkins, Wethered, Carrington, Coleman, Nixon, Mullen, Harrison, Kincheloe, Fontaine, Holleman, Gregory, Griggs, Berry, Summers, Fleet, Hooe, Robinson, Carter, Neill, Hays, Straton, Taylor of Loudoun, Harris, Ragsdale, Waggener, Rogers, Garland of Mecklenburg, Willey, Morgan, Chapman, Ingles, Sherrard, Benton, Brown of Nelson, Cooke, Leland, Fitzgerald, Chapline, Masters, Almond, Adams, M'Coy, Swanson, Witcher, Cackley, Hopkins, Carroll, Morris, Shands, Williams, Nicklin, Dorman, Leyburn, Moffett, Conrad, Jessee, M'Mullen, Bare, Rinker, Harley, Butts, Moncure, Spratley, Hargrave, Gillespie, Delashmutt, Gibson, Jett, Prentiss, Saunders, Cunningham, Brown of Petersburg, and Stanard.—107.

Ordered, That Messrs. Kincheloe, Sherrard, Wilson of Botetourt, Fontaine, Ball, Watkins, Gregory and M'Coy, be a committee to act jointly with a committee of the senate to ascertain the state of the joint vote; the committee withdrew, and after some time returned into the house, and Mr. Kincheloe reported that the said committee had, according to order, ascertained the joint vote to be for each of the nominees 132: whereupon, Charles B. Shaw, esq'r, was declared duly elected principal engineer of this commonwealth; Charles S. Morgan, esq'r, was declared duly elected superintendent of the penitentiary, and Thomas G. Moncure, esq'r, was declared duly elected general agent or storekeeper of said institution, each for one year.

Mr. Garland of Mecklenburg, from the committee of schools and colleges, presented reports upon the petition of the school commissioners of Smyth county; and upon the resolution for increasing the number of visitors to the University.

And reported with amendments, a bill appropriating the surplus revenue of the literary fund.

Which were received and laid upon the table.

On motion of Mr. Garland of Mecklenburg, *Ordered*, That 185 copies of the said bill and proposed amendments be printed for the use of the general assembly.

On motion of Mr. Garland of Mecklenburg, *Ordered*, That the committee of schools and colleges be discharged from the farther consideration of petitions of citizens of Estillville; of the trustees of St. Bride's academy; of the trustees of the Newtown Stephensburg academy; of the trustees of the Randolph academy; and of the trustees of the Upperville academy; and that the same be laid upon the table.

Mr. Brown of Petersburg, from the committee of finance, presented a report upon the petition of John M'Henry.

And a bill concerning delinquent lands, and lands not heretofore entered on the commissioners' books.

Mr. Daniel, according to order, presented a bill changing the time of holding the superior courts of Campbell, Bedford, and the town of Lynchburg.

Which report and bills were received and laid upon the table.

On motion of Mr. Madison, *Ordered*, That the committee of agriculture and manufactures be discharged from the farther consideration of the petition of the inspectors of tobacco at the city of Richmond, and towns of Lynchburg, Petersburg and Clarksville, and that the same be laid upon the table.

On motion of Mr. Carroll, the house adjourned until Monday 11 o'clock.

MONDAY, February 29th, 1836.

A communication from the senate by their clerk:

IN SENATE, February 27th, 1836.

The senate have passed the bill, entitled,

"An act to authorize the auditor to issue warrants on the treasury in satisfaction of certain judgments against the commonwealth."

They have also passed the bills, entitled,

"An act incorporating the Natural bridge turnpike company;" and

"An act providing for a geological survey of the state, and for other purposes," with amendments, in which they request the concurrence of the house of delegates.

The said amendments to the said first bill being twice read, were, on questions severally put thereupon, agreed to by the house.

Ordered, That the clerk inform the senate thereof.

The said amendment proposed by the senate to the bill, entitled, "an act providing for a geological survey of the state, and for other purposes," being twice read, a motion was made by Mr. Booker, that the said bill and amendment be indefinitely postponed, and the question being put thereupon, was determined in the negative. Ayes 27, noes 79.

The ayes and noes thereupon being required by Mr. Woolfolk, (and sustained according to the rule of the house,) were as follow:

Ayes, Messrs. Banks, (speaker,) Grinalds, Drummond, M'Clintic, Turnbull, Mallory, Booker, Austin, Hill, Hickerson, Hale of Franklin, Holland, Hail of Grayson, Avent, Coleman, Morgan, Woolfolk, Adams, Swanson, Hopkins, Nicklin, Moffett, Conrad, Bare, Rinker, Hargrave and Gibson—27.

Noes, Messrs. Gilmer, Southall, Layne, Wiley, Garland of Amherst, Brooke, Craig, Hunter of Berkeley, Henshaw, Miller, Wilson of Botetourt, Decamps, Beuhring, Daniel, Samuel, Hunter of Essex, Ball, Smith of Fauquier, Price, Strange, Steger, Bowen, Davison, Watts, Smith of Gloucester, Watkins, Wethered, Sloan, Nixon, Mullen, Harrison, Kincheloe, Fontaine, Gregory, Berry, Summers, Robinson, Carter, Hays, Straton, Beard, Harris, Ragsdale, Waggener, Rogers, Garland of Mecklenburg, Willey, Chapman, Ingles, Sherrard, Brown of Nelson, Murdaugh, Cooke, Fitzgerald, Chapline, Masters, Almond, M'Coy, Cackley, Carroll, Madison, Morris, Williams, Marteney, Dorman, Leyburn, Jessee, M'Mullen, Harley, Butts, Moncure, Gillespie, Delashmutt, Jett, Prentiss, Saunders, Cunningham, Brown of Petersburg, and Stanard.—79.

The said amendment was then, on the question put thereupon, agreed to by the house.

Ordered, That the clerk inform the senate thereof.

Mr. Southall presented a petition of citizens of the county of Albemarle, for the establishment of a bank at the town of Charlottesville, which was ordered to be referred to the committee on banks, that they do examine the matter thereof, and report their opinion thereupon to the house.

Mr. Garland of Mecklenburg, from the committee of schools and colleges, reported without amendment, a bill incorporating the trustees of the Martinsville academy, which was received and laid upon the table.

The order of the day on the state of the commonwealth, was, on motion of Mr. Watkins, ordered to be postponed until to-morrow.

Mr. Dorman presented a petition of sundry citizens of the county of Rockbridge, upon the subject of the free road from Staunton to the Warm springs, which was ordered to be laid upon the table.

Mr. Stanard presented a document to be used in evidence to support the petition of Peter J. Chevallie, which was ordered to be referred to the committee of claims.

Mr. Hill, from the committee of propositions and grievances, presented a report upon the petitions of the trustees of the town of Portsmouth; of citizens of the county of Northumberland; and of citizens of the county of Nicholas.

Also, a bill to amend the act, entitled, "an act to incorporate the Grayson Sulphur springs company;" and

A bill to change the place of holding a separate election in the county of Harrison.

Which report and bills were received and laid upon the table.

A bill forming a new county out of parts of the counties of Shenandoah and Frederick, with the amendments thereto proposed by the committee of propositions and grievances, was taken up on motion of Mr. Bare, and the said amendments being agreed to by the house, the said bill, as amended, was ordered to be again laid upon the table.

A bill to authorize a subscription on behalf of the state to the stock of the Lewisburg and Blue Sulphur springs turnpike company, was taken up on motion of Mr. Wethered, read the first and second times, and ordered to be committed to the committee which brought it in.

A bill to form a new county out of the county of Frederick, with the amendments thereto proposed by the committee of propositions and grievances, was taken up on motion of Mr. Hunter of Berkeley, and the said amendments being severally agreed to, except the second amendment, which was disagreed to by the house, the said bill, as amended, was, on motion of Mr. Smith of Frederick, ordered to be again laid upon the table.

On motion of Mr. Brown of Petersburg, *Ordered*, That leave be given to the committee of finance to sit during the session of this house on this day.

On motion of Mr. Cunningham, the following report of the committee of roads and internal navigation, was taken up:

The committee of roads and internal navigation have, according to order, had under consideration the petition of the mayor, recorder, aldermen, and common council of the borough of Norfolk, and of sundry stockholders and citizens thereof, and of other stockholders in the Portsmouth and Roanoke rail-road company, praying that the charter of the said rail-road company be so amended, as to authorize and require the said company to extend their rail-road to the borough of Norfolk, by steam boat or otherwise, and to establish a place of common deposite for produce therein; or on failure thereof, that a separate company be authorized to establish a rail-road, by steam boat or otherwise, to the borough of Norfolk, from an intersecting point of union with the Portsmouth and Roanoke rail-road, beyond the limits of the town of Portsmouth: Whereupon,

1. *Resolved as the opinion of this committee*, That so much of said petition as prays that the Portsmouth and Roanoke rail-road company be authorized and required to extend their road to the borough of Norfolk, be rejected.

2. *Resolved as the opinion of this committee*, That the residue of said petition, praying the incorporation of a company to construct a rail-road from Norfolk to a point of the Portsmouth and Roanoke rail-road beyond the limits of the town of Portsmouth, be rejected.

The said committee have also, according to order, had under consideration the counter memorial of sundry citizens of Norfolk county, and stockholders of the said Portsmouth and Roanoke rail-road company, to so much of the aforesaid petition as prays the extension of the rail-road by the erection of a bridge across the southern branch of Elizabeth river: Whereupon,

3. *Resolved as the opinion of this committee*, That said counter memorial is reasonable.

The said resolutions were, on questions severally put thereupon, agreed to by the house, an *unsuccessful* motion having been made by Mr. Cunningham, to amend the said first resolution, by striking therefrom the words "be rejected," and inserting in lieu thereof, the words "is reasonable," so as to reverse the decision of the committee.

An engrossed bill incorporating the stockholders of the Richmond and Petersburg rail-road company, was read a third time, and a blank therein was filled; whereupon, a clause by way of ryder thereto was submitted by Mr. Brown of Petersburg, which was read the first and second times, and forthwith engrossed and read a third time:

Resolved, That the bill (with the ryder,) do pass, and that the title be, " an act incorporating the stockholders of the Richmond and Petersburg rail-road company."

Ordered, That the clerk communicate the same to the senate and request their concurrence.

On motion of Mr. Hickerson, the report of the committee of claims upon the petition of Berkeley Ward, was taken up, and ordered to be recommitted to the said committee.

On motion of Mr. Craig, *Ordered,* That leave be given to John C. Wender to withdraw his petition and documents presented to the legislature some years since.

The following bills heretofore reported with amendments from the several committees to which the same had been committed, were taken up, and the said amendments being severally agreed to by the house, the same as amended were ordered to be engrossed and read a third time, viz:

A bill incorporating the Smithfield savings institution in the county of Isle of Wight.
A bill incorporating the Orange savings society; and
A bill concerning the Rappahannock company.

A bill incorporating the Laurel Hill turnpike company, was read a second time, and on motion of Mr. Marteney, ordered to be committed to the committee which brought it in.

Mr. Brown of Petersburg, from the committee of finance, presented a report upon the revenue and expenditures and debt of the commonwealth.

Also a bill imposing taxes for the support of government,
A bill appropriating the public revenue; and
A bill to amend the act concerning merchants' licenses.

Which bills, on his motion, were taken up, read the first and second times, and (together with the said report,) were ordered to be committed to a committee of the whole house on the state of the commonwealth, and 185 copies thereof were ordered to be printed for the use of the general assembly.

Resolved, That this house will, on Thursday next, resolve itself into a committee of the whole house, to take the said report and bills into consideration.

Mr. Brown of Petersburg also, from the same committee, presented a bill amending the act concerning waste tobacco, which was received and laid upon the table.

On motion of Mr. Murdaugh, the house adjourned until to-morrow 11 o'clock.

TUESDAY, March 1st, 1836.

A communication from the senate by their clerk:

IN SENATE, February 29th, 1836.

The senate have passed the bill, entitled,
" An act incorporating the Virginia towing company."

Mr. Brooke presented a petition of citizens of the counties of Augusta and Rockingham, asking the establishment of a bank at Charlottesville, which was ordered to be referred to the committee on banks, that they do examine the matter thereof, and report their opinion thereupon to the house.

On motion of Mr. Chapman, *Resolved,* That the committee of propositions and grievances be requested to enquire into the expediency of changing the time of the meeting of the general assembly of Virginia, from the first Monday in December, to the first Monday in January in every year, and that they have leave to report by bill or otherwise.

On motion of Mr. Dorman, *Ordered,* That leave be given to bring in a bill to revive an act incorporating a company to construct a turnpike road from the upper end of the Blue Ridge canal, to its intersection with the Lexington and Covington turnpike road, passed March 13th, 1832, and that Messrs. Dorman, Leyburn, Craig, Moffett, Layne, M'Clintic, and Wilson of Botetourt, prepare and bring in the same.

On motion of Mr. Moffett, *Ordered,* That leave be given to bring in a bill to change the time of holding the circuit superior courts of law and chancery for the counties of Rockingham and Pendleton, and that Messrs. Moffett, Conrad, M'Coy, Mullen, Brooke, Woolfolk, Bare and Almond, prepare and bring in the same.

A motion was made by Mr. Cunningham that the house adopt the following resolution:

Resolved, That leave be given to bring in a bill incorporating a company to connect with the Portsmouth and Roanoke rail-road, for the purpose of transporting produce, merchandize, &c., conveyed on said road to and from the borough of Norfolk; whereupon, a motion was made by Mr. Murdaugh to amend the same by substituting therefor the following:

Resolved, That the committee of roads and internal navigation be instructed to enquire into the expediency of incorporating a joint stock company to construct one or more boats to transport produce, merchandize and other articles, across Elizabeth river, between Norfolk and Portsmouth, and that said committee report by bill or otherwise.

And the question being put upon the said amendment, was determined in the negative.

The resolution was then agreed to by the house, and Messrs. Cunningham, Murdaugh, Cooke, Witcher, Butts, Morris, Benton, Holleman, Avent, Mallory and Shands, were ordered to prepare and bring in the said bill.

Mr. Murdaugh then submitted a letter from James Cornick upon the same subject, which was ordered to be referred to the said committee.

Mr. Smith of Fauquier presented a petition of citizens of the county of Fauquier, praying the establishment of a bank at Warrenton.

Mr. Moffett, a petition of citizens of Albemarle and Rockingham, asking for the location of a portion of any increase of capital of the banks in the commonwealth, at the town of Charlottesville.

Ordered, That the said petitions be referred to the committee on banks, that they do examine the matter thereof, and report their opinion thereupon to the house.

Mr. M'Mullen presented a petition of citizens of the county of Scott, asking aid in the construction of a bridge across the North fork of Holstein river, which was ordered to be referred to the committee of roads and internal navigation, that they do examine the matter thereof, and report their opinion thereupon to the house.

Mr. Dorman, from the committee for courts of justice, presented reports upon the petition of Andy; upon the resolution concerning the sheriff of Spottsylvania; concerning the extension of the jurisdiction of magistrates and the law relating to constables; and upon the charges preferred against judge Duncan.

Also, a bill to amend an act, entitled, "an act for the inspection of fish," passed the 28th of December, 1795.

A bill regulating the mode of obtaining writs of error in criminal prosecutions for misdemeanors; and

A bill prescribing the punishment of offences committed on rail-roads.

Mr. Austin, according to order, presented a bill to increase the capital stock of Booker's gold mine company, and for other purposes.

Mr. Garland of Amherst, in like manner, a bill appointing trustees of the town of New Glasgow, and for other purposes.

Mr. Watkins, from the committee of roads and internal navigation, reported with amendments, a bill incorporating the Laurel Hill turnpike company; and

A bill to authorize a subscription on behalf of the state to the stock of the Lewisburg and Blue Sulphur springs turnpike company.

Which bills and reports were received and laid upon the table.

On motion of Mr. Smith of Frederick, *Ordered*, That the committee on the militia laws be discharged from petitions of the regimental court of enquiry for the 57th regiment; of the officers of the 56th regiment; and of the court of enquiry of the 132d regiment; and that the same be laid upon the table.

The house, according to the order of the day, resolved itself into a committee of the whole house on the state of the commonwealth, Mr. Miller in the chair; and after some time spent therein, the speaker resumed the chair, and Mr. Miller reported that the said committee had, according to order, taken into consideration a bill increasing the banking capital of the commonwealth, and made some progress therein, but not having had time to go through the same, had instructed him to ask leave to sit again.

Resolved, That this house will on to-morrow, again resolve itself into a committee of the whole house to take the said bill into consideration.

On motion of Mr. Miller, the house adjourned until to-morrow 11 o'clock.

WEDNESDAY, March 2d, 1836.

A communication from the senate by their clerk:

IN SENATE, March 1st, 1836.

The senate have passed the bill, entitled,

"An act releasing the commonwealth's claim to a certain balance against the estate of Betsey Bidgood."

On motion of Mr. Cooke, *Ordered*, That leave be given to bring in a bill incorporating the Portsmouth provident society, and that Messrs. Cooke, Murdaugh, Cunningham, Benton, Morris, Butts, Servant and Hargrave, prepare and bring in the same.

On motion of Mr. Daniel, *Resolved*, That the committee on the militia laws be instructed to enquire into the expediency of providing by law for the payment to William Owens, of the price of two standards of colours, furnished the 18th regiment of Virginia militia in the year 1825, and that said committee have leave to report by bill or otherwise.

On motion of Mr. Watkins, *Ordered*, That leave be given to bring in a bill vesting in the board of public works the stock held by the state in the James river and Kanawha company, and for other purposes, and that Messrs. Watkins, Daniel, Booker, Wethered, Summers, Brown of Nelson, Stanard, Garland of Amherst, and Dorman, prepare and bring in the same.

Mr. Southall presented a petition of citizens of the county of Albemarle for the establishment of a bank at the town of Charlottesville.

Mr. Booker, a petition of citizens of the county of Buckingham for the establishment of a bank at the town of Scottsville in said county.

Ordered, That the said petitions be referred to the committee of the whole house on the state of the commonwealth.

Mr. Beard presented a petition of citizens of the town of Leesburg for an amendment of the acts incorporating that town, which was ordered to be referred to the committee of propositions and grievances, that they do examine the matter thereof, and report their opinion thereupon to the house.

Mr. Crutchfield, according to order, presented a bill incorporating the Deane iron and steel manufacturing company.

Mr. Watkins, from the committee of roads and internal navigation, presented a bill incorporating sundry companies to construct turnpike roads from Richmond to Big Bird bridge in the county of Goochland.

Mr. Hill, from the committee of propositions and grievances, presented a report upon the resolution for changing the time of meeting of the general assembly.

Mr. Moffett, according to order, presented a bill changing the times of holding the circuit superior courts of law and chancery in the counties of Rockingham and Pendleton.

Which bills and report were received and laid upon the table.

A bill to suppress the circulation of incendiary publications, and for other purposes, was taken up on motion of Mr. Garland of Mecklenburg, read the first time and ordered to be read a second time, and 185 copies thereof were ordered to be printed for the use of the general assembly.

A bill forming a new county out of parts of the counties of Shenandoah and Frederick, was taken up on motion of Mr. Almond, and, as heretofore amended, was ordered to be engrossed and read a third time.

The speaker laid before the house the following letter:

WASHINGTON, February 29, 1836.
To the Speaker and Members of the General Assembly of Virginia.

GENTLEMEN,
Certain resolutions of the general assembly, instructing their senators in the congress of the United States to introduce and to vote for a resolution to expunge the journal of a previous senate in the particular therein mentioned, and pointing out the precise manner in which the act shall be performed, has been made known to me. After the most deliberate examination which I am capable of bestowing upon them, and with a sincere desire to conform my conduct to the wishes of the general assembly, I find it impossible to reconcile the performance of the prescribed task with the obligations of the solemn oath which I have taken to support the constitution of the United States. With what promptitude I should comply with the instructions of the legislature, if compliance was permitted me, may readily be inferred from my past course of conduct. And I beg your indulgence, gentlemen, whilst I advert to the most prominent incidents of my life in connection with the great question of instructions. I was very young when I first took my seat in the house of delegates, to which I had been elected within a few days after I had attained the age of twenty-one. The then senators from Virginia (Messrs. Giles and Brent) stood obnoxious to the charge of having disregarded the instructions of the legislature, which had been adopted on the motion of a gentleman, then a distinguished member (governor Barbour), to vote against rechartering the bank of the United States. The first, while he voted against the bank, denied the right of the legislature to instruct him; the last disregarded the instructions altogether, and voted for the bank. Impelled by no other motive than to uphold the legislature in its right to instruct its deputed organs, I introduced a resolution disapproving the course which had been pursued by the senators. My motive in doing so was single and unmixed. *I was too young to seek profit by their overthrow.* The resolution thus introduced by me passed into other hands, and was substituted by other resolves, which were finally adopted by the two houses of assembly by large and overwhelming majorities. At the age of twenty-five, I took my seat in the house of representatives of the United States. The repeal of the compensation law soon came under discussion. I came in to supply a vacancy, and brought with me the wishes of my constituents in regard to that measure. I made them known, and claimed the repeal of the law as due to the well ascertained wishes of the people. This brought into discussion the obligation of instructions, and I contended for the right under the same restrictions and limitations as had been laid down in the resolutions before alluded to. I now reaffirm the opinion, at all times heretofore expressed by me, that instructions are mandatory, provided they do not require a violation of the constitution, or the commission of an act of moral turpitude. When acting under an oath, the public agent, whether a senator or a juror, is bound by obligations of a higher and more controlling character than can proceed from any earthly source. The constitution of the United States is the original and primary letter of instructions; supreme over all, and binding upon all. For the agent who is sworn to support it, to violate it knowingly and intentionally, would be an act of the grossest immorality and most unmitigated debasement. Such is the condition in which, in my view of the subject, obedience to your instructions would place me. It is known to you, gentlemen, that on my entering the senate, the only oath which I took was an oath to support the constitution of the United States; to support it in all and each of its provisions; to yield it neither to force, persuasion or expediency. No matter what the object, should its attainment confer upon me the greatest personal advantage, still to remain unseduced; not to touch that forbidden fruit. I entered into a covenant with my Creator, to break which would not fail to place in my bosom a Promethean vulture to tear and devour me. The obligation then to obey an instruction which calls upon me to break that covenant, cannot possibly exist. I should be unworthy the confidence of all honourable men, if I could be induced, under any circumstances, to commit an act of deliberate perjury. Instead of a seat in the senate, I should most richly deserve to be put in the pillory and to lose both my ears as an indelible mark of my baseness; and such would be the sentence which the laws of Virginia would pronounce against me. You have admitted the truth of

this position in the alternatives presented in your second resolution. Between those alternatives I cannot hesitate to choose. It is not for every difference of opinion between the representative and constituent, that the constituent would necessarily require the resignation of the representative. In the course of a somewhat long political life, it must have occurred that my opinions have been variant from the opinions of those I represented; but in presenting to me the alternative of resignation in this instance, you give me to be distinctly informed, that the accomplishment of your object is regarded as of such primary importance, that my resignation is desired if compliance cannot be yielded. I am bound to consider you, as in this, fairly representing the sentiments of our common constituents, the people of Virginia, to whom alone you are amenable if you have mistaken their wishes. My position in regard to this whole subject is of a character to preclude me from going into abstractions. I do not hesitate on the contrary to declare, that if you had, as the accredited organs of the people, addressed me a request to vacate my seat in the senate, your request would have had with me the force of law. Not a day or an hour could I desire to remain in the senate, beyond that day and that hour wherein I came to be informed that it was the settled wish of the people of Virginia that I should retire from their service. That people have honoured me with the highest offices within their gift. If the talents which I have brought into their service be humble, I have at least brought fidelity to their interests. No where else have I looked for reward but to their approbation. I have served under four administrations, and might doubtlessly, by a course of subserviency and sycophancy, have obtained, what is called by some, preferment. But what could have compensated for the baseness of my prostitution, and the betrayal of the confidence reposed in me by a generous people? The executive files furnish no record of my name as an applicant for any of the crumbs which have fallen from the executive table. I repeat, that I have looked exclusively to the people of Virginia; and when they extended to me their confidence for twenty odd years; when I am indebted to them for whatsoever of credit and standing I possess in the world, I cannot and will not permit myself to remain in the senate for a moment beyond the time that their accredited organs shall instruct me that my services are no longer acceptable. If gratitude for the past did not, my own conscious weakness would control my course. What would it profit the country or myself for me to remain in the senate against their wishes? By retaining my place in opposition to their fixed, declared and settled will, I should aid no cause—advance no great purpose—be powerless for good, and provoke only to harm. Reposing on my own feeble strength, I should vainly flatter myself that I could with my single arm sustain the constitution, and keep back, what I might consider, the tide of error, when in very truth I should but excite the popular prejudices more strongly, and imminently endanger the constitution by my very efforts to sustain it.

In resigning then, gentlemen, into your hands my place in the senate of the United States, to which I was called by your predecessors, I trust I shall be indulged in a brief exposition of the reasons which have led me to the conclusion, that to obey your instructions would be to violate the constitution of the United States. I shall do so boldly and fearlessly, but with all becoming respect, and with all the brevity in my power. The senate is ordered by the constitution *to keep a journal of its proceedings,* and *to publish it from time to time.* This injunction is thus solemnly imposed upon the aggregate body, and on each individual senator—whatever shall be done shall be faithfully recorded by the secretary, and shall be faithfully kept—not for an hour and then to be defaced—not for a day and then to be erased—nor for a year and then to be expunged—but forever, as a perpetual witness, a faithful history, by which the conduct, the motives, the actions of men shall be judged, not by those of the present day only, but through all time. It was a wise custom among the Chinese which required the biography of each emperor to be written before the close of his life and placed before him, so as to give him foreknowledge of what the world would think of him after his death. It was designed to restrain his evil passions—to curb the exercise of despotic sway. It addressed itself to his ambition, and excited within him a longing for an immortality in the gratitude and admiration of succeeding ages. But this provision in our constitution is still wiser. Each senator writes daily his own biography. He is required to record his own acts, and takes an oath *to keep* that record, and *to publish it from time to time.* The applause or censure of his fellow men is not postponed until he has descended to the tomb, it is then uttered by the living generation. How powerful are the inducements thus addressed to each member to be faithful to the trust confided to him. How much to be admired the wisdom of our ancestors in framing the constitution. If this was its only feature their title to immortality would be established.

This simple provision is one of the great securities of American liberty. It takes nothing upon trust. If the senate kept no journal, it would be a secret conclave, where deeds the most revolting might be performed in secrecy and darkness. The train might there be laid, the mine prepared, and the first knowledge of the treason might be the explosion, and consequent overthrow of free government; liberty could not coexist with such a state of things. There is no liberty where there is no responsibility, and there can be no responsibility where nothing is known. To have a secretary seated at the table of the senate to write down its proceedings, and to claim for itself the right to cancel, obliterate or expunge what he had written, is equivalent to having no journal at all—a mockery and a fraud. The journal of the morning may be cancelled in the evening, that of to-day may be expunged on to-morrow. Cancel it in any way, whether by black or red marks, whether with circles or by straight lines, it ceases to be a journal, and that which was, is not. The journal is to be published, but there is no journal: there was on yesterday, but ere it can reach the press it is cancelled, marked out or expunged. These are the necessary results of obedience to your instructions. If that journal contain a transaction discreditable to the senate, I would preserve it as a perpetual monument of its disgrace. If of a party leader, I will give him and his friends who may temporarily have the ascendancy, no warrant to erase or blur the page on which such act of misconduct is recorded. I should be afraid, after performing such a deed, if Virginia is what she once was, and I do not doubt it, to return within her limits. The execrations of her people would be thundered in my ears. The soil which had been trod by her heroes and statesmen, would furnish me no resting place. I should feel myself guilty, most guilty, and however I might succeed in concealing myself from the sight of men, I could not, in my view of the subject, save myself from the upbraidings of my own perjured conscience. How could I return to mix among her people, to share their hospitality and kindness, with the declaration on my lips, "I have violated my oath for office, and sooner than surrender my place in the senate, have struck down the constitution."

If the senate has a right to touch the journal under instructions, it has a right to do so without—if to cancel a part, a right to expunge the whole—if to use ink from a pen, a right to pour it from a bottle—to destroy the journal in any other way—to burn it—to make a bonfire of all that is bright and glorious in our history. I know it has been said that the process directed to be adopted by your resolution is not designed to expunge. I cannot believe this, and reject it as equally injurious to yourselves and unjust to those you represent. You direct the words "Expunged by order of the senate," to be written across the resolution on which you propose to make war. I will not believe that you merely design to ensnare my conscience—much less will I indulge for a moment the idea that you direct a falsehood to be recorded by me. Those do not understand you who make such ascriptions, and I am not misled by them. The general assembly of a proud and lofty state is incapable of a mere quibble, and such an one as would disgrace a king's jester. No, gentlemen, the act which you direct to be performed is designed to be, and is equivalent to an actual obliteration in all its practical results. The manner of accomplishing this act of cancellation is wholly immaterial. In *publishing this journal from time to time* hereafter, the resolution thus cancelled cannot be published as a part of it. It is declared to be expunged upon its face. But if in this I could possibly be mistaken—if after all it is merely child's play—the making a few flourishes, and putting the secretary of the senate to the trouble to write a few unmeaning words—the question would not be changed. Such as is the journal, so shall it be kept—unaltered in a letter, unchanged in a comma—the same as it now is, "to the last syllable of recorded time." Such is the fiat of the constitution. There is not a clerk or deputy clerk in the commonwealth of Virginia, who would execute such an order in regard to his records. The people would be alive to the question, and in vindication of their rights, would *expunge the court* sooner than permit the record containing the titles to their estates to be cancelled in any manner whatever. They surely cannot take less interest in the preservation of the constitution, the great charter of all their rights.

The effort has been made to hunt up precedents to justify this act. The pages of English parliamentary history have been ransacked, and an array has been made of examples drawn from the times of the Jameses and Georges of England. With equal force might examples be quoted to justify an American president in executing capitally a citizen of any one of the states without the form of a trial. He might equally be justified in the use of the bowstring, because such is the power of the grand seignor. The power of the English parliament is unlimited—so is that of many of the states of this Union in regard to this particular subject. No precedent can have force to overthrow an express enactment of the constitution. Under its provision the senate is directed to keep a journal of its proceedings—to preserve it, and publish it from time to time. If I was permitted to look elsewhere than to that constitution, I would go to Virginia for bright and glorious examples to conduct me in safety. The first in point of prominence, although not in point of time, is the course attempted to be adopted by the king's party in the house of burgesses in 1765, as to the celebrated resolutions of Patrick Henry of that period. These resolutions were declaratory of the rights of British America. After their adoption, many of those who voted for them left the city of Williamsburg, thereby giving to the opposite party the accidental ascendancy, and they immediately formed the resolution *to expunge* them from the journal; but, by a stroke of policy as bold as it was successful, Mr. Henry saved those resolutions from being expunged, which form at this day one of the brightest pages of Virginia history, and, recorded on any man's tomb, would eternize his fame—and yet to expunge them from the journal was regarded as much an act of duty by those who proposed it, as you, gentlemen, can esteem it to be in the case under consideration. They failed—and my prayer as a citizen of a free country is, that you too may be unsuccessful. Your posterity may have good cause to rejoice in your failure.

Another example almost as illustrious, is to be found in the conduct of Robert Beverly during the administration of lord Culpeper. The history of the incidents of that transaction are not only instructive, but highly interesting. Lord Culpeper, armed with all the authority of the king of England his master, ordered that a resolution adopted by the house of burgesses during the administration of Herbert Jeffries, should be expunged from their records, "as highly derogatory to his majesty's prerogative." Robert Beverly was clerk to the house of burgesses. Every effort was made to induce him to produce the journal, in order to have it *expunged*. He was subjected to all manner of persecutions, but he gloried in his sufferings, and his noble spirit rose in proportion to his persecutions. He peremptorily refused to comply, alleging, "that his masters the house of burgesses had alone a right to make such a demand, and that their authority alone he durst or would obey." And I too reply to these orders which are now given me, that I will not expunge the records of the senate, until the constitution, which, while it is permitted to remain, is master over all, shall be changed, altered or abolished. You will have full opportunity, gentlemen, to appoint another in my place. For my part, I will not consent to be made an instrument to accomplish such an object—nor shall I envy any successor who you may send on such a mission.

Had your resolutions directed me to repeal or rescind the resolution of the senate, I would have obeyed your orders. Although with great reluctance, I would, nevertheless, have felt myself constrained to do so, by my recognition of your right to instruct me. That proceeding would have reversed and annulled the act complained of. If your object was to vindicate the president in the authority which he assumed and still exercises over the public money, and esteemed it necessary in order to do so, to have had your opinions expressed through me in the senate chamber, they should have been faithfully represented. His vindication, after all, cannot consist in the form in which it may be urged. It is to be found alone in the legislative expression of opinion—and even if your declarations in his behalf, were confined to your own journals, the historian would not fail to avail himself of them as efficiently as if they stood emblazoned on the heavens. From my knowledge of you, I am sure that you would not be willing to pull down the constitution unnecessarily and without object.

In your effort to vindicate the president, you have cast on me, in common with others, the very reproach which you are pleased to regard as so offensive in reference to him. You have publicly, and before the world, declared a resolution for which I voted, to be "subversive of the rights of the house of representatives and the fundamental principles of free government." If you designed to charge me with impurity of motive in the vote thus given, your accusation would imply the highest censure. But this I do not ascribe to you. You intend to say no more than that your judgment and opinion differs from that expressed by me upon the subject out of which grew the resolution of the senate, and that the senate committed an error, which, in its effects, is calculated to subvert "the rights of the house of representatives and the fundamental principles of free government." The censure which your resolution conveys, implies a want of correct judgment on my part, in voting for that resolution, and nothing more. If this be your true meaning, and I will not permit myself to think otherwise, I am yet to learn how I incur the hazard of subverting "the rights of the house of representatives and the fundamental principles of free government," by having declared in substance, what, as a member of the senate, I did by my vote declare, that the president had mistaken his course, and that his conduct was "in derogation of the constitution and laws." Have I done more in this than you have done in your declaration? and if not, I submit it in all candour to your dispassionate judgment to say, whether, if I was liable to trial on impeachment before you, you would consider yourselves as having already pronounced upon my guilt in advance. I should certainly not dream of excepting to you as my judges, because resting on my integrity of motive, I should feel confident of acquittal. There can be no guilt without a criminal design—and I am sure you would be among the last to ascribe to the president any criminality of design. Am I to understand you as declaring that, because the house of representatives may originate an impeachment against the president or other officer of the government, that the senate has no right to express an opinion as to any act of the president or such other officer? No matter what may be the act, even if it annihilates the powers of the senate. Has it no power inherent in all other bodies, of self protection and defence? A Brennus may invade the body and pluck it by the beard, and yet, according to this, it has no authority to strike. Go to that venerable patriarch of Montpelier, (Mr. Madison,) and ask him whether in framing the constitution, he designed that the senate should be a mere motionless stock or a vigilant sentinel to give notice of the approach of danger, to that very constitution which it is sworn to support? Whether the representatives of the sovereign states, are such mere automata as to move only when they are bidden, and to sit in their places like statues, to record such edicts as may come to them? If the president recommends a measure, which the senate believes impolitic, shall it not say so? So, if he adopt a course which he may believe to be correct, but which the senate thinks unconstitutional, may it not say so? And does its so declaring, tend *to subvert* or *to support* "the fundamental principles of free government." You surely can be at no loss to decide. The senate in the instance of the late post master general, (Mr. Barry,) who had contracted loans in his official character, for the use of his department, without authority, declared by an *unanimous vote*, that his proceedings in this respect were in violation of the constitution. And yet no complaint has ever been uttered against that resolution of the senate. How comes it about that anathemas have not been thundered in the ears of the senate, because of that vote? Why is not that ordered to be expunged? Why is not that also declared to be "subversive of the rights of the house of representatives, and of the fundamental principles of free government." Is not the error as vital when it affects William T. Barry as when it affects Andrew Jackson? If so, every motive of generosity, prompted an interference in behalf of the first. He was powerless and is now in his grave. I had a personal regard for Mr. Barry. He was talented, and his fault lay in being too confiding. Honest himself, he did not suspect others, and they deceived him. This was the rock on which he split. In voting for that resolution, I did not design to impute to him moral guilt. I did not believe it. I designed nothing more than to vindicate the constitution. I thought that in doing so, I gave support to "the fundamental principles of free government," and never once dreamed that I had done an act in the remotest degree "subversive of the rights of the house of representatives."

But say that in all this I was wrong. In voting for the resolution of the senate against which you are now so indignant, I did no more than carry out the expressly declared views of the legislature, as expressed in their resolutions of that day, and which were passed by overwhelming majorities of more than two to one in both houses. The terms employed by the legislature were strong and decided. The conduct of the president was represented as dangerous and alarming. I was told that it could not be too strongly condemned; that he had manifested a disposition greatly to extend his official influence—and because with these declarations before me I voted for a resolution which declares, "that the president, in the late executive proceedings, has assumed upon himself authority and power not conferred by the constitution and laws, but in derogation of both," I am now ostracized by your fiat, which requires obedience or resignation. Compare the resolutions of the general assembly of that day with the above resolution, and its mildness will be entirely obvious. I submit with all due deference to yourselves what is to be the condition of a senator in future, if for yielding obedience to the wishes of one legislature, he is to be called upon to resign by another. If he disobeys the first he is condemned—if he obeys the last he violates his oath and becomes an object of scorn and contempt. I respectfully ask if this be the mode by which the great right of instructions is to be sustained?

May it not degenerate into an engine of faction—an instrument to be employed by *the outs to get in?* Instead of being directed to noble purposes—to the advancement of the cause of civil liberty, may it not be converted into a political guillotine devoted to the worst of purposes? Nor are these anticipations at all weakened by the fact, as it exists in the case now under consideration, that several of those who constitute the present majority in the general assembly, and who now call upon me to expunge the journal or to resign my seat, actually voted for the very resolutions of a previous session to which I have referred?

I have thus, gentlemen, with frankness, but without designing offence, expressed to you my opinions. With the question whether the resolution of the senate which you direct to be expunged be true or false, I have nothing in this place to do. If false, to rescind or repeal it was to annihilate its force as effectually as to cancel it. You have preferred to adopt a different course. I dare not touch the journal of the senate—the constitution forbids it. In the midst of all the agitations of party, I have heretofore stood by that sacred instrument. It is the only post of honour and of safety. Parties are continually changing. The men of to-day give place to the men of to-morrow, and the idols which one set worship, the next destroy. The only object of my political worship shall be the constitution of my country. I will not be the instrument to overthrow it. A seat in the senate is sufficiently elevated to fill the measure of any man's ambition; and as an evidence of the sincerity of my convictions, that your resolutions cannot be executed without violating my oath, I surrender into your hands three unexpired years of my term. I shall carry with me into retirement the principles which I brought with me into public life—and by the surrender of the high station to which I was called by the voice of the people of Virginia, I shall set an example to my children which shall teach them to regard as nothing place and office, when either is to be attained or held at the sacrifice of honour.

I am, gentlemen, your fellow citizen,

JOHN TYLER.

On motion of Mr. Smith of Gloucester, *Ordered,* That the said communication be laid upon the table.

A motion was made by Mr. Botts that 25,000 copies of the said communication be printed for distribution among the people of this commonwealth.

Mr. Miller proposed that 1,000 copies thereof be printed.

Mr. Watkins proposed that 185 copies thereof be printed.

The question was taken upon the largest number first, and was decided in the negative. Ayes 50, noes 78.

The ayes and noes thereupon being required by Mr. Benton, (and sustained according to the rule of the house,) were as follow:

Ayes, Messrs. Grinalds, Drummond, Gilmer, Southall, Garland of Amherst, Brooke, Craig, Campbell, Pate, Hunter of Berkeley, Henshaw, Beuhring, Christian, Wilson of Cumberland, Servant, Ball, Price, Hale of Franklin, Davison, Smith of Frederick, Smith of Gloucester, Wethered, Mullen, Botts, Gregory, Griggs, Berry, Summers, Carter, Neill, Beard, Powell, Taylor of Loudoun, Ragsdale, Waggener, Benton, Murdaugh, Cooke, Masters, Swanson, Witcher, Morris, Dorman, Leyburn, Harley, Delashmutt, Jett, Cunningham, Brown of Petersburg, and Stanard.—50.

Noes, Messrs. Banks, (speaker,) Layne, Wiley, Miller, Wilson of Botetourt, Decamps, Turnbull, Mallory, Booker, Austin, Daniel, Samuel, Richardson, Johnson, Hill, Vaughan, Hunter of Essex, Smith of Fauquier, Hickerson, Strange, Steger, Holland, Bowen, Watts, Watkins, Hail of Grayson, Avent, Carrington, Coleman, Sloan, Nixon, Goodall, Harrison, Kincheloe, Fontaine, Holleman, Fleet, Robinson, Hays, Straton, Harris, Taylor of Mathews and Middlesex, Rogers, Garland of Mecklenburg, Willey, Morgan, Chapman, Ingles, Sherrard, Brown of Nelson, Leland, Fitzgerald, Woolfolk, Almond, Adams, M'Coy, Cackley, Hopkins, Carroll, Madison, Shands, Williams, Marteney, Nicklin, Moffett, Conrad, Jessee, M'Mullen, Bare, Rinker, Butts, Crutchfield, Moncure, Hargrave, Gillespie, Gibson, Prentiss and Saunders.—78.

Mr. Miller then (with the leave of the house,) withdrew his motion, and the question being then put upon the proposition of Mr. Watkins, was determined in the affirmative.

On motion of Mr. Watkins, *Resolved,* That this house will proceed, by joint vote with the senate, on to-morrow, to the election of a United States senator, to supply the vacancy occasioned by the resignation of John Tyler, esq.

Ordered, That the clerk communicate the same to the senate and request their concurrence.

Mr. Wilson of Botetourt presented a petition of citizens of the county of Botetourt, for the location, at the town of Fincastle, of a branch of one of the banks proposed to be established, which was ordered to be referred to the committee of the whole house on the state of the commonwealth.

Mr. Dorman, according to order, presented a bill reviving an act incorporating a company to construct a turnpike road from the upper end of the Blue Ridge canal, to its intersection with the Lexington and Covington turnpike road, which was received and laid upon the table.

The house, according to the order of the day, resolved itself into a committee of the whole house on the state of the commonwealth, Mr. Miller in the chair; and after some time the speaker resumed the chair, and Mr. Miller reported that the said committee had, according to order, taken into consideration a bill increasing the banking capital of the commonwealth, and had made further progress therein, but not having had time to go through the same, had instructed him to ask leave to sit again.

Resolved, That this house will on to-morrow again resolve itself into a committee of the whole house on the state of the commonwealth.

On motion of Mr. Smith of Frederick, a bill to amend the several acts concerning the public guard in the city of Richmond, was taken up, read the first and second times, and ordered to be committed to the committee which brought it in.

On motion of Mr. Smith of Frederick, *Ordered*, That the committee on the militia laws be discharged from the resolution for enquiry into the claim of Peter Klipstine, and that the same be laid upon the table.

On motion of Mr. Watkins, *Resolved*, That when this house adjourns to-day, it will adjourn until to-morrow 10 o'clock.

And on his motion the house adjourned accordingly.

THURSDAY, March 3d, 1836.

A communication from the senate by their clerk:

IN SENATE, March 2d, 1836.

The senate have passed the bill, entitled,

"An act authorizing Jesse Sturm to erect a dam across the West Fork of Monongalia river, in the county of Harrison."

And they have agreed to the resolution for a survey of the Nottoway river, from the Petersburg and Roanoke rail-road to its mouth, or where it empties into the Meherrin river.

Mr. Wilson of Botetourt, from the committee for courts of justice, presented a bill to increase the library at Lewisburg; and

A bill authorizing appeals to be taken from the courts of certain counties therein mentioned, to the court of appeals held at Lewisburg.

Which were received and laid upon the table.

An engrossed bill forming a new county out of parts of the counties of Shenandoah and Frederick, was, on motion of Mr. Griggs, ordered to be laid upon the table.

On motion of Mr. Wethered, *Ordered*, That leave of absence from the service of this house be granted for the remainder of the session to Mr. M'Clintic from yesterday.

Mr. Crutchfield, from the committee on the militia laws, presented a bill re-organizing the Lexington arsenal, and establishing a military school in connection with Washington college.

Mr. Wiley, according to order, presented a bill to regulate the conduct of boatmen on the Appomattox river and its branches.

Mr. Watkins, from the committee of roads and internal navigation, presented a bill vesting the commonwealth's stock in the James river and Kanawha company in the board of public works, and for other purposes.

Mr. Witcher, from the committee of claims, presented a report upon the resolution concerning James Burk.

Mr. Hunter of Essex, from the committee on the penitentiary institution, presented a report upon the petition of Samuel S. Pendleton.

Which bills and reports were received and laid upon the table.

On motion of Mr. Witcher, the rule of the house was suspended for the purpose of reconsidering the vote rejecting the resolution concerning James Jenks; and the said resolution was then adopted by the house as follows:

Resolved, That the committee of finance be instructed to enquire into the expediency of allowing to James Jenks, deputy sheriff of Logan county, the sum of thirty dollars and four cents, being the amount of sundry insolvent tickets in the militia fines for 1833, not certified by the court of enquiry, and of certain claims not presented in time, in consequence of the death of said Jenks.

Mr. Adams presented a petition of citizens of the county of Patrick, asking for the appointment of an additional commissioner of the revenue for said county, which was ordered to be referred to the committee of finance, that they do examine the matter thereof, and report their opinion thereupon to the house.

A bill incorporating the trustees of the Martinsville academy, reported without amendment, from the committee of schools and colleges, was taken up, and ordered to be engrossed and read a third time.

A bill to amend the act, entitled, "an act to amend and reduce into one act, all acts, and parts of acts, to prevent the destruction of oysters," passed March 24th, 1831, was read a second time, and on motion of Mr. Taylor of Middlesex, ordered to be committed to the committee which brought it in.

A bill to authorize a subscription on behalf of the state to the stock of the Lewisburg and Blue Sulphur springs turnpike company; and

A bill incorporating the Laurel Hill turnpike company, with the amendments thereto proposed by the committee of roads and internal navigation, were taken up, and the said amendments being severally agreed to by the house, the same as amended, were ordered to be engrossed and read a third time.

A bill appropriating the surplus revenue of the literary fund, with the amendments thereto proposed by the committee of schools and colleges, was ordered to be laid upon the table on motion of Mr. Watkins.

Mr. Strange presented a petition of citizens of the county of Fluvanna, for the establishment of a bank at the town of Scottsville.

Mr. Moncure, a petition of citizens of Warrenton, for the establishment of a bank at the town of Falmouth.

Mr. Brown of Nelson, a petition of citizens of Nelson, for the establishment of a bank at the town of Scottsville.

Ordered, That the said petitions be referred to the committee of the whole house on the state of the commonwealth.

An engrossed bill incorporating the Smithfield savings institution in the county of Isle of Wight, was read a third time:

Resolved, That the bill do pass, and that the title be, "an act incorporating the Smithfield savings institution in the county of Isle of Wight."

An engrossed bill concerning the Orange savings society, was read a third time:

Resolved, That the bill do pass, and that the title be, "an act concerning the Orange savings society."

An engrossed bill concerning the Rappahannock company, was read a third time:

Resolved, That the bill do pass, and that the title be, "an act concerning the Rappahannock company."

Ordered, That the clerk communicate the same to the senate and request their concurrence.

A bill appointing commissioners to select a site for the seat of justice for the county of Ohio, was read a second time, and ordered to be committed to the committee which brought it in.

A bill to amend the several acts concerning pilots, was read the first and second times, and ordered to be committed to the committee which brought it in.

A bill to form a new county out of the county of Frederick, was taken up on motion of Mr. Griggs, amended by the house on his motion, and as amended, ordered to be engrossed and read a third time.

The following bills were read a second time, and ordered to be engrossed and read a third time, viz:

A bill concerning the county of Gloucester.

A bill changing the place of holding a separate election in the county of Kanawha.

A bill to amend the act, entitled, "an act to incorporate the Richmond manufacturing company," passed on the 12th January, 1832.

A bill declaring Pocatallico river a public highway.

A bill incorporating the Staunton and Augusta springs turnpike company.

A bill directing the sale of the stock held by the state in joint stock companies incorporated for purposes of internal improvement.

A bill to incorporate the Coal working company of Richmond and Manchester.

A bill to incorporate the Virginia insurance company.

A bill to change the time of holding the county court of Alleghany county.

A bill to authorize additions to the town of Farmville in the county of Prince Edward.

A bill to amend the act, entitled, "an act incorporating a company to erect a toll bridge over the Ohio river at Wheeling," passed February 17th, 1816.

A bill to incorporate the Red springs company.

A bill establishing a new regiment in the county of Preston.

A bill to amend the act concerning fraudulent devises.

A bill to amend the act, entitled, "an act to alter and reform the mode of proceeding in the courts of chancery."

A bill to incorporate the trustees of the Estillville academy.

A bill requiring of the inspectors of tobacco in this commonwealth to distinguish in their inspections between tobacco produced in Virginia and that produced in other states.

A bill to incorporate the United States copper mining company.

A bill to amend an act incorporating the Spring creek turnpike company.

A bill to incorporate the New Hope gold mine company.

A bill to amend the act, entitled, "an act making further provisions for completing the road from Staunton to the mouth of the Little Kanawha."

A bill to establish the town of Lovettsville in the county of Loudoun; and

A bill to incorporate the Gills mountain mining company.

The following bills were read the first and ordered to be read a second time, viz:

A bill to equalize the regimental districts in the county of Rockingham, and for other purposes.

A bill to incorporate the trustees of the Charlestown athenæum and female academy

A bill to amend the several acts concerning the Petersburg rail-road company.

A bill to amend an act, entitled, "an act to enact with amendments, 'an act of the general assembly of North Carolina, entitled, 'an act to incorporate the Greensville and Roanoke rail-road company,'" passed February 7th, 1834.

A bill to incorporate the Goochland mining company.

A bill to incorporate the Big Bird mining company.

A bill authorizing the auditor to issue a warrant in favour of James Paxton.

A bill incorporating the Fredericksburg Union manufacturing company.

A bill incorporating the American mining company.

A bill incorporating the Rappahannock marine and fire insurance company.

A bill incorporating the Great Kanawha mining, timber and lumber company.

A bill to establish an additional grade of flour in the inspections of flour in this commonwealth.

A bill to explain the act authorizing subscriptions on the part of the commonwealth to the capital of joint stock companies.

A bill directing a survey of the Dragon swamp.

A bill to amend the act, entitled, "an act concerning the Cumberland road."

A bill to amend an act, entitled, "an act to enact with amendments, an act of the general assembly of North Carolina, entitled, 'an act to incorporate the Greensville and Roanoke rail-road company.'"

A bill to amend and explain the act, entitled, "an act to reduce into one the several acts to regulate the solemnization of marriages," &c. passed 1st March, 1819.

A bill making further provision for taking depositions in certain cases.

A bill to authorize a separate election at M'Gaheysville in the county of Rockingham.

A bill concerning the legal representatives of Severn Eyre, deceased.

A bill to incorporate the Front Royal library society in the county of Frederick.

A bill to incorporate the Berkeley coal mining and rail-road company

A bill concerning William Fenn.

A bill concerning John Chew.

A bill incorporating the trustees of the Clarksville female academy.

A bill for the construction of a bridge across Jackson's river at the town of Covington.

A bill to incorporate the proprietors of the Wellsburg lyceum.

A bill concerning the subscription on behalf of the commonwealth to the stock of the Richmond, Fredericksburg and Potomac rail-road company.

A bill concerning John Pittinger, late sheriff of Brooke county.

A bill concerning the administrator of Dominie Bennehan, deceased.

A bill to amend the act, entitled, "an act incorporating the Goose creek navigation company."

A bill to authorize Thomas A. Morton to erect a dam across Appomattox river.

A bill securing to debtors a certain portion of their property.

A bill amending the laws concerning slaves, free negroes and mulattoes.

A bill to amend the act, entitled, "an act reducing into one the several acts for punishing persons guilty of certain thefts and forgeries, and the destruction or concealment of wills."

A bill to amend an act, entitled, "an act to incorporate the Augusta springs company;" and

A bill to change the time of holding the county courts of the counties of Lewis and Braxton.

The following bills were read the first and second times, and ordered to be committed to the respective committees which brought them in, viz:

A bill concerning savings institutions.

A bill changing the Hunting run gold mining company into a company for mining and manufacturing iron and steel.

A bill to incorporate the Portsmouth and Chesapeake steam-boat company.

A bill to authorize a subscription on behalf of the state to the stock of the Pittsylvania and Lynchburg turnpike company, and for other purposes.

A bill to incorporate the trustees of the Lynchburg female academy.

A bill incorporating the Lynchburg and Campbell court-house turnpike company; and

A bill repealing the law requiring lands in this commonwealth to be processioned, so far as the same may apply to the county of Patrick.

A report of the committee of claims was read as follows:

The committee of claims have, according to order, had under consideration the petition of Solomon Tomlinson, administrator *de bonis non* of Richard Kelsick, deceased, to them referred, praying the payment of a judgment recovered by the former administrator of his intestate in Norfolk county court, against Robert Gilmore, surviving partner of Logan Gilmore & Co., whose property had been confiscated, and the proceeds arising therefrom paid into the treasury, amounting to the sum of two hundred and thirty-five pounds four shillings, with interest thereon at the rate of six per centum per annum, to be computed from the 24th day of May, 1774, till paid, and eight dollars and sixty-three cents costs, and have come to the following resolution thereupon:

Resolved as the opinion of this committee, That the prayer of the said petition is reasonable.

The said resolution was, on the question put thereupon, agreed to by the house, and a bill was ordered to be brought in conformably therewith.

The following reports of the committee for courts of justice were read:

The committee for courts of justice have, according to order, had under consideration the petition of Ann Edmunds, to them referred, praying to be divorced from her husband John W. A. Edmunds, and have come to the following resolution thereupon:

Resolved as the opinion of this committee, That the prayer of the said petition is reasonable.

The committee for courts of justice have, according to order, had under consideration the petition of Ann, a free woman of colour, to them referred, praying that she may be permitted to remain in the commonwealth, and to reside in the county of Cabell, and have come to the following resolution thereupon:

Resolved as the opinion of this committee, That the prayer of the said petition is reasonable.

The said resolutions were, on questions severally put thereupon, agreed to by the house, and bills were ordered to be brought in conformably therewith.

A report of the same committee, rejecting the petition of John Barnes, was, on motion of Mr. Adams, ordered to be laid upon the table.

A report of the committee of propositions and grievances was read as follows:

The committee of propositions and grievances have, according to order, had under consideration several petitions to them referred, and have come to the following resolutions thereupon:

1. *Resolved as the opinion of this committee,* That the petition of sundry owners of property on the banks of James river, in the counties of Fluvanna and Albemarle, praying that an act may pass, placing said river on the footing of a lawful fence, so far as the same borders on said counties, is reasonable.

2. *Resolved as the opinion of this committee,* That the petition of William Townes, of the county of Mecklenburg, praying that he be authorized to erect a toll-bridge across the Roanoke river, opposite the lower part of the town of Clarksville in said county, is reasonable.

The said resolutions were, on questions severally put thereupon, agreed to by the house, and bills were ordered to be brought in conformably therewith.

A report of the select committee on banks was read as follows:

The select committee on banks, to whom was referred the memorial of citizens of Elizabethtown and Moundsville, in the county of Marshall, praying "that an act may be passed authorizing the savings institution at Elizabethtown to issue notes or bills under such restrictions as may seem necessary and proper," have had the same under consideration, and have come to the following resolution thereupon:

Resolved, That the prayer of the memorialists be rejected.

The committee have also had under consideration the memorial of the stockholders of the Wheeling savings institution, praying the passage of "an act authorizing the said institution to issue notes, and to extend its capital, under such regulations and restrictions as public policy may require," and have come to the following resolution thereupon:

Resolved, That the prayer of the memorialists be rejected.

The said resolutions were, on questions severally put thereupon, agreed to by the house.

A report of the committee on the militia laws was read as follows:

The committee upon the militia laws have had under consideration a resolution of the house of delegates, instructing them to enquire into the expediency of allowing to David Stickly, assignee of Peter Klipstine, the amount due him for three stands of colours furnished thirteenth regiment, and have come to the following resolution:

Resolved, That it is inexpedient to make the said allowance.

The same committee have also had under consideration a resolution instructing them to enquire into the expediency of allowing compensation to Peter Klipstine for sundry stands of colours furnished to several regiments, and have come to the following resolution:

Resolved, That it is inexpedient to make the said allowance.

The same committee have had under consideration a resolution instructing them to enquire into the expediency of furnishing arms to one volunteer company (whether uniformed or not) in each regiment, and have come to the following resolution thereupon:

Resolved, That it is inexpedient to do so.

The said resolutions were, on questions severally put thereupon, agreed to by the house.

Several reports of the committee for courts of justice were read as follow:

The committee for courts of justice have, according to order, enquired into the expediency of fixing by law the commissions on sales made under decrees in chancery: Whereupon,

Resolved as the opinion of this committee, That it is expedient to fix by law the said commissions.

The committee for courts of justice have, according to order, had under consideration the petition of sundry citizens of Culpeper and Madison counties, to them referred, praying that Robin, a free man of colour, may be permitted to remain in the commonwealth, and have come to the following resolution thereupon

Resolved as the opinion of this committee, That the prayer of the said petition be rejected.

The said resolutions were, on questions severally put thereupon, agreed to by the house, and a bill was ordered to be brought in conformably with the said first resolution.

A report of the committee of propositions and grievances was read as follows:

The committee of propositions and grievances have, according to order, had under consideration the petition of William H. Riggan of the county of Surry, to them referred, representing that he is the son of a certain Richard D. Riggan, late of the said county, who was the son of one Richard Drewry, deceased; that the petitioner is more generally called and known by the name of Drewry than Riggan; and, having derived all his estate from his grandfather, the said Richard Drewry, deceased, prays, therefore, that an act may pass changing his name from that of William H. Riggan to that of William H. Drewry: Whereupon,

Resolved as the opinion of this committee, That the prayer of said petition is reasonable.

The said committee have also had under consideration a resolution of the house of delegates, instructing them "to enquire into the expediency of providing by law for paying to the trustees of Estillville academy, in the county of Scott, the quota of that county, out of the fund created by act of 1833, for the removal of free persons of colour:" Whereupon,

Resolved as the opinion of this committee, That it is inexpedient so to provide by law.

The said resolutions were, on questions severally put thereupon, agreed to by the house, and a bill was ordered to be brought in conformably with the said first resolution.

A report of the committee of roads and internal navigation was read as follows:

The committee of roads and internal navigation have, according to order, had under consideration the petition of sundry citizens of the county of Kanawha, and of other counties adjacent thereto, praying the passage of an act incorporating a company to construct a rail-road from some point on the Kanawha river in the vicinity of the salt works, to some point on Coal river: Whereupon,

Resolved as the opinion of this committee, That the prayer of said petition is reasonable.

The said resolution was, on the question put thereupon, agreed to by the house, and a bill was ordered to be brought in conformably therewith.

A report of the committee of roads and internal navigation, reporting reasonable the petitions for subscribing to the stock of the Baltimore and Ohio rail-road company, was, on motion of Mr. Chapline, ordered to be laid upon the table.

A report of the committee on banks was read as follows:

The select committee on banks, to whom was referred the petition of sundry citizens of Petersburg, praying the incorporation of a savings institution, have had the same under consideration, and have come to the following resolution:

Resolved, That the prayer of the said petition is reasonable.

The said resolution was, on the question put thereupon, agreed to by the house, and a bill was ordered to be brought in conformably therewith.

A report of the committee of propositions and grievances was read as follows:

The committee of propositions and grievances have, according to order, had under consideration the petition of sundry citizens of the county of Tazewell, residing on the waters of Knox creek, and of the Louisa fork of Sandy river, to them referred, praying that an act may pass authorizing a separate election at the ginseng factory, near the mouth of Slate creek, in said county: Whereupon,

Resolved as the opinion of this committee, That the prayer of said petition is reasonable.

The said resolution was, on the question put thereupon, agreed to by the house, and a bill was ordered to be brought in conformably therewith.

A report of the committee appointed to examine the executive expenditures was read as follows:

The committee to examine the executive expenditures have performed that duty, and submit the following report:

They have, according to usage, confined their examination exclusively to the expenditures chargeable on the civil contingent fund, and disbursed within the fiscal year, commencing on the 1st of October, 1834, and ending on the 30th of September, 1835.

The whole expenditure amounts to	7,849 06
The contingent fund appropriated by an act passed the 5th March, 1835,	15,000 00
Leaving a balance unexpended of	$7,150 94

The committee have examined the various expenditures, item by item, and found them all duly sustained by vouchers, paid by the first auditor, upon the warrant of the executive, and duly receipted. The warrants and vouchers are neatly arranged, and filed in the office of the first auditor.

A full and complete list of the warrants, with a note explaining the nature of the claim upon which they issued annexed to each, is herewith presented as a part of this report.

LIST OF CLAIMS upon which Warrants have issued on the Contingent Fund from 1st October, 1834, to the 1st October, 1835, by order of the Executive.

1834—Oct'r	4—John Hamilton, cleaning public offices,	21 00
	William Evans, plaistering done at the armory,	14 81
	6—Alexander, cleaning out treasurer's office,	15 00
	11—Richard D. Sanxay, stationery, &c. furnished executive and auditor's office,	37 64
	Charles A. Mayo, books furnished the treasurer's office,	40 25
	13—Joseph Danforth, cleaning public privy,	6 00
	18—Mayo & Brown, books furnished treasurer's and auditor's offices,	14 25
Nov'r	1—Samuel Sharp, lightwood for register's and auditor's offices,	4 25
	3—Robert Poore, press, &c. for register's office,	30 50
	4—C. L. M'Coull, conveying a convict to penitentiary,	33 13
	5—C. L. M'Coull, for distributing session acts 1834,	196 19
	10—Pleasants & Abbott, advertising general orders, &c.	11 17
	12—Samuel D. Denoon, repairing locks, &c. about the capitol,	5 50
	John Hamilton, putting up coal for first and second auditor's offices,	4 00
	13—Binford, Brooks, Gay & Co. carpeting furnished for use of the hall of delegates,	128 22
	21—James Findley, putting up coal for treasurer's office,	2 50
	25—Thomas H. Wade, lightwood furnished treasurer's office,	1 50
	Joseph Danforth, cleaning library room,	12 50
	26—J. P. Taylor, carpeting, &c. furnished for use of the capitol,	242 52
	28—Wm. Evans, repairing senate chamber,	25 00

1834—Nov. 29—Charles B. Shaw, expenses incurred by him as one of the commissioners appointed to survey the coast of Delaware, Maryland and Virginia, under resolution of the general assembly, passed April 15th, 1831,		525
Dec'r 8—Thomas H. Wade, lightwood furnished the executive,		4
9—Henry Lazarus, quills for auditor's office,		6
10—Mayo & Brown, books furnished register's office,		15
12—Myers & Crow, cleaning stove pipes in the capitol,		5
13—L. W. Allen, lightwood furnished the executive,		1 68
Ryland Ford, conveying a convict to the penitentiary,		6 00
17—Thomas S. Haymond, sheriff of Monongalia, travelling to Pennsylvania and returning with a prisoner,		32 16
20—Norman Broomfield, work done about the capitol,		18 37
24—T. C. Lipscomb, work done on governor's house,		3 00
29—Walker & Booth, work done on the capitol,		6 25
30—Titus C. Rice, stove, &c. furnished hall of delegates,		74 25
1835—Jan'y 1—Joseph Danforth, sundry expenses incurred about the capitol,		29 60
2—Blair Bolling, expended by him as superintendent of public buildings,		3 50
3—Joseph Danforth, cleaning library and public privy,		18 50
Charles A. Mayo, books furnished register's office,		16 50
8—John Hamilton, cleaning out public offices,		14 00
Alexander Stewart, cleaning treasurer's and second auditor's offices,		15 00
10—C. W. M'Ginniss, putting glass in public buildings,		25 28
12—Joseph Danforth, sundry articles purchased for second auditor's office,		3 10
16—Robert Thogmorton, lightwood furnished executive,		3 00
19—Robert I. Smith, stationery for executive,		3 50
20—Gales & Seaton, subscription to National Intelligencer,		10 00
A. & A. Wooldridge & Co., coal furnished for the offices in the capitol,		503 50
R. D. Sanxay, stationery for the executive,		27 37
Norman Broomfield, work done on the capitol and governor's house,		43 92
26—Charles B. Shaw, for services and expenses as commissioner appointed to survey the sounds, &c. under resolution 15th April, 1831,		432 90
27—William Drew, making up fires in the room occupied by the keeper of the rolls,		10 00
28—Robert Thogmorton, lightwood for the executive,		3 00
Feb'y 2—Binford, Brooks, Gay & Co., cloth to cover tables in the hall of delegates,		11 38
12—Thomas A. Rust, lead furnished for use of the senate chamber,		19 84
Robert I. Smith, stationery furnished register's office,		3 50
16—A. Stewart, lightwood furnished register's office,		1 00
19—I. A. Goddin, repairing offices in the capitol,		8 69
Feb'y 20—B. W. Crow, work done on the armory,		12 00
21—Robert Thogmorton, lightwood furnished the public offices,		4 50
24—R. D. Sanxay, parchment for the register's office,		156 83
Norman Broomfield, painting a case for the clock at the guard-house,		16 00
Mayo & Davis, stationery furnished the agent for revolutionary claims,		6 00
March 5—A. Bargamin, sheet iron aprons for fireplaces in capitol,		9 40
6—John Hill, clock for the guard-house,		21 00
11—Thomas Jones, commission allowed him for collecting an execution,		60 00
12—T. G. Broughton, subscription to the Norfolk Herald,		6 00
18—John A. Eacho, conveying a convict to the penitentiary,		21 87
21—John Hamilton, cleaning register's office,		4 25
R. Thogmorton, lightwood for the executive,		1 50
25—Editor of the New York Courier and Enquirer, subscription to paper three years,		30 00
April 4—John Hamilton, cleaning public offices,		15 00
6—Alexander Stewart, cleaning public offices,		22 50
13—J. W. Randolph, stationery for use of the agent for revolutionary claims,		6 00
May 5—Mayo & Davis, quills for use of the register's office,		6 00
6—Duff Green, subscription to the Telegraph four years,		40 00
14—William Hutchinson, advance payment for distributing the laws,		100 00
18—John A. Eacho, for distributing the laws,		70 00
19—Barton Smoot, ditto ditto,		100 00
20—John Ford, ditto ditto,		100 00
21—Ryland Ford, ditto ditto,		60 00
C. L. M'Coull, ditto ditto,		100 00
June 1—Geo. W. Munford, keeper of the rolls, copies of laws furnished the executive,		10 50
3—John Warrock, printing and binding journals for the senate,		19 50
6—Blair Bolling, sundries for use of the public,		2 75
10—R. D. Sanxay, stationery for use of agent for revolutionary claims,		3 62
15—Thomas G. Moncure, pick axe for use of the public guard,		1 15

1835—June	20—William Hutchinson, balance for distributing laws,						157	17
	24—Barton Smoot, distributing the laws,						167	32
	27—J. A. Eacho, ditto ditto,						121	10
	30—C. W. M'Ginniss, putting glass in the capitol,						5	70
	John S. Gallaher, advertising boring mill for lease,						2	75
July	1—Norman Broomfield, work done in senate chamber,						1	25
	John Ford, for distributing the laws,						138	94
	John Ford, bringing convict to the penitentiary,						4	16
	3—John A. Eacho, ditto ditto,						29	61
	6—John Hamilton, cleaning out public offices,						15	00
	7—Walter D. Blair, stationery for use of the agent for revolutionary claims,						2	00
	8—Alexander Stewart, cleaning out public offices,						22	50
	11—Thomas P. Butler, repairing public warehouse,						24	83
	R. D. Sanxay, stationery furnished register's office,						34	19
	13—Ryland Ford, distributing the laws,						61	89
	18—R. D. Sanxay, stationery furnished the executive and auditor's office,						230	89
	24—A. Grant, work done at the public warehouse,						4	00
	25—Mayo & Frayser, binding books for auditor's office,						24	75
	Henry Johnston, repairing public bell,						7	00
	27—John Young, work done on the public warehouse,						12	50
	30—Micajah Bates, surveying public lands attached to armory,						12	00
	31—John A. Eacho, conveying a convict to the penitentiary,						60	07
Aug.	5—Mayo & Frayser, revenue book for auditor,						7	50
	7—Anderson Barret, work done in auditor's office,						90	01
	John Goddin, work done on public warehouse,						84	82
	8—R. D. Sanxay, stationery furnished,						9	38
	S. Greenhow, whitewashing done in the capitol,						19	50
	John Hamilton, putting up coal in auditor's office,						2	50
	B. W. Crow, work done in the capitol,						4	87
	13—Alexander Stewart, cleaning treasurer's office,						2	50
	14—Samuel Shepherd, printing done for the executive, library, register's and treasurer's offices,						432	40
	15—Charles H. Hyde, powder furnished the Fayette artillery to fire salutes,						68	17
	28—C. Hall, stationery for auditor's office,						7	50
Sept.	1—A. & A. Wooldridge & Co., coal for the public offices,						130	00
	21—J. T. Swann, putting up coal in the register's office,						2	00
1834—Oct'r	28—Joseph Danforth, in advance, to pay postage to and from the executive,						100	00
Dec'r	3	Do.	do.	do.	do.	do.	100	00
1835—Jan'y	24	Do.	do.	do.	do.	do.	100	00
March	30	Do.	do.	do.	do.	do.	100	00
April	13	Do.	do.	do.	do.	do.	100	00
May	6	Do.	do.	do.	do.	do.	100	00
	19	Do.	do.	do.	do.	do.	100	00
June	6	Do.	do.	do.	do.	do.	100	00
	19	Do.	do.	do.	do.	do.	100	00
July	25	Do.	do.	do.	do.	do.	100	00
Aug't	8	Do.	do.	do.	do.	do.	100	00
Sept'r	16	Do.	do.	do.	do.	do.	100	00
1835—Jan'y	12—J. A. Smith, in advance, to pay postage to and from the auditor of public accounts,						100	00
May	19	Do.	do.	do.	do.	do.	100	00
June	24	Do.	do.	do.	do.	do.	100	00
July	6	Do.	do.	do.	do.	do.	200	00
Aug't	4	Do.	do.	do.	do.	do.	200	00
	27	Do.	do.	do.	do.	do.	200	00

$7,849 06

Ordered, That the same be laid upon the table.

A report of the committee of agriculture and manufactures was read as follows:

The committee of agriculture and manufactures, to whom was referred the petition of the inspectors of tobacco in the town of Farmville, asking for an increase of their salaries, having had the same under consideration, have come to the following resolution thereupon:

Resolved, That the prayer of said petitioners is reasonable.

The said resolution was, on the question put thereupon, agreed to by the house, and a bill was ordered to be brought in conformably therewith.

A further report of the committee of roads and internal navigation was read as follows:

The committee of roads and internal navigation, to whom was referred the petition of a committee of the stockholders of the James river and Kanawha company, asking a modification of the charter of the company in the following particulars:

First, authorizing the purchase or condemnation of land along the general line of improvement, of greater breadth than one hundred feet, under proper limitations and restrictions.

Secondly, authorizing the company to purchase small parcels of land, along the line of improvement, under proper limitations and restrictions, even though such parcels of land may not be necessary for the construction of the works of the company, or for abutments, or for the use of their buildings; and

Thirdly, that the mode of assessing damages for land condemned, which is provided by the charter, may be so changed, as that in lieu of the assessors which the county courts are required to appoint, a board of assessors, having jurisdiction over the whole line of improvement, may be organized, and their proceedings regulated in such manner as to the general assembly may seem expedient, have had the same under consideration and have come to the following resolution thereupon:

Resolved as the opinion of this committee, That the prayer of the said petition is reasonable.

The said resolution was, on the question put thereupon, agreed to by the house, and a bill was ordered to be brought in conformably therewith.

A further report of the committee for courts of justice was read as follows:

The committee for courts of justice have, according to order, enquired into the expediency of re-enacting the act, passed the 24th day of January, 1824, entitled, "an act concerning the processioning of lands in certain counties:" Whereupon,

Resolved as the opinion of this committee, That it is expedient to re-enact the said act.

The said resolution was, on the question put thereupon, agreed to by the house, and a bill was ordered to be brought in conformably therewith.

The several orders of the day being read, were, on motions made by Mr. Brown of Petersburg, and Mr. Dorman, ordered to be postponed until to-morrow.

A message from the senate by Mr. Rives:

Mr. SPEAKER,—The senate agree to the resolution for proceeding by joint vote on this day, to the election of a senator to represent this state in the congress of the United States, to supply the vacancy occasioned by the resignation of John Tyler, esq.—And then he withdrew.

The house then proceeded accordingly to execute the said joint order; whereupon Mr. Garland of Mecklenburg, nominated William C. Rives, esq., and the senate being informed thereof by Mr. Wilson of Botetourt, and no person having been added to the nomination in that house, the names of the members were called by the clerk, when the vote appeared to be for Mr. Rives 76, scattering 32.

The names of the gentlemen who voted for Mr. Rives, are Messrs. Banks, (speaker,) Layne, Wiley, Miller, Wilson of Botetourt, Decamps, Turnbull, Mallory, Booker, Austin, Daniel, Samuel, Richardson, Hill, Vaughan, Smith of Fauquier, Hickerson, Strange, Steger, Holland, Bowen, Davison, Watts, Watkins, Hail of Grayson, Avent, Carrington, Coleman, Sloan, Nixon, Goodall, Harrison, Kincheloe, Fontaine, Holleman, Robinson, Neill, Hays, Straton, Harris, Taylor of Mathews and Middlesex, Rogers, Garland of Mecklenburg, Willey, Morgan, Chapman, Ingles, Sherrard, Brown of Nelson, Leland, Fitzgerald, Woolfolk, Almond, Adams, M'Coy, Cackley, Hopkins, Carroll, Madison, Shands, Williams, Marteney, Nicklin, Moffett, Conrad, Jessee, M'Mullen, Bare, Rinker, Harley, Crutchfield, Moncure, Hargrave, Gillespie, Gibson and Saunders.—76.

Messrs. Grinalds, Craig, Henshaw, Beuhring, Servant, Hunter of Essex, Ball, Wethered, Fleet, Taylor of Loudoun, Benton, Chapline, Masters, Dorman, Jett, Prentiss, Cunningham, and Brown of Petersburg, voted for Thomas W. Gilmer.—18.

Messrs. Southall, Garland of Amherst, Smith of Gloucester, and Cooke, voted for John Tyler.—4.

Messrs. Gilmer, Swanson and Butts, voted for John T. Brown.—3.

Messrs. Drummond and Beard, voted for Chapman Johnson.—2.

Messrs. Price, and Hail of Franklin, voted for Joseph S. Watkins.—2.

Mr. Smith of Frederick voted for Linn Banks.—1.

Mr. Botts voted for Absalom Hickerson.—1.

And Mr. Powell voted for Thomas H. Benton.—1.

Ordered, That Messrs. Garland of Mecklenburg, Harris, Wilson of Botetourt, Mallory, Watkins, Hopkins, Strange, Sherrard, Harley, Chapman and Kincheloe, be a committee to act jointly with a committee of the senate, to ascertain the state of the joint vote; the committee then withdrew, and after some time returned into the house, and Mr. Garland of Mecklenburg reported that the said committee had, according to order, ascertained the joint vote to be, for Mr. Rives 95, scattering 44; whereupon, William C. Rives, esq. was declared duly elected a senator to represent this state in the congress of the United States, to supply the vacancy occasioned by the resignation of John Tyler, esq.

On motion, the house adjourned until to-morrow morning 10 o'clock.

FRIDAY, March 4th, 1836.

On motion of Mr. Mullen, *Ordered*, That leave be given to bring in a bill to amend an act, entitled, "an act incorporating the town of Moorfield in the county of Hardy," and that Messrs. Mullen, Hunter of Berkeley, Berry, Sherrard, Bare, Almond and Davison, prepare and bring in the same.

Mr. Crutchfield reported without amendment, a bill changing the Hunting run gold mining company into a company for mining and manufacturing iron and steel.

Mr. Booker, from the committee for courts of justice, reported with amendments, a bill repealing the law requiring lands in this commonwealth to be processioned, so far as the same may apply to the county of Patrick.

And presented a bill concerning Ann, a free woman of colour.

Mr. Dorman, according to order, presented a bill making certain changes in the general road law, passed March 3d, 1835, so far as the county of Rockbridge is concerned.

Which were severally received and laid upon the table.

An engrossed bill to incorporate the city of Wheeling, was taken up on motion of Mr. Chapline; whereupon, a clause by way of ryder thereto, was offered by Mr. Watkins, which was read the first and second times, and forthwith engrossed and read a third time;

Resolved, That the bill (with the ryder,) do pass, and that the title be, "an act to incorporate the city of Wheeling."

Ordered, That the clerk communicate the same to the senate and request their concurrence.

An engrossed bill forming a new county out of parts of the counties of Shenandoah and Frederick, was taken up on motion of Mr. Bare, and sundry blanks therein were filled, and the question being put upon its passage, was determined in the affirmative. Ayes 80, noes 44.

The ayes and noes thereupon being required by Mr. Smith of Frederick, (and sustained according to the rule of the house,) were as follow:

Ayes, Messrs. Banks, (speaker,) Layne, Wiley, Garland of Amherst, Pate, Hunter of Berkeley, Henshaw, Decamps, Booker, Austin, Beuhring, Richardson, Vaughan, Smith of Fauquier, Hickerson, Strange, Steger, Holland, Watts, Watkins, Hail of Grayson, Wethered, Avent, Sloan, Nixon, Goodall, Mullen, Harrison, Kincheloe, Botts, Fontaine, Holleman, Gregory, Griggs, Berry, Hooe, Straton, Taylor of Loudoun, Harris, Ragsdale, Taylor of Mathews and Middlesex, Waggener, Rogers, Garland of Mecklenburg, Willey, Morgan, Chapman, Ingles, Brown of Nelson, Murdaugh, Leland, Chapline, Masters, Almond, Adams, Swanson, Witcher, Cackley, Hopkins, Carroll, Madison, Shands, Williams, Marteney, Nicklin, Dorman, Moffett, Conrad, Jessee, M'Mullen, Bare, Rinker, Crutchfield, Moncure, Hargrave, Gillespie, Delashmutt, Gibson, Prentiss and Saunders.—80.

Noes, Messrs. Grinalds, Gilmer, Southall, Brooke, Craig, Campbell, Wilson of Botetourt, Turnbull, Mallory, Daniel, Samuel, Christian, Johnson, Hill, Wilson of Cumberland, Servant, Hunter of Essex, Ball, Hale of Franklin, Bowen, Davison, Smith of Frederick, Smith of Gloucester, Carrington, Coleman, Summers, Fleet, Robinson, Carter, Neill, Beard, Powell, Sherrard, Benton, Fitzgerald, M'Coy, Morris, Leyburn, Harley, Butts, Jett, Cunningham, Brown of Petersburg, and Stanard.—44.

Resolved, That the bill do pass, and that the title be, "an act forming a new county out of parts of the counties of Shenandoah and Frederick."

Ordered, That the clerk communicate the same to the senate and request their concurrence.

Mr. Holleman, from the committee of privileges and elections, presented a report, which, on his motion, was read as follows:

The committee of privileges and elections, to whom were referred the petitions of Alexander Rives and Thomas J. Randolph, with the accompanying documents, contesting the elections of Thomas W. Gilmer and Valentine W. Southall, delegates returned from the county of Albemarle, to the present general assembly, have had the same under consideration, and have agreed to the following report:

From an examination of the poll books of said county, it appears to your committee, that at the close of the election the poll stood thus:

For Thomas W. Gilmer,	658 votes.
Valentine W. Southall,	650
Alexander Rives,	646
Thomas J. Randolph,	635
Alexander Rives challenged on the poll of Thomas W. Gilmer,	113 votes.
And on the poll of V. W. Southall,	111
Thomas J. Randolph challenged on the poll of Thomas W. Gilmer,	114 votes.
And on the poll of V. W. Southall,	110
Thomas W. Gilmer challenged on the poll of Alexander Rives,	108 votes.
And on the poll of Thomas J. Randolph,	106
Valentine W. Southall challenged on the poll of Alexander Rives,	109 votes.
And on the poll of Thomas J. Randolph,	107
Thomas W. Gilmer's poll as above,	658
From which deduct illegal votes admitted, or so decided by the committee,	44
Carried forward,	614

Brought forward,	614
To which add votes transferred from the back of the poll,	3
Making of legal votes,	617
Valentine W. Southall's poll as above,	650
From which deduct illegal votes, admitted, or so decided by the committee,	40
	610
To which add votes transferred from the back of the poll,	3
Making of legal votes,	613
Alexander Rives's poll as above,	646
From which deduct illegal votes, admitted, or so decided by the committee,	52
Remaining legal votes,	594
Thomas J. Randolph's poll as above,	635
From which deduct illegal votes, admitted, or so decided by the committee,	52
Remaining legal votes,	583

Your committee are of opinion that the polls as corrected, should stand thus:

For Thomas W. Gilmer,	617
Valentine W. Southall,	613
Alexander Rives,	594
Thomas J. Randolph,	583

Therefore resolved, That Thomas W. Gilmer and Valentine W. Southall were duly elected as delegates from the county of Albemarle, to serve in the present general assembly.

The said resolution was, on the question put thereupon, agreed to by the house.

The house, according to the order of the day, resolved itself into a committee of the whole house on the state of the commonwealth, Mr. Miller in the chair; and after some time spent therein, the speaker resumed the chair, and Mr. Miller reported that the said committee had taken into consideration a bill increasing the banking capital of this commonwealth, and made sundry amendments thereto, which, together with the said bill, were laid upon the table.

The remaining orders of the day were ordered to be postponed until to-morrow.

On motion of Mr. Miller, the house adjourned until to-morrow 10 o'clock.

SATURDAY, March 5th, 1836.

A communication from the senate by their clerk:

IN SENATE, March 4th, 1836.

The senate have passed the bill, entitled,

"An act concerning the Rappahannock company."

They have also passed the bills, entitled,

"An act for incorporating the Medical College at Richmond, in Virginia;" and

"An act to change the times of holding the courts in the third judicial circuit, and for other purposes," with amendments, in which they request the concurrence of the house of delegates.

On motions severally made, the said bills and amendments were ordered to be laid upon the table.

On motion of Mr. Dorman, *Resolved,* That the committee for courts of justice be discharged from the further consideration of the claim of Laurent Buzadone's heirs, without prejudice to said claim either here or elsewhere, said committee not having time during the present session to investigate the same, and that leave be given to withdraw the memorial and accompanying documents.

On motion of Mr. Watkins, the committee of roads and internal navigation were ordered to be discharged from the duty of bringing in bills incorporating a company to improve the navigation of the Pamunkey river; and amending the act incorporating the Cartersville bridge company, so as to enable them to hold real estate not exceeding five acres of land.

On motion of Mr. Madison, *Ordered,* That the committee of agriculture and manufactures be discharged from the consideration of proceedings of the agricultural convention of Albemarle and Fredericksburg, and that the same be laid upon the table.

Mr. Dorman, from the committee for courts of justice, presented a bill divorcing Ann Edmunds from her husband John W. A. Edmunds.

Mr. Witcher, from the committee of claims, presented reports upon petitions of Milly Cooper; of Peter J. Chevallie; of Abner Robinson; of Edward Goodwin; and of Berkeley Ward.

And a bill concerning the administrator of Richard Kelsick, deceased.

Mr. Watkins, from the committee of roads and internal navigation, reported without amendment, a bill incorporating the Lynchburg and Campbell court-house turnpike company.

And presented a bill incorporating the Glen Leonard rail-road company.

A bill to amend the charter of the James river and Kanawha company; and

A bill to authorize a change of location of the Warm springs and Harrisonburg turnpike, and for other purposes.

Also, reports upon the petition of citizens of Scott; and upon the resolution for subscribing to the stock of the Lexington and Richmond turnpike company.

And reported without amendment, a bill to authorize a subscription on behalf of the state to the stock of the Pittsylvania and Lynchburg turnpike company, and for other purposes.

Mr. Hill, from the committee of propositions and grievances, reported without amendment, a bill to incorporate the Portsmouth and Chesapeake steam boat company.

A bill to incorporate the Wythe watering company, in the county of Wythe; and

A bill concerning the town of Leesburg in the county of Loudoun.

Mr. Mullen, according to order, presented a bill to amend the act, entitled, "an act concerning the town of Moorfield in the county of Hardy."

Mr. Cooke in like manner, presented a bill to alter and increase the terms of the circuit superior court of law and chancery for the county of Norfolk; and

A bill incorporating the Portsmouth provident society.

Mr. Madison, from the committee on agriculture and manufactures, presented a report upon petitions of citizens of Farmville.

Which bills and reports were received and laid upon the table.

Mr. Dorman, presented a memorial of George Hay Lee, in behalf of Judge Edwin S. Duncan, asking the legislature to investigate the charges against said Duncan during the present session, which was ordered to be laid upon the table.

A bill to regulate the conduct of boatmen on the Appomattox river, and its branches, was taken up on motion of Mr. Wiley, read the first and second times, and ordered to be committed to the committee which brought it in.

The speaker laid before the house the following, which were read:

RICHMOND, 24th February, 1836.

The honourable B. W. LEIGH.

SIR,—In obedience to a joint resolution adopted by the general assembly on this day, we herewith transmit to you a preamble and resolutions "upon the subject of expunging from the journals of the senate of the United States a resolution of that body, and relative to the right of instruction," with a request that you will lay the same before the senate of the United States.

We have the honour to be, with great respect, your ob't servants,

(Signed,)   STAFFORD H. PARKER, *Speaker of the Senate.*
LINN BANKS, *Speaker H. D.*

SENATE CHAMBER, WASHINGTON, March 2d, 1836.

To the honourable STAFFORD H. PARKER, *Speaker of the Senate,*
and the honourable LINN BANKS, *Speaker of the House of Delegates of Virginia.*

GENTLEMEN,—I am honoured with your letter of the 24th ultimo, enclosing me a copy of the preamble and resolutions of the general assembly, upon the subject of expunging from the journal of the senate of the United States, a resolution of that body, and requesting me to lay the same before the senate.

I adhere to the doctrine of the right of instruction, as laid down in the resolutions of the general assembly of February, 1812, taken in the plain and obvious sense, and in the full extent, in which it is there expressed; and I shall continue, not only to respect, but also to maintain it, to the utmost of my ability. I deem it, indeed, an important part of the great right of state interposition, as explained and enforced in the memorable resolutions which have illustrated the session of the general assembly of 1799-1800; and, in my opinion, this right of instruction will be found of inestimable value on all occasions that may arise, presenting questions concerning the just boundaries of power between the federal and state governments. If, then, the general assembly had instructed me to give a vote, according to its sense of propriety, on any constitutional question which I could consider as at all doubtful, especially, on a question on which the public mind had been long and deliberately exercised, on which men's judgments had been formed under the influence of no party or temporary excitement, but of dispassionate reason, and yet remained divided and balanced; I should, in such a case, have followed the judgment of the general assembly, though it had been contrary to my own. For this would not be to violate my oath of office, but only to renounce all vainglorious pretensions to infallibility, and to pay a proper and conscientious deference to the wisdom of the general assembly. If the general assembly had instructed me *not* to vote for a particular measure, on the ground that it held the measure unconstitutional, then, as it could hardly be unconstitutional to comply with such negative instruction, I should have had no hesitation in yielding obedience to it, however clearly the measure so disapproved, might appear to my mind constitutional and wise. And as to questions of mere policy, involving no point of constitutional right, I can hardly conceive a case in which I should find difficulty in conforming my vote with instructions given me by the general assembly. But I do not hold myself bound to obey, and I cannot obey, any instruction that commands me to do an act, which, in my conscientious opinion, would be, in itself, a plain violation of the constitution, and, in its consequences, dangerous and mischievous in the extreme.

While I thus declare my adherence to the doctrine of the right of instruction asserted by the general assembly in 1812, which, sincerely believing it to be just and true, I then lent my humble aid to maintain, I beg it may be distinctly understood, that if upon more mature reflection I thought the principle wrong, neither the pride of opinion, nor a sense of the advantages which public men usually derive from maintaining their consistency, nor a fear of the reproaches which inconsistency always incurs (unless, indeed, it be backed with power), would withhold me from renouncing it.

The first of the resolutions you have transmitted to me, instructs the senators from Virginia in the congress of the United States "to introduce and vote for a resolution, directing the resolution of the senate of the 28th March, 1834, declaring 'that the president, in the late executive proceedings in relation to the public revenue, has assumed upon himself authority and power not conferred by the constitution and laws, but in derogation of both,'—to be expunged from the journal of the senate of the United States, by causing black lines to be drawn around the said resolution, as it stands on the original manuscript journal, and these words plainly written across the face of the said resolution and entry,—Expunged by order of the senate of the United States."

I have reconsidered the resolution of the senate disapproved of by the general assembly, in reference as well to its intrinsic propriety, as to the constitutional competency of the senate to adopt it; I have reflected on the question, whether the resolution of the senate, supposing it wrong, can constitutionally be expunged from the journal; I have, in doing so, earnestly endeavoured to discard from my memory, the circumstances belonging to the history both of the resolution condemned, and of the resolution condemnatory; indeed, I was called upon to consider the proposition to expunge the resolution of the senate, before I thought it possible I could ever be personally concerned in the result: and in every view I have been able to take of the subject, I find it absolutely impossible to obey the instruction now given to me. I cannot obey it, without committing an act, which, to my judgment and conscience, would be a plain violation of the constitution of the United States. I cannot obey it, without descending to a degree of slavish baseness that would render me justly despicable, and expose me to the scorn even of those who have commanded the deed. I cannot obey it, without forfeiting my own self-respect forever.

The constitution of the United States contains a provision (such as is to be found in few if any of the state constitutions) that "each house" [of congress] "shall keep a journal of its proceedings, and from time to time publish the same, excepting such parts as may in their judgment require secrecy; and the yeas and nays of the members of either house on any question, shall, at the desire of one fifth of those present, be entered on the journal." The purpose of the provision is most obvious. It requires each house to record "its" trans*ctions,—to record them all, truly, exactly and fully—to record them for the information of present and future generations; to furnish evidence, to which the constituent may refer in the examination of the conduct of the representative, or the representative resort for his justification; and to hand down to our posterity, a certain knowledge of all the acts of their ancestors, which may often serve as a guide to direct them, and sometimes a beacon to warn. And unless the provision can be complied with by keeping a partial, false, and garbled record of the proceedings of the two houses—unless this duty to record the truth, can be fulfilled without recording the whole truth,—or unless the injunction to *keep* the journal, can be understood as not commanding us to *preserve* it; it is impossible, I should think, to maintain, that the record of any resolution or proceeding of the senate can be *expunged* from its journal, in the literal sense and true acceptation of that word; that is, wholly blotted out or erased. Indeed, it would be difficult so to expunge any part of the journal, without impairing the record of something else, which all would wish to preserve truly and fairly recorded.

The general assembly itself, sensible (as I humbly venture to suppose) that the resolution of the senate in question, cannot be actually expunged from the journal without a violation of the constitution, proposes, that it shall be expunged "by causing black lines to be drawn around the said resolution, as it stands on the original manuscript journal, and these words plainly written across the face of the said resolution and entry—'Expunged by order of the senate.'" In other words, if I mistake not the meaning and principle of the instructions, the general assembly, admitting that the resolution of the senate cannot, consistently with the constitution, be expunged from the journal *literally*, yet thinks, that it may be expunged *figuratively*. I pray the general assembly to consider the danger and the mischief that must flow from a precedent of this kind—which would, in effect, elude a positive injunction of the constitution by a metaphorical use of words, and what is more, a typical doing of deeds. I doubt whether there is a single provision of the constitution, which may not be eluded, and set at nought, by a similar process; and I must add, that this typical method of expunction is more abhorrent from my feelings of constitutional duty and propriety, than the literal. Undoubtedly, the precedent admits of a broader and easier, and therefore more mischievous, application. I pray the general assembly to consider, too, the hardship of imposing upon the consciences of men acting under the sanction of an official oath, the duty of conforming their official conduct with the rhetoric of their constituents. In the framing of laws, and in legislative proceedings of all kinds, it has always been found wise and necessary to discard all figures of speech, and to adopt the plainest language in its plainest literal acceptation. If I rightly understand the meaning and purpose of the instruction given me, the general assembly would have me propose and vote for an expunction of the obnoxious resolution of the senate from its journal, in such a manner, that it shall not be expunged after all, in whole or in part. Now, in the first place, I doubt very much, whether this could be done, even in the method prescribed; and, in the next place, if, entertaining the opinions I do on the subject, I should vote for any such process of expunging, I should be guilty of mental equivocation in the discharge of my official duty. I humbly hope for the pardon of the general assembly, and of all good men, if I cannot, at its command, extinguish the knowledge I have acquired of my mother tongue; much more, if I cannot disregard the dictates of reason and conscience, which God has planted in my breast, to be the ruler and monitor of all my actions.

I find myself constrained to say, that I cannot obey the instruction for expunging the resolution of the senate, in any manner, literally or figuratively.

This brings me to the consideration of the second resolution of the general assembly, which declares, that "the assembly regards the right of instruction 'as resting on the broad basis of the nature of representation,' and one of the vital principles of our free institutions; and that it is the duty of the representative to obey the instructions of his constituents, or resign the trust with which they have clothed him, in order that it may be transferred to the hands of those who will carry into effect the wishes and instructions of the constituent body."

And here, in considering the alternative proposed to me, I cannot but advert to the very peculiar nature of the act which the instruction requires of me, and to some remarkable circumstances in the history of the subject.

The resolution which the general assembly proposes to expunge, is only the expression of an opinion held by the majority of the senate for the time being, and the entry of it on the journal, only the record of the fact that such was the opinion of the body.. It must be obvious to the minds of all men, that the expunction of the resolution from the journal of the senate, can no wise affect the main questions,—whether the opinion therein declared was just or erroneous,—and whether or no it was within the competency of the senate to determine on the subject of the resolution; nor can the defacement of the record of a historical fact, in whatever manner it may be effected, annul or alter the fact itself, or, in the present case, impair in the slightest degree, the memory of the transaction. Some hundreds of copies of the journal containing this resolution, have been printed; some deposited in the public archives, and some delivered to members of congress for the time being, which have thus become private property, and been dispersed throughout the Union: the resolution was published, too, in all the public journals of the day: it stands recorded on the journals of all the state legislatures that have thought proper to take the subject into their consideration: the general assembly of Virginia has itself recorded it, in the very resolutions in which it directs the senators of the state in congress, to vote for expunging it from the manuscript journal of the senate. For any direct purpose, therefore, which the expunction of it can serve, viewing the act apart from the intention, nothing can be more absolutely nugatory. The resolution itself, the evidence of it, and the opinion it declares, will all be handed down to posterity by faithful history; nay, even by the very record of the proceeding to expunge it. It is vain to say, as the general assembly has said in the preamble to its resolutions, that the resolution of the senate is "an assumption of power not warranted by the constitution, and calculated to subvert the rights of the house of representatives and the fundamental principles of our free institutions;" for, if this were really the case, the general assembly should have levelled some of its censures against the house of representatives, for neglecting its high trust—for neglecting to vindicate "the fundamental principles of our free institutions," and, especially, its own rights and privileges, against the encroachment of the senate. I am not aware, that that house has made any complaint: perhaps, it understood the subject too well, to do so. It is the executive only that has protested against this proceeding of the senate; and the only conceivable purpose which the proposed expunction of it can answer, will be to signalize the triumph of executive power over a department of the legislative that has had the firmness to oppose its measures—to set a mark of disgrace and humiliation upon the senate, and to bind a wreath of inglorious victory around the brow of the president. And even for this purpose, no stroke of the pen was ever more vain, than that which shall mark those black lines around the resolution of the senate, and write that sentence of expunction on its face—if, indeed, it be not calculated to work the direct contrary effect to that intended. The victory of the president over the senate may be as complete without it. And if, unhappily, the fruits of that victory shall ripen into their full maturity of bitterness—in times to come, when the constitution of the senate shall be subverted—when the check it was ordained to hold upon the power of the executive, and of the popular national branch of the legislature, shall be removed—when the substance of the constitution shall be destroyed, and nothing but its empty forms remain; history will paint those black lines drawn around this resolution, and those fatal words of condemnation written across its face, and hold them up as a mournful memento to ourselves of departed liberty, and a warning to some happier race of mankind. If, on the other hand, the senate shall, by the blessing of Providence, continue to maintain its place in the system,—still exercising the functions for which it was designed,—enjoying freedom of deliberation and independence of action; then will the manuscript volume of the journal, and indeed the single page, containing those memorable circular black lines, be the only volume, and the only page, that will ever be sought after, or read. The process of expunging the resolution, is the surest way to render the memory of it immortal.

It cannot be forgotten, that very shortly before I was first elected to the senate, the general assembly of Virginia, upon long and solemn deliberation, resolved, " 1. That the recent act of the president of the United States, exerting a control over the public deposites, by causing them to be withheld and withdrawn on his own responsibility, from the United States bank, in which they had been ordered to be placed by the act of congress chartering the said bank, is, in the judgment of the general assembly, a dangerous and alarming assumption of power by that officer, which cannot be too strongly condemned. 2. That, while the general assembly will ever be ready to sustain the president in the exercise of all such powers as the constitution has confided to him, they, nevertheless, cannot but regard with apprehension and distrust, the disposition to extend his official authority beyond its just and proper limits, which he has so clearly manifested in his recent interference with the treasury department of the federal government, in the exercise of a sound discretion which congress had confided to the head of that department alone. 3. That our senators in congress be instructed, and our representatives requested, to use their best endeavours to procure the adoption, by congress, of proper measures for restoring the public moneys to the bank of the United States, or at least causing them to be deposited therein for the future, according to the direction and stipulation of the act of congress chartering the said bank, if at the time of their action on the subject, the said bank be, in their opinion, a safe depository of the public treasure." Thus, the general assembly, at that session, expressly affirmed the very proposition, (and in far stronger terms,) contained in the resolution of the senate, which the present general assembly condemns ; and the resolutions of the former session manifestly pre-suppose, that it was within the competency of the senate, as well as the house of representatives, to act upon that proposition, then in fact pending in the senate. In consequence of those resolutions, one of the senators from Virginia resigned his seat; a resignation certainly most unexpected to me; equally unexpected, I believe, to the general assembly. Neither have I ever believed, that the resolutions it had adopted, were designed to produce any such result. I was, soon after, elected to fill the vacancy. I shall not say, that the resolutions which had recently been adopted by the general assembly, constituted my motive for voting for the resolution passed by the senate some few weeks after I took my seat : for, in truth, this resolution expressed the sentiment I myself had all along entertained and expressed. But, surely, I have a right to refer to the instructions of the general assembly of 1833-4, requiring me to vote for the resolution which the present general assembly instructs me to expunge, and to vindicate and sustain myself by their authority : otherwise, no senator can ever safely obey any instructions: he must incur the danger of being driven to the alternative now presented to me, of dishonouring himself by voting against his conscience, or of resigning his place, whenever, in the vicissitudes of party warfare, a subsequent legislature shall think the instruction wrong. It is with the deepest conviction and heartfelt pain, that I say, as I must say, that the proceedings of the general assembly of Virginia on the present occasion, are calculated, above all things, to impair the right of instruction itself.

I should have a right, too, after having acted in conformity with instructions given by the general assembly at one session, and seeing the same opinions prevail at a succeeding session, to appeal from the mandate of the present assembly, to the people, at the next elections. And this would seem the more reasonable, if it should be considered, that some of the state legislatures have, at their sessions of 1834-5, instructed their senators to vote for expunging the resolution of the senate in question ; and, though their instructions have been disregarded, have, at their last sessions, declined to repeat and enforce them. But I choose to place myself, at once, upon different and higher ground, and to act up to the principles, reasons and motives, which, in reality, dictate the conduct I am going to pursue.

It cannot escape observation, that, while the general assembly instructs *me* to *expunge* the resolution of the senate, which I voted for in conformity with the instructions of the assembly of 1833-4, the *present* assembly has not *expunged* the resolutions of the *former* assembly. And though (if I am rightly informed) a proposition has been made to *rescind* the former resolutions, even that proposition had not yet been acted on. So that I am to understand, that the general assembly is instructing me to do, in respect to a former resolution of the senate, that which it will not do itself, in respect to resolutions passed at a former session of its own body. I must bespeak pardon for remarking, further, that, though proceedings have been had in congress, and some laws have been passed, violating, in the opinion of the general assembly, *the dearest rights of the people*—take, for example, the sedition law ; and though, too, many laws have been passed by the federal legislature, which, in the opinion of the general assembly, transcended its constitutional powers, and encroached on *the rights of the states;* yet it has never, heretofore, occurred to the general assembly, in any case, or at any time, to assert and vindicate *the rights of the people*, or *the rights of the states*, against such assumptions of power by congress, by an expunction (literal or typical) of the obnoxious proceedings from the journals of the two houses. And now, for the first time, when a simple resolution of the senate is supposed (by some unaccountable misconception of its import and intention) to encroach upon the rights of the national branch of the federal legislature, which, probably, has not perceived, and certainly has not complained of the encroachment—or (to speak plainly) when the senate has presumed to question the rights and powers claimed for the executive department by the president, who alone has complained and protested against its proceedings—I see the general assembly of Virginia coming forward to vindicate *the rights and powers claimed by the president*, by this process of expunction, which it has never thought of resorting to, for the vindication either of *the rights of the people*, or *the rights of the states*. I mention these strange contrasts, because they have raised the gloomiest apprehensions, in my mind, of approaching danger to our republican institutions, and because those apprehensions have had an important influence in determining my judgment, and my conduct, under the extraordinary instructions which the general assembly has thought proper to give me.

The general assembly can have no reason to doubt, and I am quite sure, does not doubt, that I voted for the resolution of the senate, which it condemns as unconstitutional and mischievous, under a sincere conviction, that it was constitutional, wise, and even necessary to assert and vindicate the authority of the laws ; neither can it doubt, that this is still my opinion. Yet, without deigning to suggest any reasons to enlighten and convince my understanding, the general assembly gives me a peremptory instruction to propose and vote for the expunction of this resolution from the journal of the senate : and it insists, that I must obey its will and command—or resign my office. It instructs me to vote to expunge from the journal, that which it knows, as well as I do, is there truly recorded: it instructs me to deface, and in a manner to falsify, a public record, which it knows the constitution explicitly requires the senate to keep ; and (to remove my scruples) it prescribes the expunction of the resolution from the journal, figuratively and typically, in such a manner as can only serve to elude the positive injunction of the constitution, and to signalize the humiliation and disgrace of the senate, without at all affecting the historical evidence of the fact: it instructs me to do this—or resign. It instructs me so to expunge, as *not* to expunge, the resolution : it requires of me, in a word, a jesuitical equivocation with my oath and conscience; and (considering the knowledge it must have of the opinions I entertain) it commands me to incur dishonour, shame and guilt—or resign. It requires me, in effect, to give my recorded sanction to the prerogatives claimed by the president, in his memorable protest against the proceedings of the senate, and to the limitations he thinks proper to set upon the rights, powers and privileges of this body: well knowing the opinions I have avowed on the questions of constitutional right, and, I hope, not doubting their sincerity, the general assembly commands me to inflict this (in my sense of things) vital blow upon the constitution of my country—or resign. I cannot shut my eyes against the truth—plain and glaring upon the very face of the transaction—that such instructions were not given me, with any expectation, or view, or perhaps even wish, that I should yield obedience to them. There is, in truth, no choice between the alternatives proposed to me; and I believe, most undoubtingly, that it was not designed to leave me any choice; that the real and the only purpose of the instruction, was to compel me to resign—" to instruct me out of my seat." Indeed, it seems to me, that this design is almost avowed in the preamble and resolutions you have transmitted to me. For the preamble recites, as a motive for the proceeding, that "the assembly deem it *their solemn duty* again to reassert the *duty* of the representative to *obey* or *resign*;" and then after giving me an instruction which the assembly knew that *I* could not *obey* without crime and foul disgrace, it resolves,—" that it is the DUTY of the representative to *obey* the instructions of his constituents, or to resign the trust with which they have clothed him, in order that it may be transferred into the hands of those who will carry into execution the wishes and instructions of the constituent body."

It was impossible that I should have remained ignorant, and it is equally impossible for me to forget, the political operations in Virginia during the past year. I know, that the design of "instructing me out of my seat"—or (in courtly phrase) "giving me a walking ticket"—was early and openly avowed and recommended; that it was an advantage not a little vaunted, which the victors promised themselves from the success they achieved at the last annual elections; that the scheme of the instruction was proposed and discussed, and the very method of typical expunction which the general assembly has adopted, strenuously recommended, as the proper and sure means of driving me to a resignation, in the public prints, which are sometimes the organs, and sometimes the dictators, of party plans. I know, moreover, that the proceeding was aimed at *me*—particularly at *me;* and that, to insure its success, no effort has been spared, to exaggerate my faults, such as they are; to falsify the history of my life, simple and obscure, as hitherto it had been, and barren of incident; to misrepresent all my motives, sentiments and actions, and to raise such a storm of public indignation against me, as should make me bend like the willow in the fable, and preserve a worthless existence by yielding, rather than be torn up by the roots like the sturdy oak, and laid forever prostrate on the earth. I shall fulfil my destiny with firmness and composure. Let me thank my enemies, for having given me a consequence which my own merits would never have achieved, that enables me to act a conspicuous and useful part in the defence of the "free institutions" of my country. I ought to be grateful to the general assembly, for placing me, as it were, at the head of a forlorn hope, in the contest now waging for the preservation of the constitution and the laws; and though I am as sensible of the danger, as I am of the honour, of the post assigned me, I hope, with the blessing of God, to approve myself not altogether unworthy of it.

If the general assembly had any object at heart, pursued directly for its own value, and not as a means of accomplishing, by indirection, other objects, plainly unjust and unconstitutional,—and should give me an instruction to use my endeavours, in my official station, to promote its views—an instruction, which it believed I could conscientiously obey—an instruction framed with no design to force me to a resignation; and if, in such a case, I should think the end aimed at unconstitutional, and should be, therefore, unwilling to be an active agent in accomplishing it, the case would be a very strong one, indeed, and attended with very peculiar circumstances, in which I would retain my seat, and stand as an obstruction to the accomplishment of the measure desired. But regarding the present instruction, as mainly directed to the purpose of forcing me "to resign the trust with which" the general assembly "has clothed me, in order that it may be transferred into the hands of those who will carry into execution the wishes and instructions of the constituent body"—which wishes and instructions I think plainly contrary to the letter and spirit of the constitution; and deeply convinced, as I am, that my resignation would more vitally affect the integrity of the constitution, than even an implicit obedience to the instructions, I have, therefore, come to a resolution, that I cannot, ought not, and will not resign.

I pray the general assembly to accompany me for a brief space, and to accompany me with patience, in a consideration of the practical consequences of the precedent, and of the doctrine (for precedent will soon grow into doctrine), which it proposes to establish—namely, that the state legislatures may give instructions to their senators in congress, which they believe they cannot obey without conscious dishonour and crime, and therefore will not obey, in order to force them to the alternative of resignation.

The unavoidable effect will be, to change the tenure of the senatorial office, from a term of six years, which the constitution has ordained, to a tenure during the pleasure of the respective state legislatures that elect them; to make the senate, which was plainly designed, and that for the most obvious purposes, to be the most permanent body in the government, in effect and in practice, the most fluctuating, transient, and unstable.

The senate, constructed on the federative principle, to represent the sovereignties of the states, which, from the nature of sovereignty, are co-equal, is so essential to their existence and preservation, that if the senate were abolished from the system,—the other branches of the government, both of which are national in their character, remaining in full force,—it is hard to imagine how the state governments, or any thing more than the forms of them, could long endure. And whatever tends to diminish the weight of the senate in the system, must tend to impair, in exactly the same proportion, the state sovereignties themselves, and to a general consolidation of them all into one empire. The federative senate, representing the states, was designed as the balance of the system—as a check on the popular branch of the legislature, and on the executive, both of which are almost entirely national in their constitution—and, in matters of important and permanent interest, it is a check that can very rarely operate for a longer time than may suffice to mature the judgment of the people on sober dispassionate reflection. The senate cannot, if it would, counteract the permanent will, the deliberate settled judgment of the nation. The house of representatives, elected for two years, representing the people immediately, and therefore more exactly representing their opinions and wishes for the time being, and more apt also to represent their passions, is, in that way, endued with a power and influence, which the shortness of its term of office hardly suffices to countervail. The president, elected for four years, clothed with all the powers necessary for the executive of a government charged with the foreign relations of the nation, with his veto on the acts of the legislature, and the whole patronage of government in his hands, is far more than the equal in power of either branch of the legislature, and, in the opinion of many, more powerful than both combined. His very unity is a principle of strength. The only means of making the senate co-ordinate with the other departments, was that which has been resorted to; namely, to make it more permanent: and hence it was, that the senatorial term of office was made three times as long as that of the representatives, and half as long again as that of the president. If the senatorial term of office be reduced, the power of its check on the national branches of the government, will be proportionally impaired; if it be made to depend on the pleasure of the state legislatures, the check will be almost annihilated: and the state sovereignties must share its fate, and be impaired or annihilated with it. To me, therefore, it seems, that the state governments would commit an imprudent act, if they should consent to shorten the term of the senatorial office, and a suicidal one, if they should establish the principle, in theory or in practice, that their senators shall hold their offices only during pleasure.

But whether these views are wise or not, all will agree, that the tenure of the senatorial office, being for a term of six years fixed by the constitution, is not now, and was not designed to be, dependent on the pleasure of the state legislatures, and can be nowise authoritatively made so, but by an amendment of the constitution of the United States, perfected according to the provisions of the 5th article; and that such an amendment would work a vital change in the whole constitution of the federal government, and in the relations between that and the state governments. If the doctrine, which the general assembly now asserts, and which it calls upon me to give my aid to establish, by setting the example of conforming with it, shall become generally prevalent in the other states of the Union as well as in Virginia, then will that vital change be wrought in our institutions, as effectually as it could be by an amendment of the constitution, and this, by means the most irregular, and the most contrary that can well be conceived, to the cautious spirit of the provision for future amendments.

The doctrine is, that a senator in congress is bound to yield implicit obedience to any instruction, which the state legislatures that elected him may give him, or to resign—no matter how plainly unconstitutional, no matter how base and criminal, the act which he is enjoined to perform, may be, *in his own judgment*—that he has no right to exercise his own judgment at all, or consult his own conscience: he is not, in this case, a moral agent: he has no alternative but to obey or resign.

If this doctrine shall become generally adopted and established throughout the United States, by the assertion and exercise of it on the one part, and submission to it on the other, I pray the general assembly to consider, for a moment, the probable workings of the principle in practice. Whenever the president shall feel the check of senatorial opposition—if the senators in opposition shall have the firmness to continue refractory to his will, unmoved and unawed by his power—especially, if there should be nearly a balance of parties in the body, so that a few changes may reverse the majority—the president will be placed under the strongest temptations to have recourse to the state legislatures, in order to disembarrass himself of the opposition. Suitable, nay even plausible, pretexts will never be wanting, to justify or excuse their interference. There will be no difficulty, at any time, much more in times of violent party excitement, to select some prominent measure, involving a question of constitutional right, and to frame an instruction upon it to the refractory senator, which it is known he cannot conscientiously obey, and therefore will not obey; and to require him, nevertheless, to obey or resign. And to obtain the instruction, we may surely expect to see all the mighty influence of presidential power and patronage, brought to bear upon the state legislatures, and upon the elections to them—to delude and demoralize the people,—to tamper with, corrupt and seduce, the state assemblies, whose senators in congress it may be deemed most important, or most feasible, to remove. Fit instruments and agents for the work will always abound, and volunteer in the service,—the venal panders of power, the whole tribe of parasites and sycophants zealous to conciliate favour,—the vain aspirants after political importance, honour and notoriety—all will crowd into the president's train, and vie with each other in doing his biddings. I am speaking of the probable, natural, inevitable effects of political causes put into action. I do not believe, and therefore I am not insinuating, that the general assembly intends to open the field for these abominations. I speak with freedom, but not without sincere respect. It is the firm conviction of my mind, that there never was, and cannot be, a process invented, better calculated than that which I am now called upon to take an active part in establishing, to place the federal executive under the strongest temptation to employ its influence, power and patronage, in the purchase of subservient senators; and to place the state assemblies under temptation to provide the commodity for market; to destroy the purity of the people, upon which all depends at last; to destroy the purity of the state assemblies, and to prostrate their dignity, authority and influence, in the dust. As to the senate, that will soon be, to all purposes of useful service, which it was intended to answer in the system of the federal government, absolutely annihilated.

And if this doctrine shall, in practice, be confined to Virginia, as perhaps it may be, and, judging from present appearances, probably will be, then these abominations will be confined to her alone: her people alone will be exposed to the process of demoralization, her assembly to the arts of corruption and seduction: and her ancient dignity and pristine glory will only be remembered to point the tauntings of scorn at her fallen condition.

Many there are, I know, many good and thinking men, especially in Virginia, who differ with me on this subject; who approve the doctrine I have been controverting, in principle, and hope the most beneficial results from it, in practice; who are as firm in the conviction, that it is necessary to the maintenance of the state sovereignties, as I am in the belief, that its probable and indeed unavoidable effect will be, to impair, degrade and prostrate them; and whose minds are, therefore, predisposed to condemn my opinions, and my conduct, on this occasion. I do not presume to censure *them;* and I must patiently abide the censure they will pronounce on me. If, with the sentiments I entertain concerning this doctrine, and the pernicious consequences that are likely to flow from it, I should consent to become an active instrument in establishing it, by setting an example of conforming with it, I could not ask the forgiveness of my country, and should hardly hope for mercy from Heaven.

I see, with no little surprize, that it is declared, in the preamble to the resolutions of the general assembly, which you have transmitted to me, that "the assembly deem it their duty *again to re-assert*, in behalf of themselves and the people of Virginia, the *right* of the constituent to *instruct*, and the *duty* of the representative *to obey or resign:*" from which I infer, that the general assembly supposes, that this same doctrine has been asserted more than once before. I can only say, that if this peculiar doctrine ever was asserted before, I do not know when, where, or on what occasion, it was asserted. It certainly is not asserted, nor was it intended to be asserted, in the preamble and resolutions, adopted by the general assembly in February, 1812, on the subject of the right of instruction. That paper was the work of my own hands, without assistance from any other person whatever, and drawn up, (as I but too well remember,) with a haste, which, in my own apprehension at the time, materially impaired its value; yet, upon a recent and careful review of it, I do not find myself inclined to retract, or to modify, in any essential point, the propositions there asserted and maintained; and, therefore, I am willing, and even desirous, that my present opinions and conduct shall be tested by them. I was, then, a young statesman, but not a very young man; and it had been fixed in my mind, by reflection and by the lessons of history, as a rudiment in ethics and in politics, that no proposition can be stated in either, however just and true, when properly understood and applied, that may not, if abused, misapplied, or pushed to extremes, result in vice or folly. Sensible that the right of instruction, and the correlative duty of obedience, might be abused to the purpose of commanding violations of the constitution and even acts of moral turpitude—so abused, under the influence of excitement and passion, to which the constituent body, as well as the representative, like all other men, might sometimes be subject—I took the utmost pains to guard the doctrine against such abuses. Let us see how I accomplished the object. The very claim which I understand the general assembly now to assert, to power in itself, and to obedience from me,—absolute power on the one hand, and blind obedience on the other,—is stated as an objection to the reasoning of the preamble, and answered as follows:

"But it has been said, that a state government may instruct its senators to violate the constitution of the United States—that a state, in actual insurrection against the general government, may instruct its senators to promote the cause of rebellion: and it is asked, *whether the senator would be bound by such instruction, to violate the constitution he had sworn to preserve,* and to overthrow the government he had sworn to defend? It may be answered, in the first place, that the particular instruction, which forms the subject of present consideration, could by no possibility involve a breach of the constitution of the United States. It might, and in the opinion of this assembly, would have been, unconstitutional to charter the Bank of the United States anew; but, surely, it could not possibly be deemed unconstitutional not to charter it. As to the rest, without determining the point which has been taken for granted, that a state in open rebellion against the general government, would still be entitled to its representation in the senate, which, to say the least, is extremely doubtful—it is admitted without difficulty, that *if a state instruct its senator to give a vote plainly unconstitutional, or to raise the standard of rebellion, the senator is not bound to obey such instruction.* Every case, such as that supposed, must stand upon its own peculiar circumstances: it supposes all bounds of right transcended, all legitimate rule prostrated; and *the propriety of opposition*, must be determined *by the nature of the injustice, the extent of the mischief, and the prudence of resistance.* But it is no argument against the exercise of a lawful power, that it may be made the pretext for the assumption of an unlawful power. The right of instruction, rightfully exercised, with no evil intention, to no pernicious object, cannot be affected by the admission, that if a state government, or the general government, become corrupt and ambitious, and usurp tyrannical power, it may of right and ought to be resisted. The admission is cheerfully made. *The general assembly of Virginia is incapable of affirming the exploded doctrine of non-resistance.*" And upon this reasoning in the preamble, the two resolutions of a general nature, with which that paper concludes, assert—"That it is the indubitable right of the state legislatures to instruct their senators in congress, on all points, either constitutional or politic, whenever the magnitude of the occasion shall require such interference, and that by consequence, it is the bounden duty of the senators to obey such instructions; *provided the instructions to be given and obeyed, require not the senator to commit a violation of the constitution, or an act of moral turpitude.* That, after this solemn expression of the opinion of the general assembly, on the right of instruction, and the duty of obedience thereto, no man ought henceforth to accept the appointment of a senator of the United States from Virginia, who doth not hold himself bound to obey such instructions"—meaning, obviously, such legitimate instructions as those mentioned in the previous resolution.

The resolutions, then, which are the conclusions resulting from the reasoning of the preamble, expressly declare, that the instructions which the state legislatures have a right to give their senators in congress, and which it is the bounden duty of the senators to obey, are such only, as "require not the senator to commit a violation of the constitution, or an act of moral turpitude." And it is expressly stated in the preamble, "that if a state instruct its senator to give a vote plainly unconstitutional"—"the senator is not bound to obey such instruction"—that every case of the kind "must stand on its own peculiar circumstances"—and that "the propriety of opposition must be determined by the nature of the injustice, the extent of the mischief, and the prudence of resistance." The alternative here proposed to the senator, is not *obedience or resignation*, but *obedience or resistance*; to be determined by the considerations by which all resistance to the authority of government must ever be determined.

If an instruction were given me to vote for a measure of no very material consequence,—a measure, which, if adopted, would not lead to any serious permanent evil,—and yet I could not, for reasons of any kind, conscientiously vote for the proposed measure; in such a case, I might very properly, and should without hesitation, resort to a resignation, in order to evade the painful alternative of disobedience or resistance. Or, if an instruction were given me, which I could not obey without violence to my conscience, and the "peculiar circumstances" of the case should nevertheless be such, that my resignation would be attended with far less of evil than the accomplishment of the object of the instruction, and would not be itself a source of equal or greater evil; in such a case as this, too, I might, consistently with my sense of duty, and very gladly should, disembarrass myself of the alternative of obedience or resistance, by a resignation. In truth, resignation is a *privilege*, not a *duty*—a privilege allowed the senator, by which he may wholly avoid the alternative of obedience or resistance, as expounded in the preamble and resolutions of February 1812.

Here, the general assembly has instructed me to do that which, in my judgment and conscience, would be a crime, and of course, *in me*, an act of moral turpitude: I cannot obey without crime: and, in my opinion, formed upon long and anxious deliberation, resignation would inflict a more vital blow on the constitution, because it would be followed by far more serious and mischievous consequences to both the federal and the state government, than a literal obedience to the instruction. The alternative is, then, forced upon me, of obedience or resistance; an alternative which would be painful enough in itself, and is rendered doubly so to me, by considerations which I shall mention in the sequel.

He that would judge my conduct fairly, should suppose himself in my situation, and bring home to his own bosom the opinions *I* entertain and the motives by which *I* am actuated. If the views I have unfolded, as to the nature of the instruction that has been given to me, the real object at which it was aimed, the turpitude and criminality, which, entertaining the sentiments I do, I should incur by yielding obedience to it, and the impossibility of resigning without giving my aid to a dangerous innovation on the constitution,—be not wholly groundless, then, I apprehend, there is no man who can think, that "the nature of the injustice, and the extent of the mischief," does not justify, and call for, resistance. I have understood it has been supposed, that all the moral responsibility rests on the constituent body, and the senator is relieved from any portion of it; that it is the province of the constituent to judge and command, and *his* to believe and obey. Can it be really thought, that the official oath of a senator to support the constitution of the United States, is subject to an exception which exempts him from the duty of supporting it against infringements attempted by the state legislature that has elected him? That the senator may and ought to take the oath with a mental reservation, that he will support the constitution, unless he shall be commanded by the constituent body to violate it? Surely, the general assembly is not going to give its high sanction to doctrines of this kind, which would sap the foundations of all public virtue. The truth is, that, in all contests between those who exercise authority, and those over whom it is exercised, as to the rightful exercise of such authority,—as to the duty of obedience, or the right of resistance,—both parties must, in the nature of things, judge for themselves; and the only difference between them is, that the party resisting power, resists at his peril; which alone suffices, in general, to determine him against resistance, except in extreme cases. To say, that those who hold power have the sole right to exercise judgment, and that those over whom power is exercised, have no right to judge for themselves whether they are oppressed or not, were to affirm the very doctrine of passive obedience and non-resistance, maintained by the university of Oxford in the reign of James II. The commands of the constituent legislature cannot justify, or even excuse, the senator, in a palpable violation of the constitution, or in an act of moral turpitude. The servant, nay, even the slave, is not bound to obey, and more, is not excusable for obeying, the unlawful commands of his master.

Then, as to "the prudence of resistance" in this case. All questions of resistance to authority present a compound consideration of right and expediency. However just and right resistance may be in itself, yet it ought never to be resorted to, unless there be a reasonable hope of correcting the mischief, and securing some good end; nor ought any man, however strong his sense of wrong, and injustice, to involve others with himself, in a hopeless, useless, dangerous effort of resistance. This last objection to the course I have resolved to pursue, I have taken the most effectual care to obviate. I have asked the advice of no man, much as I desired the advice of my friends, and willingly as I should have sought it, if I could have done so, without danger of committing them, as men of honour, to share my fate: I have, indeed, communicated my purpose to very few, and to them in the strictest confidence: I have held no correspondence with any member of the general assembly on this subject, since the commencement of its present session, and, in fact, have written only one short note on a different topic to one of them, lest correspondence commenced on other subjects might lead to correspondence on this. This line of conduct had its inconveniences, to which I was not insensible, but I could not depart from it, without abandoning the system of action I had prescribed for myself, and involving others in my difficulties. No man, for aught that I have done, stands committed to share my fate: for aught that I have done to draw others to my support, I stand alone, sustained only by the conscious virtue of my motives and purposes, and a confidence in my own firmness to meet and abide the result. I *trust* I am actuated by no false pride, and no vainglorious opinion of my own importance (for, if I am, the fault is not owing to the want of a most careful self-examination and scrutiny) in thinking, and declaring my belief and humble hope, that the sacrifice I am making of myself, of all prospects of political honours and distinction in future, and even of the affectionate regards of many whose esteem and confidence I have hitherto enjoyed, may have some slight effect, in saving the constitution of my country from violation; saving the senate from subversion, and with it saving the state sovereignties from utter prostration; and even placing the right of instruction itself, upon the only stable grounds on which it can be rested, by so guarding it from abuse and misapplication, that it may appear to all men's minds, an agent of good, worthy to be respected and preserved, not an evil principle, to be eschewed and rooted out.

I see from the vote of the two houses of the general assembly on the second of the resolutions transmitted to me, that most of my own friends approved the principle therein declared—that it is the duty of the senator to obey, implicitly obey, the instruction of the state legislature, or resign. All these will, of course, disapprove the resolution I have taken. This is ominous, probably decisive, of the destiny that awaits me. In all likelihood, before the heats that now inflame the public mind, shall be extinguished, I shall attain to an age, which will render me unfit for any active public service. I have the clearest perception of all these consequences. But I hope I shall be pardoned for saying, that I cannot, and will not, do what I think wrong in principle, and mischievous, fatal, in its effects, to comply with the wishes of my friends, and to retain their approbation and support, any more than to avert or escape from the rage of my enemies. I do not pretend to be insensible to popularity, especially to the favour of my native state; but if I know myself, my love of popularity has its source rather in my own attachment to the people, than in the hope or desire of any rewards they can bestow; and I would not betray what I think the interest of Virginia, to gain her favour, dear as it is to me. I care for no fame, but that which I have little prospect of obtaining—the renown of good and useful deeds, which survives the author of them.

It is proper that I should tell the general assembly and the public, that when I returned home, after the termination of the session of congress of 1834-5, I had come to the resolution to leave the senate—that I would keep it in my power to take my seat, under my last election to this body, in case an extra session of congress should be called by the president; but that I would resign the office, or (which was the same thing) decline the acceptance of it, at the commencement of the then next session of the general assembly. This resolution, dictated by a sense of the duty I owed my family, was so openly announced, that I suppose it must have been generally known, at least in the city of Richmond. It was not until the scheme of "instructing me out of my seat," was agitated, after the result of the spring elections was ascertained, that I saw, that if I should decline to take my seat under my new appointment, it would have precisely the same pernicious consequences, which would result from a forced resignation, under instructions which I could not in conscience obey—that I changed the resolution I had previously formed, and determined to accept the appointment, and abide the consequences. I shall hold my seat, only long enough to signalize my resistance to what I honestly believe to be unconstitutional instructions. I say now, that I shall, in all events, resign it, at the commencement of the next session of the general assembly.

I beg leave also to explain the reason, that induced me not to divulge the course I intended to pursue, until the final action of the general assembly on the expunging resolutions, was announced. I did not think it proper or respectful to the general assembly, to invite a contest with it, which it might possibly be not unwilling to avoid, by declaring in anticipation, that I would not obey such instructions, as I understood were in contemplation, if they should be given me.

I have only to add, that, as to the merits of the resolution of the senate of the 28th March, 1834, which the general assembly condemns,—both in respect to the truth of the proposition it contains, and the right of the senate to act upon the subject,—these are points which ought properly to be discussed in the senate; and that I shall endeavour to vindicate the resolution, in both aspects, if and whenever it shall be brought under consideration.

Praying you, gentlemen, to lay this letter before the two houses of the general assembly in which you respectively preside,

I have the honour to be, with all respect, your and their humble servant,

B. W. LEIGH.

On motion of Mr. Stanard, the same was ordered to be laid upon the table, and 185 copies thereof were ordered to be printed for the use of the general assembly, on motion of Mr. Griggs.

The orders of the day on the state of the commonwealth, were, on motion of Mr. Gilmer, ordered to be postponed until Monday.

An engrossed bill, forming a new county out of the county of Frederick, was read a third time, a blank therein was filled, and the question being put upon its passage, was determined in the affirmative. Ayes 84, noes 29.

The ayes and noes thereupon being required by Mr. Smith of Frederick, (and sustained according to the rule of the house,) were as follow:

Ayes, Messrs. Banks, (speaker,) Drummond, Layne, Wiley, Garland of Amherst, Pate, Hunter of Berkeley, Henshaw, Miller, Decamps, Mallory, Booker, Austin, Beuhring, Samuel, Richardson, Johnson, Vaughan, Hickerson, Steger, Holland, Watts, Smith of Gloucester, Watkins, Hail of Grayson, Wethered, Avent, Nixon, Mullen, Kincheloe, Bouts, Fontaine, Holleman, Griggs, Berry, Summers, Hooe, Carter, Neill, Hays, Straton, Taylor of Loudoun, Harris, Ragsdale, Waggener, Rogers, Garland of Mecklenburg, Willey, Morgan, Chapman, Ingles, Benton, Brown of Nelson, Chapline, Masters, Woolfolk, Adams, M'Coy, Swanson, Witcher, Cackley, Carroll, Madison, Morris, Shands, Williams, Marteney, Nicklin, Dorman, Moffett, Conrad, Jessee, M'Mullen, Bare, Rinker, Crutchfield, Moncure, Hargrave, Gillespie, Delashmutt, Gibson, Jett, Prentiss and Saunders.—84.

Noes, Messrs. Grinalds, Brooke, Craig, Wilson of Botetourt, Turnbull, Daniel, Christian, Hill, Servant, Hunter of Essex, Ball, Price, Bowen, Davison, Smith of Frederick, Carrington, Coleman, Sloan, Robinson, Beard, Sherrard, Fitzgerald, Almond, Leyburn, Harley, Butts, Cunningham, Brown of Petersburg, and Stanard.—29.

Resolved, That the bill do pass, and that the title be, "an act forming a new county out of the county of Frederick."

Ordered, That the clerk communicate the same to the senate and request their concurrence.

Mr. Brown of Petersburg, from the committee of finance, presented a report upon the petition of William I. Frazer, and Mary Ann Anthony.

And a bill providing for the repairs and preservation of the public arms, the armory buildings, and for other purposes.

Mr. Cooke, according to order, presented a bill to increase the number of the trustees in the town of Portsmouth, and to enlarge their powers and privileges.

Mr. Taylor of Middlesex, reported with amendment, an act to amend the act, entitled, "an act to amend and reduce into one act, all acts and parts of acts to prevent the destruction of oysters," passed March 24th, 1831.

Which were received and laid upon the table.

On motion of Mr. Brown of Petersburg, *Ordered,* That leave be given to bring in a bill appropriating money to pay the purchase money of Brown's warehouse, lately purchased by the executive in pursuance of an act of assembly, and that Messrs. Brown of Petersburg, Stanard, Carter, Witcher, Carrington, Johnson, Mallory, and Taylor of Middlesex, prepare and bring in the same; and that they have leave to sit during the session of this house.

Mr. Brown of Petersburg, subsequently presented the said bill, which on his motion, was read the first and second times, and (by general consent,) ordered to be engrossed and read a third time.

A bill prescribing the punishment of offences committed on rail-roads, was taken up on motion of Mr. Dorman, read the first and second times, and (by general consent,) ordered to be engrossed and read a third time.

Mr. Garland of Mecklenburg, from the committee of schools and colleges, reported without amendment, a bill to incorporate the trustees of the Lynchburg female academy, which was received and laid upon the table.

An engrossed bill to incorporate the Virginia insurance company was read a third time, and a blank therein was filled:

Resolved, That the bill do pass, and that the title be, "an act to incorporate the Virginia insurance company."

An engrossed bill to change the time of holding the county court of Alleghany county, was read a third time:

Resolved, That the bill do pass, and that the title be, "an act to change the time of holding the county court of Alleghany county."

An engrossed bill to authorize additions to the town of Farmville in the county of Prince Edward, was read a third time:

Resolved, That the bill do pass, and that the title be, "an act to authorize additions to the town of Farmville in the county of Prince Edward."

An engrossed bill to incorporate the Red springs company, was read a third time:

Resolved, That the bill do pass, and that the title be, "an act to incorporate the Red springs company."

Ordered, That the clerk communicate the same to the senate and request their concurrence.

On motion of Mr. Daniel, the house adjourned until Monday morning 10 o'clock.

MONDAY, March 7th, 1836.

On motion of Mr. Carter, *Resolved unanimously by the general assembly of Virginia,* That the governor of this commonwealth be, and he is hereby requested to procure a sword with appropriate devices and inscriptions, and to cause the same to be presented to the son of lieutenant colonel George Armistead, late of the army of the United States, as an evidence of the high esteem and admiration entertained by his native state, for the courage and soldierlike conduct of colonel Armistead in the cannonade of Fort George by Niagara, and in the gallant defence of Fort M'Henry on the 14th of September, 1814.

Ordered, That the clerk communicate the said resolution to the senate and request their concurrence.

On motion of Mr. Murdaugh,

Whereas, Elie A. F. Valette, a native citizen of this commonwealth, while acting as a lieutenant in the navy of the United States, in the memorable action fought on Lake Champlain, on the eleventh of September, 1814, between the squadron of the United States and that of Great Britain, "*nobly distinguished*" himself, by discharging the duties of his station with such "*able effect,*" as to receive the special approbation of his commander: Therefore,

Resolved unanimously by the general assembly of the commonwealth of Virginia, That the governor be requested, in the name of the general assembly, to present to captain E. A. F. Valette of the United States navy, a sword, ornamented with suitable devices, emblematical of the action between the two squadrons, as a testimonial of their high regard for the gallantry and distinguished patriotism which he displayed on that occasion.

Ordered, That the clerk communicate the same to the senate and request their concurrence.

Mr. Dorman, from the committee for courts of justice, presented a bill limiting recoveries on certain judgments therein mentioned.

And a bill suspending the processioning of lands in counties therein mentioned.

Mr. Carter, from the committee on banks, reported with amendment, a bill concerning savings institutions.

And presented a bill incorporating the Petersburg savings institutions.

Mr. Servant reported without amendment, a bill to amend the several acts concerning pilots.

Which bills were received and laid upon the table.

An engrossed bill to provide for the construction of the eastern section of the road on the route surveyed from Huntersville to Parkersburg, was taken up on motion of Mr. Price, and read a third time:

Resolved, That the bill do pass, and that the title be, "an act to provide for the construction of the eastern section of the road on the route surveyed from Huntersville to Parkersburg."

Ordered, That the clerk communicate the said bill to the senate and request their concurrence.

An engrossed bill to provide for the payment of the purchase money of Brown's warehouse, was taken up on motion of Mr. Stanard, and read a third time:

Resolved, That the bill do pass, and that the title be, "an act to provide for the payment of the purchase money of Brown's warehouse."

An engrossed bill incorporating the Laurel Hill turnpike company, was read a third time:

Resolved, That the bill do pass, and (the title being amended on motion of Mr. Marteney,) that the title be, "an act providing for the construction of a turnpike road from the town of Beverley in Randolph county, to the town of Clarksburg in Harrison county."

An engrossed bill to amend the act, entitled, "an act incorporating a company to erect a toll-bridge over the Ohio river at Wheeling," passed February 17th, 1816, was read a third time.

Resolved, That the bill do pass, and that the title be, "an act to amend the act, entitled, 'an act incorporating a company to erect a toll-bridge over the Ohio river at Wheeling,'" passed February 17th, 1816.

An engrossed bill to authorize a subscription on behalf of the state, to the stock of the Lewisburg and Blue Sulphur springs turnpike company, was read a third time:

Resolved, That the bill do pass, and that the title be, "an act to authorize a subscription on behalf of the state to the stock of the Lewisburg and Blue Sulphur springs turnpike company."

An engrossed bill to amend the act concerning fraudulent devises, was read a third time:

Resolved, That the bill do pass, and that the title be, "an act to amend the act concerning fraudulent devises."

An engrossed bill to incorporate the trustees of the Estillville academy, was read a third time:

Resolved, That the bill do pass, and that the title be, "an act to incorporate the trustees of the Estillville academy."

Ordered, That Mr. Wethered carry the same to the senate and request their concurrence.

An engrossed bill to amend the act, entitled, "an act to alter and reform the mode of proceeding in the courts of chancery," was read a third time:

Resolved, That the bill do pass, and that the title be, "an act to amend the act, entitled, 'an act to alter and reform the mode of proceeding in the courts of chancery.'"

An engrossed bill establishing a new regiment in the county of Preston, was read a third time:

Resolved, That the bill do pass, and that the title be, "an act establishing a new regiment in the county of Preston."

Ordered, That Mr. Wethered carry the same to the senate and request their concurrence.

An engrossed bill to incorporate the United States copper mining company, was read a third time:

Resolved, That the bill do pass, and that the title be, "an act to incorporate the United States copper mining company."

An engrossed bill requiring of the inspectors of tobacco in this commonwealth to distinguish in their inspections between tobacco produced in Virginia and that produced in other states, was read a third time:

Resolved, That the bill do pass, and that the title be, "an act requiring of the inspectors of tobacco in this commonwealth to distinguish in their inspections between tobacco produced in Virginia and that produced in other states."

An engrossed bill to amend an act incorporating the Spring creek turnpike company, was read a third time:

Resolved, That the bill do pass, and that the title be, "an act to amend an act incorporating the Spring creek turnpike company."

An engrossed bill to incorporate the coal working company of Richmond and Manchester, was read a third time

Resolved, That the bill do pass, and that the title be, "an act to incorporate the coal working company of Richmond and Manchester."

An engrossed bill concerning the county of Gloucester, was read a third time:

Resolved, That the bill do pass, and that the title be, "an act concerning the county of Gloucester."

Ordered, That the clerk communicate the said bills to the senate and request their concurrence.

An engrossed bill directing the sale of the stock held by the state in joint stock companies incorporated for purposes of internal improvement, was read a third time, and the question being put upon its passage, was determined in the negative. Ayes 21, noes 90.

The ayes and noes thereupon being required by Mr. Woolfolk, (and sustained according to the rule of the house,) are as follow:

Ayes, Messrs. Layne, Garland of Amherst, Price, Strange, Watkins, Wethered, Sloan, Harrison, Kincheloe, Holleman, Griggs, Hays, Harris, Morgan, Brown of Nelson, Murdaugh, M'Coy, Oackley, Moffett, Rinker and Prentiss.—21.

Noes, Messrs. Banks, (speaker,) Grinalds, Wiley, Craig, Campbell, Pate, Henshaw, Miller, Wilson of Botetourt, Decamps, Turnbull, Mallory, Booker, Austin, Beuhring, Daniel, Samuel, Christian, Richardson, Hill, Wilson of Cumberland, Vaughan, Hunter of Essex, Ball, Hickerson, Steger, Holland, Bowen, Davison, Watts, Smith of Gloucester, Hail of Grayson, Avent, Coleman, Nixon, Mullen, Botts, Fontaine, Berry, Summers, Fleet, Hooe, Robinson, Carter, Neill, Straton, Taylor of Loudoun, Ragsdale, Taylor of Mathews and Middlesex, Rogers, Garland of Mecklenburg, Chapman, Ingles, Sherrard, Benton, Cooke, Leland, Fitzgerald, Chapline, Masters, Woolfolk, Almond, Adams, Swanson, Witcher, Carroll, Madison, Morris, Shands, Williams, Marteney, Nicklin, Dorman, Leyburn, Conrad, Jessee, M'Mullen, Bare, Harley, Crutchfield, Moncure, Hargrave, Gillespie, Delashmutt, Gibson, Jett, Saunders, Cunningham, Brown of Petersburg, and Stanard.—90.

Resolved, That the said bill be rejected.

The house, according to the orders of the day, resolved itself into a committee of the whole house on the state of the commonwealth, Mr. Holleman in the chair; and after some time spent therein, the speaker resumed the chair, and Mr. Holleman reported that the said committee had, according to order, taken into consideration a report of the committee of finance upon the revenue and expenditures and debt of the commonwealth; also a bill imposing taxes for the support of government; and a bill appropriating the public revenue, and made sundry amendments thereto; and a bill to amend the act concerning merchants' licenses, which he was instructed to report without amendment.

On motion of Mr. Carter, the said report and bills were ordered to be laid upon the table.

On motion of Mr. Hunter of Berkeley, the house adjourned until to-morrow 10 o'clock.

TUESDAY, March 8th, 1836.

A communication from the senate by their clerk:

IN SENATE, March 7th, 1836.

The senate have passed the bill, entitled,

"An act to change the time of holding the county court of Alleghany county," with an amendment, in which they request the concurrence of the house of delegates.

The said amendment being twice read, was, on the question put thereupon, agreed to by the house.

Ordered, That the clerk inform the senate thereof.

On motion of Mr. Gregory, a bill, entitled, "an act to change the times of holding the courts in the third judicial circuit, and for other purposes," with the amendments thereto proposed by the senate, was taken up, and the said amendments being twice read, were, on questions severally put thereupon, agreed to by the house.

Ordered, That the clerk inform the senate thereof.

Mr. Shands, from the committee for courts of justice, presented a bill regulating the commissions on sales made under decrees in chancery, and for other purposes, which was received and laid upon the table.

The following bills, heretofore reported with amendments from the several committees to which the same had been committed, were taken up, and the said amendments being severally agreed to by the house, the said bills as amended, were ordered to be engrossed and read a third time.

A bill to amend the act, entitled, "an act to amend and reduce into one act, all acts and parts of acts, to prevent the destruction of oysters," passed March 24th, 1831; and

A bill concerning savings institutions.

A bill repealing the law requiring lands in this commonwealth to be processioned so far as the same may apply to the county of Patrick, with the amendments thereto proposed by the committee for courts of justice, was taken up, and amendments having been offered to the said amendments, the same was, on motion of Mr. Crutchfield, ordered to be laid upon the table.

A bill to suppress the circulation of incendiary publications, and for other purposes, was read a second time, and on motion of Mr. Stanard, ordered to be committed to a committee of the whole house on the state of the commonwealth.

Resolved, That this house will, on to-morrow, resolve itself into a committee of the whole house, to take said bill into consideration.

A bill to amend the several acts concerning pilots, was ordered to be laid upon the table, on motion of Mr. Stanard.

The following bills, heretofore reported without amendment, were taken up, and ordered to be engrossed and read a third time.

A bill to incorporate the Portsmouth and Chesapeake steam-boat company.

A bill incorporating the Lynchburg and Campbell court-house turnpike company.

A bill to authorize a subscription on behalf of the state to the stock of the Pittsylvania and Lynchburg turnpike company, and for other purposes.

A bill to incorporate the trustees of the Lynchburg female academy; and

A bill changing the Hunting run gold mining company into a company for mining and manufacturing iron and steel.

The following bills were read a second time, and ordered to be engrossed and read a third time, viz:

A bill to incorporate the Goochland mining company.

A bill to equalize the regimental districts in the county of Rockingham, and for other purposes.

A bill to incorporate the trustees of Charlestown athenæum and female academy; and

A bill to amend the several acts concerning the Petersburg rail-road company.

A bill to amend an act, entitled, "an act to enact with amendments an act of the general assembly of North Carolina, entitled, 'an act to incorporate the Greensville and Roanoke rail-road company,'" passed February 7th, 1834, was, on motion of Mr. Cooke, ordered to be laid upon the table.

A message from the senate by Mr. M'Mahon:

MR. SPEAKER,—The senate have passed a bill, entitled, "an act forming a new county out of the county of Frederick." They have also passed a bill, entitled, "an act forming a new county out of parts of the counties of Shenandoah and Frederick," with amendments, in which they request the concurrence of the house of delegates. And then he withdrew.

The said bill and amendments were received and laid upon the table.

An engrossed bill incorporating the Staunton and Augusta springs turnpike company, was read a third time:

Resolved, That the bill do pass, and that the title be, "an act incorporating the Staunton and Augusta springs turnpike company."

Ordered, That the clerk communicate the said bill to the senate and request their concurrence.

A bill appropriating the surplus revenue of the literary fund, together with the amendments thereto proposed by the committee of schools and colleges, was taken up on motion of Mr. Watkins; whereupon, a motion was made by him that the farther consideration of the said bill be indefinitely postponed; and the question being put thereupon, was determined in the negative. Ayes 11, noes 100.

The ayes and noes thereupon being required by Mr. Dorman, (and sustained according to the rule of the house,) were as follow:

Ayes, Messrs. Banks, (speaker,) Mallory, Hill, Strange, Watkins, Ragsdale, Chapman, Brown of Nelson, Shands, Nicklin and Gillespie.—11.

Noes, Messrs. Grinalds, Layne, Wiley, Garland of Amherst, Brooke, Craig, Campbell, Páte, Hunter of Berkeley, Miller, Wilson of Botetourt, Decamps, Turnbull, Booker, Austin, Beuhring, Samuel, Christian, Richardson, Johnson, Wilson of Cumberland, Vaughan, Hunter of Essex, Ball, Hickerson, Price, Steger, Hale of Franklin, Holland, Bowen, Davison, Watts, Smith of Gloucester, Hail of Grayson, Wethered, Avent, Coleman, Sloan, Nixon, Goodall, Mullen, Harrison, Kincheloe, Botts, Fontaine, Holleman, Gregory, Griggs, Summers, Fleet, Hooe, Robinson, Neill, Hays, Straton, Beard, Taylor of Loudoun, Harris, Waggener, Rogers, Garland of Mecklenburg, Morgan, Sherrard, Benton, Murdaugh, Cooke, Leland, Chapline, Masters, Woolfolk, Almond, Adams, M'Coy, Swanson, Witcher, Cackley, Madison, Morris, Williams, Marteney, Dorman, Leyburn, Moffett, Conrad, Jessee, M'Mullen, Bare, Rinker, Butts, Crutchfield, Moncure, Hargrave, Delashmutt, Gibson, Jett, Prentiss, Saunders, Cunningham, Brown of Petersburg, and Stanard.—100.

A motion was then made by Mr. Garland of Mecklenburg, that the said bill and amendments be recommitted to the said committee; and the question being put thereupon, was determined in the negative. Ayes 38, noes 77.

The ayes and noes thereupon being required by Mr. Harrison, (and sustained according to the rule of the house,) were as follow:

Ayes, Messrs. Banks, (speaker,) Wiley, Hunter of Berkeley, Miller, Wilson of Botetourt, Decamps, Samuel, Christian, Johnson, Hill, Wilson of Cumberland, Strange, Smith of Gloucester, Watkins, Coleman, Goodall, Botts, Fontaine, Summers, Hooe, Robinson, Carter, Harris, Taylor of Mathews and Middlesex, Rogers, Garland of Mecklenburg, Sherrard, Benton, Brown of Nelson, Cooke, Witcher, Madison, Dorman, Leyburn, Harley, Cunningham, Brown of Petersburg, and Stanard.—38.

Noes, Messrs. Grinalds, Layne, Brooke, Craig, Henshaw, Turnbull, Mallory, Booker, Austin, Beuhring, Richardson, Vaughan, Servant, Hunter of Essex, Ball, Hickerson, Price, Steger, Hale of Franklin, Holland, Bowen, Davison, Smith of Frederick, Watts, Hail of Grayson, Wethered, Avent, Sloan, Nixon, Mullen, Harrison, Kincheloe, Holleman, Gregory, Fleet, Neill, Hays, Straton, Beard, Taylor of Loudoun, Ragsdale, Waggener, Morgan, Chapman, Ingles, Murdaugh, Leland, Chapline, Masters, Woolfolk, Almond, Adams, M'Coy, Swanson, Carroll, Morris, Shands, Williams, Marteney, Nicklin, Moffett, Conrad, Jessee, M'Mullen, Bare, Rinker, Butts, Crutchfield, Moncure, Hargrave, Gillespie, Delashmutt, Gibson, Jett, Prentiss and Saunders.—77.

The said amendments proposed by the said committee, were then agreed to by the house; whereupon, a substitute was offered thereto by Mr. Prentiss, and the said bill and proposed substitute was, on motion of Mr. Garland of Mecklenburg, ordered to be laid upon the table.

On motion of Mr. Carter, a bill increasing the banking capital of this commonwealth, together with the amendments thereto proposed by the committee of the whole house, was taken up, and the said amendments being amended, on motions made by Mr. Brown of Petersburg, and as amended agreed to by the house; and the said bill being further amended, on motions severally made, a motion was then made by Mr. Carter, that the said bill and amendments be recommitted, with instructions to report the bill with amendments reducing the increase of capital to five millions, distributed to the places designated by the present bill, by the following means: first, by a new bank to be located at   , with branches; second, by an increase of the capital of the Farmers bank of Virginia, and the Bank of Virginia; third, by increasing the capital of the Bank of the Valley, the North-western bank, and the Merchants and Mechanics bank of Wheeling.

The said bill and amendments, together with the said motion, were then ordered, on motion of Mr. Carter, to be laid upon the table.

And then, on motion of Mr. Mullen, the house adjourned until to-morrow 10 o'clock.

WEDNESDAY, March 9th, 1836.

The bill, entitled, "an act forming a new county out of parts of the counties of Shenandoah and Frederick," with the amendments thereto proposed by the senate, was taken up, and the said amendments being twice read, were, on questions severally put thereupon, agreed to by the house.

Ordered, That the clerk inform the senate thereof.

On motion, *Ordered,* That leave of absence from the service of this house for the remainder of the session be granted to Mr. Ingles, from to-day, and to Mr. Powell, from Saturday last.

Mr. Wiley reported without amendment, a bill to regulate the conduct of boatmen on the Appomattox and Roanoke rivers, and their branches, which was received and laid upon the table.

Mr. Morgan presented a petition of the trustees of the Monongalia academy, praying that a sum supposed to be forfeited to the commonwealth, by the breach of a recognizance of bail given by Jacob Rush and his securities in a case of felony, be released to said trustees, which was ordered to be referred to the committee for courts of justice, that they do examine the matter thereof, and report their opinion thereupon to the house.

Mr. Southall presented petitions of citizens of Albemarle and Buckingham, for the establishment of a bank or branches of some bank at the towns of Charlottesville and Scottsville, which were ordered to be laid upon the table.

A report of the committee on the militia laws was read as follows:

The committee upon the militia laws, have had under consideration the petitions of the citizens of Lexington and the county of Rockbridge, and of the town of Fairfield, praying a change in the organization of the Lexington arsenal, by giving to that establishment a collegiate as well as military character, and have come to the following resolution thereupon:

Resolved, That the said petition is reasonable.

The same committee have also had under consideration the petition of Cornelius C. Baldwin and three others, praying for a change of the mode of preserving and protecting the public arms at the Lexington arsenal, by transferring the same from the arsenal, and establishing a "deaf and dumb asylum" at the said arsenal, and have come to the following resolution thereupon:

Resolved, That the said petition be rejected.

The same committee have also had under consideration a resolution of the house of delegates, instructing them to enquire into the expediency of so amending the 65th section of the militia laws, as to grant the privilege to the commandant of the 147th regiment to appoint a place for training the officers thereof, within the bounds of said regiment, and have come to the following resolution thereupon:

Resolved, That it is inexpedient so to amend the said section of the militia laws.

The said resolutions were, on questions severally put thereupon, agreed to by the house, and a bill was ordered to be brought in conformably with the said first resolution.

A report of the committee of privileges and elections was read as follows:

The committee of privileges and elections, to whom was referred a resolution directing them to enquire into the expediency of so "amending the general election law, as to provide that all the elections in this commonwealth be held on the same day," have had the same under consideration, and have adopted the following resolution thereupon:

Resolved as the opinion of this committee, That it is inexpedient so to amend the general law.

The said resolution was, on the question put thereupon, agreed to by the house, an unsuccessful motion having been made by Mr. Wilson of Botetourt to reverse the decision of the said committee.

The following reports of the committee for courts of justice were read:

The committee for courts of justice have, according to order, had under consideration the petition of Jacob Boush and Toney Boush, free men of colour, to them referred, praying to be permitted to remain in the commonwealth, and have come to the following resolution thereupon:

Resolved as the opinion of this committee, That the prayer of the said petitioners is reasonable.

The committee for courts of justice have, according to order, inquired into the expediency of so amending the act, entitled, "an act requiring the clerks of the county and corporation courts to keep process books," passed the 11th day of March, 1835, as to authorize the clerks of the courts aforesaid to charge for such services the same fees which the clerks of the circuit superior courts of law and chancery are authorized to charge for similar services: Whereupon,

Resolved as the opinion of this committee, That it is expedient so to amend the said act.

The said first resolution was disagreed to, and the last was agreed to by the house, and a bill was ordered to be brought in conformably therewith.

A further report of said committee, rejecting the petition of James D. Grigsby, was, on motion of Mr. M'Mullen, ordered to be laid upon the table.

The following reports of the committee of claims were read:

The committee of claims have, according to order, had under consideration the petition of Levi Simms, to them referred, praying the remission of certain fines imposed upon him for retailing spirituous liquors without license, and have come to the following resolution thereupon:

Resolved as the opinion of this committee, That the prayer of the said petition is reasonable.

The committee of claims have, according to order, had under consideration the petition of John Jordan and

Frederick H. Murrell, partners, trading under the firm of Jordan and Murrell, to them referred, praying compensation of a horse belonging to them that died whilst in the service of the state, in conveying to the penitentiary a criminal sentenced to confinement therein by the circuit superior court of law and chancery for the town of Lynchburg, and have come to the following resolution thereupon:

Resolved as the opinion of this committee, That the prayer of the said petition be rejected.

The said first resolution was disagreed to, and the last was agreed to by the house.

A further report of said committee rejecting the petition of Thomas Byrne, was, on motion of Mr. Hays, ordered to be laid upon the table.

The following reports of the committee of roads and internal navigation were read

The committee of roads and internal navigation have, according to order, had under consideration the petition of John Crouch, Richard Crouch, Thomas Crouch, John Barr and Jesse Snead, praying the incorporation of a joint stock company to construct a rail-road from some point on the James river canal near the Tuckahoe aqueduct, on the western side of Tuckahoe creek in the county of Goochland, to the coal pits on the lands of Temple Redd in the county of Henrico, crossing the works of the Tuckahoe canal company, if necessary; also, the memorial and remonstrance of the president and stockholders of the said Tuckahoe canal company, for and on behalf of the company, in opposition to the prayer of the aforesaid petition: Whereupon,

1. *Resolved as the opinion of this committee,* That the prayer of said petition is reasonable.
2. *Resolved as the opinion of this committee,* That the said memorial and remonstrance be rejected.

The committee of roads and internal navigation have, according to order, had under consideration a resolution to them referred, to inquire into the expediency of changing the mode of constructing the North-western turnpike road, and the superintendence thereof: Whereupon,

Resolved as the opinion of this committee, That it is inexpedient to change the mode of construction of said road and the superintendence thereof.

The said resolutions were, on questions severally put thereupon, agreed to by the house, and a bill was ordered to be brought in conformably with the said first resolution.

A report of the committee of schools and colleges was read as follows:

The committee of schools and colleges have, according to order, had under consideration the petition of the directors of the Female orphan asylum at Fredericksburg, praying an appropriation to said institution, from the unappropriated income of the literary fund, of twelve hundred dollars per annum, or such other sum as may be deemed just and proper: Whereupon,

Resolved as the opinion of this committee, That said petition be rejected.

The said resolution was, on the question put thereupon, agreed to by the house, an unsuccessful motion having been made by Mr. Crutchfield to reverse the decision of the committee.

The following reports of the committee for courts of justice were read:

The committee for courts of justice have, according to order, had under consideration the petition of Charles Williams, a free man of colour, to them referred, praying to be permitted to remain in the commonwealth a limited time, and have come to the following resolution thereupon

Resolved as the opinion of this committee, That the prayer of the said petition is reasonable.

The committee for courts of justice have, according to order, had under consideration the petition of Daniel Starks, a free man of colour, to them referred, praying to be permitted to remain in the commonwealth a limited time, and have come to the following resolution thereupon:

Resolved as the opinion of this committee, That the prayer of the said petition is reasonable.

The committee for courts of justice have, according to order, had under consideration the petition of Stephen, a free man of colour, to them referred, praying to be permitted to remain in the commonwealth, and have come to the following resolution thereupon:

Resolved as the opinion of this committee, That the prayer of the said petition is reasonable.

The said resolutions were, on questions severally put thereupon, agreed to by the house, and bills were ordered conformably therewith.

A report of the committee of propositions and grievances was read as follows:

The committee of propositions and grievances have, according to order, had under consideration several petitions to them referred, and have come to the following resolutions thereupon:

1. *Resolved as the opinion of this committee,* That the petition or memorial of sundry citizens and voters of the county of Princess Anne, praying the repeal of the act, entitled, "an act to authorize a separate election at Kempsville in the county of Princess Anne," passed March 10th, 1835, be rejected, for want of notice.

2. *Resolved as the opinion of this committee,* That the petition of sundry citizens of the county of Page, praying that so much of the act, entitled, "an act forming a new county out of parts of the counties of Shenandoah and Rockingham," passed March 30th, 1831, as requires the county court of the said county to be holden on the *fourth* Monday in every month, may be repealed, and that an act may pass directing that the county court of said county be holden on the *first* Monday in every month, be rejected.

3. *Resolved as the opinion of this committee,* That the petition of sundry property holders and citizens of the town of Petersburg, praying that such an act may pass as will enable the mayor, aldermen, and common councilmen of the town of Petersburg, to proceed in the usual manner to open and graduate a street not exceeding sixty feet in width, from a point at or near the north termination of Union street, running in a direct line, nearly due west, to

Market street, a distance of about six hundred feet, and passing through the southern portion of the improved lot of land belonging to the estate of the late Archibald Moore, and now in the occupancy of John Thompson Robertson, esq., being held by him in virtue of the life interest of his wife (late widow of said Moore,) in the same, be rejected.

4. *Resolved as the opinion of this committee,* That the memorial of John T. Robertson of the town of Petersburg, remonstrating "against a grant of power to the common hall of the town of Petersburg, authorizing them to open a new street somewhere through the lot of the memorialist, so as to connect Union street on the east, with Market street on the west," is reasonable.

5. *Resolved as the opinion of this committee,* That the memorial of Daniel Zane and Ebenezer Zane, proprietors of the island in the Ohio river, opposite the town of Wheeling, commonly called Zane's island, praying that so much of the act passed at the present session, extending and defining the corporation limits of the town of Wheeling, as extends the corporation limits of said town over the territory of the said island may be repealed, be rejected.

The said resolutions were, on questions severally put thereupon, agreed to by the house, except the third and fourth, which were amended on motion of Mr. Brown of Petersburg, so as to reverse the decision of the committee, and as amended, were also agreed to by the house, and a bill was ordered to be brought in conformably with the said third resolution.

Reports of the committee of roads and internal navigation were read as follow:

The committee of roads and internal navigation have, according to order, had under consideration the memorial of the Chesapeake and Ohio canal company, asking further aid to their improvements on the part of this commonwealth: Whereupon,

Resolved as the opinion of this committee, That the said memorial is reasonable.

The committee of roads and internal navigation have, according to order, had under consideration the petition of sundry citizens of the county of Chesterfield and city of Richmond, praying the incorporation of a joint stock company to construct a rail-road from the Chesterfield coal mines, to some point on James river above Bosher's dam; also, the memorial of the president and directors of the Chesterfield rail-road company, in opposition to the prayer of the said petition: Whereupon,

Resolved as the opinion of this committee, That the prayer of said petition is reasonable.

Resolved as the opinion of this committee, That said counter memorial be rejected.

The first resolution was disagreed to, and the remaining resolutions were agreed to by the house, and a bill was ordered to be brought in conformably with the said second resolution.

A further report of the same committee was read as follows:

The committee of roads and internal navigation have, according to order, enquired into "the expediency of incorporating a joint stock company to complete the road from Staunton to the Warm springs, commonly called the 'free road,' and known by that name:" Whereupon,

Resolved as the opinion of this committee, That it is not expedient to incorporate a joint stock company for such purpose.

The said resolution was, on the question put thereupon, agreed to by the house, an unsuccessful motion having been made by Mr. Craig to reverse the decision of the said committee.

A report of the committee of propositions and grievances was read as follows:

The committee of propositions and grievances have, according to order, had under consideration several petitions to them referred, and have come to the following resolutions thereupon:

1. *Resolved as the opinion of this committee,* That the petition of sundry citizens of the county of Henrico, praying the general assembly to establish, in addition to the one central position of the county court-house, two places for holding separate elections, at points convenient to the people of the upper and lower sections of the county, be rejected, for want of sufficient notice.

2. *Resolved as the opinion of this committee,* That the petition of sundry citizens of the county of Harrison, praying that the general assembly will establish a separate election at the house of Robert Reed, on Booth's creek, for the convenience of the persons living between Tygart's Valley and the West Fork rivers, be rejected, for want of notice.

The said resolution was, on the question put thereupon, agreed to by the house.

A report of the committee on the penitentiary institution was read as follows:

The committee on the penitentiary institution have had under consideration petitions of citizens of the counties of Botetourt and Franklin, praying that Eli Blankenship, a prisoner in said institution, may be released from confinement, and be pardoned: Whereupon,

Resolved as the opinion of this committee, That the said petition be rejected.

The said resolution was, on motion of Mr. Wilson of Botetourt, ordered to be laid upon the table.

A bill to authorize a separate election at the house of William Pulliam, in the county of Henry, was taken up on motion of Mr. Fontaine, read the first, and ordered to be read a second time.

A report of the committee of propositions and grievances, reporting reasonable the petition of citizens of the county of Fayette, for submitting to the people of said county the question of the location of their seat of justice, was, on motion of Mr. Price, ordered to be laid upon the table.

A report of the committee of roads and internal navigation, rejecting petitions of citizens of Richmond, Buckingham and Powhatan, for a rail-road on the ridge between Richmond and Lynchburg, was, on motion of Mr. Booker, ordered to be laid upon the table.

The house, according to the order of the day, resolved itself into a committee of the whole house on the state of the commonwealth, Mr. Summers in the chair; and after some time spent therein, the speaker resumed the chair, and Mr. Summers reported, that the said committee had, according to order, taken into consideration a bill to suppress the circulation of incendiary publications, and for other purposes, and instructed him to report the same with sundry amendments.

The said amendments were amended by the house, and as amended, on questions severally put thereupon, agreed to.

A motion was then made by Mr. Gregory further to amend the said bill, by inserting after the first section the following:

"*Be it enacted*, That no citizen or resident of this state shall hereafter purchase from or sell to any member of an abolition or anti-slavery society within the limits of this state, his or her factors or agents, knowing them to be such, any article or commodity whatsoever, within the limits of this state, nor directly nor indirectly engage in any traffic, dealing or partnership with any such members, their factors or agents; and any person herein offending shall, on conviction, forfeit and pay the sum of   dollars, one moiety to the use of the commonwealth, for the benefit of the literary fund, and the other to the informer, or the person who will sue for the same, to be recovered with costs, by action of debt or information, in any court of record in this commonwealth."

And the question being put thereupon, was determined in the negative. Ayes 9, noes 91.

The ayes and noes thereupon having been required by Mr. Gregory, (and sustained according to the rule of the house,) are as follow:

Ayes, Messrs. Drummond, Wiley, Booker, Strange, Watkins, Avent, Gregory, Garland of Mecklenburg, and Moncure.—9.

Noes, Messrs. Banks (speaker), Grinalds, Southall, Layne, Garland of Amherst, Craig, Hunter of Berkeley, Henshaw, Wilson of Botetourt, Decamps, Turnbull, Mallory, Austin, Beuhring, Daniel, Samuel, Johnson, Hill, Wilson of Cumberland, Vaughan, Hunter of Essex, Ball, Smith of Fauquier, Hickerson, Price, Steger, Holland, Davison, Watts, Hail of Grayson, Coleman, Sloan, Nixon, Goodall, Mullen, Harrison, Kincheloe, Botts, Fontaine, Holleman, Summers, Fleet, Hooe, Robinson, Neill, Hays, Straton, Beard, Taylor of Loudoun, Harris, Taylor of Mathews and Middlesex, Waggener, Morgan, Chapman, Sherrard, Benton, Brown of Nelson, Murdaugh, Cooke, Fitzgerald, Chapline, Masters, Adams, M'Coy, Swanson, Witcher, Cackley, Hopkins, Morris, Shands, Marteney, Nicklin, Dorman, Leyburn, Moffett, Conrad, Jessee, M'Mullen, Bare, Harley, Butts, Crutchfield, Hargrave, Gillespie, Delashmutt, Gibson, Jett, Prentiss, Saunders, Cunningham, Brown of Petersburg, and Stanard.—91.

The said bill was then further amended on motions severally made, and as amended, ordered to be engrossed and read a third time.

An engrossed bill to incorporate the Gills mountain mining company, was read a third time:

Resolved, That the bill do pass, and that the title be, "an act to incorporate the Gills mountain mining company."

Ordered, That the clerk communicate the same to the senate and request their concurrence.

Mr. Botts presented a petition of the officers constituting the court martial held in the city of Richmond, on the trial of ensign Bentley, asking to be allowed compensation for certain days attendance on said court, which has been refused by the executive, which was ordered to be referred to the committee on the militia laws, that they do examine the matter thereof, and report their opinion thereupon to the house.

On motion of Mr. Botts, the house adjourned until to-morrow morning 10 o'clock.

THURSDAY, March 10th, 1836.

A communication from the senate by their clerk:

IN SENATE, March 9th, 1836.

The senate have passed the bills, entitled,
"An act to provide for the payment of the purchase money of Brown's warehouse."
"An act to incorporate the Red springs company."
"An act requiring the inspectors of tobacco in this commonwealth to distinguish in their inspections between tobacco produced in Virginia and that produced in other states."
"An act to amend the act, entitled, 'an act to alter and reform the mode of proceeding in the courts of chancery.'"
"An act to authorize a subscription on behalf of the state to the stock of the Lewisburg and Blue Sulphur springs turnpike company."
"An act to amend the act concerning fraudulent devises."
"An act concerning the county of Gloucester."
"An act to incorporate the trustees of the Estillville academy."
"An act to authorize additions to the town of Farmville, in the county of Prince Edward."
"An act establishing a new regiment in the county of Preston;" and
"An act to amend an act incorporating the Spring creek turnpike company.".

And they have agreed to the resolution voting a sword to the son of lieutenant colonel George Armistead of the army of the United States.

On motion of Mr. Crutchfield, *Ordered*, That leave be given to bring in a bill to authorize the common council of Fredericksburg to subscribe for stock of the Rappahannock and Blue Ridge rail-road, and that Messrs. Crutchfield, Hill, Heoe, Woolfolk, Harris, Nicklin, Moncure and Williams, prepare and bring in the same.

Mr. Harrison, from the joint committee on the penitentiary institution, presented a report upon the state of that institution, which was received and laid upon the table.

On motion of Mr. Brooke, *Ordered*, That leave be given to bring in a bill for a further appropriation of money to complete the additional buildings and cross walls of the Western lunatic asylum, and that Messrs. Brooke, Craig, Dorman, Summers, M'Coy, Wilson of Botetourt, Conrad and Leyburn, prepare and bring in the same.

On motion of Mr. Davison, *Ordered*, That leave be given to bring in a bill to establish a new regiment in the county of Warren, and that Messrs. Davison, Bowen, Smith of Frederick, Mullen, Sherrard, Bare, Almond and Rinker, prepare and bring in the same.

On motion of Mr. Hill, *Ordered*, That the committee of propositions and grievances be discharged from the consideration of the petition of citizens of Leesburg, and that the same be laid upon the table.

Mr. Hill, from the committee of propositions and grievances, reported with amendment, a bill appointing commissioners to select a site for the seat of justice for the county of Ohio.

And presented a bill changing the name of William H. Riggan to that of William H. Drewry.

A bill placing James river on the footing of a lawful fence so far as concerns the counties of Fluvanna and Albemarle.

A bill to authorize a separate election in the county of Tazewell; and

A bill to authorize Elisha B. Williams to erect a wool carding machine on Jackson's river, near the town of Covington, in the county of Alleghany.

Mr. Stanard, from the committee for courts of justice, presented a report upon the resolution concerning the residence of jailors.

Which bills and report were received and laid upon the table.

Mr. Moffett presented a petition of citizens of the counties of Augusta, Albemarle and Rockingham, asking that a part of the banking capital of the state may be located at the town of Charlottesville, which was ordered to be laid upon the table.

On motion of Mr. Garland of Amherst, *Resolved*, That the committee for courts of justice be requested to report a bill to repeal the law creating the office of vaccine agent.

An engrossed bill to incorporate the Narrow falls turnpike company, was taken up on motion of Mr. Summers, and the question being put upon its passage, together with the ryder heretofore attached thereto, was determined in the negative.

Resolved, That the said bill be rejected.

A bill to amend the several acts concerning pilots, was taken up on motion of Mr. Servant, and the same having been amended on motions severally made, was, as amended, ordered to be engrossed and read a third time.

A bill appropriating the surplus revenue of the literary fund, as amended, together with the substitute thereto proposed by Mr. Prentiss, was taken up on his motion, and the said substitute having been amended on his motion, a motion was made by Mr. Garland of Mecklenburg, further to amend the same.

The said substitute is as follows:

"*Be it enacted*, That all the revenue of the literary fund, unappropriated at this time, shall be added to the fund granted to the primary schools, and be appropriated amongst the several counties and corporations entitled thereto, in the same manner and in the same ratio as is now directed by law: *Provided*, That the school commissioners in any of the counties or corporations may be authorized to apply the additional fund created by this act to the higher branches of literature within their respective counties or corporations: *And provided also*, That a majority of all the commissioners in any county or corporation shall concur therein.

"*Be it further enacted*, That if the school commissioners of any county or corporation shall think proper to appropriate the portion of the fund hereby directed to be distributed, to which said county or corporation may be entitled, or any part thereof, to the support or in aid of any college or academy which may be situated in said county or corporation, it shall be the duty of the trustees of such college or academy, to make annual report to the president and directors of the literary fund of the manner in which such appropriation is employed by them. And it shall be lawful for the said president and directors, at any time, for good cause, to suspend or revoke such appropriation, and direct the same to the use of the primary schools within said county."

Mr. Garland of Mecklenburg proposed to substitute for the foregoing the following:

"*Be it enacted by the general assembly*, That the surplus revenue annually arising from the literary fund, shall be distributed among the several counties and corporations entitled thereto, in the same manner and in the same ratio as is now directed by law, to be applied to the purposes of education in the said counties and corporations, in the manner hereinafter prescribed.

"*Be it further enacted*, That the county or corporation court, they having been summoned for that purpose, and not less than a majority being present, shall be and they are hereby constituted a board of examination, to decide all claims that may be presented by any academy, and should it appear to them by satisfactory evidence, that there exists no corporate academy worthy the benefits of this act, the said court are hereby authorized and directed to appropriate the fund to such schools, within their respective counties or corporations, as to them shall seem best, and they shall report their proceedings to the second auditor, who shall lay the same before the next succeeding general assembly."

And the question being put upon adopting the said last substitute, was determined in the negative. Ayes 31, noes 80.

The ayes and noes thereupon, being required by Mr. Carroll, (and sustained according to the rule of the house,) are as follow:

Ayes, Messrs. Wiley, Garland of Amherst, Brooke, Craig, Hunter of Berkeley, Wilson of Botetourt, Decamps, Daniel, Richardson, Wilson of Cumberland, Smith of Gloucester, Watkins, Botts, Fontaine, Holleman, Griggs, Robinson, Garland of Mecklenburg, Chapman, Benton, Cooke, Leland, Witcher, Hopkins, Madison, Dorman, Leyburn, Jett, Cunningham, Brown of Petersburg, and Stanard.—31.

Noes, Messrs. Banks, (speaker,) Gilmer, Southall, Layne, Campbell, Henshaw, Turnbull, Mallory, Booker, Beuhring, Samuel, Johnson, Hill, Vaughan, Hunter of Essex, Ball, Smith of Fauquier, Hickerson, Price, Steger, Hale of Franklin, Holland, Bowen, Smith of Frederick, Watts, Hail of Grayson, Wethered, Avent, Sloan, Nixon, Goodall, Mullen, Harrison, Kincheloe, Gregory, Summers, Fleet, Carter, Neill, Hays, Straton, Beard, Harris, Ragsdale, Taylor of Mathews and Middlesex, Waggener, Rogers, Willey, Morgan, Sherrard, Brown of Nelson, Murdaugh, Fitzgerald, Masters, Woolfolk, Almond, Adams, M'Coy, Swanson, Cackley, Carroll, Morris, Shands, Williams, Marteney, Nicklin, Moffett, Conrad, Jessee, M'Mullen, Bare, Rinker, Butts, Crutchfield, Moncure, Hargrave, Gillespie, Gibson, Prentiss and Saunders.—80.

The said substitute proposed by Mr. Prentiss, was then amended, on motions severally made, and as amended, is the following:

"*Be it further enacted,* That all the surplus revenue of the literary fund unappropriated at this time, or which may hereafter accrue, shall be annually added to the fund granted to the primary schools, and be appropriated amongst the several counties and corporations entitled thereto, in the same manner and in the same ratio as is now directed by law: *Provided,* That the county or corporation courts in any of the counties or corporations, a majority of the acting magistrates being summoned therefor, may be authorized to apply the additional fund created by this act, or any part thereof, to the colleges or academies within their respective counties or corporations: *And provided also,* That a majority of all the justices in any county or corporation shall concur therein.

"*Be it further enacted,* That if the county or corporation court shall think proper to appropriate the portion of the fund hereby directed to be distributed, to which the said county or corporation may be entitled, or any part thereof, to the support or in aid of any college or academy which may be situated in said county or corporation, it shall be the duty of the trustees of such college or academy to make annual report to the president and directors of the literary fund of the manner in which such appropriation is employed by them. And it shall be lawful for the said president and directors, at any time, for good cause, to suspend or revoke such appropriation, and direct the same to the use of the primary schools within said county or corporation."

And the question being put upon adopting the said substitute as amended, was determined in the affirmative. Ayes 83, noes 20.

The ayes and noes being required thereupon by Mr. Woolfolk, (and sustained according the rule of the house,) are as follow:

Ayes, Messrs. Banks, (speaker,) Layne, Wiley, Campbell, Henshaw, Wilson of Botetourt, Mallory, Booker, Beuhring, Samuel, Richardson, Johnson, Hill, Wilson of Cumberland, Vaughan, Hunter of Essex, Ball, Smith of Fauquier, Hickerson, Price, Steger, Hale of Franklin, Holland, Bowen, Smith of Frederick, Watts, Smith of Gloucester, Hail of Grayson, Wethered, Avent, Coleman, Sloan, Nixon, Goodall, Mullen, Harrison, Kincheloe, Fontaine, Gregory, Neill, Hays, Straton, Beard, Harris, Waggener, Rogers, Morgan, Chapman, Sherrard, Benton, Brown of Nelson, Chapline, Masters, Woolfolk, Almond, Adams, M'Coy, Swanson, Witcher, Cackley, Hopkins, Carroll, Morris, Shands, Williams, Marteney, Nicklin, Moffett, Conrad, Jessee, M'Mullen, Bare, Rinker, Butts, Crutchfield, Moncure, Hargrave, Gillespie, Delashmutt, Gibson, Jett, Prentiss and Saunders.—83.

Noes, Messrs. Gilmer, Southall, Garland of Amherst, Brooke, Craig, Hunter of Berkeley, Decamps, Daniel, Davison, Watkins, Holleman, Garland of Mecklenburg, Murdaugh, Cooke, Leland, Madison, Leyburn, Cunningham, Brown of Petersburg, and Stanard.—20.

The said bill as amended, was then ordered to be engrossed and read a third time.

The speaker laid before the house a communication from John H. Smith esq., which was read as follows:

RICHMOND, March 10th, 1836.

To the Speaker of the House of Delegates of Virginia.

SIR,—I have acted as commissioner of revolutionary claims for the last two years, under an appointment by the legislature. The course of conduct pursued by the governor of this commonwealth in regard to applications for bounty lands for revolutionary services, has put it out of my power to perform the duties which the legislature has imposed on me. I do not wish to hold an office, the duties of which I am not permitted to perform.

Since the first day of September last, (as I have heretofore reported to the general assembly,) no claim for bounty land has been referred to me by the governor. I have had much else to do (besides attention to that branch of my business,) between that time and the present. But if this state of things shall be permitted to exist, the commissioner of revolutionary claims will hereafter have no employment but to receive and reply to letters; to give information respecting claims for military bounty land to those who may call upon him for it; and to investigate and adjust claims against the state of Virginia, for and on account of supplies and advances to the Illinois regiment in the war of the revolution. If the executive proceedings, respecting claims for military land bounties, shall be sanctioned and legalized by legislative action, or, under existing circumstances, by legislative inaction, on the subject, the office of commissioner of revolutionary claims will be almost useless.

I should have been wanting in self-respect, and in the respect which is due to the legislature, (who appointed me,) if I had resigned the office of commissioner before it was known whether the legislature approved or disapproved of the course of executive proceeding above spoken of, and which has been spoken of more at large in my report to the general assembly of the 10th of December, 1835. But the inaction of the legislature on this subject until this late period of its session, and a bill, which, I have been informed, has been reported by a committee of the house of delegates, to abolish the office of commissioner of revolutionary claims, ought to relieve me of all difficulty or doubt respecting the propriety of my resignation. I shall resign the office of commissioner, but I owe it to myself, before resigning, to ask, as I now do respectfully, through you, that a committee of the house of delegates may be appointed to examine my office, and to enquire into the manner in which I have discharged the duties of commissioner.

As soon as this request shall be complied with or refused, (if the house of delegates should think fit to refuse to comply with it,) I shall resign the office of commissioner of revolutionary claims, being firmly convinced, that, under present circumstances, I can do but little good by holding it longer.

I am, very respectfully, yours,

JOHN H. SMITH.

On motion of Mr. Murdaugh, the same was ordered to be laid upon the table.

Mr. Watkins, from the committee of roads and internal navigation, presented a bill incorporating the Chesterfield and James river canal rail-road company; and

A bill incorporating the Tuckahoe rail-road company.

Which were received and laid upon the table.

On motion of Mr. Price, the house adjourned until to-morrow 10 o'clock.

FRIDAY, March 11th, 1836.

A communication from the senate by their clerk:

IN SENATE, March 10th, 1836.

The senate have passed the bills, entitled,

"An act to enact an act of the general assembly of North Carolina, entitled, 'an act to incorporate the Roanoke, Danville and Junction rail-road company.'"

"An act to provide for the construction of the eastern section of the road on the route surveyed from Huntersville to Parkersburg."

"An act concerning the Orange savings society."

"An act to amend the act, entitled, 'an act incorporating a company to erect a toll-bridge over the Ohio river at Wheeling,'" passed February 17th, 1816.

"An act to incorporate the Coal working company at Richmond and Manchester;" and

"An act incorporating the Smithfield savings institution in the county of Isle of Wight."

They have also passed the bills, entitled,

"An act incorporating the Staunton and Augusta springs turnpike company;" and

"An act to incorporate the stockholders of the Lynchburg and Tennessee rail-road company, and to authorize them, or the James river and Kanawha company, to construct a rail road from Lynchburg to Richmond," with amendments, in which they request the concurrence of the house of delegates.

The said amendment proposed by the senate to the bill entitled, "an act incorporating the Staunton and Augusta springs turnpike company," being twice read, was, on the question put thereupon, agreed to by the house.

Ordered, That the clerk inform the senate thereof.

The said amendments to the remaining bill being also twice read, the first six amendments were, on questions severally put thereupon, agreed to by the house; the seventh amendment being read, a motion was made by Mr. Booker to amend the same.

The senate proposed to amend the said bill in the nineteenth section, so as to make the part amended read:

"But if the James river and Kanawha company shall not elect to construct the rail-road from '*Lynchburg to Richmond hereby authorized within five years, and actually and* bona fide *commence the construction of the aforesaid rail-road from Lynchburg to Richmond within seven years, and diligently prosecute the work so that the same shall be completed within twelve years after the passage of this act*,' then the privilege hereby granted to the James river and Kanawha company shall cease," &c.

Mr. Booker proposed to amend the said amendment of the senate by inserting after the word "act," the following:

"Or if the said company shall fail or refuse, by a majority of the votes which can be given by the stockholders for the time being other than the commonwealth, duly ascertained at a special meeting, after due notice, or at the next annual meeting of the said stockholders, to agree and consent that at all future general meetings of the stockholders of the said company, the proxy of the state shall be entitled to one vote on every ten shares of stock owned by the commonwealth in the said company, and shall have the right to vote in all other matters which may be presented to the said meeting, except the election of the directors, and that from and after the next annual meeting of the stock-

And a bill suspending the processioning of lands in counties therein mentioned.

Mr. Carter, from the committee on banks, reported with amendment, a bill concerning savings institutions.

And presented a bill incorporating the Petersburg savings institutions.

Mr. Servant reported without amendment, a bill to amend the several acts concerning pilots.

Which bills were received and laid upon the table.

An engrossed bill to provide for the construction of the eastern section of the road on the route surveyed from Huntersville to Parkersburg, was taken up on motion of Mr. Price, and read a third time:

Resolved, That the bill do pass, and that the title be, "an act to provide for the construction of the eastern section of the road on the route surveyed from Huntersville to Parkersburg."

Ordered, That the clerk communicate the said bill to the senate and request their concurrence.

An engrossed bill to provide for the payment of the purchase money of Brown's warehouse, was taken up on motion of Mr. Stanard, and read a third time:

Resolved, That the bill do pass, and that the title be, "an act to provide for the payment of the purchase money of Brown's warehouse."

An engrossed bill incorporating the Laurel Hill turnpike company, was read a third time:

Resolved, That the bill do pass, and (the title being amended on motion of Mr. Marteney,) that the title be, "an act providing for the construction of a turnpike road from the town of Beverley in Randolph county, to the town of Clarksburg in Harrison county."

An engrossed bill to amend the act, entitled, "an act incorporating a company to erect a toll-bridge over the Ohio river at Wheeling," passed February 17th, 1816, was read a third time.

Resolved, That the bill do pass, and that the title be, "an act to amend the act, entitled, 'an act incorporating a company to erect a toll-bridge over the Ohio river at Wheeling,'" passed February 17th, 1816.

An engrossed bill to authorize a subscription on behalf of the state, to the stock of the Lewisburg and Blue Sulphur springs turnpike company, was read a third time:

Resolved, That the bill do pass, and that the title be, "an act to authorize a subscription on behalf of the state to the stock of the Lewisburg and Blue Sulphur springs turnpike company."

An engrossed bill to amend the act concerning fraudulent devises, was read a third time:

Resolved, That the bill do pass, and that the title be, "an act to amend the act concerning fraudulent devises."

An engrossed bill to incorporate the trustees of the Estillville academy, was read a third time:

Resolved, That the bill do pass, and that the title be, "an act to incorporate the trustees of the Estillville academy."

Ordered, That Mr. Wethered carry the same to the senate and request their concurrence.

An engrossed bill to amend the act, entitled, "an act to alter and reform the mode of proceeding in the courts of chancery," was read a third time:

Resolved, That the bill do pass, and that the title be, "an act to amend the act, entitled, 'an act to alter and reform the mode of proceeding in the courts of chancery.'"

An engrossed bill establishing a new regiment in the county of Preston, was read a third time:

Resolved, That the bill do pass, and that the title be, "an act establishing a new regiment in the county of Preston."

Ordered, That Mr. Wethered carry the same to the senate and request their concurrence.

An engrossed bill to incorporate the United States copper mining company, was read a third time:

Resolved, That the bill do pass, and that the title be, "an act to incorporate the United States copper mining company."

An engrossed bill requiring of the inspectors of tobacco in this commonwealth to distinguish in their inspections between tobacco produced in Virginia and that produced in other states, was read a third time:

Resolved, That the bill do pass, and that the title be, "an act requiring of the inspectors of tobacco in this commonwealth to distinguish in their inspections between tobacco produced in Virginia and that produced in other states."

An engrossed bill to amend an act incorporating the Spring creek turnpike company, was read a third time:

Resolved, That the bill do pass, and that the title be, "an act to amend an act incorporating the Spring creek turnpike company."

An engrossed bill to incorporate the coal working company of Richmond and Manchester, was read a third time:

Resolved, That the bill do pass, and that the title be, "an act to incorporate the coal working company of Richmond and Manchester."

An engrossed bill concerning the county of Gloucester, was read a third time:

Resolved, That the bill do pass, and that the title be, "an act concerning the county of Gloucester."

Ordered, That the clerk communicate the said bills to the senate and request their concurrence.

An engrossed bill directing the sale of the stock held by the state in joint stock companies incorporated for purposes of internal improvement, was read a third time, and the question being put upon its passage, was determined in the negative. Ayes 21, noes 90.

The ayes and noes thereupon being required by Mr. Woolfolk, (and sustained according to the rule of the house,) are as follow:

Ayes, Messrs. Layne, Garland of Amherst, Price, Strange, Watkins, Wethered, Sloan, Harrison, Kincheloe, Holleman, Griggs, Hays, Harris, Morgan, Brown of Nelson, Murdaugh, M'Coy, Cackley, Moffett, Rinker and Prentiss.—21.

Noes, Messrs. Banks, (speaker,) Grinalds, Wiley, Craig, Campbell, Pate, Henshaw, Miller, Wilson of Botetourt, Decamps, Turnbull, Mallory, Booker, Austin, Beuhring, Daniel, Samuel, Christian, Richardson, Hill, Wilson of Cumberland, Vaughan, Hunter of Essex, Ball, Hickerson, Steger, Holland, Bowen, Davison, Watts, Smith of Gloucester, Hail of Grayson, Avent, Coleman, Nixon, Mullen, Botts, Fontaine, Berry, Summers, Fleet, Hooe, Robinson, Carter, Neill, Straton, Taylor of Loudoun, Ragsdale, Taylor of Mathews and Middlesex, Rogers, Garland of Mecklenburg, Chapman, Ingles, Sherrard, Benton, Cooke, Leland, Fitzgerald, Chapline, Masters, Woolfolk, Almond, Adams, Swanson, Witcher, Carroll, Madison, Morris, Shands, Williams, Marteney, Nicklin, Dorman, Leyburn, Conrad, Jessee, M'Mullen, Bare, Harley, Crutchfield, Moncure, Hargrave, Gillespie, Delashmutt, Gibson, Jett, Saunders, Cunningham, Brown of Petersburg, and Stanard.—90.

Resolved, That the said bill be rejected.

The house, according to the orders of the day, resolved itself into a committee of the whole house on the state of the commonwealth, Mr. Holleman in the chair; and after some time spent therein, the speaker resumed the chair, and Mr. Holleman reported that the said committee had, according to order, taken into consideration a report of the committee of finance upon the revenue and expenditures and debt of the commonwealth; also a bill imposing taxes for the support of government; and a bill appropriating the public revenue, and made sundry amendments thereto; and a bill to amend the act concerning merchants' licenses, which he was instructed to report without amendment.

On motion of Mr. Carter, the said report and bills were ordered to be laid upon the table.

On motion of Mr. Hunter of Berkeley, the house adjourned until to-morrow 10 o'clock.

TUESDAY, March 8th, 1836.

A communication from the senate by their clerk:

IN SENATE, March 7th, 1836.

The senate have passed the bill, entitled,

"An act to change the time of holding the county court of Alleghany county," with an amendment, in which they request the concurrence of the house of delegates.

The said amendment being twice read, was, on the question put thereupon, agreed to by the house.

Ordered, That the clerk inform the senate thereof.

On motion of Mr. Gregory, a bill, entitled, "an act to change the times of holding the courts in the third judicial circuit, and for other purposes," with the amendments thereto proposed by the senate, was taken up, and the said amendments being twice read, were, on questions severally put thereupon, agreed to by the house.

Ordered, That the clerk inform the senate thereof.

Mr. Shands, from the committee for courts of justice, presented a bill regulating the commissions on sales made under decrees in chancery, and for other purposes, which was received and laid upon the table.

The following bills, heretofore reported with amendments from the several committees to which the same had been committed, were taken up, and the said amendments being severally agreed to by the house, the said bills as amended, were ordered to be engrossed and read a third time.

A bill to amend the act, entitled, "an act to amend and reduce into one act, all acts and parts of acts, to prevent the destruction of oysters," passed March 24th, 1831; and

A bill concerning savings institutions.

A bill repealing the law requiring lands in this commonwealth to be processioned so far as the same may apply to the county of Patrick, with the amendments thereto proposed by the committee for courts of justice, was taken up, and amendments having been offered to the said amendments, the same was, on motion of Mr. Crutchfield, ordered to be laid upon the table.

A bill to suppress the circulation of incendiary publications, and for other purposes, was read a second time, and on motion of Mr. Stanard, ordered to be committed to a committee of the whole house on the state of the commonwealth.

Resolved, That this house will, on to-morrow, resolve itself into a committee of the whole house, to take said bill into consideration.

A bill to amend the several acts concerning pilots, was ordered to be laid upon the table, on motion of Mr. Stanard.

The following bills, heretofore reported without amendment, were taken up, and ordered to be engrossed and read a third time.

A bill to incorporate the Portsmouth and Chesapeake steam-boat company.

A bill incorporating the Lynchburg and Campbell court-house turnpike company.

A bill to authorize a subscription on behalf of the state to the stock of the Pittsylvania and Lynchburg turnpike company, and for other purposes.

A bill to incorporate the trustees of the Lynchburg female academy; and

A bill changing the Hunting run gold mining company into a company for mining and manufacturing iron and steel.

The following bills were read a second time, and ordered to be engrossed and read a third time, viz:

A bill to incorporate the Goochland mining company.

A bill to equalize the regimental districts in the county of Rockingham, and for other purposes.

A motion was made by Mr. Murdaugh that the house adopt the following resolution:

Resolved, That leave be given to bring in a bill to establish an independent bank in the town of Portsmouth.

And the question being put thereupon, was determined in the negative.

A bill to amend the act, entitled, "an act incorporating the Goose creek navigation company," was taken up on motion of Mr. Beard, read a second time, and ordered to be engrossed and read a third time.

An engrossed bill changing the times of holding the spring terms of the circuit superior courts of law and chancery in the fifth circuit and third judicial district, and for other purposes, was taken up on motion of Mr. Crutchfield, and read a third time; whereupon, a clause by way of ryder thereto, was submitted by Mr. Stanard, which was read the first and second times, and forthwith engrossed and read a third time:

Resolved, That the bill do pass, and (the title being amended on motion of Mr. Stanard,) that the title be, "an act to change the times of holding the courts in the fifth and seventh judicial circuits, and of the counties of Henrico and Powhatan, and the hustings court of the city of Richmond, and for other purposes."

Ordered, That the clerk communicate the same to the senate and request their concurrence.

On motion of Mr. Coleman, the house adjourned until to-morrow 10 o'clock.

SATURDAY, March 12th, 1836.

A communication from the senate by their clerk:

IN SENATE, March 11th, 1836.

The senate have passed the bills, entitled,
"An act to incorporate the city of Wheeling in Ohio county;" and
"An act to incorporate the Gills mountain mining company."

They have also passed the bill, entitled,
"An act to incorporate the United States copper mining company," with amendments, in which they request the concurrence of the house of delegates.

The said amendments being twice read, were, on questions severally put thereupon, agreed to by the house.

Ordered, That the clerk inform the senate thereof.

On motions severally made, *Ordered*, That leave of absence from the service of this house for the remainder of the session, be granted to Mr. Morris from Wednesday next, and to Mr. Avent from to-day.

Mr. Crutchfield, from the committee on the militia laws, reported with amendment, a bill to amend the several acts concerning the public guard in the city of Richmond, which was received and laid upon the table.

And according to order, presented a bill authorizing the common council of Fredericksburg to subscribe for stock in the Rappahannock and Blue Ridge rail-road company.

Mr. Stanard, from the committee for courts of justice, presented a bill allowing Stephen, a man of colour, to remain in the commonwealth.

A bill allowing Charles Williams, a free man of colour, to remain in the commonwealth a limited time.

A bill allowing Daniel Starks, a free man of colour, to remain in the commonwealth a limited time; and

A bill authorizing the county and corporation court clerks to charge fees for certain services performed by them.

Mr. Hill, from the committee of propositions and grievances, presented a bill to incorporate the town of Salem, in the county of Botetourt.

And a bill to authorize William Townes to erect a toll-bridge across the Roanoke river, opposite the town of Clarksville, in the county of Mecklenburg.

Which bills were received, and subsequently read the first and ordered to be read a second time.

On motion of Mr. Stanard, *Ordered*, That the committee for courts of justice be discharged from the consideration of the petition of Littlepage Anderson and his wife Eliza, and that the same be laid upon the table.

A bill repealing the law requiring lands in this commonwealth to be processioned, so far as the same may apply to the county of Patrick, together with the amendments thereto proposed, was taken up, and the said amendments being agreed to by the house, the question was put upon engrossing the same as amended, and reading it a third time, and was determined in the negative.

Resolved, That the said bill be rejected.

The bill, entitled, "an act for incorporating the medical college at Richmond, in Virginia," with the amendments thereto proposed by the senate, was taken up on motion of Mr. Gregory; whereupon a motion was made by Mr. Miller that the farther consideration of the said bill and amendments be indefinitely postponed; and the question being put thereupon, was determined in the affirmative.

Resolved, That the said bill be rejected.

On motion of Mr. Hunter of Berkeley, *Resolved*, That this house will proceed on Tuesday next by joint vote with the senate, to the election of a major general of the third division of militia of this commonwealth, to supply the vacancy occasioned by the death of major general John Smith.

Ordered, That the clerk communicate the same to the senate and request their concurrence.

On motion of Mr. Almond, the fifth rule of the house was suspended for the purpose of reconsidering the vote rejecting the resolution of the committee of roads and internal navigation reporting reasonable the petition of the

Chesapeake and Ohio canal company, and the said resolution was then agreed to by the house, and a bill was ordered to be brought in conformably therewith.

Ordered, That Messrs. Sherrard, Garland of Amherst, Hunter of Berkeley, Griggs, Almond, Willey, Mullen, Davison, Sloan, Nixon, Beard, Chapline and Harrison, prepare and bring in the said bill.

On motion of Mr. Dorman, the following report of the committee for courts of justice was taken up and read as follows:

The committee for courts of justice, to whom were referred the charges preferred by the member from Harrison against judge Duncan, together with the memorial of the judge, and his accompanying explanations, with instructions to enquire into the expediency of enquiring into the truth of the said charges, and if in their opinion it was expedient to make the enquiry, then to enquire into the most regular and convenient mode of conducting the enquiry, have had the same under consideration, and have come to the following resolutions thereupon:

1. *Resolved as the opinion of this committee,* That the first specification is insufficient to ground any proceedings thereon, and it is therefore inexpedient to recommend to the house any action on the said first specification.

2. *Resolved as the opinion of this committee,* That the second specification is insufficient to ground any proceedings thereon, and it is therefore inexpedient to recommend to the house any action on said second specification.

3. *Resolved as the opinion of this committee,* That it is expedient to enquire into the truth of the charge contained in the third specification.

4. *Resolved as the opinion of this committee,* That it is inexpedient to enquire into the matter mentioned in the fourth specification, and in the explanation of the judge in regard thereto.

5. *Resolved as the opinion of this committee,* That it is expedient to enquire into the truth of the charge contained in the fifth specification.

6. *Resolved,* That the session of the legislature is so far advanced that the notice required by the constitution cannot be given to the judge in time to proceed with the investigation this session, without protracting the session to an unusual length, and it is therefore inexpedient to enquire into the truth of the charges at this time.

The said first and second resolutions were, on questions severally put thereupon, agreed to by the house; thereupon, a motion was made by Mr. Price to reverse the decision made by the committee in the third resolution, and then a motion was made by Mr. Gregory, that the said report and resolutions be indefinitely postponed, and the question being put thereupon, was determined in the affirmative. Ayes 69, noes 29.

The ayes and noes thereupon, being required by Mr. Price, (and sustained according to the rule of the house,) are as follow:

Ayes, Messrs. Banks, (speaker,) Grinalds, Drummond, Gilmer, Southall, Wiley, Brooke, Campbell, Pate, Hunter of Berkeley, Henshaw, Miller, Decamps, Turnbull, Mallory, Beuhring, Johnson, Hill, Wilson of Cumberland, Vaughan, Servant, Hunter of Essex, Smith of Fauquier, Price, Steger, Hale of Franklin, Holland, Smith of Gloucester, Watkins, Wethered, Coleman, Sloan, Goodall, Mullen, Kincheloe, Fontaine, Gregory, Griggs, Berry, Summers, Hooe, Robinson, Carter, Neill, Hays, Straton, Taylor of Loudoun, Ragsdale, Waggener, Brown of Nelson, Cooke, Leland, Chapline, Masters, Swanson, Witcher, Carroll, Morris, Dorman, Leyburn, Conrad, Harley, Hargrave, Delashmutt, Jett, Prentiss, Cunningham, Brown of Petersburg, and Stanard.—69.

Noes, Messrs. Layne, Wilson of Botetourt, Booker, Austin, Richardson, Hickerson, Bowen, Davison, Watts, Hail of Grayson, Nixon, Botts, Holleman, Harris, Taylor of Mathews and Middlesex, Sherrard, Woolfolk, Adams, M'Coy, Cackley, Hopkins, Williams, Nicklin, Moffett, Jessee, M'Mullen, Bare, Rinker and Gillespie.—29.

The following bills were read the second time and ordered to be engrossed and read a third time, viz:

A bill to incorporate the Big Bird mining company.

A bill incorporating the Fredericksburg Union manufacturing company.

A bill incorporating the American mining company.

A bill incorporating the Rappahannock marine and fire insurance company.

A bill to explain the act authorizing subscriptions on the part of the commonwealth to the capital of joint stock companies.

A bill directing a survey of the Dragon swamp.

A bill to amend the act, entitled, "an act concerning the Cumberland road."

A bill to amend an act, entitled, "an act to enact with amendments an act of the general assembly of North Carolina, entitled, 'an act to incorporate the Greensville and Roanoke rail-road company.'"

A bill to amend and explain the act, entitled, "an act to reduce into one the several acts to regulate the solemnization of marriages," &c. passed 1st March, 1819.

A bill making further provision for taking depositions in certain cases.

A bill to authorize a separate election at M'Gaheysville in the county of Rockingham.

A bill concerning the legal representatives of Severn Eyre, deceased.

A bill to incorporate the Front Royal library society in the county of Frederick.

A bill to incorporate the Berkeley coal mining and rail-road company.

A bill concerning William Fenn.

A bill incorporating the trustees of the Clarksville female academy.

A bill for the construction of a bridge across Jackson's river at the town of Covington.

A bill to incorporate the proprietors of the Wellsburg lyceum.

A bill concerning John Chew.

A bill concerning John Pittinger, late sheriff of Brooke county; and

A bill concerning the administrator of Dominie Bennehan, deceased.

A bill to regulate the conduct of boatmen on the Appomattox and Roanoke rivers and their branches, heretofore reported from the committee to which the same had been committed, without amendment, was taken up, and ordered to be engrossed and read a third time.

A bill appointing commissioners to select a site for the seat of justice for the county of Ohio, with the substitute thereto proposed by the committee of propositions and grievances, was taken up, and the said substitute being agreed to by the house, the said bill, as amended, was ordered to be engrossed and read a third time.

The following bills were read the first and ordered to be read a second time, viz:

A bill to incorporate the Etna coal company.

A bill to add a part of the county of Tazewell to the county of Giles.

A bill to establish the town of Meadowville in the county of Greensville.

A bill to incorporate the Potomac silk and agricultural company.

A bill to authorize Richard Barton Haxall to construct additional wharves at and near the town of Bermuda Hundred.

A bill to amend and explain the 96th, 99th and 100th sections of an act for the better organization of the militia, passed March 8th, 1834.

A bill to change the place of holding a separate election in the county of Cabell.

A bill incorporating the Fredericksburg mining company.

A bill to prevent slaves, free negroes and mulattoes from trading beyond the limits of the city, county or town in which they reside.

A bill incorporating the Marshall and Ohio turnpike company.

A bill to enlarge the powers of the county courts of Albemarle and Nelson, for the purpose of opening a road from Scottsville to the head waters of Rockfish river.

A bill incorporating the stockholders of the Smithfield rail-road company.

A bill to authorize the Dismal swamp canal company to increase their capital stock, and to authorize the loans of the state to said company to be converted into stock.

A bill incorporating the stockholders of the Eastern Shore rail-road company.

A bill to prevent frauds in the packing of cotton.

A bill incorporating the Virginia silk company.

A bill to authorize Richard Lorton to surrender his interest in the museum property.

A bill authorizing the auditor of public accounts to issue a warrant on the treasury in favour of John H. Gwathmey, administrator of Richard Clark, deceased, in pursuance of a judgment of the superior court of Henrico county, for commutation of five years full pay with interest.

A bill providing further security for the payment of jailors' fees.

A bill to incorporate the trustees of Saint Bride's academy in Norfolk county.

A bill concerning Amos Johnson.

A bill concerning the Matoaca manufacturing company.

A bill constituting a portion of the margin of the Potomac river in Berkeley county a legal fence.

A bill to amend an act incorporating the Fredericksburg mechanics association.

A bill to repeal the act to provide for the appointment of a commissioner to examine and report upon claims for unsatisfied military land bounties, and for other purposes, passed March 11th, 1834.

A bill changing the time of holding the county courts in the counties of Marshall and Ohio, and to amend the act establishing the town of Moundsville in Ohio (now Marshall) county.

A bill changing the punishment of slaves convicted of hog-stealing.

A bill to change the time of holding a quarterly term of the county court of the county of Shenandoah.

A bill to amend the act, entitled, "an act to incorporate a rail-road company from the city of Richmond to the town of York."

A bill changing the terms of the circuit superior court of law and chancery in and for the county of Stafford.

A bill to change the place of holding a separate election in the county of Pittsylvania.

A bill incorporating the Sweet springs and Price's mountain turnpike company.

A bill concerning Robert W. Christian, treasurer of the late charity school of Charles City, and the overseers of the poor of said county.

A bill to incorporate a company to construct a toll-bridge across the Shenandoah river at Harper's Ferry.

A bill to prevent the destruction of oysters in Nansemond river, and Chuckatuck creek in the county of Nansemond.

A bill concerning delinquent lands and lands not heretofore entered on the commissioners' books.

A bill to change the place of holding a separate election in the county of Harrison.

A bill to amend the act, entitled, "an act to incorporate the Grayson Sulphur springs company."

A bill to incorporate the town of Waterford in the county of Loudoun.

A bill amending the act concerning waste tobacco.

A bill regulating the mode of obtaining writs of error in criminal prosecutions for misdemeanors

A bill appointing trustees to the town of New Glasgow, and for other purposes.

A bill to increase the capital stock of Booker's gold mine company, and for other purposes.

A bill incorporating the Deane iron and steel manufacturing company.

A bill changing the times of holding the circuit superior court of law and chancery in the counties of Rockingham and Pendleton.

A bill incorporating sundry companies to construct turnpike roads from Richmond to Big Bird bridge in the county of Goochland.

A bill authorizing appeals to be taken from the courts of certain counties therein mentioned in the court of appeals held at Lewisburg.

A bill to increase the library at Lewisburg.

A bill reviving an act incorporating a company to construct a turnpike road from the upper end of the Blue Ridge canal to its intersection with the Lexington and Covington turnpike road.

A bill vesting the commonwealth's stock in the James river and Kanawha company in the board of public works, and for other purposes.

A bill making certain changes in the general road law, passed March 3d, 1835, so far as the county of Rockbridge is concerned.

A bill concerning Ann, a free woman of colour.

A bill incorporating the Portsmouth provident society.

A bill to amend the act, entitled, "an act concerning the town of Moorfield in the county of Hardy."

A bill incorporating the Glen Leonard rail-road company.

A bill to authorize a change of location of the Warm springs and Harrisonburg turnpike, and for other purposes.

A bill to incorporate the Wythe watering company in the county of Wythe.

A bill providing for the repairs and preservation of the public arms, the armory buildings, and for other purposes.

A bill concerning the administrator of Richard Kelsick, deceased.

A bill divorcing Ann Edmunds from her husband John W. A. Edmunds.

A bill to increase the number of trustees in the town of Portsmouth, and to enlarge their powers and privileges.

A bill concerning the town of Leesburg in the county of Loudoun.

A bill to amend the charter of the James river and Kanawha company.

A bill regulating the commissions on sales made under decrees in chancery, and for other purposes.

A bill incorporating the Petersburg savings institution.

A bill limiting recoveries on certain judgments therein mentioned.

A bill suspending the processioning of lands in counties therein mentioned.

A bill to authorize Elisha B. Williams to erect a wool carding machine on Jackson's river near the town of Covington in the county of Alleghany.

A bill changing the name of William H. Riggan to that of William H. Drewry.

A bill placing James river on the footing of a lawful fence, so far as concerns the counties of Fluvanna and Albemarle.

A bill incorporating the Chesterfield and James river canal rail-road company.

A bill incorporating the Tuckahoe rail-road company; and

A bill appropriating a further sum of money for completing the improvements of the Western lunatic hospital.

The following bills were read the first, and on motions severally made, the second time, and (by general consent) ordered to be engrossed and read a third time, viz:

A bill to amend an act, entitled, "an act incorporating the trustees of the Bedford female academy."

A bill re-organizing the Lexington arsenal, and establishing a military school in connexion with Washington college.

A bill to alter and increase the terms of the circuit superior court of law and chancery for the county of Norfolk; and

A bill to authorize a separate election in the county of Tazewell.

The following bills were read the first and second times, and on motions severally made, ordered to be committed to the respective committees which brought them in, viz:

A bill incorporating the Mayo's bridge company.

A bill to amend an act, entitled, "an act for the inspection of fish," passed the 28th December, 1795; and

A bill changing the time of holding the superior courts of Campbell, Bedford and the town of Lynchburg.

Mr. Daniel subsequently reported the said last bill with an amendment, which was received and laid upon the table.

A bill incorporating the Great Kanawha mining, timber and lumber company; and

A bill to establish an additional grade of flour in the inspections of flour in this commonwealth, were severally read the second time, and ordered, on motions made, to be laid upon the table.

Mr. Sherrard, according to order, presented a bill concerning the Chesapeake and Ohio canal company, which was subsequently read the first and second times, and on his motion, ordered to be committed to the committee which brought it in.

The following report of the committee for courts of justice was read:
The committee for courts of justice have, according to order, had under consideration the petition of the clerk of the circuit superior court of law and chancery of the county of Fairfax, and attornies at law practising in that court, praying that the said court may be held on the Tuesday after the first Monday in April and September, instead of the time now fixed by law, and have come to the following resolution thereupon:
Resolved as the opinion of this committee, That the prayer of the said petition is reasonable.
The said resolution was, on the question put thereupon, agreed to by the house, and a bill was ordered to be brought in conformably therewith.
An engrossed bill to amend the act, entitled, "an act incorporating the Goose creek navigation company, was taken up on motion of Mr. Beard, and read a third time, and sundry blanks therein were filled:
Resolved, That the bill do pass, and that the title be, "an act to amend the act, entitled, 'an act incorporating the Goose creek navigation company.'"
Ordered, That the clerk communicate the same to the senate and request their concurrence.
Mr. Davison, according to order, presented a bill creating a new regiment within the county of Warren, and for other purposes.
Mr. Brown of Petersburg, from the committee of finance, presented a report upon the petition of Henry Anderson.
And a bill concerning the executor of James Jenks, deceased.
Which bills and report were received and laid upon the table.
On motion of Mr. Brown of Petersburg, *Ordered*, That the committee of finance be discharged from the consideration of the petitions of P. Keenan; and of T. W. Graves; and from the resolutions for assigning a room in the capitol for the office of the attorney general; for the use of the principal engineer; and for another apartment for the auditor of public accounts; and that the same be laid upon the table.
On motion of Mr. Holleman, *Ordered*, That leave be granted to Alexander Rives to withdraw from among the papers filed in the contested election from the county of Albemarle, the original lease from Meriwether and others to John Thomas, and the report and registry of George Toole, an alien.
On motion of Mr. Prentiss, the house adjourned until Monday morning 10 o'clock.

MONDAY, March 14th, 1836.

A communication from the senate by their clerk:

IN SENATE, March 12th, 1836.
The senate have passed the bills, entitled,
"An act allowing Richard Bolling, a free man of colour, to remain in the commonwealth."
"An act allowing Daniel Higginbotham, a free man of colour, to remain in the commonwealth a limited time;" and
"An act to incorporate the Virginia insurance company."
They have also passed the bill, entitled,
"An act incorporating the stockholders of the Richmond and Petersburg rail-road company," with amendments, in which they request the concurrence of the house of delegates.
And they have rejected the bill, entitled,
"An act to incorporate the stockholders of the Cartersville and Farmville rail-road company."
Their committee appointed to examine the enrolled bills have examined sundry other such bills, which being found truly enrolled, have been signed by their speaker, and are herewith returned to the house of delegates.
The said amendments being twice read, were, on questions severally put thereupon, agreed to by the house.
Ordered, That the clerk inform the senate thereof.
Mr. Sherrard reported without amendment, a bill concerning the Chesapeake and Ohio canal company.
Mr. Brown of Petersburg, from the committee of finance, presented a bill to amend the act concerning the overseers of the poor, passed 20th February, 1829; and
A bill regulating the allowances in cases of arrest for criminal offences.
Which were received and laid upon the table.
On motion of Mr. Brooke, the rule of the house was suspended, and the vote adopting a resolution on Saturday last, was reconsidered, and the following resolution was adopted in lieu thereof:
Resolved, That the auditor of public accounts be requested to transmit to this house as soon as practicable, a copy of the report of the treasurer of the Western lunatic hospital, of the expenditures for the cross walls and additional buildings of that institution during the last year.
On motion of Mr. Watkins, *Resolved*, That the speakers of the senate and of the house of delegates, be requested to transmit a copy of the expunging resolutions to William C. Rives, esqr., senator from this state to the congress of the United States, with a request to lay the same before the senate.
Ordered, That the clerk communicate the same to the senate and request their concurrence.
Mr. Watkins, from the committee of roads and internal navigation, reported with amendment, a bill incorporating the Mayo's bridge company.

Mr. Stanard, from the committee for courts of justice, presented a bill to define the duties and regulate the fees of the attorney general.

Which were received and laid upon the table.

Mr. Watkins, from the select committee on banks, reported with a substitute, a bill increasing the banking capital of the commonwealth, which, on his motion was ordered to be recommitted to the said committee.

A bill to establish an additional grade of flour in the inspections of flour in this commonwealth, was taken up on motion of Mr. Davison, amended on his motion, and as amended, ordered to be engrossed and read a third time.

A bill to amend an act, entitled, "an act to enact with amendments an act of the general assembly of North Carolina, entitled, 'an act to incorporate the Greensville and Roanoke rail-road company,'" passed February 7th, 1834, was taken up on motion Mr. Cooke, amended on his motion, and as amended, ordered to be engrossed and read a third time.

An engrossed bill declaring Pocatallico river a public highway, was read a third time ;

Resolved, That the bill do pass, and that the title be, "an act declaring Pocatallico river a public highway."

An engrossed bill to amend the act, entitled, "an act to incorporate the Richmond manufacturing company," passed January 12th, 1832, was read a third time:

Resolved, That the bill do pass, and that the title be, "an act to amend the act, entitled, 'an act to incorporate the Richmond manufacturing company, passed January 12th, 1832.'"

An engrossed bill changing the place of holding a separate election in the county of Kanawha, was read a third time :

Resolved, That the bill do pass, and that the title be, "an act changing the place of holding a separate election in the county of Kanawha."

An engrossed bill to incorporate the New Hope gold mine company, was read a third time :

Resolved, That the bill do pass, and that the title be, "an act to incorporate the New Hope gold mine company."

An engrossed bill to amend the act, entitled, "an act making further provision for completing the road from Staunton to the mouth of the Little Kanawha," was read a third time :

Resolved, That the bill do pass, and that the title be, "an act to amend the act, entitled, 'an act making further provision for completing the road from Staunton to the mouth of the Little Kanawha.'"

An engrossed bill incorporating the trustees of the Martinsville academy, was read a third time:

Resolved, That the bill do pass, and that the title be, "an act incorporating the trustees of the Martinsville academy."

An engrossed bill to establish the town of Lovettsville in the county of Loudoun, was read a third time :

Resolved, That the bill do pass, and that the title be, "an act to establish the town of Lovettsville in the county of Loudoun."

An engrossed bill to incorporate the Portsmouth and Chesapeake steam-boat company, was read a third time ;

Resolved, That the bill do pass, and that the title be, "an act to incorporate the Portsmouth and Chesapeake steam-boat company."

An engrossed bill to authorize a subscription on behalf of the state to the stock of the Pittsylvania and Lynchburg turnpike company, and for other purposes, was read a third time :

Resolved, That the bill do pass, and that the title be, "an act to authorize a subscription on behalf of the state to the stock of the Pittsylvania and Lynchburg turnpike company, and for other purposes."

An engrossed bill incorporating the Lynchburg and Campbell court-house turnpike company, was read a third time :

Resolved, That the bill do pass, and that the title be, "an act incorporating the Lynchburg and Campbell courthouse turnpike company"

An engrossed bill to incorporate the trustees of the Lynchburg female academy, was read a third time :

Resolved, That the bill do pass, and that the title be, "an act to incorporate the trustees of the Lynchburg female academy."

An engrossed bill changing the Hunting run gold mining company into a company for mining and manufacturing iron and steel, was read a third time:

Resolved, That the bill do pass, and that the title be, "an act changing the Hunting run gold mining company into a company for mining and manufacturing iron and steel."

An engrossed bill to amend the act, entitled, "an act to amend and reduce into one act, all acts and parts of acts to prevent the destruction of oysters," passed March 24th, 1831, was read a third time :

Resolved, That the bill do pass, and that the title be, "an act to amend the act, entitled, 'an act to amend and reduce into one act all acts and parts of acts to prevent the destruction of oysters,'" passed March 24th, 1831.

An engrossed bill concerning savings institutions, was read a third time ; whereupon, a clause by way of ryder thereto was submitted by Mr. Carter, which was read the first and second times, and forthwith engrossed and read a third time :

Resolved, That the bill (with the ryder) do pass, and that the title be, "an act concerning savings institutions."

An engrossed bill to equalize the regimental districts in the county of Rockingham and for other purposes, was read a third time :

Resolved, That the bill do pass, and that the title be, "an act to equalize the regimental districts in the county of Rockingham and for other purposes."

An engrossed bill to incorporate the trustees of the Charlestown athenæum and female academy, was read a third time:

Resolved, That the bill do pass, and that the title be, "an act to incorporate the trustees of the Charlestown athenæum and female academy."

Ordered, That the clerk communicate the said bills to the senate and request their concurrence.

A bill imposing taxes for the support of government, with the amendment thereto proposed by the committee of the whole house, was taken up on motion of Mr. Brown of Petersburg, and the said amendment being agreed to by the house, motions were made by Mr. M'Mullen further to amend the said bill by reducing the age of slaves to be taxed from twelve years to ten years, and by providing that horses, mules and asses should not be taxed until three years old, and on the questions put thereupon the said amendments were disagreed to by the house, and the said bill as previously amended, was ordered to be engrossed and read a third time.

The report of the committee of finance, together with the amendments thereto proposed by the committee of the whole house, was taken up on motion of Mr. Brown of Petersburg, and the said amendments having been amended by the house, were as amended agreed to.

The said report as amended is the following:

The committee of finance have, according to order, examined into the state of the debts due from the commonwealth, the probable revenue and expenses of the government during the fiscal year, ending the 30th of September, 1836, and also the probable expenses of the ensuing year, and have prepared a report thereupon, which they now respectfully submit:

ESTIMATE OF THE EXPENSES OF GOVERNMENT DURING THE CURRENT FISCAL YEAR.

Expenses of the general assembly,		90,000 00
Civil list,		75,000 00
Commissioners of the revenue, and clerks of courts for examining commissioners' books,		31,000 00
Criminal charges, including guards of jails,		35,000 00
Contingent expenses of courts,		25,000 00
Civil contingent fund,		12,000 00
Military contingent fund,		1,000 00
Civil prosecutions,		100 00
Militia establishment, including pay of the adjutant general,		11,000 00
Pensioners,		2,500 00
Sinking fund, for the redemption of the old 6 per cent. military debt certificates,		100 00
Interest on the public debt, to wit:		
7 per cent. debt due the literary fund,	22,330 00	
6 per cent. ditto, held by ditto,	1,442 34	
		23,772 34
One year's interest on $250,000 of 5 per cent. stock, created to pay the state's subscription to the Chesapeake and Ohio canal company, by an act of the 20th of February, 1833,		12,500 00
Public guard in the city of Richmond,		21,000 00
Public arsenal at Lexington,		6,000 00
Collection and transportation of arms,		500 00
Rent of water for armory from James river company,		1,280 00
Pay of artificers at the armory, repairs of arms, &c.,		8,000 00
Slaves executed and transported,		12,000 00
Penitentiary, to wit: Internal charges,	3,500 00	
Officers' salaries,	8,080 00	
Transportation of convicts,	6,000 00	
		17,580 00
Lunatic hospital at Williamsburg,		13,522
Ditto at Staunton,		7,493
Expense of transportation and maintenance of lunatics in county jails,		5,000
Public warehouses, pay of superintendents, repairs, &c.,		1,200
Expense of representation in congress and state senate,		600
Reports of decisions in the court of appeals and general court,		4,000
Vaccine agent,		500
Commissions to agent for settling revolutionary claims at Washington,		500 50
Agent and his clerk, for settling revolutionary claims,		1,800 00
Balances of appropriations unexpended on the 1st of October, to wit:		
For furniture and repairs of the governor's house,	1,407 20	
For a geological reconnoissance of the state,	1,500 00	
		2,907 20
Amount carried forward,		$422,855 73

JOURNAL OF THE HOUSE OF DELEGATES. 215

Amount brought forward,		422,855 73
Sinking fund, for the final redemption of the public debt, authorized by the act of the 10th of March, 1835,		50,000 00
Probable expenditure for the removal of free persons of colour,		1,000 00
Appropriations for the construction of public roads, to wit:		
Road from Monroe county to the Kentucky line,	1,000 00	
Road across the Cheat mountain in Randolph county,	11,000 00	
Road in Bath and Alleghany counties, (from M'Avoy's,)	500 00	
Road from Staunton to the Little Kanawha,	500 00	
Road from Pendleton to Rockingham,	500 00	
		13,500 00
The state's subscription for three hundred copies of the Statutes at Large, published by Samuel Shepherd, in continuation of Hening's Statutes at Large, by act of 21st February, 1835,		3,150 00
Judgments against the commonwealth, on account of revolutionary services, for which appropriations will probably be made, viz		
In favour of Walls's representatives,	13,532 53	
Ditto Paxton's ditto,	2,381 26	
		15,913 79
For a geological survey of the state,		5,000 00
For purchase of Brown's warehouse,		21,500 00
		$532,919 52

PROBABLE RECEIPTS DURING THE CURRENT FISCAL YEAR.

From taxes on lands,		148,391 49
lots,		31,088 68
slaves,		59,464 25
houses,		17,760 84
studs,		12,900 75
coaches,		10,977 69
stages,		40 50
carryalls,		2,443 29
gigs,		4,420 02
merchants, brokers, jewellers and auctioneers,		67,247 43
pedlars,		6,345 18
ordinary keepers,		18,176 72
keepers of houses of private entertainment,		3,461 31
venders of lottery tickets,		5,938 34
exhibitors of shows,		1,530 00
		389,286 49
Add estimated amount of tax of counties of Pittsylvania and Tyler		5,798 43
		395,084 92
Deduct as the estimated amount of insolvents, overcharges, &c.,	3,000 00	
sheriffs' commissions of 5 per cent.,	19,604 24	
Ditto of 2½ per cent. for prompt payment,	6,902 30	
		29,506 24
		365,578 38
Deduct the portion of the revenue of 1835 paid into the treasury previous to the 1st of October, 1835,		36,931 71
		328,645 67
Add the portion of the revenue of 1836 expected to be paid into the treasury prior to the 1st of October, 1836,		38,000 00
		366,646 67
From militia fines and arrearages,		10,000 00
tax on law process and seals of courts,		15,000 00
tax on the great seal and notarial seals,		3,000 00
Amount carried forward,		$394,646 67

Amount brought forward,	394,646 67
From duties on tobacco shipped and sales of waste tobacco,	5,500 00
land office fees,	3,000 00
sales of unappropriated land,	1,500 00
redemption of delinquent land,	500 00
sales of penitentiary manufactures,	6,000 00
sales of condemned slaves for transportation,	5,000 00
miscellaneous receipts,	5,000 00
	421,146 67
Add the balance reported to be in the treasury on the 1st of October, 1835, applicable to the ordinary expenses of government, exclusive of the sum of $162 09 standing to the credit of the Washington monument fund,	118,091 04
And the total estimated receipts will be	539,237 71
Deduct estimated expenses for the same period,	532,919 52
And the probable balance in the treasury on the 1st of October, 1836, will be	$ 6,318 19

DEBT OF THE COMMONWEALTH OF VIRGINIA, 30TH OF SEPTEMBER, 1835.

INTERNAL IMPROVEMENT DEBT.

James river company certificates of loan, to wit:	$1,021,200, at 6 per cent.	
	25,300, at 5½ per cent.	
	278,000, at 5 per cent.	1,324,500 00
North-western turnpike road certificates of loan, at 5 per cent.,		121,000 00
Petersburg rail-road company certificates of loan, at 5 per cent.,		80,000 00
Portsmouth and Roanoke rail-road company certificates of loan, at 5 per cent.,		190,000 00
Richmond, Fredericksburg and Potomac rail-road company certificates of loan, at 5 per cent.,		110,000 00
Winchester and Potomac rail-road company certificates of loan, to wit: $30,000, at 6 per cent.		
	70,000, at 5 per cent.	100,000 00
		1,925,500 00

The annual interest on the foregoing debts amounts to $106,913 50; for the payment of which, and for the redemption of the principal, the following pledges and appropriations are made:

1st. For the James river company loan, the profits of their works, after paying expenses and repairs, and setting apart $21,000 annually forever for the dividends at 15 per cent. to the original stockholders, are pledged to the public creditors, who, on the faith of that pledge, have lent money to the James river company for the use of the commonwealth; but, by the act of March 16th, 1832, the works and property of the James river company have been transferred to the James river and Kanawha company, and the faith of the state is thereby pledged to the new company that they shall be protected from the payment of any part of the interest or principal of the loans aforesaid, (except the perpetual annuity of $21,000,) for which the profits of the commonwealth's stock in the new company are in the first instance pledged; for the North-western turnpike road loan, the profits, after paying expenses and repairs, are pledged; for the loans for the Petersburg, the Portsmouth and Roanoke, the Richmond, Fredericksburg and Potomac, and the Winchester and Potomac rail-road companies, the dividends of the stock, and the stock itself held by the state in those companies respectively, are pledged.

2dly. If such profits and dividends shall be insufficient for the payment of interest and redemption of the principal of the said loans, the state is pledged to provide other and adequate funds.

3dly. Until such other and adequate funds shall have been provided, the revenues of the fund for internal improvement are pledged and appropriated, except in regard to a portion of the James river company loan, amounting to $77,000, as to which the fund is pledged for interest only, and not the redemption of the principal.

Chesapeake and Ohio canal company certificates of loan, at 5 per cent. for paying the state's subscription,	250,000 00

This loan not having been charged, by the act creating it, on any specific fund, is chargeable on the public treasury, and the interest is payable out of the ordinary revenue.

Amount carried forward,	$2,175,500 00

Amount brought forward, - - - - 2,175,500 00

LITERARY FUND DEBT.

Consisting of the following state stocks purchased by the fund, to wit:
7 per cent. bank debt of 1814, - - -	319,000 00
6 per cent. old military debt, - - -	24,039 17

343,039 17

This debt is also chargeable on the ordinary revenue, and the interest is provided for by annual appropriation.

LIBRARY FUND DEBT,

Consisting of a 6 per cent. from the literary fund, for the interest and principal of which the library fund and half of its proceeds are pledged and appropriated,   10,000 00

Total debt of the commonwealth, exclusive of the perpetual annuity of $21,000 to the old James river company stockholders, the payment of which is devolved, by the act of March 16th, 1832, on the James river and Kanawha company, and exclusive of a small unascertained balance of the old 6 per cent. military debt certificates, - - - - $2,528,539 17

Of the foregoing public debt, there is held by the literary fund the sum of $869,372 50, and by the fund for internal improvement, $90,000, leaving the amount of certificates of debt held by individuals and corporate bodies, $1,569,166 67.

The board of public works are authorized to borrow the additional sums of $2,500, to pay outstanding claims for the James river improvements; $90,000 for the North-western turnpike road; $30,000 for the Winchester and Potomac rail-road company; $170,000 for the Richmond, Fredericksburg and Potomac rail-road company; and $40,000 for the construction of a road from Price's turnpike to Cumberland gap. The commonwealth has also become a subscriber, by the act of the 24th of February, 1835, for stock in the James river and Kanawha company, to the amount of $3,000,000, one million of which has been paid by the transfer of the works and property of the James river company, and the other two millions will become due and payable in money, in the proportions in which other stockholders shall be required to pay the residue of their subscriptions, after those other stockholders shall have previously paid one third of their subscriptions. It is not probable that any portion of this two millions will be required during the current fiscal year, and no provision has been made for the payment of it on the part of the commonwealth.

The nominal amount of the fund for internal improvement, permanent and disposable, including an uninvested balance, was, at the end of the last fiscal year, 30th September, 1835, $3,223,484 60, yielding, annually, a revenue from profits, and dividends on stocks, and interest on loans, of $120,477 36. The amount of interest, annually charged on this revenue, on account of the above mentioned loans for internal improvements, is $106,913 50; and when the residue of the loans authorized by existing laws shall have been made, the whole revenue of the fund will be but little more than sufficient to meet the charge for interest. No further provision is at this time necessary for the payment of interest on these loans, the profits of the several improvements and the revenue of the fund, being adequate to the purpose; nor is any portion of those loans, as yet, redeemable. The general assembly, however, at the last session, set apart the sum of $50,000 as a sinking fund, to be placed in the hands of commissioners, and applied to the purchase of such certificates of the above loans, held by individuals or corporations, as might be offered for sale at par, and if none such were offered, then the fund to be otherwise invested and improved until such time as the commonwealth may become entitled to redeem such loans. The debt of $343,039 17, due to the literary fund, bearing an interest of 7 per cent., and payable out of the ordinary revenue, is redeemable at the pleasure of the general assembly, but as the redemption would materially lessen the resources devoted to the purposes of education, which it is presumed there was no inclination to do, the act creating this sinking fund expressly prohibited the redemption of any part of the literary fund debt. The debts held against the state by individuals and corporate bodies, other than the literary fund, are those for the reimbursement of which it would seem expedient to make the earliest provision. Some portion of them will be redeemable in the year 1841, and the sum placed during the current fiscal year, under the act of the last assembly, to the credit of the commissioners, will, it is anticipated, form a foundation upon which, through the aid of interest when invested, and of occasional additions of unemployed balances, may be gradually accumulated a fund adequate to the object ultimately in view. It is a subject of regret that the present state of the finances does not admit of a farther contribution, at this time, to this sinking fund.

The estimated receipts of the current fiscal year, on account of the ordinary revenue, including the balance in the treasury on the 1st of October last, subject to the expenses of the government, amount to $537,237 71; and the estimated disbursements during the same period, amount to $532,919 52; leaving a probable balance at the end of the current fiscal year, applicable to the support of government, of $6,318 19.

The additional sum of $13,961 50, not embraced in the foregoing estimates of disbursements, because not likely to be called for during the current fiscal year, is appropriated by existing laws from the treasury, for the construction of public roads, to wit: for the road across the Alleghany, between Pendleton and Pocahontas, $6,000; for a road near the Great Falls in Bath county, $600; residue for the Pendleton and Rockingham road, $500; residue for the Staunton and Little Kanawha road, $861 50; and for the road from Lewis to Kanawha county, by act of the present assembly, $6,000. There is also an annual appropriation of $18,000, for the removal of free persons of colour, of which, it is supposed in the preceding estimates, not more than $1,000 will be expended during the year.

It is deserving of notice, that the appropriations which may be authorized during the residue of the session of the general assembly, except such as relate to judgments heretofore rendered against the commonwealth, have not been taken into consideration, because they are wholly conjectural and uncertain. Applications for appropriations, and money claims against the state, to a considerable amount, are pending before the assembly, and should they be allowed, the abovementioned balance of $6,318 19 may be greatly reduced, if not wholly absorbed.

Should the extraordinary and temporary appropriations of the future part of the present session be small in amount, the estimated probable balance at the end of the fiscal year will be a sufficient one, but not greater than it is deemed necessary to retain in the treasury to meet unforeseen demands, or to supply such deficiencies as may arise from fluctuations in the revenue. Nor is there any probability that this balance will be increased in future years, the rates of taxation remaining the same; for it will be seen, by an inspection of the foregoing estimates of the ordinary expenses of government, and of the usual receipts at the present rates of taxation, that the revenue will not be more than sufficient to meet the expenditures, supposing both the revenue and expenditures to continue uniform. The considerable balances exhibited for a few years past have arisen from other causes than an excess of the ordinary revenue beyond the usual expenditures, being composed entirely of the sums reimbursed by the United States on account of the payments made by this state in compensation for services during the revolutionary war. It may be remarked, moreover, that the gain of the ordinary revenue, without any change of the rates of taxation, through the expansion and improvement of the resources of the commonwealth for some years past, amounted annually to little less than $10,000; but, during the fiscal year of 1835, it was almost entirely checked, exhibiting an increase of only about $1,500. This may have been owing in a great measure to the extensive emigration from this state to the south-western quarter of the Union, and the consequent removal and sale of slaves and other kinds of taxable property. It appears from the returns of taxable property in 1835, that the number of taxable slaves of that year, as compared with the previous year, was diminished 2,649; and from the increased emigration which it is believed has since occurred, it is not improbable that the ensuing returns may shew a diminution of 10,000 taxable slaves. It is supposed that at least an equal number of slaves not taxable have been removed during the same time; and as these were taken from those classes which gradually swell the lists as they arrive at an age to be liable to taxation, it is obvious that those lists, in future years, in the absence of countervailing causes, must be affected in a progressive ratio much greater than the decrease disclosed in the taxable subjects of a particular year. Seeing, then, that the ordinary receipts, at the present rates of taxation, are not more than sufficient to cover the ordinary expenditures, and that no improvement in the revenue can for some time be reasonably expected, if indeed a decline shall not occur, the committee cannot recommend a reduction of the taxes. On the contrary, should the expenses and appropriations of the current session be made much to exceed the usual amount, a moderate increase of the taxes may be deemed expedient, in anticipation of the wants of the ensuing year, if not of the present. Such an increase is further recommended by the consideration of the means it would furnish of adding something to the sinking fund for the eventual redemption of the public debt. Should the two millions of dollars subscribed by the state to the stock of the James river and Kanawha company, be called for during the ensuing fiscal year, and the necessary provision for the payment thereof impose any additional charge on the revenue, it would seem that the present rates of taxation should be considerably increased, or new subjects of taxation be put in requisition. But, considering the contingent character of the demand, the uncertainty as to what portion of it, if any, may be called for during the ensuing year, and the probability that no resort will be had to the treasury until the fund dedicated to the purposes of internal improvement shall have been found inadequate, the committee think it unnecessary to suggest at this time any measures in relation to it, further than to refer to the magnitude of the engagement as an argument in favour of prudence and economy in the distribution of the public funds, which will soon be burthened with so considerable a charge. In accordance with the foregoing views, and with reference to the probable amount of expenditure as at present appearing, the committee recommend the adoption of the following resolution:

Resolved, That it is not necessary to increase the existing rates of taxation.

The said resolution was, on the question put thereupon, agreed to by the house, an *unsuccessful* motion having been made by Mr. Brown of Petersburg to reverse the decision of the committee, so as to declare that a moderate increase of the taxes is expedient.

A bill appropriating the public revenue, with the amendments thereto proposed by the committee of the whole house, was taken up on motion of Mr. Brown of Petersburg, and the said amendments being agreed to by the house, the said bill as amended, was ordered to be engrossed and read a third time.

A bill to amend the act concerning merchants' licenses, was taken up on motion of Mr. Brown of Petersburg, and ordered to be engrossed and read a third time.

The speaker laid before the house the following letter from the auditor of public accounts:

AUDITOR'S OFFICE, March 14, 1836.

SIR,—In compliance with a resolution of the house of delegates of this date, I herewith transmit copies of the accounts of the Western lunatic hospital, embracing the expenditures of that institution for the last year, on account of additional buildings and cross walls.

I have the honour to be, very respectfully, yours,   JA'S E. HEATH, *Auditor.*

To LINN BANKS, Esq. *Speaker of the House of Delegates.*

On motion of Mr. Brooke, *Ordered,* That the same be laid upon the table, and that 185 copies thereof be printed for the use of the general assembly.

Mr. Holleman, from the committee of privileges and elections, presented a report upon the qualifications of the members and returns of elections to the present legislature, which was received and laid upon the table.

On motion of Mr. Holleman, *Ordered,* That the clerk to the said committee be discharged from further attendance on said committee, the committee having no business before them.

On motion of Mr. Brown of Petersburg, *Ordered,* That leave be given to bring in a bill to repeal the act of the present session authorizing the payment of a judgment against the commonwealth in favour of Thomas Walls's representatives on account of revolutionary services, and that Messrs. Brown of Petersburg, Campbell, Coleman, Holland, Austin, Hopkins, Mallory, Neill, Richardson, Fitzgerald, and Hunter of Berkeley, prepare and bring in the same.

A bill to amend the several acts concerning the public guard in the city of Richmond.

A bill changing the time of holding the superior courts of Campbell, Bedford, and the town of Lynchburg, with the amendments thereto proposed, were taken up, and the said amendments being agreed to, the said bills as amended, were ordered to be engrossed and read a third time.

The following bills were read the second time, and ordered to be engrossed and read a third time, viz:

A bill concerning the subscription on behalf of the commonwealth to the stock of the Richmond, Fredericksburg and Potomac rail-road company.

A bill to authorize Thomas A. Morton to erect a dam across Appomattox river.

A bill authorizing the auditor to issue a warrant in favour of James Paxton

A bill amending the laws concerning slaves, free negroes and mulattoes.

A bill to amend the act, entitled, "an act reducing into one the several acts for punishing persons guilty of certain thefts and forgeries, and the destruction or concealment of wills."

A bill to incorporate the Etna coal company.

A bill to add a part of the county of Tazewell to the county of Giles.

A bill to establish the town of Meadowville in the county of Greenbrier.

A bill to incorporate the Potomac silk and agricultural company.

A bill to authorize Richard Barton Haxall to construct additional wharves at and near the town of Bermuda Hundred.

A bill to amend an act, entitled, "an act to incorporate the Augusta springs company."

A bill to change the time of holding the county courts of the counties of Lewis and Braxton; and

A bill to authorize a separate election at the house of William Pulliam in the county of Henry.

A bill securing to debtors a certain portion of their property, was read a second time; whereupon a substitute was offered therefor by Mr. Fleet, and on motion of Mr. Gregory, the said bill and amendment was ordered to be laid upon the table.

An engrossed bill to amend the several acts concerning pilots, was read a third time, and sundry blanks therein were filled; and the question being put upon its passage, was determined in the affirmative. Ayes 52, noes 24.

The ayes and noes thereupon being required by Mr. Brown of Petersburg, (and sustained according to the rule of the house,) are as follow:

Ayes, Messrs. Grinalds, Craig, Hunter of Berkeley, Turnbull, Mallory, Booker, Austin, Hill, Servant, Ball, Price, Steger, Holland, Bowen, Davison, Smith of Gloucester, Watkins, Wethered, Mullen, Holleman, Gregory, Fleet, Neill, Straton, Waggener, Rogers, Morgan, Benton, Murdaugh, Cooke, Leland, Masters, Almond, Adams, M'Coy, Cackley, Carroll, Morris, Nicklin, Moffett, Jessee, M'Mullen, Bare, Rinker, Butts, Crutchfield, Hargrave, Delashmutt, Gibson, Jett, Prentiss and Cunningham.—52.

Noes, Messrs. Campbell, Decamps, Beuhring, Wilson of Cumberland, Vaughan, Smith of Fauquier, Hickerson, Coleman, Sloan, Nixon, Harrison, Fontaine, Hays, Harris, Sherrard, Brown of Nelson, Fitzgerald, Chapline, Hopkins, Shands, Leyburn, Moncure, Brown of Petersburg, and Stanard.—24.

Resolved, That the bill do pass, and that the title be, "an act to amend the several acts concerning pilots."

Ordered, That the clerk communicate the same to the senate and request their concurrence.

On motion of Mr. Sherrard, the house adjourned until to-morrow 10 o'clock.

TUESDAY, March 15th, 1836.

A communication from the senate by their clerk:

IN SENATE, March 14th, 1836.

The senate have passed the bill, entitled,

"An act allowing Judy Johnson, a free woman of colour, to remain in the commonwealth."

"An act providing for the construction of a turnpike road from the town of Beverley in Randolph county, to the town of Clarksburg in Harrison county;" and

"An act to amend the act, entitled, 'an act incorporating the Goose creek navigation company.'"

They have also passed the bill, entitled,

"An act to provide for the construction of a road from the Ohio river by Morgantown, to the Maryland line," with amendments, in which they request the concurrence of the house of delegates.

They have agreed to the resolution for the election of a major general of the third division of Virginia militia.

They have also agreed to the resolution directing a survey of a route for a rail-road from Buford's gap to the Tennessee line, by Walker's creek and the North fork of Holstein river, with an amendment, in which they request the concurrence of the house of delegates.

The said amendments being twice read, were, on questions severally put thereupon, agreed to by the house.

Ordered, That the clerk inform the senate thereof.

A bill securing to debtors a certain portion of their property, together with the amendment thereto proposed by Mr. Fleet, was taken up, and the said amendment having been amended on motion of Mr. Gregory, and as amended agreed to by the house, the said bill, as amended, was ordered to be engrossed and read a third time.

Mr. Stanard, from the committee for courts of justice, presented a bill to amend the act, entitled, "an act for the relief of creditors against fraudulent devises."

A bill to explain the act, entitled, "an act to reduce into one the several acts concerning grand juries and petit juries;" and

A bill changing the time of holding the circuit superior court of Fairfax county, which were received and laid upon the table.

He also from the same committee, reported with amendment, a bill to amend an act, entitled, "an act for the inspection of fish," passed 28th December, 1795, which, on his motion was taken up, and the first amendment being agreed to by the house, and the second disagreed to, the said bill, as amended, was ordered to be engrossed and read a third time.

Mr. Brown of Petersburg, according to order, presented a bill to repeal part of an act passed on the 27th February, 1836, "entitled, an act to authorize the auditor to issue warrants on the treasury in satisfaction of certain judgments against the commonwealth," which was received and laid upon the table.

An engrossed bill to amend the several acts concerning the Petersburg rail-road company, was read a third time; whereupon, a clause by way of ryder thereto was offered by Mr. Brown of Petersburg, which was read the first and second times, and forthwith engrossed and read a third time

Resolved, That the said bill, (with the ryder,) do pass, and that the title be, "an act to amend the several acts concerning the Petersburg rail-road company."

An engrossed bill prescribing the punishment of offences committed on rail-roads, was read a third time; whereupon, a clause by way of ryder thereto, was offered by Mr. Dorman, which was read the first and second times, and forthwith engrossed and read a third time :

Resolved, That the bill (with the ryder,) do pass, and that the title be, "an act prescribing the punishment of offences committed on rail-roads."

An engrossed bill to incorporate the Goochland mining company, was read a third time :

Resolved, That the bill do pass, and that the title be, "an act to incorporate the Goochland mining company."

An engrossed bill to suppress the circulation of incendiary publications, and for other purposes, was read a third time, and sundry blanks therein were filled :

Resolved, That the bill do pass, and that the title be, "an act to suppress the circulation of incendiary publications, and for other purposes."

An engrossed bill appropriating the surplus revenue of the literary fund, was read a third time ; whereupon a clause by way of ryder thereto was offered by Mr. Prentiss, which was read the first and second times, engrossed and read a third time, and the question being put upon the passage of the said bill and ryder, was determined in the affirmative. Ayes 82, noes 29.

The ayes and noes thereupon being required by Mr. Prentiss, (and sustained according to the rule of the house,) are as follow :

Ayes, Messrs. Grinalds, Layne, Wiley, Garland of Amherst, Campbell, Henshaw, Wilson of Botetourt, Decamps, Austin, Beuhring, Christian, Richardson, Hill, Ball, Smith of Fauquier, Price, Strange, Steger, Hale of Franklin, Holland, Bowen, Smith of Frederick, Watts, Smith of Gloucester, Hail of Grayson, Carrington, Coleman, Sloan, Nixon, Goodall, Mullen, Harrison, Kincheloe, Fontaine, Holleman, Gregory, Berry, Summers, Fleet, Hooe, Robinson, Neill, Hays, Straton, Beard, Taylor of Loudoun, Harris, Ragsdale, Taylor of Mathews and Middlesex, Rogers, Morgan, Sherrard, Benton, Brown of Nelson, Chapline, Masters, Woolfolk, Almond, Adams, M'Coy, Swanson, Witcher, Cackley, Hopkins, Carroll, Williams, Marteney, Nicklin, Moffett, Conrad, Jessee, M'Mullen, Bare, Rinker, Harley, Butts, Moncure, Gillespie, Delashmutt, Gibson, Jett and Prentiss.—82.

Noes, Messrs. Banks, (speaker,) Gilmer, Southall, Brooke, Craig, Hunter of Berkeley, Miller, Turnbull, Mallory, Daniel, Wilson of Cumberland, Vaughan, Hunter of Essex, Watkins, Botts, Griggs, Carter, Garland of Mecklenburg, Cooke, Leland, Fitzgerald, Madison, Shands, Dorman, Leyburn, Crutchfield, Hargrave, Cunningham and Stanard.—29.

Resolved, That the bill (with the ryder,) do pass, and that the title be, "an act appropriating the surplus revenue of the literary fund."

Ordered, That Mr. Hunter of Berkeley, carry the said bills to the senate and request their concurrence.

The house according to the joint order of the day, proceeded by joint vote with the senate to the election of a major general of the third division of militia, to supply the vacancy occasioned by the death of major general John Smith; whereupon, Mr. Hunter of Berkeley nominated general Elisha Boyd, and Mr. Brooke nominated general Briscoe G. Baldwin, and the senate having been informed thereof by Mr. Hunter of Berkeley, and no person being added to the nomination in that house, the names of the members were called by the clerk, and the vote was for Baldwin 99; for Boyd 8.

The names of the gentlemen voting for general Baldwin, are Messrs. Banks, (speaker,) Gilmer, Southall, Layne, Wiley, Brooke, Craig, Campbell, Miller, Wilson of Botetourt, Decamps, Turnbull, Mallory, Austin, Beuhring, Daniel, Christian, Hill, Wilson of Cumberland, Vaughan, Hunter of Essex, Smith of Fauquier, Price, Strange, Steger, Hale of Franklin, Holland, Bowen, Watts, Smith of Gloucester, Watkins, Hail of Grayson, Carrington, Coleman, Sloan, Nixon, Goodall, Kincheloe, Botts, Fontaine, Holleman, Gregory, Berry, Summers, Fleet, Hooe, Robinson, Carter, Neill, Straton, Taylor of Loudoun, Harris, Ragsdale, Taylor of Mathews and Middlesex, Rogers, Garland of Mecklenburg, Morgan, Chapman, Sherrard, Benton, Brown of Nelson, Murdaugh, Cooke, Leland, Fitzgerald, Chapline, Masters, Woolfolk, Almond, Adams, M'Coy, Swanson, Hopkins, Carroll, Madison, Morris, Shands, Williams, Marteney, Nicklin, Dorman, Leyburn, Moffett, Conrad, Jessee, M'Mullen, Rinker, Harley, Butts, Crutchfield, Moncure, Hargrave, Gillespie, Delashmutt, Gibson, Jett, Prentiss, Cunningham, and Brown of Petersburg.—99.

And the gentlemen voting for general Boyd, are Messrs. Grinalds, Hunter of Berkeley, Henshaw, Richardson, Mullen, Harrison, Griggs and Beard.—8.

Ordered, That Messrs. Hunter of Berkeley, Brooke, Wilson of Botetourt, Dorman, Harrison, Moffett, Cackley and Mullen, be a committee to act jointly with a committee from the senate to ascertain the state of the joint vote: the committee then withdrew, and after some time returned into the house, and Mr. Hunter of Berkeley reported that they had ascertained the joint vote to be for Baldwin 115; for Boyd 12; scattering 1; whereupon, Briscoe G. Baldwin, esq., was declared duly elected a major general of the third division of militia.

A message from the senate by Mr. Patteson:

MR. SPEAKER,—The senate have passed a bill, entitled, "an act to change the times of holding the courts in the fifth and seventh judicial circuits, and of the counties of Henrico and Powhatan, and the hustings court of the city of Richmond, and for other purposes," with amendments, in which they request the concurrence of this house. And then he withdrew.

The said amendments being twice read, were, on questions severally put thereupon, agreed to by the house.

Ordered, That the clerk inform the senate thereof.

A message from the senate by Mr. Fontaine:

MR. SPEAKER,—The senate agree to the resolution for transmitting a copy of the expunging resolutions to William C. Rives, esq. And then he withdrew.

On motion, *Ordered*, That leave of absence from the service of this house be granted to Messrs. Witcher and Swanson, each for the balance of the session from to-morrow.

Mr. Hill, from the committee of propositions and grievances, presented a bill to authorize the opening a new street in the town of Petersburg, which was received and laid upon the table.

Mr. Watkins reported with a substitute, a bill increasing the banking capital in this commonwealth, which was taken up on his motion; whereupon a motion was made by Mr. Mallory, that the further consideration of the said bill and substitute be indefinitely postponed; and the question being put thereupon, was determined in the negative. Ayes 49, noes 65.

The ayes and noes thereupon being required by Mr. Botts, (and sustained according to the rule of house,) are as follow:

Ayes, Messrs. Banks, (speaker,) Gilmer, Southall, Wiley, Campbell, Pate, Turnbull, Mallory, Booker, Austin, Daniel, Richardson, Hill, Wilson of Cumberland, Vaughan, Hunter of Essex, Steger, Hale of Franklin, Smith of Gloucester, Hail of Grayson, Carrington, Coleman, Nixon, Botts, Gregory, Fleet, Hooe, Robinson, Neill, Harris, Rogers, Garland of Mecklenburg, Leland, Fitzgerald, Woolfolk, Hopkins, Shands, Nicklin, Dorman, Jessee, M'Mullen, Bare, Rinker, Butts, Hargrave, Gillespie, Delashmutt, Cunningham and Stanard.—49.

Noes, Messrs. Grinalds, Layne, Garland of Amherst, Brooke, Craig, Hunter of Berkeley, Henshaw, Miller, Wilson of Botetourt, Decamps, Christian, Servant, Ball, Smith of Fauquier, Hickerson, Price, Strange, Holland, Bowen, Davison, Smith of Frederick, Watts, Watkins, Wethered, Sloan, Goodall, Mullen, Harrison, Kincheloe, Fontaine, Holleman, Berry, Summers, Carter, Hays, Straton, Beard, Taylor of Loudoun, Taylor of Mathews and Middlesex, Morgan, Sherrard, Benton, Brown of Nelson, Murdaugh, Cooke, Chapline, Masters, Adams, M'Coy, Swanson, Cackley, Madison, Morris, Williams, Marteney, Leyburn, Moffett, Conrad, Harley, Crutchfield, Moncure, Gibson, Jett, Prentiss, and Brown of Petersburg.—65.

The said substitute was then amended on motions of Mr. Brown of Petersburg, and Mr. Cunningham; whereupon,

On motion of Mr. Daniel, the house adjourned until to-morrow 10 o'clock.

WEDNESDAY, March 16th, 1836.

A communication from the senate by their clerk:

IN SENATE, March 15th, 1836.

The senate have passed the bills, entitled,
"An act to amend the act, entitled, 'an act to incorporate the Richmond manufacturing company.'"
"An act to incorporate the Portsmouth and Chesapeake steamboat company."
"An act to incorporate the trustees of the Charleston athenæum and female academy."
"An act to incorporate the trustees of the Lynchburg female academy."
"An act to incorporate the Goochland mining company."
"An act to establish the town of Lovettsville."
"An act changing the place of holding a separate election in the county of Kanawha;" and
"An act incorporating the trustees of the Martinsville academy."

They have also passed the bills, entitled,
"An act directing the survey and location of a route for a road from Moorfield to the North-western turnpike;" and
"An act concerning savings institutions," with amendments, in which they request the concurrence of the house of delegates.

The said amendments being twice read, were, on questions severally put thereupon, agreed to by the house.

Ordered, That the clerk inform the senate thereof.

On motion of Mr. Hill, *Ordered,* That leave be given to bring in a bill to amend an act passed March 1st, 1834, incorporating the town of Fairfax in the county of Culpeper, and that Messrs. Hill, Woolfolk, Nicklin, Smith of Fauquier, Harris and Crutchfield, prepare and bring in the same.

Mr. Mallory reported that the committee appointed to examine enrolled bills, had examined sundry other such bills and found them truly enrolled.

Ordered, That the clerk communicate the same to the senate.

A motion was made by Mr. Woolfolk, that the house adopt the following resolution:

Resolved by the general assembly, That the *commissioner of revolutionary claims* be directed to proceed to investigate all claims that may be presented to him, and report as required by law to the governor, and that the governor be requested to proceed to decide upon the same according to the laws of the land.

A motion was made by Mr. Miller, to amend the same by striking therefrom in the first line, the words "commissioner of revolutionary claims," and inserting in lieu thereof, the word "executive;" whereupon, on motion of Mr. Stanard, the said resolution and amendment were indefinitely postponed.

A report of the committee of finance, was read as follows:

The committee of finance have, according to order, had under consideration the petition of John M'Henry of the county of Cabell, to them referred, praying that an act may pass authorizing him to receive from the treasury the sum of twenty-five dollars, the amount of a fine which he alleges was improperly imposed upon him, and which he has paid: Whereupon,

Resolved as the opinion of this committee, That the prayer of said petition be rejected.

The said resolution was, on the question put thereupon, agreed to by the house.

A bill increasing the banking capital of this commonwealth, together with the substitute thereto, was taken up on motion of Mr. Woolfolk; whereupon, a motion was made by Mr. Daniel, further to amend the said substitute, so as to establish an independent bank at the town of Lynchburg, with a capital of $500,000; a motion was then made by Mr. Hunter of Essex, that the farther consideration of the said bill, proposed substitute, and amendment thereto, be indefinitely postponed; and the question being put thereupon, was determined in the affirmative. Ayes 68, noes 48.

The ayes and noes being required thereupon by Mr. M'Mullen, (and sustained according to the rule of the house,) are as follow:

Ayes, Messrs. Banks, (speaker,) Gilmer, Southall, Layne, Wiley, Campbell, Miller, Turnbull, Mallory, Booker, Austin, Samuel, Richardson, Johnson, Hill, Vaughan, Hunter of Essex, Smith of Fauquier, Hickerson, Strange, Steger, Hale of Franklin, Holland, Watts, Watkins, Hail of Grayson, Carrington, Coleman, Sloan, Nixon, Goodall, Fontaine, Holleman, Gregory, Fleet, Hooe, Robinson, Neill, Harris, Ragsdale, Taylor of Mathews and Middlesex, Rogers, Garland of Mecklenburg, Morgan, Chapman, Brown of Nelson, Leland, Woolfolk, Almond, Adams, Hopkins, Carroll, Shands, Williams, Nicklin, Moffett, Conrad, Jessee, M'Mullen, Bare, Rinker, Butts, Crutchfield, Hargrave, Gillespie, Delashmutt, Gibson and Cunningham.—68.

Noes, Messrs. Garland of Amherst, Brooke, Craig, Pate, Hunter of Berkeley, Henshaw, Wilson of Botetourt, Decamps, Beuhring, Daniel, Wilson of Cumberland, Price, Bowen, Davison, Smith of Frederick, Smith of Gloucester, Wethered, Mullen, Harrison, Kincheloe, Botts, Griggs, Berry, Summers, Carter, Hays, Straton, Beard, Taylor of Loudoun, Waggener, Sherrard, Benton, Murdaugh, Cooke, Fitzgerald, Chapline, Masters, M'Coy, Cackley, Madison, Marteney, Dorman, Leyburn, Moncure, Jett, Prentiss, Brown of Petersburg, and Stanard.—48.

Resolved, That the said bill be rejected.

A motion was made by Mr. Summers, that the rule of the house be suspended for the purpose of permitting him to introduce the following resolution:

Resolved, That leave be given to bring in a bill authorizing the stockholders of the Bank of Virginia to increase their capital stock $250,000, to be added to the present capital of the branch of said bank at Charleston in the county of Kanawha; also authorizing the stockholders of the Bank of the Valley to increase their capital stock $400,000, and to place a branch of said bank at Staunton in the county of Augusta, with a capital of $175,000, with leave also to establish an agency of said bank at Moorfield in the county of Hardy; also authorizing the North-western bank to increase its capital stock $200,000, and authorizing the Merchants and Mechanics bank of Wheeling to increase its capital stock $100,000.

And the question being put upon suspending the said rule, was determined in the negative. Ayes 36, noes 74. The ayes and noes being required thereupon by Mr. Hopkins, (and sustained according to the rule of the house,) are as follow:

Ayes, Messrs. Garland of Amherst, Brooke, Craig, Hunter of Berkeley, Henshaw, Decamps, Beuhring, Price, Bowen, Davison, Smith of Frederick, Wethered, Mullen, Griggs, Berry, Summers, Hays, Straton, Beard, Taylor of Loudoun, Waggener, Sherrard, Benton, Murdaugh, Cooke, Chapline, Masters, M'Coy, Cackley, Madison, Leyburn, Moncure, Delashmutt, Prentiss, Brown of Petersburg, and Stanard.—36.

Noes, Messrs. Banks, (speaker,) Gilmer, Southall, Layne, Wiley, Campbell, Miller, Wilson of Botetourt, Turnbull, Mallory, Booker, Austin, Daniel, Samuel, Richardson, Johnson, Hill, Wilson of Cumberland, Vaughan, Hunter of Essex, Smith of Fauquier, Hickerson, Strange, Steger, Hale of Franklin, Holland, Watts, Smith of Gloucester, Watkins, Hail of Grayson, Carrington, Coleman, Sloan, Nixon, Goodall, Harrison, Kincheloe, Botts, Fontaine, Holleman, Gregory, Fleet, Hooe, Robinson, Neill, Harris, Ragsdale, Taylor of Mathews and Middlesex, Rogers, Garland of Mecklenburg, Brown of Nelson, Leland, Fitzgerald, Woolfolk, Almond, Adams, Hopkins, Carroll, Shands, Williams, Marteney, Nicklin, Dorman, Moffett, Conrad, M'Mullen, Bare, Rinker, Butts, Crutchfield, Hargrave, Gillespie, Jet and Cunningham.—74.

Reports of the committee for courts of justice were read as follow:

The committee for courts of justice have, according to order, had under consideration the petition of sundry persons to them referred, praying that Jim Smith and Synthia his wife, and Betsy, Ann and Susan, their infant children, free persons of colour, may be permitted to remain in the commonwealth, and have come to the following resolution thereupon:

Resolved as the opinion of this committee, That the prayer of the said petition is reasonable.

The committee for courts of justice have, according to order, had under consideration the petition of Hugh M'Gavock, to them referred, praying to be allowed a balance of full pay due to him on account of services rendered during the revolutionary war, with interest thereon from the first January, 1782, and have come to the following resolution thereupon:

Resolved as the opinion of this committee, That the prayer of the said petition be rejected, it appearing that the amount claimed has been received by the petitioner.

The first resolution was, on the question put thereupon, agreed to by the house, and a bill was ordered conformably therewith.

The second resolution was, on motion of Mr. Gillespie, ordered to be laid upon the table.

Reports of the committee of roads and internal navigation were read as follow:

The committee of roads and internal navigation have, according to order, had under consideration the petition of sundry citizens of the town of Lynchburg, praying the passage of an act, giving to the hustings court of said town, power to let out the public roads within the corporation, annually, at public auction, to the lowest bidder, taking bond and good security to have them kept in good repair, and paying the expense thereof out of the ordinary revenue of the said town: Whereupon,

Resolved as the opinion of this committee, That the prayer of said petition is reasonable.

The committee of roads and internal navigation have, according to order, enquired into "the expediency of increasing the capital stock of the Richmond, Fredericksburg and Potomac rail-road company:" Whereupon,

Resolved as the opinion of this committee, That it is not expedient to increase the capital of said company.

The committee of roads and internal navigation have, according to order, had under consideration the petition of Samuel S. Williams and Henry H. Evans, representing that the petitioner Williams, undertook the construction of the turnpike road, at the canal of the Blue Ridge; that owing to the hidden ledges of rock, and other unforeseen difficulties, the contract has proved a hard one, and has resulted in his utter ruin. That the road is nearly a quarter of a mile longer than he understood it to be at the time he took the contract. That he has sunk entirely $200, which he had in hand at the commencement of his undertaking, and after its completion is left at least $300 in debt. That the said Williams let out a part of the road to the petitioner Evans, who met with similar difficulties in the execution of his contract, and is now left $200 in debt; and praying that the said petitioners be paid at least what they have lost on their contracts, if not for their severe and incessant personal labour: Whereupon,

Resolved as the opinion of this committee, That the said petition be rejected.

The committee of roads and internal navigation have, according to order, had under consideration the petition of sundry citizens of the county of Smyth, asking that the revenue of said county for the year 1836, or one moiety of the revenue of the county for each of the years 1836 and 1837, be appropriated to the completion of a wagon road from Smyth court-house, across Walker's mountain, to the plaister banks in said county: Whereupon,

Resolved as the opinion of this committee, That said petition be rejected.

The said resolutions were, on questions put thereupon, agreed to by the house, and a bill was ordered conformably with the first resolution.

A further report of the same committee was read as follows:

The committee of roads and internal navigation have, according to order, enquired into "the expediency of authorizing Lavender London and William H. Garland to erect a dam across Tye river, in the county of Nelson, from their own land, for the purpose of working a saw-mill and other machinery:" Whereupon,

Resolved as the opinion of this committee, That it is not expedient to authorize the erection of said dam.

The said resolution was amended, on motion of Mr. Garland of Amherst, by striking therefrom the word "*not*," so as to reverse the decision of the committee, and as amended, was agreed to by the house, and a bill was ordered conformably therewith.

A report of the committee of claims was read as follows:

The committee of claims have, according to order, had under consideration the petition of Berkeley Ward, to them referred, praying the remission of a fine imposed by the circuit superior court of law and chancery of Fauquier county upon John B. Armistead, sheriff of the said county, and have come to the following resolution thereupon:

Resolved as the opinion of this committee, That the prayer of the said petition be rejected.

The said resolution was amended, on motion of Mr. Hickerson, by striking therefrom the words "be rejected," and inserting in lieu thereof the words "is reasonable," and as amended, was agreed to by the house, and a bill was ordered conformably therewith.

An engrossed bill imposing taxes for the support of government, was read a third time, and sundry blanks therein were filled:

Resolved, That the bill do pass, and that the title be, "an act imposing taxes for the support of government."

An engrossed bill appropriating the public revenue, was read a third time, and sundry blanks therein were filled; whereupon, a clause by way of ryder thereto, was offered by Mr. Brown of Petersburg, which was read twice, and engrossed and read a third time:

Resolved, That the bill (with the ryder) do pass, and that the title be, "an act appropriating the public revenue."

An engrossed bill to amend the act concerning merchants' licenses, was read a third time:

Resolved, That the bill do pass, and that the title be, "an act to amend the act concerning merchants' licenses."

An engrossed bill directing a survey of the Dragon swamp, was read a third time:

Resolved, That the bill do pass, and that the title be, "an act directing a survey of the Dragon swamp."

An engrossed bill to regulate the conduct of boatmen on the Appomattox and Roanoke rivers and their branches, was read a third time:

Resolved, That the bill do pass, and that the title be, "an act to regulate the conduct of boatmen on the Appomattox and Roanoke rivers and their branches."

An engrossed bill appointing commissioners to select a site for the seat of justice for the county of Ohio, was read a third time:

Resolved, That the bill do pass, and that the title be, "an act appointing commisssioners to select a site for the seat of justice for the county of Ohio."

An engrossed bill incorporating the Big Bird mining company, was read a third time:

Resolved, That the bill do pass, and that the title be, "an act incorporating the Big Bird mining company."

An engrossed bill incorporating the Fredericksburg Union manufacturing company, was read a third time:

Resolved, That the bill do pass, and that the title be, "an act incorporating the Fredericksburg Union manufacturing company."

An engrossed bill incorporating the American mining company, was read a third time:

Resolved, That the bill do pass, and that the title be, "an act incorporating the American mining company."

An engrossed bill incorporating the Rappahannock marine and fire insurance company, was read a time:

Resolved, That the bill do pass, and that the title be, "an act incorporating the Rappahannock marine and fire insurance company."

An engrossed bill to incorporate the Berkeley coal mining and rail-road company, was read a third time:

Resolved, That the bill do pass, and that the title be, "an act to incorporate the Berkeley coal mining and rail-road company."

An engrossed bill to amend the act, entitled, "an act concerning the Cumberland road," was read a third time:

Resolved, That the bill do pass, and that the title be, "an act to amend the act, entitled, 'an act concerning the Cumberland road.'"

An engrossed bill to amend an act, entitled, "an act to enact with amendments, an act of the general assembly of North Carolina, entitled, 'an act to incorporate the Greensville and Roanoke rail-road company,'" was read a third time:

Resolved, That the bill do pass, and that the title be, "an act to amend an act, entitled, 'an act to enact with amendments, an act of the general assembly of North Carolina, entitled, 'an act to incorporate the Greensville and Roanoke rail-road company.'"

An engrossed bill to amend and explain the act, entitled, "an act to reduce into one, the several acts to regulate the solemnization of marriages," was read a third time:

Resolved, That the bill do pass, and that the title be, "an act to amend and explain the act, entitled, 'an act to reduce into one the several acts to regulate the solemnization of marriages.'"

Ordered, That the clerk communicate the said bills to the senate and request their concurrence.

An engrossed bill making further provision for taking depositions in certain cases, was read a third time, whereupon, on motion of Mr. Price, the farther consideration thereof was indefinitely postponed.

Resolved, That the said bill be rejected.

Mr. Stanard, from the committee for courts of justice, presented a report upon the petition of Frederick Moore, which was received and laid upon the table.

On motion of Mr. Servant, the house adjourned until to-morrow 10 o'clock.

THURSDAY, March 17th, 1836.

A communication from the senate by their clerk:

IN SENATE, March 16th, 1836.

The senate have passed the bills, entitled,

"An act to amend the act, entitled, 'an act to amend and to reduce into one act all acts and parts of acts to prevent the destruction of oysters,'" passed March 24th, 1831.

"An act to incorporate the New Hope gold mine company."

"An act changing the Hunting Run gold mining company into a company for mining and manufacturing iron and steel."

"An act to amend the several acts concerning the Petersburg rail-road company."

"An act to authorize a subscription on behalf of the state to the stock of the Pittsylvania and Lynchburg turnpike company, and for other purposes."

"An act incorporating the Lynchburg and Campbell court-house turnpike company;" and

"An act to amend the act, entitled, 'an act making further provision for completing the road from Staunton to the mouth of the Little Kanawha.'"

They have also passed the bills, entitled,

"An act declaring Pocatallico river a public highway;" and

"An act to equalize the regimental districts in the county of Rockingham, and for other purposes," with amendments, in which they request the concurrence of the house of delegates.

And they have agreed to the resolution voting a sword to captain E. A. F. Valette of the United States navy.

The said amendments being twice read, were, on questions severally put thereupon, agreed to by the house.

Ordered, That the clerk inform the senate thereof.

Mr. Shands, from the committee for courts of justice, presented a bill allowing Jim Smith and wife and their infant children, free persons of colour, to remain in the commonwealth a limited time, which was received and laid upon the table.

On motion, *Ordered,* That leave of absence from the service of this house, for the remainder of the session, be granted to Messrs. Chapman, and Garland of Mecklenburg.

On motion of Mr. Goodall, *Resolved by the general assembly of Virginia,* That the board of public works be, and they are hereby instructed to cause a survey to be made of the Pamunkey river, from New Castle in the county of Hanover, to the junction of the north and south branches, and also of the south branch up to Darricott's mills in the county of Hanover; and if the engagements of the principal engineer of the state will not permit him to perform the service, that they are hereby authorized to employ some competent engineer for that purpose, who shall report to the next general assembly an estimate of the cost of making the same navigable for boats, on the most practicable plan.

Ordered, That the clerk communicate the same to the senate and request their concurrence.

Mr. Hill, according to order, presented a bill to amend and explain an act, entitled, "an act to prescribe the mode of electing trustees for the town of Fairfax in the county of Culpeper, and vesting them with corporate powers."

Mr. Stanard, from the committee for courts of justice, presented a report upon the petition of Lucy and Delila.

And a bill abolishing the vaccine agency of this commonwealth.

Which were received and laid upon the table.

A motion was made by Mr. Wilson of Cumberland, to suspend the rule of the house, for the purpose of introducing a resolution for leave to bring in a bill to construct a rail-road from Cartersville to Farmville; whereupon, on motion of Mr. Shands, the said motion was ordered to be laid upon the table.

A bill concerning the Chesapeake and Ohio canal company, was taken up and ordered to be engrossed and read a third time.

A bill incorporating the Mayo's bridge company, with the substitute thereto proposed by the committee of roads and internal navigation, was taken up, and the said amendment being agreed to by the house, the said bill, as amended, was ordered to be engrossed and read a third time.

The following bills were read a second time, and ordered to be engrossed and read a third time, viz:

A bill concerning Robert W. Christian, treasurer of the late charity school of Charles City, and the overseers of the poor of said county.

A bill to amend the act, entitled, "an act to incorporate the Grayson Sulphur springs company;" and

A bill authorizing appeals to be taken from the courts of certain counties therein mentioned to the court of appeals at Lewisburg.

A bill to amend and explain the 96th, 99th and 100th sections of an act for the better organization of the militia, was, on motion of Mr. Watkins, ordered to be laid upon the table.

The following bills were read a second time, and ordered to be engrossed and read a third time:

A bill to change the place of holding a separate election in the county of Cabell.

A bill incorporating the Fredericksburg mining company.

A bill to prevent slaves, free negroes and mulattoes, from trading beyond the limits of the city, county or town in which they reside.

A bill incorporating the Marshall and Ohio turnpike company.

A bill to enlarge the powers of the county courts of Albemarle and Nelson, for the purpose of opening a road from Scottsville to the head waters of Rockfish river.

A bill to prevent frauds in the packing of cotton.

A bill incorporating the stockholders of the Smithfield rail-road company.

A bill to authorize the Dismal Swamp canal company to increase their capital stock, and to authorize the loans of the state to said company to be converted into stock.

A bill incorporating the stockholders of the Eastern Shore rail-road company.

A bill incorporating the Virginia silk company.

A bill to authorize Richard Lorton to surrender his interest in the museum property.

A bill authorizing the auditor of public accounts to issue a warrant on the treasury in favour of John H. Gwathmey, administrator of Richard Clarke, deceased, in pursuance of a judgment of the superior court of Henrico county, for commutation of five years full pay with interest.

A bill providing further security for the payment of jailors' fees.

A bill to incorporate the trustees of St. Bride's academy in Norfolk county.

A bill concerning Amos Johnston.

A bill constituting a portion of the margin of the Potomac river in Berkeley county a legal fence.

A bill changing the punishment of slaves convicted of hog stealing.

A bill to amend an act incorporating the Fredericksburg mechanics association.

A bill to repeal the act to provide for the appointment of a commissioner to examine and report upon claims for unsatisfied military land bounties, and for other purposes, passed March 11th, 1834.

A bill changing the time of holding the county courts in the counties of Marshall and Ohio, and to amend the act establishing the town of Moundsville in Ohio (now Marshall) county.

A bill concerning the Matoaca manufacturing company.

A bill to change the time of holding a quarterly term of the county court of the county of Shenandoah.

A bill to amend the act, entitled, "an act to incorporate a rail-road company from the city of Richmond to the town of York."

A bill changing the terms of the circuit superior court of law and chancery in and for the county of Stafford.

A bill to change the place of holding a separate election in the county of Pittsylvania.

A bill incorporating the Sweet springs and Price's mountain turnpike company.

A bill amending the act concerning waste tobacco.

A bill to incorporate a company to construct a toll-bridge across the Shenandoah river at Harper's Ferry.

A bill to prevent the destruction of oysters in Nansemond river, and Chuckatuck creek in the county of Nansemond.

A bill to change the place of holding a separate election in the county of Harrison.

A bill to amend the act, entitled, "an act to incorporate the Grayson Sulphur springs company."

A bill to incorporate the town of Waterford in the county of Loudoun.

A bill appointing trustees to the town of New Glasgow, and for other purposes.

A bill to increase the capital stock of Booker's gold mine company, and for other purposes.

A bill regulating the mode of obtaining writs of error in criminal prosecutions for misdemeanors; and

A bill incorporating the Deane iron and steel manufacturing company.

An engrossed bill to amend an act, entitled, "an act to incorporate the Augusta springs company," was read a third time:

Resolved, That the bill do pass, and that the title be, "an act to amend an act, entitled, 'an act to incorporate the Augusta springs company.'"

An engrossed bill to authorize Thomas A. Morton to erect a dam across Appomattox river, was read a third time:

Resolved, That the bill do pass, and that the title be, "an act to authorize Thomas A. Morton to erect a dam across Appomattox river."

An engrossed bill to incorporate the Etna coal company, was read a third time:

Resolved, That the bill do pass, and that the title be, "an act to incorporate the Etna coal company."

Ordered, That Mr. Wilson of Botetourt, carry the same to the senate and request their concurrence.

An engrossed bill concerning the administrator of Dominic Bennehan, deceased, was read a third time, and on motion of Mr. Crutchfield, ordered to be laid upon the table.

An engrossed bill concerning William Fenn, was read a third time:

Resolved, That the bill do pass, and that the title be, "an act concerning William Fenn."

An engrossed bill concerning John Chew, was read a third time:

Resolved, That the bill do pass, and that the title be, "an act concerning John Chew."

An engrossed bill incorporating the trustees of the Clarksville female academy, was read a third time:

Resolved, That the bill do pass, and that the title be, "an act incorporating the trustees of the Clarksville female academy."

An engrossed bill for the construction of a bridge across Jackson's river at the town of Covington, was read a third time:

Resolved, That the bill do pass, and (the title being amended on motion of Mr. Layne,) that the title be, "an act to change the site for the erection of a bridge across Jackson's river opposite the town of Covington from second to third street, in accordance with the act, entitled, 'an act for the erection of said bridge,'" passed 23d January, 1833.

An engrossed bill to incorporate the proprietors of the Wellsburg lyceum, was read a third time:

Resolved, That the bill do pass, and that the title be, "an act to incorporate the proprietors of the Wellsburg lyceum."

An engrossed bill to amend an act, entitled, "an act incorporating the trustees of the Bedford female academy," was read a third time:

Resolved, That the bill do pass, and that the title be, "an act to amend an act, entitled, 'an act incorporating the trustees of the Bedford female academy.'"

An engrossed bill re-organizing the Lexington arsenal and establishing a military school in connexion with Washington college, was read a third time:

Resolved, That the bill do pass, and that the title be, "an act re-organizing the Lexington arsenal and establishing a military school in connexion with Washington college."

An engrossed bill to alter and increase the terms of the circuit superior court of law and chancery for the county of Norfolk, was read a third time:

Resolved, That the bill do pass, and (the title being amended on motion of Mr. Cooke,) that the title be, "an act to alter the terms of the circuit superior court of law and chancery for the county and borough of Norfolk."

An engrossed bill to authorize a separate election in the county of Tazewell, was read a third time; whereupon, a clause by way of ryder thereto was offered by Mr. Jessee, which being read the first and second times, and forthwith engrossed and read a third time:

Resolved, That the bill, with the ryder, do pass, and the title being amended on motion of Mr. Jessee, that the title be, "an act to authorize a separate election in the county of Tazewell, *and one in the county of Russell.*"

An engrossed bill to add a part of the county of Tazewell to the county of Giles, was read a third time:

Resolved, That the bill do pass, and that the title be, "an act to add a part of the county of Tazewell to the county of Giles."

An engrossed bill to authorize a separate election at the house of William Pulliam, in the county of Henry, was read a third time:

Resolved, That the bill do pass, and that the title be, "an act to authorize a separate election at the house of William Pulliam, in the county of Henry."

An engrossed bill to amend the act, entitled, "an act reducing into one the several acts for punishing persons guilty of certain thefts and forgeries, and the destruction or concealment of wills," was read a third time:

Resolved, That the bill do pass, and that the title be, "an act to amend the act, entitled, 'an act reducing into one the several acts for punishing persons guilty of certain thefts and forgeries, and the destruction or concealment of wills.'"

An engrossed bill to authorize Richard Barton Haxall to construct wharves at and near the town of Bermuda Hundred, was read a third time:

Resolved, That the bill do pass, and that the title be, "an act to authorize Richard Barton Haxall to construct wharves at and near the town of Bermuda Hundred."

An engrossed bill to incorporate the Potowmac silk and agricultural company, was read a third time:

Resolved, That the bill do pass, and that the title be, "an act to incorporate the Potowmac silk and agricultural company."

An engrossed bill to authorize a separate election at M'Gaheysville in the county of Rockingham, was read a third time:

Resolved, That the bill do pass, and that the title be, "an act to authorize a separate election at M'Gaheysville in the county of Rockingham."

Ordered, That Mr. Wilson of Botetourt carry the said bills to the senate and request their concurrence.

An engrossed bill concerning the legal representatives of Severn Eyre, deceased, was read a third time, and on motion of Mr. Dorman, ordered to be laid upon the table.

An engrossed bill to incorporate the Front Royal library society in the county of Frederick, was read a third time:

Resolved, That the bill do pass, and that the title be, "an act to incorporate the Front Royal library society in the county of Frederick."

An engrossed bill to explain the act authorizing subscriptions on the part of the commonwealth to the capital of joint stock companies, was read a third time:

Resolved, That the bill do pass, and that the title be, "an act to explain the act authorizing subscriptions on the part of the commonwealth to the capital of joint stock companies."

An engrossed bill concerning John Pittinger, late sheriff of Brooke county, was read a third time:

Resolved, That the bill do pass, and that the title be, "an act concerning John Pittinger, late sheriff of Brooke county."

An engrossed bill to establish the town of Meadowville in the county of Greenbrier, was read a third time:

Resolved, That the bill do pass, and that the title be, "an act to establish the town of Meadowville in the county of Greenbrier."

An engrossed bill to change the time of holding the county courts of the counties of Lewis and Braxton, was read a third time; whereupon, a clause by way of ryder thereto was offered by Mr. Ball, which was read the first and second times, and forthwith engrossed and read a third time:

Resolved, That the bill do pass, and the title being amended on motion of Mr. Hays, that the title be, "an act to change the time of holding the county courts of the county of Lewis and Braxton, *and the circuit superior courts of law and chancery for the county of Fairfax.*"

An engrossed bill changing the time of holding the superior courts of Campbell, Bedford and the town of Lynchburg, was read a third time:

Resolved, That the bill do pass, and that the title be, "an act changing the time of holding the superior courts of Campbell, Bedford and the town of Lynchburg."

An engrossed bill concerning the subscription on behalf of the commonwealth to the stock of the Richmond, Fredericksburg and Potowmac rail-road company, was read a third time:

Resolved, That the bill do pass, and that the title be, "an act concerning the subscription on behalf of the commonwealth to the stock of the Richmond, Fredericksburg and Potowmac rail-road company."

Ordered, That Mr. Wilson of Botetourt carry the said bills to the senate and request their concurrence.

An engrossed bill to amend an act, entitled, "an act to enact with amendments an act of the general assembly of North Carolina, entitled, 'an act to incorporate the Greensville and Roanoke rail-road company,'" passed February 7th, 1834, was read a third time; whereupon, Mr. Brown of Petersburg, offered a clause thereto by way of ryder, which was read twice and forthwith engrossed and read a third time:

Resolved, That the bill do pass, and that the title be, "an act to amend an act, entitled, 'an act to enact with amendments an act of the general assembly of North Carolina, entitled, 'an act to incorporate the Greensville and Roanoke rail-road company,'" passed February 7th, 1834.

Ordered, That the clerk communicate the same to the senate and request their concurrence.

A bill to amend the charter of the James river and Kanawha company, was taken up on motion of Mr. Miller, and read a second time; whereupon, a motion was made by Mr. Garland of Amherst, to strike from the first section the following clause:

"For the purpose of assessing the damages to the owner from the condemnation of his land for the use of the road or canal, or any feeder of the canal, or for any abutment of a dam, or for the sites of toll-houses, stables and other buildings, there shall be appointed by the board of public works, five assessors, being discreet, intelligent and impartial men, neither stockholders of the company nor owners of any land through which the improvements of the company will pass; who, or any three or more of them, shall constitute a board for the assessment of such damages throughout the whole line of the improvement. All vacancies in the board of assessors shall be filled by the board of public works. These assessors shall hold their offices during the pleasure of the board of public works, and shall receive as a compensation for their services five dollars each, for every day that he shall be engaged in the performance of his duties, and twenty cents for every mile he shall necessarily travel to and from the place of performing his duties, to be paid by the company."

And the question being put upon striking out the clause, was determined in the negative. Ayes 48, noes 53.

The ayes and noes thereupon being required by Mr. Garland of Amherst, (and sustained according to the rule of the house,) are as follow:

Ayes, Messrs. Gilmer, Southall, Wiley, Garland of Amherst, Miller, Wilson of Botetourt, Turnbull, Mallory, Booker, Austin, Daniel, Samuel, Hill, Wilson of Cumberland, Hunter of Essex, Smith of Fauquier, Strange, Holland, Coleman, Sloan, Goodall, Fontaine, Holleman, Fleet, Hooe, Robinson, Taylor of Loudoun, Harris, Ragsdale, Rogers, Benton, Brown of Nelson, Almond, Hopkins, Madison, Shands, Williams, Nicklin, Moffett, Conrad, Jessee, Bare, Rinker, Butts, Crutchfield, Hargrave, Gibson and Stanard.—48.

Noes, Messrs. Banks, (speaker,) Layne, Brooke, Hunter of Berkeley, Henshaw, Decamps, Beuhring, Johnson, Vaughan, Servant, Ball, Price, Steger, Hale of Franklin, Davison, Smith of Frederick, Watts, Smith of Gloucester, Watkins, Hail of Grayson, Wethered, Nixon, Mullen, Kincheloe, Botts, Gregory, Griggs, Berry, Summers, Neill, Hays, Straton, Beard, Waggener, Morgan, Sherrard, Murdaugh, Cooke, Fizgerald, Chapline, Masters, Adams, M'Coy, Cackley, Carroll, Marteney, Leyburn, M'Mullen, Moncure, Gillespie, Delashmutt, Jett and Cunningham.—53.

A motion was made by Mr. Stanard to amend the said bill, by inserting therein the following clause:

"*Provided however*, That in the event the provisions of this act changing the mode of assessing damages, shall not be confirmed by the next general assembly, the same shall from and after the adjournment of the next general assembly cease and determine, and the clauses of the original charter herein mentioned as repealed, shall be reinstated, and form a part of the charter of the company, in like manner as though this act had not been passed."

A motion was then made by Mr. Watkins, to amend the said amendment, by substituting therefor the following: "*Provided however*, That nothing herein contained shall prevent the general assembly from hereafter altering or repealing the mode of assessing damages as provided for in this act."

And the question being put upon the said amendment to the amendment, was determined in the affirmative. Ayes 55, noes 35.

The ayes and noes thereupon being required by Mr Austin, (and sustained according to the rule of the house,) are as follow:

Ayes, Messrs. Banks, (speaker,) Southall, Layne, Brooke, Hunter of Berkeley, Henshaw, Miller, Wilson of Botetourt, Decamps, Turnbull, Beuhring, Daniel, Johnson, Vaughan, Price, Steger, Hale of Franklin, Holland, Smith of Frederick, Smith of Gloucester, Watkins, Hail of Grayson, Wethered, Nixon, Mullen, Kincheloe, Gregory, Griggs, Berry, Summers, Fleet, Carter, Hays, Beard, Ragsdale, Waggener, Sherrard, Cooke, Fitzgerald, Masters, Adams, M'Coy, Cackley, Carroll, Leyburn, Jessee, M'Mullen, Butts, Hargrave, Gillespie, Delashmutt, Gibson, Jett, Cunningham, and Brown of Petersburg.—55.

Noes, Messrs. Gilmer, Wiley, Garland of Amherst, Booker, Austin, Samuel, Wilson of Cumberland, Hunter of Essex, Ball, Smith of Fauquier, Strange, Davison, Coleman, Sloan, Goodall, Botts, Fontaine, Holleman, Robinson, Neill, Harris, Rogers, Morgan, Benton, Brown of Nelson, Murdaugh, Almond, Hopkins, Madison, Williams, Nicklin, Bare, Crutchfield, Moncure and Stanard.—35.

The said amendment, as amended, was then agreed to by the house, and the said bill, as amended, was ordered to be engrossed and read a third time.

The speaker laid before the house a communication from the governor, which was read as follows:

EXECUTIVE DEPARTMENT, March 17, 1836.

SIR,—Enclosed is a communication for the house of delegates, which you will be pleased to lay before that body.

Respectfully your obedient servant,
LITT'N W. TAZEWELL.

To the Speaker of the House of Delegates.

EXECUTIVE DEPARTMENT, March 17th, 1836.

To the House of Delegates.

I have just received the enclosed letter from the governor of the state of Ohio, which I have the honour to submit to the general assembly.

LITT'N W. TAZEWELL.

EXECUTIVE OFFICE, OHIO,
COLUMBUS, 4th March, 1836.

SIR,—In compliance with the request of the general assembly, I have the honour to transmit you the annexed resolutions, passed by that body on the 29th ult.

Very respectfully, your obedient servant,
ROBERT LUCAS.

His Excellency the Governor of Virginia.

Resolutions relating to the election of President and Vice President.

Be it resolved by the general assembly of the state of Ohio, That our senators in congress be instructed, and our representatives requested, to use their exertions to procure an amendment of the constitution of the United States, so as to prevent any future election of president of the United States, by the house of representatives, and of vice president of the United States, by the senate; and so that the election can in no case be taken from the people.

Be it further resolved, That his excellency the governor be requested to forward a copy of the foregoing resolution to each of our senators and representatives in congress, and to each of the governors of the several states of this Union.

WILLIAM MEDILL,
Speaker pro tem. of the House of Representatives.

ELIJAH VANCE,
Speaker of the Senate.

February 29, 1836.

STATE OF OHIO, SECRETARY'S OFFICE,
Columbus, March 2, 1836.

I certify that the foregoing resolutions is a correct copy of the original roll remaining on file in this office.

C. B. HARLAN, *Secretary of State.*

On motion of Mr. Wilson of Botetourt, *Ordered*, That the said communication be laid upon the table; and on motion of Mr. Wethered, 185 copies thereof were ordered to be printed for the use of the general assembly.

An engrossed bill to establish an additional grade of flour in the inspections of flour in this commonwealth, was, on motion of Mr. Southall, ordered to be laid on the table.

A bill concerning delinquent lands, and lands not heretofore entered on the commissioners' books, was amended on motion of Mr. Hays, and as amended, ordered to be engrossed and read a third time.

On motion of Mr. Holleman, the following report of the committee of schools and colleges was taken up:

The committee of schools and colleges have, according to order, had under consideration the petition of Richard H. Edwards, treasurer of the school commissioners of the county of Surry, representing that in transferring from his record into his day book, the amount which was stated in the annual report of 1834, as being in his hands, he entered the sum of $210 43 instead of $110 43, and not being apprized of the error, he expended the said sum of $210 43, whereby he became a creditor of the literary fund to the amount of $108 50, as appears by the report of the board of school commissioners for the said county; that the said board of school commissioners have decided that they are not authorized by law to afford relief to the petitioner; and praying that the auditor of public accounts, or any other proper authority, be directed to issue a warrant in his favour for the said sum of $108 50, or that the board of school commissioners of said county be directed to pay the same out of any money which may come into their hands: Whereupon,

Resolved as the opinion of this committee, That said petition be rejected.

On motion of Mr. Holleman, the said resolution was amended, by substituting therefor the following:

Resolved, That so much of the said petition as prays that the school commissioners of the county of Surry refund to the said petitioner the sum of one hundred dollars, out of the annual quota from the literary fund, is reasonable.

The said resolution, as amended, was then agreed to by the house.

Ordered, That Messrs. Holleman, Garland of Amherst, Murdaugh, Madison, Hargrave, Shands and Turnbull, prepare and bring in a bill conformably with said resolution, as amended.

On motion of Mr. Crutchfield, the house adjourned until to-morrow 10 o'clock.

FRIDAY, March 18th, 1836.

A communication from the senate by their clerk:

IN SENATE, March 17th, 1836.

The senate have passed the bills, entitled,

"An act to amend and explain the act, entitled, 'an act to reduce into one act, the several acts to regulate the solemnization of marriages.'"

"An act incorporating the Fredericksburg Union manufacturing company."

"An act appointing commissioners to select a site for the seat of justice for the county of Ohio."

"An act incorporating the American mining company."

"An act incorporating the Rappahannock marine and fire insurance company."

"An act incorporating the Big Bird mining company;" and

"An act to authorize a separate election in the county of Tazewell, and one in the county of Russell."

And they have agreed to the resolution for surveying the Pamunkey river from New Castle to the junction of the North and South branches of said river, and of the South branch thereof to Darricott's mills.

Mr. Stanard, from the committee for courts of justice, presented a bill to prevent more effectually persons trading with slaves.

Mr. Henshaw, from the committee of claims, presented a report upon the petition of John B. Findley and John Rogers.

And a bill concerning John B. Armistead, sheriff of Fauquier county.

Which were received and laid upon the table.

On motions severally made, *Ordered*, That leave of absence from the service of this house, be granted to Messrs. Pate, Campbell and Coleman from to-day; to Messrs. Mallory, Richardson, Brown of Nelson, and Griggs from to-morrow, and to Mr. Holland from Monday next.

On motion of Mr. Henshaw, *Ordered*, That the committee of claims be discharged from the consideration of the petition of Peter Kremer, and that the same be laid upon the table.

The following reports of the committee of roads and internal navigation were read:

The committee of roads and internal navigation have, according to order, enquired into "the expediency of authorizing the board of public works to subscribe for two fifths of the capital stock of the Lexington and Richmond turnpike company:" Whereupon,

Resolved as the opinion of this committee, That it is not expedient to authorize said subscription.

The committee of roads and internal navigation have, according to order, had under consideration the petition of sundry citizens of the county of Scott, praying the appropriation of a sum of money to aid in building a bridge across the North fork of Holston river, near the site where one lately stood, on the main western road leading through Moccason gap in Clinch mountain: Whereupon,

Resolved as the opinion of this committee, That said petition be rejected.

The said resolutions were, on motions of Mr. M'Mullen and Mr. Dorman, ordered to be laid upon the table.

A report of the committee of schools and colleges was read as follows:

The committee of schools and colleges have, according to order, enquired into "the expediency of increasing the number of visitors of the University of Virginia:" Whereupon,

Resolved as the opinion of this committee, That it is not expedient to increase the number of said visitors.

The said resolution was, on motion of Mr. Wilson of Botetourt, ordered to be laid upon the table.

A report of the committee of schools and colleges was read as follows:

The committee of schools and colleges have, according to order, had under consideration the petition of the school commissioners of Smyth county, representing that there remains due to said county, and undrawn from the literary fund, the sum of four hundred and twenty-seven dollars and twenty-five cents, and praying that they be authorized by law to draw the same from the literary fund: Whereupon,

Resolved as the opinion of this committee, That said petition be rejected.

The said resolution was, on the question put thereupon, agreed to by the house.

A report of the committee of finance was read as follows:

The committee of finance have, according to order, had under consideration the petition of Henry Anderson, to them referred, representing:

That a certain Lewis Eisenmenger, deceased, was the owner of many tracts of land lying in the counties of Bath, Grayson, Russell and Randolph, on which a large amount of tax was due and unpaid; that said lands became vested in the literary fund prior to the 22d day of February, 1830; that on that day an act was passed, authorizing the president and directors of the literary fund to make an equitable arrangement with said Eisenmenger, and accordingly on the 27th day of April, 1831, the term of five years from that date was allowed him, within which to pay the taxes, exclusive of damages due on said lands; that said Eisenmenger died in January 1833, no payment having been made then or at the present time of any part of said taxes; that said Eisenmenger made a will, (an office copy of which accompanies the petition,) in which are sundry bequests to persons in this country and in Europe; that said Eisenmenger has no personal estate sufficient to pay said taxes; that said Eisenmenger was a native of Germany, a stranger to the laws, customs and language of Virginia, and therefore employed the petitioner, from the year 1826 to the time of his death, (near seven years,) to aid him in the investigation and prosecution of his land titles and business; that since the death of said Eisenmenger, the petitioner has obtained a judgment against his administrator with the will annexed, for the sum of five hundred dollars and costs; that all the other lands of said Eisenmenger, (besides those referred to as being vested as aforesaid,) were at the time of his death, and still are, conveyed by him in trust: and thereupon the petitioner prays, that an act may pass, "authorizing him, at any time within the year 1836, to pay the taxes on the said lands which remain due and unpaid, and when so paid, that the petitioner may be *invested* with all the right, title and interest, in and to the said lands, which would have been vested in the said Eisenmenger, had he lived and redeemed the same, under the act of assembly and resolutions of the president and directors of the literary fund above referred to:" Whereupon,

1. *Resolved as the opinion of this committee,* That the prayer of the petitioner, so far as it asks that he may be permitted to redeem the said lands and apply the same to the payment of his debt, be rejected.

2. *Resolved also as the opinion of this committee,* That it is reasonable to extend the privilege of redemption to the representatives and creditors of Lewis Eisenmenger, generally, for the period of one year beyond the 27th day of April, 1836.

The said resolutions were, on questions put thereupon, agreed to by the house, and a bill was ordered to be brought in conformably with the said last resolution.

A report of the committee of propositions and grievances was read as follows:

The committee of propositions and grievances have, according to order, had under consideration several petitions to them referred, and have come to the following resolutions thereupon:

1. *Resolved as the opinion of this committee,* That the petition or memorial of the trustees of the town of Portsmouth, praying that the act passed on the 10th of March, 1832, amending an act of the 4th of April, 1831, declaring that an avenue in the said town, on the eastern border, called and known by the name of Water street, should be made a street, under the direction of the trustees of said town, may be so amended as to provide, that if any person or persons whatsoever, owning or having any interest in any land on the said avenue, should refuse to consent to the said street being laid off, that so much of his or her land may be taken as may be necessary to form the same, and that his or her damages may be ascertained by a writ of *ad quod damnum,* to be issued from the county court of Norfolk county, on application in that behalf; and that said street may be made forty feet, instead of thirty feet wide, as is provided in the acts aforesaid, is reasonable.

2. *Resolved as the opinion of this committee,* That the petition of sundry citizens of the county of Northumberland, and of that part of said county commonly known as Upper Saint Stephen's parish, and freeholders and voters therein, praying that an act may pass authorizing a separate election in said parish, at the place called the Burn'd Chimneys, in said county, is reasonable.

3. *Resolved as the opinion of this committee,* That the petition of sundry citizens of the county of Nicholas, residing on the waters of Twenty Mile creek and Gauley river, and adjoining the county of Fayette, praying that so much of the territory of the county of Nicholas as lies within a line commencing at the mouth of Meadow river, (which empties into Gauley river,) thence a straight line to the residence of William Bird, on Twenty Mile creek,

(including the house of said Bird,) thence a straight line to Rock camp, on Bell creek, where it will intersect the Nicholas, Fayette and Kanawha boundary lines, may be attached to, and made a part of the county of Fayette, be rejected for want of notice.

The said resolutions were, on questions severally put thereupon, agreed to by the house, and bills were ordered to be brought in conformably with the first and second resolutions.

Reports of the committee for courts of justice were read as follow:

The committee for courts of justice have, according to order, had under consideration the petition of Frederick Moore of the county of Cabell, to them referred, praying the passage of a law granting to him all the rights, privileges and advantages that he would have been entitled to under the deed executed to him in the year 1818, from Robert Webb, for twenty acres of land lying in the said county of Cabell, (which deed was delivered to the clerk for record, and by him lost without having been recorded,) had the deed been recorded at the time of the delivery aforesaid, and have come to the following resolution thereupon:

Resolved as the opinion of this committee, That the prayer of the said petition is reasonable.

The committee for courts of justice, to whom was recommitted a report of the committee of claims, rejecting the petition of Stapleton Crutchfield, deputy sheriff of the county of Spottsylvania, praying such compensation as may be deemed reasonable, in consideration of services rendered by him, as deputy sheriff aforesaid, in attending upon the circuit superior court of law and chancery of the said county, have had the same under consideration, and have come to the following resolution thereupon:

Resolved as the opinion of this committee, That it is expedient to make an additional allowance to the sheriff of Spottsylvania county, in future, in consideration of his attendance upon the circuit superior court of law and chancery of that county.

The committee for courts of justice have, according to order, had under consideration the petition of Andy, a free man of colour, to them referred, praying that he may be permitted to remain in the commonwealth, and have come to the following resolutions thereupon:

Resolved as the opinion of this committee, That so much of the prayer of the said petitioner as prays to be permitted to remain in the commonwealth be rejected.

Resolved as the opinion of this committee, That so much of the prayer of the said petitioner as prays to be permitted to remain in the commonwealth a limited time, is reasonable.

The said resolutions were, on questions severally put thereupon, agreed to by the house, and bills were ordered conformably with the first and last two resolutions.

Reports of the committee on the penitentiary were read as follow:

The committee on the penitentiary institution, have had under consideration the petition of Samuel S. Pendleton, to them referred, praying to be released from confinement for the residue of his term of imprisonment, and asking to be pardoned, and have come to the following resolution thereupon:

Resolved as the opinion of this committee, That the prayer of the said petition be rejected.

The joint committee appointed to examine the penitentiary institution, beg leave to submit the following report:

They have discharged the duty assigned to them, and have examined the prison and store. They found every thing in excellent order. The books connected with the institution had been accurately kept, and the internal police seemed to have been regulated with system, skill and a due regard to the health of the prisoners. Experience, which has been gradually developing the wants of our penitentiary system, has shown the propriety of certain changes which are respectfully recommended to the house. It has been found that the assistant keepers, delivery clerk, sergeant and porter, each receives a compensation too small to reward him adequately for his services, and to secure hereafter the labours of such men as are fitted for the office. It is, therefore, respectfully recommended, that each of these officers be allowed the value of one hundred dollars per annum in manufactures of the institution; the price to be fixed by the directors, and the addition to be made only upon condition that the income of the institution shall amount to $32,000 for the year; it being deemed probable by the committee, that this conditional increase may operate as a wholesome stimulus upon the zeal and activity of these officers.

The necessity for some changes in our criminal code has been perceived by the general assembly for some years past. Two years ago a board of jurists was appointed, whose existence has expired, without their having acted upon the subject. There were defects in its constitution, which prevented their action. It is believed that a board constituted of a smaller number of jurists, and vested with the power of employing a clerk to aid them in the manual labours attendant upon the discharge of their duties, would accomplish the end which the general assembly had in view. There is one change in the system of punishments so immediately connected with the efficient operation of our penitentiary institution, that the committee has deemed it a duty respectfully to recommend the subject to the consideration of this body. Experience has shown, that a confinement for two years in the penitentiary has signally failed in accomplishing the ends proposed by that mode of punishment. It is too short to impose an efficient check upon crime, by operating through the fears of the offender. And the convict for this period of confinement is discharged, before he has acquired any trade which can be useful to him afterwards. During the period of his stay, he is in most cases a charge upon the institution, because it requires an apprenticeship of two years to enable him to attain the degree of skill necessary for making his labours profitable. It is believed that three years constitute the best period for which offenders should be confined in the penitentiary. But a just attention to the graduation of punishments to crimes would require, that such a change should be accompanied with several others in our criminal code: a subject which will suggest itself to the consideration of the proposed board of jurists, should it be the pleasure of this general assembly to create such a board.

The committee submit the following resolutions:
1. *Resolved,* That it is expedient that the assistant keepers, delivery clerk, sergeant and porter of the penitentiary, shall each be allowed an additional compensation of one hundred dollars per annum, to be paid in the manufactures of the institution, at a price to be fixed by the directors, provided the income of the institution shall amount to $32,000 yearly.
2. *Resolved,* That an early revision of the criminal code of this commonwealth is expedient and necessary.
All which is respectfully submitted.

WM. M'MAHON, *C. C. S.*
R. M. T. HUNTER, *C. C. H. D.*

The said resolutions were, on questions severally put thereupon, agreed to by the house, and bills were ordered conformably with the said second and third resolutions.

Reports of the committee of claims were read as follow:

The committee of claims have, according to order, had under consideration the petition of Meilly Cooper, the only heir of Archy Cooper, to them referred, praying that such claim as the commonwealth may have upon the estate of the said Archy, her son, who was a lunatic, and died several years past in the lunatic hospital at Williamsburg, may be released to her, and have come to the following resolution thereupon:
Resolved as the opinion of this committee, That the prayer of the said petition is reasonable.

The committee of claims have, according to order, had under consideration the petition of Peter J. Chevallie, to them referred, praying to have refunded to him certain water rents paid by him to the James river company, between the destruction of his mills by fire in February 1833, and the completion of his present mills in July 1834, when the use of the said water was resumed by him, and have come to the following resolution thereupon:
Resolved as the opinion of this committee, That the prayer of the said petition is reasonable.

The committee of claims have, according to order, enquired into the expediency of authorizing the auditor of public accounts to issue a warrant in favour of James Burk, in payment of two stands of colours furnished the 128th regiment, should the fines of said regiment be sufficient, if not, for such amount as may have been paid in by said regiment: Whereupon,
Resolved as the opinion of this committee, That it is expedient to grant the authority aforesaid.

The committee of claims have, according to order, had under consideration the petition of Edward Goodwin, to them referred, praying compensation for nine months services, as a soldier, in guarding the frontier settlements of Virginia against the Indians, and have come to the following resolution thereupon:
Resolved as the opinion of this committee, That the prayer of the said petition be rejected.

The committee of claims have, according to order, had under consideration the petition of Abner Robinson, to them referred, praying to have refunded to him, the sum of two hundred and twenty-five dollars, paid by him in the year 1825, as the purchase money for a convict then in the penitentiary, condemned to sale and transportation beyond the limits of the United States, named Alexander Sparrow, who escaped from the petitioner on his way out of the United States, was thereafter arrested upon a charge of felony, and convicted upon such charge, was again condemned to imprisonment in the penitentiary, was afterwards pardoned by the executive, and finally lost to the petitioner, by reason (as is alleged by him), of such pardon, and have come to the following resolution thereupon:
Resolved as the opinion of this committee, That the prayer of the said petition be rejected.

The committee of claims have, according to order, had under consideration the petition of John B. Findley and John Rogers, to them referred, praying remuneration for expenses incurred by them, in arresting in the state of Tennessee, a criminal named William N. Antony, who had been committed to the jail of Nottoway county upon a charge of murder, and from which he had escaped, in conveying the said criminal to the jail aforesaid, and have come to the following resolution thereupon:
Resolved as the opinion of this committee, That the prayer of the said petition be rejected.

The said resolutions were, on questions severally put thereupon, agreed to by the house, and bills were ordered conformably with the three first resolutions.

A report of the committee on agriculture and manufactures was read as follows:

The committee of agriculture and manufactures, to whom was referred the petition of citizens of the town of Farmville, praying for the appointment of a person to weigh all loose and unprized tobacco sold in that town, having had the same under consideration, have come to the following resolution thereupon:
Resolved, That the prayer of the said petition is reasonable.

The said resolution was, on the question put thereupon, agreed to by the house, and a bill was ordered to be brought in conformably therewith.

A further report of the committee for courts of justice was read as follows:

The committee for courts of justice have, according to order, enquired into the expediency of extending magistrates' jurisdiction, and into the expediency of amending the several laws relating to constables: Whereupon,
Resolved as the opinion of this committee, That it is inexpedient to extend the jurisdiction of magistrates and to amend the laws in relation to constables.

On motion of Mr. Hickerson, the said resolution was ordered to be laid upon the table.

A report of the committee of propositions and grievances was read as follows:

The said resolutions were, on questions put thereupon, agreed to by the house, and a bill was ordered conformably with the first resolution.

A further report of the same committee was read as follows:

The committee of roads and internal navigation have, according to order, enquired into "the expediency of authorizing Lavender London and William H. Garland to erect a dam across Tye river, in the county of Nelson, from their own land, for the purpose of working a saw-mill and other machinery:" Whereupon,

Resolved as the opinion of this committee, That it is not expedient to authorize the erection of said dam.

The said resolution was amended, on motion of Mr. Garland of Amherst, by striking therefrom the word "*not,*" so as to reverse the decision of the committee, and as amended, was agreed to by the house, and a bill was ordered conformably therewith.

A report of the committee of claims was read as follows:

The committee of claims have, according to order, had under consideration the petition of Berkeley Ward, to them referred, praying the remission of a fine imposed by the circuit superior court of law and chancery of Fauquier county upon John B. Armistead, sheriff of the said county, and have come to the following resolution thereupon:

Resolved as the opinion of this committee, That the prayer of the said petition be rejected.

The said resolution was amended, on motion of Mr. Hickerson, by striking therefrom the words "be rejected," and inserting in lieu thereof the words "is reasonable," and as amended, was agreed to by the house, and a bill was ordered conformably therewith.

An engrossed bill imposing taxes for the support of government, was read a third time, and sundry blanks therein were filled:

Resolved, That the bill do pass, and that the title be, "an act imposing taxes for the support of government."

An engrossed bill appropriating the public revenue, was read a third time, and sundry blanks therein were filled; whereupon, a clause by way of ryder thereto, was offered by Mr. Brown of Petersburg, which was read twice, and engrossed and read a third time:

Resolved, That the bill (with the ryder) do pass, and that the title be, "an act appropriating the public revenue."

An engrossed bill to amend the act concerning merchants' licenses, was read a third time:

Resolved, That the bill do pass, and that the title be, "an act to amend the act concerning merchants' licenses."

An engrossed bill directing a survey of the Dragon swamp, was read a third time:

Resolved, That the bill do pass, and that the title be, "an act directing a survey of the Dragon swamp."

An engrossed bill to regulate the conduct of boatmen on the Appomattox and Roanoke rivers and their branches, was read a third time:

Resolved, That the bill do pass, and that the title be, "an act to regulate the conduct of boatmen on the Appomattox and Roanoke rivers and their branches."

An engrossed bill appointing commissioners to select a site for the seat of justice for the county of Ohio, was read a third time:

Resolved, That the bill do pass, and that the title be, "an act appointing commissioners to select a site for the seat of justice for the county of Ohio."

An engrossed bill incorporating the Big Bird mining company, was read a third time:

Resolved, That the bill do pass, and that the title be, "an act incorporating the Big Bird mining company"

An engrossed bill incorporating the Fredericksburg Union manufacturing company, was read a third time:

Resolved, That the bill do pass, and that the title be, "an act incorporating the Fredericksburg Union manufacturing company."

An engrossed bill incorporating the American mining company, was read a third time:

Resolved, That the bill do pass, and that the title be, "an act incorporating the American mining company."

An engrossed bill incorporating the Rappahannock marine and fire insurance company, was read a time:

Resolved, That the bill do pass, and that the title be, "an act incorporating the Rappahannock marine and fire insurance company."

An engrossed bill to incorporate the Berkeley coal mining and rail-road company, was read a third time:

Resolved, That the bill do pass, and that the title be, "an act to incorporate the Berkeley coal mining and rail-road company."

An engrossed bill to amend the act, entitled, "an act concerning the Cumberland road," was read a third time:

Resolved, That the bill do pass, and that the title be, "an act to amend the act, entitled, 'an act concerning the Cumberland road.'"

An engrossed bill to amend an act, entitled, "an act to enact with amendments, an act of the general assembly of North Carolina, entitled, 'an act to incorporate the Greensville and Roanoke rail-road company,'" was read a third time:

Resolved, That the bill do pass, and that the title be, "an act to amend an act, entitled, 'an act to enact with amendments, an act of the general assembly of North Carolina, entitled, 'an act to incorporate the Greensville and Roanoke rail-road company.'"

An engrossed bill to amend and explain the act, entitled, "an act to reduce into one, the several acts to regulate the solemnization of marriages," was read a third time:

Resolved, That the bill do pass, and that the title be, "an act to amend and explain the act, entitled, 'an act to reduce into one the several acts to regulate the solemnization of marriages.'"

Ordered, That the clerk communicate the said bills to the senate and request their concurrence.

An engrossed bill making further provision for taking depositions in certain cases, was read a third time, whereupon, on motion of Mr. Price, the farther consideration thereof was indefinitely postponed.

Resolved, That the said bill be rejected.

Mr. Stanard, from the committee for courts of justice, presented a report upon the petition of Frederick Moore, which was received and laid upon the table.

On motion of Mr. Servant, the house adjourned until to-morrow 10 o'clock.

THURSDAY, March 17th, 1836.

A communication from the senate by their clerk:

IN SENATE, March 16th, 1836.

The senate have passed the bills, entitled,

"An act to amend the act, entitled, 'an act to amend and to reduce into one act all acts and parts of acts to prevent the destruction of oysters,'" passed March 24th, 1831.

"An act to incorporate the New Hope gold mine company."

"An act changing the Hunting Run gold mining company into a company for mining and manufacturing iron and steel."

"An act to amend the several acts concerning the Petersburg rail-road company."

"An act to authorize a subscription on behalf of the state to the stock of the Pittsylvania and Lynchburg turnpike company, and for other purposes."

"An act incorporating the Lynchburg and Campbell court-house turnpike company;" and

"An act to amend the act, entitled, 'an act making further provision for completing the road from Staunton to the mouth of the Little Kanawha.'"

They have also passed the bills, entitled,

"An act declaring Pocatallico river a public highway;" and

"An act to equalize the regimental districts in the county of Rockingham, and for other purposes," with amendments, in which they request the concurrence of the house of delegates.

And they have agreed to the resolution voting a sword to captain E. A. F. Valette of the United States navy.

The said amendments being twice read, were, on questions severally put thereupon, agreed to by the house.

Ordered, That the clerk inform the senate thereof.

Mr. Shands, from the committee for courts of justice, presented a bill allowing Jim Smith and wife and their infant children, free persons of colour, to remain in the commonwealth a limited time, which was received and laid upon the table.

On motion, *Ordered,* That leave of absence from the service of this house, for the remainder of the session, be granted to Messrs. Chapman, and Garland of Mecklenburg.

On motion of Mr. Goodall, *Resolved by the general assembly of Virginia,* That the board of public works be, and they are hereby instructed to cause a survey to be made of the Pamunkey river, from New Castle in the county of Hanover, to the junction of the north and south branches, and also of the south branch up to Darricott's mills in the county of Hanover; and if the engagements of the principal engineer of the state will not permit him to perform the service, that they are hereby authorized to employ some competent engineer for that purpose, who shall report to the next general assembly an estimate of the cost of making the same navigable for boats, on the most practicable plan.

Ordered, That the clerk communicate the same to the senate and request their concurrence.

Mr. Hill, according to order, presented a bill to amend and explain an act, entitled, "an act to prescribe the mode of electing trustees for the town of Fairfax in the county of Culpeper, and vesting them with corporate powers."

Mr. Stanard, from the committee for courts of justice, presented a report upon the petition of Lucy and Delila.

And a bill abolishing the vaccine agency of this commonwealth.

Which were received and laid upon the table.

A motion was made by Mr. Wilson of Cumberland, to suspend the rule of the house, for the purpose of introducing a resolution for leave to bring in a bill to construct a rail-road from Cartersville to Farmville; whereupon, on motion of Mr. Shands, the said motion was ordered to be laid upon the table.

A bill concerning the Chesapeake and Ohio canal company, was taken up and ordered to be engrossed and read a third time.

A bill incorporating the Mayo's bridge company, with the substitute thereto proposed by the committee of roads and internal navigation, was taken up, and the said amendment being agreed to by the house, the said bill, as amended, was ordered to be engrossed and read a third time.

The following bills were read a second time, and ordered to be engrossed and read a third time, viz:

A bill concerning Robert W. Christian, treasurer of the late charity school of Charles City, and the overseers of the poor of said county.

A bill to amend the act, entitled, "an act to incorporate the Grayson Sulphur springs company;" and

A bill authorizing appeals to be taken from the courts of certain counties therein mentioned to the court of appeals at Lewisburg.

A bill to amend and explain the 96th, 99th and 100th sections of an act for the better organization of the militia, was, on motion of Mr. Watkins, ordered to be laid upon the table.

The following bills were read a second time, and ordered to be engrossed and read a third time:

A bill to change the place of holding a separate election in the county of Cabell.

A bill incorporating the Fredericksburg mining company.

A bill to prevent slaves, free negroes and mulattoes, from trading beyond the limits of the city, county or town in which they reside.

A bill incorporating the Marshall and Ohio turnpike company.

A bill to enlarge the powers of the county courts of Albemarle and Nelson, for the purpose of opening a road from Scottsville to the head waters of Rockfish river.

A bill to prevent frauds in the packing of cotton.

A bill incorporating the stockholders of the Smithfield rail-road company.

A bill to authorize the Dismal Swamp canal company to increase their capital stock, and to authorize the loans of the state to said company to be converted into stock.

A bill incorporating the stockholders of the Eastern Shore rail-road company.

A bill incorporating the Virginia silk company.

A bill to authorize Richard Lorton to surrender his interest in the museum property.

A bill authorizing the auditor of public accounts to issue a warrant on the treasury in favour of John H. Gwathmey, administrator of Richard Clarke, deceased, in pursuance of a judgment of the superior court of Henrico county, for commutation of five years full pay with interest.

A bill providing further security for the payment of jailors' fees.

A bill to incorporate the trustees of St. Bride's academy in Norfolk county.

A bill concerning Amos Johnston.

A bill constituting a portion of the margin of the Potomac river in Berkeley county a legal fence.

A bill changing the punishment of slaves convicted of hog stealing.

A bill to amend an act incorporating the Fredericksburg mechanics association.

A bill to repeal the act to provide for the appointment of a commissioner to examine and report upon claims for unsatisfied military land bounties, and for other purposes, passed March 11th, 1834.

A bill changing the time of holding the county courts in the counties of Marshall and Ohio, and to amend the act establishing the town of Moundsville in Ohio (now Marshall) county.

A bill concerning the Matoaca manufacturing company.

A bill to change the time of holding a quarterly term of the county court of the county of Shenandoah.

A bill to amend the act, entitled, "an act to incorporate a rail-road company from the city of Richmond to the town of York."

A bill changing the terms of the circuit superior court of law and chancery in and for the county of Stafford.

A bill to change the place of holding a separate election in the county of Pittsylvania.

A bill incorporating the Sweet springs and Price's mountain turnpike company.

A bill amending the act concerning waste tobacco.

A bill to incorporate a company to construct a toll-bridge across the Shenandoah river at Harper's Ferry.

A bill to prevent the destruction of oysters in Nansemond river, and Chuckatuck creek in the county of Nansemond.

A bill to change the place of holding a separate election in the county of Harrison.

A bill to amend the act, entitled, "an act to incorporate the Grayson Sulphur springs company."

A bill to incorporate the town of Waterford in the county of Loudoun.

A bill appointing trustees to the town of New Glasgow, and for other purposes.

A bill to increase the capital stock of Booker's gold mine company, and for other purposes.

A bill regulating the mode of obtaining writs of error in criminal prosecutions for misdemeanors; and

A bill incorporating the Deane iron and steel manufacturing company.

An engrossed bill to amend an act, entitled, "an act to incorporate the Augusta springs company," was read a third time:

Resolved, That the bill do pass, and that the title be, "an act to amend an act, entitled, 'an act to incorporate the Augusta springs company.'"

An engrossed bill to authorize Thomas A. Morton to erect a dam across Appomattox river, was read a third time:

Resolved, That the bill do pass, and that the title be, "an act to authorize Thomas A. Morton to erect a dam across Appomattox river."

An engrossed bill to incorporate the Etna coal company, was read a third time:

Resolved, That the bill do pass, and that the title be, "an act to incorporate the Etna coal company."

Ordered, That Mr. Wilson of Botetourt, carry the same to the senate and request their concurrence.

An engrossed bill concerning the administrator of Dominie Bennehan, deceased, was read a third time, and on motion of Mr. Crutchfield, ordered to be laid upon the table.

An engrossed bill concerning William Fenn, was read a third time:

Resolved, That the bill do pass, and that the title be, "an act concerning William Fenn."

An engrossed bill concerning John Chew, was read a third time:

Resolved, That the bill do pass, and that the title be, "an act concerning John Chew."

An engrossed bill incorporating the trustees of the Clarksville female academy, was read a third time:

Resolved, That the bill do pass, and that the title be, "an act incorporating the trustees of the Clarksville female academy."

An engrossed bill for the construction of a bridge across Jackson's river at the town of Covington, was read a third time:

Resolved, That the bill do pass, and (the title being amended on motion of Mr. Layne,) that the title be, "an act to change the site for the erection of a bridge across Jackson's river opposite the town of Covington from second to third street, in accordance with the act, entitled, 'an act for the erection of said bridge,'" passed 23d January, 1833.

An engrossed bill to incorporate the proprietors of the Wellsburg lyceum, was read a third time:

Resolved, That the bill do pass, and that the title be, "an act to incorporate the proprietors of the Wellsburg lyceum."

An engrossed bill to amend an act, entitled, "an act incorporating the trustees of the Bedford female academy," was read a third time:

Resolved, That the bill do pass, and that the title be, "an act to amend an act, entitled, 'an act incorporating the trustees of the Bedford female academy.'"

An engrossed bill re-organizing the Lexington arsenal and establishing a military school in connexion with Washington college, was read a third time:

Resolved, That the bill do pass, and that the title be, "an act re-organizing the Lexington arsenal and establishing a military school in connexion with Washington college."

An engrossed bill to alter and increase the terms of the circuit superior court of law and chancery for the county of Norfolk, was read a third time:

Resolved, That the bill do pass, and (the title being amended on motion of Mr. Cooke,) that the title be, "an act to alter the terms of the circuit superior court of law and chancery for the county and borough of Norfolk."

An engrossed bill to authorize a separate election in the county of Tazewell, was read a third time; whereupon, a clause by way of ryder thereto was offered by Mr. Jessee, which being read the first and second times, and forthwith engrossed and read a third time:

Resolved, That the bill, with the ryder, do pass, and the title being amended on motion of Mr. Jessee, that the title be, "an act to authorize a separate election in the county of Tazewell, *and one in the county of Russell.*"

An engrossed bill to add a part of the county of Tazewell to the county of Giles, was read a third time:

Resolved, That the bill do pass, and that the title be, "an act to add a part of the county of Tazewell to the county of Giles."

An engrossed bill to authorize a separate election at the house of William Pulliam, in the county of Henry, was read a third time:

Resolved, That the bill do pass, and that the title be, "an act to authorize a separate election at the house of William Pulliam, in the county of Henry."

An engrossed bill to amend the act, entitled, "an act reducing into one the several acts for punishing persons guilty of certain thefts and forgeries, and the destruction or concealment of wills," was read a third time:

Resolved, That the bill do pass, and that the title be, "an act to amend the act, entitled, 'an act reducing into one the several acts for punishing persons guilty of certain thefts and forgeries, and the destruction or concealment of wills.'"

An engrossed bill to authorize Richard Barton Haxall to construct wharves at and near the town of Bermuda Hundred, was read a third time:

Resolved, That the bill do pass, and that the title be, "an act to authorize Richard Barton Haxall to construct wharves at and near the town of Bermuda Hundred."

An engrossed bill to incorporate the Potowmac silk and agricultural company, was read a third time:

Resolved, That the bill do pass, and that the title be, "an act to incorporate the Potowmac silk and agricultural company."

An engrossed bill to authorize a separate election at M'Gaheysville in the county of Rockingham, was read a third time:

Resolved, That the bill do pass, and that the title be, "an act to authorize a separate election at M'Gaheysville in the county of Rockingham."

Ordered, That Mr. Wilson of Botetourt carry the said bills to the senate and request their concurrence.

An engrossed bill concerning the legal representatives of Severn Eyre, deceased, was read a third time, and on motion of Mr. Dorman, ordered to be laid upon the table.

An engrossed bill to incorporate the Front Royal library society in the county of Frederick, was read a third time:

Resolved, That the bill do pass, and that the title be, "an act to incorporate the Front Royal library society in the county of Frederick."

Resolved, That his excellency the lieutenant and acting governor, be requested to transmit a copy of this report and resolutions to the executive of each state, and to each of our senators and representatives in congress, with a request to said executive, to lay the same before their respective legislatures.

JOHN L. HELM,
Speaker of the House of Representatives.
CYRUS WINGATE,
Speaker of the Senate.

Approved 1st March, 1836.

J. T. MOREHEAD.

By the lieutenant and acting governor,
A. P. COX, *Secretary.*

On motion of Mr. Murdaugh, *Ordered,* That the said communication be laid upon the table, and on motion of Mr. Gregory, 185 copies thereof were ordered to be printed for the use of the general assembly.

The speaker laid before the house a further communication from the governor, which was also read as follows:

EXECUTIVE DEPARTMENT, March 18, 1836.

SIR,—Inclosed is a communication for the house of delegates, which you will be pleased to lay before that body.

Respectfully, your obedient servant,
LITT'N W. TAZEWELL.

To the Speaker of the House of Delegates.

EXECUTIVE DEPARTMENT, March 18, 1836.

To the House of Delegates.

In compliance with his request, I have the honour to lay before you the inclosed communication from the honourable Henry A. Wise, one of the representatives of the state of Virginia, in the congress of the United States.

LITT'N W. TAZEWELL.

H. REPRESENTATIVES,
WASHINGTON CITY, March 15th, 1836.

SIR,—Various causes have delayed until this time an answer to the communication, dated the 18th, which I had the honour to receive from you, forwarding "a copy of certain resolutions," adopted on the 16th of February last "by both houses of the general assembly of Virginia."

In reply to your communication of these resolutions, I deem it no less my privilege than my duty to respond fully. It is all important at this time that every man at every outpost of the public service should truly and accurately report the knowledge and information he possesses of the state and condition of the vital interests of the people whom he represents, intrusted to his care and watchfulness; and no interests are more vital to the people of Virginia, and no interests of the people of Virginia are more in jeopardy, than those of *slavery.* And more especially do I consider it a precious privilege to avail myself of this mode of making my report fully on that subject to the legislature and people of Virginia, now that I was, by a late act of the speaker of the house of representatives in congress, deprived of the freedom of speech at my post as a slaveholding representative.

I need not recount the history of the abolition question. For more than twenty years, even to the termination of the last session of congress, the subject had been regarded by slaveholding representatives as too delicate and dangerous for them to raise any question upon petitions praying for the abolition of slavery; and they abided under the assurance of safety, from the impression that such petitions could never assume character or influence sufficient ever to become subjects of legislation. The mode of disposing of these petitions by congress was altogether a negative or passive mode. To prevent the effects of agitation and excitement upon both extremes of the country, they had been silently received and referred, without resistance, invariably to the committee of the District of Columbia, a committee appointed for a great number of years by a speaker of the house from a slave state, and by which they were never, by a tacit understanding, reported on, and never permitted to disturb the peace and harmony and safety of the nation. Slaveholding representatives, in fact, were mainly induced, by non-slaveholding representatives themselves, not to resist in any other way these attacks upon the rights and interests of their constituents, for reasons which seemed then to constitute this course itself the best mode of resistance. It surely never can be fairly said that the slaveholding representatives had acquiesced in, and consented to the reception of, these petitions to deprive them and their constituents of their private property.

Thus for many years, until the events of the past year opened new scenes, did the slaveholding representatives in congress desist merely from taking more decisive steps of resistance to this encroachment upon the compromises of the constitution, and the rights and interests of their people. The events of last summer were of so alarming a character as to arouse and painfully excite the public mind of the slaveholding states. The authors of petitions for the abolition of slavery in the District of Columbia, aided by a mercenary foreigner, who is now heralding his triumphs in the cause of *universal emancipation,* on this side of the atlantic, to the people of a European power, which has just by one fell swoop emancipated all the slaves of its citizens in the West India islands, began to throw the firebrands of incendiarism into the southern *states* of the Union. They caused insurrection and massacre, the destruction of vast amounts of property, and the prostration of the reign of law in several counties of one southern state, endangered the peace and safety of other states, roused the slaveholding people to meet in primary assemblies to resolve upon the means of protection and self-preservation, excited the popular fury against one of the most useful institutions of the government, the post-office, and abusing its uses, threatened its existence in many places, together with the lives and fortunes of the people every where in the south.

This the slaveholding states were led to suppose had produced a general conviction every where in the country, of the necessity of demolishing anti-slavery societies, and of resisting their effects and proceedings. There was much evidence given of this conviction, as well by the meetings of the people of the non-slaveholding states as of the south. Consequent upon these meetings, upon the assembling of the different state legislatures, several governors of the states made the subject of suppressing abolition a special topic of recommendation to their respective legislatures—the post-master general brought it to the notice of the president of the United States, and he made it a part of his annual message to congress. Such was the late history and the new aspect of this subject at the earliest period of the present session of congress. The president's message had just been read to us, followed by the publication of an impudent and daring protest by the rich and powerful New York *state* anti-slavery society, when petition upon petition, hundreds signed by thousands, began again to pour in upon congress in increased numbers from the north, praying still, in defiance of what had appeared to be public sentiment in the north, for the abolition of slavery and the slave trade in the District of Columbia.

The evil thus within an almost incredibly short period, had become the alarming cause of general excitement, and forced itself upon the serious consideration of the whole country and its official agents. This was enough, I humbly thought, to cause the slaveholding representatives in congress to assume stronger grounds of opposition to the incendiary means of annoying and ruining their constituents. In reflecting and advising upon the course of opposition to be pursued, I concluded that the time had come for the slaveholding states to act boldly, firmly and decisively, in resistance to the *first steps* of legislation by congress on the subject, and to go farther and obtain a declaration, if possible, of the full extent of the guarantee with which the slaveholding states are assured by the federal constitution in their rights of property in slaves. I was forced to this conclusion by two prominent reasons, the one social, and the other political, to which I could not shut my eyes. The first reason too obvious to any mind at all acquainted with the character of the non-slaveholding population, and with the certain tendency of moral causes, is, that it was wholly unphilosophical to suppose that the anti-slavery advocates of abolition would not sooner or later, be in a majority in the non-slaveholding states. They have already hundreds of societies, hundreds of pulpits, hundreds of schools, thousands of zealots, thousands of publications, (many of them now printed and stamped on *cotton fabric*,) and thousands of money, actively operating on an entire free population, living under and imbibing the spirit of democratic institutions, with no interests or associations of slavery, and only mutual friends at best of slaveholders among them, to oppose the most strenuous exertions on the side of abolition, or to correct false impressions on the popular mind constantly inflamed and abused by appeals of the press and the preacher, to the love of liberty and the love of God and man, in a land of civil liberty and christian religion! How can the slaveholding states be lulled or deluded into the hope even that these fanatics will not soon snatch the reins of government? With me it was a certain and a fearful looking forward to a day of wrath soon to come. Indeed, I was informed by members of congress from the north, and by other sources on which I can equally rely, that there are two causes which conceal and restrain the full extent of abolition opinions and proceedings at this time; the advocates of anti-slavery do not themselves desire *immediate* abolition in the District of Columbia, because they desire to preserve a bone of contention for awhile, until they can, by discussing the evils of slavery *there*, more deeply and widely affect public sentiment on the subject in the *states*; and, many of these advocates of anti-slavery do not show themselves, and are not active *now*, because they are *politicians* as well as *abolitionists*, and they do not wish, *at this particular juncture*, to injure the prospects of their particular favourite candidate for the presidency in the slaveholding states. They can, in perfect accordance with these two reasons of the policy of their anti-slavery cause, wait a few months, until the presidential election is over, and then of a sudden, show their real sentiments, under the easy pretext, *that agitation has made them abolitionists*. The real truth is, that the population of the non-slaveholding states is a mass of material out of which abolition is formed as naturally as the sparks fly upwards; and that was the first reason which operated on my mind, a reason deduced from the social condition of the non-slaveholding states.

The other reason I have called a *political* reason. God forbid, that I should ever look at this question in any point of view, as a political *party* question. No; but I freely admit that I was anxiously disposed, as wisdom and policy required of me, to make the state of political parties available in obtaining for the slaveholding states and for the whole country, a permanent good, in the complete settlement of this dangerous controversy, upon the weakest point of our government. I knew that the lust for power was a stronger passion with politicians than that of fanaticism itself, and therefore could plainly foresee that the dominant political party in congress would not dare to vote *against* the slaveholding states on so vital a question, and I hoped that it might, under the influence of its ruling passion to make a president, be induced or compelled to vote *with them* on a question of far greater consequence to their welfare than all the offices to be won or lost by any course of policy. The second reason which influenced my mind then, was the state of parties at the time, which characterized this as the most auspicious period, perhaps, for all time to come, for the slaveholding states to obtain a declaration by congress of the permanent guarantee in the constitution, which they claim *for all slaveholders in the Union*, of their inviolable rights of private property in slaves.

The problem then was reduced to this; that from the course of events and the tendency of causes, good policy required us to act, and act speedily, whilst it was yet day; and that, being protected by the adventitious state of political parties, we had every thing to gain and nothing to lose, by acting boldly, *provided the representatives of the slaveholding states were united, and true to themselves and their constituents.* Accordingly, my course was taken with those whom I considered the true advocates of slaveholding rights, of southern safety, and of the nation's welfare, *in resisting the reception, not the hearing, of abolition petitions.*

This resistance was in vindication of the true right of petition, and founded upon the true construction of the constitution in relation to the power in congress of abolishing slavery. *The right of petition,* it was contended, belonged only to *petitioners praying to a government having the power of legislating over themselves; in cases where they had a direct interest themselves in the subject of their prayer for legislation; where they petitioned in a peaceable manner, not subversive of the rights of the legislative body to whom they prayed; for no* OBJECT HOSTILE TO THE PUBLIC SAFETY; *and where* THE GOVERNMENT TO WHICH THEY PETITIONED HAD THE POWER TO GRANT THEIR PRAYERS.

In these cases the petitioners were not citizens of the District of Columbia, and they prayed to the government of the District of Columbia, distinct from the government of the United States, and from any or either of the state governments. It was contended that the people of Maine had as much right to petition the legislature of Virginia to abolish slavery in Virginia, which would not be claimed or conceded by any, as they or the people of any state had to petition the local legislature of the District of Columbia to abolish slavery in that district.

That the right to petition carried with it the right to have the petition considered and granted, if reasonable and just; and it would be unreasonable and unjust that petitions, of people *whose own rights and interests* could not be affected either for good or for evil by the grant of their prayers, should be received, considered or granted, to affect the rights and interests of *others* which might be injured or destroyed against their own consent.

That one limitation, universally admitted, was, that the petition should be decorous and respectful, and not subversive of the rights of the body to whom it was addressed; that these petitions were direct attacks upon the moral character of slaveholders and their representatives, and personally insulting, by opprobriously denominating them "*men stealers and land pirates;*" that the "*salus populi*" and the public weal were greater considerations than the personal dignity of legislatures or legislators, and that "*a fortiori,*" a stronger limitation upon the right of petition than the preceding, founded on the necessity of self-preservation in every legislative body, was *that which is founded upon the public safety, and the necessity of preserving the government and its citizens and their property under its protection;* and these petitions struck at the compromises of the constitution, at the peace and safety of the people of the states, and at the existence of the union of the confederacy.

And lastly, that even though these petitioners were citizens of the District of Columbia, yet they could not petition their local legislature to abolish slavery, *because that local legislature, consisting of congress, has no constitutional power to abolish slavery in the District of Columbia.* It has no such power for the reason that it cannot take private property *except for public use;* that to take *slaves for emancipation* is for *no use* whatever in the sense of the constitution; that if taken for public use, they cannot be taken *without just compensation,* and the local legislature for the district *cannot make compensation* for want of power to raise a revenue; it cannot touch the treasury of the United States for such an object; it cannot *tax the inhabitants of the district to compensate themselves,* for that would be *no compensation,* and it cannot, especially, tax the inhabitants of the district to pay themselves, *without representation elected by themselves,* which is denied them by the constitution.

It was further contended, *that to refuse to receive petitions, after hearing their contents stated or read,* was not *a denial* in any sense of the right of petition. That the constitution restrained congress from *making any "law* prohibiting the right of the people *peaceably to assemble,* and *to petition* the government *for a redress of grievances;*" that *a refusal to receive* these petitions was *the making of "no law;*" that it prohibited not the right "*to assemble,*" that it prevented not and hindered not the right "*to petition,*" or even the right to have the petition *heard;* that these petitions for abolition were not for "*redress*" of their own "*grievances,*" but of the grievances of *others* who did not and could not themselves petition or complain; and that the rights of congress, as a legislative body, to receive or reject these petitions, commenced only where the right of petition ended. That if petitioners had the *absolute* right to have their petitions *received,* by the same course of reasoning they had the right absolutely to have them *considered* and *granted.*

It was, therefore, admitted, that these petitions might be *presented* or *offered,* and *their contents might be stated or read;* but if *upon the hearing* of them, they proved to be addressed from their very nature to the local legislature of the District of Columbia, by persons not citizens of that district, over whom that local legislature could pass no laws, having no direct or common interest in the subject of legislation, in a manner insulting to the dignity of congress or any of its members—hostile to the public peace and safety—injurious to the government and its citizens, and for the passage of a law in violation of the constitution and of the rights of private property, congress might not only refuse to *receive* them, consistently with the right of petition, but *could not* receive them without impairing rights and interests as sacred as that of petition, and without assuming powers dangerous to the government and destructive of public harmony. Such was the argument upon the right of petition, and the power of congress to abolish slavery in the District of Columbia. When, therefore, the petitions were presented and stated or read, *the question was demanded on their reception,* and *the motion to receive* was, in a number of cases which first occurred, *laid on the table* by large majorities. Thus then, the slaveholding representatives had so far succeeded *in excluding every petition* offered to the house of representatives, and even so far as to *reconsider* a motion to receive, which had been made (by Mr. Adams) and inadvertently carried.

Such was the successful course of proceeding, when a northern representative (Mr. Jarvis of Maine) offered a series of *resolutions*, declaring the *inexpediency* and *impolicy* merely of abolishing slavery in the District of Columbia. This necessarily compelled me to offer an amendment. After the events and the discussion which had already taken place, and the offering of these resolutions by Mr. Jarvis, it would have been an entire dereliction of the whole ground occupied by the slaveholding states, if their representatives had failed to offer an amendment, denying the *power* in congress, as well as the *expediency* of abolishing slavery in the District of Columbia, or in any of the territories of the United States. To say that it was *inexpedient* or *impolitic* or *dangerous* alone *to exercise the power*, was to say directly that there *was such a power* to be exercised, and that it *might* be exercised whenever, in the opinion of a majority, neither policy or expediency or safety would forbid—aye, though all three should forbid its exercise. To assign any other objection than a constitutional objection, was to admit the possibility at least of the exercise of the power. To say alone that the acts of cession by Virginia and Maryland of the district, forbad the exercise of the power, by an implied or even expressed covenant of faith, was to leave the mere faith of statute laws to the tender mercies of a strong majority, and to say that the constitution did not forbid its exercise, upon the common principle of construction, that the expression of one cause or reason would have been an exclusion of every other cause or reason. If congress has the power, it has it by the constitution, which is the supreme, uniform and permanent law; and no state act or acts can give or take away any of the *powers* of the federal government, which are not or are granted by that constitution, in which alone must the trust of slaveholders be placed. Every other barrier to fanaticism will be broken down, and I fear even for that, in the general crush of every thing secured by it. I therefore deemed it my imperative duty, as a representative of Virginia, not to permit her rights to be pretermitted or prejudiced by any negative conclusions. I had no alternative left but to offer an amendment, declaring that congress had *no power* to abolish slavery in the District of Columbia.

It was my desire and expectation, that these views, and this course, would meet the approbation and co-operation of all the representatives of the slaveholding states, or that they would meet with no opposition at least from that quarter, certainly not after they were expressed and pursued, and considering too the great necessity of union and concert among the representatives of the slave interest now in a fearful minority. But I and those who acted with me were doomed to disappointment, and the slaveholding interest to total defeat and the loss of every inch of ground which had been gained, and that too by a blow struck from the south.

A member from South Carolina, (Mr. Pinckney) representing the city of Charleston, actually obtained a vote of two thirds to suspend the rules for the purpose of offering the following resolution, which, I consider, yielded more of southern rights, and compromitted more of southern claims, than the abolitionists themselves expected:

"*Resolved*, That all the memorials which have been offered, or may hereafter be presented to this house, praying for the abolition of slavery in the District of Columbia; and also the resolutions offered by an honourable member from Maine, (Mr. Jarvis) with the amendment thereto proposed by an honourable member from Virginia, (Mr. Wise) and every other paper or proposition that may be submitted in relation to that subject, be referred to a select committee, with instructions to report, that congress possesses no constitutional authority to interfere in any way with the institution of slavery in any of the *states* of this confederacy; and that in the opinion of this house, congress ought not to interfere in any way with slavery in the District of Columbia, because it would be a violation of the public faith, unwise, impolitic and dangerous to the Union; assigning such reasons for these conclusions as, in the judgment of the committee, may be best calculated to enlighten the public mind, to allay excitement, to sustain and preserve the just rights of the slaveholding states and of the people of this district, and to establish harmony and tranquillity amongst the various sections of the Union."

Immediately upon the suspension of the rules, the *previous question*, now odious from its slavish uses, was moved and seconded, *in part by the representatives of slave states*, and this resolution, without debate, without deliberation, and without precedent, was referred to its *select* committee, carrying with it every species of abolition memorials, papers and propositions, which had been offered, presented or submitted, those off and those on the table, past, present and to come, without distinction or discrimination, *except avoiding most studiously to carry with it any instruction to report the amendment which I had offered!!* It yielded the point which had been contended for and practically gained, that congress could not *receive* or *refer* and *act* upon such petitions. It assumed that congress had the power to legislate on the subject of the abolition of slavery in the District of Columbia, and at once prostrated the rights of slaveholding members, the dignity of the house of representatives and every rule of order and decorum before the infamous and scurrilous memorials and extravagant and horrid pretensions of fanatics, false philanthropists and foul impostors.

In the first place it *referred*, and of course *received*, "*all* the memorials *which had been offered*," including, by the expressed intention of the mover, and by the deliberate construction of the house, *all memorials on which the motion to receive had been laid on the table*; and *all*, however false, foul, slanderous, insulting or indecorous to slaveholders and their representatives!

It *referred all memorials thereafter to be presented*, without knowledge of their contents or of their authors, though their contents might be worse than any already condemned, and *though their authors might be foreigners*, whose signatures had been procured by Thompson since his return to England!

It referred the resolutions of Mr. Jarvis, denying the *expediency* merely of abolition in the district, *with instructions to the committee to report all in them contained*; and it referred the amendment to these resolutions, offered by me, denying the *power* of congress on the subject, *without instructions* to report any such amendment or resolution, thus in effect denying the proposition it contained.

And it referred "*every other paper or proposition that might be submitted*" on the subject of abolition, in like manner, regardless of its character or its source.

By one general sweeping act it obtained for the abolitionists on *all* memorials, of every description, presented or to be presented, what they had already failed to obtain in a single case, *their reception, their reference, and the action of congress upon them;* and what was still more goading to the slaveholding representatives, it not only deprived them of the power of speech and of motion against its iniquitous operation in disposing of the petitions of abolitionists in the way most favourable and flattering to them, but it arbitrarily deprived these representatives of the privilege of disposing of *their* own memorials, papers or propositions on the same subject, in *their* own way, *in defiance of a vote of the majority, without a vote of two-thirds!*

Its *instructions* to the committee were worse for the slaveholding states, than its clause to receive and refer. They were well calculated, and were no doubt intended, to entrap every slaveholding representative, and to force them against their principles, their feelings and their strongest wishes, to vote for them to avoid denying them.

First, it instructed the committee to report the proposition, that congress has no *authority to interfere with* slavery in the *states*. I had no difficulty *in refusing to vote on such a question-at all;* for the very reason that *congress had no authority to affirm or deny* such a proposition. If it may *affirm* it, it may *deny* it. And if I had voted upon it at all, I should have voted with my worthy colleague (Mr. Robertson) in the *negative*, to exclude, as far as such a vote could, all assumption of power by congress to affirm or deny the proposition, without meaning to deny it myself, as I am sure he did not by his vote.

In the next place, whilst it instructed the committee immediately preceding to deny the "*authority*" of congress to "interfere" with slavery *in the states*, by the second instruction, directly contrasted with the first, it required the committee to report that, "*in the opinion of the house*" merely, "congress *ought* not to *interfere in any way* with slavery *in the District of Columbia ,*" saying, by the plainest implication, that congress *might*, if it saw fit in its opinion, abolish slavery in the District of Columbia. For that reason I retired, and did not vote upon that proposition, and too, for another reason equally as strong, *that its terms do not import its sense*. For, whilst I deny that congress has power to *abolish*, I claim that it *has* the power "*to interfere in*" *some way* with slavery in the district, as to pass laws, for instance, *to prevent the effects of abolition societies on the relation of master and slave*.

Lastly, it expresses various *reasons* for this latter instruction, not one of which can be tortured into a *denial* of the *power* of congress to abolish slavery, and the expression of which, without any kind of guard, is an exclusion of the strongest reason of all, that congress has *no constitutional power* to do what this instruction says merely it ."*ought not*" to do. And by the adroit use of the words, "reasons for THESE conclusions," in the latter clause, the committee was denied the power of assigning reasons for *any other* conclusions than those they were instructed to report by the resolution.

Such was the extraordinary character of this resolution, offered by a representative of a slaveholding state. If asked to account for it, I must answer that it was to afford a dominant political party of the north the *pretext for avoiding a direct vote upon the constitutional question of power;* and that such a pretext would not have been complete, if such a resolution had not been offered *by a representative of slaveholders, from a slaveholding state in a peculiar political position, and professing to be of an opposite party to the one seeking the means of blinding slaveholders in prospect of a presidential election.*

After this resolution had been adopted, a gentleman of Massachusetts, (Mr. Briggs,) *presented* a memorial praying for the abolition of slavery. The question was demanded on its *reception*. The speaker decided, very properly, that such a question might be demanded, still notwithstanding Mr. Pinckney's resolution. The house, by an overwhelming majority reversed this decision of the speaker, and decided that by the resolution of Mr. Pinckney, the memorial *was received and referred* immediately on presentation, in anticipation of any other motion whatever. Numbers of slaveholding representatives voting to overrule the chair, and to sustain this enormous decision and precedent by the house.

Such was the dilemma in which slaveholding rights and interests were involved when your communication of the resolutions of the legislature of Virginia was received; and, upon its reception we found to our sorrow, that state pride and state sovereignty were alike involved in the same vortex of abolition, aided by party influence in congress. My colleague, (Mr. Patton,) submitted the copy of your communication addressed to him, and moved to refer it to the usual committee of the District of Columbia, with the instruction to report one of the resolutions of your legislature, declaring that "congress has no constitutional power to abolish slavery in the District of Columbia or in any of the territories of the United States." The speaker *then* decided that *this* motion was *not* in order, that it was "*a paper*" *on the subject of the abolition of slavery*, and "*submitted*," and was therefore taken by the resolution of Mr. Pinckney, and immediately carried to the "*select committee*," and too, *without the instruction moved*. From this decision, there was an appeal. Upon this appeal, I attempted to show the absurd *consequences* of the speaker's decision: that it would do what was never before attempted to be done by congress, *refer the legislative acts of a state of the Union to a committee of congress, to be supervised and reported on by it, and on a subject too, where that very state by its very act to be referred, denied all power in congress to touch the subject involved!* I was called to order by the speaker, for *the irrelevancy of this argument*, ordered to take *my seat and silenced by a majority of the house!* For the first time since the foundation of the government, was a direct and sustained attack made upon the *freedom of debate* in congress, and that *in the instance of a representative of slaveholders, defending the sovereign rights of his state and the private rights of his constituents from direct aggression;* on a debateable question, in order before the house, and for *arguments irrelevant in the speaker's opinion merely, not for words insulting or indecorous!*

The world knows the latitude of debate heretofore allowed in congress. I cite the debate on Foot's resolution in the senate. The present house of representatives is conscious of the wide indulgence allowed this session in every case both before and since the instance in which I was denied the right of speech even *in order*. I cite the cases of Mr. Dutee J. Pearce, on the New York fire bill, and of Mr. Adams and Mr. Bynum on *a motion which the house had actually decided,* relating to the contested election from North Carolina. Before this time, I had claimed that the *freedom of debate and of speech*, was the last vestige of *political liberty* left us by the mal-administration and the abuses of the federal government. That gone, it only remains for abolition to make its threatened attack upon *civil liberty* in the District of Columbia, in its onward march against *private property and personal rights in the slaveholding states,* to awaken the people of the United States to a faithful reform of their government or to a bloody revolution in a country where a free and wise constitution was established less than fifty years ago.

After my colleague saw that the speaker was sustained in his decision by the house, and the direction that was about to be forcibly given to the resolutions of Virginia, he faithfully endeavoured to withdraw them from actual violence and disgrace. That indulgence was refused by a majority, and I have to inform you, sir, *that the resolutions of Virginia are now under the supervision and control of a committee of congress,* which is not likely to give them any additional sanction or force, even though it may treat them with more respect than did the house of representatives. That committee is composed of *nine* gentlemen, appointed *by a slaveholding speaker, five* of whom are representatives of non-slaveholding states, all of the opinion that congress *has the power* to abolish slavery in the district, and *four* of whom are representatives of slave states, with one or two of that number even agreeing with the other *five* against Virginia on the constitutional question.

The next day after my colleague had submitted the copy of your communication transmitted to him, I presented the memorial of a citizen of the district, protesting against the right of petition and the power of congress to abolish slavery in the district, which I moved to refer, *by a written "paper" "submitted" to the select committee with instructions to report the resolution of Virginia, declaring that congress has no constitutional power to abolish slavery in the District of Columbia, or in the territories of the United States.* Strange to tell, the speaker decided this motion *not to be in order,* though like the Virginia resolutions, it was *a written "paper" on the subject of abolition "submitted," and the house sustained his decision;* thus excluding in every form, the instruction as to the question of *power,* in the teeth of the decision of the chair and the house, both made within the preceding twenty-four hours!

I then read in my place to the house of representatives the copy of your communication addressed to me, but withheld it from the clerk of the house, from the company of abolition memorials, and from the ignominy which I knew awaited its *submission* to congress.

Before I conclude, I deem it my duty to state, it is no longer to be concealed, that the senators and representatives in congress from the non-slaveholding states, composing a large majority in both houses, are nearly united in the opinion that congress *has the power* to abolish slavery in the District of Columbia and in the territories of the United States. And a majority of them believe that congress has power to abolish the slave trade not only in the district, but, *between the states* of the Union, by the clause of the constitution "to regulate *commerce* among the several states," in conformity with the opinions of the north advanced and urged in 1819.

How long before these opinions will be acted on in congress depends upon the rapidity of the increase of abolitionists, now *admitted* to be fast multiplying in the non-slaveholding states, where there is no mode or means of resisting their influence. And how long before the Missouri question, especially, will again show itself, depends upon the order, perhaps, of the question of admitting Arkansas as a state, now before congress.

But the present aspect of the slavery question in congress, is not owing to the non-slaveholding representatives alone. It is partly, if not mainly owing to the *union with them* of many representatives of the *slave states* themselves. Whilst they are united to a man, we are divided and distracted. *Some of the representatives of the slave states,* I know, actually joined with the representatives of the non-slaveholding states, *because they were with them, conscientiously of the opinion that congress has the power to abolish slavery in the District of Columbia.* But I must say, that I believe others of them, *who were not of that opinion, and yet united with the non-slaveholding interest,* were influenced by their attachment to a northern political party, which is now seeking to elect a northern candidate to the presidency.

Thus, sir, I have detailed to you, and the legislature of Virginia, the whole history of this subject before congress; and I hope I have done nothing more than my duty, in reporting fully and truly upon measures of the general government and opinions of public men, affecting interests of my state of the greatest magnitude; less I could not have said by way of apology, for not *"submitting,"* as I was requested, the resolutions of Virginia to the legislative body of which I am a member, and in which I have been deprived of the rights of a member in a late instance of the freedom of speech.

With the deepest solicitude for the welfare of Virginia, the security of her rights, and the peace and happiness of her citizens, and with the highest respect for her governor and legislature,

I am, sir, your humble servant,

HENRY A. WISE.

Litt. W. Tazewell, *Governor of Virginia.*

P. S. I beg, sir, that this communication may be laid before the legislature of Virginia.

HENRY A. WISE.

On motion of Mr. Prentiss, *Ordered*, That the said communication be laid upon the table, and that 185 copies thereof be printed for the use of the members of the general assembly.

Mr. Holleman, according to order, presented a bill concerning Richard H. Edwards, which was received and laid upon the table.

A motion was made by Mr. Morgan, that the fifth rule of the house be suspended, for the purpose of reconsidering the vote rejecting a bill for increasing the banking capital of the commonwealth, and the question being put thereupon, was determined in the negative. Ayes 32, noes 64.

The ayes and noes thereupon being required by Mr. Watkins, (and sustained according to the rule of the house,) are as follow:

Ayes, Messrs. Drummond, Garland of Amherst, Brooke, Hunter of Berkeley, Henshaw, Wilson of Botetourt, Decamps, Beuhring, Servant, Ball, Price, Bowen, Davison, Smith of Frederick, Mullen, Kincheloe, Summers, Hays, Beard, Waggener, Willey, Morgan, Sherrard, Benton, Brown of Nelson, Murdaugh, Cooke, Masters, Carroll, Madison, Moncure, Gibson, and Brown of Petersburg.—32.

Noes, Messrs. Banks, (speaker,) Gilmer, Southall, Layne, Turnbull, Mallory, Booker, Austin, Daniel, Samuel, Richardson, Johnson, Hill, Wilson of Cumberland, Vaughan, Hunter of Essex, Smith of Fauquier, Hickerson, Strange, Steger, Holland, Watts, Smith of Gloucester, Watkins, Hail of Grayson, Sloan, Nixon, Holleman, Gregory, Berry, Carter, Neill, Straton, Taylor of Loudoun, Harris, Ragsdale, Taylor of Mathews and Middlesex, Rogers, Leland, Fitzgerald, Woolfolk, Almond, Adams, M'Coy, Cackley, Hopkins, Shands, Williams, Marteney, Nicklin, Leyburn, Moffett, Jessee, M'Mullen, Bare, Rinker, Butts, Crutchfield, Hargrave, Gillespie, Jett, Saunders, Cunningham and Stanard.—64.

Mr. Carter, from the committee on banks, presented a bill declaratory of the sixteenth section of the act incorporating the Farmers bank of Virginia, and directing the distribution of the contingent or reserved fund in conformity thereto.

Mr. Hunter of Essex, from the committee on the penitentiary, presented a bill to amend an act to provide for a revision of the criminal code, and for other purposes.

Mr. Madison, from the committee of agriculture and manufactures, presented a bill to increase the salaries of the inspectors of tobacco at Farmville in the county of Prince Edward.

Mr. Hill, from the committee of propositions and grievances, presented a bill to amend the act, entitled, "an act to amend an act, entitled, 'an act to establish Water street in the town of Portsmouth,'" passed April 4th, 1831.

Which bills were received and laid upon the table.

A motion was made by Mr. Taylor of Middlesex, that the fifth rule of the house be suspended, for the purpose of reconsidering the vote rejecting a resolution for leave to bring in a bill establishing an independent bank in the town of Portsmouth, and the question being put thereupon, was determined in the negative. Ayes 22, noes 64.

The ayes and noes thereupon being required by Mr. Austin, (and sustained according to the rule of the house,) are as follow:

Ayes, Messrs. Drummond, Garland of Amherst, Brooke, Henshaw, Wilson of Botetourt, Beuhring, Servant, Ball, Price, Smith of Gloucester, Berry, Summers, Hays, Beard, Taylor of Mathews and Middlesex, Sherrard, Murdaugh, Cooke, Masters, Moncure, Prentiss, and Brown of Petersburg.—22.

Noes, Messrs. Banks, (speaker,) Southall, Layne, Decamps, Turnbull, Mallory, Booker, Austin, Daniel, Samuel, Richardson, Johnson, Hill, Wilson of Cumberland, Vaughan, Hunter of Essex, Smith of Fauquier, Hickerson, Strange, Steger, Holland, Bowen, Davison, Watts, Watkins, Hail of Grayson, Sloan, Nixon, Kincheloe, Holleman, Gregory, Fleet, Carter, Neill, Straton, Taylor of Loudoun, Harris, Ragsdale, Rogers, Leland, Fitzgerald, Woolfolk, Almond, Adams, M'Coy, Hopkins, Madison, Shands, Marteney, Nicklin, Leyburn, Moffett, Jessee, M'Mullen, Bare, Butts, Crutchfield, Hargrave, Gillespie, Gibson, Jett, Saunders, Cunningham and Stanard.—64.

An engrossed bill to incorporate the Eastern Shore rail-road company, was read a third time:

Resolved, That the bill do pass, and that the title be, " an act to incorporate the Eastern Shore rail-road company."

An engrossed bill incorporating the Mayo's bridge company, was read a third time:

Resolved, That the bill do pass, and that the title be, " an act incorporating the Mayo's bridge company."

An engrossed bill to change the place of holding a separate election in the county of Cabell, was read a third time:

Resolved, That the bill do pass, and that the title be, " an act to change the place of holding a separate election in the county of Cabell."

An engrossed bill incorporating the Fredericksburg mining company, was read a third time:

Resolved, That the bill do pass, and that the title be, " an act incorporating the Fredericksburg mining company."

Ordered, That the clerk communicate the said bills to the senate and request their concurrence.

An engrossed bill to prevent slaves, free negroes and mulattoes, from trading beyond the limits of the city, county or town, in which they reside, was read a third time; whereupon, on motion of Mr. Watkins, the farther consideration thereof was indefinitely postponed.

Resolved, That the said bill be rejected.

On motion of Mr. Hunter of Essex, the house adjourned until to-morrow 10 o'clock.

SATURDAY, March 19th, 1836.

A communication from the senate by their clerk:

IN SENATE, March 18th, 1836.

The senate have passed the bills, entitled,
"An act to incorporate the proprietors of the Wellsburg lyceum."
"An act to change the time of holding the county courts of the counties of Lewis and Braxton, and the circuit superior courts of law and chancery for the county of Fairfax."
"An act incorporating the trustees of the Clarksville female academy."
"An act to authorise Richard Barton Haxall to construct additional wharves at and near the town of Bermuda Hundred."
"An act to amend an act, entitled, 'an act to incorporate the Augusta springs company.'"
"An act to amend an act, entitled, 'an act incorporating the trustees of the Bedford female academy.'"
"An act to incorporate the Etna coal company."
"An act concerning John Pettinger, late sheriff of Brooke county."
"An act to add a part of the county of Tazewell to the county of Giles."
"An act directing a survey of the Dragon swamp."
"An act concerning William Fenn."
"An act to incorporate the Berkeley coal mining and rail-road company."
"An act to authorize a separate election at the house of William Pulliam in the county of Henry."
"An act changing the time of holding the superior courts of Campbell, Bedford and the town of Lynchburg."
"An act to explain the act authorizing subscriptions on the part of the commonwealth to the capital of joint stock companies."
"An act to authorize Thomas A. Morton to erect a dam across Appomattox river;" and
"An act to incorporate the Potomac silk and agricultural company."

They have also passed the bills, entitled,
"An act to incorporate the Front Royal library company in the county of Frederick."
"An act to authorize a separate election at M'Gaheysville in the county of Rockingham."
"An act to establish the town of Meadowville in the county of Greenbrier;" and
"An act to amend an act, entitled, 'an act to enact with amendments, an act of the general assembly of North Carolina, entitled, 'an act to incorporate the Greensville and Roanoke rail-road company,'" with amendments, in which they request the concurrence of the house of delegates.

The said amendments being twice read, were, on questions severally put thereupon, agreed to by the house.

Ordered, That the clerk inform the senate thereof.

Mr. Summers, from the committee for courts of justice, presented a bill concerning Frederick Moore of the county of Cabell, which was received and laid upon the table.

Mr. Hill, from the committee of propositions and grievances, presented a report upon the petition of citizens of Gloucester, and upon the resolution for increasing the inspector's salary at Dixon's warehouse in Falmouth.

And a bill to authorize a separate election at the place called the Burned Chimneys in the county of Northumberland.

Which report and bill were received and laid upon the table.

An engrossed bill further to provide for the construction of a turnpike road across the Alleghany mountain in the counties of Pendleton and Pocahontas, was taken up on motion of Mr. M'Coy, and the question being put upon its passage, was determined in the negative.

Resolved, That the said bill be rejected.

An engrossed bill concerning the administrator of Dominie Bennehan, deceased, was taken up on motion of Mr. Carter, and read a third time, and the question being put upon its passage, was determined in the negative.

Resolved, That the said bill be rejected.

A bill incorporating the Great Kanawha mining, timber and lumber company, was taken up on motion of Mr. Crutchfield, and read a second time; whereupon, on motion of Mr. Price, the farther consideration of the said bill was indefinitely postponed.

Resolved, That the said bill be rejected.

An engrossed bill to authorize the Dismal swamp canal company to increase their capital stock and to authorize the loans of the state to said company to be converted into stock, was, on motion of Mr. Gregory, ordered to be laid upon the table.

An engrossed bill to prevent frauds in the packing of cotton, was, on motion of Mr. Shands, ordered to be laid upon the table.

An engrossed bill authorizing the auditor of public accounts to issue a warrant on the treasury in favour of John H. Gwathmey, administrator of Richard Clark, deceased, in pursuance of a judgment of the superior court of Henrico county, for commutation of five years full pay with interest, was, on motion of Mr. Sherrard, ordered to be laid upon the table.

An engrossed bill incorporating the Marshall and Ohio turnpike company, was read a third time:

Resolved, That the bill do pass, and that the title be, "an act incorporating the Marshall and Ohio turnpike company."

An engrossed bill to enlarge the powers of the county courts of Albemarle and Nelson, for the purpose of opening a road from Scottsville to the head waters of Rockfish river, was read a third time:

Resolved, That the bill do pass, and that the title be, "an act to enlarge the powers of the county courts of Albemarle and Nelson, for the purpose of opening a road from Scottsville to the head waters of Rockfish river."

An engrossed bill incorporating the stockholders of the Smithfield rail-road company, was read a third time:

Resolved, That the bill do pass, and that the title be, "an act incorporating the stockholders of the Smithfield rail-road company."

An engrossed bill to authorize Richard Lorton to surrender his interest in the museum property, was read a third time:

Resolved, That the bill do pass, and that the title be, "an act to authorize Richard Lorton to surrender his interest in the museum property."

An engrossed bill providing further security for the payment of jailors' fees, was read a third time:

Resolved, That the bill do pass, and that the title be, "an act providing further security for the payment of jailors' fees."

An engrossed bill to amend an act incorporating the Fredericksburg mechanics association, was read a third time:

Resolved, That the bill do pass, and that the title be, "an act to amend an act incorporating the Fredericksburg mechanics association."

An engrossed bill constituting a portion of the margin of the Potomac river in Berkeley county, a legal fence, was read a third time:

Resolved, That the bill do pass, and that the title be, "an act constituting a portion of the margin of the Potomac river in Berkeley county, a legal fence."

An engrossed bill concerning the Matoaca manufacturing company, was read a third time:

Resolved, That the bill do pass, and that the title be, "an act concerning the Matoaca manufacturing company."

An engrossed bill to incorporate the trustees of Saint Bride's academy in Norfolk county was read a third time; whereupon, a clause by way of ryder thereto, was offered by Mr. Murdaugh, which was read twice and forthwith engrossed and read a third time:

Resolved, That the bill (with the ryder) do pass, and that the title be, "an act to incorporate the trustees of Saint Bride's academy in Norfolk county, and the trustees of the Suffolk academy in the county of Nansemond."

Ordered, That Mr. Shands carry the same to the senate and request their concurrence.

An engrossed bill concerning Amos Johnson, was read a third time, and the question being put upon its passage, was determined in the negative.

Resolved, That the said bill be rejected.

An engrossed bill changing the punishment of slaves convicted of hog stealing, was read a third time, and the question being put upon its passage, was determined in the negative.

Resolved, That the said bill be rejected.

An engrossed bill to change the time of holding a quarterly term of the county court of the county of Shenandoah, was read a third time:

Resolved, That the bill do pass, and that the title be, "an act to change the time of holding a quarterly term of the county court of the county of Shenandoah."

An engrossed bill changing the time of holding the county courts in the counties of Marshall and Ohio, and to amend the act establishing the town of Moundsville in Ohio, now Marshall county, was read a third time:

Resolved, That the bill do pass, and that the title be, "an act changing the time of holding the county courts in the counties of Marshall and Ohio, and to amend the act establishing the town of Moundsville in Ohio, now Marshall county."

An engrossed bill to repeal the act to provide for the appointment of a commissioner to examine and report upon claims for unsatisfied military land bounties, and for other purposes, passed March 11th, 1834, was read a third time:

Resolved, That the bill do pass, and that the title be, "an act to repeal the act to provide for the appointment of a commissioner to examine and report upon claims for unsatisfied military land bounties, and for other purposes, passed March 11th, 1834."

An engrossed bill changing the terms of the circuit superior court of law and chancery in and for the county of Stafford, was read a third time:

Resolved, That the bill do pass, and that the title be, "an act changing the terms of the circuit superior court of law and chancery in and for the county of Stafford."

Ordered, That Mr. Shands carry the said bills to the senate and request their concurrence.

An engrossed bill to change the place of holding a separate election in the county of Pittsylvania, was read a third time:

Resolved, That the bill do pass, and that the title be, "an act to change the place of holding a separate election in the county of Pittsylvania."

Ordered, That Mr. Sherrard carry the same to the senate and request their concurrence.

An engrossed bill incorporating the Sweet springs and Price's mountain turnpike company, was read a third time:

Resolved, That the bill do pass, and that the title be, "an act incorporating the Sweet springs and Price's mountain turnpike company."

An engrossed bill to amend the act, entitled, "an act to incorporate a rail-road company from the city of Richmond to the town of York," was read a third time:

Resolved, That the bill do pass, and that the title be, "an act to amend the act, entitled, 'an act to incorporate a rail-road company from the city of Richmond to the town of York.'"

Ordered, That Mr. Shands carry the said bills to the senate and request their concurrence.

An engrossed bill concerning Robert W. Christian, treasurer of the late charity school of Charles City and the overseers of the poor of said county, was read a third time:

Resolved, That the bill do pass, and that the title be, "an act concerning Robert W. Christian, treasurer of the late charity school of Charles City and the overseers of the poor of said county."

An engrossed bill concerning delinquent lands and lands not heretofore entered on the commissioners' books, was read a third time:

Resolved, That the bill do pass, and that the title be, "an act concerning delinquent lands and lands not heretofore entered on the commissioners' books."

Ordered, That Mr. Sherrard carry the said bills to the senate and request their concurrence.

An engrossed bill to prevent the destruction of oysters in Nansemond river and Chuckatuck creek in the county of Nansemond, was read a third time:

Resolved, That the bill do pass, and that the title be, "an act to prevent the destruction of oysters in Nansemond river and Chuckatuck creek in the county of Nansemond."

Ordered, That Mr. Shands carry the same to the senate and request their concurrence.

An engrossed bill to change the place of holding a separate election in the county of Harrison, was read a third time:

Resolved, That the bill do pass, and that the title be, "an act to change the place of holding a separate election in the county of Harrison."

An engrossed bill amending the act concerning waste tobacco, was read a third time:

Resolved, That the bill do pass, and that the title be, "an act amending the act concerning waste tobacco."

An engrossed bill to amend the act, entitled, "an act to incorporate the Grayson sulphur springs company," was read a third time:

Resolved, That the bill do pass, and that the title be, "an act to amend the act, entitled, 'an act to incorporate the Grayson sulphur springs company.'"

An engrossed bill appointing trustees to the town of New Glasgow, and for other purposes, was read a third time:

Resolved, That the bill do pass, and that the title be, "an act appointing trustees to the town of New Glasgow, and for other purposes."

An engrossed bill regulating the mode of obtaining writs of error in criminal prosecutions for misdemeanors, was read a third time:

Resolved, That the bill do pass, and that the title be, "an act regulating the mode of obtaining writs of error in criminal prosecutions for misdemeanors."

An engrossed bill to increase the capital stock of Booker's gold mine company, and for other purposes, was read a third time:

Resolved, That the bill do pass, and that the title be, "an act to increase the capital stock of Booker's gold mine company, and for other purposes."

An engrossed bill authorizing appeals to be taken from the courts of certain counties therein mentioned, to the court of appeals held at Lewisburg, was read a third time:

Resolved, That the bill do pass, and that the title be, "an act authorizing appeals to be taken from the courts of certain counties therein mentioned, to the court of appeals held at Lewisburg."

Ordered, That Mr. Sherrard carry the said bills to the senate and request their concurrence.

An engrossed bill incorporating the Virginia silk company, was read a third time:

Resolved, That the bill do pass, and that the title be, "an act incorporating the Virginia silk company."

Ordered, That Mr. Shands carry the same to the senate and request their concurrence.

An engrossed bill to incorporate the town of Waterford in the county of Loudoun, was read a third time:

Resolved, That the bill do pass, and that the title be, "an act to incorporate the town of Waterford in the county of Loudoun."

An engrossed bill incorporating the Fredericksburg iron and steel manufacturing company, was read a third time:

Resolved, That the bill do pass, and that the title be, "an act incorporating the Fredericksburg iron and steel manufacturing company."

An engrossed bill to incorporate a company to construct a toll-bridge across the Shenandoah river at Harper's Ferry, was read a third time:

Resolved, That the bill do pass, and that the title be, "an act to incorporate a company to construct a toll-bridge across the Shenandoah river at Harper's Ferry."

Ordered, That Mr. Sherrard carry the said bills to the senate and request their concurrence.

An engrossed bill allowing Charlotte Morgan, a free woman of colour, to remain in the commonwealth, was taken up on motion of Mr. Mullen, and read a third time:

Resolved, That the bill do pass, and that the title be, "an act allowing Charlotte Morgan, a free woman of colour, to remain in the commonwealth."

Ordered, That the clerk communicate the same to the senate and request their concurrence.

The following bills were read a second time and ordered to be engrossed and read a third time, viz:

A bill changing the times of holding the circuit superior courts of law and chancery in the counties of Rockingham and Pendleton.

A bill reviving an act incorporating a company to construct a turnpike road from the upper end of the Blue Ridge canal, to its intersection with the Lexington and Covington turnpike road.

A bill to incorporate the Wythe watering company in the county of Wythe.

A bill incorporating sundry companies to construct turnpike roads from Richmond to Big Bird bridge in the county of Goochland.

A bill vesting the commonwealth's stock in the James river and Kanawha company in the board of public works, and for other purposes.

A bill making certain changes in the general road law, passed March 3d, 1835, so far as the county of Rockbridge is concerned.

A bill to increase the number of trustees in the town of Portsmouth, and to enlarge their powers and privileges.

A bill to increase the library at Lewisburg.

A bill concerning Ann, a free woman of colour.

A bill incorporating the Portsmouth provident society; and

A bill to authorize a change of location of the Warm springs and Harrisonburg turnpike, and for other purposes, was ordered, on motion of Mr. Moffett, to be laid upon the table.

The following bills were also read a second time, and ordered to be engrossed and read a third time:

A bill incorporating the Glen Leonard rail-road company.

A bill to amend the act, entitled, "an act concerning the town of Moorefield in the county of Hardy."

A bill divorcing Ann Edmunds from her husband John W. A. Edmunds.

A bill providing for the repairs and preservation of the public arms, the armory buildings, and for other purposes.

A bill concerning the administrator of Richard Kelsick, deceased.

A bill concerning the town of Leesburg in the county of Loudoun.

A bill incorporating the Petersburg savings institution.

A bill limiting recoveries on certain judgments therein mentioned.

A bill suspending the processioning of lands in counties therein mentioned.

A bill regulating the commissions on sales made under decrees in chancery, and for other purposes.

A bill to authorize Elisha B. Williams to erect a wool carding machine on Jackson's river, near the town of Covington in the county of Alleghany.

A bill changing the name of William H. Riggan to that of William H. Drewry.

A bill placing James river on the footing of a lawful fence, so far as concerns the counties of Fluvanna and Albemarle.

A bill incorporating the Chesterfield and James river canal rail-road company.

A bill incorporating the Tuckahoe rail-road company.

A bill appropriating a further sum of money for completing the improvements of the Western lunatic hospital.

A bill to authorize William Townes to erect a toll-bridge across the Roanoke river, opposite the town of Clarksville in the county of Mecklenburg.

A bill to incorporate the town of Salem in the county of Botetourt.

A bill authorizing the common council of Fredericksburg to subscribe for stock in the Rappahannock and Blue Ridge rail-road company.

A bill authorizing the county and corporation court clerks to charge fees for certain services performed by them.

A bill allowing Daniel Starks, a free man of colour, to remain in the commonwealth a limited time; and

A bill allowing Charles Williams, a free man of colour, to remain in the commonwealth a limited time.

A bill allowing Stephen, a man of colour, to remain in the commonwealth, was read a second time, and on motion of Mr. Gregory, ordered to be laid upon the table.

On motion of Mr. Brown of Petersburg, *Ordered,* That the rule of the house limiting the number of the committee of finance, be suspended, and that Messrs. Crutchfield and Ball be added to the said committee, and that leave be granted them to sit during the session of the house.

On motion of Mr. Layne, *Ordered,* That the committee on enrolled bills have leave to sit during the session of this house.

The following bills were read the first time and ordered to be read a second time, viz:

A bill creating a new regiment within the county of Warren, and for other purposes.

A bill concerning the executor of James Jenks, deceased.

A bill to define the duties and regulate the fees of the attorney general.

A bill regulating the allowances in cases of arrest for criminal offences; and

A bill to amend the act concerning the overseers of the poor, passed 20th February, 1829.

A bill changing the time of holding the circuit superior court of Fairfax county, was, on motion of Mr. Price, ordered to be laid upon the table.

The following bills were also read the first and ordered to be read a second time:

A bill to repeal part of an act passed on the 27th February, 1836, entitled, "an act to authorize the auditor to issue warrants on the treasury in satisfaction of certain judgments against the commonwealth."

A bill to authorize the opening a new street in the town of Petersburg.

A bill to amend the act, entitled, "an act for the relief of creditors against fraudulent devises."

A bill to explain the act, entitled, "an act to reduce into one the several acts concerning grand juries and petit juries."

A bill abolishing the vaccine agency of this commonwealth.

A bill allowing Jim Smith and wife, and their infant children, free persons of colour, to remain in the commonwealth a limited time.

A bill to amend and explain an act, entitled, "an act to prescribe the mode of electing trustees for the town of Fairfax in the county of Culpeper, and vesting them with corporate powers."

A bill to prevent more effectually persons trading with slaves.

A bill concerning John B. Armistead sheriff of Fauquier county.

A bill to increase the salaries of the inspectors of tobacco at Farmville in the county of Prince Edward.

A bill to amend an act to provide for a revision of the criminal code, and for other purposes.

A bill declaratory of the 16th section of the act incorporating the Farmers bank of Virginia, and directing the distribution of the contingent or referred fund in conformity thereto; and

A bill concerning Richard H. Edwards.

A bill to amend the act, entitled, "an act to amend an act, entitled, 'an act to establish Water street in the town of Portsmouth,'" passed April 4th, 1831, was read the first and second times, and by general consent ordered to be engrossed and read a third time.

A report of the committee of privileges and elections was read as follows:

The committee of privileges and elections to whom was referred a resolution of the house of delegates, instructing them "to enquire whether a stockholder in a corporation, which incorporation holds lands, can by virtue of his stock be a freeholder, or so possessed of said land, or any part thereof, as to entitle him to the right of suffrage under the constitution, and report their opinion, with their reasons, to the house," beg leave to submit the following report:

Your committee deem the enquiry submitted to them to be of great importance to the interest of the commonwealth, and intimately connected with the rights and interests of her citizens in reference to election and representation. If that class of persons be entitled to vote under the constitution, that right should not be abridged nor its exercise denied to them; but, if on the other hand, they are not entitled, the exercise should be prohibited as an interference with the rights and privileges of others.

In deciding the question, it is essentially necessary to discard all considerations growing out of the party politics of the day, and view it as it must operate throughout all time, not as it may affect this or that individual or county, but in reference to the whole commonwealth; not as political partisans, to effect particular purposes, but as impartial statesmen deciding the great question of political rights under the constitution.

The constitution provides, that "every white male citizen of the commonwealth, resident therein, aged twenty-one years and upwards, being qualified to exercise the right of suffrage according to the former constitution and laws; and every such citizen, being possessed, or whose tenant for years, at will or at sufferance, is possessed of an estate of freehold in land of the value of twenty-five dollars, and so assessed to be, if any assessment thereof be required by law; and every such citizen, being possessed as tenant in common, joint tenant or parcener, of an interest in, or share of land, and having an estate of freehold therein, such interest or share being of the value of twenty-five dollars, and so assessed to be, if any assessment thereof be required by law; and every such citizen being entitled to a reversion or vested remainder in fee, expectant on an estate for life or lives, in land of the value of fifty dollars, and so assessed to be, if any assessment thereof be required by law,"—"shall be qualified to vote for members of the general assembly in the county, city, town or borough, respectively," &c.

And the question arises whether a stockholder in an incorporated company is entitled to the right of suffrage under any of the foregoing provisions?

A corporation is an *artificial* body, created by law, capable of suing and being sued, of buying, selling and transferring property, and of holding estates real and personal. It is the representative by and through which the business and interests of the several individuals composing it are conducted and managed, over which no one individual has any control. He cannot demand his separate interest to be set apart to him, nor can he obtain any redress in his own name for any injury or injustice done to the corporate rights. The whole property is vested in the corporation and not in the individuals composing it. The only power existing in the individual, is the right of buying and selling the stock of the corporation, and voting under its charter and by-laws. The corporation being thus vested with the whole estate, would, generally, be entitled to the right of suffrage, but that the constitution requires the voter to be a "white male citizen of the commonwealth"—a corporation is not a citizen, and therefore cannot vote. If the whole property of the corporation is thus vested in the artificial body, created by law, it would at once appear that the individuals could not be *possessed* of any portion thereof, and therefore could not be entitled to the right of suffrage, for it is difficult to conceive how the same thing could be vested in an artificial body and a natural person at the same time. If it be vested in one, it is not vested in the other.

It is no doubt true, that the individuals have an interest in the corporate property, but it is an interest beyond their control and management. The question recurs, are the individuals *possessed* of this interest as required by the constitution, or is it in the possession of the corporation, which alone has the power to sell and transfer the same in their corporate capacity?

The individuals can maintain no action, for all suits must be instituted in the corporate name. If trespass be committed on the corporate property, the corporation (and not the individual stockholders) can alone seek redress. The individuals have no more right to interfere with the management of its affairs, than a stockholder in a bank has to assume authority and control over the moneys of the institution. The whole management is vested in the president and directors, as the representatives of the corporate power; the possession of the property is in them and not in the stockholders. The possession of the corporate property being in the corporate body, the stockholders, whether as individuals simply, or as joint tenants, or tenants in common, or parceners, are precluded from voting under the constitution, for want of *possession*, for that is required in all those cases.

It may possibly be supposed that the stockholders have the right of suffrage as reversioners or remaindermen, after the expiration of the charter, in case the estate should not be sold or transferred during its existence. It may well be questioned, whether the stockholders, under such circumstances, would be entitled to any interest whatever in the estate. The artificial body having ceased to exist, the estate could not descend and pass to heirs, for there could be none to inherit; it would be left without any legal owner, and might perhaps be forfeited to the commonwealth. It is, however, not necessary to decide this question, inasmuch as it can be clearly shewn that there exists in the stockholders no right of "reversion or vested remainder in fee, expectant on an estate for life or lives," as required by the constitution. A reversion is defined in law to be, "the residue of an estate left in the grantor to commence in possession after the determination of some particular estate granted out by him." Now the corporation becomes entitled to the property, either by the act of incorporation, or by purchase afterwards, and if any reversion can thereby be created, it must be vested in the original grantor, and not in those who may have become stockholders. It is possible that a charter might be so framed as to leave an estate in reversion in the original owners, but this could not apply to the stockholders generally, who have only become owners of stock by purchase.

The right of voting as remaindermen is believed to be entirely without foundation. The constitution requires "a vested remainder in fee, expectant on an estate for life or lives." If there be any remainder at all in the corporate estate, it must necessarily be *contingent*, and *not vested*. The corporation can at any time defeat the remainder by a transfer of the estate in any mode prescribed by the charter, and the charter always presumes that a disposition and sale of all the effects and estate of the corporation shall be made during the period of its existence; for, so soon as that time elapses, all its powers cease, unless again authorized to exist by the power that created it. Even if it were possible thus to create a remainder, still it would not be a "remainder expectant on an estate for life or lives," and would, therefore, not give the right of suffrage.

It is believed that if stockholders in corporate companies can have any claim to the right of suffrage, it must be based on some of the foregoing clauses of the constitution; as it cannot be sustained on these grounds, it cannot exist at all.

Resolved therefore as the opinion of this committee, That "a stockholder in a corporation holding lands," cannot, "by virtue of his stock, be a freeholder, or so possessed of said land, or any part thereof, as to entitle him to the right of suffrage under the constitution."

On motion of Mr. Gregory, *Ordered*, That the same be laid upon the table.

On motions severally made, *Ordered*, That leave of absence from the service of this house be granted for the remainder of the session to Messrs. Waggener, Southall and Gillespie, from to-day, and to Messrs. Bare and Rinker, from Tuesday next.

Mr. Carter, from the committee on banks, presented a report upon the state of the Bank of Virginia, and the Farmers bank of Virginia, which was received and laid upon the table, and on motion of Mr. Cunningham, 185 copies thereof were ordered to be printed for the use of the general assembly.

Mr. Watkins, from the committee of roads and internal navigation, presented a bill to provide for keeping in repair the public roads within the corporation of Lynchburg; and

A bill authorizing Lavender London and William H. Garland, to erect a dam across Tye river in the county of Nelson.

Mr. Henshaw, according to order, presented a bill releasing the commonwealth's claim upon the estate of Archy Cooper, a lunatic.

Mr. Brown of Petersburg, from the committee of finance, presented a bill allowing further time to the representatives and creditors of Lewis Eisenmenger, deceased, to redeem certain lands vested in the literary fund for the nonpayment of taxes.

Which were severally received and laid upon the table.

A bill to authorize a separate election at the place called the Burn'd Chimneys in the county of Northumberland, was read the first and second times, and, by general consent, ordered to be engrossed and read a third time.

A bill concerning Frederick Moore of the county of Cabell, was read the first, and ordered to be read a second time:

The following report of the committee of propositions and grievances was read:

The committee of propositions and grievances have, according to order, had under consideration the petition of sundry citizens of the county of Gloucester, to them referred, praying that an act may pass authorizing a separate election to be holden at the store house of Joel Hayes, situate in the lower part of said county: Whereupon,

Resolved as the opinion of this committee, That the prayer of said petition be rejected for want of notice.

The said committee have also had under consideration a resolution of the house of delegates, "requesting them to enquire into the expediency of increasing the wages of the inspectors of tobacco at Dixon's warehouse in the town of Falmouth:" Whereupon,

Resolved as the opinion of this committee, That it is *inexpedient* to increase the wages of the inspectors of tobacco at said warehouse.

The said resolutions were, on questions put thereupon, agreed to by the house.

On motion of Mr. Watkins, the house adjourned until Monday 10 o'clock.

MONDAY, March 21st, 1836.

A communication from the senate by their clerk:

IN SENATE, March 19th, 1836.

The senate have passed the bills, entitled,
"An act to amend the charter of the James river and Kanawha company."
"An act incorporating the Mayo's bridge company."
"An act to amend an act, entitled, 'an act for the inspection of fish,'" passed the 28th of December, 1795.
"An act to incorporate the trustees of Saint Bride's academy in Norfolk county, and the trustees of the Suffolk academy in the county of Nansemond."
"An act concerning Robert W. Christian, treasurer of the late charity school of Charles City and the overseers of the poor of said county."
"An act to amend the act, entitled, 'an act to incorporate a rail-road company from the city of Richmond to the town of York.'"
"An act to change the place of holding a separate election in the county of Cabell."
"An act to change the time of holding a quarterly term of the county court of the county of Shenandoah."
"An act to prevent the destruction of oysters in Nansemond river and Chuckatuck creek in the county of Nansemond."
"An act to amend the act, entitled, 'an act to incorporate the Grayson sulphur springs company.'"
"An act to change the site for the erection of a bridge across Jackson's river, opposite the town of Covington, from second to third street, in accordance with the act, entitled, 'an act for the erection of said bridge,'" passed 23d January, 1833.
"An act to amend the act, entitled, 'an act reducing into one the several acts for punishing persons guilty of certain thefts and forgeries, and the destruction or concealment of wills.'"
"An act to increase the capital stock of Booker's gold mine company, and for other purposes."
"An act constituting a portion of the margin of the Potowmac river in Berkeley county a lawful fence;" and
"An act concerning the Matoaca manufacturing company."

They have also passed the bill, entitled,
"An act to amend an act, entitled, 'an act to enact with amendments an act of the general assembly of North Carolina, entitled, 'an act to incorporate the Greensville and Roanoke rail-road company,'" passed February 7th, 1834, with amendments to the title, in which they request the concurrence of the house of delegates.

And they have rejected the bill, entitled,
"An act to amend the act concerning merchants' licenses."

Their committee appointed to examine the enrolled bills, have examined sundry other such bills, which being found truly enrolled, have been signed by their speaker, and are herewith returned to the house of delegates.

The said amendments being twice read, were, on questions severally put thereupon, agreed to by the house.

Ordered, That the clerk inform the senate thereof.

Mr. Brooke, from the joint library committee, presented a report on the state of the library, which was read as follows:

The joint committee on the public library respectfully report:

That they have examined the librarian's report for the past year, together with his accounts therein referred to, (herewith submitted,) and have found them correct.

From these documents, it appears that the receipts of the fund during the year, were $ 1,926 90, making with the former balance (of $ 824 11,) the sum of $ 2,751 01: and the expenditures for the purchase of books and contingencies during the same period, were $ 1,844, 10, and for interest on the debt due to the literary fund $ 600; making the sum of $ 2,444 10, and leaving a balance in hand on the 31st of December last, of $ 306 91.

There have been added to the library during the past year, 134 folios and quartos, and 139 octavos and duodecimos, making 273 volumes. Among them are several volumes of reports of the supreme courts of Kentucky, Indiana and Missouri, which the governor of the commonwealth received from the governors of these states, and caused to be lodged in the library; and the committee have with great pleasure acknowledged the courtesy of these donations by directing copies of Leigh's reports to be transmitted in like manner through the executive, to the said governors respectively, feeling satisfied that in thus reciprocating the civilities of those sister states, they were only executing the wishes of the general assembly.

The library being now very nearly sufficient for all the purposes of its creation, the committee have appropriated only the small sum of $200 for further purchases of books for the current year, and have directed the librarian to pay over all the balance of the accruing receipts, (after paying for the books already ordered, when received,) to the literary fund, on account of the debt owing from the library fund to that fund.

The committee have only to add that the librarian has continued to discharge the duties of his office during the past year to their entire satisfaction.

The committee respectfully submit the following resolution:

Resolved, That the account of the librarian ending on the 31st of December, 1835, be received and allowed.

Report of the Librarian to the joint Library Committee, December 31st, 1835.

In conformity to the provisions of an act of the general assembly, which requires that the librarian shall annually render to the joint library committee a report of his proceedings, and an account of the receipts and disbursements of the library fund, I have the honour to submit the following report

On the 1st day of January, 1835, there was on hand,	824 11
From the 1st day of January, to the 31st day of December 1835, inclusive, the receipts were,	1,926 90
Amounting together to	$2,751 01
Which amount has been applied to payment of interest on debt due literary fund,	600 00
To purchases of books ordered by the committee, and contingent expenses,	1,844 10
Leaving an unexpended balance on the 31st December, 1835, of	306 91
	$2,751 01

All which is stated more fully and at large in the account of receipts and disbursements herewith submitted, marked A.

The committee during the last session, by resolution, appropriated a sum not exceeding $800, to the purchase of additional books, and directed that the balance, whatever it might be, should be paid over on account of the debt due to the literary fund; but by a subsequent resolution, they also directed the purchase of all the books remaining upon the catalogue of purchases for the year 1834, which had not been obtained. This last mentioned list comprised such books as could only be obtained by importation, and it was not possible to ascertain before sending out the order what would be the cost. The amount greatly exceeded the anticipations of the committee, but it included all the purchases ordered, although the books have not all been received—a part, comprising between 4 and 500 volumes, which by advices should have been shipped in the month of October last, has not yet come to hand. The funds of the library for the present year, except the interest of the debt due to the literary fund, and the balance of $306 91 before mentioned, have been applied to the payment for that portion of the books which have already arrived and been placed in the library; and there will be due for the remainder, when received, the sum of $986 66, which the funds for the ensuing year will be adequate to meet at an early day.

These purchases constitute a splendid and valuable addition to the library; and I beg leave again respectfully to suggest for the consideration of the committee, whether that institution is not now so far complete in all its departments as for the present to answer the purposes the legislature had in view in its establishment, and whether it is not most adviseable to disencumber the fund of the debt due to the literary fund, before any further additions are made.

As connected in some measure with the interests of the library, it is perhaps my duty to advert to a subject which has heretofore received the attention of the committee, viz: a continuation of the statutes at large of this state. By an act of the 21st February last, (p. 16,) the governor is authorized to contract for the printing of 300 copies of a continuation of Hening's statutes at large to the year 1806, proposed to be published by Mr. Samuel Shepherd. In the annual report at the session of 1830-31, I stated to the committee that there were frequent calls for various acts of assembly, and for complete series of the sessions acts from the termination of Hening's publication; and the committee in their report to the general assembly "earnestly recommended that arrangements be made in order to fill up the chasm between the last volume of Hening and the commencement of the session of 1829." By the act of February 22, 1830, the legislature had already directed that 300 copies of the sessions acts, and 25 copies of the journals of both houses shall annually be added to the library fund. Consequently, the library fund, besides 462 copies of Hening's statutes at large, has 300 copies of the sessions acts from 1829-30 to the present time, and is entirely deficient in the acts from the year 1792 to the year 1829, which are no where to be obtained. I beg leave, therefore, respectfully, to propose to the committee again to recommend that the publication of the statutes at large be made complete, and that so much of such publication as may be necessary to connect Hening's statutes at large with the acts from the year 1829, be added to the library fund. There are strong reasons for the belief that public benefit would result from it; and as regards the library fund, it would obviously create a demand for Hening's statutes at large, now the least productive part of it, though, as connected with the early history of the state, perhaps not the least valuable. It may well be doubted whether a partial publication of the statutes will materially promote the public convenience or answer any valuable purpose. If, however, it shall be the pleasure of the legislature to make the publication complete, and to direct a sale of it for any object, it would seem from a recurrence to the consequences of a partial subscription to the first series of the reports, that the state ought to take the whole. The expense would be altogether inconsiderable; purchasers might be supplied at a moderate price, and the various seminaries of learning throughout the state, gratuitously.

The governor has received the following donations to the state, which he has directed me to place in the library, viz: A report on the geology, mineralogy, botany and zoology of Massachusetts; Dana's reports select cases in the court of appeals of Kentucky, 2 vols.; Pertle's digest of the same, 2 vols.; Blackford's reports supreme court of judicature of Indiana, 2 vols.; and Decisions of the supreme court of Missouri, 3 vols.

And the following donations to the library have also been received, viz: From Edward Colston, esq., a history of the Chesapeake and Ohio canal; from Matthew Carey, esq., Memoirs of the Pennsylvania agricultural society; from the common council of the city of Richmond, a plan of the city; from Benjamin W. Leigh, esq., Documents of the post office committee, and statistical view of the population of the United States from 1790 to 1830; from John Robertson, esq., Geological report of an examination of the country between Missouri and Red rivers, and a chart of the harbour of Charleston; from James Brown, jr. esq., a very ancient copy of Sheppard's touchstone; and a copy of the 2d volume of Robinson's practice from the author.

Document A. is an account of the receipts and disbursements of the library fund; B. a tabular statement of the books and maps which constitute the fund; and C. an account of disbursements of an appropriation of $1,200, by an act of the 10th March, 1835, entitled, "an act to increase the library for the use of the court of appeals at Lewisburg."

All which is respectfully submitted.

WH. H. RICHARDSON,
Sec'y Com'th and Librarian.

December 31*st*, 1835.

A.

DR. WM. H. RICHARDSON, *Secretary Commonwealth and Librarian—In account with the* COMMONWEALTH, CR.

1835.				1835.		
Jan. 1	—To balance from last year's account,		824 11	Jan. 1	—By cash, interest on debt to literary fund, per No. 1,	300 00
	To cash received from J. M. Brome & Co. agents at Winchester,		86 40	July 1	—By cash, interest on debt to date, per No. 2,	300 00
Dec. 31	—To sales of books and maps at Richmond, from 1st January to 31st December, 1835, viz:				By cash, subscription to writings of Washington, per No. 3,	21 00
	1 sett Hening's statutes at large,	13 00			By cash, subscription to Nile's register, per No. 4,	5 00
	8 copies Gilmer's reports, at $2 50,	20 00			By cash, subscription to Farmers register, vols. 2 and 3, per No. 5,	10 00
	3 copies 1st vol. Randolph's reports, at $2 50,	7 50			By cash, subscription to Southern Literary Messenger, vols. 1 and 2, per No. 6,	10 00
	6 copies 2d vol. Randolph's reports, at $2 50,	15 00			By cash paid for advertising books and maps, per No. 7,	3 00
	2 copies 4th vol. Randolph's reports, at $2 50,	5 00			By cash paid for printing catalogue, per No. 8,	93 52
	3 setts Randolph's reports, at $25,	75 00			By cash paid for books purchased and imported from London, per order joint committee, per No. 9,	1,635 93
	20 copies 1st vol. Leigh's reports, $5 50,	110 00			By cash paid R. I. Smith for books, per No. 10,	9 00
	27 copies 2d vol. Leigh's reports, at $6,	162 00			By cash paid R. D. Sanxay for binding, per No. 11,	7 43
	42 copies 3d vol. Leigh's reports, at $6,	252 00			By cash paid J. Danforth for cleaning and making fires in library part of the year, and sundry small expenses of freight, drayage, &c. per No. 12,	40 59
	210 copies 4th vol. Leigh's reports, at $6,	1,260 00				
	7 copies large map, at $10,	70 00				
	8 copies small map, at $4,	32 00				
	1 copy journal convention, 1775-6,	3 50				
	1 sett of journals house of delegates, 1776 to 1792,	20 00			By cash paid for cleaning and taking down books in library, and freight on 3 boxes from Philadelphia,	8 63
		2,045 00		Dec. 31	—By balance on hand,	306 91
	Deduct discount to booksellers, and agents' commissions 10 per cent.,	204 50				
			1,840 50			
			$2,751 01			$2,751 01

The above is a just and full account of the receipts and disbursements of the library fund, from the 1st day of January, to the 31st day of December, 1835.

WM. H. RICHARDSON,
Sec'y Com'th and Librarian.

(B.)

Account of the BOOKS AND MAPS *which constitute the Library Fund, December 31, 1835.*

Books and Maps which constitute the Library Fund.	On hand January 1, 1835.	Received since January 1, 1835.	Sold since January 1, 1835.	Donations since January 1, 1835.	In hands of agents Dec. 31, 1835.	On hand at Richmond Dec. 31, 1835.	Total unsold Dec'r 31, 1835.	Value per sett or copy.	Aggregate value of Total Dec. 31, 1835.
Hening's statutes at large, setts of 13 vols.,	464	1	1		12	450	462	$13 00 per sett,	6006 00
Gilmer's reports,	381	8			11	362	373	2 50 per copy,	932 50
Randolph's reports, setts of 6 vols.,	290	3			11	276	287	25 00 per sett,	7175 00
Do. surplus copies of vol. 1st,	70	3				67	67	2 50 per copy,	167 50
Do. do. of vol. 2d,	81	6				75	75	2 50 do.	187 50
Do. do. of vol. 3d,	5					5	5	2 50 do.	12 50
Do. do. of vol. 4th,	19	2				17	17	2 50 do.	42 50
Do. do. of vol. 5th,	130					130	130	2 50 do.	325 00
Do. do. of vol. 6th,	14				14		14	6 00 do.	84 00
Leigh's reports, vol. 1st,	300	20			33	247	280	5 50 do.	1540 00
Do. vol. 2d,	379	27			20	332	352	6 00 do.	2112 00
Do. vol. 3d,	434	42				392	392	6 00 do.	2352 00
Do. vol. 4th,	675	210				465	465	6 00 do.	2790 00
Large map of Virginia,	105	7	1	30	67	97	10 00 do.	970 00
Small map,	384	8		77	299	376	4 00 do.	1504 00
Journal of convention 1775-6,	141	1	1		139	139	3 50 do.	486 50
Setts of journals containing								
Journal convention 1788, 1 small vol. 8vo.								
Do. senate 1778-9, 1 vol. do.								
Do. do. 1785 to 1790, 1 vol. do.								
Do. house delegates 1776, 1 vol. 4to.	235	1	1		233	233	20 00 per sett,	4660 00
Do. do. 1777 to 1780, 1 vol. do.								
Do. do. 1781 to 1786, 1 vol. do.								
Do. do. 1786 to 1790, 1 vol. do.								
Do. do. 1829-30, 1 vol. do.	25				25	25		
Do. do. 1830-31, 1 vol. do.	25				25	25		
Do. do. 1831-32, 1 vol. do.	25				25	25		
Do. do. 1832-33, 1 vol. do.	25				25	25		
Do. do. 1833-34, 1 vol. do.	25				25	25		
Do. do. 1834-35, 1 vol. do.		25			25	25		
Do. senate 1830-31, 1 vol. 8vo.	25				25	25		
Do. do, 1831-32, 1 vol. do.	25				25	25		
Do. do. 1832-33, 1 vol. do.	25				25	25		
Do. do. 1833-34, 1 vol. do.	25				25	25		
Do. do. 1834-35, 1 vol. do.		25			25	25		
Acts of assembly 1829-30,	300				300	300		
Do. 1830-31,	300				300	300		
Do. 1831-32,	300				300	300		
Do. 1832-33,	300				300	300		
Do. 1833-34,	300				300	300		
Do. 1834-35,		300			300	300		

	31347 00
Deduct for expense of sales and over estimates, 25 per cent.,	7836 75
Balance, chargeable with debt of $10,000 to literary fund,	$23510 25

The donations stated above were to the historical and philosophical society of Virginia, by resolution of the joint committee. None of the agencies have been closed since the last report.

WM. H. RICHARDSON,
Sec'y Com'th and Librarian.

C.

DR.   WM. H. RICHARDSON, *Secretary Commonwealth and Librarian—In account with the* COMMONWEALTH,   CR.

1835.			1835.		
Jan. 1	—To cash, balance last year's appropriation to purchase a library for the use of the court of appeals at Lewisburg,	15 75		By cash paid for books, per voucher No. 1,	598 11
				By cash paid for books, per voucher No. 2,	489 54
				By cash paid for books, per voucher No. 3,	42 65
	To cash appropriated by act of March 10th, 1835, to increase the library,	1,200 00		By cash, expenses of librarian to Philadelphia, and freight of books to Richmond,	45 91
			Dec. 31	—By balance on hand,	39 54
		$1,215 75			$1,215 75

A small portion of the books for this library were imported from London with those for the state library at Richmond, and the expense of that importation is not included in this account. These books were received in October, and have not yet been sent to Lewisburg.

They cost, as per invoice,	173 90
From which deduct balance above stated,	39 54
Leaving to be provided for, if the legislature shall think proper,	$134 36

It is proper to state that the judges desired that these books should be first purchased, or if not to be had otherwise, imported, and the omission to reserve as much of the appropriation as would cover the purchase, was, on my part, accidental, and was not discovered until after the order was sent to London.

WM. H. RICHARDSON.

December, 31st, 1835.

The said resolution was, on the question put thereupon, agreed to by the house.

Mr. Shands, from the committee for courts of justice, presented a bill allowing Andy, a man of colour, to remain in the commonwealth a limited time; and

A bill concerning the sheriff of Spotsylvania county.

Mr. Prentiss, from the committee of claims, presented a bill concerning Peter J. Chevallie; and

A bill concerning James Burk.

Which several bills were subsequently read the first and ordered to read a second time.

On motion, *Ordered*, That leave of absence from the service of this house be granted for the remainder of the session, to Messrs. Hale of Franklin, and Steger, each from to-day; and to Messrs. Butts, Hunter of Berkeley, Saunders, Willey and M'Mullen, each from to-morrow.

Mr. Watkins submitted the following preamble and resolutions, which, on his motion, were ordered to be laid upon the table:

Whereas the general assembly of Virginia did, on the 20th day of February, adopt certain resolutions, instructing their senators to vote for expunging from the journals of the senate of the United States, the resolution adopted by that body on the 28th of March, 1834, in relation to the president of the United States, and which the general assembly regarded as subversive of the rights of the house of representatives, and the fundamental principles of free government:

And whereas Benjamin Watkins Leigh, one of the said senators, did address to the general assembly, on the second instant, a letter, declaring his determination neither to obey the said instructions nor to resign his office of senator:

And whilst this assembly can never be so devoid of self-respect as to enter into an altercation with its own servants, it yet believes that there may be occasions when it would not only be proper, but incumbent on them, to express their disapprobation of the conduct of their servants; and that the present is one of those occasions:

1. *Therefore, resolved by the general assembly of Virginia*, That the letter of Benjamin Watkins Leigh, one of the senators of this state, addressed to this assembly on the second of March, 1836, is sophistical and unsatisfactory; and that this assembly doth highly disapprove of the conduct of the said Benjamin Watkins Leigh, in relation to the expunging resolution, and to the instructions concerning the same, given to the said senator by the general assembly, during the present session thereof.

2. *Resolved*, (the letter of the said senator to the contrary notwithstanding,) That this assembly doth solemnly repeat their regard for the right of instruction, as resting on the broad basis of the nature of representation, and one of the vital principles of our free institutions, and that it is the duty of the representative to obey the instructions of his constituents, or resign the trust with which they have clothed him, in order that it may be transferred into the hands of those who will carry into execution the wishes and instructions of the constituent body.

3. *Resolved*, That after the solemn expression of the opinion of the general assembly, on the right of instruction, and the duty of obedience thereto, no man ought henceforth to accept or retain the appointment of senator of the United States, from Virginia, who doth not hold himself bound to obey such instructions, or to resign the trust with which he is clothed.

Mr. Sherrard submitted the following resolution:

Whereas the general assembly of Virginia regards the improvement of the navigation of the Cacapehon river from its junction with the Potomac to its highest point susceptible of navigation in the county of Hardy, and its union with the main stem of the Chesapeake and Ohio canal, as of such great interest and importance to this state, that those improvements should be provided for by it, without unnecessary delay:

Be it therefore resolved, That the Chesapeake and Ohio canal company be requested, and the proxy or proxies representing the stock held by this state in said company, be instructed, to take all necessary and proper measures for uniting the waters of the Cacapehon river with the Chesapeake and Ohio canal, by constructing a navigable feeder from the mouth of said river to the said canal, by means of an aqueduct across the Potomac river, with a waterway at least six feet deep and twenty feet wide, and equal to the aqueducts now constructed on said canal.

On motion of Mr. Garland of Amherst, the same was amended by adding thereto the words, "provided the cost thereof shall not exceed one hundred thousand dollars."

On motion of Mr. Brown of Petersburg, the said resolution as amended, was ordered to be laid upon the table.

On motion of Mr. Brown of Petersburg, an engrossed bill to prevent frauds in the packing of cotton, was taken up, and the question being put upon its passage, was determined in the negative

Resolved, That the said bill be rejected.

Mr. Layne, from the committee appointed to examine enrolled bills, reported that they had examined sundry other such bills and found them truly enrolled.

Ordered, That Mr. Layne carry the same to the senate.

The speaker laid before the house the following letter which was read:

To the Speaker of the House of Delegates.

SIR,—You will receive enclosed my letter of resignation of the office of commissioner of revolutionary claims, which you are respectfully requested to lay before the house of delegates.

Most respectfully, yours,

JOHN H. SMITH.

March 21st, 1836.

To the General Assembly of Virginia.

I respectfully requested of the house of delegates, on the 10th instant, an enquiry into the manner in which I have performed the duties of commissioner of revolutionary claims for the last two years. My request has not been complied with. It is, therefore, to be inferred, that my conduct in office has not been disapproved; and I may now resign, without being subject hereafter to the suspicion of having failed to perform the duties which were assigned me.

For the reasons which were given in my communication to the speaker of the house of delegates of the 10th instant, I now tender my resignation of the office of commissioner of revolutionary claims.

I have the honour to be, very respectfully,

JOHN H. SMITH.

March 21st, 1836.

On motion of Mr. Wilson of Botetourt, *Ordered*, That the same be laid upon the table.

On motion of Mr. Brown of Petersburg, *Ordered*, That leave be given to bring in a bill to provide for the purchase of additional copies of the statutes at large, published in continuation of Hening's statutes at large, and that Messrs. Brown of Petersburg, Woolfolk, Brooke, Christian, Beuhring, Marteney, Willey, Moncure, and Hunter of Essex, prepare and bring in the same, and have leave to sit during the session of this house.

Mr. Brown of Petersburg, subsequently presented the said bill, which was read the first and ordered to be read a second time.

A bill abolishing the vaccine agency of this commonwealth, was read a second time; whereupon, on motion of Mr. Crutchfield, the farther consideration thereof, was indefinitely postponed.

Resolved, That the said bill be rejected.

An engrossed bill changing the times of holding the circuit superior courts of law and chancery in the counties of Rockingham and Pendleton, was read a third time:

Resolved, That the bill do pass, and that the title be, "an act changing the times of holding the circuit superior courts of law and chancery in the counties of Rockingham and Pendleton."

An engrossed bill reviving an act incorporating a company to construct a turnpike road from the upper end of the Blue Ridge canal to its intersection with the Lexington and Covington turnpike, was read a third time:

Resolved, That the bill do pass, and that the title be, "an act reviving an act incorporating a company to construct a turnpike road from the upper end of the Blue Ridge canal to its intersection with the Lexington and Covington turnpike."

An engrossed bill to incorporate the Wythe watering company in the county of Wythe, was read a third time:

Resolved, That the bill do pass, and that the title be, "an act to incorporate the Wythe watering company in the county of Wythe."

An engrossed bill incorporating sundry companies to construct turnpike roads from Richmond to Big Bird bridge in the county of Goochland, was read a third time:

Resolved, That the bill do pass, and that the title be, "an act incorporating sundry companies to construct turnpike roads from Richmond to Big Bird bridge in the county of Goochland."

An engrossed bill vesting the commonwealth's stock in the James river and Kanawha company in the board of public works, and for other purposes, was read a third time:

Resolved, That the bill do pass, and that the title be, "an act vesting the commonwealth's stock in the James river and Kanawha company in the board of public works, and for other purposes."

Ordered, That Mr. Shands carry the said bills to the senate and request their concurrence.

An engrossed bill making certain changes in the general road law, passed March 3d, 1835, so far as the county of Rockbridge is concerned, was read a third time, and on motion of Mr. Brooke, ordered to be laid upon the table.

An engrossed bill to increase the number of trustees in the town of Portsmouth, and to enlarge their powers and privileges, was read a third time:

Resolved, That the bill do pass, and that the title be, "an act to increase the number of trustees in the town of Portsmouth, and to enlarge their powers and privileges."

An engrossed bill to increase the library at Lewisburg, was read a third time:

Resolved, That the bill do pass, and that the title be, "an act to increase the library at Lewisburg."

An engrossed bill concerning Ann, a free woman of colour, was read a third time:

Resolved, That the bill do pass, and that the title be, "an act concerning Ann, a free woman of colour."

An engrossed bill incorporating the Portsmouth provident society, was read a third time:

Resolved, That the bill do pass, and that the title be, "an act incorporating the Portsmouth provident society."

An engrossed bill incorporating the Glen Leonard rail-road company, was read a third time:

Resolved, That the bill do pass, and that the title be, "an act incorporating the Glen Leonard rail-road company."

An engrossed bill to amend the act, entitled, "an act concerning the town of Moorefield in the county of Hardy," was read a third time:

Resolved, That the bill do pass, and that the title be, "an act to amend the act, entitled, 'an act concerning the town of Moorefield in the county of Hardy.'"

An engrossed bill divorcing Ann Edmunds from her husband John W. A. Edmunds, was read a third time:

Resolved, That the bill do pass, and that the title be, "an act divorcing Ann Edmunds from her husband John W. A. Edmunds."

Ordered, That Mr. Shands carry the said bills to the senate and request their concurrence.

An engrossed bill providing for the repairs and preservation of the public arms, the armory buildings, and for other purposes, was read a third time; whereupon, on motion of Mr. Watkins, the farther consideration thereof was indefinitely postponed.

Resolved, That the said bill be rejected.

An engrossed bill concerning the administrator of Richard Kelsick, deceased, was read a third time; whereupon, a clause by way of ryder thereto, was offered by Mr. Cooke, which was twice read, and forthwith engrossed and read a third time, and on motion of Mr. Garland of Amherst, the said bill and ryder was ordered to be laid upon the table.

An engrossed bill concerning the town of Leesburg in the county of Loudoun, was read a third time:

Resolved, That the bill do pass, and that the title be, "an act concerning the town of Leesburg in the county of Loudoun."

An engrossed bill incorporating the Petersburg savings institution, was read a third time:

Resolved, That the bill do pass, and (the title being amended,) that the title be, "an act incorporating the Petersburg *and Norfolk* savings institutions."

An engrossed bill limiting recoveries on certain judgments therein mentioned, was read a third time:

Resolved, That the bill do pass, and (the title being amended,) that the title be, "an act limiting recoveries on judgments in other states."

An engrossed bill suspending the processioning of lands in counties therein mentioned, was read a third time:

Resolved, That the bill do pass, and that the title be, "an act suspending the processioning of lands in counties therein mentioned."

An engrossed bill regulating the commissions on sales made under decrees in chancery, and for other purposes, was read a third time:

Resolved, That the bill do pass, and that the title be, "an act regulating the commissions on sales made under decrees in chancery, and for other purposes."

An engrossed bill incorporating the Chesterfield and James river canal rail-road company, was read a third time:

Resolved, That the bill do pass, and that the title be, "an act incorporating the Chesterfield and James river canal rail-road company."

Ordered, That Mr. Shands carry the same to the senate and request their concurrence.

An engrossed bill incorporating the Tuckahoe rail-road company, was read a third time, and the question being put upon its passage, was determined in the negative.

Resolved, That the said bill be rejected.

An engrossed bill placing James river on the footing of a lawful fence, so far as concerns the counties of Fluvanna and Albemarle, was read a third time:

Resolved, That the bill do pass, and that the title be, "an act placing James river on the footing of a lawful fence, so far as concerns the counties of Fluvanna and Albemarle."

Ordered, That Mr. Shands carry the said bill to the senate and request their concurrence.

An engrossed bill to authorize Elisha B. Williams to erect a wool carding machine on Jackson's river, near the town of Covington in the county of Alleghany, was read a third time, and on motion of Mr. Layne, ordered to be laid upon the table.

An engrossed bill changing the name of William H. Riggan to that of William H. Drewry, was read a third time:

Resolved, That the bill do pass, and that the title be, "an act changing the name of William H. Riggan to that of William H. Drewry."

An engrossed bill appropriating a further sum of money for completing the improvements of the Western lunatic hospital, was read a third time:

Resolved, That the bill do pass, and that the title be, "an act appropriating a further sum of money for completing the improvements of the Western lunatic hospital."

An engrossed bill to authorize William Townes to erect a toll-bridge across the Roanoke river, opposite the town of Clarksville in the county of Mecklenburg, was read a third time:

Resolved, That the bill do pass, and that the title be, "an act to authorize William Townes to erect a toll-bridge across the Roanoke river, opposite the town of Clarksville in the county of Mecklenburg."

An engrossed bill to incorporate the town of Salem in the county of Botetourt, was read a third time:

Resolved, That the bill do pass, and that the title be, "an act to incorporate the town of Salem in the county of Botetourt."

An engrossed bill authorizing the common council of Fredericksburg to subscribe for stock in the Rappahannock and Blue Ridge rail-road company, was read a third time:

Resolved, That the bill do pass, and that the title be, "an act authorizing the common council of Fredericksburg to subscribe for stock in the Rappahannock and Blue Ridge rail-road company."

An engrossed bill authorizing the county and corporation court clerks to charge fees for certain services performed by them, was read a third time:

Resolved, That the bill do pass, and that the title be, "an act authorizing the county and corporation court clerks to charge fees for certain services performed by them."

An engrossed bill allowing Daniel Starks, a free man of colour, to remain in the commonwealth a limited time, was read a third time:

Resolved, That the bill do pass, and that the title be, "an act allowing Daniel Starks, a free man of colour, to remain in the commonwealth a limited time."

An engrossed bill allowing Charles Williams, a free man of colour, to remain in the commonwealth a limited time, was read a third time:

Resolved, That the bill do pass, and that the title be, "an act allowing Charles Williams, a free man of colour, to remain in the commonwealth a limited time."

An engrossed bill to amend the act, entitled, "an act to amend an act, entitled, 'an act to establish Water street in the town of Portsmouth,'" passed April 4th, 1831, was read a third time:

Resolved, That the bill do pass, and that the title be, "an act to amend the act, entitled, 'act act to amend an act, entitled, 'an act to establish Water street in the town of Portsmouth,'" passed April 4th, 1831.

An engrossed bill to authorize a separate election at the place called the Burned Chimneys in the county of Northumberland, was read a third time:

Resolved, That the bill do pass, and that the title be, "an act to authorize a separate election at the place called the Burned Chimneys in the county of Northumberland."

Ordered, That Mr. Shands carry the same to the senate and request their concurrence.

The following bills were read a second time, and ordered to be engrossed and read a third time, viz:

A bill creating a new regiment in the county of Warren, and for other purposes.

A bill concerning the executor of James Jenks, deceased.

A bill to define the duties and regulate the fees of the attorney general.

A bill regulating the allowances in cases of arrest for criminal offences.

A bill to amend the act concerning the overseers of the poor, passed 20th February, 1829.

A bill to repeal part of an act passed on the 27th February, 1836, entitled, "an act to authorize the auditor to issue warrants on the treasury in satisfaction of certain judgments against the commonwealth."

A bill to authorize the opening a new street in the town of Petersburg.

A bill to amend the act, entitled, "an act for the relief of creditors against fraudulent devises."

A bill to explain the act, entitled, "an act to reduce into one the several acts concerning grand juries and petit juries."

A bill abolishing the vaccine agency of this commonwealth.

A bill allowing Jim Smith and wife and their infant children, free persons of colour, to remain in the commonwealth a limited time.

A bill to amend and explain an act, entitled, "an act to prescribe the mode of electing trustees for the town of Fairfax in the county of Culpeper, and vesting them with corporate powers."

A bill to prevent more effectually persons trading with slaves.

A bill concerning John B. Armistead sheriff of Fauquier county.

A bill to increase the salaries of the inspectors of tobacco at Farmville in the county of Prince Edward; and

A bill to amend an act to provide for a revision of the criminal code, and for other purposes.

A bill declaratory of the 16th section of the act incorporating the Farmers bank of Virginia, and directing the distribution of the contingent or referred fund in conformity thereto, was, on motion of Mr. Cunningham, ordered to be laid upon the table.

A bill concerning Richard H. Edwards; and

A bill concerning Frederick Moore of the county of Cabell, were also read a second time and ordered to be engrossed and read a third time.

The following bills were read the first and ordered to be read a second time, viz:

A bill allowing further time to the representatives and creditors of Lewis Eisenmenger, deceased, to redeem certain lands vested in the literary fund for the non-payment of taxes.

A bill authorizing Lavender London and William H. Garland to erect a dam across Tye river in the county of Nelson.

A bill to provide for keeping in repair the public roads within the corporation of Lynchburg; and

A bill releasing the commonwealth's claim upon the estate of Archy Cooper, a lunatic.

A bill concerning Peter J. Chevallie, was read a second time on motion of Mr. Stanard, amended, and as amended, ordered to be engrossed and read a third time.

On motion of Mr. Layne, a bill concerning James Burk, was ordered to be laid upon the table.

On motion of Mr. Gibson, a resolution of the committee for courts of justice, reporting reasonable the petition of Lucy and Delila, was taken up, and on the question put thereupon, agreed to by the house, and a bill was ordered to be brought in conformably therewith.

On motion of Mr. Sherrard, *Resolved*, That when this house adjourns to-day, it will adjourn until to-morrow 11 o'clock.

On motion of Mr. Watkins, the house adjourned accordingly.

TUESDAY, March 22d, 1836.

A communication from the senate by their clerk:

IN SENATE, March 21st, 1836.

The senate have passed the bills, entitled,

"An act authorizing the auditor to issue a warrant in favour of James Paxton."

"An act incorporating the Virginia silk company."

"An act incorporating the Fredericksburg iron and steel manufacturing company."

"An act incorporating the Sweet springs and Price's mountain turnpike company."

"An act incorporating the Fredericksburg mining company."

"An act to change the place of holding a separate election in the county of Pittsylvania."

"An act to change the place of holding a separate election in the county of Harrison."

"An act changing the terms of the circuit superior court of law and chancery in and for the county of Stafford."

"An act to alter the terms of the circuit superior court of law and chancery for the county and borough of Norfolk."

"An act to amend an act incorporating the Fredericksburg mechanics association."

"An act regulating the commissions on sales made under decrees in chancery, and for other purposes."

"An act to increase the number of trustees in the town of Portsmouth and to enlarge their powers and privileges."

"An act incorporating the Portsmouth provident society."

"An act to amend the act, entitled, 'an act to amend an act, entitled, 'an act to establish Water street in the town of Portsmouth,'" passed April 4th, 1831.

"An act changing the time of holding the circuit superior courts of law and chancery in the counties of Rockingham and Pendleton."

"An act allowing Daniel Starke, a free man of colour, to remain in the commonwealth a limited time."

"An act to incorporate the Wythe watering company in the county of Wythe."

"An act authorizing the common council of Fredericksburg to subscribe for stock in the Rappahannock and Blue Ridge rail-road company."

"An act concerning the town of Leesburg in the county of Loudoun."

"An act to incorporate the town of Salem in the county of Botetourt."

"An act regulating the mode of obtaining writs of error in criminal prosecutions for misdemeanors."
"An act changing the name of William H. Riggin to that of William H. Drewry."
"An act to increase the library at Lewisburg."
"An act concerning Ann, a free woman of colour."
"An act to repeal the act to provide for the appointment of a commissioner to examine and report upon claims for unsatisfied military land bounties, and for other purposes, passed March 11th, 1834 ;" and
"An act authorizing appeals to be taken from the courts of certain counties therein mentioned, to the court of appeals held at Lewisburg."

They have also passed the bills, entitled,
"An act to amend the several acts concerning the public guard in the city of Richmond."
"An act to incorporate a company to construct a toll-bridge across the Shenandoah river at Harper's Ferry."
"An act to authorise Richard Lorton to surrender his interest in the museum property."
"An act changing the time of holding the county courts in the counties of Marshall and Ohio, and to amend the act establishing the town of Moundsville in Ohio, now Marshall county."
"An act to incorporate the town of Waterford in the county of Loudoun."
"An act to regulate the conduct of boatmen on the Appomattox and Roanoke rivers and their branches."
"An act appropriating the surplus revenue of the literary fund."
"An act to amend the act, entitled, 'an act concerning the Cumberland road ;'" and
"An act imposing taxes for the support of government," with amendments, in which they request the concurrence of the house of delegates.

The said amendment proposed by the senate to the said bill, entitled, "an act appropriating the surplus revenue of the literary fund," was twice read, as follows:

Strike out from the word "the" in the 5th line, to the word "it" in the 13th line, and insert "school commissioners in the several counties, cities, towns or boroughs *shall* when there are colleges or academies, or where they may be hereafter established by law, apply the additional fund created by this act to the colleges or academies within their respective counties or corporations : *Provided*, That no portion of the sum herein appropriated shall be used or applied to the building of any academy or college : *And provided also*, That where there are more than one incorporated academy or college in any county, city, town or borough, then the said commissioners *shall* divide the same rateably in their discretion between such colleges and academies."

A motion was then made by Mr. Prentiss, to amend the said amendment by striking out the word "shall" where it first and last occurs in the said amendment, and inserting in lieu thereof the word "may."

Whereupon, a motion was made by Mr. Madison, that the farther consideration of the said bill and proposed amendments be indefinitely postponed, and the question being put thereupon, was determined in the negative. Ayes 12, noes 64.

The ayes and noes thereupon being required by Mr. Jessee, (and sustained according to the rule of the house,) are as follow:

Ayes, Messrs. Turnbull, Daniel, Hunter of Essex, Watkins, Summers, Taylor of Mathews and Middlesex, Madison, Crutchfield, Hargrave, Cunningham, Brown of Petersburg, and Stanard.—12.

Noes, Messrs. Banks, (speaker,) Grinalds, Drummond, Layne, Wiley, Garland of Amherst, Brooke, Henshaw, Miller, Booker, Austin, Beuhring, Samuel, Christian, Hill, Servant, Ball, Smith of Fauquier, Price, Strange, Davison, Watts, Smith of Gloucester, Hail of Grayson, Nixon, Kincheloe, Botts, Fontaine, Berry, Fleet, Robinson, Neill, Hays, Straton, Beard, Taylor of Loudoun, Harris, Rogers, Willey, Morgan, Sherrard, Cooke, Leland, Chapline, Masters, Woolfolk, Almond, Adams, M'Coy, Cackley, Hopkins, Carroll, Marteney, Nicklin, Moffett, Conrad, Jessee, M'Mullen, Bare, Rinker, Gibson, Jett, Prentiss and Saunders.—64.

The said amendments proposed by Mr. Prentiss, were then agreed to, and the said amendment, as amended, was agreed to by the house.

Ordered, That Mr. Brown of Petersburg inform the senate thereof and request their concurrence in the said amendments.

The amendments proposed by the senate to the residue of the said bills, being twice read, were, on questions severally put thereupon, agreed to by the house.

Ordered, That the clerk inform the senate thereof.

A message from the senate by Mr. Patteson:

MR. SPEAKER,—The senate have passed a bill, entitled, "an act re-organizing the Lexington arsenal, and establishing a military school in connexion with Washington college." And then he withdrew.

A motion was made by Mr. Woolfolk, that the fifth rule of this house be suspended for the purpose of reconsidering the vote rejecting an engrossed bill incorporating the Tuckahoe canal company, and the question being put thereupon, was determined in the negative.

On motion of Mr. Miller, the same having been amended on motion of Mr. Woolfolk,

Resolved by the general assembly, That the public librarian be, and he is hereby instructed to deliver free of charge, to each of the judges of the court of appeals and general court, a copy of the forthcoming volume, and of all future volumes, of the reports of the decisions of the court of appeals and the general court, and also to the clerks of the circuit superior courts of law and chancery, for the use of their respective courts.

Ordered, That Mr. Watkins carry the same to the senate and request their concurrence.

On motions severally made, *Ordered,* That leave of absence from the service of this house for the remainder of the session, be granted to Messrs. Grinalds, Drummond, Gibson, Ragsdale, Madison, Watts and Shands.

Similar leave was refused to Messrs. Davison, Nixon, Jessee and Moncure.

On motion of Mr. Stanard, *Ordered,* That the committee for courts of justice be discharged from the farther consideration of the resolution in relation to the acts concerning executions and insolvents; concerning the publication of county levies; from the petitions of citizens of the county of Morgan, and citizens of the 13th judicial circuit for an increase of the compensation to the judges; from the resolution in relation to process against absconding debtors; in relation to limitations of actions, &c.; concerning counsel and attorneys concerning the expenses attending the arrest and prosecution of criminals; from the petitions of citizens of Fauquier and Loudoun, in relation to free negroes owning and driving market carts; of citizens of the county of Ohio, in relation to limited partnerships; of Jonas Baker, Bassett Saunders and Milly, free persons of colour, to remain in the commonwealth; from the resolutions in relation to slaves, free negroes and mulattoes; concerning transcripts of patents; from the petition of David Skurry, to remain in the commonwealth; from the resolution concerning slaves, free negroes and mulattoes; from the petitions of Jesse Winn, asking a restoration of lands forfeited; of Jane Carter, praying that her husband, Richard Binns, may be permitted to remain in the commonwealth; from the resolution concerning United States convicts; from the petition of Stephen Turner, asking the appointment of a trustee; from the resolution concerning the delivery by clerks of courts of original wills; concerning special bail; from the petitions of citizens of Fauquier; concerning free negroes; of citizens of Fredericksburg in relation to the statute of limitations concerning real estate; from the resolutions in relation to revolutionary claims; in relation to Revised Code and Supplement; and from the petitions of the heirs of Thomas Carter, John Stackhouse, James Johnson, John Nicholas, Robert Millinor, Randal Chivis, Francis F. Dunlap, Thomas Warring, Reuben Butler, William Ramsey, William Rumney, Robert Fauntleroy, Joseph Blackwell, Lincefield Sharp, David Rogers, William Brooke and William Lewis, asking compensation for revolutionary services; of the trustees of Monongalia academy, praying an appropriation of the amount of a forfeited recognizance, and that the said resolutions and petitions be laid upon the table.

Mr. Stanard, from the said committee, presented a bill allowing Lucy and Delila, free persons of colour, to remain in the commonwealth; which was subsequently read the first and second times, and by general consent, ordered to be engrossed and read a third time.

On motion of Mr. Stanard, *Ordered,* That leave be given to bring in a bill permitting sundry free persons of colour therein named to remain in the commonwealth a limited time, and that Messrs. Stanard, Berry, Gibson, Mullen, Woolfolk, Austin and Williams, prepare and bring in the same, and have leave to sit during the session of this house.

Mr. Stanard subsequently presented the said bill, which was read the first and second times, and by general consent, ordered to be engrossed and read a third time.

On motion of Mr. M'Coy, *Resolved by the general assembly,* That the board of public works be, and they are hereby authorized, to cause the eastern section of the turnpike road across the Alleghany mountain, from Heavnor's store in Pendleton county to the Greenbrier river, to be put under contract and constructed as soon as practicable, so far as the appropriation made by an act passed March 4th, 1834, will extend, provided the same can be done on terms which to them shall appear reasonable; and that they are also hereby required to report to the next session of the general assembly, what further appropriation will in their opinion, be required to complete the construction of the said road to the Greenbrier river.

Ordered, That Mr. Watkins carry the same to the senate and request their concurrence.

On motion of Mr. Watkins, *Resolved by the general assembly,* That the superintendent of the public buildings be, and he is hereby authorized, to rent out the old public stable and carriage house on such terms and conditions as he shall deem expedient, for the term of one year.

Ordered, That Mr. Watkins carry the same to the senate and request their concurrence.

On motion of Mr. Carter, *Ordered,* That the committee on banks be discharged from the farther consideration of the resolutions adopted by a meeting of citizens of the borough of Norfolk, and the reply thereto by the president of the bank of Virginia, and that the same be laid upon the table.

On motion of Mr. Smith of Frederick, *Ordered,* That the committee on the militia laws be discharged from the farther consideration of the petition of the officers who sat upon the court martial for the trial of ensign Bentley; and from the resolutions for increasing the pay of musicians; for providing for the better instruction, discipline and organization of the militia; and for paying William Owens for stands of colours, and that the said petition and resolutions be laid upon the table.

On motion of Mr. Cooke, an engrossed bill concerning the administrator of Richard Kelsick, deceased, with the ryder thereto, was taken up:

Resolved, That the bill (with the ryder) do pass, and that the title be, "an act concerning the administrator of Richard Kelsick, deceased."

An engrossed bill concerning the executor of James Jenks, deceased, was read a third time:

Resolved, That the bill do pass, and that the title be, "an act concerning the executor of James Jenks, deceased."

An engrossed bill to repeal part of an act passed on the 27th February, 1836, entitled, "an act to authorize the auditor to issue warrants on the treasury in satisfaction of certain judgments against the commonwealth, was read a third time:

Resolved, That the bill do pass, and that the title be, " an act to repeal part of an act passed on the 27th February, 1836, entitled, ' an act to authorize the auditor to issue warrants on the treasury in satisfaction of certain judgments against the commonwealth.' "

An engrossed bill to define the duties and regulate the fees of the attorney general, was read a third time:

Resolved, That the bill do pass, and that the title be, " an act to define the duties and regulate the fees of the attorney general."

An engrossed bill to amend the act concerning overseers of the poor, passed 10th February, 1829, was read a third time:

Resolved, That the bill do pass, and that the title be, " an act to amend the act concerning overseers of the poor," passed 10th February, 1829.

An engrossed bill regulating the allowances in cases of arrest for criminal offences, was read a third time:

Resolved, That the bill do pass, and that the title be, " an act regulating the allowances in cases of arrest for criminal offences."

An engrossed bill to increase the salaries of the inspectors of tobacco at Farmville in the county of Prince Edward, was read a third time:

Resolved, That the bill do pass, and that the title be, " an act to increase the salaries of the inspectors of tobacco at Farmville in the county of Prince Edward."

An engrossed bill creating a new regiment within the county of Warren, and for other purposes, was read a third time:

Resolved, That the bill do pass, and that the title be, " an act creating a new regiment within the county of Warren, and for other purposes."

An engrossed bill to amend an act to provide for a revision of the criminal code, and for other purposes, was read a third time:

Resolved, That the bill do pass, and that the title be,. " an act to amend an act to provide for a revision of the criminal code, and for other purposes."

Ordered, That Mr. Brown of Petersburg, carry the said bills to the senate and request their concurrence.

An engrossed bill to prevent more effectually persons trading with slaves, was read a third time, and the question being put upon its passage, was determined in the negative.

Resolved, That the said bill be rejected.

An engrossed bill concerning John B. Armistead, sheriff of Fauquier county, was read a third:

Resolved, That the bill do pass, and that the title be, " an act concerning John B. Armistead, sheriff of Fauquier county."

An engrossed bill to amend and explain an act, entitled, " an act to prescribe the mode of electing trustees for the town of Fairfax in the county of Culpeper, and vesting them with corporate powers," was read a third time:

Resolved, That the bill do pass, and that the title be, " an act to amend and explain an act, entitled, ' an act to prescribe the mode of electing trustees for the town of Fairfax in the county of Culpeper, and vesting them with corporate powers.' "

An engrossed bill to authorize the opening a new street in the town of Petersburg, was read a third time:

Resolved, That the bill do pass, and that the title be, " an act to authorize the opening a new street in the town of Petersburg."

An engrossed bill to amend the act, entitled, " an act for the relief of creditors against fraudulent devises," was read a third time:

Resolved, That the bill do pass, and that the title be, " an act to amend the act, entitled, ' an act for the relief of creditors against fraudulent devises.' "

An engrossed bill allowing Jim Smith and wife and their infant children, free persons of colour, to remain in the commonwealth a limited time, was read a third time:

Resolved, That the bill do pass, and that the title be, " an act allowing Jim Smith and wife and their infant children, free persons of colour, to remain in the commonwealth a limited time."

An engrossed bill concerning Richard H. Edwards, was read a third time:

Resolved, That the bill do pass, and that the title be, " an act concerning Richard H. Edwards."

An engrossed bill to explain the act, entitled, " an act to reduce into one the several acts concerning grand juries and petit juries," was read a third time:

Resolved, That the bill do pass, and that the title be, " an act to explain the act, entitled, ' an act to reduce into one the several acts concerning grand juries and petit juries.' "

An engrossed bill concerning Peter J. Chevallie, was read a third time:

Resolved, That the bill do pass, and that the title be, " an act concerning Peter J. Chevallie."

An engrossed bill concerning Frederick Moore of the county of Cabell, was read a third time

Resolved, That the bill do pass, and that the title be, " an act concerning Frederick Moore of the county of Cabell."

Ordered, That Mr. Watkins carry the same to the senate and request their concurrence.

The following bills were read a second time, and ordered to be engrossed and read a third time, viz:

A bill to provide for the purchase of additional copies of the statutes at large, published in continuation of Hening's statutes at large.

A bill concerning the sheriff of Spottsylvania.
A bill allowing Andy, a man of colour, to remain in the commonwealth a limited time.
A bill releasing the commonwealth's claim upon the estate of Archy Cooper, a lunatic.
A bill to provide for keeping in repair the public roads within the corporation of Lynchburg; and
A bill authorizing Lavender London and William H. Garland to erect a dam across Tye river in the county of Nelson.

On motion of Mr. Sherrard, *Resolved*, That when this house adjourns to-day, it will adjourn until to-morrow 12 o'clock.

And then the house adjourned accordingly.

WEDNESDAY, March 23d, 1836.

A communication from the senate by their clerk:

IN SENATE, March 22d, 1836.

The senate have passed the bills, entitled,

"An act allowing Charlotte Morgan, a free woman of colour, to remain in the commonwealth."

"An act appointing trustees to the town of New Glasgow, and for other purposes."

"An act to enlarge the powers of the county courts of Albemarle and Nelson, for the purpose of opening a road from Scottsville to the head waters of Rockfish river."

"An act placing James river on the footing of a lawful fence so far as concerns the counties of Fluvanna and Albemarle."

"An act to amend the act, entitled, 'an act concerning the town of Moorefield in the county of Hardy.'"

"An act appropriating a further sum of money for completing the improvements of the Western lunatic hospital."

"An act concerning John Chew."

"An act incorporating sundry companies to construct turnpike roads from Richmond to Big bird bridge in the county of Goochland."

"An act incorporating the Glen Leonard rail-road company."

"An act incorporating the stockholders of the Smithfield rail-road company."

"An act vesting the commonwealth's stock in the James river and Kanawha company in the board of public works, and for other purposes."

"An act incorporating the stockholders of the eastern shore rail-road company."

"An act incorporating the Marshall and Ohio turnpike company."

"An act to authorize William Townes to erect a toll-bridge across the Roanoke river opposite the town of Clarksville, in the county of Mecklenburg."

"An act reviving an act incorporating a company to construct a turnpike road from the upper end of the Blue Ridge canal to its intersection with the Lexington and Covington turnpike company."

"An act divorcing Ann Edmunds from her husband John W. A. Edmunds."

"An act allowing Charles Williams, a free man of colour, to remain in the commonwealth a limited time."

"An act limiting recoveries on judgments in other states."

"An act incorporating the Petersburg and Norfolk savings institutions."

"An act incorporating the Chesterfield and James river canal rail-road company."

"An act suspending the processioning of lands in counties therein mentioned."

"An act authorizing the county and corporation court clerks to charge fees for certain services performed by them."

"An act regulating the allowances in cases of arrest for criminal offences."

"An act to repeal part of an act passed on the 27th of February, 1836, entitled, 'an act to authorize the auditor to issue warrants on the treasury in satisfaction of certain judgments against the commonwealth.'"

"An act amending the act concerning waste tobacco."

They have also passed the bill, entitled,

"An act concerning delinquent lands, and land not heretofore entered on the commissioners' books," with an amendment, in which they request the concurrence of the house of delegates.

They agree to the amendments proposed by the house of delegates to their amendment to the bill, entitled, "an act appropriating the surplus revenue of the literary fund."

They agree to the resolution providing for renting out the old stable and carriage house attached to the public square.

And they have rejected the bills, entitled,

"An act amending the laws concerning slaves, free negroes and mulattoes."

"An act concerning Frederick Moore of the county of Cabell;" and

"An act providing further security for the payment of jailors' fees"

And they have disagreed to the resolution providing certain courts with reports of the decisions of the court of appeals and general court.

The said amendment being twice read, was, on the question put thereupon, agreed to by the house.
Ordered, That the clerk inform the senate thereof.

On motion of Mr. Wilson of Botetourt, *Resolved,* That when this house adjourns to-morrow, it will, with the consent of the senate, adjourn *sine die.*

Ordered, That Mr. Brown of Petersburg carry the same to the senate and request their concurrence.

On motion of Mr. Layne, the following report of the committee for courts of justice was taken up and read:

The committee for courts of justice have, according to order, had under consideration the petition of Arthur Lee, a free man of colour, to them referred, praying that himself and family may be permitted to remain in the commonwealth, and have come to the following resolution thereupon:

Resolved as the opinion of this committee, That the prayer of the said petition be rejected.

The said resolution was amended on motion of Mr. Layne, by striking therefrom the words "be rejected," and inserting in lieu thereof the words "is reasonable," and as amended, agreed to by the house.

On motion of Mr. Hunter of Berkeley, *Resolved,* That this house will proceed on this day by joint vote with the senate, to the election of four visitors, pursuant to the provisions of an act "re-organizing the Lexington arsenal and establishing a military school in connexion with Washington college," passed March 22d, 1836.

Ordered, That Mr. Hunter of Berkeley carry the same to the senate and request their concurrence.

An engrossed bill releasing the commonwealth's claim upon the estate of Archy Cooper, a lunatic, was read a third time, and on motion of Mr. Crutchfield, ordered to be laid upon the table.

An engrossed bill to provide for keeping in repair the public roads within the corporation of Lynchburg, was read a third time:

Resolved, That the bill do pass, and that the title be, "an act to provide for keeping in repair the public roads within the corporation of Lynchburg."

An engrossed bill authorizing Lavender London and William H. Garland to erect a dam across Tye river in the county of Nelson, was read a third time:

Resolved, That the bill do pass, and that the title be, "an act authorizing Lavender London and William H. Garland to erect a dam across Tye river in the county of Nelson."

An engrossed bill to provide for the purchase of additional copies of the statutes at large, published in continuation of Hening's statutes at large, was read a third time:

Resolved, That the bill do pass, and that the title be, "an act to provide for the purchase of additional copies of the statutes at large, published in continuation of Hening's statutes at large."

Ordered, That Mr. Brown of Petersburg carry the said bills to the senate and request their concurrence.

An engrossed bill concerning the sheriff of Spottsylvania county, was read a third time, and the question being put upon its passage, was determined in the negative:

Resolved, That the bill be rejected.

An engrossed bill allowing Andy, a man of colour, to remain in the commonwealth a limited time, was read a third time:

Resolved, That the bill do pass and that the title be, "an act allowing Andy, a man of colour, to remain in the commonwealth a limited time."

An engrossed bill allowing Lucy and Delila, free persons of colour, to remain in the commonwealth, was read a third time:

Resolved, That the bill do pass, and that the title be, "an act allowing Lucy and Delila, free persons of colour, to remain in the commonwealth."

An engrossed bill permitting sundry free persons of colour, therein named, to remain in the commonwealth a limited time, was read a third time; whereupon, on motion of Mr. Sherrard, the rule of the house was suspended, and the vote ordering the said bill to be engrossed was reconsidered; the said bill was then amended on motions severally made, and as amended, again ordered to be engrossed and read a third time; the same was forthwith engrossed and read a third time:

Resolved, That the bill do pass, and that the title be, "an act permitting sundry free persons of colour, therein named, to remain in the commonwealth a limited time."

Ordered, That Mr. Brown of Petersburg carry the said bills to the senate and request their concurrence.

A message from the senate by Mr. Patteson:

Mr. Speaker,—The senate agree to the resolution for proceeding on this day to the election of visitors to the military school in connexion with Washington college. And then he withdrew.

On motion, the speaker signed the following enrolled bills:

An act to revive the inspection of tobacco at Spring warehouse in the town of Lynchburg.

An act incorporating a company for the purpose of improving the navigation of Little and Big Deep creeks in the county of Powhatan.

An act to amend the act, entitled, "an act concerning William Brown."

An act to incorporate the Phœnix mining company.

An act to authorize the president and directors of the Portsmouth and Roanoke rail-road company to increase their capital stock or to borrow a sum of money.

An act to incorporate the Falmouth mining company.

An act to incorporate the Deep run mining company.

An act to change the place of holding a separate election in the county of Marshall.
An act to change the place of holding a separate election in the county of Preston.
An act to incorporate the Virginia mills manufacturing company.
An act to change the place of holding a separate election in the county of Wythe.
An act incorporating the Great Falls manufacturing company in the county of Fayette.
An act to authorize the appointment of a third commissioner of the superior court of Petersburg.
An act to authorize William Chapline and others to construct wharves on Wheeling creek and the Ohio river adjoining the town of South Wheeling in Ohio county.
An act to amend the act establishing the town of Grandville in the county of Monongalia.
An act to enlarge, define and establish the corporate boundaries and limits of the town of Wheeling in the county of Ohio.
An act concerning Smith's river.
An act to incorporate the Petersburg navigation company.
An act to authorize the mayor and commonalty of the town of Wheeling to subscribe for stock of the Baltimore and Ohio rail-road company.
An act to amend an act, entitled, "an act for cutting a navigable canal from the waters of Elizabeth river in the state of Virginia, to the waters of Pasquotank river in North Carolina."
An act to revive and amend the act, entitled, "an act incorporating the Richmond rail-road company."
An act providing for the better security of persons charged with criminal offences.
An act to amend an act, entitled, "an act to incorporate the Midlothian coal mining company."
An act to amend the act, entitled, "an act to reduce into one the several acts for the settlement and regulation of ferries," passed January 30th, 1819.
An act to authorize a separate election at Greenfield in the county of Nelson.
An act to amend an act, entitled, "an act to incorporate the Staunton and Potomac rail-road company."
An act to revive and amend an act incorporating the Belle Isle manufacturing company, passed 19th March, 1832.
An act fixing the school quotas of the counties of Ohio and Marshall, York, James City, and the city of Williamsburg.
An act to incorporate the Fleet's manufacturing company.
An act to incorporate the Ettrick manufacturing company.
An act to provide for the enlargement of the public warehouse for the storage and inspection of tobacco in the city of Richmond.
An act to amend an act, entitled, "an act incorporating the stockholders of the Winchester and Potomac rail-road company."
An act directing a change of location of the North-western turnpike through the town of Evansville.
An act directing the survey and location of routes for certain roads therein mentioned.
An act directing the survey of a route for a road from the North-western road to some point on Leading creek in the county of Randolph.
An act to incorporate the Newburn and Red Sulphur springs turnpike company.
An act to prevent trespasses by non-resident herdsmen in the county of Preston.
An act concerning the fire and marine insurance company of Wheeling.
An act forming a new county out of parts of the counties of Lewis, Kanawha and Nicholas.
An act to dispose of certain moneys heretofore raised by lottery in the county of Monroe.
An act to reduce and regulate the tolls on the North-western turnpike.
An act to incorporate the Sweet springs company.
An act incorporating the Red and Blue Sulphur springs turnpike company.
An act to provide for the construction of a road between Weston in the county of Lewis, and Charleston in the county of Kanawha.
An act incorporating the stockholders of the Rappahannock and Blue Ridge rail-road company.
An act to incorporate the stockholders of the City Point rail-road company.
An act concerning the town of Portsmouth.
An act to amend the act, entitled, "an act incorporating the Falmouth and Alexandria rail-road company."
An act to incorporate the Union Potomac company.
An act incorporating the Lexington and Richmond turnpike company.
An act to incorporate the Fluvanna mining company.
An act to change the place of holding a separate election in the county of Hampshire.
An act further to amend the act, entitled, "an act to amend the act, entitled, 'an act establishing a ferry from Onancock town in the county of Accomac to Norfolk, and for other purposes,'" passed March 5th, 1833.
An act authorizing the sale of the estate of John Haskins, senior, a lunatic.
An act to authorize the county court of Southampton to appoint processioners of lands, at the session of their court in the months of February, March or April of the present year, and thereafter as required by the general law upon the subject.
An act to amend an act, entitled, "an act to limit the assessment upon titheables, and to authorize a tax upon

property for the purpose of defraying county expenditures within the county of Berkeley," passed March 5th, 1835.
An act authorizing James Martin to hold and convey certain real estate.
An act releasing to William Fisher the commonwealth's right to one thousand acres of land in the county of Nicholas.
An act to establish the town of Hedgesville in the county of Berkeley.
An act to provide an index to the journals of the house of delegates.
An act to authorize a separate election at the tavern house of William Irwin in the county of Cumberland.
An act to incorporate the trustees of the Halifax academy.
An act to authorize a separate election at Hedgesville in the county of Berkeley.
An act to enlarge the town of Clarksville in the county of Mecklenburg.
An act concerning Duff Green.
An act to alter the terms of the circuit superior courts of law and chancery for the seventh district and thirteenth circuit of this commonwealth.
An act to authorize the common council of the town of Fredericksburg to make an advancement upon the stock of the corporation in the Rappahannock canal company.
An act incorporating the stockholders of the Louisa rail-road company.
An act to change the place of holding a separate election in the county of Tyler.
An act changing the time of holding the circuit superior courts of law and chancery for the counties of Monroe, Giles and Montgomery.
An act to incorporate the trustees of the Upperville academy, in the county of Fauquier.
An act to incorporate the Mechanics manufacturing company.
An act to authorize the judge of the second circuit to appoint a time for holding the courts thereof in certain cases.
An act authorizing an increase of the capital stock of the Merchants manufacturing company.
An act to incorporate the Kanawha slave insurance company.
An act to incorporate the Newtown Stephensburg library company.
An act to revive the charter of the Nelson and Albemarle Union factory company.
An act to amend an act, entitled, "an act to incorporate the Manchester wool and cotton manufacturing company," passed March 13th, 1832.
An act to establish an inspection of flour and Indian meal at the town of Winchester.
An act to authorize a separate election at Triadelphia in the county of Ohio.
An act to authorize a separate election at the house of Michael Snodgrass in the county of Monongalia.
An act relating to the Greensville and Panther gap turnpike road.
An act to amend an act, entitled, "an act for opening and improving the navigation of the Dragon swamp."
An act to incorporate the Stafford mining company.
An act to incorporate the Heth manufacturing company.
An act to provide for the construction of a road across the Blue Ridge at Milam's gap.
An act to incorporate the Fauquier White Sulphur springs.
An act to incorporate the Virginia fire insurance company.
An act to incorporate the Suffolk rail-road company.
An act to change the place of holding a separate election in the county of Lunenburg.
An act incorporating the literary and scientific mechanics institute of Norfolk and Portsmouth.
An act to amend an act, entitled, "an act to incorporate the Cold Brook company of colliers," passed January 23d, 1835."
An act to authorize the auditor to issue warrants on the treasury in satisfaction of certain judgments against the commonwealth.
An act incorporating the Natural Bridge turnpike company.
An act providing for a geological survey of the state, and for other purposes.
An act incorporating the Virginia towing company.
An act releasing the commonwealth's claim to a certain balance against the estate of Betsy Bidgood.
An act authorizing Jesse Sturm to erect a dam across the west fork of Monongalia river in the county of Harrison.
An act concerning the Rappahannock company.
An act to change the time of holding the county court of Alleghany county.
An act to change the times of holding the courts in the third judicial circuit.
An act forming a new county out of the county of Frederick.
An act forming a new county out of parts of the counties of Shenandoah and Frederick.
An act to amend "an act incorporating the Spring creek turnpike company."
An act to provide for the payment of the purchase money of Brown's warehouse.
An act to incorporate the Red springs company in the county of Alleghany.
An act requiring of the inspectors of tobacco in this commonwealth to distinguish in their inspections between tobacco produced in Virginia, and that produced in other states.
An act to amend the act, entitled, "an act to alter and reform the mode of proceeding in the courts of chancery."

An act to authorize a subscription on behalf of the state to the stock of the Lewisburg and Blue Sulphur springs turnpike company.
An act to amend the act concerning fraudulent devises.
An act concerning the county of Gloucester.
An act to incorporate the trustees of the Estillville academy in the county of Scott.
An act to authorize additions to the town of Farmville in the county of Prince Edward.
An act establishing a new regiment in the county of Preston.
An act incorporating the Smithfield savings institution in the county of Isle of Wight.
An act to incorporate the coal working company of Richmond and Manchester.
An act to amend the act, entitled, "an act incorporating a company to erect a toll-bridge over the Ohio river at Wheeling," passed February 17th, 1816.
An act concerning the Orange savings institution.
An act to provide for the construction of the eastern section of the road on the route surveyed from Huntersville to Parkersburg.
An act to enact an act of the general assembly of North Carolina, entitled, "an act to incorporate the Roanoke, Danville and Junction rail-road company."
An act incorporating the Staunton and Augusta springs turnpike company.
An act to incorporate the stockholders of the Lynchburg and Tennessee rail-road company, and to authorize them or the James river and Kanawha company to construct a rail-road from Lynchburg to Richmond.
An act to incorporate the Gills mountain mining company.
An act to incorporate the city of Wheeling.
An act to incorporate the United States copper mining company.
An act allowing Richard Bolling, a free man of colour, to remain in the commonwealth.
An allowing Daniel Higginbotham, a free man of colour, to remain in the commonwealth a limited time.
An act to incorporate the Virginia insurance company.
An act incorporating the stockholders of the Richmond and Petersburg rail-road company.
An act allowing Judy Johnson, a free woman of colour, to remain in the commonwealth.
An act providing for the construction of a turnpike road from the town of Beverley, in Randolph county, to the town of Clarksburg, in Harrison county.
An act to amend the act, entitled, "an act incorporating the Goose creek navigation company."
An act to provide for the construction of a road from the Ohio river, by Morgantown, to the Maryland line.
An act to change the times of holding the courts in the fifth and seventh judicial circuits, and of the counties of Henrico and Powhatan, and the hustings court of the city of Richmond, and for other purposes.
An act incorporating the trustees of the Martinsville academy.
An act changing the place of holding a separate election in the county of Kanawha.
An act to establish the town of Lovettsville in the county of Loudoun.
An act to incorporate the Goochland mining company.
An act to incorporate the trustees of the Lynchburg female academy.
An act to incorporate the trustees of the Charlestown athenæum and female academy.
An act to incorporate the Portsmouth and Chesapeake steamboat company.
An act to amend the act, entitled, "an act to incorporate the Richmond manufacturing company," passed on the 12th January, 1832.
An act directing the survey of a route for a road from Moorfield to the North-western turnpike.
An act concerning savings institutions.
An act to amend the act, entitled, "an act to amend an act to reduce into one act all acts and parts of acts to prevent the destruction of oysters," passed March 24th, 1831.
An act changing the Hunting run gold mining company into a company for mining and manufacturing iron and steel.
An act to incorporate the New Hope gold mine company.
An act to amend the several acts concerning the Petersburg rail-road company.
An act to authorize a subscription on behalf of the state to the stock of the Pittsylvania and Lynchburg turnpike company, and for other purposes.
An act incorporating the Lynchburg and Campbell court-house turnpike company.
On motion of Mr. Wilson of Botetourt, *Resolved*, That when this house adjourns to-day, it will adjourn until to-morrow, 10 o'clock.
On motion of Mr. Hunter of Essex, the house adjourned accordingly.

THURSDAY, March 24th, 1836.

A communication from the senate by their clerk:

IN SENATE, March 23d, 1836.

The senate have passed the bills, entitled,
"An act appropriating the public revenue."
"An act allowing Jim Smith and wife, and their infant children, free persons of colour, to remain in the commonwealth a limited time."
"An act creating a new regiment within the county of Warren, and for other purposes."
"An act concerning the subscription on behalf of the commonwealth to the stock of the Richmond, Fredericksburg and Potowmac rail-road company."
"An act to define the duties and regulate the fees of the attorney general."
"An act concerning the executor of James Jenks, deceased."
"An act to amend and explain an act, entitled, 'an act to prescribe the mode of electing trustees for the town of Fairfax in the county of Culpeper, and vesting them with corporate powers.'"
"An act concerning Richard H. Edwards."
"An act to authorize the opening a new street in the town of Petersburg."
"An act authorizing Lavender London and William H. Garland to erect a dam across Tye river in the county of Nelson."
"An act concerning John B. Armistead, sheriff of Fauquier county."
"An act allowing Lucy and Delila, free persons of colour, to remain in the commonwealth."
"An act to increase the salaries of the inspectors of tobacco at Farmville in the county of Prince Edward."
"An act concerning Peter J. Chevallie."
"An act to amend the several acts concerning pilots."
"An act permitting sundry free persons of colour, therein named, to remain in the commonwealth a limited time."
"An act to authorize a separate election at the Burned Chimneys, in the county of Northumberland."
"An act allowing Andy, a man of colour, to remain in the commonwealth a limited time."
"An act to explain the act, entitled, 'an act to reduce into one the several acts concerning grand juries and petit juries.'"
"An act prescribing the punishment of offences committed on rail-roads."
"An act to provide for keeping in repair the public roads within the corporation of Lynchburg."
"An act to suppress the circulation of incendiary publications, and for other purposes."
"An act concerning the administrator of Richard Kelsick, deceased;" and
"An act to amend an act to provide for the revision of the criminal code, and for other purposes."

They have agreed to the resolution requiring the eastern section of the turnpike road across the Alleghany mountain, from Heavnor's store to the Greenbrier river to be put under contract and constructed.

And to the resolution for an adjournment of the house of delegates *sine die*.

And they have rejected the bill, entitled, "an act to amend the act concerning the overseers of the poor, passed 20th February, 1829."

Their committee appointed to examine the enrolled bills, have examined sundry other such bills, which being found truly enrolled, have been signed by their speaker, and are herewith returned to the house of delegates.

Ordered, That Messrs. Woolfolk, Wilson of Botetourt, and Watkins, be added to the committee appointed to examine enrolled bills.

Mr. Woolfolk, from the said committee, reported that they had examined all bills which had been passed and found them truly enrolled.

Ordered, That Mr. Woolfolk carry the same to the senate.

A message from the senate by Mr. Keller:

Mr. SPEAKER,—The committee on behalf of the senate have examined the residue of the enrolled bills, which, having been found truly enrolled, have been signed by the speaker of the senate. And then he withdrew.

On motion, the speaker signed the residue of the enrolled bills:

An act to amend the act, entitled, "an act making further provision for completing the road from Staunton to the mouth of the Little Kanawha."
An act declaring Pocatallico river a public highway, from its mouth to Droddy's mill.
An act to equalize the regimental districts in the county of Rockingham, and for other purposes.
An act to amend and explain the act, entitled, "an act to reduce into one the several acts to regulate the solemnization of marriages."
An act to incorporate the Fredericksburg Union manufacturing company.
An act appointing commissioners to select a site for the seat of justice for the county of Ohio.
An act incorporating the American mining company.
An act to incorporate the Rappahannock marine and fire insurance company.
An act to incorporate the Big Bird mining company.
An act to authorize a separate election in the county of Tazewell, and one in the county of Russell.

An act to incorporate the proprietors of the Wellsburg lyceum.
An act to change the time of holding the county courts of the counties of Lewis and Braxton, and the circuit superior courts of law and chancery for the county of Fairfax.
An act incorporating the trustees of the Clarksville female academy.
An act to authorize Richard Barton Haxall to construct additional wharves at and near the town of Bermuda Hundred.
An act to amend an act, entitled, "an act to incorporate the Augusta springs company."
An act to amend an act, entitled, "an act incorporating the trustees of the Bedford female academy."
An act to incorporate the Etna coal company.
An act concerning John Pittinger, late sheriff of Brooke county.
An act to add a part of the county of Tazewell to the county of Giles.
An act directing a survey of the Dragon swamp.
An act concerning William Fenn.
An act to incorporate the Berkeley coal mining and rail-road company.
An act to authorize a separate election at the house of William Pulliam, in the county of Henry.
An act changing the time of holding the superior courts of Campbell, Bedford and the town of Lynchburg.
An act to explain the act authorizing subscriptions on the part of the commonwealth to the capital of joint stock companies.
An act to authorize Thomas A. Morton to erect a dam across Appomattox river.
An act to incorporate the Potomac silk and agricultural company.
An act to establish the town of Meadowville, in the county of Greenbrier.
An act concerning the Greensville and Roanoke rail-road company.
An act to authorize a separate election at M'Gaheysville, in the county of Rockingham.
An act to incorporate the Front Royal library society, in the county of Warren.
An act to amend an act, entitled, "an act for the inspection of fish," passed the 28th of December, 1795.
An act incorporating the Mayo's bridge company.
An act to amend the act, entitled, "an act reducing into one the several acts for punishing persons guilty of certain thefts and forgeries, and the destruction or concealment of wills."
An act to incorporate the trustees of Saint Bride's academy in Norfolk county, and the trustees of the Suffolk academy in the county of Nansemond.
An act concerning Robert W. Christian, treasurer of the late charity school of Charles City and the overseers of the poor of the said county.
An act to change the place of holding a separate election in the county of Cabell.
An act to amend the act, entitled, "an act to incorporate a rail-road company from the city of Richmond to the town of York."
An act to change the time of holding a quarterly term of the county court of the county of Shenandoah.
An act to amend the act, entitled, "an act to incorporate the Grayson Sulphur springs company."
An act to prevent the destruction of oysters in Nansemond river and Chuckatuck creek in the county of Nansemond.
An act to change the site for the erection of a bridge across Jackson's river opposite the town of Covington.
An act concerning the Matoaca manufacturing company.
An act constituting a portion of the margin of the Potomac river in Berkeley county, a lawful fence.
An act to increase the capital stock of Booker's gold mine company, and for other purposes.
An act to amend the charter of the James river and Kanawha company.
An act concerning the Greensville and Roanoke rail-road company.
An act incorporating the Fredericksburg iron and steel manufacturing company.
An act changing the terms of the circuit superior court of law and chancery in and for the county of Stafford.
An act to alter the terms of the circuit superior courts of law and chancery for the county and borough of Norfolk.
An act incorporating the Fredericksburg mining company.
An act incorporating the Sweet springs and Price's mountain turnpike company.
An act to change the place of holding a separate election in the county of Harrison.
An act to change the place of holding a separate election in the county of Pittsylvania.
An act authorizing the auditor to issue a warrant in favour of James Paxton.
An act incorporating the Virginia silk company.
An act to amend the act incorporating the Fredericksburg mechanics association.
An act authorizing the common council of Fredericksburg to subscribe for stock in the Rappahannock and Blue Ridge rail-road company.
An act allowing Daniel Starke, a free man of colour, to remain in the commonwealth a limited time.
An act changing the time of holding the circuit superior courts of law and chancery in the counties of Rockingham and Pendleton.
An act to incorporate the Wythe watering company in the county of Wythe.

An act act authorizing appeals to be taken from the courts of certain counties therein mentioned, to the court of appeals held at Lewisburg.

An act regulating the commissions on sales under decrees in chancery, and for other purposes.

An act to increase the number of trustees in the town of Portsmouth, and to enlarge their powers and privileges.

An act incorporating the Portsmouth provident society.

An act to amend the act, entitled, "an act to amend an act, entitled, 'an act to establish Water street, in the town of Portsmouth,'" passed April 4th, 1831.

An act to incorporate the town of Salem in the county of Botetourt.

An act concerning the town of Leesburg in the county of Loudoun.

An act changing the name of William H. Riggan to that of William H. Drewry.

An act to increase the library at Lewisburg.

An act concerning Ann, a free woman of colour.

An act imposing taxes for the support of government.

An act regulating the mode of obtaining writs of error in criminal prosecutions for misdemeanors.

An act to repeal the act to provide for the appointment of a commissioner to examine and report upon claims for unsatisfied military land bounties, and for other purposes, passed March 11th, 1834.

An act to amend the several acts concerning the public guard in the city of Richmond, and for other purposes.

An act to incorporate a company to construct a toll-bridge across the Shenandoah river at Harper's Ferry.

An act to authorize Richard Lorton to surrender his interest in the museum property.

An act changing the time of holding the county courts in the counties of Marshall and Ohio, and to amend the act establishing the town of Moundsville in Ohio, now Marshall county.

An act to incorporate the town of Waterford in the county of Loudoun.

An act to regulate the conduct of boatmen on the Appomattox and Roanoke rivers, and their branches.

An act re-organizing the Lexington arsenal and establishing a military school in connexion with Washington college.

An act incorporating the Chesterfield and James river canal rail-road company.

An act concerning John Chew.

An act divorcing Ann Edmunds from her husband John W. A. Edmunds.

An act incorporating sundry companies to construct turnpike roads from Richmond to Big Bird bridge in the county of Goochland.

An act incorporating the Glen Leonard rail-road company.

An act incorporating the stockholders of the Smithfield rail-road company.

An act to amend the act, entitled, "an act concerning the town of Moorfield, in the county of Hardy."

An act placing James river on the footing of a lawful fence, so far as concerns the counties of Fluvanna and Albemarle.

An act to enlarge the powers of the county courts of Albemarle and Nelson

An act appointing trustees to the town of New Glasgow, and for other purposes.

An act appropriating a further sum of money for completing the improvements of the Western lunatic hospital.

An act allowing Charlotte Morgan, a free woman of colour, to remain in the commonwealth.

An act reviving an act incorporating a company to construct a turnpike road from the upper end of the Blue Ridge canal to its intersection with the Lexington and Covington turnpike road.

An act incorporating the Marshall and Ohio turnpike company.

An act incorporating the Petersburg and Norfolk savings institutions.

An act to authorize William Townes to erect a toll-bridge across the Roanoke river, opposite the town of Clarksville, in the county of Mecklenburg.

An act limiting recoveries on judgments in other states.

An act allowing Charles Williams, a free man of colour, to remain in the commonwealth a limited time.

An act vesting the commonwealth's stock in the James river and Kanawha company in the board of public works, and for other purposes, together with all dividends and other profits thereon.

An act incorporating the stockholders of the Eastern Shore rail-road company.

An act appropriating the surplus revenue of the literary fund.

An act suspending the processioning of lands in counties therein mentioned.

An act authorizing the county and corporation court clerks to charge fees for certain services performed by them.

An act to repeal part of an act passed on the 27th February, 1836, entitled, "an act to authorize the auditor to issue warrants on the treasury in satisfaction of certain judgments against the commonwealth."

An act amending the act concerning waste tobacco.

An act regulating the allowances in cases of arrest for criminal offences.

An act concerning delinquent lands and land not heretofore entered on the commissioners' books.

An act to amend the several acts concerning pilots.

An act concerning Peter J. Chevallie.

An act allowing Lucy and Delila, free persons of colour, to remain in the commonwealth.

An act concerning John B. Armistead, sheriff of Fauquier county.

An act authorizing Lavender London and William H. Garland to erect a dam across Tye river in the county of Nelson.
An act to increase the salaries of the inspectors of tobacco at Farmville in the county of Prince Edward.
An act to authorise the opening a new street in the town of Petersburg.
An act to amend and explain an act, entitled, "an act to prescribe the mode of electing trustees for the town of Fairfax in the county of Culpeper, and vesting them with corporate powers."
An act concerning the subscription on behalf of the commonwealth to the stock of the Richmond, Fredericksburg and Potomac rail-road company.
An act to define the duties and regulate the fees of the attorney general.
An act concerning the executor of James Jenks, deceased.
An act creating a new regiment within the county of Warren, and for other purposes.
An act allowing Jim Smith and wife and their infant children, free persons of colour, to remain in the commonwealth a limited time.
An act concerning Richard H. Edwards.
An act appropriating the public revenue.
An act prescribing the punishment of offences committed on rail-roads.
An act to amend an act to provide for a revision of the criminal code, and for other purposes.
An act concerning the administrator of Richard Kelsick, deceased.
An act to suppress the circulation of incendiary publications, and for other purposes.
An act to provide for keeping in repair the public roads within the corporation of Lynchburg.
An act permitting sundry free persons of colour, therein named, to remain in the commonwealth a limited time.
An act to authorize a separate election at the place called the Burned Chimneys, in the county of Northumberland.
An act allowing Andy, a man of colour, to remain in the commonwealth a limited time.
An act to explain the act, entitled, "an act to reduce into one the several acts concerning grand juries and petit juries."

The speaker laid before the house the following letter from the governor, which was read:

EXECUTIVE DEPARTMENT, March 24, 1836.

SIR,—Inclosed is a communication for the house of delegates, which you will please lay before that body.
Respectfully, your obedient servant,

LITT'N W. TAZEWELL.

To the Speaker of the House of Delegates.

EXECUTIVE DEPARTMENT, March 24, 1836.

To the House of Delegates:

I have the honour to communicate the inclosed resolutions of the legislature of Pennsylvania, relative to the distribution of the proceeds arising from the sales of the public lands, and for other purposes.

LITT'N W. TAZEWELL.

EXECUTIVE CHAMBER,
HARRISBURG, 19th March, 1836.

SIR,—For the purpose therein mentioned, I have the honour to transmit to you the accompanying resolutions of the legislature of Pennsylvania, adopted on the 15th instant.

JOS. RITNER,
Governor of Pennsylvania.

*To his Excellency the Governor
of the State of Virginia, at Richmond.*

Resolutions relative to the distribution of the proceeds arising from the sale of the public lands, and for other purposes.

Whereas, by the official statements from the treasury department of the United States, it appears there will be an unappropriated balance in the treasury, above the ordinary demands of the government, subject to the action of congress during the present session: And whereas, it is presumed that the wisdom of congress will not suffer that fund to accumulate in the treasury without devising means by which it can be usefully employed for the benefit of the people of this Union: And whereas, some of our sister states deny to congress the constitutional power of making internal improvements in the several states, while all seem to admit the power and propriety of distributing the proceeds arising, or which may have arisen, from the sale of the public lands, amongst the several states, subject to the control of their respective legislatures: And whereas, the proportion to which Pennsylvania would be entitled, should such distribution be made, would enable her to complete her public works, and establish a fund for the support of common schools, which would preclude the necessity of taxation for either purpose: And whereas, it is the policy of our government to guard against the increase of executive patronage, and especially against the accumulation of large sums of money in the treasury unappropriated: And whereas, a very large proportion of surplus revenue arises from the sales of the public lands, the joint property of all the states, which is regarded as a source of revenue which ought to be applied in the promotion of education, by establishing a system of common schools,—to the purposes of internal improvement,—or such other purposes as will best promote the interests of the states respectively: Therefore,

Resolved by the senate and house of representatives of the commonwealth of Pennsylvania, in general assembly met, That our senators in congress be instructed, and our representatives be recommended, to use their influence to procure the passage of a law to distribute the proceeds arising, or which may have arisen, from the sale of the public lands, amongst the several states, in proportion to the number of members from each state, in the house of representatives of the United States.

Resolved, That our senators in congress be instructed, and our representatives be recommended, to vote for a liberal and judicious expenditure of public money for the completion and construction of fortifications for the common defence.

Resolved, That the governor be requested to forward to each of our senators and members of congress from Pennsylvania, a copy of the foregoing preamble and resolutions; and also to the governors of the several states, with a request that they shall be laid before their state legislatures, requesting their co-operation.

NER MIDDLESWARTH,
Speaker of the House of Representatives.
THOMAS S. CUNNINGHAM,
Speaker of the Senate.

Approved: the fifteenth day of March, A. D. eighteen hundred and thirty-six.
JOSEPH RITNER.

SECRETARY'S OFFICE,
HARRISBURG, March 16, 1836.

I hereby certify the above to be a true copy of the original resolutions now remaining on file and of record in this office. Witness my hand and seal of office, the day and year aforesaid.

THO. H. BURROWES,
Secretary of the Commonwealth.

On motion of Mr. Wilson of Botetourt, *Ordered,* That the same be laid upon the table.

On motion of Mr. Hill, *Resolved,* That the thanks of this house be presented to its speaker, Linn Banks, for the prompt and impartial manner in which he has discharged the duties of the chair during the present session of the legislature.

Ordered, That Mr. Sherrard inform the senate that this house having finished the business before it, is now ready to adjourn *sine die.*

A message from the senate by Mr. Patteson:

MR. SPEAKER,—The senate have adopted a resolution for the adjournment of the senate, in which they request the concurrence of the house of delegates. And then he withdrew.

The said resolution was read as follows:

Resolved, That when the senate adjourns to-day, it will, with the consent of the house of delegates, adjourn until the first Monday in December next.

The said resolution was, on the question put thereupon, agreed to by the house.

Ordered, That Mr. Watkins inform the senate thereof.

On motion of Mr. Watkins, the house then adjourned *sine die.*

LIST OF DELEGATES FOR THE SESSION OF 1835-36.

Accomack,	Southey Grinalds,	*Botetourt,*	Fleming B. Miller,
	John P. Drummond.		George W. Wilson.
Albemarle,	Thomas W. Gilmer,	*Brooke,*	Jacob Decamps.
	Valentine W. Southall.	*Brunswick,*	Charles Turnbull,
Alleghany,	Douglass B. Layne.		James B. Mallory.
Amelia,	John F. Wiley.	*Buckingham,*	George Booker,
Amherst,	David S. Garland.		Archibald Austin.
Augusta,	Robert S. Brooke,	*Cabell,*	Frederick G. L. Beuhring.
	John J. Craig.	*Campbell,*	Oden G. Clay,
Bath,	William M'Clintic.		William Daniel, jr.
Bedford,	Robert Campbell,	*Caroline,*	Archibald Samuel.
	Edmund Pate.	*Charles City and*	Robert Christian.
Berkeley,	Edmund P. Hunter,	*New Kent,*	
	Levi Henshaw.	*Charlotte,*	John D. Richardson.

JOURNAL OF THE HOUSE OF DELEGATES.

Chesterfield,	William R. Johnson.	*Mason & Jackson,*	Andrew Waggener.
Culpeper,	Ambrose P. Hill.	*Mecklenburg,*	George Rogers,
Cumberland,	Allen Wilson.		Hugh A. Garland.
Dinwiddie,	John L. Scott.*	*Monongalia,*	William J. Willey,
Elizabeth City & }	Samuel B. Servant.		Stephen H. Morgan.
Warwick,		*Monroe,*	Aug's A. Chapman.
Essex,	R. M. T. Hunter.	*Montgomery,*	John Ingles.
Fairfax,	Spencer M. Ball.	*Morgan,*	John Sherrard.
Fauquier,	William R. Smith,	*Nansemond,*	John B. Benton.
	Absalom Hickerson.	*Nelson,*	Alexander Brown.
Fayette and Nicholas,	Hudson M. Dickinson.†	*Norfolk County,*	John W. Murdaugh,
Fluvanna,	Gideon A. Strange.		Mordecai Cooke.
Floyd,	Thomas H. Steger.	*Northampton,*	Severn E. Parker.
Franklin,	Samuel Hale,	*Northumberland,*	John D. Leland.
	John M. Holland.	*Nottoway,*	Robert Fitzgerald, jr.
Frederick,	James Bowen,	*Ohio and Marshall,*	Moses W. Chapline,
	John S. Davison,		Zadock Masters.
	John B. D. Smith.	*Orange,*	John Woolfolk.
Giles,	Reuben F. Watts.	*Page,*	William R. Almond.
Gloucester,	Thomas Smith.	*Patrick,*	Haman Critz.‖
Goochland,	Joseph S. Watkins.	*Pendleton,*	William M'Coy, jr.
Grayson,	Lewis Hail.	*Pittsylvania,*	William Swanson,
Greenbrier,	Pere B. Wethered.		Vincent Witcher.
Greensville,	Tamlin Avent.	*Pocahontas,*	William Cackley.
Halifax,	John B. Carrington,	*Powhatan,*	Henry L. Hopkins.
	Thomas G. Coleman.	*Preston,*	William Carroll.
Hampshire,	Thomas Sloan,	*Prince Edward,*	James Madison.
	William Nixon.	*Princess Anne,*	Jesse Morris, jr.
Hanover,	Charles P. Goodall.	*Prince George,*	William Shands.
Hardy,	John Mullen.	*Prince William,*	John W. Williams.
Harrison,	William A. Harrison,	*Randolph,*	William Marteney.
	Daniel Kincheloe.	*Rappahannock,*	Joseph Nicklin.
Henrico,	William B. Randolph.‡	*Rockbridge,*	Charles P. Dorman,
Henry,	Patrick H. Fontaine.		Alfred Leyburn.
Isle of Wight,	Joel Holleman.	*Rockingham,*	Anderson Moffett,
James City, York & }	John M. Gregory.		Jacob Conrad.
Williamsburg,		*Russell,*	William Jessee.
Jefferson,	Thomas Griggs, jr.,	*Scott,*	Fayette M'Mullen.
	Henry Berry.	*Shenandoah,*	Samuel Bare,
Kanawha,	George W. Summers.		Absalom Rinker.
King & Queen,	Alexander Fleet.	*Smyth,*	William R. Harley.
King George,	John Hooe.	*Southampton,*	Edward Butts.
King William,	Samuel Robinson.	*Spottsylvania,*	Oscar M. Crutchfield.
Lancaster and }	Robert W. Carter.	*Stafford,*	John Moncure.
Richmond,		*Surry,*	Peter T. Spratley.
Lee,	Stephen T. Neill.	*Sussex,*	Jesse Hargrave.
Lewis,	Samuel L. Hays.	*Tazewell,*	Robert Gillespie.
Logan,	Joseph Straton.	*Tyler,*	Van B. Delashmutt.
Loudoun,	Lewis Beard,	*Washington,*	John Gibson.
	George C. Powell,	*Westmoreland,*	James Jett.
	Timothy Taylor, jr.	*Wood,*	Henry L. Prentiss.
Louisa,	George Harris.	*Wythe,*	John A. Saunders.
Lunenburg,	Joel M. Ragsdale	*Norfolk Borough,*	William E. Cunningham.
Madison,	Linn Banks.	*Petersburg,*	John T. Brown.
Mathews & Middlesex,	John R. Taylor.	*Richmond City,*	Robert Stanard.

*Alfred J. Vaughan succeeded Mr. Scott, who resigned January 2d; took his seat January 23d.
† Samuel Price succeeded Mr. Dickinson, prevailing in his contest for the seat December 30th.
‡ John M. Botts succeeded Mr. Randolph, prevailing in his contest for the seat on the 24th December.
‖ Isaac Adams succeeded Mr. Critz, prevailing in his contest for the seat January 7th.

INDEX.

A

ABINGDON.
Petition of citizens, 33
ABOLITION.
Governor's message, 6-8
So much of governor's message as relates to, referred, 15
Select committee, 15
Mr. Holleman excused from serving on committee, 20
Mr. Coleman added in his stead, 20
Committee to collect and have printed proceedings of counties, 21
Documents referred to in governor's message committed, 21
Select committee discharged from collecting and publishing proceedings of counties, and subject referred to general committee, 23
Committee to employ a clerk, 23
Mr. Gilmer's resolution directing governor to correspond with other states upon the subject, laid on table, 29
Motion to take up; ayes and noes called, 29
Mr. Gilmer's resolution taken up, discussed, 30
Motion to refer to committee, 33
Resolution taken up, discussed, 34
Motion to postpone indefinitely, 35-36
Question on postponement decided, vote, 37
Resolutions transmitted by governor from the state of South Carolina, 38
Governor transmits resolutions of North Carolina on subject, 51
Report of select committee, 61
Resolutions of committee, 62
Report of minority presented, 62
Motion to insert report of minority on journal, laid on table, 64
Report of committee; motion to take up; vote recorded, 74
First resolution—attachment to union; agreed to, 74
Mr. Garland's substitute for residue of report presented, 74
Consideration postponed, 74
Report and substitute taken up, 75
Resolution, vote recorded, 75-76
Question divided, first on striking out second resolution, 76
Motion to lay on table by Mr. Watkins, vote recorded, 77
Motion by Mr. Watkins to recommit, vote recorded, 79
Substitute of Mr. Garland withdrawn, 79
Motion by Mr. Watkins to amend second resolution, 79
Mr. Watkins's amendment to second resolution, 81
Mr. Woolfolk's motion to amend Mr. Watkins's amendment: constitutional question of right to abolish slavery in the District of Columbia, vote recorded, 81
Report and amendment laid on table and printed, 81
Governor communicates resolutions of Georgia on movements of abolitionists, 81
Report of committee taken up and discussed, 81
Question on striking out second resolution of committee, vote recorded, 83
Mr. Stanard proposed to amend Mr. Watkins's amendment, 84

Speaker decided it out of order, Mr. Stanard appeals, 84
Motion to adjourn pending appeal, vote recorded, 84
Report of committee and appeal laid on table, 86
Mr. Miller's proposed amendment submitted, 86
Mr. Miller's amendment taken up, vote recorded, 87
Mr. Stanard's motion to amend amendment of Mr. Miller, 87
Mr. Watkins called previous question; vote on previous question recorded, 87-88
Question on Mr. Stanard's amendment to amendment of Mr. Miller, vote recorded, 88
Question on second resolution in Mr. Miller's amendment; Mr. Woolfolk called previous question; vote recorded, 88
Motion by Mr. Gregory to postpone indefinitely, vote recorded, 88
Question on second resolution; Mr. Parker moved to amend; vote recorded, 89
Second resolution agreed to, 89
Third resolution adopted, 89
Fourth resolution adopted, 89
Fifth resolution adopted, 89
Mr. Miller's motion to amend raising constitutional question of abolishing slavery in district, vote recorded, 89
Sixth resolution adopted, 89
Preamble changed to resolution, 89
Further amended and adopted, vote recorded, 89, 90
Resolutions as finally adopted, 90
Alterations in laws relating to the post office department, 100
Resolution to prevent free negroes who go out of state from returning, 100
Resolution amended and adopted, 102
Report of committee agreed to by senate, 109
Governor transmits address and resolutions of Alabama,
Amendments of senate to resolutions of house taken up; first amendment, Mr. Parker moves to disagree; vote recorded, 122
Amendment to second resolution agreed, 123
Third amendment of senate, Mr. Parker moves to disagree, vote recorded, 123
Amendment to sixth resolution, Mr. Parker moves to disagree; vote recorded, 123, 124
Fifth amendment agreed, 124
Senate recede from 1st and 3d, and insist on 4th amendment, 131
House recede from disagreement to 4th amendment, 145
Amendment amended by house, 145
Agreed to by senate, 146
Resolutions of state of Mississippi presented, 153
Resolutions of state of Kentucky, 236-238
Letter from Henry A. Wise, 238-243
Letter to governor from New York on subject of excitement, Doc. No. 1, p. 9
Resolutions of South Carolina, Doc. No. 11
Proceedings of counties in Virginia and several of non-slaveholding states, Doc. No. 12.
Accomack, Amelia, Augusta, 1, 2, 3
Buckingham, Campbell, 3
Caroline and Charles City, 4
Charlotte, Cumberland, 5
Elizabeth City, Hampton, Fairfax, 6
Fluvanna, Fredericksburg, 7

Gloucester, Greensville, 8
Halifax, Hanover, Henry, 9
Isle of Wight, 10
James City, Williamsburg, King & Queen, King William, 11
Louisa, 12
Lynchburg, 13
Mecklenburg, Middlesex, 14
Norfolk borough, Northampton, 15, 17
Nottoway, Pittsylvania, 18
Powhatan, 19
Prince Edward, 20
Prince George, Petersburg, 21
Richmond and Henrico, 22
Smithfield, Southampton, Spottsylvania, 23
Surry, 24
Albany, (New York,) 25
Hamilton college, New York city, (Park,) 26
New York city, (Tammany,) Plattsburg, 27
Rochester, Syracuse, 28
Troy, (New York,) 29
Utica, (New York,) Newark, (New Jersey,) 30
Harrisburg, (Penn.) Philadelphia, 31
Hartford, (Conn.) 32
Meridan, (Conn.) 33
New Haven, 34
Boston, Lowell, (Mass.) Brunswick, (Me.) 35
Concord, (N. H.) Franklin, (N. H.) 36, 37
Portsmouth, (N. H.) Charleston, (S. C.) 38
Resolutions of North Carolina on subject of incendiary publications, Doc. No 13.
Report of select committee, Doc. No. 20.
Report of minority, Doc. No. 21.
Amendment proposed by Mr. Watkins to report of committee, Doc. No. 25.
Resolutions of state of Georgia, Doc. No. 26.
Amendment proposed by Mr. Miller to report of committee, Doc. No. 29.
Resolutions relative to the interference of associations in northern states with slavery in the south, as passed by house, Doc. No. 40.
Amendments proposed by senate, Doc. No. 40.
Resolutions of state of Alabama, Doc. No. 42.
Resolutions of state of Mississippi, Doc. No. 51.
Resolutions of state of Kentucky, Doc. No. 54.
Communication of Henry A. Wise, Doc. No. 53.
Bill to suppress circulation of incendiary publications, printed bills, No. 9, in documents.

ABSCONDING DEBTORS.
Resolution for amending attachment laws to authorize sheriffs to serve process against, wherever found, 69
Committee discharged from resolution relating to process against, 262

ABSENCE.
See Rule 1, 3
See Rule 9, 4
When revoked, rule 12, 4
Granted to Mr. Carrington, 35
to Mr. Garland of Amherst, 35
to Mr. Richardson, 35
to Mr. Brown of Nelson, 35
to Mr. Booker, 35
to Mr. Madison, 35
to Mr. Jett, 36
to Mr. Ragsdale, 36
to Mr. Hopkins, 37
to Mr. Fitzgerald, 37

INDEX.

Granted to Mr. Wiley, 37
to Mr. Booker, 37
to Mr. Taylor of Middlesex, 37
to Mr. Holleman, 42
to Mr. Spratley, 42
to Mr. Clay, 85
to Mr. Fleet, 121
to Mr. Samuel, 121
to Mr. Parker, 163
to Mr. M'Clintic, 176
to Mr. Ingles, 199
to Mr. Powell, 199
to Mr. Morris, 208
to Mr. Avent, 208
to Messrs. Witcher and Swanson, 221
to Mr. Chapman, 225
to Mr. Garland of Mecklenburg, 225
to Messrs. Pate, Campbell and Coleman, 230
to Messrs. Mallory, Richardson, Brown of Nelson, and Griggs, 230
to Mr. Holland, 230
to Messrs. Waggener, Southall, Gillespie, Bare and Rinker, 250
to Messrs. Hale of Franklin, Steger, Butts, Hunter of Berkeley, Saunders, Willey and M'Mullen, 256
to Messrs. Grinalds, Gibson, Drummond, Ragsdale, Madison, Watts and Shands,
Refused to Messrs. Davison, Nixon, Jessee and Moncure, 262
ACADEMIES.
Report of literary fund relative to, presented, 54
Resolution for distributing surplus revenue of literary fund, 63
See *Colleges and Academies.*
ACTIONS, PERSONAL.
For amending provision for obtaining bail, 76
ADAMS, (ISAAC.)
His petition, 13. 38. 64. 66. 67
Report on his contested election presented, 64
Special report taken up and acted on, 66, 67
Resolution declaring him elected, 67
Added to committee, 67
ADJOURNMENT.
See Rule 9, 4
Time for, fixed, 12
Resolution for temporary adjournment of senate, 21
Amended by house, 21
Second resolution for adjournment of senate rejected, 28
Question to take up Mr. Gilmer's resolution on abolition; motion to adjourn; vote recorded, 29
Senate agree to amendment to first resolution for adjournment, 31
Temporary adjournment of house from 24th December till 28th, 37
Motion by Mr. Austin to adjourn; vote recorded, 44
Motion to adjourn pending appeal from speaker's decision on abolition resolution; vote recorded, 84
Question on second of the expunging resolutions; previous question called; Mr. Gregory moved to adjourn; vote recorded, 116, 117
Question on second expunging resolution; Mr. Gregory moved to adjourn, 117
Motion to adjourn pending resolution for displaying flag of United States; vote recorded, 155, 156
Resolution for, *sine die*, 265
Agreed to by senate, 269
Of senate till first Monday in December, agreed to, 273
Of house *sine die,* 273
ADJUTANT GENERAL.
His report referred, 28
Return of militia, arms, accoutrements and ammunition, Doc. No. 1, pp. 22, 23
AGRICULTURAL CONVENTION;
Of Albemarle and Fredericksburg, petition, 80

Of Albemarle and Fredericksburg, committee discharged from proceedings of, 185
Memorial of societies of Albemarle and Fredericksburg, Doc. No. 30.
AGRICULTURE AND MANUFACTURES.
Number of committee on, rule 28, 5
Committee appointed, 13
ALBEMARLE COUNTY.
Petition of citizens, 34. 60. 78, 79. 156. 160. 166. 168. 170
ALBEMARLE AND BUCKINGHAM.
Petition of citizens, 199
ALBEMARLE AND FLUVANNA.
Petition of citizens, 78. 179
ALBEMARLE AND NELSON.
Petition of citizens, 22. 61. 93. 107. 136. 148
See Bills No. 226, concerning road.
ALBEMARLE AND ROCKINGHAM.
Petition of citizens, 170. 203
ALLEGHANY COUNTY.
Petition of citizens, 101
Court day changed. See Bills No. 118.
ALLEGHANY, ROCKBRIDGE AND BOTETOURT.
Petition of citizens, 38. 63. 71
ALLEGHANY MOUNTAIN ROAD.
Resolution for putting it under contract and for further appropriation, 262
Agreed to by senate, 269
See Bills No. 99.
ALLEGHANY TURNPIKE.
Resolution for appropriating money to complete, 63
AMELIA COUNTY.
Petition of citizens, 16
AMELIA, PRINCE EDWARD, &c.
Petition of citizens, 83
AMERICAN MINING COMPANY.
See Bills No. 175.
ANDERSON, (DAVID.)
Leave to withdraw petition, 104
ANDERSON, (HENRY.)
His petition, 26
ANDERSON, (ISABELLA.)
Her petition, 45
ANDERSON, (LITTLEPAGE.)
His petition, 142
ANDY.
His petition, 142
ANN.
Her petition, 94. 110. 178
See Bills No. 281.
ANTHONY AND FRAZIER.
Their petition, 105. 195. 234
APPEALS, (Court of.)
Resolution for requiring appeals from courts of Shenandoah, Hardy and Page to be taken to court of appeals at Lewisburg, 59
See Bills No. 278.
APPOMATTOX COMPANY, (UPPER.)
Resolution for subscribing to stock, 26
Resolution for amending act concerning, 28
Report on resolution, 33
Petition of trustees, 36. 41. 76. 100. 107
See Bills No. 73.
ARMISTEAD, (GEORGE.)
Sword voted his son, 195
Agreed to by senate, 202
ARMISTEAD, (JOHN B.)
See Bills No. 324.
ARMORY.
Number of committee on, rule 28, 5
Committee appointed, 13
Mr. Ragsdale added to committee, 13
Report of superintendent transmitted by governor, 27
Superintendent's report to be be printed, 76
Report of joint committee, 105
Report of committee on, 149, 150
Resolutions agreed to, 150
See Bills No. 289.
Superintendent's report, Doc. No. 27.
Arms and accoutrements received and issued 1834-1835, Doc. No. 27, p. 3

Arms, &c. at armory, Doc. No. 27, p. 4
Ordnance at armory, 5
Report of joint committee, Doc. No. 39.
ARMS.
See Bills No. 289.
See Doc. No. 27.
ARRESTS.
To provide for paying guards conveying prisoners before commitment, 78
Committee discharged from resolution, 262
See Bills No. 314.
ARTILLERY COMPANIES.
See Bills No. 140.
ASSEMBLY, (GENERAL.)
For changing time of meeting, 169
Report on resolution, 171
Report on resolution acted on, 234
ATTACHMENTS.
See *Absconding Debtors,* 69
ATTORNEY GENERAL.
Room for him in capitol, 149
Duties defined and fees regulated, 162
Resolution agreed to, 166
Room for him, committee discharged, 212
See Bills No. 315.
ATTORNIES AT LAW.
Resolution for repealing act prohibiting those who commence suits from prosecuting appeals, 76
Committee discharged from resolution, 262
AUDITOR'S OFFICE.
Number of committee, rule 28, 5
Committee appointed, 13
Rule suspended to enlarge committee, 22
Report of committee on, 97
Report referred to committee finance, 97
AUDITOR OF PUBLIC ACCOUNTS.
His annual communication, 12
To be printed, 13
His communication referred, 32
To furnish copy of journal and report of commissioners to ascertain losses by burning Norfolk and Portsmouth, 59
List of balances transmitted to house, 79
Transmits copies of reports of commissioners on losses by burning of Norfolk, &c. 90
Resolution for electing, 90
Communication on burning of Norfolk, &c. referred, 91
Resolution for electing, agreed to by senate, 94
Election made, vote recorded, 99
To transmit report of treasurer of Western lunatic hospital, 206. 212
Rooms for him, committee discharged, 212
Accounts of Western lunatic hospital transmitted, 218
Annual report, Doc. No. 2, p. 1
Statement of receipts, 3, 4
Of disbursements, 5, 6, 7
Statement of taxes on lands, lots, &c. 8, 9, 10
Commonwealth's funds in treasury, 12, 13
Estimate of receipts and expenses, 14, 15, 16
Correspondence with secretary of treasury of United States, under act directing moneys to be refunded, 17
State of accounts between Virginia and United States, 18
State of advances to officers of state line on account of half pay in 1783-1784, 18
State of balances paid by Virginia on account of half pay, 19
Letter to secretary of treasury, 20
Secretary Woodbury's answer, 20
J. L. Edwards's letter to auditor, 20
List of accounts remaining on books in his office on 30th September, 1835. Doc. No. 32.
AUGUSTA COUNTY.
Petition of citizens, 33
AUGUSTA AND ROCKINGHAM.
Petition of citizens, 169. 203
AUGUSTA SPRINGS COMPANY.
See Bills No. 194.
AYES AND NOES.
Right to demand, rule 13,
See *Subjects on which votes recorded.*

B

BACK BAY.
Survey between, and Linkhorn bay, 146
Agreed to by senate, 160

BAIL.
Resolution for amending provision for obtaining bail in personal actions, 76
Committee discharged from resolution, 262
To authorise sheriffs to take principals upon written direction of bail, 154

BAILEY, (JOSEPH.)
His petition, 16. 76. 135

BAKER, (JONAS.)
Petition in his favour, 95. 262

BALANCES.
List on auditor's books, presented, 79
See Doc. No. 32.

BALTIMORE AND OHIO RAIL-ROAD.
Memorial of Brownsville convention for subscription to stock, Doc. No. 10.

BALDWIN, (CORNELIUS C.)
Petition for him, 147. 199

BANKING CAPITAL.
Resolution for raising committee on subject, 14
Committee appointed, 15
Committee discharged from petitions; referred to standing committee, 16
Governor's message on subject referred, 21
Committee increased, 31
Report of committee taken up, 124
Postponed, 124
Report of committee in favour of increase, taken up, 126
Spread on journal, 126, 127, 128, 129, 130, 131
Resolutions agreed to, 131
Vote agreeing to resolutions for increasing capital, reconsidered, 143
Motion by Mr. M'Mullen to postpone indefinitely, vote recorded, 143
Question on adopting first resolution, vote recorded, 143
Second resolution adopted, 143
Capital allotted to Petersburg, 207
For capital at Lynchburg, 207
For bail for the bank at Portsmouth, 208
See Bills, No. 255.
Mr. Summers's resolution for increasing capital at Charleston, at Staunton, at Moorfield, and at Wheeling, 223
Vote recorded, 223
Motion to reconsider vote rejecting bill, lost, vote, 244
Motion to suspend rule to reconsider vote rejecting leave for a bill establishing bank at Portsmouth, vote recorded, 244
Report of committee on increasing amount in state, Doc. No. 22.
Statement of amount of capital of the United States in 1834 and 1835, with population of each state, and imports and exports, *Ibid.* p. 6
Statement of value of imports and exports to and from Massachusetts, New York,

Pennsylvania, Maryland and Louisiana, during nine months, Doc. No. 22, p. 6
Table of currency of United States, England, France and Holland, 7
Population of states in relation to square mile, 7
Statements of exports of domestic products of several states, their population and banking capital, 8

BANK OF THE UNITED STATES.
Governor's message, 9, 10
See *Rescinding Resolutions.*

BANK OF THE VALLEY.
Governor transmits returns from, 25
Referred, 25
Petition of stockholders, 32
Returns of bank, Doc. No. 55, pp. 11-17

BANK OF VIRGINIA.
To prepare statement of dividends, &c. 20
Communication of president in answer to resolution of December 11th, 39
To furnish statements of capital, contingent funds, &c. 82
Information called for furnished by president of bank, 98
Taken up and referred, 99
Resolution relative to distribution of surplus fund, &c. 125
Answer of president to proceedings of citizens of Norfolk, 146
Report of state of bank, presented, 250
Annual dividends on capital, Doc. No. 17.
Nett annual profits of bank and branches, 5, 6, 7
Statement of president shewing nett profits of branch at Norfolk, Doc. No. 33.
Report of joint committee, Doc. No. 55.
State of bank, *Ibid.* pp. 3, 4, 5

BANKS.
Number of committee on, rule 28, 5
Joint committee appointed, 13
Special committees raised, 14, 15
Discharged from petitions and referred to standing committee, 15
Governor's message, 9, 10
Report of committee on increasing banking capital presented, 63
Committee to enquire into expediency of amending act incorporating Fredericksburg mechanics association, 85
Select committee leave sit during session, 146
Report of committee on state of Bank of Virginia and Farmers bank of Virginia, 250
Committee discharged from resolutions of meeting of citizens of Norfolk and reply thereto of president of Virginia bank, 262
Report of joint committee on Farmers and Virginia banks, Doc. No. 55.
State of Bank of Virginia, 3, 4, 5
State of Farmers bank, 6-10
Returns of Bank of Valley, 11-17

BANKS, (LINN.)
Elected speaker, vote recorded, 3
Thanks voted him as speaker, 273

BARNES, (JOHN.)
His petition, 26. 110. 178

BASSETT.
His petition, 95. 262

BATH COUNTY.
Petition of citizens, 18. 23. 30, 31

BEDFORD COUNTY.
Petition of citizens, 16. 19. 20. 26. 35. 73. 95. 106. 139
BEDFORD, BOTETOURT, GREENBRIER, &c.
Petition of citizens, 57

BEDFORD FEMALE ACADEMY.
See Bills No. 236.

BELLE ISLE MANUFACTURING COMPANY.
See Bills No. 61.

BENNEHAN, (DOMINIE.)
See Bills No. 231.

BENSON, (JOHN.)
His petition, 131

BERKELEY COAL MINING AND RAIL-ROAD COMPANY.
See Bills No. 202.

BERKELEY COUNTY.
Petition of citizens, 14. 26. 31, 32. 42. 45. 53. 84. 98
Leave to bring in bill amending act limiting assessment upon titheables. See Bills No. 5. No. 97.
Separate elections. See Bills No. 52. No. 53.

BERKELEY AND JEFFERSON.
Petition of citizens, 105

BERRYVILLE AND WINCHESTER ROAD.
Resolution for extending North-western road from Winchester to Berryville, 21

BEVERLEY AND NORTH-WESTERN ROAD.
See Bills No. 26. 29

BIDGOOD, (BENJAMIN or BETSY.)
His petition, 22. 72
See Bills No. 115.

BIG BIRD MINING COMPANY.
See Bills No. 165.

BILLS.
How disposed of, rule 17, 4
When delivered to members, rule 18, 4
Regulating and reducing expenses of collecting money under execution, Doc. Bills No. 1.
Incorporating stockholders of the Lynchburg and Tennessee rail-road company, Doc. Bills No. 2.
Amending charter of James river and Kanawha company, Doc. Bills No. 3.
Increasing banking capital, Doc. Bills No. 4
Appropriating surplus literary fund, Doc. Bills No. 5.
Amendments thereto. *Ibid.*
Concerning merchants' licenses, Doc. Bill No. 6.
Imposing taxes, Doc. Bill No. 7.
Appropriating revenue, Doc. Bill No. 8.
To suppress circulation of incendiary publications, Doc. Bill No. 9.

Number.	BILLS.	Leave to introduce.	When presented.	Different readings.	Laid on table.	Rejected in house.	Passed in house.	Rejected in senate.	Passed in senate.	Enrolled and signed.
1	A bill to amend an act, entitled, an act to incorporate the Midlothian coal mining company,	14	29	39, 57, 60			60		68	266
2	A bill to amend an act, entitled, an act to incorporate the Staunton and Potowmac rail-road company,	15	28	39, 43, 44, 51, 61	55, 57		61		72	266
3	A bill to amend the act, entitled, an act establishing the town of Mount Crawford, and for appointing trustees thereof,	15									
4	A bill to revive the inspection of tobacco at Spring warehouse, in the town of Lynchburg,	15	20	20, 22, 24,			24		30	265
5	A bill to amend an act passed March 5th, 1835, entitled, an act to limit										

Number	BILLS	Leave to introduce	When presented	Different readings	Laid on table	Rejected in house	Passed in house	Rejected in senate	Passed in senate	Enrolled and signed
	the assessment upon titheables, and to authorize a tax upon property, for the purpose of defraying county expenditures within the county of Berkeley,	15	66	132, 148			153		160	267
6	A bill explanatory of the 99th section of the act, entitled, an act for the better organization of militia,	15	150	210, 226	226					
7	A bill to incorporate the Falmouth mining company,	18	26	26, 30, 32			32, 35		34	265
8	A bill to incorporate the Deep run mining company,	18	26	26, 30, 32			32, 35		35	265
9	A bill to change the time of holding the courts in the third judicial circuit,	18	63	70, 91, 143, 150, 153	91		162		185, 197	267
10	A bill to re-organize the first and second judicial districts of the circuit superior courts of law and chancery,	18	63	70, 80, 91	104	148				
11	A bill to amend an act, entitled, an act incorporating the Falmouth and Alexandria rail-road company,	21	27	27, 38, 39, 42, 44, 51, 79, 81, 91	38, 55		99		105	266
12	A bill changing the place of holding a separate election in the county of Marshall,	21	33	39, 43			51		65	266
13	A bill incorporating the Sweet springs company,	23	27	39, 57, 60	27		65		83	266
14	A bill incorporating the Phœnix mining company,	23	26	26, 30, 32			32		34	265
15	A bill to incorporate the Red spring company, in the county of Alleghany,	23	91	132, 177			195		202	267
16	A bill to alter the terms of the circuit superior courts of law and chancery in the seventh district and thirteenth circuit of this commonwealth,	23	32	39, 106, 122			126		146	267
17	A bill incorporating the stockholders of the Louisa rail-road company,	18	23	27, 30, 31, 38, 51	23, 43, 92, 106, 107		55	•	99, 104, 105, 151	267
18	A bill incorporating the stockholders of the Rappahannock and Blue Ridge rail-road company,	14	23	27, 30, 32	23		32		90	266
19	A bill to amend the act, entitled, an act concerning William Brown,		23	23, 27, 30			30		33	265
20	A bill incorporating a company for the purpose of improving the navigation of Little and Big Deep creeks, in the county of Powhatan,		23	23, 27, 30			30		33	265
21	A bill directing the survey and location of routes for certain roads therein mentioned,		23	24, 38, 43			49		77	266
22	A bill incorporating the Great falls manufacturing company, in the county of Fayette,		25	35	51, 57, 60		60		65	266
23	A bill to amend the act, entitled, an act to reduce into one the several acts for the settlement and regulation of ferries,		26	45	52, 60, 63		63		73	266
24	A bill to authorize a separate election at Greenfield, in the county of Nelson,		27	38, 43			43		73	266
25	A bill regulating the respective quotas of the primary school fund to which the counties of Ohio and Marshall are entitled, and for other purposes,		28	38	52, 54		58		73	266
26	A bill to authorize the appointment of a third commissioner in chancery for the circuit superior court of law and chancery for the town of Petersburg,		28	30	39, 43		49		65	266
27	A bill authorizing the mayor and commonalty of the town of Wheeling to take and subscribe for 2,500 shares of the capital stock of the Baltimore and Ohio rail-road company,		28	31	39, 44		51		65	266
28	A bill directing the survey of a route for a road from the north-western road in the direction of Beverley, in the county of Randolph,			29	39, 51, 55		58		77	266
29	A bill incorporating the stockholders of the Richmond and Petersburg rail-road company,		23	29	39, 51, 68, 150, 166	153		166, 169		212	268
30	A bill to enlarge, define and establish the corporate boundaries and limits of the town of Wheeling, in the county of Ohio,			29	39, 45, 51		55		65	266
31	A bill to amend the act establishing the town of Grandville, in the county of Monongalia,			30	39, 43		49		65	266
32	A bill authorizing the board of public works to subscribe on behalf of the commonwealth to the stock of the Smith's river navigation company,			30	39, 43, 51, 54, 57, 60	49		60		68	266
33	A bill to authorize the president and directors of the Portsmouth and Roanoke rail-road company to borrow a sum of money,			29	30, 31, 32			32		34	265
34	A bill providing for the better security of persons charged with criminal offences,		15	31	32, 33, 38, 43			43		68	266
35	A bill authorizing Jesse Sturm to erect a dam across the west fork of Monongalia river, in the county of Harrison,			31	143, 151, 153	51, 162		163		176	267
36	A bill to regulate the conduct of boatmen on the Roanoke river and its branches. (See bills No. 107,)			31	39, 43, 122		144				
37	A bill concerning the fire and marine insurance company of Wheeling,		23	31	39, 44, 51, 65, 67	60		67		81	266
38	A bill to incorporate the Virginia mills manufacturing company,			31	39, 43			49		65	266

INDEX.

Number	BILLS.	Leave to introduce.	When presented.	Different readings.	Laid on table.	Rejected in house.	Passed in house.	Rejected in senate.	Passed in senate.	Enrolled and signed.
39	A bill to amend an act, entitled, an act for incorporating the stockholders of the Winchester and Potowmac rail-road company,	32	35	39, 43	51		57		77	266
40	A bill incorporating the Lexington and Richmond turnpike company,		32	39, 43, 51			51		106	266
41	A bill to incorporate the Newtown Stevensburg library company,	33	73	125, 131			146		152	267
42	A bill to vest the trustees of the town of Portsmouth with certain additional powers,	35	76	86, 91, 94			94		104	266
43	A bill incorporating the Red and Blue sulphur springs turnpike company,		35	51, 54, 60, 64, 70	58		82		84	266
44	A bill to revive and amend the act, entitled, an act incorporating the Richmond rail-road company,	33	35	51, 54			58		68	266
45	A bill to provide for the construction of a road between Weston, in the county of Lewis, and Charleston in the county of Kanawha,		38	52, 54, 56, 60, 63			83		86	266
46	A bill to change the place of holding a separate election in the county of Preston,		43	52, 54			58		65	266
47	A bill to change the place of holding a separate election in the county of Wythe,		43	52, 54, 56			58		65	266
48	A bill to authorise William Chapline and others to construct wharves on Wheeling creek and the Ohio river, adjoining the town of South Wheeling in Ohio county,		43	52, 54			58		65	266
49	A bill further to amend the act, entitled, an act to amend the act, entitled, an act establishing a ferry from Onancock town, in the county of Accomack, to Norfolk, and for other purposes, passed March 5th, 1833,		45	52, 54	58		109		118	266
50	A bill directing the survey and location of a route for a road from the Pennsylvania line, to its intersection with the road from Clarksburg to Beverly,		45	52			219		219	268
51	A bill to incorporate the Narrow Falls turnpike company,		45	52, 53	58, 145	203				
52	A bill to authorise a separate election at Hedgesville in the county of Berkeley,		45	52, 53	58		121		144	267
53	A bill to change the place of holding a separate election in the county of Berkeley,		45	52, 54	58					
54	A bill to incorporate the Fluvanna mining company,	49	61	70, 92			104		107	266
55	A bill to incorporate the Petersburg navigation company,		50	52, 54			58		68	266
56	A bill to incorporate the stockholders of the Lynchburg and Tennessee rail-road company, and to authorise them, or the James river and Kanawha company, to construct a rail-road from Lynchburg to Richmond,		50	54, 107, 131, 141, 156, 157, 164, 165	155, 163		165		205, 206	268
57	A bill forming a new county out of parts of the counties of Lewis and Nicholas,		53	60, 65			65		81	266
58	A bill directing a change of location of the North-western turnpike through the town of Evansville,		54	57, 60			60		68	266
59	A bill to amend an act, entitled, an act for cutting a navigable canal from the waters of Elizabeth river, in the state of Virginia, to the waters of Pasquotank river in North Carolina,		54	57, 60			60		68	266
60	A bill to provide for the enlargement of the public warehouse for the storage and inspection of tobacco in the city of Richmond,		54	57, 60			60		76	266
61	A bill to revive and amend an act, entitled, an act to incorporate the Belle Isle manufacturing company, passed 19th March, 1832,	55	58	61, 65, 67			67		73	266
62	A bill to reduce and regulate the tolls on the North-western turnpike,		55	57, 61, 64, 70			82		84	266
63	A bill to incorporate the Suffolk rail-road company,		57	73, 147, 153	155		161		165	267
64	A bill to incorporate the stockholders of the City Point rail-road company,		57	61, 64, 68, 70	61		91		98	266
65	A bill to incorporate the stockholders of the Cartersville and Farmville rail-road company,		57	61, 64, 70, 143	70, 148		164	212		
66	A bill to prevent trespasses by non-resident herdsmen in the county of Preston,		57	61, 65, 67			67		77	266
67	A bill to incorporate the Ettrick Banks manufacturing company,		58	61, 65, 67			67		67	266
68	A bill to incorporate the Fleets' manufacturing company,		58	61, 65, 67			67		67	266
69	A bill to change the place of holding the Cundiff precinct election in the county of Hampshire,	58	63	70, 92			109		118	266
70	A bill to amend an act, entitled, an act to incorporate the Cold Brook company of colliers, passed January 23d, 1835,	59	78	132, 148			153		165	267
71	A bill to amend an act, entitled, an act to incorporate the Manchester wool and cotton manufacturing company, passed March 13th, 1832,	59	73	125, 132			148		154	267
72	A bill to incorporate the Newburn and Red Sulphur springs turnpike company,		60	70, 74			74		77	266
73	A bill to authorize a subscription on behalf of the commonwealth to the enlarged capital stock of the Upper Appomattox company,		60	65, 70	82	145				
74	A bill to dispose of certain moneys heretofore raised by lottery in the county of Monroe,		60	60, 63			63		83	266
75	A bill to enact an act of the general assembly of North Carolina, en-									

INDEX.

№	BILLS.	Leave to introduce.	When presented.	Different readings.	Laid on table.	Rejected in house.	Passed in house.	Rejected in senate.	Passed in senate.	Enrolled and signed.
	titled, an act to incorporate the Roanoke, Danville and Junction rail-road company,		60	78, 91, 104, 141, 148	98		151		205	268
76	A bill to amend an act incorporating the Spring creek turnpike,	61	94	132, 177			196		202	267
77	A bill to provide an index to the journals of the house of delegates,		61	70, 92			109		125	267
78	A bill concerning Shelton Ford,		61	70, 92		109				
79	A bill concerning George Johnson,		61	70, 92	104	109				
80	A bill concerning James Wysong,		61	70, 91						
81	A bill for the construction of a road across the Blue Ridge at Milam's gap,	33	64	70, 73, 91, 101		98, 101	148		164	267
82	A bill directing the survey and location of a route for a road from Moorfield to the North-western turnpike,	53	64	70, 92		109			222	268
83	A bill to establish the town of Hedgesville, in the county of Berkeley,		64	70, 92	109		112		125	267
84	A bill allowing Charlotte Morgan to remain in the commonwealth,		64	70, 92, 118, 122	143		247, 248		264	271
85	A bill concerning Duff Green,		64	70, 92			112		146	267
86	A bill allowing Richard Bolling to remain in the commonwealth,		64	70, 92			112		212	268
87	A bill allowing Daniel Higginbotham to remain in the commonwealth,		64	70, 92			112		212	268
88	A bill allowing Judy Johnson to remain in the commonwealth,		64	70, 92			112		219	268
89	A bill authorizing James Martin to hold and convey real estate,		64	70, 92			112		125	267
90	A bill regulating and reducing the expenses incident to the collection of money under execution,		64	70, 91, 126	91	102				
91	A bill authorizing the sale of the estate of John Haskins, senior, a lunatic,		64	70, 92			119		118	266
92	A bill releasing to William Fisher the commonwealth's right to certain lands,		64	70, 92			112		125	267
93	A bill changing the time of holding courts in the 8th district and 16th circuit,	65								
94	A bill to incorporate the trustees of the Upperville academy, in Fauquier,	65	72	125, 132			146		159	267
95	A bill to authorise a separate election at the tavern house of William Irwin, in the county of Cumberland,		65	70, 92			121		144	267
96	A bill to enlarge the town of Clarksville in the county of Mecklenburg,		66	70, 92			121		144	267
97	A bill to amend an act to limit the assessment upon tithables, and to authorise a tax upon property for the purpose of defraying county expenditures in Berkeley,	15	66	70, 92			109		121	266, 267
98	A bill to incorporate the Stafford gold mining company,	68	76	132, 148			153		160	267
99	A bill further to provide for the construction of a turnpike road across the Alleghany mountain, in the counties of Pendleton and Pocahontas,		68	70, 92	122	245				
100	A bill to increase the capital of the Merchants manufacturing company,		68	70, 92			122		152	267
101	A bill to incorporate the Mechanics manufacturing company,		68	70, 122			145		152	267
102	A bill to revive the charter of the Nelson and Albemarle Union factory company,		68	70, 92			121		152	267
103	A bill to authorise the judge of the second circuit to appoint a time for holding the courts thereof in certain cases,	68	73	125, 132			146		152	267
104	A bill incorporating the Kanawha slave insurance company,	68	104	141, 143			143		152	267
105	A bill to incorporate the Fauquier White Sulphur springs,	68	76	132, 148			153		164	267
106	A bill to incorporate the Virginia insurance company,	68	82	125, 132, 177			195		212	268
107	A bill to regulate the conduct of boatmen navigating the Appomattox river above the town of Petersburg,		69	105, 176, 186, 192, 210			224		261	271
108	A bill to change the time of holding the circuit courts in Monroe, Giles and Montgomery,		73	125, 132			146		152	267
109	A bill incorporating the Virginia towing company,		73	125, 131			148		169	267
110	A bill to provide for the construction of the eastern section of the road from Huntersville to Parkersburg,		75	140, 141, 148	151		196		205	268
111	A bill to incorporate the Virginia fire insurance company,		75	141, 148			152		164	267
112	A bill to change the place of holding a separate election in the county of Lunenburg,		76	132, 148			153		165	267
113	A bill to authorize a separate election at the house of Michael Snodgrass, in the county of Monongalia,		76	132, 148			153		160	267
114	A bill to authorise a separate election at Triadelphia, in the county of Ohio,		76	132, 148			153		160	267
115	A bill releasing the commonwealth's claim to a certain balance against the estate of Betsey Bidgood,		76	140, 141, 148	151		152		170	267
116	A bill to change the place of holding a separate election in Tyler county,		76	125, 126, 131			146		152	267
117	A bill to amend the act for opening and improving the navigation of the Dragon swamp,	78	82	132, 142, 144, 148			151		160	267
118	A bill to change the time of holding the county court of Alleghany county,	78	85	132, 177			195		197	267
119	A bill to incorporate the Union Potowmac company,		78	85, 86, 91	86, 99, 101		109		105	266

INDEX. 281

Number	BILLS.	Leave to introduce	When presented	Different readings	Laid on table	Rejected in house	Passed in house	Rejected in senate	Passed in senate	Enrolled and signed
120	A bill to provide for the construction of a road from the line of Preston county to the Ohio river,		78	141, 148			153		220	269
121	A bill incorporating the Natural bridge turnpike company,		80	132, 149			153		167	267
122	A bill to explain the act to reduce into one the several acts concerning the county and other inferior courts, and the jurisdiction of justices of the peace within this commonwealth,		80	132, 149, 151	149					
123	A bill to establish an inspection of flour and indian meal in the town of Winchester,		81	132, 149			153		156	267
124	A bill to incorporate the United States copper mining company,	82	93	132, 177			196		208	268
125	A bill to incorporate the Great Kanawha timber, lumber and mining company,	82	126	177	211	245				
126	A bill to incorporate the New Hope gold mining company,	85	96	132, 177			213		225	268
127	A bill to amend an act reducing into one the several acts concerning pilots, and regulating their fees,	85	118	177, 196, 208	197		219		209	271
128	A bill to authorise additions to the town of Farmville, in the county of Prince Edward,		85	132, 177			195		202	268
129	A bill to amend the act incorporating a company to erect a toll bridge over the Ohio river at Wheeling,		85	132, 177			196		205	268
130	A bill establishing a new regiment in the county of Preston,		91	132, 177			196		202	268
131	A bill to amend the act concerning fraudulent devises,		91	132, 177			196		202	268
132	A bill giving to the circuit courts of law and chancery concurrent jurisdiction with the county and corporation courts in all actions of forcible entry and detainer,		91	140, 150, 153		163				
133	A bill to alter and reform the mode of proceeding in the courts of chancery,		91	177			196		202	267
134	A bill to incorporate the trustees of the Estillville academy,		92	132, 177			196		202	268
135	A bill requiring the inspectors of tobacco in this commonwealth to distinguish in their inspections between tobacco produced in Virginia and that produced in other states,		93	132, 177			196		202	267
136	A bill incorporating the Laurel Hill turnpike,		94	132, 169, 170, 176			196		219	268
137	A bill to authorise the county court of Southampton to appoint processioners of lands in said county,	95	97	101, 109			110		116	266
138	A bill incorporating the Gills mountain gold mining company in Halifax,	96	103	132, 177			202		208	268
139	A bill providing for a geological survey of the state, and for other purposes,		96	105, 107, 122			143		167, 168	267
140	A bill to amend act directing the governor to cause houses or shelters to be erected for the protection of the equipments of the Richmond Fayette artillery and Portsmouth artillery companies,	100								
141	A bill to amend act making further provision for completing the road from Staunton to the mouth of Little Kanawha,		101	132, 177			213		225	269
142	A bill to establish the town of Lovettsville in the county of Loudoun,		101	132, 177			213		222	268
143	A bill to amend and extend the provisions of an act making appropriations for the removal of free persons of colour,	102								
144	A bill appointing commissioners to select a site for the seat of justice for the county of Ohio,		102	132, 177, 203, 210			224		230	269
145	A bill to incorporate the city of Wheeling,		104	132, 153	161		184		208	268
146	A bill for incorporating the medical college at Richmond in Virginia,		105	105, 107, 112		208	121		185 Rejected afterwards in house.	
147	A bill to incorporate the trustees of the Halifax academy,		105	107, 110			121		144	267
148	A bill incorporating the literary and scientific mechanics institute of Norfolk and Portsmouth,		105	132, 153			161		165	267
149	A bill to amend the act to reduce into one all acts and parts of acts to prevent the destruction of oysters,		105	132, 176, 195, 197			213		225	268
150	A bill incorporating the Front Royal library society in the county of Frederick,	106	141	178, 209			227		245	270
151	A bill to change the place of holding the separate election at Colesmouth, in county of Kanawha,	106	107	132, 177			213		2	268
152	A bill declaring Pocatallico river a public highway,	106	107	132, 177			213		225	269
153	A bill incorporating the Orange savings society in the county of Orange,	106	109	141, 155, 169			177		205	268
154	A bill to incorporate the coal working company of Richmond and Manchester,		107	108	132, 177			196		205	268
155	A bill incorporating the trustees of the Charlestown athenæum and female academy,		107	112	177, 198			214		222	268
156	A bill to amend the act to incorporate the Richmond manufacturing company,	107		132, 177			213		222	268
157	A bill concerning the county of Gloucester,		107	132, 177			196		202	268
158	A bill incorporating the Smithfield savings institution in Isle of Wight,		108	140, 155, 169			177		205	262

Number	BILLS.	Leave to introduce	When presented	Different readings	Laid on table	Rejected in house	Passed in house	Rejected in senate	Passed in senate	Enrolled and signed
159	A bill to amend an act incorporating the Hunting run mining company,	108	110	178, 184, 197			213		225	268
160	A bill incorporating the Goochland mining company,	108	121	177, 197			220		222	268
161	A bill to revive and amend an act to incorporate the Gallego manufacturing company,	108	124	126			145, 146, 147		160	267
162	A bill changing the times of holding the spring terms of the circuit superior courts of law and chancery in the 5th circuit and 3d judicial district,		108	108	122		208		221	268
163	A bill incorporating the Staunton and Augusta springs turnpike company,		108	132, 177			198		205	268
164	A bill directing the sale of the stock held by the state in joint stock companies incorporated for purposes of internal improvement,		108	132, 177		196				
165	A bill incorporating the Big Bird mining company,	110	121	177, 209			224		230	269
166	A bill concerning savings institutions,		110	178, 196, 197			213		222	268
167	A bill to add a part of the county of Tazewell to the county of Giles,	111	147	210, 219			227		245	270
168	A bill to incorporate the Eastern Shore rail-road company,	111	151	210, 226			244		264	271
169	A bill to equalize the regimental districts in the county of Rockingham, and for other purposes,		111	177, 197			213		225	269
170	A bill concerning the Greensville and Roanoke rail-road company,	56	118	178, 196, 213			228		245	270
171	A bill to amend the several acts concerning the Petersburg rail-road company,	56	118	177, 196			220		225	268
172	A bill authorizing the auditor to issue a warrant in favour of James Paxton,	121	126	177, 219			235		260	270
173	A bill incorporating the Rappahannock marine and fire insurance company,		121	126	177, 209			224		230	269
174	A bill incorporating the Fredericksburg Union manufacturing company,	124	126	177, 209			224		230	269
175	A bill incorporating the American mining company,	121	126	177, 209			224		230	269
176	A bill to establish an additional grade of flour in the inspections of flour in this commonwealth,		121	177, 213	211, 230		235			
177	A bill to incorporate the Fredericksburg mining company,	125	150	210, 226			244		260	270
178	A bill concerning the subscription on behalf of the state to the stock of the Richmond, Fredericksburg and Potomac rail-road company,	125	147	178, 219			226		269	270
179	A bill appointing trustees for the town of New Glasgow, in the county of Amherst,		126	170	210, 226			247		264	271
180	A bill to suppress the circulation of incendiary publications, and for other purposes,		126	171	197, 202			220		269	272
181	A bill to incorporate the Portsmouth and Chesapeake steam-boat company,		126	178, 186, 197			213		222	268
182	A bill to explain the act authorizing subscriptions on the part of the commonwealth to the capital of joint stock companies,		126	177, 209			228		245	270
183	A bill to authorise the auditor to issue warrants on the treasury in satisfaction of certain judgments against the commonwealth,		126	147, 153	157		164		167	267
184	A bill to authorize the common council of Fredericksburg to make an advancement upon the stock of the corporation in the Rappahannock canal company,	131	142	142			145		148	267
185	A bill to amend the several acts concerning the public guard in the city of Richmond,		131	175, 206, 219			235		261	271
186	A bill concerning the Cumberland road,		141	177, 209			224		261	271
187	A bill concerning the Greensville and Roanoke rail-road company,		141	177, 209			224		251	270
188	A bill directing a survey of the Dragon swamp,		141	177, 209			224		245	270
189	A bill to authorise a subscription on behalf of the state to the stock of the Pittsylvania and Lynchburg turnpike company, and for other purposes,		141	178, 197			213		225	268
190	A bill to authorise a subscription on behalf of the state to the stock of the Lewisburg and Blue Sulphur springs turnpike company,		141	168, 170, 176			196		202	268
191	A bill to amend and explain the act to reduce into one the several acts to regulate the solemnization of marriages,		141	177, 209			225		230	269
192	A bill to authorize a separate election at M'Gaheysville in the county of Rockingham,		141	178, 209			227		245	270
193	A bill concerning the legal representatives of Severn Eyre, deceased,		141	178, 209	227					
194	A bill to amend an act to incorporate the Augusta springs company,	141	146	178, 196, 219			226		245	270
195	A bill changing the time of holding the courts in the counties of Lewis and Braxton,	142	147	178, 219			228		245	270
196	A bill to change the place of holding a separate election in the county of Cabell,	142	150	210, 226			244		251	270
197	A bill making further provision for taking depositions in certain cases,		142	178, 209		225				
198	A bill incorporating the trustees of the Clarksville female academy,		144	178, 209			227		245	270
199	A bill to incorporate the proprietors of the Wellsburg lyceum,		144	178, 209			227		245	270
200	A bill concerning William Penn,		144	178, 209			227		245	270
201	A bill concerning John Chew,		144	178, 209			227		264	271
202	A bill to incorporate the Berkeley coal mining and rail-road company,		144	178, 209			224		245	270
203	A bill for the construction of a bridge across Jackson's river at the town of Covington,		144	178, 209			227		251	270

INDEX.

Number	BILLS.	Leave to introduce	When presented	Different readings	Laid on table	Rejected in house	Passed in house	Rejected in senate	Passed in senate	Enrolled and signed
204	A bill extending the time for the commencement of the work of the Greensville and Panther gap turnpike company,	146	151	151			153		160	267
205	A bill to prevent frauds in the packing of cotton,	146	152	210, 226	245	257				
206	A bill to amend the act incorporating Booker's gold mine company,	146	170	211, 226			247		251	270
207	A bill securing to debtors a certain portion of their property,		147	178, 219, 220	219		235			
208	A bill repealing the law requiring lands in this commonwealth to be processioned, so far as concerns the county of Patrick,		147	178, 184, 197	197	208				
209	A bill to amend the act reducing into one the several acts for punishing persons guilty of thefts and forgeries, and the destruction and concealment of wills,		147	178, 219			227		251	270
210	A bill amending the laws concerning slaves, free negroes and mulattoes,		147	178, 219			235	264		
211	A bill incorporating the Lynchburg and Campbell courthouse turnpike company,		147	178, 186, 197			213		225	268
212	A bill to authorise Thomas A. Morton to erect a dam across Appomattox river,		147	178, 219			226		245	270
213	A bill to incorporate the Goose creek navigation company,		147	178, 208			212		219	268
214	A bill concerning the Rappahannock company,		147	147, 153, 169			177		185	267
215	A bill to establish the town of Meadowville in the county of Greenbrier,		147	210, 219			228		245	270
216	A bill to authorize a separate election at the house of William Pulliam in the county of Henry,		147	201, 219			227		245	270
217	A bill to authorize Richard Barton Haxall to construct additional wharves at and near the town of Bermuda Hundred,		147	210, 219			227		245	270
218	A bill to incorporate the Potowmac silk and agricultural company,		147	210, 219			237		245	270
219	A bill to incorporate the Etna coal company,		147	210, 219			226		245	270
220	A bill to amend and explain the 96th, 99th and 100th sections of an act for the better organization of the militia,	15	150	210, 226	226					
221	A bill to prevent slaves, free negroes and mulattoes, from trading beyond the limits of the city, county or town, in which they reside,		150	210, 226, 230		244				
222	A bill forming a new county out of parts of the counties of Shenandoah and Frederick,		150	162, 166, 171	168, 176		184		198, 199	267
223	A bill forming a new county out of the county of Frederick,		150	162, 166, 177	168		194		198	267
224	A bill to incorporate the trustees of the Lynchburg female academy,		150	178, 195, 197			213		222	268
225	A bill incorporating the trustees of the Martinsville academy,		150	166, 168, 176			213		222	268
226	A bill to enlarge the powers of the county courts of Albemarle and Nelson, for the purpose of opening a road from Scottsville to the head waters of Rock fish river,		151	210, 226			246		264	271
227	A bill incorporating the Marshall and Ohio turnpike company,		151	210, 226			245, 246		264	271
228	A bill to authorize the Dismal swamp canal company to increase their capital stock, and to authorise the loans of the state to said company to be converted into stock,		151	210, 226	245					
229	A bill incorporating the stockholders of the Smithfield rail-road company,		151	210, 226			246		264	271
230	A bill concerning John Pittinger, late sheriff of Brooke county,		151	178, 210			227		245	270
231	A bill concerning the administrator of Dominie Bonnehan, deceased,		151	178, 210	227	245				
232	A bill to amend the charter incorporating the stockholders of the Richmond and Yorktown rail-road company,	152, 160	163	210, 226			247		251	270
233	A bill to change the quarterly court of Shenandoah county,	152	160	210, 226			246		251	270
234	A bill to authorize the Matoaca manufacturing company to increase their capital stock,	152	159	210, 226			246		251	270
235	A bill changing the time of holding the county courts in the counties of Marshall and Ohio, and to amend the act establishing the town of Moundsville in Ohio,	152	160	210, 226			246		261	271
236	A bill to amend the act incorporating the trustees of the Bedford female academy,	154	164	211			227		245	270
237	A bill authorising the auditor to issue a warrant in favour of John H. Gwathmey, administrator of Richard Clarke, deceased, in pursuance of a judgment of the superior court of Henrico, for commutation pay,	154	155	210, 226	245					
238	A bill to authorise Richard Lorton to surrender his interest in the museum property,		154	210, 226			246		261	271
239	A bill incorporating the Virginia silk company,		154	210, 226			247		260	270
240	A bill authorizing certain changes in the road law, so far as the county of Rockbridge is concerned,	155	184	211, 248	258					
241	A bill to alter and increase the terms of the circuit superior court of law and chancery for the county of Norfolk,	155	186	211			227		260	270
242	A bill providing further security for the payment of jailors' fees,		155	210, 226			246	264	260	270
243	A bill to increase the number of trustees in the town of Portsmouth, and to enlarge their powers and privileges,		195	211, 248			258		260	271
244	A bill to amend an act incorporating the Fredericksburg mechanics association,	156	156	210, 226			246		260	270

INDEX.

Number	BILLS.	Leave to introduce	When presented	Different readings	Laid on table	Rejected in house	Passed in house	Rejected in senate	Passed in senate	Enrolled and signed
245	A bill concerning Amos Johnson,		156	210, 226		246				
246	A bill constituting a portion of the margin of the Potowmac river, in Berkeley county, a legal fence,		156	210, 226			246		251	270
247	A bill appropriating the surplus revenue of the literary fund,		159	164, 198, 203, 204	176, 198		220		261, 264	271
248	A bill to incorporate the trustees of Saint Bride's academy in Norfolk,		159	210, 226			246		251	270
249	A bill to change the terms of the circuit superior court of law and chancery in and for the county of Stafford,	160	162	210, 226			246		260	270
250	A bill changing the punishment of slaves convicted of hog stealing,		160	210, 226		246				
251	A bill to repeal the act to provide for the appointment of a commissioner to examine and report upon claims for unsatisfied military land bounties,		160	210, 226			246		261	271
252	A bill incorporating the Mayo's bridge company,		160	211, 212, 225			244		251	270
253	A bill to change the place of holding a separate election in the county of Pittsylvania,		162	210, 226			246		260	270
254	A bill incorporating the Sweet springs and Price's mountain turnpike,		163	210, 226			246		260	270
255	A bill increasing the banking capital of this commonwealth,		163	170, 175, 185, 206, 207, 213, 221		222				
256	A bill to authorize Robert W. Christian, treasurer of the late charity school of Charles City county, to pay over to the overseers of the poor of that county the funds in his hands of that institution,	164	165	210, 226			247		251	270
257	A bill to incorporate the Deane iron and steel manufacturing company,	164, 165	171	211, 226			247		260	270
258	A bill to incorporate the town of Waterford in Loudoun,		166	210, 226			247		261	271
259	A bill to prevent the destruction of oysters in Nansemond river and Chuckatuck creek, in the county of Nansemond,		166	210, 226			247		251	270
260	A bill to incorporate a company to construct a toll-bridge across the Shenandoah river at Harper's Ferry,		166	210, 226			247		261	271
261	A bill changing the time of holding the superior courts of Campbell, Bedford, and the town of Lynchburg,		167	211, 219			228		245	270
262	A bill to incorporate the Grayson Sulphur springs company,		168	210, 226			247		251	270
263	A bill to change the place of holding a separate election in the county of Harrison,		168	210, 226			247		260	270
264	A bill imposing taxes for the support of government,		169	197, 214			224		261	271
265	A bill appropriating the public revenue,		169	197, 218			224		269	272
266	A bill to amend the act concerning merchants' licenses,		169	197, 218			224	251		
267	A bill amending the act concerning waste tobacco,		169	210, 226			247		264	271
268	A bill to revive an act incorporating a company to construct a turnpike road from the upper end of the Blue Ridge turnpike road to its intersection with the Lexington and Covington turnpike,	169	175	211, 248			257		264	271
269	A bill to change the time of holding the circuit superior courts of law and chancery for the counties of Rockingham and Pendleton,	169	171	211, 248			257		260	270
270	A bill to incorporate a company to connect with the Portsmouth and Roanoke rail-road, for the purpose of transporting produce, merchandize, &c.,	169								
271	A bill to amend the act for the inspection of fish,		170	211, 220			235		251	270
272	A bill regulating the mode of obtaining writs of error in criminal prosecutions for misdemeanors,		170	210, 226			247		261	271
273	A bill prescribing the punishment of offences committed on rail-roads,		170	195, 220			230		269	272
274	A bill incorporating the Portsmouth provident society,	170	186	211, 248			258		260	271
275	A bill vesting in the board of public works the stock held by the state in the James river and Kanawha company,	170	176	211, 248			258		264	271
276	A bill incorporating sundry companies to construct turnpike roads from Richmond to Big Bird bridge,		171	211, 248			258		264	271
277	A bill to increase the library at Lewisburg,		176	211, 248			258		261	271
278	A bill authorizing appeals to be taken from the courts of certain counties therein mentioned, to the court of appeals held at Lewisburg,		176	211, 226			247		261	271
279	A bill re-organizing the Lexington arsenal, and establishing a military school in connexion with Washington college,		176	211			227		261	271
280	A bill to amend an act incorporating the town of Moorfield in the county of Hardy,	184	186	211, 248			258		264	271
281	A bill concerning Ann, a free woman of colour,		184	211, 248			258		261	271
282	A bill divorcing Ann Edmonds from her husband John W. A. Edmunds,		185	211, 248			258		264	271
283	A bill concerning the administrator of Richard Kelsick, deceased,		186	211, 248			262		269	272
284	A bill incorporating the Glen Leonard rail-road company,		186	211, 248	258		258		264	271
285	A bill to amend the charter of the James river and Kanawha company,		186	211, 228, 229			235		251	270
286	A bill to authorize a change of location of the Warm springs and Harrisonburg turnpike,		186	211, 248	248					
287	A bill to incorporate the Wythe watering company in the county of Wythe,		186	211, 248			257		260	270
288	A bill concerning the town of Leesburg in the county of Loudoun,		186	211, 248			258		260	271
289	A bill providing for the repairs and preservation of the public arms, the armory buildings, and for other purposes,		195	211, 248		258				

INDEX.

Number.	BILLS.	Leave to introduce.	When presented.	Different readings.	Laid on table.	Rejected in house.	Passed in house.	Rejected in senate.	Passed in senate.	Enrolled and signed.
290	A bill appropriating money to pay the purchase money of Brown's warehouse,	195	195	195			195		202	
291	A bill limiting recoveries on judgments therein mentioned,		195	211, 248			258		264	271
292	A bill suspending the processioning of lands in counties therein mentioned,		196	211			258		264	271
293	A bill incorporating the Petersburg savings institutions,		196	211, 248			258		264	271
294	A bill regulating the commissions on sales made under decrees in chancery, &c.		197	211, 248			258		260	271
295	A bill to authorize the common council of Fredericksburg to subscribe for stock of the Rappahannock and Blue Ridge rail-road,	203	206	248			259		260	270
296	A bill for a further appropriation of money to complete the additional buildings and cross walls of the Western lunatic asylum,	203	206	211, 248			259		264	271
297	A bill to establish a new regiment in the county of Warren,	203	212	248, 259			263		269	272
298	A bill changing the name of William H. Riggan to that of William H. Drewry,		203	211, 248			259		261	271
299	A bill placing James river on the footing of a lawful fence, so far as concerns the counties of Fluvanna and Albemarle,		203	211, 248			259		264	271
300	A bill to authorize a separate election in the county of Tazewell,		203	211			227		230	269
301	A bill to authorize Elisha B. Williams to erect a wool carding machine on Jackson's river, near the town of Covington,		203	211, 248	259					
302	A bill incorporating the Chesterfield and James river canal rail-road company,		205	248			258		264	271
303	A bill incorporating the Tuckahoe rail-road company,		205	211, 248		259, 261				
304	A bill allowing Stephen to remain in the commonwealth,		208	208, 248						
305	A bill allowing Charles Williams to remain in the commonwealth a limited time,		208	208, 248			259		264	271
306	A bill allowing Daniel Starks to remain in the commonwealth a limited time,		208	208, 248			259		260	270
307	A bill authorizing the county and corporation court clerks to charge fees for certain services performed by them,		208	208, 248			259		264	271
308	A bill to incorporate the town of Salem in the county of Botetourt,		208	208, 248			259		260	271
309	A bill to authorize William Townes to erect a toll-bridge across the Roanoke river opposite the town of Clarksville,		208	208, 248			259		264	271
310	A bill concerning delinquent lands, and lands not heretofore entered on the commissioners' books,			210, 230			247		264	271
311	A bill concerning the Chesapeake and Ohio canal company,		211	212, 225		236				
312	A bill concerning the executor of James Jenks, deceased.		212	248, 259					269	272
313	A bill to amend the act concerning the overseers of the poor,		212	248, 259				269		
314	A bill regulating the allowances in cases of arrest for criminal offences,		212	248, 259			263		264	271
315	A bill to define the duties and regulate the fees of the attorney general,		213	248, 259			263		269	272
316	A bill to repeal the act of the present session authorizing the payment of a judgment against the commonwealth in favour of Thomas Walls's representatives,	219	220	220, 249, 259			262		264	271
317	A bill to amend the act for the relief of creditors against fraudulent devises,		220	249, 259			263			
318	A bill to explain the act to reduce into one the several acts concerning grand juries and petit juries,		220	249, 259			263		269	272
319	A bill changing the time of holding the circuit superior court of Fairfax county,		220	248	248					
320	A bill to authorize the opening of a new street in the town of Petersburg,		221	249, 259			263		269	272
321	A bill to amend an act incorporating the town of Fairfax in the county of Culpeper,	222	225	249, 260			263		269	272
322	A bill allowing Jim Smith and wife and their infant children to remain in the commonwealth a limited time,		225	249, 260			263		269	272
323	A bill abolishing the vaccine agency of this commonwealth,		225	249, 259		257				
324	A bill concerning John B. Armistead, sheriff of Fauquier county,		230	249, 260			263		269	271
325	A bill concerning Richard H. Edwards,		244	249, 260			263		269	272
326	A bill declaratory of the sixteenth section of the act incorporating the Farmers bank of Virginia, and directing the distribution of the contingent or reserved fund in conformity thereto,		244	249	260					
327	A bill to amend an act to provide for a revision of the criminal code,		244	249, 260			263		269	272
328	A bill to amend the act to establish Water street in the town of Portsmouth,		244	249			259		260	271
329	A bill to increase the salaries of the inspectors of tobacco at Farmville, in the county of Prince Edward,		244	249, 260			263		269	272
330	A bill concerning Frederick Moore of the county of Cabell,		245	250, 260			263	264		
331	A bill to authorize a separate election at the place called the Burned Chimneys, in the county of Northumberland,		245	250			259		269	272
332	A bill incorporating the Fredericksburg iron and steel manufacturing company,	164, 165	171	211, 226			247		260	270
333	A bill to prevent more effectually persons trading with slaves,			249, 260		263				
334	A bill to provide for keeping in repair the public roads within the corporation of Lynchburg,		250	260, 264			265		269	272

INDEX.

Number	BILLS.	Leave to introduce.	When presented.	Different readings.	Laid on table.	Rejected in house.	Passed in house.	Rejected in senate.	Passed in senate.	Enrolled and signed.
335	A bill authorizing Lavender London and William H. Garland to erect a dam across Tye river, in the county of Nelson,	250	260,264			265		269	272	
336	A bill releasing the commonwealth's claim upon the estate of Archy Cooper, a lunatic,	250	260,264	265						
337	A bill allowing further time to the representatives and creditors of Lewis Eisenmenger to redeem certain lands vested in the literary fund,	250	260							
338	A bill allowing Andy, a man of colour, to remain in the commonwealth,	256	256,264			265		269	272	
339	A bill concerning the sheriff of Spottsylvania,	256	256,264		265					
340	A bill concerning Peter J. Chevallie,	256	256,260			263		269	271	
341	A bill concerning James Burk,	256	256	260						
342	A bill to provide for the purchase of additional copies of the Statutes at large,	257	257	257,263			265			
343	A bill allowing Lucy and Delila, free persons of colour, to remain in the commonwealth,	269	269			265		269	271	
344	A bill permitting sundry free persons of colour therein named to remain in the commonwealth a limited time,	262	262	262			265		269	272

BINNS, (RICHARD.)
Petition of Jane Carter for him, 104. 262
BLACKWELL, (JOSEPH,) Heirs.
Their petition, 94. 262
BLANKENSHIP, (ELI.)
Petition of Botetourt and Franklin citizens in his favour, 77. 160. 201
BLUE AND RED SULPHUR SPRINGS ROAD.
Resolution for incorporating company, 25
BLUE RIDGE, LEXINGTON AND COVINGTON TURNPIKE.
See Bills No. 268.
BOARD OF PUBLIC WORKS.
Twentieth annual report presented, 145
Its funds, &c., 217
See Bills No. 275.
See *Internal Improvement Fund.*
Twentieth annual report, Doc. No. 47.
Statement in relation to joint stock companies, p. 7
Letter of principal engineer, 8
Report of principal engineer, 9
Chesapeake and Ohio canal, 11
Winchester and Potowmac rail-road, 11
North-western turnpike, 12
South branch Potowmac, 13
Road from Moorfield to North-western road, 13, 14
Charleston and Parkersburg road, 14
Staunton and James river turnpike, 15
Rail-road from Scottsville to Staunton, 15. 18
Rivanna and Valley rail-road, 18
Road from Lexington to Richmond, 18, 19
Report of John Couty, assistant engineer, 19. 21
Report of Thomas H. De Witt, assistant engineer, 22. 24
Reports of James D. Drown, assistant engineer, 24-26
Returns of joint stock companies, 27
Lower Appomattox company, 29
Upper Appomattox company, 30
Ashby's gap turnpike, 31
Berryville turnpike, 32
Cartersville bridge company, 33
Dismal swamp canal company, 34
Fairfax turnpike company, 37
Fallsbridge turnpike, 38
Fincastle and Blue Ridge turnpike, 39
James river and Kanawha company, 40-48
Jackson's river turnpike, 49
Leesburg and Snicker's gap turnpike, 49, 50
Leesburg turnpike, 50
Lexington and Covington turnpike, 51
Little river turnpike, 52, 53

Lynchburg and Salem turnpike,
Doc. No. 47, p. 64
Manchester and Petersburg turnpike, 55
Millboro' and Carr's creek turnpike, 56
Petersburg rail-road, 57
Portsmouth and Roanoke rail-road, 58-65
Rappahannock company, 66
Rivanna navigation company, 67
Richmond, Fredericksburg and Potowmac rail-road, 69-72
Richmond dock company, 73
Roanoke navigation company, 74-77
Slate river company, 78
Staunton and James river turnpike, 78
Shepherdstown and Smithfield turnpike, 79
Snicker's gap turnpike, 80
Smithfield, Charlestown and Harper's Ferry turnpike, 81
Swift run gap turnpike, 82
Tye river and Blue Ridge turnpike, 83
Warm spring and Harrisonburg turnpike, 83-85
Wellsburg and Washington turnpike, 85-86
Winchester and Potowmac rail-road, 86-88
Propriety of disposing of stocks, 96
BOATMEN ON APPOMATTOX.
See Bills No. 107.
BOATMEN ON ROANOKE.
See Bills No. 36.
BOLLING, (BLAIR.)
Communication from him relative to flag, 162, 163
BOLLING, (RICHARD.)
His petition, 26. 33. 40
See Bills No. 86.
BONDS OF PUBLIC OFFICERS.
Number of committee; rule 28, 5
Committee appointed, 13
BOOKER'S GOLD MINE COMPANY.
See Bills No. 206.
BOOMER, (LUCY.)
Her petition, 36. 82. 136
BOOTH, (WILLIAM and others.)
Their petition, 18. 23
BOTETOURT COUNTY.
Petition of citizens, 27. 64. 75. 76. 83. 92. 95. 175
BOTETOURT, BEDFORD, MONROE, &c.
Petition of citizens, 57
BOTETOURT AND FRANKLIN.
Petition of citizens, 77. 160. 201
BOTETOURT, ROCKBRIDGE AND ALLEGHANY.
Petition of citizens, 38. 57. 63. 71
BOTTS, (JOHN M.)
His petition, 13. 36. 37

Prevails in his contest, 37
Added to various committees, 37
His protest against expunging, 124
BOUNDARY.
See *Maryland Boundary.*
BOUSH, (JACOB AND TONEY.)
Their petition, 26. 150. 199
BRADEN, (NOBLE S.)
His petition, 19. 81. 134
BRADLEY, (ROBERT.)
Elected door-keeper, 3
BRAXTON & LEWIS.
Court days changed. See Bills No. 195.
BRIDGES.
Aid for constructing, across north fork of Holstein river in Scott, 105
Report of committee, 107
Report taken up, 140
Over Ohio at Wheeling. See Bills No. 129.
Across Jackson's river at Covington. See Bills No. 203.
Across Shenandoah river at Harper's Ferry. See Bills No. 260.
William Townes's bridge. See Bills No. 309.
BRIGADIER GENERAL.
Governor's message, 12
Resolution for supplying vacancy occasioned by death of general M'Coy, 56
Agreed to by senate with amendment, 68
Amendment agreed to by house, 68
Election made; vote recorded, 102, 103
BRIGGS, (ROBERT and others.)
Their petition, 36. 92. 103
BROCKENBROUGH, (JOHN.)
President of Bank of Virginia; his communication in answer to resolution of December 11th, 39
Furnishes information relative to Bank of Virginia, 98
Taken up and referred, 99
Answers proceedings of Norfolk relative to bank, 146
BROCK, (ISAAC.)
His petition, 66. 91. 135
BROOKE ACADEMY.
Petition of trustees, 19
BROOKE COUNTY.
Petition of citizens, 53. 73. 124
BROOKE, (WILLIAM,) Heirs.
Their petition, 104. 262
BROWNSVILLE CONVENTION.
Their *Memorial,* 36
Printed documents, No. 10.
BROWN'S WAREHOUSE.
See Bills No. 290.

INDEX. 287

BROWN, (WILLIAM.)
Petition of citizens, 14
Report thereon, 17
Report acted on, 20
See Bills No. 19.
BROWNE, (WILLIAM and others.)
Their petition, 110
BUCKINGHAM COUNTY.
Petition of citizens, 131. 142. 160. 170. 201
BUCKINGHAM AND ALBEMARLE.
Petition of citizens, 199
BUCKINGHAM, NELSON AND FLUVANNA.
Petition of citizens, 34
BURK, (JAMES.)
His claim enquired into, 161
Report presented, 176
Acted on, 233
See Bills No. 341.
BURNING OF NORFOLK.
See *Eyre, (Severn,)* 56
Auditor to furnish copy of report of commissioners ascertaining losses, 59
Auditor transmits copies of reports of commissioners on losses by, 90
Communication of auditor referred, 91
Report of commissioners to ascertain losses, printed, 110
Journal of commissioners to ascertain losses, Doc. No. 43.
Schedule of claims entered for losses sustained in Norfolk, pp. 8-14
Report of commissioners containing special reports on claims numbered in schedule, 15-18
Further report of commissioners, 19, 20
Schedule of valuation of houses burnt and destroyed at Portsmouth, 21, 22
Schedule of valuation of sundry houses in Norfolk remaining unvalued, or valuation disallowed by legislature, 21
Schedule ascertaining damages sustained by houses in Suffolk, 22
Total amount of different valuations, 23
BUSINESS
Of house, how disposed of, rule 17, 4
BUTLER, (REUBEN,) Heirs.
Their petition, 94. 202
BUZADONE, (LAURIEUT.)
Petition, 160. 185
BYRNE, (THOMAS.)
His claim enquired into, 28
His petition, 34. 151. 200

C

CABELL COUNTY.
Separate action. See Bills No. 196.
CACAPEHON RIVER.
Resolution for uniting with Chesapeake and Ohio canal, 257
CALE, (JAMES B.)
Report of committee of elections on his vote, 46
Disagreed to by house, 48
CALL OF HOUSE.
See rule 9, 4
See rule 11, 4
CAMPBELL COUNTY.
Petition of citizens, 16. 20. 69. 73. 124
CANALS.
Resolution for amending act for cutting canal from Elizabeth river to Pasquotank river, 44
See Bills No. 59.
CAROLINE, KING & QUEEN AND ESSEX.
Petition of citizens, 34. 78. 132
CARPER & ROSSON.
Their petition, 57. 73
CARTER, (JANE.)
Her petition, 104. 262
CARTER, (THOMAS,) Heirs.
Their petition, 22. 61. 262

CARTERSVILLE AND FARMVILLE RAIL-ROAD.
Motion to suspend rule to bring in bill to incorporate company, 225
See Bills No. 65.
CARTERSVILLE BRIDGE COMPANY.
Amending act incorporating, 78
Committee discharged from bringing in bill allowing company to hold real estate, 185
CAUFIELD, (MOSES.)
Report of committee of elections on his vote, 47
Laid on table, 48
CENSURE.
See rule 9, 4
CESSION OF PUBLIC LANDS.
Documents to be printed relating to, 59
See Doc. No. 36.
CHANCERY COURTS.
Time for hearing causes on reports of commissioners lessened, 85
See Bills No. 133.
CHAPLINE, (WILLIAM and others.)
Their petition, 24
His wharves on Wheeling creek. See Bills No. 48.
CHARLESTON AND WESTON ROAD.
Resolution for constructing road, 26
CHARLESTOWN ATHENÆUM AND FEMALE ACADEMY.
See Bills No. 155.
CHARLOTTE.
Her petition, 14. 29
To remain in state. See Bills No. 84.
CHAVIS, (RANDAL.)
His petition, 86. 262
CHESAPEAKE AND OHIO CANAL COMPANY.
Report of Charles B. Fisk presented, 73
of probable revenue presented, 110
Petition of citizens,
73. 107. 136. 145. 150. 201. 208. 209
Resolution for uniting improvements of Cacapehon river with canal by aqueduct, 257
See Bills No. 311.
Report of Charles B. Fisk, engineer, Doc. No. 23.
Report of probable revenue after it reaches coal mines near Cumberland, and after its completion to Pittsburg, Doc. No. 41.
CHESTERFIELD AND JAMES RIVER CANAL RAIL-ROAD.
See Bills No. 302.
CHESTERFIELD RAIL-ROAD COMPANY.
Petition, 118. 201
CHEVALLIE, (PETER J.)
His petition, 142. 168. 186. 233
See Bills No. 340.
CHEW, (JOHN.)
His petition, 76, 77. 85. 136
See Bills No. 201.
CHRISTIAN, (ROBERT W.)
See Bills No. 256.
CINCINNATI FUND.
State of, Doc. No. 3, pp. 12, 13
CIRCUIT COURTS.
Joint resolution for electing judge of fourth circuit, 15
Amended by senate, 19
Amendment amended by house, 19
Amendment of house agreed to by senate, 21
Election proceeded in; John B. Christian elected, 31
Resolution for giving them concurrent jurisdiction with county and corporation courts in cases of forcible entry and detainer, 44
Concerning session of Spottsylvania court, 99
Leave bill to change times in third circuit. See Bills No. 9.
Leave bill to re-organize first and second districts. See Bills No. 10.
To alter terms in seventh district, thirteenth circuit. See Bills No. 16.
To alter terms in eighth district, sixteenth circuit. See Bills No. 93.

Judge of second circuit to appoint time for holding courts. See Bills No. 103.
Fifth circuit, third district. See Bills No. 162.
Terms of Stafford court changed. See Bills No. 249.
Terms of Campbell, Bedford and Lynchburg courts. See Bills No. 261.
Terms of Norfolk superior court altered and increased. See Bills No. 241.
Terms of Stafford superior court changed. See Bills No. 249.
Terms changed in Rockingham and Pendleton. See Bills No. 269.
Changed for Monroe, Giles and Montgomery. See Bills No. 108.
Of Fairfax. See Bills No. 319.
CIRCUITS.
Petition of citizens of thirteenth circuit, 77. 202
CITY POINT RAIL-ROAD.
See Bills No. 64.
CLAIMS.
Number of committee, rule 28, 5
Committee, of whom composed, 12
Appointment of clerk to committee postponed, 13
Joshua W. Fry appointed clerk, 15
CLARKE COUNTY.
See Bills No. 223.
CLARKSBURG AND BEVERLEY ROAD.
See Bills No. 50.
CLARKSBURG AND MIDDLEBOURN ROAD.
Resolution for constructing, 18
CLARKSBURG AND WHEELING ROAD.
Resolution for constructing, 18
CLARKSVILLE.
Petition of citizens, 33. 38. 45. 52. 86. 92. 140
Town enlarged. See Bills No. 96.
CLARKSVILLE FEMALE ACADEMY.
See Bills No. 198.
CLARKSVILLE, PETERSBURG, RICHMOND, &c.
Petition of inspectors, 109. 167
CLERK TO HOUSE.
George W. Munford elected, 3
To note absence, and disallow pay, rule 12, 4
See rule 13—taking ayes and noes, 4
See rule 18—papers, &c. not to be taken from custody, 4
See rule 19—journal, 4
See rule 20—laws, resolutions, 4
Messages between clerks interchanged, rule 21, 4
To prepare schedule of petitions, rule 22, 4
How petitions withdrawn, rule 26, 5
To refer petitions to committees, rule 27, 5
Number of committee to examine office, rule 28, 5
Committee appointed, 13
Report of committee on his office presented, 31
Report read, 42
To make index to journal, 42
CLERKS OF COMMITTEES
To keep lists of petitions, rule 21, 4
To deliver them to clerk of house, 4
Hugh N. Pendleton appointed clerk to committee of roads, &c. and of schools, &c. 13
Philip S. Fry appointed clerk to committee for courts of justice, 13
Thomas Vanneman appointed clerk to committee of propositions, &c. and of finance, 13
Edward V. Sparhawk appointed clerk to committee of agriculture and manufactures, 13
Appointment of clerk to committee, &c. and claims postponed, 13
Joshua W. Fry appointed said clerk, 15
CLERKS OF COURTS.
Resolution for allowing fees for process books, 18
Report on resolution concerning process books, 150
Taken up and acted on, 199
See Bills No. 307.

INDEX.

Resolution for delivering to them, for the use of their courts, certain reports and books, 261
Rejected by senate, 264
COLD BROOK COLLIERS.
See Bills No. 70.
COLLEGES AND ACADEMIES.
Report of literary fund relative to, presented, 54
Resolution for distributing surplus revenue of literary fund, 63
Report of president and directors of the literary fund respecting their condition, &c. Doc. No. 31.
University, p. 5-10
William and Mary college, 10-23
Washington college, 24-30
Hampden Sydney college, 30-40
Randolph Macon college, 40-41
Ann Smith academy, 41
Abingdon academy, 42
Berryville academy, 42, 43
Brooke academy, 43, 44
Danville female academy, 44-46
Ebenezer academy, 46, 47
Franklin academy, 47
Fincastle female academy, 47
Jefferson academy, (Culpeper,) 48
Margaret academy, (Accomack,) 48-50
Martinsville academy, (Henry,) 50, 51
Monongalia academy, 51
New London academy, 53
Newtown academy, 53, 54
Newington academy, 54
Northumberland academy, 56-59
Norfolk academy, 59-61
Patrick Henry academy, 61
Pittsylvania academy, 62
Portsmouth academy, 63
Rappahannock academy, 63-65
Rehoboth academy, 65
Richmond academy, 66-70
Rockingham academy, 70, 71
Rumford academy, 71
Strasburg academy, 72
Staunton academy, 72
Smithfield academy, 73
Union academy, 73
Washington academy, (Westmoreland,) 74-77
Waynesborough academy, 77
Washington Henry academy, 78
White Post academy, 79
COLSTON, (EDWARD.)
His petition, 85. 96. 140
COMMISSIONERS IN CHANCERY.
See Bills No. 26.
Time for hearing causes on their reports lessened, 85
COMMISSIONER OF REVOLUTIONARY CLAIMS.
Resolution for abolishing office, 59
Conditional resignation, 204, 205
To proceed to investigate claims, and report to governor, 222
Resolution indefinitely postponed, 222
Letter of final resignation of commissioner, 257
See Bills No. 251.
His report, Doc. No. 6.
List of claims for bounty land examined and reported on, pp. 8, 9, 10
List of claims against Virginia for supplies to Illinois regiment, 11
Memorandum of claims against Virginia examined and adjusted in 1834, 11
Commissioner's adjustment of the claim of the heir of Philip Barbour, deceased, 13-32
Claim of colonel Francis Vigo, 33-46
Claim of Pierre Menard, 46-50
Claim of Antoine Renno, 50-54
Statement and adjustment of the claims of Pierre Menard, 55-64
Claim of Joseph Bogy, heir of Joseph Placy, 64, 65
Claim of Antoine Peltier, 66-69

Statement and adjustment of claim of Joseph Bogy, 70-74
List of officers of Virginia state line and navy and of continental line, 75-118
COMMISSIONS.
Resolution for prescribing, for sales under decrees in chancery, 69
Report on resolution, 179
COMMITTEES.
Rule requiring appointment of standing, rule 28, 5
Quorum for business, rule 29, 5
Reports how made, rule 30, 5
Select committees, their number, rule 31, 5
Report of privileges and elections in contested elections, rule 32, 5
Committee of schools to report on literary fund, rule 33, 5
Committee of finance to report debt, revenue, &c. rule 34, 5
Standing committees appointed, 12, 13
Clerks appointed, 13. 15
On revolutionary claims added to standing committees, 82
Rule requiring committee on revolutionary claims, rescinded, 110
CONSTABLES.
Resolution for amending laws relating to, 18
Report on resolution presented, 170
Acted on, 233
CONTESTED ELECTIONS.
Person contesting, when entitled to pay, rule 36, 5
Documents from Henrico referred, 28
Report in Henrico case presented, 36
Taken up and read, 36
See *Fayette and Nicholas*, 45-48
Report on contested election between Adams and Critz, 64
Acted on, and Adams declared elected, 66, 67
Report on Albemarle contest recommitted, 155
Again presented and acted on, 184, 185
CONTINENTAL LINE.
List of officers of state line and navy and continental line, Doc. No. 6, pp. 75-118
CONVICTS.
Resolution for making provision for confining convicts of federal courts in the penitentiary, 125
Committee discharged from resolution, 262
COOPER, (ARCHY.)
See Bills No. 336.
COOPER, (MILLY.)
Her petition, 16. 186. 233
COPARCENERS.
Resolution for making partition of personal as well as real estate, 44
COPELAND, (HEZEKIAH B.)
Report of committee of privileges on his vote, 46
Motion to amend, negatived, vote recorded, 48
CORNICK, (JAMES.)
His letter, 170
CORPORATIONS.
Resolution enquiring whether stockholders have right of suffrage, 44
COSTS.
Resolution for reducing costs on collection of money recovered by judgments, &c. 15
COTTON.
See Bills No. 205.
COUNCIL.
Resolution for electing member, 21
Senate agree to resolution, 25
Election entered into; vote recorded; Peter V. Daniel elected, 27
COUNSEL.
Resolution for repealing section prohibiting attorney who commenced suit from prosecuting appeals, 76
COUNTERFEITING.
Amendment to criminal laws relating to, 110
COUNTY LEVY.
Resolution for publication of levy annually, 64

Committee discharged from resolution, 262
COURT OF APPEALS
At Lewisburg; appeals from counties of Shenandoah, Hardy and Page to be taken to, 59
Library at Lewisburg enlarged, 78
See Bills No. 278.
COURTS OF CHANCERY.
See Bills No. 133.
COURTS OF JUSTICE.
Number of committee, rule 28, 5
Committee, of whom to consist, 12
Committee enlarged, 124
COURTS MARTIAL.
Governor's message, 11.12
Petition of officers on trial of ensign Bentley, 202. 262
COVINGTON.
Petition of citizens, 104-137
COVINGTON BRIDGE.
See Bills No. 203.
CREDITORS.
Resolution for requiring security from, for jail fees of debtors, 40
CRIMINAL CODE.
Revision of. See Bills No. 327.
CRIMINAL OFFENCES.
See Bills No. 314.
CRIMINAL PROSECUTIONS.
Writs of error in, 59
CRIMINALS.
Resolution for removal, where jails destroyed, 15
See Bills No. 34.
CRITZ, (HAMAN.)
Report on his contested election presented, 64
Special report acted on, 66, 67
Resolution declaring his competitor elected, 67
CRUTCHFIELD, (STAPLETON.)
His petition, 80. 93. 136. 151. 232
CULPEPER COUNTY.
Petition of citizens, 74
CULPEPER AND MADISON.
Petition in favour of Robin, 95. 179
CULPEPER, STAFFORD AND FAUQUIER.
Petition of citizens, 74
CULPEPER, (THOMAS.)
His petition, 16. 76. 135
CUMBERLAND COUNTY.
Petition of citizens, 16. 34, 35. 52, 53. 147. 163
Separate election. See Bills No. 95.
CUMBERLAND. AMELIA AND PRINCE EDWARD.
Petition of citizens, 83
CUMBERLAND ROAD.
See Bills No. 186.
CURRENCY.
Governor's message, 9, 10

D

DALLAS, (Captain.)
Communication of sheriff of Norfolk on his refusing to permit service of process on board his ship, Doc. No. 1, p. 10
DANVILLE RAIL-ROAD CONVENTION.
Proceedings referred, 98. 108
DANVILLE.
Petition of citizens, 14
Report on, 20
DAVIS, (THOMAS.)
Elected door-keeper, 3
DEANE IRON MANUFACTURING COMPANY.
See Bills No. 257, or No. 332.
DEBATE.
Order, mode, &c., rules 2, 3, 4, 3
DEBT
Of state, 216, 217
DEBTORS.
Resolution for exempting certain property from execution, 36
Reported on, 124
See Bills No. 207.

INDEX.

Resolution for requiring security from creditors for jail fees of debtors,		49
Reported on,		135
DECREES IN CHANCERY.		
See *Costs*,		15
Resolution for prescribing fees for sales under,		69. 126
Reported on,		179
See Bills No. 204.		
DEEP CREEKS, (LITTLE AND BIG.)		
See Bills No. 20,		23
DEEP RUN MINING COMPANY.		
Leave to bring in bill to incorporate company.		
See Bills No. 8,		18
DELEGATES.		
List of,		273, 274
DELILA AND LUCY.		
Their petition,	33. 225. 235. 260	
See Bills No. 343.		
DELINQUENT LANDS.		
Resolution to continue in force 17th section of act 1831,		85
Committee for courts of justice discharged from resolution, and referred to finance,		86
See Bills No. 310.		
DEPOSITES.		
See *Rescinding Resolutions*.		
DEPOSITIONS.		
Resolution for amending act prescribing mode of obtaining commissions for,		21
Reported on,		135
See Bills No 197.		
DETINUE.		
Resolution for authorizing executions or distringas in detinue,		57
DEVISES.		
Resolution for amending act concerning fraudulent devises,		15. 152
See Bills No. 131.		
See Bills No. 317.		
DICKINSON, (HUDSON M.)		
Report on his contested election recommitted,		43
Report again presented and acted on,		45-48
Election decided against,		49
DINWIDDIE COUNTY.		
John L. Scott (member elect) resigns,		56
Writ of election issued,		56
New delegate takes his seat,		94
DISMAL SWAMP CANAL.		
Resolution for amending act for cutting canal from Elizabeth river to Pasquotank river,		44
Petition of company,		98. 136
See Bills No. 59.		
To increase capital. See Bills No. 228.		
DISTRICT FREE SCHOOLS.		
Reports of school commissioners on operations of,	Doc. No. 4,	p. 17
DISTRICTS.		
Petition of citizens of seventh district,		77
DISTRINGAS.		
Resolution for authorizing distringas or other executions in detinue,		57
DIXON'S WAREHOUSE		
For increase of inspectors' salaries,		154
Resolution reported on,		245
Taken up and acted on,		251
DIVISION OF HOUSE		
See rule 37,		5
DOCUMENTS.		
How printed, rule 3d,		5, 6
ABOLITION.		
Resolutions of South Carolina, Doc. No. 11.		
Proceedings of counties in Virginia, Doc. No. 12.		
Of Accomack county, Amelia,	pp.	1, 2
Augusta,		2, 3
Buckingham and Campbell,		3
Caroline and Charles City,		4
Charlotte and Cumberland,		5
Elizabeth City, Hampton and Fairfax,		6
Fluvanna and Fredericksburg,		7
Gloucester and Greensville,		8

Halifax, Hanover, Henry,	Doc. No. 12,	p. 9
Isle of Wight,		10
James City, Williamsburg, King & Queen, King William,		11
Louisa,		12
Lynchburg,		13
Mecklenburg, Middlesex,		14
Norfolk borough, Northampton,		15-17
Nottoway, Pittsylvania,		18
Powhatan,		19
Prince Edward,		20
Prince George, Petersburg,		21
Richmond and Henrico,		22
Smithfield, Southampton, Spottsylvania,		23
Surry,		24
Proceedings of non-slaveholding states, Doc. No. 12.		
Albany,		25
Hamilton college, New York city, (Park,)		26
New York city, (Tammany hall,) Plattsburg,		27
Rochester, Syracuse,		28
Troy, (New York,)		29
Utica, (New York,) Newark, (N. Jersey,)		30
Harrisburg, (Penn.) Philadelphia,		31
Hartford, (Conn.)		32
Meridon, (Conn.)		33
New Haven,		34
Boston, Lowell, (Mass.) Brunswick, (Maine,)		35
Concord, (N. H.)		36
Franklin, (N. H.)		37
Portsmouth, (N. H.) Charleston, (S. C.)		38
Report of select committee of house on abolition, Doc. No. 20.		
Report of minority of committee, Doc. No. 21.		
Amendment proposed by Mr. Watkins to report of committee, Doc. No. 25.		
Amendment of Mr. Miller, Doc. No. 29.		
Resolutions as passed by house, Doc. No. 40.		
Amendments proposed by senate, Doc. No. 40.		
Resolutions of *Georgia*, Doc. No. 26.		
Resolutions of *Alabama*, Doc. No. 42.		
Resolutions of *Mississippi*, Doc. No. 51.		
Resolutions of *Kentucky*, Doc. No. 54.		
Resolutions of *North Carolina*, Doc. No. 13.		
ADJUTANT GENERAL.		
Return of militia; arms, accoutrements and ammunition,	Doc. No. 1,	pp. 22, 23
AGRICULTURAL CONVENTION.		
Memorial of convention of societies of Albemarle and Fredericksburg, Doc. No. 30.		
ARMORY.		
Report of joint committee, Doc. No. 39.		
AUDITOR OF PUBLIC ACCOUNTS.		
His annual report to legislature, Doc. No. 2,		1
His statement of receipts,		3, 4
Of disbursements,		5, 6, 7
His statement of taxes on lands, lots, slaves, &c.		8, 9, 10
His statement of the commonwealth's funds in the treasury,		12, 13
His estimate of probable receipts and expenses,		14, 15, 16
Auditor's correspondence with the secretary of the treasury of the United States under act directing moneys to be refunded to the United States,		17
State of accounts between the United States and state of Virginia,		18
State of advances to officers of state line on account of half pay in 1783, 1784.		
State of balances paid by Virginia on account of half pay,		19
Letter of auditor to secretary of treasury,		20
Secretary Woodbury to auditor,		20
J. L. Edwards, commissioner of pensions, letter to auditor,		20
List of accounts remaining on his books September 1835, Doc. No. 32.		
SECOND AUDITOR'S ANNUAL REPORT, Doc. No 4.		
State of literary fund,		5
Permanent capital literary fund,		6
Stocks and loans belonging to permanent capital of literary fund,		7

Revenue derived from interest, dividends and rents,	Doc. No. 4,	p. 8
Charges on this fund,		9
Statement of school quotas,		10
His estimate of receipts and disbursements on account of the revenue,		11
Abstract of accounts of treasurers of school commissioners,	12,	13, 14
Abstract of school commissioners' reports for the year 1834,		15, 16
School commissioners' reports, shewing the operations of the district free schools,		17
Extracts from the reports of school commissioners relating to the state of the primary schools for 1834, in each county,		19-29
Accounts of *fund for internal improvement*, Doc. No. 5.		
State of the fund,		5
Permanent funds,		6
Disposable funds in stocks and loans,		7
Receipts,		8. 10
Disbursements,		9. 11
Estimate of certain and probable receipts,		12
Disbursements on account of the disposable funds,		13
Prospective statement relating to the funds of the board of public works,		14
Table of instalments due on subscriptions to stocks,		15
Summary statement of loans,		16
BANKS.		
Statement of annual dividends on capital of Bank of Virginia, Doc. No. 17.		
Nett annual profit of bank and branches,	5,	6, 7
Statement of president, shewing annual nett profits of branch at Norfolk, Doc. No. 33.		
Statement of stock of Farmers bank of Virginia and its branches, Doc. No. 16.		
Statement, shewing nett annual profit of its branch at Norfolk, Doc. No. 34.		
Annual statement of *Merchants and Mechanics bank of Wheeling*, and its branch at Morgantown, Doc. No. 46.		
Report of joint committee appointed to examine Bank of Virginia and Farmers bank of Virginia, Doc. No. 55.		
State of Bank of Virginia,		3, 4, 5
State of Farmers bank,		6-10
Returns of the *Bank of the Valley*,		11-17
Statement of condition of *North-western bank*, Doc. No. 8.		
BANKING CAPITAL.		
Report of committee on increasing capital of state, Doc. No. 22.		
Statement, shewing amount of banking capital of the United States in 1834 and 1835, with population of each state, and imports and exports,		6
Statement of value of imports and exports to and from Massachusetts, New York, Pennsylvania, Maryland and Louisiana, during nine months,		6
Table, shewing currency of United States, England, France and Holland,		7
Population of states in relation to square miles,		7
Statements of exports of domestic products of several states, their population, and banking capital,		8
BILLS PRINTED.		
Regulating and reducing expenses of collecting money under execution, Bill No. 1 in documents.		
Incorporating stockholders of the Lynchburg and Tennessee rail-road company, &c. Bill No. 2 in documents.		
Amending charter of James river and Kanawha company, Bill No. 3 in documents.		
Increasing banking capital, Bill No. 4 in documents.		
Appropriating surplus literary fund, Bill No. 5 in documents.		
Amendments of committee to Bill No. 5 in documents.		

INDEX.

Concerning merchants' licenses, Bill No. 6 in documents.
Imposing taxes, Bill No. 7 in documents.
Appropriating revenue, Bill No. 8 in documents.
To suppress circulation of incendiary publications, Bill No. 9 in documents.
BOARD OF PUBLIC WORKS.
Twentieth annual report, Doc. No. 47.
Statement in relation to joint stock companies, p. 7
Letter of principal engineer, 8
Report of principal engineer, 9
Chesapeake and Ohio canal, 11
Winchester and Potowmac rail-road, 11
North-western turnpike, 12
South branch Potowmac, 13
Road from Moorfield to North-western turnpike, 13, 14
Charleston and Parkersburg road, 14
Staunton and James river turnpike, 15
Rail-road from Scottsville to Staunton, 15, 18
Rivanna and Valley rail-road, 18
Road from Lexington to Richmond, 18, 19
Report of John Couty, assistant engineer, 19-21
Report of Thomas H. De Witt, assistant engineer, 22, 24
Reports of James D. Brown, assistant engineer, 24-26
Returns of joint stock companies
Lower Appomattox company, 29
Upper Appomattox company, 30
Ashby's gap turnpike, 31
Berryville turnpike, 32
Cartersville bridge company, 33
Dismal swamp canal company, 34
Fairfax turnpike company, 37
Fallsbridge turnpike company, 38
Fincastle and Blue Ridge turnpike, 39
James river and Kanawha company, 40-48
Jackson's river turnpike, 49
Leesburg and Snicker's gap turnpike, 49, 50
Leesburg turnpike, 50
Lexington and Covington turnpike, 51
Little river turnpike, 52, 53
Lynchburg and Salem turnpike, 54
Manchester and Petersburg turnpike, 55
Millboro' and Carr's creek turnpike, 56
Petersburg rail-road, 57
Portsmouth and Roanoke rail-road, 58-65
Rappahannock company, 66
Rivanna navigation company, 67
Richmond, Fredericksburg and Potowmac rail-road, 69-72
Richmond dock company, 73
Roanoke navigation company, 74-77
Slate river company, 78
Staunton and James river turnpike, 78
Shepherdstown and Smithfield turnpike, 79
Snicker's gap turnpike, 80
Smithfield, Charlestown and Harper's Ferry turnpike, 81
Swift run gap turnpike, 82
Tye river and Blue Ridge turnpike, 83
Warm spring and Harrisonburg turnpike, 83-85
Wellsburg and Washington turnpike, 85-86
Winchester and Potowmac rail-road, 86-88
BROWNSVILLE CONVENTION.
Their memorial in favour of a subscription by the state to the stock of the Baltimore and Ohio rail-road company, Doc. No. 10.
BURNING OF NORFOLK AND PORTSMOUTH.
Journal of commissioners to ascertain losses occasioned by burning in 1776, Doc. No. 43, 3-7
Schedule of claims entered for losses sustained by inhabitants of Norfolk, 8-14
Report of commissioners containing special reports on claims numbered in schedule, 15-18
Further report of commissioners, 19, 20
Schedule of valuation of houses burnt and destroyed at Portsmouth, 21, 22
Schedule of valuation of sundry houses in Norfolk remaining unvalued, or valuation not allowed by assembly, 21

Schedule ascertaining damages sustained by houses in Suffolk, Doc. No. 43, p. 22
Total amount of different valuations, 23
CHESAPEAKE AND OHIO CANAL.
Report of Charles B. Fisk, engineer, Doc. No. 23.
Report of probable revenue, Doc. No. 41.
COLLEGES AND ACADEMIES.
Report of president and directors of the literary fund respecting their condition, &c. Doc. No. 31.
University, 5-10
William and Mary college, 10-23
Washington college, 24-30
Hampden Sydney college, 30-40
Randolph Macon college, 40-41
Ann Smith academy, 47
Abingdon academy, 42
Berryville academy, 42, 43
Brooke academy, 43, 44
Danville female academy, 44-46
Ebenezer academy, 46, 47
Franklin academy, 47
Fincastle female academy, 47
Jefferson academy, (Culpeper,) 48
Margaret academy, (Accomack,) 48-50
Martinsville academy, (Henry,) 50, 51
Monongalia academy, 51
New London academy, 53
Newtown academy, 53, 54
Newington academy, 54
Northumberland academy, 55-59
Norfolk academy, 59-61
Patrick Henry academy, 61
Pittsylvania academy, 62
Portsmouth academy, 63
Rappahannock academy, 63-65
Rehoboth academy, 65
Richmond academy, 66-70
Rockingham academy, 70-71
Rumford academy, 71
Strasburg academy, 72
Staunton academy, 72
Smithfield academy, 73
Union academy, 73
Washington academy, (Westmoreland,) 74-77
Waynesborough academy, 77
Washington Henry academy, 78
White Post academy, 79
SCHOOL COMMISSIONERS.
Reports of the several counties, 80-87
COMMISSIONER OF REVOLUTIONARY CLAIMS.
His report, Doc. No. 6.
List of claims for bounty land for revolutionary services examined and reported on by him, 8, 9, 10
List of claims against Virginia for supplies to Illinois regiment, 11
Memorandum of claims against Virginia presented to him, examined and adjusted in 1834, 11
Commissioner's adjustment of the claim of the heir of Philip Barbour, deceased; evidence filed, 13-32
Claim of colonel Francis Vigo, 33-46
Claim of colonel Pierre Menard, 46-50
Claim of administrator of Antoine Renno, 50-54
Statement and adjustment of the claims of Pierre Menard. 55
Claim of Joseph Bogy, heir of Joseph Placy, 64, 65
Claim of Antoine Peltier, 66-69
Statement and adjustment of claim of Joseph Bogy, 70-74
List of officers of Virginia state line and navy, and of continental line, 75-118
JUDGE DUNCAN.
Charges preferred by William A. Harrison against him as judge, Doc. No. 44.
His memorial, Doc. No. 45.
EXPUNGING.
Report of select committee, Doc. No. 15.
FINANCE.
Report of committee on revenue, expenditures and debt of state, Doc. No. 48.

GEOLOGICAL RECONNOISSANCE.
Report by professor William B. Rogers, Doc. No. 24.
General geological division of the state, p. 4
Tertiary marl region, 5
Miocene marl district, 6
Condition of shells in tertiary deposits, 7, 8
Disposition of the fossils, 8, 9
Description of the cliffs at York town, 9, 10, 11
Nature and varieties of the Miocene shell marl, 11, 12
Shells least useful, and most suited for marling, 12
Green sand, sulphate of iron, sulphur and other matters associated with marl beds, 13, 14
Table, shewing per cent. of carbonate of lime in Miocene marls, 14, 15
Eocene marl district, 15
Of the Miocene over the Eocene, 16
Of the Eocene or lower tertiary marl, 17
Description of the Eocene strata on the Pamunkey, 17, 18, 19
Eocene strata of the James river, 19
Eocene deposits of the Potowmac, Rappahannock and Mattapony, 19
Of the several beds composing the Eocene formation, 19
Eocene on the rivers; existence throughout whole breadth of state, 20
Value of Eocene green sand marl in agriculture, 20
Composition of green sand; Eocene marls, 21
Region between head of tide and western flank of the Blue Ridge, 22, 23
Bituminous coal field in primary region, 23-26
Sandstone over primary rocks along their eastern boundary, 26, 27
Of the primary rocks, 27, 28
Of the auriferous rocks, 28, 29, 30
Of the micaceous and garnet slates, silicious slate, whetstone beds, roofing slate, steaschist iron ore, of the gneiss region, 30
Micaceous garnet slate, or birdseye maple slate, 30, 31
Limestone and marble east of South-west and Green mountains, 31, 32
Rocks, ores, soils of the region west of the limestone as far as west flank of the Blue Ridge, 32-35
Rocks of the Blue Ridge at Turk's gap, 35-37
Of the Valley of Virginia, 37-39
Of the North mountain and Alleghany region, 39-46
South-western district of state, 46-47
Western bituminous coal and salt region, 47-50
Plan of geological survey, 51-52
GOVERNOR'S MESSAGE, Doc. No. 1.
Letter to governor from New York on subject of abolition excitement, Doc. No. 1, p. 9
Communication of William B. Manning, sheriff of Norfolk, relative to the refusal of captain Dallas to permit the service of process upon a man on board his ship, 10
Letter of governor to the president of the United States on the subject of the letter from the sheriff of Norfolk county, 11
Answer of secretary of the navy thereto, 11
Letter from governor Thomas of Maryland relative to disputed boundary, 12
Report and resolutions of state of Maryland upon subject of disputed boundary, 12, 13, 14
Answer of governor Tazewell to letter of governor Thomas relating to disputed boundary, 14, 15
Continuation of correspondence by governor Thomas, 16, 17
Letter of attorney general of Maryland announcing the discontinuance of the suit of Maryland against Virginia in the supreme court, 18
Governor Tazewell to governor Thomas in reply to letter of 15th October, 1835, 18
Governor Thomas to governor Tazewell in reply, 19

INDEX. 291

Governor Tazewell to governor Thomas,
  Doc. No. 1, pp. 19, 20
INSTRUCTIONS.
Preamble and resolutions asserting the right,
  adopted in 1812, Doc. No. 9.
LANDS, SALES OF PUBLIC.
Resolutions of Mr. Dorman relating to distribution of proceeds, Doc. No. 14.
LUNATIC HOSPITALS.
Report of directors of *Western hospital*, Doc. No. 19.
Accounts of Western hospital, Doc. No. 52.
Report of directors at *Williamsburg*, Doc. No 37.
Second report of same directors, Doc. No. 38.
MARYLAND BOUNDARY.
Correspondence between governors Tazewell and Thomas,   Doc. No. 1, 12-20
Letter from governor Thomas to governor Tazewell, Doc. No. 18.
NORTH-WESTERN TERRITORY.
Respecting the cession of the territory, Doc. No. 36.
PENITENTIARY.
Report of board of directors, Doc. No. 7.
General agent's account current,   2, 3
Superintendent's report,   4-7
Penitentiary in account with state,   8, 9
Manufacturing operations of the shoe and
  tailors' apartment,   10, 11
Operations of weaving apartment,   12, 13
Number of prisoners remaining in 1834, and
  received, pardoned, died and discharged
  since,   14
Number of prisoners received since 1834,   15
Number confined on 30th September, 1835,   16
Natives and foreigners remaining at that
  time,   17
Ages of convicts,   17
Hospital returns,   18
Number since opened,   19
Condition and employments of convicts,   20
Cost of building shed for timber, &c.   21
Physician's and superintendent's report,   22
PRESIDENT AND VICE-PRESIDENT OF UNITED STATES.
Resolution of state of Ohio, Doc. No. 56.
RESCINDING RESOLUTIONS.
To rescind resolutions censuring the president for removing the deposites, Doc. No. 35.
SENATORS.
John Tyler's resignation, Doc. No. 49.
Benjamin W. Leigh's letter, Doc. No. 50.
SUPERINTENDENT OF ARMORY.
His report, Doc. No. 27.
Arms and accoutrements,   3, 4
Ordnance,   5
TREASURER.
His annual report, Doc. No. 3.
Statement of receipts and disbursements on
  account of commonwealth,   4, 5
Receipts and disbursements of various funds, 6, 7
State of treasury end of each quarter, 8, 9, 10, 11
Cincinnati fund,   12, 13
Washington monument fund,   14
Report of joint committee on his accounts,
  Doc. No 28.
HENRY A. WISE.
His communication on abolition, Doc. No. 53.
DOORKEEPERS.
John Stubblefield elected,   3
Thomas Davis elected,   3
Robert Bradley elected,   3
DRAGON SWAMP.
Petition of president and directors, 66. 78. 98. 101
Resolution for improving navigation,   78
Reported on,   107. 139
See Bills No. 117.
See Bills No. 168.
DUFFY, (PETER.)
Report of committee of elections on his vote, 47
Laid on table,   48

DUNCAN, (EDWIN S.)
Charges preferred against him,   142
His petition,   142. 186
Charges and memorial referred,   151
Additional specification,   154
Reported on by committee,   170
Acted on; indefinitely postponed,   209
See Documents No. 44, No. 45.
DUNLAP, (FRANCIS F.)
His petition   93. 262
DUPEY, (ANTHONY M.)
Encloses proceedings of Danville rail-road
  convention,   98

E

EASTERN SHORE RAIL-ROAD.
See Bills No. 168.
EDITORS OF PAPERS.
Allowed seats at bar,   3
EDMUNDS, (ANN.)
Her petition,   105. 110. 178
See Bills No. 232.
EDWARDS, (RICHARD H.)
His petition,   34. 92. 140. 230
See Bills No. 325.
EISENMENGER, (LEWIS.)
See Bills No. 337.
ELECTIONS.
One vacancy filled at a time, rule 43,   6
Joint vote, how conducted, rule 44,   6
Resolution requiring elections to be held on
  same day,   141
Report thereon,   148
Acted on,   199
ELECTORAL DISTRICTS.
Motion to bring in bill arranging, for electors
  of president and vice-president, laid on
  table.   68
ELIZABETH CITY COUNTY.
Petition of citizens,   107. 142. 144
ELIZABETHTOWN AND MOUNDSVILLE.
Petition of citizens,   98. 118. 179
ELIZABETHTOWN AND WHEELING ROAD.
Resolution for incorporating company to
  construct road,   49. 63. 71
ENGINEER, (PRINCIPAL.)
To provide him an office in capitol,   154
Resolution for election,   160
Agreed to by senate,   164
Election made; vote recorded,   166, 167
ENROLLED BILLS
Number of committee on, rule 28,   5
Committee appointed,   13
Reports of committee,   107. 165. 222. 257
Examined and signed in senate,   165. 212. 251
Signed,   265, 266, 267, 268, 269, 270, 271, 272
See *Delinquent Lands*,   85
ESSEX, CAROLINE AND KING & QUEEN.
Petition of citizens,   34. 78
ESTILLVILLE.
Petition of citizens,   26. 71. 167
ESTILLVILLE ACADEMY.
Resolution for giving to academy the quota
  due Scott county for removal of free negroes, 63
Reported on,   126
Report acted on,   179
See Bills No. 134.
ETNA COAL COMPANY.
See Bills No. 219.
ETTRICK MANUFACTURING COMPANY.
See Bills No. 67.
EVANSHAM.
Petition of citizens,   101. 104. 137
EVANSHAM AND JEFFERSONVILLE ROAD.
Survey directed,   96
Agreed to by senate,   103
EVANS & WILLIAMS.
Their petition,   151. 163. 223

EXECUTIONS.
Certain portion of debtor's property exempted from, 36
Reported on,   72
Report acted on,   124
See Bills No. 207.
Resolution for amending act so as to authorize in detinue a distringas or other execution, 57
See Bills No. 90, reducing expenses for collecting money, 64
Committee discharged from resolution concerning executions and insolvents, 262
EXECUTIVE COUNCIL.
Call for journal,   18
Resolution for electing member,   21
Senate agree to resolution,   25
Election made; vote recorded; Peter V.
  Daniel elected,   27
EXECUTIVE EXPENDITURES.
Number of committee, rule 28,   5
Committee appointed,   13
Report of committee,   141
Report acted on,   160
List of warrants and vouchers for claims, 180-182
EXPUNGING RESOLUTIONS.
Resolution of senate of United States relative to executive proceedings, referred, 24
Motion to lay on table negatived; vote,   24
Motion to amend by Mr. Hickerson,   24-25
Vote thereon,   25
Committee appointed,   25
Report of committee presented,   55
Taken up; motion to refer to committee of
  whole house; vote recorded,   67
Motion of Mr. Carter to postpone execution
  of order of day upon resolutions of committee; vote recorded, 93
House in committee of whole,   93-94
Reported without amendment,   94
Taken up and discussed, 95, 96. 98, 99. 102, 103,
                                            104, 105, 106. 108, 109, 110
Motion of Mr. Mallory to amend, so as to rescind, &c. 111
Taken up; question on Mr. Mallory's motion; Mr. Daniel called division of question; question on striking out taken; vote
  recorded,   112
Motion of Mr. Parker to amend; vote recorded, 113
Mr. Witcher's motion to amend first resolution; vote recorded, 113
Second motion to amend by Mr. Witcher;
  vote,   113
Mr. Brown's motion to amend first resolution; vote recorded, 114
Mr. Hayes's motion to amend; vote recorded, 114
Second motion by Mr. Parker to amend;
  vote recorded,   114
Mr. Gilmer's motion to amend,   115
Motion by Mr. Craig to lay on table; vote
  recorded,   115
Motion to amend by Mr. Murdaugh,   115
Vote recorded thereon,   116
Previous question called by Mr. Madison,   116
First resolution adopted; vote recorded,   116
Question on second resolution,   116
Mr. Madison called previous question,   116
Motion by Mr. Gregory to adjourn; vote
  corded,   116, 117
Previous question withdrawn,   117
Second resolution; Mr. Stanard moved to
  amend,   117
Mr. Daniel divide question; question on striking out taken; vote recorded, 117
Motion by Mr. Gregory to adjourn; vote recorded, 117
Second resolution taken up; motion by Mr.
  Parker to amend; vote recorded,   118
Motion by Mr. Price to amend; vote,   119
Previous question called by Mr. Watkins;
  vote recorded,   119
Question on second resolution taken; vote,
                                            119, 120

INDEX.

Third resolution amended, 120
Motion to amend by Mr. Parker; vote recorded, 120
Third resolution adopted, 120
Question on preamble; vote recorded, 120
Mr. Botts's protest; laid on table, 124
Preamble and resolution agreed to by senate, 155
Communication from governor refusing to transmit resolutions to senators, 158, 159
Mr. Watkins's resolution requiring speakers to transmit resolutions to senators, 159
Vote on preamble recorded, 159
Agreed to by senate, 161
Resignation of John Tyler, 171
Letter from B. W. Leigh, 186, 194
Speakers to transmit to W. C. Rives, 212
Agreed to by senate, 221
Mr. Watkins's resolution expressing sense of legislature upon disobedience of B. W. Leigh to instructions, 256, 257
Report of select committee, printed Doc. No. 15.
John Tyler's resignation, Doc. No. 49.
B. W. Leigh's letter, Doc. No. 50.
EYRE, (SEVERN,) *Representative.*
Committee to provide for paying for his losses by burning of Norfolk 1776, 56
Report of committee, 103
Acted on, 139
See Bills No. 193.

F

FAIRFAX COUNTY.
Petition of citizens, 18. 44. 95. 162. 212
Circuit court. See Bills No. 319, No. 196.

FAIRFAX.
Town of. See Bills No. 321.

FAIRFIELD.
Petition of citizens, 79. 147. 199

FALLSBRIDGE TURNPIKE.
Petition of company, 96. 107. 137

FALMOUTH.
Petition of citizens, 13

FALMOUTH AND ALEXANDRIA RAIL-ROAD.
Survey for rail-road, 144
Agreed to by senate, 160
Leave bill to amend charter. See Bills No 11.

FALMOUTH MINING COMPANY.
Leave to bring in bill to incorporate company. See Bills No. 7.

FARMERS BANK OF VIRGINIA.
To prepare statement of dividends, &c. 20
Statement communicated, 38
To furnish statement of capital, contingent funds, &c. 82
Information afforded by president, 99
Referred to committee on banks, 100
Resolution relative to distribution of surplus fund, &c. 195
Report of state of bank presented, 250
See Bills No. 326.
Statement of stock of bank and branches, Doc. No. 16.
Statement, shewing nett annual profits of branch at Norfolk, Doc. No. 34.
Report of joint committee, Doc. No. 55.
State of bank, pp. 6-10

FARMVILLE.
Petition of citizens, 13. 16. 34. 41. 71. 106. 142. 157. 186. 233
See Bills No. 198.
Inspectors' salaries. See Bills No. 329.

FAUNTLEROY, (HENRY.)
His petition, 94. 262

FAUQUIER COUNTY.
Petition of citizens, 74. 81. 154. 170. 269

FAUQUIER WHITE SULPHUR SPRINGS.
See Bills No. 105.

FAYETTE COUNTY.
Petition of citizens, 22. 35. 52. 53. 147. 201. 231

FAYETTE AND KANAWHA.
Petition of citizens, 22. 31. 41

FAYETTE AND NICHOLAS.
Report on contested election presented and recommitted, 43
Report again presented and considered, 45-48
Votes on resolutions, 48
Third resolution; motion to amend; vote recorded, 48
Samuel Price declared elected, 49

FEDERAL COURTS.
Convicts of, to be confined in state penitentiary, 125

FEDERAL GOVERNMENT.
See governor's message, 8, 9

FENN, (WILLIAM.)
His petition, 29. 73. 125
Document to support his petition, 37

FERRIES.
See Bills No. 23, amending general act.
See Bills No. 49, Onancock ferry.

FINANCE.
Number of committee, rule 28, 5
Report on debts, revenue and expenses, rule 36, 5
Committee appointed, 13
Governor's message, 11
Mr. Ragsdale added to committee, 22
Committee increased, 164
To sit during session, 168
Report on revenue, expenses and debt of state, 169
Acted on in committee of whole; amended, 197
Report of committee on estimates, &c. 214
Estimate of expenses, 214-215
Estimate of receipts, 215-216
Debt of state, 216
Literary fund debt, 217
Fund of internal improvement, 217
Resolution for increasing taxes, 218
Committee enlarged, 248
Report of committee on revenue, expenditures and debt of commonwealth, Doc. No. 48.

FINDLEY & ROGERS.
Their petition, 29. 230. 233

FIRE AND MARINE COMPANY, (WHEELING.)
See Bills No. 37, 23

FISH.
Concerning inspection, size of barrels, &c. 141
See Bills No. 271.

FISHER, (WILLIAM.)
His petition, 19. 31. 40
See Bills No. 92.

FISK, (CHARLES B.)
His report to the Chesapeake and Ohio canal company presented, 73
Printed documents No. 23.

FLAG OF THE UNITED STATES.
Resolution requesting it to be displayed on public buildings, 155
Motion to adjourn pending resolution, vote recorded, 155, 156
Resolution withdrawn, 156
Speaker to direct sergeant to request superintendent of edifices to display it, 156
Motion to lay on table; vote recorded, 156
Resolution agreed, 156
Mr. Dorman's resolution to procure flag, 156
Reconsidered, amended, and sent to senate, 161
Communication of superintendent of public edifices, 162, 163

FLEET'S MANUFACTURING COMPANY.
See Bills No. 68.

FLOUR.
Resolution for new grade, 65
Report of committee thereon, 81
Report recommitted, 94
See Bills No. 176.
Inspection at Winchester. See Bills No. 123.

FLOYD COUNTY.
Petition of citizens, 14
Report on, 20

FLUVANNA COUNTY.
Petition of citizens, 176

FLUVANNA AND ALBEMARLE.
Petition of citizens, 78. 179

FLUVANNA, BUCKINGHAM AND NELSON.
Petition of citizens, 34

FLUVANNA MINING COMPANY.
See Bills No. 54.

FORCIBLE ENTRY AND DETAINER.
Resolution for giving circuit courts concurrent jurisdiction with county and corporation courts, in cases of, 44
See Bills No. 132.

FORD, (SHELTON.)
His petition, 29. 32. 39
See Bills No. 78.

FORGERIES.
See Bills No. 209.

FOSTER, (TURLEY.)
Report of committee of elections on his vote, 46
Agreed to by house, 48

FRAME, (JOHN.)
Report of committee of privileges on his vote, 45, 46
Agreed to by house, 48

FRANKLIN COUNTY.
Petition of citizens, 14
Report on, 20

FRANKLIN AND BOTETOURT.
Petition of citizens, 77. 160. 201

FRAUDULENT DEVISES.
Resolution for amending act, 15
Mr. Boothall's resolution further to amend, 152
See Bills No. 131.
See Bills No. 317.

FRAZIER & ANTHONY.
Their petition, 105. 196. 234

FREDERICK COUNTY.
Petition of citizens, 14. 16. 32. 35. 41. 45. 69. 73, 74. 80. 83, 84. 95. 103. 140. 145
New county of Clarke formed. See Bills No. 223.

FREDERICK AND SHENANDOAH.
Petition of citizens, 14. 50. 73, 74. 93. 101. 140. 144
New county of Warren formed. See Bills No. 222.

FREDERICK AND JEFFERSON.
Petition of citizens, 77

FREDERICKSBURG.
Petition of citizens, 13. 16. 17. 30. 161. 262
Common council to make advance on stock held in Rappahannock canal company, 131
See Bills No. 184.
To subscribe for stock in Rappahannock canal company. See Bills No. 205.

FREDERICKSBURG AND BLUE RIDGE RAIL-ROAD.
Resolution for chartering company, 14
See Bills No. 18.

FREDERICKSBURG FEMALE ORPHAN ASYLUM.
Petition of managers, 32. 154. 200

FREDERICKSBURG IRON AND STEEL MANUFACTURING COMPANY.
See Bills No. 332, or No. 256.

FREDERICKSBURG MECHANIC ASSOCIATION.
For further amending charter to grant banking privileges, 83
See Bills No. 244.

FREDERICKSBURG MINING COMPANY.
See Bills No. 177.

FREDERICKSBURG UNION MANUFACTURING COMPANY.
See Bills No. 174.

FREE NEGROES.
Resolution for amending law to remove them from state, 32
Resolution for providing that upon failing to leave state they shall forfeit freedom and pass to next of kin, 49

INDEX. 293

Resolution for requiring them to be hired out, 59
For their removal from state, 59
Resolution for preventing their return into state, 100
Resolution amended and adopted, 102
For removing them from state, 102
For amending act appropriating money to remove them, 102
Report on resolution for forfeiting freedom for failing to remove, 135
FREE ROAD.
To incorporate a company to complete the Staunton and Warm springs road, 103
FRIEND, (ISRAEL A.)
Report of committee of elections on his vote, 46
Disagreed to by house, 48
FRONT ROYAL LIBRARY SOCIETY.
See Bills No. 150.
FRY, (PHILIP S.)
Clerk to committee for courts of justice, 13
of revolutionary claims, 85
FUND FOR INTERNAL IMPROVEMENT.
See *Internal Improvement Fund.*

G

GALLEGO MANUFACTURING COMPANY.
See Bills No. 161.
GARLAND & LONDON.
Their dam, 152
Report of committee, 163
Acted on, 224
See Bills No. 335.
GARY, (BETSY.)
Resolution for appropriating money for her; rejected, 56
GENERAL AGENT OF PENITENTIARY.
See *Penitentiary.*
Resolution for election, 160
Agreed to by senate, 164
Election made; vote recorded, 166, 167
GENERAL ASSEMBLY.
Resolution for changing time of meeting, 169
Report on resolution, 171
Report acted on, 224
GENERAL COURT.
See *Circuit Courts.*
GENERALS.
Resolution for electing major general for third division, 208
Agreed to by senate, 220
Election made; vote recorded, 221
GEOLOGICAL RECONNOISSANCE.
Professor Rogers's report transmitted by governor, 76
Report and governor's message on subject referred, 79
Profile accompanying report to be engraved and printed, 82
Professor Rogers authorised to publish his report and use plates, 152
See Bills No. 139.
Report of professor Rogers, Doc. No. 24.
General geological division of the state, p. 4
Tertiary marl region, 5
Miocene marl district, 6
Condition of shells in tertiary deposits, 7, 8
Disposition of the fossils, 8, 9
Description of the cliffs at York town, 9, 10, 11
Nature and varieties of the Miocene shell marl, 11, 12
Shells least useful, and most suited for marling, 12
Green sand, sulphate of iron, sulphur and other matters associated with marl beds, 13, 14
Table, shewing per cent. of carbonate of lime in Miocene marls, 14, 15
Eocene marl districts, 15
Of the Miocene over the Eocene, 16
Of the Eocene or lower tertiary marl, 17
Description of the Eocene strata on the Pamunkey, 17-19
Eocene strata of the James river, 19

Eocene deposits of the Potowmac, Rappahannock and Mattapony, Doc. No. 24, p. 19
Of the several beds composing the Eocene formation, 19
Eocene on the rivers; existence throughout whole breadth of state, 20
Value of Eocene green sand marl in agriculture, 20
Composition of Eocene green sand marls, 21
Region between head of tide and western flank of the Blue Ridge, 22, 23
Bituminous coal field in primary region, 23-26
Sandstone over primary rocks along their eastern boundary, 26, 27
Of the primary rocks, 27, 28
Of the auriferous rocks, 28-30
Of the micaceous and garnet slates, silicious slate, whetstone beds, roofing slate, steaschist iron ore, of the gneiss region, 30
Micaceous garnet slate, or birdseye maple slate, 30, 31
Limestone and marble east of South-west and Green mountains, 31, 32
Rocks, etc., soils of the region west of the limestone as far as west flank of the Blue Ridge, 32-35
Rocks of the Blue Ridge at Turk's gap, 35-37
Of the Valley of Virginia, 37-39
Of the North mountain and Alleghany region, 39-46
South-western district of state, 46, 47
Western bituminous coal and salt region, 47-50
Plan of geological survey, 51, 52
GILES AND TAZEWELL.
Line dividing. See Bills No. 167.
GILL'S MOUNTAIN GOLD MINE.
See Bills No. 138.
GILMER AND SOUTHALL.
Report on contested election, 184, 185
GLEN LEONARD RAIL-ROAD.
See Bills No. 284.
GLOUCESTER COUNTY.
Petition of citizens, 78. 80. 245. 250
See Bills No. 157.
GOOCHLAND COUNTY.
Petition of citizens, 57. 63. 71. 147. 163
GOOCHLAND MINING COMPANY.
See Bills No. 160.
GOODMAN, (GEORGE W.)
Petition in favour of Stephen, 75
GOODWIN, (EDWARD.)
Leave to withdraw his petition, 111
Petition presented and acted on, 121. 186. 233
GOOSE CREEK NAVIGATION COMPANY
See Bills No. 213.
GORDONSVILLE AND CHARLOTTESVILLE RAIL-ROAD.
Resolution for survey, 94
Amended and adopted, 106
Agreed to by senate, 111
GORDONSVILLE AND HARRISONBURG RAIL-ROAD.
Resolution for survey, 94
Amended and adopted, 106
Agreed to by senate, 111
GOVERNOR.
Communicates annual message, 6-12
To be printed, 12
Transmits report of the superintendent of the penitentiary, 23
Returns of the Bank of the Valley; referred, 25
Communicates two reports of the captain of the public guard, 27
Communicates returns of North-western bank, 34
Transmits resolutions of South Carolina on abolition, 38
Communicates letter from governor of Maryland relative to disputed boundary, 44
Transmits resolutions from North Carolina on subject of abolition, 51
Communicates report of the board of the literary fund relative to University, colleges and academies, 54

Transmits professor Rogers's report of the geological reconnoissance of the state, 76
Communicates resolutions of Georgia on movements of abolitionists, 81
Communicates address and resolutions of legislature of Alabama on abolition, 111
Communicates annual statement of Merchants and Mechanics bank of Wheeling, 144
Communicates twentieth annual report of the board of public works, 145
Transmits resolution of Mississippi on abolition, 153
Refuses to transmit expunging resolutions to senators, 158, 159
Communicates resolutions of state of Ohio relating to the election of president and vice-president, 229
Transmits resolutions of state of Kentucky respecting abolition societies, 236-238
Communicates letter from Henry A. Wise on subject of abolition, 238-243
Communicates resolutions of Pennsylvania concerning sales of public lands, 272, 273
His annual message, Doc. No. 1.
Letter to him from New York on subject of abolition excitement, p. 9
Communication of William B. Manning, sheriff of Norfolk, relative to the refusal of captain Dalles to permit the service of process upon a man on board his ship, 10
Letter of governor to the president of the United States on the subject of the letter from the sheriff of Norfolk county, 11
Answer of secretary of the navy thereto, 11
Letter from governor Thomas of Maryland relative to disputed boundary, 12
Report and resolutions of state of Maryland upon subject of disputed boundary, 12, 13, 14
Answer of governor Tazewell to letter of governor Thomas relating to disputed boundary, 14, 15
Continuation of correspondence by governor Thomas, 16, 17
Letter of attorney general of Maryland announcing the discontinuance of the suit of Maryland against Virginia in the supreme court, 18
Governor Tazewell to governor Thomas in reply to letter of 15th October, 1835, 18
Governor Thomas to governor Tazewell in reply, 19
Governor Tazewell to governor Thomas, 19, 20
Adjutant general's return of militia, 22, 23
Governor Thomas in conclusion, Doc. No 18
GRAND JURIES.
Resolution for amending act concerning, 61
GRANDVILLE.
Petition of citizens, 16
See Bills No. 31.
GRAVES, (T. W.)
His petition, 126. 212
GRAYSON COUNTY.
Petition of citizens, 93. 101. 139
GRAYSON SULPHUR SPRINGS.
See Bills No. 262.
GREAT FALLS MANUFACTURING COMPANY.
See Bills No. 22.
GREENBRIER, MONROE, BOTETOURT.
Petition of citizens, 57
GREEN, (DUFF.)
His petition, 16. 29. 40. 66. 70
See Bills No. 85.
GREENFIELD.
Separate election established at, in Nelson.
See Bills No. 24, 27
GREENSVILLE.
Petition of citizens, 96. 107. 139
GREENSVILLE AND PANTHER GAP TURNPIKE.
See Bills No. 204.
GREENSVILLE RAIL-ROAD COMPANY.
See Bills No. 170.
See Bills No. 167.

INDEX.

GREGORY, (WILLIAM S.)
Report of committee of elections on his vote, 47
Laid on table, 48
GRIGSBY, (J. D.)
His petition, 98. 150. 199
GUARDIANS AD LITEM.
Resolution for giving courts of law power to appoint, 63
Report thereon, 91
Report acted on, 135
GUARD, (PUBLIC.)
Governor's message, 11, 12
See Bills No. 185.
GUARDS.
For providing for pay for guarding prisoners before commitment, 78

H

HALIFAX COUNTY.
Petition of citizens, 14. 20. 34. 35. 22. 103
See Bills No. 147.
HALL OF HOUSE.
Resolution for altering arrangement of seats, &c. and for accommodation of officers and visitors, 69
HAMPSHIRE COUNTY.
Petition of citizens, 14. 32. 41
Separate election. See Bills No. 69.
HAMPTON ACADEMY.
Report on petition, 107. 142. 144
HARDY COUNTY.
Petition of citizens, 16. 22. 40
HARPER'S FERRY.
Petition of citizens, 34
HARRISON COUNTY.
Petition of citizens, 24. 68. 72. 78. 104. 162. 137. 201
Separate election. See Bills No. 263.
HARRISON, RANDOLPH AND MONONGALIA.
Petition of citizens, 50. 63. 72
HARRISON AND TYLER.
Petitions of citizens withdrawn, 28
HASKINS, (JAMES.)
His petition, 19. 29. 41
See Bills No. 91.
HAXALL, (RICHARD B.)
His petition, 92. 104. 187
See Bills No. 217.
HAYES & MOORE.
Their petition, 84
HEDGESVILLE.
Town established. See Bills No. 83.
HENING'S JUSTICE.
Further number of last edition desired, 85
HENRICO COUNTY.
Petition of citizens, 36. 162. 201
Contested election reported on, 36
See Bills No. 162.
HENRY COUNTY.
Petition of citizens, 14
Report on, 20
Resolution for separate election, 14
See Bills No. 216.
HERDSMEN IN PRESTON.
See Bills No. 66.
HETH, (JOHN and others.)
Their petition, 93. 94. 201
HETH MANUFACTURING COMPANY.
See Bills No. 161.
HIGGINBOTHAM, (DANIEL.)
His petition, 16
See Bills No. 86.
HINES, (HIRAM.)
Report of committee of elections on his vote, 46
Agreed to by house, 48
HITE, (WILLIAM AND JACOB.)
Their petition, 74. 93. 136
HIXON, (FLEMING.)
His petition, 19. 124
HOG STEALING.
Resolution for amending act on subject, 59
See Bills No. 250.

HOLEMAN & TONEY.
Their petition, 81. 86. 136
HOLSTEIN RIVER, (NORTH FORK.)
Resolution for improving navigation, 33
Aid for constructing bridge across, 105
Report of committee, 140
HOOMES, (NELLY.)
Her petition, 101
HOPE, (JOHN.)
His petition, 61. 108. 137
HORSES, &c.
Resolution for altering taxes on, 43
HOUSE OF DELEGATES.
Resolution for altering arrangement of seats in hall, and for accommodating visitors and officers, 69
HUNTERSVILLE AND OHIO RIVER ROAD.
Resolution for opening eastern portion, 64
See Bills No. 110.
HUNTING RUN MINING COMPANY.
See Bills No. 159.

I

IDIOTS AND LUNATICS.
Amending law concerning, 142
INCENDIARY PUBLICATIONS.
See Abolition.
Governor's message, 6. 8
Message referred, 15
See Bills No. 180.
INDEX.
To journal. See Bills No. 77.
INSPECTORS.
Of tobacco, for increase of salaries of, at Dixon's warehouse, 154
Reported on, 245
Salaries of inspectors at Farmville. See Bills No. 329.
INSTRUCTIONS.
See Expunging Resolutions.
Resolutions of 1812, Doc. No. 9.
Resolutions on right, to be printed, 36
Letter of resignation of John Tyler, 171. 175
Vote on printing his letter recorded, 175
Letter of B. W. Leigh in answer to expunging resolutions, 186. 194
Mr. Watkins's resolutions expressing disapprobation of legislature to course of Mr. Leigh in disobeying instructions, 255
INTERNAL IMPROVEMENTS.
Act of incorporation no pledge to subscribe to stock by state, 106
Its funds, 217
INTERNAL IMPROVEMENT FUND.
Accounts of, Doc. No. 5.
State of fund, p. 5
Permanent funds, 6
Disposable funds, 7
Receipts, 8. 10
Disbursements, 9. 11
Estimate of certain and probable receipts, 12
Disbursements on account of the disposable funds, 13
Prospective statement relating to funds of board of public works, 14
Table of instalments due on subscriptions to stocks, 15
Summary of loans, 16
ISLE OF WIGHT.
Petition of citizens, 101

J

JACOBS, (JOHN J.)
Administrator of David Rogers; his petition, 98
JAILS.
Resolution for requiring security from creditors for fees of debtors, 49
Reported on, 135
Jailors to reside in dwellings attached to jails, 100
Reported on, 203
Last report acted on, 235
See Bills No. 242.

JAILS DESTROYED.
Resolution for removing criminals, 15
See Bills No. 34.
JAMES RIVER.
Lawful fence. See Bills No. 299.
JAMES RIVER COMPANY.
Governor's message, 11
JAMES RIVER AND KANAWHA COMPANY.
Governor's message, 11
Petition of stockholders, 103. 144. 183
Bill to be printed, 147
See Bills No. 285, also No. 275.
JAMES RIVER LANDHOLDERS.
Their petition, 112. 154. 163. 179
JEFFERSON COUNTY.
Petition of citizens, 34. 61. 134
JEFFERSON AND BERKELEY.
Petition of citizens, 105
JEFFERSON AND FREDERICK.
Petition of citizens, 77
JENKS, (JAMES.)
His claim enquired into; negatived, 162
Vote reconsidered; resolution agreed, 176
See Bills No. 312.
JEWETT, (SIMEON B.)
His petition, 81. 85. 134
JOHNSON, (AMOS.)
His petition, 26. 85. 136
See Bills No. 245.
JOHNSON, (GEORGE.)
His petition, 16. 32. 39
See Bills No. 79.
JOHNSON, (JAMES.)
His petition, 24. 61. 262
Report of committee of elections on his vote, 46
Agreed to by house, 48
JOHNSON, (JOHN.)
Report of committee of elections on his vote, 46
Agreed to by house, 48
JOHNSON, (JUDY.)
Her petition, 19
See Bills No. 88.
JOINT COMMITTEES.
Appointment required, rule 29, 5
Appointed, 13
Senate appointed committees on their part, 17
JOINT RESOLUTIONS.
See Surveys.
Mr. Dorman's resolution for distributing revenue arising from sales of public lands among states, 49, 50
On subject of expunging resolution of senate of the United States, 55, 56
On right of instruction, 56
See Expunging.
Survey of Richmond and York rail-road required, 86
Resolution agreed to by senate, 92
Survey of Smith's river, 94
Agreed to by senate, 100
Survey of road from Evansham to Jeffersonville, 96
Survey of roads from Gordonsville to Harrisonburg and Charlottesville, 94. 106. 111
Resolution for survey of Evansham and Jeffersonville road, agreed to by senate, 103
JOINT STOCK COMPANIES.
Passage of acts incorporating, no pledge by state to subscribe, 106
See Bills No. 182.
Report of committee of privileges against right to vote in elections, 249, 250
JOINT TENANTS.
Resolution for making partition of personal as well as of real estate, 44
JOINT VOTES.
See rule 44, 6
JORDAN & MURRELL.
Their petition, 38. 151. 199, 200
JORDAN & RUFF.
Their petition, 45. 80. 136
JOURNALS.
How kept, rule 19, 4

Documents bound up with, rule 38, 5, 6
Index to be made. See Bills No. 77.
Call for journal of executive council, 18
JUDGES.
Governor's message, 12
Resolution for electing judge in lieu of judge Semple, deceased, 15
Election of judge in fourth circuit postponed by senate, 19
Amendment amended by house, 19
Amendment agreed to by senate, 21
Election of judge proceeded in, 31
John B. Christian elected, 31
Resolution requiring librarian to deliver to them certain reports, 263
Rejected by senate, 264
JUDGMENTS.
Resolution for reducing costs on collection of money recovered by judgments and decrees, 15
See Bills No. 183.
See Bills No. 291.
JURIES.
Resolution for amending act concerning, 61
See Bills No. 318.
JURISDICTION OF MAGISTRATES.
Resolution for extending, 18
Report on resolution, 170
Taken up and acted on, 233
JUSTICES.
See *Magistrates*.

K

KANAWHA COUNTY.
Petition of citizens, 38. 121. 126. 180
Separate election. See Bills No. 151.
KANAWHA AND FAYETTE.
Petition of citizens, 22. 31. 41
KANAWHA LUMBER AND MINING COMPANY.
See Bills No. 125.
KANAWHA SLAVE INSURANCE COMPANY.
See Bills No. 104.
KEENAN, (PATRICK.)
His petition, 86. 212
KELSICK, (RICHARD'S ADM'R.)
His petition, 96. 110. 178
See Bills No. 283.
KENTUCKY.
Resolution on subject of abolition communicated by governor, 236. 238
KERN, (JAMES.)
To increase the height of his dam, 96
KING & QUEEN, CAROLINE AND ESSEX.
Petition of citizens, 34. 78
KLIPSTINE, (PETER.)
His claim for colours enquired into, 49. 121. 161
Committee discharged, 176
Report on resolution, 179
KNOX, (THOMAS F.)
His petition, 110
KREMER, (PETER.)
His petition, 50. 230

L

LAND BOUNTY.
Register to report quantity of land due by Virginia to officers and soldiers of revolution, 154
LANDS, (PUBLIC.)
Resolutions of Pennsylvania concerning distribution of proceeds of sales, 272, 273
See *Delinquent Lands*.
Mr. Dorman's resolution for distributing revenue arising from sales among states, 49, 50
Printed, Doc. No. 14.
Documents relating to the cession of the north-west territory, Doc. No. 36, 59
LAUREL HILL ROAD.
Resolution for providing for its construction, 74
See Bills No. 136.

LAWS.
Clerk to publish, rule 20, 4
LEE, (ARTHUR.)
His petition, 38. 72. 124. 126. 265
LEE, (GEORGE H.)
His memorial in behalf of judge Duncan, 186
LEESBURG.
Petition of citizens, 85. 102. 137. 155. 171. 203
See Bills No. 238.
LEIGH, (BENJAMIN W.)
Letter from him in answer to expunging resolutions, 186. 194
See Doc. No. 50.
Resolutions of Mr. Watkins disapproving his course in disobeying instructions, 256. 257
LEVY.
Resolution for annual publication of county levies, 64
LEWIS, (ANDREW.)
Report of committee of elections on his vote, 46
Disagreed to by house, 48
LEWIS AND BRAXTON.
Court days changed. See Bills No. 195.
LEWIS AND NICHOLAS COUNTIES.
Petition of citizens, 24. 28. 39
New county formed. See Bills No, 57.
LEWIS & SHANKS.
Their petition, 26. 33. 41
LEWISBURG AND BLUE SULPHUR SPRINGS COMPANY.
Petition of company, 83. 86. 135
See Bills No. 190.
LEWIS, (WILLIAM,) *Heirs*.
Their petition, 103. 262
LEXINGTON.
Petition of citizens, 79. 86. 96. 147. 199
LEXINGTON ARSENAL.
Military school to be established. See Bills No. 279, 82
Resolution for electing visitors to military school, 265
Agreed to by senate, 265
LEXINGTON AND RICHMOND TURNPIKE.
Resolution for incorporating company, 15
Reported on, 20
Resolution for subscription to stock, 154
Reported on, 186
Report acted on, 230
See Bills No. 40.
LIBRARY.
Number of committee on, rule 28, 5
Joint committee appointed, 13
For court of appeals at Lewisburg enlarged, 78
Resolution for electing librarian, 95
Agreed to by senate, 98
Election made ; vote recorded, 99
Amendment to rules enquired into, 100
Report of joint committee, 251
Librarian's report to committee, 252. 253
Account with librarian, 254
Books, &c. constituting library fund, 255
Further account of librarian, 256
LIBRARIAN.
Resolution requiring him to deliver to judges and clerks of superior courts certain books and reports, 261
Rejected by senate, 264
See Bills No. 277.
LICENSES TO RETAIL SPIRITS.
Resolution for amending act regulating, 57
See Bills No. 266.
LIMITATION OF ACTIONS.
Resolution to amend act limiting recoveries on judgments in other states, 18
Resolution for amending provision for obtaining bail in personal actions, 76
Committee discharged from resolution, 262
LINKHORN BAY.
Survey between, and Buck bay, 146
Agreed to by senate, 160
LITERARY FUND.
Report of board relative to University, colleges and academies, presented, 54

Resolution for distributing surplus, 63
See Bills No. 247.
Its debt, 217
State of fund, Doc. No. 4, p. 5
Permanent capital, 6
Stocks and loans, 7
Revenue, 8
Charges on fund, 9
Statement of school quotas, 10
Estimate of receipts and disbursements, 11
Abstract of accounts of treasurers of school commissioners, 12, 13, 14
Abstract of school commissioners' reports for 1834, 15, 16
School commissioners' reports of operations of district free schools, 17
Extracts from reports of school commissioners relating to primary schools in each county, 19-29
See *Colleges and Academies*.
LITTLE AND BIG DEEP CREEKS.
See Bills No. 20.
LLOYD, (WILSON.)
Report of committee of privileges on his vote, 46
Motion to amend negatived ; vote recorded, 48
LONDON & GARLAND.
Their dam, 152
Report of committee, 163
Acted on, 244
See Bills No. 335.
LORTON, (RICHARD *and others*.)
Their petition, 50
See Bills No. 238.
LOTTERIES.
Money disposed of, raised in Monroe. See Bills No. 74
LOUDOUN COUNTY.
Petition of citizens, 30. 45. 53. 59. 69. 95. 104. 133
LOUDOUN AND FAUQUIER.
Petition of citizens, 79. 81. 102. 136
LOUISA RAIL-ROAD.
Resolution for chartering company, 18
Cost of estimates for constructing, called for, 124
See Bills No. 17.
LOVETTSVILLE.
Petition of citizens, 57. 71
See Bills No. 142
LUCY AND DELILA.
Their petition, 33. 235. 235. 260
See Bills No. 343.
LUNATIC HOSPITALS.
Report of directors for Western, presented, 36
Report of directors at Williamsburg, 104
Additional report, 106
List of directors and officers, and other information required at Williamsburg, 85
See *Western Lunatic Hospital*.
See *Williamsburg Lunatic Hospital*.
LUNENBURG COUNTY.
Petition of citizens, 36. 69
Separate election. See Bills No. 112.
LYNCHBURG.
Petition of citizens, 16. 20. 29. 96. 103. 110. 140. 161. 163. 223
LYNCHBURG AND CAMPBELL TURNPIKE.
See Bills No. 211.
LYNCHBURG FEMALE ACADEMY.
See Bills No. 224.
LYNCHBURG ROADS.
See Bills No. 334.
LYNCHBURG AND PITTSYLVANIA TURNPIKE.
Petition of company, 104. 108. 140
LYNCHBURG AND TENNESSEE RAILROAD.
See Bills No. 56.
LYNHAVEN BAY.
Survey between, and North river, 146
Agreed to by senate, 160

M

M'COLGIN, (DAVID.)
Report of committee of elections on his vote, 46
Agreed to by house, 48
M'COY, (WILLIAM, General.)
Death announced, governor's message, 12
M'GAVOC, (HUGH.)
His petition, 26. 61. 126. 162. 223
M'HENRY, (JOHN.)
His petition, 161. 167. 222
M'LURE, (JOHN and others.)
Their petition, 86. 107. 137
MADISON AND CULPEPER
Petition in favour of Robin, 95. 179
MAGISTRATES.
Resolution for extending jurisdiction, 18
Resolution for amending or explaining the law concerning county courts and jurisdiction of justices, allowing appeals from their decisions, 44
MAJOR GENERAL.
Resolution for election for third division, 208
Agreed to by senate, 220
Election made; vote recorded, 221
MANCHESTER AND PETERSBURG TURNPIKE.
Petition of company, 68. 89. 135
MANCHESTER WOOL AND COTTON MANUFACTORY.
See Bills No. 71.
MANNING, (WILLIAM B.)
See *Sheriff of Norfolk.*
MARRIAGES.
Resolution for amending act concerning, 28
See Bills No. 191.
MARSHALL COUNTY.
Petition of citizens, 24. 30. 39
Leave bill separate election in. See Bills No. 12, 21
MARSHALL AND OHIO.
County courts changed. See Bills No. 235.
MARSHALL AND OHIO TURNPIKE.
See Bills No. 227.
MARTIN, (JAMES and others.)
Their petition, 16. 50. 59
See Bills No. 89.
MARTINSVILLE ACADEMY.
Resolution enquiring into expediency of incorporating, 15
Report of committee, 92
Acted on, 140
See Bills No. 225.
MARYLAND BOUNDARY.
See governor's message, 9
Letter from governor of Maryland, 44
Mr. Hopkins's resolution for referring governor's message relating to, 68
Taken up, 73
Committee discharged and laid on table, 105
Letter from governor Thomas relative to, Doc. No. 1, p. 12
Report and resolutions of Maryland, 12, 13, 14
Answer of governor Tazewell to letter of governor Thomas, 14, 15
Governor Thomas in reply, 16, 17
Letter of attorney general of Maryland, 18
Governor Tazewell to governor Thomas, 18
Governor Thomas in reply, 19
Governor Tazewell, rejoinder, 19, 20
Governor Thomas to governor Tazewell, Doc. No. 18.
MATHEWS COUNTY.
Petition of citizens, 96
MATOACA MANUFACTURING COMPANY.
See Bills No. 234.
MAYO'S BRIDGE.
To be incorporated into a joint stock company, 91
See Bills No. 252.
MEADOWVILLE.
See Bills No. 215.

MECHANICS ASSOCIATION OF FREDERICKSBURG.
Resolution for amending act, 59
MECHANICS INSTITUTE.
Of Norfolk and Portsmouth. See Bills No. 148.
MECHANICS MANUFACTURING COMPANY.
Resolution to incorporate, 49
See Bills No. 101.
MECKLENBURG.
Petition of citizens, 14
Report on, 20
MEDICAL COLLEGE, (RICHMOND.)
See Bills No. 146.
MEMBERS.
Not to be absent unless sick, rule 1, 3
Order in debate, rules 2, 3, 4, 3
When to vote when not, rules 7, 8, 4
To keep seats till speaker passes, rule 10, 4
See rule 11, 4
When absence revoked, rule 12, 4
Right to call for ayes and noes, rule 13, 4
Right to papers by giving receipts, rule 18, 4
Rule for presenting petitions, rule 26, 5
List of members, 273, 274
MERCHANTS' LICENSES.
See Bills No. 266.
MERCHANTS AND MECHANICS BANK OF WHEELING.
Annual statement of bank and branches, 144
Doc. No. 46.
MERCHANTS MANUFACTURING COMPANY.
Petition of president and directors, 50. 61
See Bills No. 100.
MESSAGES.
Between houses interchanged by clerks, rule 21, 4
See *Governor.*
MICHAELS, (ALBERT.)
His petition, 96. 105. 140
MIDDLEBOURN AND NORTH-WESTERN ROAD.
Resolution for constructing, 18
MIDLOTHIAN COAL COMPANY.
Leave to introduce bill. See Bills No. 1, 14
MILAM'S GAP ROAD.
Resolution for appropriating money, 33
See Bills No. 81.
MILITARY LAND BOUNTY.
Governor's message, 9
MILITARY SCHOOL.
To be established in connexion with Washington college, 82
Resolution for electing visitors, 265
Agreed to by senate, 265
See Bills No. 279.
MILITIA.
Number of committee, rule 28, 5
Committee appointed, 12
Governor's message, 12
Message referred, 18
Leave bill explaining act. See Bills Nos. 6 and 230.
Petition of officers of 58th regiment, 17. 72
of court of enquiry for 132d regiment, 17. 170
of officers of 56th regiment, 18. 170
Resolution of officers of 57th regiment, 18. 170
Resolution for supplying vacancy in 18th brigade by death of general M'Coy, 56
Resolution for enrolment of persons subject to duty, 94
Committee discharged therefrom, 147
Resolution for providing for better organization, instruction, &c. 61
Committee discharged therefrom, 61
Rule limiting committee suspended, and committee enlarged, 64
Resolution to amend or explain the 96th and 100th sections of general law, 82
See Bills No. 299.
Arms to volunteer companies, 118

Resolution for authorizing commandant of
147th regiment to fix place for training, 22
Reported on, 147
Acted on, 199
Resolution for increasing pay of musicians, 154
New regiment in Preston. See Bills No. 130
Return of strength of militia; arms, accoutrements and ammunition,
Doc. No. 1, pp. 22, 23
MILLINER, (ROBERT,) Heirs.
Allowance of bounty land enquired into, 74
MILLY.
Her petition, 95. 262
MISDEMEANORS.
In criminal prosecutions for, writs of error awardable, 59
MOLLOHON, (GEORGE G.)
Report of committee on his vote, 45
Agreed to by house, 46
MONONGALIA COUNTY.
Petition of citizens, 16, 17. 19, 20. 22. 26. 40. 59. 71
Separate election. See Bills 113.
MONONGALIA ACADEMY.
Petition of trustees, 199. 262
MONONGALIA, PRESTON AND TYLER.
Petition of citizens, 43. 55
MONONGALIA, RANDOLPH AND HARRISON.
Petition of citizens, 50. 63. 72
MONONGALIA, RANDOLPH AND PRESTON.
Petition of citizens, 26. 29. 40
MONROE COUNTY.
Petition of citizens, 18. 24. 45. 51. 55
Money raised by lottery disposed of. See Bills No. 74.
MONROE, BOTETOURT, BEDFORD, &c.
Petition of citizens, 57
MONTGOMERY COUNTY.
Petition of citizens, 16
MONTGOMERY, (THOMAS.)
His remonstrance, 61
MOORE, (FREDERICK.)
His petition, 161. 225. 232
See Bills No. 330.
MOORE & HAYES.
Their petition, 84
MOORFIELD.
See Bills No. 290.
MOORFIELD AND NORTH-WESTERN TURNPIKE.
Resolution for survey, 53
See Bills No. 82.
MOORFIELD AND WARDENSVILLE ROAD.
Resolution for appropriating money to aid in constructing, 55
Report of committee, 107
MORGAN, (CHARLOTTE.)
See Bills No. 84.
MORGAN COUNTY.
Petition of citizens, 66. 262
MORTON, (THOMAS A.)
His petition, 53. 76. 134
His dam. See Bills No. 212.
MOUNDSVILLE.
Petition of citizens, 96. 179
See Bills No. 235.
MOUNT CRAWFORD TOWN.
Leave to bring in bill amending act establishing town. See Bills No. 5, 15
MUNFORD, (GEORGE W.)
Elected clerk to house, 3
MURRELL & JORDAN.
Their petition, 36. 151. 199, 200
MUSEUM.
See Bills No. 296.
MUSICIANS.
Increase of pay, 154
Committee discharged from resolution, 262

N

NANSEMOND COUNTY.
Petition of citizens, 59. 81. 134
NARROW FALLS TURNPIKE.
See Bills No. 51.
NATURAL BRIDGE TURNPIKE.
See Bills No. 121.
NAVAL OFFICERS.
See governor's message, 8, 9
Referred, 25
NAVIGATION COMPANIES.
Form for general law, 96
NEILL, (BERNARD O.)
His petition, 35. 93
NELSON COUNTY.
Petition of citizens, 14. 24. 34. 176
Separate election. See Bills No. 24.
NELSON AND ALBEMARLE.
Petition of citizens, 22. 58. 61. 148
NELSON AND ALBEMARLE UNION FACTORY COMPANY.
See Bills No. 102.
NELSON, BUCKINGHAM AND FLUVANNA.
Petition of citizens, 34
NEWBURN AND RED SULPHUR SPRINGS TURNPIKE.
See Bills No. 72.
NEW COUNTIES.
Formed of Lewis and Nicholas. See Bills No. 57.
NEW GLASGOW.
See Bills No. 179.
NEW HOPE GOLD MINE COMPANY.
See Bills No. 126.
NEWTOWN (STEPHENSBURG) ACADEMY.
Petition of trustees, 16. 167
NEWTOWN STEPHENSBURG LIBRARY COMPANY.
See Bills No. 41.
NICHOLAS COUNTY
Petition of citizens, 107
NICHOLAS AND LEWIS.
Petition of citizens, 24. 23. 39. 168. 231
NICHOLAS, (JOHN.)
His petition, 64. 262
NICHOLAS, (PHILIP N.)
President of Farmers bank of Virginia in answer to resolution of December 11th, 38
Furnishes information called for, 99
Referred to committee, 100
NORFOLK ACADEMY.
Petition of trustees, 34
NORFOLK BOROUGH.
Petition of citizens, 13, 14. 22. 75
Proceedings of meeting relative to communication from president of Bank of Virginia, 142
Answer of John Brockenbrough, 146
NORFOLK COUNTY.
Petition of citizens, 14. 20. 91. 96. 136. 168
Terms of superior court altered and increased. See Bills No. 241.
NORFOLK AND PORTSMOUTH MECHANICS INSTITUTE.
Petition of managers, 34. 63. 71
NORFOLK SAVINGS INSTITUTION.
See Bills No. 293.
NORTHAMPTON COUNTY.
Proceedings of citizens on abolition subject, 33
NORTH CAROLINA.
Governor transmits resolutions from, on subject of abolition, 51
NORTH RIVER.
Survey between, and Lynhaven bay, 146
Agreed to by senate, 160
NORTHUMBERLAND COUNTY.
Petition of citizens, 94. 168. 231
Separate election. See Bills No. 331.
NORTH-WESTERN BANK.
Returns transmitted by governor, 34
Petition of president and directors, 96
Statement of condition, Doc. No. 8.

NORTH-WESTERN AND BEVERLEY OR LEADING CREEK ROAD.
See Bills No. 28.
NORTH-WESTERN AND MIDDLEBOURN ROAD.
Resolution for constructing, 18
NORTH-WESTERN TERRITORY.
Respecting its cession by Virginia to United States, Doc. No. 36.
NORTH-WESTERN TURNPIKE.
Mode of constructing to be changed, 85
Superintendence, 85
Report on expediency of changing route, 163
Report on resolution concerning superintendence, 200
See Bills No. 58.
Tolls regulated. See Bills No. 62.
NOTTOWAY RIVER.
Resolution for survey, 161
Agreed to by senate, 176

O

OFFENCES ON RAIL-ROADS.
Resolution providing for punishing, 73
See Bills No. 273.
OFFICERS OF NINETEENTH REGIMENT.
Their petition, 202. 262
OFFICERS OF FIFTY-SIXTH REGIMENT.
Their petition, 18. 170
OFFICERS OF FIFTY-SEVENTH REGIMENT.
Their petition, 18. 170
OFFICERS OF FIFTY-EIGHTH REGIMENT.
Their petition, 17. 72
OFFICERS OF ONE HUNDRED AND FOURTH REGIMENT.
Their petition, 66. 69
OFFICERS OF ONE HUNDRED AND SIXTEENTH AND ONE HUNDRED AND FOYTY-FIFTH REGIMENTS.
Their petition, 110. 121
OFFICERS OF ONE HUNDRED AND THIRTY-SECOND REGIMENT.
Their petition, 170
OFFICERS OF VIRGINIA STATE LINE AND NAVY.
List of, Doc. No. 6, pp. 75-118
OHIO COUNTY.
Petition of citizens, 19. 24. 35. 53. 65. 72. 91. 95. 262
Separate election. See Bills No. 114.
Seat of justice. See Bills No. 144.
OHIO AND MARSHALL.
School quotas. See Bills No. 25, 29
County courts changed. See Bills No. 235.
OHIO RIVER, MORGANTOWN AND MARYLAND ROAD.
See Bills No. 120; title changed.
OHIO, (STATE OF.)
Resolutions relating to the election of president and vice-president of the United States, 229
OLINGER, (JOHN C.)
His petition, 43
ONANCOCK FERRY.
See Bills No. 49.
ORANGE COUNTY.
Petition of citizens, 59. 91. 93. 95. 140
ORANGE SAVINGS SOCIETY.
See Bills No. 153.
ORDERS.
In debate, rules 2, 3, 4, 3
ORDERS OF DAY.
See rule 14, 4
OVERSEERS OF POOR.
Resolution for requiring them to hire out free negroes, 59
See Bills No. 313.

OWENS, (WILLIAM.)
His claim enquired into, 170
Committee discharged from resolution concerning, 262
OYSTERS.
To amend act for protecting, 96
See Bills No. 149.
In Nansemond River. See Bills No. 259.

P

PACKING COTTON.
See Bills No. 205.
PAGE COUNTY.
Petition of citizens, 142. 156. 200
PALMER, (JOSEPH,) *Administrator*.
His petition, 14. 104. 136
PAMUNKEY RIVER.
For incorporating company to improve navigation, 154
Committee of roads discharged from bringing in bill concerning, 185
Resolution for survey, 225
Agreed to by senate, 230
PARKER, (HENRY.)
His petition, 26. 32. 42
PARKERSBURG.
Petition of citizens, 38
PARRIOTT, (CHRISTOPHER.)
His petition, 19. 73. 194
PARTITION.
Resolution for extending provision of law for making partition of real estate where parties are interested or unknown, to personal estate, 44
PATENTS.
Transcript of number, dates, &c. to be furnished county court offices, 95
Committee discharged from resolution, 262
PATRICK COUNTY
Petition of citizens, 14. 20. 64. 108. 135. 176
Documents in contested election, 38
Report upon contested election, 64
Special report, 66. 67
PAXTON, (JAMES.)
See Bills No. 172.
PEARISBURG.
Petition of citizens, 43. 71
PENDLETON, (HUGH N.)
Appointed clerk to committees of roads, &c. and of schools and colleges, 13
PENDLETON, (SAMUEL S.)
His petition, 118. 176. 232
PENITENTIARY.
Number of committee on, rule 28, 5
Committee appointed, 13
Report of superintendent presented, 23
Committee to examine, enlarged, 85
Resolution for making provision for confining convicts of federal courts, 125
Resolution for electing superintendent and general agent, 160
Election made; vote recorded, 166, 167
Report of joint committee presented, 203
Report of joint committee, 232
Resolution for increasing compensation of assistant keepers, clerk, sergeant and porter, 233
Report of directors, Doc. No. 7.
General agent's account current, pp. 2, 3
Superintendent's report, 4-7
In account with state, 8, 9
Operations of shoe and tailors' apartment, 10, 11
Operations of weaving apartment, 12, 13
Prisoners remaining in 1834, and received, pardoned, dead and discharged since, 14
Prisoners received since 1834, 15
Confined on 30th September, 1835, 16
Natives and foreigners remaining then, 17
Ages of convicts, 17
Hospital returns, 19
Condition and employments of convicts, 20
Cost of shed, 21
Physician's and superintendent's reports, 22

INDEX.

PENNSYLVANIA.
Resolutions concerning distribution of proceeds of sales of public lands, 272, 273
PENNSYLVANIA, CLARKSBURG AND BEVERLEY ROAD.
See Bills No. 50.
PERSONS OF COLOUR.
See Bills No. 344.
PETERSBURG.
Petitions of citizens, 14. 16. 20. 35. 40, 41. 57. 69. 93. 95. 106. 141. 156. 180. 200
Petition of merchants, 14. 29. 40. 44. 122
Commissioner in chancery. See Bills No. 26.
New street opened. See Bills No. 320.
PETERSBURG NAVIGATION COMPANY.
See Bills No. 55.
PETERSBURG AND PRINCE GEORGE.
Petition of citizens, 32. 33. 86. 91. 107. 140
PETERSBURG RAIL-ROAD COMPANY.
See Bills No. 171.
PETITIONS.
Once rejected, when allowed to be presented, rule 23, 4
Notice of presentation, rule 24, 4
For claims to be accompanied with reasons for rejection from executive or auditor, rule 25, 4
When allowed to be withdrawn, rule 26, 5
Not read unless required; rule for presenting, rule 27, 5
Abingdon, 23
Adams, (Isaac,) 13. 38. 64. 66. 67
Albemarle, 34. 60. 78, 79. 102. 156. 160. 166. 168. 170
Albemarle and Buckingham, 199
Albemarle and Fluvanna, 78. 179
Albemarle and Fredericksburg agricultural society, 89
Albemarle and Nelson, 22. 61. 93. 107. 136. 148
Albemarle and Rockingham, 170. 203
Alleghany, 101
Alleghany and Rockbridge, 38. 63. 71
Amelia, 16
Amelia, Prince Edward and Cumberland, 83
Anderson, (David,) 104
Anderson, (Henry,) 26. 106. 140. 212. 231
Anderson, (Isabella,) 45. 81
Anderson, (Littlepage,) 142. 208
Anderson, (Richard,) 50. 63. 71
Andy, 142. 170. 232
Ann, 94. 110. 178
Anthony and Frazier, 105. 195. 234
Appomattox company, 36. 76. 100. 107
Augusta, 33
Augusta and Rockingham, 169. 203
Bailey, (Joseph,) 16. 76. 135
Baker, (Jonas,) 95. 262
Baldwin, (Cornelius C.) 147. 199
Bank of the Valley stockholders, 32
Barns, (John, 26. 110. 178
Bassett, 95. 262
Bath county, 18. 23. 30, 31
Bedford county, 16. 19. 20. 26. 35 73 95. 106. 139
Bedford, Botetourt, Greenbrier, &c. 57
Benson, (John,) 131
Berkeley county, 14. 31. 26. 32. 42. 45. 53. 84. 93
Berkeley and Jefferson, 105
Bidgood, (Benjamin,) 22. 72
Binns, (Richard,) 104. 262
Blackwell, (Joseph,) 94. 262
Blankenship, (Eli,) 77. 160. 201
Bolling, (Richard,) 26. 33. 40
Boomer, (Lucy,) 36. 62. 136
Booth, (William,) 18. 23
Botetourt county, 27. 64. 75, 76. 83. 92. 95. 108. 175
Botetourt, Bedford, Monroe, &c. 57
Botetourt and Franklin, 77. 160 201
Botetourt, Rockbridge and Alleghany, 38. 57. 63. 71
Botts, (John M.) 13. 36. 37
Bough, (Toney and Jacob,) 26. 150. 199
Braden, (Noble B.) 19. 81. 134
Briggs, (Robert and others,) 36. 92. 103
Brook, (Isaac,) 66. 91. 135

Brooke academy, 19
Brooke county, 53. 73. 124
Brooke, (William,) 104. 262
Brownsburg convention, 36. 141. 180
Brown, (William,) 14. 17. 20
Brown, (William and others,) 110
Buckingham county, 131. 142. 160. 170. 201
Buckingham and Albemarle, 199
Buckingham, Nelson and Fluvanna, 34
Butler, (Reuben,) 94. 262
Buzadone, (Laurieut,) 160. 165
Byrne, (Thomas,) 34. 151. 200
Campbell county, 16. 20. 69. 73. 124
Caroline, King & Queen and Essex, 34. 7d. 132
Carper and Rosson, 57. 73
Carter, (Jane,) 104. 262
Carter, (Thomas,) heirs, 22. 61. 262
Chaplins, (William and others,) 24
Charlotte, 14. 29
Chavis, (Randal,) 86. 262
Chesapeake and Ohio canal company, 73. 107. 136. 145. 159. 201 208, 209
Chesterfield rail-road company, 118. 201
Chevallie, (Peter J.) 142. 168. 186. 233
Chew, (John,) 76, 77. 85. 135
Circuit, thirteenth, 77. 262
Clarksville, 33. 38. 45. 59. 86. 96. 140
Clarksville, Petersburg, Richmond, &c. 109. 167
Colston, (Edward,) 85. 96. 140
Cooper, (Milly,) 16. 186. 233
Covington, 104. 137
Crouch, (John and others, 32. 59. 151. 200
Crutchfield, (Stapleton,) 80. 93. 136. 151. 232
Culpeper and Madison, 95. 179
Culpeper, Stafford, Fauquier, &c. 74
Culpeper, (Thomas,) 16. 76. 135
Cumberland county, 16. 34. 35. 52. 53. 147. 163
Cumberland, Amelia and Prince Edward, 83
Danville, 14. 20
Danville convention, 98. 106
Delila and Lucy, 33. 225. 235. 260
Dismal swamp canal company, 98. 136
District the seventh, 77
Dragon swamp canal company, 66. 78. 96. 101
Duncan, (Edwin B.) 142. 186
Dunlap, (Francis F.) 93. 262
Edmonds, (Ann,) 105. 110. 178
Edwards, (Richard H.) 34. 92. 140. 232
Elizabeth City county, 107. 142. 144
Elizabethtown and Moundsville, 98. 118. 179
Essex, Caroline, &c. 34. 35. 78
Estillville, 26. 71. 167
Evans and Williams, 151. 163. 223
Evansham, 101. 104. 137
Eyre, (Severn,) 56. 103. 139
Fairfax county, 18. 44. 95. 162. 212
Fairfield, 79. 147. 199
Fallsbridge turnpike, 96. 107. 137
Falmouth and Fredericksburg, 13
Farmville, 13. 16. 34. 41. 71. 106. 142. 157. 186. 192. 233
Fauntleroy, (Henry,) 94. 262
Fauquier county, 154. 262
Fauquier and Loudoun, 79. 81. 136. 262
Fauquier, Stafford, Culpeper, &c. 74
Fayette county, 22. 35. 52. 53. 147. 201. 231
Fayette and Kanawha, 22. 31. 41
Fenn, (William,) 29. 37. 73. 125
Findley and Rogers, 29. 230. 233
Fisher, (William,) 19. 31. 40
Floyd county, 14. 20
Fluvanna county, 176
Fluvanna and Albemarle, 78. 179
Fluvanna, Buckingham and Nelson, 34
Ford, (Shelton,) 29. 32. 39
Franklin county, 14. 20
Franklin and Botetourt, 77. 160. 201
Frazier and Anthony, 105. 195. 234
Frederick county, 14. 16. 32. 36. 41. 45. 69. 73. 80. 83, 84. 95. 103. 145
Frederick and Jefferson, 77
Frederick and Shenandoah, 14. 50. 73, 74. 93. 101. 140. 144
Fredericksburg, 17. 30. 161. 262

Fredericksburg and Albemarle agricultural society, 80
Fredericksburg female orphan asylum, 32. 154. 200
Gloucester, 78. 80. 245. 250
Goochland, 57. 63. 71. 147. 163
Goodman, (George W.) 75
Goodwin, (Edward,) 111. 121. 186. 233
Grandville, 16. 27
Graves, (T. W.) 126. 212
Grayson county, 93. 101. 139
Greenbrier, Monroe, Botetourt, &c. 57
Green, (Duff,) 16. 29. 40. 66. 70
Greeneville county, 96. 107. 139
Grigsby, (J. D.) 98. 150 199
Halifax county, 14. 20. 34, 35. 92. 103
Hampshire county, 14. 32. 41
Hardy and Rockingham, 16. 22. 40
Harper's Ferry citizens, 34
Harrison county, 24. 36. 68. 72. 78. 104. 137. 162. 201
Harrison, Monongalia and Randolph, 50. 63. 72
Harrison and Tyler, 29
Haskins, (James,) 19. 29. 41
Hazall, (Richard B.) 92. 104. 137
Hayes and Moore, 84
Henrico county, 36. 162. 201
Henry county, 14. 20
Heth, (John and others,) 93, 94. 201
Higginbotham, (Daniel,) 16. 33. 41
Hite, (Jacob and William,) 74. 33. 136
Hixon and Braden, 19. 134
Holeman and Toney, 81. 96. 136
Hoomes, (Nelly,) 101
Hope, (John,) 61. 108. 137
Isle of Wight county, 101
Jacobs, (John J.) 98
James river and Kanawha company, 103. 144. 163
James river owners of property, 112. 154. 162. 179
Jefferson county, 34. 81. 134
Jefferson and Berkeley, 105
Jefferson and Frederick, 77
Jewett, (Simeon B.) 81. 85. 134
Johnson, (Amos,) 26. 85. 136
Johnson, (George,) 16. 22. 39
Johnson, (James,) 24. 61. 262
Johnson, (Judy,) 19. 29. 41
Jordan & Murrell, 38. 151. 199, 200
Jordan and Ruff, 45. 80. 136
Kanawha county, 38. 121. 126. 180
Kanawha and Fayette, 22. 31. 41
Keenan, (Patrick,) 86. 212
Kelsick, (Richard,) administrator, 96. 110. 178
King & Queen, Caroline and Essex, 34. 78
Klipstine, (Peter,) 121
Knox, (Thomas F.) 110
Kremer, (Peter,) 50. 230
Lee, (Arthur,) 38. 72. 124. 126. 265
Lee, (George Hay,) 186
Leesburg, 85. 102. 137. 155. 171. 203
Lewis and Nicholas counties, 24. 28. 39
Lewis and Shanks, 26. 33. 41
Lewis, (William,) 103. 262
Lewisburg and Blue Sulphur springs company, 83. 86. 135
Lexington, 79. 86. 92. 147. 199
Lorton, (Richard) and others, 50. 81. 134
Loudoun county, 30. 45. 53. 59. 69. 81. 95. 104. 133
Loudoun and Fauquier, 79. 81. 102. 136. 262
Lovettsville, 57. 71
Lucy and Delila, 33. 225. 235. 260
Lunenburg county, 36. 69
Lynchburg, 16. 20. 29. 96. 103. 140. 161. 163. 223
Lynchburg and Pittsylvania turnpike, 104. 106. 140
Lynchburg, Richmond, Petersburg and Clarksville, 109. 167
M'Gavoc, (Hugh,) 26. 61. 126. 162. 223
M'Henry, (John,) 161. 167. 222
M'Lure, (John,) 86. 107. 137

Madison and Culpeper,	95. 179	Ramsay, (William,)	94. 262
Manchester and Petersburg turnpike,	68. 82. 135	Randolph academy,	75. 167
Marshall county,	24. 30. 39	Randolph, Harrison and Monongalia,	50. 63. 72
Martin, (James,)	16. 50. 52	Randolph, Monongalia and Preston,	26. 29. 40
Mathews county,	96	Randolph and Preston,	19. 21, 22
Mecklenburg county,	14. 20	Randolph and Rives,	13. 155. 184, 185
Merchants manufacturing company,	50. 61	Rappahannock canal company,	126
Michaels, (Albert,)	98. 105. 140	Rappahannock county,	74
Millinor, (Robert,)	262	Read, (Anderson,)	19. 95. 139
Milly,	95. 262	Richmond city, 22. 37. 43. 50. 53. 71. 78. 86. 105,	
Monongalia county, 16, 17. 19, 20. 26. 40. 59. 71		109. 118. 142. 160. 201	
Monongalia academy,	199. 262	Richmond, Lynchburg, Petersburg and	
Monongalia, Harrison and Randolph,	50. 63. 72	Clarksville,	109. 167
Monongalia, Preston and Tyler,	43. 55	Richmond and Petersburg,	85
Monongalia, Randolph and Preston,	26. 29. 40	Riggan, (William H.)	106. 126. 179
Monroe county,	18. 24. 45- 51. 55	Rives and Randolph,	13. 155. 184. 185
Monroe, Greenbrier, Botetourt, &c.	57	Roanoke navigation company,	78. 86
Montgomery county,	18	Robertson, (John T.)	93. 156. 201
Montgomery, (Thomas,)	61	Robin,	95. 126
Moore, (Frederick,)	161. 225. 232	Robinson, (Abner,)	156. 186. 233
Moore and Hayes,	84	Rockbridge county,	45. 169
Morgan, (Charlotte,)	14. 39	Rockbridge and Botetourt,	38. 67. 63. 71
Morgan county,	66 262	Rockingham county,	16. 64. 82. 83. 134
Morton, (Thomas A.)	53. 76. 134	Rockingham and Albemarle,	170. 203
Moundsville and Elizabethtown,	98. 179	Rockingham and Augusta,	169. 203
Murrell and Jordan,	38. 151. 199, 200	Rockingham and Hardy,	16. 22
Nansemond county,	59. 81. 134	Rogers's administrator,	98. 262
Neill, (Bernard O.)	35. 93	Rogers and Findley,	29. 230. 233
Nelson county,	14. 24. 34. 176	Rowson and Carper,	57. 73
Nelson and Albemarle,	22. 56. 61. 146	Ruff and Jordan,	45. 80. 136
Nelson, Buckingham and Fluvanna,	34	Rumney, (William,)	94. 262
Newtown Stephensburg academy,	16. 167	Saint Bride's academy,	142. 167
Nicholas and Lewis,	24. 28. 39. 168. 231	Salem,	95. 139
Nicholas, (John,)	64. 262	Saunders, (Bassett,)	95. 262
Norfolk academy,	74	Scott county,	16. 20. 63. 170. 186. 230
Norfolk borough,	13, 14. 22. 75	Scottsville,	34
Norfolk county,	91. 96. 136. 168	Scott, (William,)	38. 54
Norfolk and Portsmouth mechanics institute,		Shanks and Lewis,	26. 33. 41
	34. 63. 71	Sharpe, (Linceford,)	94. 262
Northumberland county,	94. 168. 231	Shaver, (John,)	18. 23
North-western bank,	95	Shenandoah county,	14. 84
Officers of 19th regiment,	202. 262	Shenandoah and Frederick,	14. 50. 93. 144
Officers of 56th regiment,	18. 170	Simms, (Levi,)	118. 151. 199
Officers of 57th regiment,	18. 170	Skurry, (David,)	101. 202
Officers of 58th regiment,	17. 72	Smithfield,	107. 137
Officers of 104th regiment,	66. 69	Smith, (James,)	36. 162. 222
Officers of 116th and 145th regiments,	110. 191	Smyth county, 45. 59. 118. 163. 167. 223. 231	
Officers of 132d regiment,	170	Smyth school commissioners,	14
Ohio county,	19. 24. 35. 53. 65. 72. 91. 262	Snead, (Jesse,)	32. 59. 200
Olinger, (John C.)	43	Snodgrass, (Michael,)	64
Orange county,	59. 91. 93. 95. 140	Stackhouse, (John and Nancy,)	29. 61. 262
Page county,	142. 156. 200	Stafford, Culpeper, Fauquier,	74
Palmer, (Joseph,)	14. 104. 136	Stafford county,	19. 32. 42
Parker, (Henry F.)	26. 32. 42	Starks, (Daniel,)	35. 155. 200
Parkersburg,	29	Stephen,	19 75 79. 155. 220
Parriott, (Christopher,)	19. 73. 194	Sturm, (Jesse,)	16. 20
Patrick county,	14. 20. 84. 106. 135. 176	Suffolk,	25. 54
Pearisburg,	43. 71	Tazewell county,	121. 141. 180
Pendleton, (Samuel S.)	118. 176. 232	Tomlinson, (Solomon,)	96. 178
Petersburg,	14. 16. 20. 29. 35. 40, 41. 57. 69. 93	Toney and Holeman,	81. 86. 136
	95. 108. 141. 156. 180. 200	Townes, (William,)	64. 112. 179
Petersburg merchants,	14. 40. 44. 122	Tuckahoe canal company,	50
Petersburg and Prince George,	66. 91. 107	Turner, (Stephen,)	142. 162
Petersburg, Richmond, Lynchburg and		Tutt, (Ann M.)	16. 50. 51
Clarksville,	109. 167	Tyler county,	64. 69
Pittsylvania county,	14. 20. 85. 106. 139	Tyler and Harrison,	28
Pittsylvania and Lynchburg turnpike,		Tyler, Preston and Monongalia,	43. 55
	104. 108. 140	Upper Appomattox company,	36. 76. 100. 107
Portsmouth,	13, 14. 20. 29. 32. 42. 104. 168. 231	Upperville,	154. 167
Portsmouth and Roanoke rail-road company,		Wallace, (Celinda C.)	19. 108. 136
	14. 17. 20. 91. 96. 168	Walls, (George and Thomas,)	98. 100. 108. 124
Powhatan county,	16, 17. 20. 110. 142. 160. 201	Ward, (Berkley,)	16. 73. 125. 169. 186. 224
Preston county,		Warrenton,	176
	16. 17. 19. 21. 26. 28, 29. 31. 39, 40, 41. 43	Waring, (Thomas,) heirs,	59. 76. 134
Preston, Monongalia and Randolph,		Waterford,	22. 50. 51. 139
	26. 29. 40. 43. 55	Wedderburn, (William,)	19. 73. 124
Preston and Randolph,	19. 22	Wells, (Ephraim,)	169
Price, (George) and others,	96. 126	Wender, (John C.)	19. 28. 30. 34. 40. 78. 84
Price, (Jacob,)	34. 54	Wheeling,	34. 69
Price, (Samuel,)	13. 43. 45. 49	Wheeling and Belmont bridge company,	30. 118. 179
Prince Edward, Amelia and Cumberland,	87	Wheeling savings institution,	35. 155. 200
Prince George and Petersburg,	32, 33. 91. 140	Williams, (Charles,)	33. 85. 134
Princess Anne county,	142. 156. 200	Williams, (Elisha B.)	151. 163. 223
Ramsay, (Benjamin,)	131	Williams and Evans,	

Winchester,	59. 68. 72
Winn, (Jesse,)	102. 262
Wood, (John,)	28. 33. 41
Wythe county,	14. 19, 20 28. 40
Zane, (Daniel and Ebenezer,)	94. 156. 201
Zull, (William,)	78. 84. 134
PHENIX MINING COMPANY.	
See Bills No. 14,	23
PILOTS.	
See Bills No 127.	
PITTENGER, (JOHN.)	
His claim enquired into,	105
See Bills No. 230.	
PITTSYLVANIA COUNTY.	
Petition of citizens,	14. 20. 85. 106. 139
Separate election. See Bills No. 253.	
PITTSYLVANIA AND LYNCHBURG TURNPIKE.	
See Bills No. 189.	
POCATALICO RIVER.	
See Bills No. 152.	
PORTSMOUTH.	
Petition of citizens,	
13, 14. 20. 29. 32. 42. 104. 168. 231	
See Bills No. 42	
Trustees increased and powers enlarged.	
See Bills No. 243.	
Water street. See Bills No. 328.	
PORTSMOUTH ARTILLERY COMPANY.	
See Bills No. 140.	
PORTSMOUTH AND CHESAPEAKE COMPANY.	
To incorporate transportation company,	99
See Bills No. 181.	
PORTSMOUTH PROVIDENT SOCIETY.	
See Bills No. 274.	
PORTSMOUTH AND ROANOKE RAILROAD COMPANY.	
Petition of company, 14. 17. 20. 22. 91. 96. 168	
See Bills No. 33.	
POTOWMAC RIVER.	
Portion of margin in Berkeley legal fence.	
See Bills No. 246.	
Resolution for aqueduct,	257
POTOWMAC SILK AND AGRICULTURAL COMPANY.	
See Bills No. 218.	
POWHATAN COUNTY.	
Petition of citizens, 16, 17. 20. 110. 142. 160. 201	
See Bills No. 162.	
PRESIDENT AND VICE-PRESIDENT OF THE UNITED STATES.	
Resolution of state of Ohio concerning their election presented,	229
See Document No. 56.	
PRESIDENT OF THE UNITED STATES.	
Letter of governor to him on subject of refusal of captain Dallas to permit process to be served on board his ship, Doc. No. 1, p. 11	
PRESTON COUNTY.	
Petition of citizens,	
16, 17. 19. 21. 26. 28, 29. 31. 39, 40, 41. 43	
Separate election. See Bills No. 46.	
New regiment. See Bills No. 130.	
PRESTON, MONONGALIA AND TYLER.	
Petition of citizens,	26. 29. 40. 43. 55
PRESTON AND OHIO RIVER ROAD.	
See Bills No. 120.	
PRESTON AND RANDOLPH.	
Report of committee on petition,	19. 22
PRICE, (GEORGE) AND OTHERS.	
Their petition,	96. 126
PRICE, (JACOB.)	
His petition,	34. 54
PRICE, (SAMUEL.)	
	13. 43
Report on contested election acted on,	45. 49
PRICE'S MOUNTAIN TURNPIKE.	
See Bills No. 254.	
PRICE'S AND SWEET SPRINGS MOUNTAIN.	
Committee of roads discharged from petitions for road across mountain,	73
For incorporating joint stock company,	73

INDEX.

PRIMARY SCHOOLS.
Extracts from reports of school commissioners relating to, in each county, Doc. No. 4, pp. 19-29

PRINCE EDWARD, AMELIA, &c.
Petition of citizens, 83

PRINCE GEORGE AND PETERSBURG.
Petition of citizens, 32, 33. 91. 140

PRINCESS ANNE COUNTY.
Instructions to delegate to vote for extending Portsmouth and Roanoke rail-road presented, 75
Petition of citizens, 142. 156. 200

PRINCIPAL ENGINEER.
Resolution to provide him an office in capitol, 154
Committee discharged therefrom, 212
Resolution for election, 160
Agreed to by senate, 164
Election made; vote recorded, 166, 167

PRINTER, (PUBLIC.)
How to print journal and documents, rule 38, 5, 6
Joint resolution for electing, 14
Senate agree to resolution, 17
Election made; vote recorded; Thomas Ritchie elected, 17

PRISONERS.
Resolution for removal where jails destroyed, 15
See Bills No. 34.

PRIVILEGE.
When persons taken in custody for breach of, rule 42.

PRIVILEGED SEATS.
See rule 16, 4
Within bar of house, 84

PRIVILEGES AND ELECTIONS.
Number of committee, rule 28, 5
To report their reasons in contested elections, rule 32, 5
To examine qualifications of members and sheriffs' returns, rule 33, 5
Committee, of whom to consist, 12
Appointment of clerk to committee postponed, 13
Joshua W. Fry elected clerk to committee, 15
Required to take up petitions, 15
Documents referred to committee, 17
Committee granted authority to send for persons and papers, 17
Leave to committee to sit during session, 21
Resolution enquiring whether stockholders in corporations have right of suffrage, 44
Report upon contested election from Patrick presented, 64
Special report acted on, 66, 67
Report of committee on qualifications of members and returns of elections, 219
Clerk discharged, 219
Report of committee on qualifications and returns of elections acted on, 234
Report on resolution concerning right of stockholders in companies to exercise suffrage, 235
Taken up and read; laid on table, 249. 250

PROCESS.
Service prevented by naval officer, governor's message, 8, 9
Referred to committee, 25
Resolution for authorizing sheriffs to serve process any where against absconding debtors, 69

PROCESS BOOKS.
Fees to clerks of counties, &c. for keeping, 18
Report on resolution, 150
Acted on, 199

PROCESSIONING.
For amending act concerning, 111
Report thereon, 183
See Bills No. 137. Southampton county.
Repealing law requiring, in certain counties. See Bills No. 208.
Report on resolution, 147
See Bills No. 292.

PROPOSITIONS AND GRIEVANCES.
Number of committee, rule 28, 5
Committee, of whom composed, 12

PROTEST.
To expunging resolutions submitted by Mr. Botts, 124

PUBLIC GUARD.
Governor's message, 11, 12
See Bills No. 185.

PUBLIC LANDS.
Mr. Dorman's resolution for distributing revenue, arising from sales of public lands, among states, 49, 50

PUBLIC PROPERTY.
Superintendent of public buildings to rent out old stable, &c. 262
Resolution agreed to by senate, 264

PUBLIC WAREHOUSE.
Resolution for enlarging, in Richmond, 28
See Bills No. 60.

Q

QUALIFICATIONS.
Report of committee on oaths of members, 234

QUESTIONS.
Determined, to stand, rule 5, 4
Order when speaker reporting, rule 6, 4
When members not to vote, rule 7, 4
When to be counted, rule 8, 4
How determined, rule 9, 4
How taken by ayes and noes, rule 13, 4
Division of house, rule 37, 5

QUORUM.
See rule 9, 4

R

RAIL-ROADS.
See Surveys.
Resolution for punishing offences on, 73
See Bills No. 273.

RAMSAY, (BENJAMIN.)
His petition, 131

RAMSEY, (JAMES R.)
Report of committee of elections on his vote, 47
Laid on table, 48

RAMSAY, (WILLIAM.)
Petition of his heirs, 94. 262

RANDOLPH ACADEMY.
Petition of trustees, 75. 167

RANDOLPH COUNTY.
Petition of citizens, 19. 21, 22

RANDOLPH, HARRISON AND MONONGALIA.
Petition of citizens, 50. 63. 72

RANDOLPH, MONONGALIA AND PRESTON.
Petition of citizens, 26. 29. 40

RANDOLPH AND RIVES.
Report on contested election, 13. 155. 184, 185

RANDOLPH, (THOMAS J.)
His petition, 13

RANDOLPH, (WILLIAM B.)
His election contested; report on, 36, 37

RAPPAHANNOCK AND BLUE RIDGE RAIL-ROAD.
Resolution for chartering company, 14
See Bills No 18.

RAPPAHANNOCK CANAL COMPANY.
Petition of stockholders, 126
Common council of Fredericksburg to subscribe for stock, 203
See Bills No. 295.
See Bills No. 214.

RAPPAHANNOCK COUNTY.
Petition of citizens, 74

RAPPAHANNOCK MARINE AND FIRE INSURANCE COMPANY.
See Bills No. 173.

READ, (ANDERSON.)
Petition of citizens of Bedford in his favour, 19. 95. 139

RECOVERIES ON JUDGMENTS.
In courts of other states, limited, 18
See Bills No 201.

RED AND BLUE SULPHUR SPRINGS.
See Bills No. 43.

RED SPRINGS COMPANY.
See Bills No. 15.

RED SULPHUR SPRINGS AND NEWBURN ROAD.
Resolution for incorporating company to construct road, 43

REGIMENTS.
See Bills No. 130, No. 297 and No. 169.
Communication from court of enquiry for 132d regiment, 170

REGISTER.
Number of committee to examine office, rule 28, 5
Committee appointed, 13
Committee added to, 38
Report of committee presented, 76
Acted on, 132. 133
Resolution for electing, 90
Agreed to by senate, 94
Election made, vote recorded, 99
Resolution for furnishing clerks' offices with the number, dates, &c. of patents, 95
Required to report quantity of land due from the state to officers and soldiers of the revolution, 154
Communicates the information required, 161

REMOVAL OF PRISONERS.
Resolution for removal where jails injured or destroyed, 15
See Bills No. 34.

RESCINDING RESOLUTIONS.
Mr. Watkins's resolutions for rescinding resolutions on subject of deposits, 100
Laid on table, vote recorded, 101
Resolutions printed. See Doc. No. 35.

RESOLUTIONS.
Clerk to publish, rule 20, 4
To be offered one hour after meeting of house, 162
See various subjects upon which offered

RETURNS OF ELECTIONS.
Report of committee on sheriffs' returns, 234

REVENUE, (PUBLIC.)
See Bills No. 265.

REVISED CODE.
Resolution for supplying justices, 161
Committee discharged therefrom, 262
For revision of criminal code. See Bills No. 327.

REVOLUTIONARY CLAIMS.
See Commissioner of Revolutionary Claims.
Report of commissioner presented, 21
Resolution for abolishing office of commissioner, 59
Committee added to standing committees, 82
Philip S. Fry assigned as clerk to committee, 85
Governor's message relating to, referred, 95
Resolution for providing some other tribunal, 95
Resolution requesting reasons of executive for rejecting petitions, 103
See Bills No. 251.
Rule requiring standing committee, rescinded, 110
Resolution for referring subjects to committee, 121
Referred to committee for courts of justice, 160
Committee for courts of justice discharged, 262
Register transmits information relative to land due officers and soldiers of revolution, 161

RICHMOND AND BIG BIRD TURNPIKE COMPANIES.
See Bills No. 276.

RICHMOND CITY.
Petition of citizens, 22. 37. 43. 50. 53. 71. 78. 86. 108, 109. 118. 142. 160. 201

RICHMOND FAYETTE ARTILLERY COMPANY.
See Bills No. 140.

RICHMOND, FREDERICKSBURG AND POTOWMAC RAIL-ROAD.
Resolution for increasing capital stock, 78
Reported on, 108

Recommitted,	121	
State's subscription. See Bills No. 178.		
Report of committee on increasing capital,	166	
Acted on,	223	
RICHMOND HUSTINGS COURT.		
See Bills No. 162.		
RICHMOND AND MANCHESTER COAL WORKING COMPANY.		
See Bills No. 154.		
RICHMOND MANUFACTURING COMPANY.		
See Bills No. 156.		
RICHMOND MEDICAL COLLEGE.		
See Bills No. 146.		
RICHMOND AND PETERSBURG.		
Petition of citizens,	85	
RICHMOND AND PETERSBURG RAIL-ROAD.		
Resolution for incorporating company,	23	
See Bills No. 29.		
RICHMOND RAIL-ROAD.		
Resolution for amending charter,	33	
See Bills No. 44.		
RICHMOND AND TUCKAHOE BRIDGE ROAD.		
Resolution for incorporating company,	23	
RICHMOND AND YORK RAIL-ROAD.		
Survey required,	86	
Resolution for survey agreed to by senate,	92	
See Bills No. 232.		
RIGGAN, (WM. H.)		
His petition,	108	
See Bills No. 296.		
RIGHT OF INSTRUCTION.		
Resolutions of 1812, Doc. No. 9.		
RIGHT OF SUFFRAGE.		
Resolution enquiring whether stockholders in corporations have this right,	44	
RIVES, (ALEXANDER.)		
His petition,	13. 165. 184, 185	
Leave to withdraw papers,	212	
ROADS.		
Number of committee, rule 28,	5	
Committee appointed,	12	
Resolution for chartering Rappahannock and Blue Ridge rail-road,	14	
Lexington and Richmond turnpike,	15	
Louisa rail-road,	18	
Clarksburg and Middlebourn road,	18	
Wheeling and Clarksburg road,	18. 54	
Winchester and Berryville road,	21	
Report on,	54	
Bill for survey and location of certain roads.		
See Bills No. 21,		
Blue and Red Sulphur springs road,	24	
Weston and Charleston road,	24	
See Bills No. 45.		
Rule of house limiting committee suspended; committee enlarged,	28. 50. 55	
North-western and Beverley road. See Bills No. 23,		
Milam's gap road,		
Richmond rail road company,		
Richmond and Tuckahoe bridge turnpike,		
Committee added to,		
Red Sulphur springs and Newbern road,	29	
From Pennsylvania line to road from Clarksburg to Beverley. See Bills No. 50,	45	
From Elizabethtown through the Narrows to Wheeling,	49, 63, 71	
Staunton and Augusta springs road,	50	
From Moorfield to North-western road,	53. 60	
From Moorfield to Wardensville,	55. 107	
Report of committee on,	137	
For completing Alleghany turnpike,	63	
For opening eastern portion of road from Huntersville to Ohio river,	64	
Warm springs and Harrisonburg turnpike,	64	
Across Alleghany mountain in Pendleton and Pocahontas,	68	
Committee discharged from bringing in bills for road across Price's mountain,	73	
Joint stock company for said road,	73	
Across Laurel hill in Randolph,	74	

Changing mode of constructing North-western turnpike and its superintendence,	85	
Survey of rail road from Richmond to York,	86	
Staunton and Little Kanawha road,	93	
Survey of rail-road routes from Gordonsville to Harrisonburg and Charlottesville,	94	
Resolution amended and adopted,	106	
Survey from Evansham to Jeffersonville,	96	
Agreed to by senate,	103	
Form for a general law for rail-roads and navigation companies,	96	
Staunton and Warm springs road,	103	
Across Alleghany mountain from Heavner's store in Pendleton to Greenbrier river,	262	
ROAD LAW,	X	
See Bills No. 240.		
ROANOKE, DANVILLE AND JUNCTION RAIL-ROAD.		
See Bills No. 75.		
ROANOKE NAVIGATION COMPANY.		
Their petition,	78. 86	
ROBERTSON, (JOHN T.)		
His petition,	93. 156. 201	
ROBIN.		
Petition in his favour,	95	
ROBINSON, (ABNER.)		
His petition,	156. 186. 233	
ROCKBRIDGE, BOTETOURT AND ALLEGHANY.		
Petition of citizens,	38. 57. 63. 71	
ROCKBRIDGE COUNTY.		
Petition of citizens,	45. 168	
Road law changed. See Bills No. 240.		
ROCKINGHAM COUNTY.		
Petition of citizens,	16. 64. 62, 83. 134	
Regimental districts. See Bills No. 160.		
Separate election. See Bills No. 192.		
ROCKINGHAM AND ALBEMARLE.		
Petition of citizens,	3. 175. 203	
ROCKINGHAM AND AUGUSTA.		
Petition of citizens,	169. 203	
ROCKINGHAM AND BOTETOURT.		
Petition of citizens,	38. 57. 63. 71	
ROCKINGHAM AND HARDY.		
Report of committee on petition,	16. 22	
ROGERS, (DAVID,) adm'r.		
His petition,	92. 262	
ROGERS AND FINDLEY.		
Their petition,	29. 230. 233	
ROGERS, (WM. B.)		
See Geological Reconnoissance.		
Authorized to publish geological report, and use plates of profile, &c.	152	
ROSSON AND CARPER.		
Their petition,	57. 73	
RUFF AND JORDAN.		
Their petition,	45. 80. 136	
RULES AND REGULATIONS.		
Adopted,	3 to 6	
Resolutions to be offered one hour after meeting of house; postponed,	162	
RUMNEY, (WILLIAM,) reps.		
His petition,	94. 262	
RUSSELL COUNTY.		
Separate election. See Bills No. 300.		
RYON, (WILLIAM.)		
Report of committee of elections on his vote,	46	
Laid on table,	48	

S

ST. BRIDE'S ACADEMY.		
For incorporating,	141	
Petition of trustees,	142. 167	
See Bills No. 246.		
SALEM.		
See Bills No. 308.		
SALES OF PUBLIC LANDS.		
Governor communicates resolutions of Pennsylvania concerning distribution of proceeds,	272, 273	
Resolution of Mr. Dorman relating to distribution of proceeds, Doc. No. 14.		

SAUNDERS, (BASSETT.)		
His petition,	95. 262	
SAVINGS INSTITUTIONS.		
Whether deal in bonds, &c.	107	
See Bills No. 166.		
SCHEDULE.		
Of petitions to be prepared by clerk. rule 22,	4	
SCHOOL COMMISSIONERS.		
Abstract of treasurer's accounts, Doc. No. 4,	pp. 12, 13, 14	
Abstract of commissioners' reports for 1834,	15. 16	
Reports of operations of district free schools,	17	
Extracts from reports relating to primary schools in each county,	19 to 29	
Reports of the several counties,	30 to 67	
SCHOOL QUOTAS.		
Of Ohio and Marshall. See Bills No. 25,	26	
Statement of school quotas of counties, Doc. No. 4,	p. 10	
SCHOOLS AND COLLEGES.		
Number of committee, rule 29,	5	
To examine and report state of literary fund, rule 34,	5	
Committee of whom to consist,	12	
Rule limiting committee suspended, and Mr. Madison added,	27	
Committee increased,	35	
Resolution for distributing surplus revenue of literary fund,	63	
See Military School.		
SCOTT COUNTY.		
Petition of citizens,	16. 20. 63. 170. 186. 230	
See Estillville academy,	63	
SCOTT, (JOHN L.)		
Member from Dinwiddie resigns,	56	
SCOTT, (WILLIAM.)		
His petition,	38. 54	
SCOTTSVILLE.		
Petition of citizens,	34	
SCOTTSVILLE AND ROCKFISH RIVER ROAD.		
See Bills No. 226.		
SEATS.		
See rule 16,	4	
Resolution for altering arrangements in hall, and for accommodating visitors, &c.	69	
Within bar, to be set apart by speaker,	84	
SECOND AUDITOR'S OFFICE.		
Number of committee, rule 28,	5	
Committee appointed,	13	
His annual report presented,	12	
Resolution for electing,	90	
Agreed to by senate,	94	
Election made, vote recorded,	99	
Annual report, Doc. No. 5.		
State of literary fund,	p. 5	
Permanent capital literary fund,	6	
Stocks and loans belonging to it,	7	
Its revenue,	8	
Charges on the fund,	9	
Statement of school quotas,	10	
Estimate of receipts and disbursements on account of the revenue,	11	
Abstract of accounts of treasurers of school commissioners,	12 to 14	
Abstract of school commissioners' reports for 1834,	15, 16	
School commissioners' reports shewing the operations of the district free schools,	17	
Extracts from the reports of school commissioners relating to the state of the primary schools for 1834, in each county,	19 to 29	
Accounts of fund for internal improvement, Doc. No. 5.		
State of the fund,		
Permanent funds,		
Disposable funds,		
Receipts,	8. 10	
Disbursements,	9. 11	
Estimate of certain and probable receipts,	12	
Disbursements on account of disposable funds,	13	
Prospective statement relating to funds of board of public works,	14	

302   INDEX.

Table of instalments due on subscriptions to stocks,	15	
Summary statement of loans,	16	
SECRETARY TO COMMONWEALTH.		
Resolution for electing,	95	
Agreed to by senate,	98	
Election made, vote recorded,	99	
SECRETARY OF NAVY.		
Answer to governor's letter on subject of refusal of captain Dallas to permit service of civil process on board his ship, Doc. No. 1, p. 11		
SELECT COMMITTEES.		
Quorum for business, rule 29,	5	
Number of members to compose, rule 31,	5	
SEMPLE, (JAMES,) *Judge.*		
His death announced, governor's message, vacancy supplied,	12	
SENATE.		
Resolution for temporary adjournment,	21	
Amended by house,	21	
Second resolution for adjournment,	28	
Amendment to first resolution agreed,	31	
SENATE UNITED STATES.		
Resolution relative to proceedings of executive referred to committee. See *Expunging*,	24	
SENATORS OF UNITED STATES.		
Letter of John Tyler resigning,	171. 175	
Vote on printing his letter recorded,	175	
Resolution for electing, to supply vacancy of Mr. Tyler,	175	
Agreed to by senate,	183	
Election proceeded in, vote recorded,	183	
Letter from B. W. Leigh in answer to expunging resolutions,	186. 194	
Senator Tyler's letter printed, Doc. No. 49.		
Senator Leigh's letter printed, Doc. No. 50.		
SEPARATE ELECTIONS.		
Resolution for establishing one in Henry county.	14	
In Marshall. See Bills No. 12.		
In Preston. See Bills No. 46.		
In Wythe. See Bills No. 47.		
In Berkeley established. See Bills No. 52.		
In Berkeley changed. See Bills No. 53.		
In Hampshire. See Bills No. 69.		
In Cumberland. See Bills No. 95.		
In Lunenburg. See Bills No. 112.		
In Monongalia. See Bills No. 113.		
In Ohio. See Bills No. 114.		
In Tyler. See Bills No. 116.		
In Kanawha. See Bills No. 151.		
In Rockingham. See Bills No. 192.		
In Cabell. See Bills No. 196.		
In Henry. See Bills No. 216.		
In Pittsylvania. See Bills No. 253.		
In Harrison. See Bills No. 263.		
In Tazewell. See Bills No. 300.		
In Russell. See Bills No. 300.		
In Northumberland. See Bills No. 331.		
SERGEANT AT ARMS.		
Samuel J. Winston elected,	3	
When to take persons in custody for breach of privilege, rule 42,	6	
SHANKS AND LEWIS.		
Their petition,	26. 33. 41	
SHANKS, (ROBERT.)		
See *Mechanics Manufacturing Company,*	49	
SHARPE, (LINCEFIELD,) *heirs.*		
Their petition,	94. 262	
SHAVER, (JOHN,) *and others.*		
Their petition,	18. 23	
SHENANDOAH COUNTY.		
Petition of citizens,	14. 50. 64. 93. 144	
Quarterly court changed. See Bills No. 233.		
SHENANDOAH AND FREDERICK.		
New county of Warren formed. See Bills No. 229.		
SHERIFF OF NORFOLK.		
Process prevented from being served by naval commander; governor's message,	8, 9	
His communication to governor printed, Doc. No. 1,	p. 10	

SHERIFF OF SPOTTSYLVANIA.		
See Bills No. 339.		
SHERIFFS.		
To take body of principal upon written request of bail,	154	
SIMMS, (LEVI.)		
His petition,	118. 151. 199	
SINKING FUND.		
Governor's message,	11	
SKURRY, (DAVID.)		
His petition,	101. 262	
SLAVERY.		
See *Abolition.*		
SLAVES, FREE NEGROES, &c.		
Resolution to amend law to provide for removal from commonwealth,	32. 76	
Committee discharged from,	262	
Resolution for providing that free negroes shall forfeit freedom and pass to next of kin, for failing to leave state,	49	
Reported on,	135	
Resolution for amending act relating to hog stealing by them,	59	
See Bills No. 250.		
Rights of creditors to services of slaves emancipated,	95	
For preventing the return of free negroes into state,	100	
Resolution amended and adopted,	102	
For removing free negroes from the state,	102	
Amending the laws concerning. See Bills No. 219.		
To prevent them from trading beyond city, county, &c. See Bills No. 221.		
To prevent trading with. See Bills No. 333		
SMITHFIELD RAIL-ROAD.		
See Bills No. 229.		
SMITHFIELD SAVINGS INSTITUTION.		
See Bills No. 158.		
SMITH, (JAMES.)		
His petition,	36. 162. 223	
See Bills No. 322.		
SMITH, (JOHN H.)		
His report as commissioner of revolutionary claims,	21	
Letter communicating conditional resignation as commissioner of revolutionary claims,	204, 205	
Letter of final resignation,	257	
SMITH'S RIVER.		
Survey required,	94	
Agreed to by senate,	100	
SMITH'S RIVER NAVIGATION COMPANY.		
Resolution for amending act incorporating company—to authorize subscription by state,	18	
See Bills No. 32.		
SMYTH COUNTY.		
Petition of school commissioners,	14	
Petition of citizens, 45. 59. 118. 163. 167. 223. 231		
SNEAD, (JESSE *and others.)*		
Their petition,	32. 59. 200	
SOUTHALL, (VALENTINE W.)		
Excused from voting in contested election from Fayette and Nicholas,	48	
SOUTHALL AND GILMER.		
Report on contested election,	184, 185	
SOUTHAMPTON COUNTY.		
See Bills No. 137. Processioning.		
SPARHAWK, (EDWARD V.)		
Clerk to committee of agriculture, &c.	13	
SPARR, (JOHN.)		
Report of committee of elections on his vote,	47	
Laid on table,	48	
SPEAKER.		
Linn Banks elected; vote,	3	
May call members to chair, rule 15,	4	
To set apart privileged seats, rule 16,	4	
To examine journal, rule 19,	4	
To appoint committees, rule 28,	5	
Division of house, rule 37,	5	
Thanks voted,	273	

SPIRITS.		
Resolution for amending act regulating licenses for retailing,	57	
SPRING CREEK TURNPIKE		
See Bills No. 76.		
SPRING WAREHOUSE.		
Inspection of tobacco revived. See Bills No. 4,	15	
STABLES.		
Superintendent of public buildings to rent out old stable,	262	
Resolution agreed to by senate,	264	
STACKHOUSE, (JOHN AND NANCY.)		
Their petition,	29. 61. 262	
STAFFORD COUNTY.		
Petition of citizens,	19. 32. 42. 74	
Circuit courts changed. See Bills No. 249.		
STAFFORD GOLD MINING COMPANY.		
See Bills No. 98.		
STARKS, (DANIEL.)		
His petition,	35. 155. 200	
See Bills No. 306.		
STATE LINE.		
List of officers of Virginia, Doc. No. 6, pp. 75-118		
STATE NAVY.		
List of officers of line and navy, Doc. No. 6, pp. 75-118		
STATUTES AT LARGE.		
See Bills No. 342.		
STAUNTON AND AUGUSTA SPRINGS ROAD.		
Resolution to incorporate company,	50	
STAUNTON AND LITTLE KANAWHA ROAD.		
Further provision for completing,	93	
See Bills No. 141.		
STAUNTON AND POTOWMAC RAIL-ROAD.		
Leave to introduce bill concerning. See Bills No. 2,	15	
STAUNTON AND WARM SPRINGS ROAD.		
To incorporate a company to complete,	103	
Reported on,	160	
Acted on,	201	
STENOGRAPHERS.		
Allowed seats in house,	3	
STEPHEN.		
His petition,	19. 75. 79. 155. 200	
See Bills No. 304.		
STICKLEY, (DAVID.)		
Allowance for colours,	94	
Reported on,	179	
STOCKS, (PUBLIC.)		
Propriety of directing board of public works to dispose of,	96	
STUBBLEFIELD, (JOHN.)		
Elected doorkeeper,	3	
STURM, (JESSE.)		
His petition,	16	
Report acted on,	20	
See Bills No. 35.		
SUBPOENAS.		
How sueable against members, rule 39,	6	
SUFFOLK.		
Petition of citizens,	35. 54	
Schedule ascertaining damages sustained by houses in, Doc. No. 43, p. 22		
SUFFOLK ACADEMY.		
See Bills No. 243.		
SUFFOLK RAIL-ROAD.		
See Bills No. 63.		
SUFFRAGE, (RIGHT OF.)		
See *Right of Suffrage,*	44	
Report against stockholders in companies exercising,	249	
SUPERINTENDENT OF ARMORY.		
See *Armory.*		
His report presented,	27	
To be printed,	76	
SUPERINTENDENT OF PENITENTIARY.		
See *Penitentiary.*		
His report presented,	23	
Resolution for election,	160	

INDEX.

303

Agreed to by senate,	164	Their report,	80
For adding him to committee of revisors,	164	Acted on,	138
Election made; vote recorded,	166, 167	**TREASURER.**	
SUPERINTENDENT OF PUBLIC EDIFICES.		His annual communication,	12
		To be printed.	12
His report transmitted by governor,	27	Resolution for electing,	90
Communication relative to flag,	162, 163	Agreed to by senate,	94
Resolution requiring old stable to be rented,	262	Election made; vote recorded,	99
Agreed to by senate,	264	Annual report, Doc. No. 3.	
SUPPLEMENT TO CODE.		Statement of receipts and disbursements on account of commonwealth,	pp. 4, 5
Resolution for supplying justices,	161	Statement of receipts and disbursements of various funds,	6, 7
Committee discharged therefrom,	262	Cincinnati fund,	12, 13
SURPLUS REVENUE.		Washington monument fund,	14
Mr. Dorman's resolution for distributing revenue, arising from sales of public lands, among states,	49, 50	Report of joint committee on his accounts, Doc. No 28.	
SURVEYS.		**TRESPASSES BY HERDSMEN.**	
Of rail-roads from Falmouth to Alexandria, and from Warrenton, to intersect said road,	144	See Bills No. 66.	
Agreed to by senate,	160	Remonstrance,	50
Between Back bay and Linkhorn bay, and between North river and Lynhaven bay,	146	**TUCKAHOE CANAL COMPANY.**	
Agreed to by senate,	160	**TUCKAHOE RAIL-ROAD.**	
For rail-road from Buford's gap to Tennessee line, by Walker's creek and north fork of Holstein,	155	See Bills No. 303.	
		TURNER, (STEPHEN.)	
Agreed to by senate,	220	His petition,	142, 162
Resolution for survey of Nottoway river,	161	**TUTT, (ANN M.)**	
Agreed to by senate,	176	Her petition,	16. 50, 51
Of Pamunkey river,	225	**TYLER COUNTY.**	
Agreed to by senate,	230	Petition of citizens,	64, 69
SWEET SPRINGS COMPANY.		See Bills No. 116.	
See Bills No. 13.	23	**TYLER AND HARRISON.**	
SWEET SPRINGS AND PRICE'S MOUNTAIN TURNPIKE.		Leave to withdraw petitions of citizens,	28
See Bills No. 254.		**TYLER, (JOHN.)**	
SWORDS.		His resignation as senator,	171-175
Voted son of lieutenant colonel George Armistead,	195	Vote on printing letter recorded,	175
Agreed to by senate,	202	Letter printed, Doc. No. 49.	
Voted captain E. A. F. Valette,	202	**TYLER, MONONGALIA AND PRESTON.**	
Agreed to by senate,	225	Petition of citizens,	43. 55

T

TAXES.

See Finance.
Resolution for altering taxes on horses and mules, 43
See Bills No. 264.

TAZEWELL.

Petition of citizens, 121. 141. 180
Separate election. See Bills No. 300.
Line dividing Giles and Tazewell. See Bills No. 167.

TENANTS IN COMMON.

Resolution for making partition of personal as well as real estate, 44
TERRY, (WILLIAM.)
Report of committee of elections on his vote, 47
Laid on table, 48
THEFTS AND FORGERIES.
See Bills No. 209.

TOBACCO.
Inspection at Spring warehouse revived. See Bills No. 4, 15
Inspectors to designate between that produced in and out of state, 56
See Bills No. 135.
See Bills No. 267.

TOMLINSON, (SOLOMON.)
His petition, 96. 178
TONEY AND HOLEMAN.
Their petition, 81. 86. 136
TOWNES, (WILLIAM.)
His petition, 64. 112. 179
His bridge. See Bills No. 309.
TRANSPORTATION COMPANY.
Between Norfolk and Portsmouth, 99
TREASURER'S ACCOUNTS.
Number of committee, rule 28, 5
Joint committee appointed, 13

U

UNDERWOOD, (GEORGE.)
Report of committee of elections on his vote, 47
Laid on table, 48
UNION FACTORY COMPANY
Of Nelson and Albemarle, 22
UNION POTOWMAC COMPANY.
See Bills No. 119.
UNITED STATES COPPER MINING COMPANY.
See Bills No. 194.
UNITED STATES GOVERNMENT.
See governor's message, 8, 9
UNIVERSITY.
Report of literary fund relative to, presented, 54
Resolution for increasing visitors, 110
Reported on, 167
Acted on, 231
UPPER APPOMATTOX COMPANY
Resolution for subscription to stock, 26
Resolution for amending act concerning, 28
Report on resolution, 33
Petition of trustees, 36. 41. 76. 100. 107
See Bills No. 73.
UPPERVILLE ACADEMY.
See Bills No. 94.
UPPERVILLE.
Petition of citizens, 154. 167

V

VACCINE AGENT.
See Bills No. 323.
VALETTE, (E. A. F.)
Sword voted him, 202
Agreed to by senate, 225
VALLEY BANK.
Governor transmits returns from, 25
Referred, 25
Returns of, Doc. No. 55, pp. 11-17
VAN BIBBER, (JAMES.)
His ferry. See Bills No. 23, 26

VANNERSON, (THOMAS.)
Clerk to committees of propositions, &c. and of finance, 13
VAUGHAN, (ALFRED J.)
Elected from Dinwiddie—takes his seat, 94
Added to committees, 94
VIOLATION OF LAWS.
By naval officer of United States government. See governor's message, 8, 9
VIRGINIA FIRE INSURANCE COMPANY.
See Bills No. 111.
VIRGINIA INSURANCE COMPANY.
See Bills No. 106.
VIRGINIA MILLS MANUFACTURING COMPANY.
Resolution for incorporating, 28
See Bills No. 38.
VIRGINIA SILK COMPANY.
See Bills No. 239.
VIRGINIA STATE LINE.
List of officers, Doc. No. 6, pp. 75-118
VIRGINIA TOWING COMPANY.
See Bills No. 109.
VOLUNTEER COMPANIES.
Arms to volunteer companies, 118
Reported on, 179

W

WAGES.
When member contesting election entitled to, rule 36, 5
WALLACE, (CELINDA C.)
Her petition, 19
WALLS, (GEORGE AND THOMAS.)
Petition of administrator, 96
Committee discharged, and referred to finance, 100
See Bills No. 183.
See Bills No. 316.
WARD, (BERKELEY.)
His petition, 16. 73. 125. 169. 186. 224
WAREHOUSES.
Resolution for enlarging public, 28
See Bills No. 60.
WARING, (THOMAS,) Heirs.
Their petition, 94
WARM SPRINGS AND HARRISONBURG TURNPIKE.
Resolution for amending charter of company, 64
Reported on, 101
Report recommitted, 103
See Bills No. 286.
WARREN COUNTY.
New regiment. See Bills No. 222.
WARREN, (JAMES C.)
Report of committee of elections on his vote, 48
Laid on table, 48
WARRENTON.
Petition of citizens, 176
WARRENTON RAIL-ROAD.
Survey for rail-road from Warrenton, to intersect Falmouth and Alexandria rail-road, 144
Agreed to by senate, 160
WASHINGTON COLLEGE.
See Military School.
WASHINGTON MONUMENT FUND.
State of, Doc. No. 3, p. 14
WASTE TOBACCO.
See Bills No. 267.
WATERFORD.
Petition of citizens, 59. 76. 134
See Bills No. 258.
WEDDEBURN, (WILLIAM.)
His petition, 22. 50, 51. 139
WELLSBURG LYCEUM.
See Bills No. 199.
WELLS, (EPHRAIM.)
His petition, 19. 73. 124
WELLS, (THOMAS.)
Report of committee of elections on his vote, 46
Agreed to by house, 48

WESTERN LUNATIC HOSPITAL.
See Bills No. 296
Report of directors presented, 36
Auditor to transmit report of treasurer, 206
Accounts of treasurer transmitted, 218
Report of directors printed, Doc. No. 19.
Accounts printed, Doc. No. 52.

WESTON AND CHARLESTON ROAD.
Resolution for constructing road, 26
See Bills No. 45.

WHARVES.
William Chapline's, on Wheeling creek.
See Bills No. 48.

WHEELING.
Petition of citizens, 19. 28. 30. 34. 40. 78. 84
Mayor, &c. to subscribe to stock of the Baltimore and Ohio rail-road company. See Bills No. 27, 28
Corporate boundaries defined. See Bills No. 30,
City incorporated. See Bills No. 145. 29

WHEELING AND BELMONT BRIDGE COMPANY.
Petition of stockholders, 34. 69

WHEELING FIRE AND MARINE COMPANY.
See Bills No. 37, 23

WHEELING AND CLARKSBURG ROAD.
Resolution for constructing, 18
Report on resolution, 54

WILLIAMSBURG HOSPITAL.
Information called for, 85
Report of directors, 104
Additional report, 108
Report printed, Doc. No. 37.
Second report, Doc. No. 38.

WILLIAMS, (CHARLES.)
His petition, 35. 155. 200
See Bills No. 305.

WILLIAMS, (ELISHA B.)
His petition, 33. 85. 134
See Bills No. 301.
Report of committee of elections on his vote, 47
Laid on table, 48

WILLIAMS AND EVANS.
Their petition, 154. 163. 223

WILLS.
For clerks to deliver original, 152
Committee discharged from resolution, 262
See Bills No. 209.

WINCHESTER.
Petition of common council, 59. 68. 72
Inspection of flour. See Bills No. 123.

WINCHESTER AND BERRYVILLE ROAD.
Resolution for extending North-western road from Winchester to Berryville, 21
Reported on, 54

WINCHESTER AND POTOWMAC RAIL-ROAD.
See Bills No. 39.

WINN, (JESSE.)
His petition, 102. 262

WINSTON, (SAMUEL J.)
Elected sergeant at arms, 3

WISE, (HENRY A.)
His letter on the subject of abolition, 233. 243
See also Doc. No. 53.

WITNESSES.
Privilege of, rule 40, 6
Pay and attendance on house or committees, 6
Not to be tampered with, rule 41, 6

Resolution for amending act prescribing mode of obtaining commissions for depositions, 21
Reported on, 94
Acted on, 135

WOOD, (JOHN.)
His petition, 28. 33. 41

WRIT OF ELECTION.
Issued to sheriff of Dinwiddie, 56

WRITS.
How suable against members, rule 39, 6

WRITS OF ERROR.
In criminal prosecutions, 59
See Bills No. 272.

WYSONG, (JAMES.)
Resolution for refunding money to him, 26
Report on his claim, 35
Acted on, 52
See Bills No. 80.

WYTHE COUNTY.
Petition of citizens, 14. 19, 20. 28. 40
Separate election. See Bills No. 47.

WYTHE WATERING COMPANY.
See Bills No. 287.

Y

YOUNG, (JOSEPH.)
Report of committee of elections on his vote, 47
Laid on table, 48

Z

ZANE, (DANIEL AND EBENEZER.)
Their petition, 94. 156. 201

ZULL, (WM.)
His petition, 78. 84. 134

CPSIA information can be obtained
at www.ICGtesting.com
Printed in the USA
LVOW10s0711260617
539372LV00010B/135/P